JUDITH FLANDERS is the author of the critically acclaimed biography, *Circle of Sisters*, which was nominated for the Guardian First Book Award, and of the bestselling *The Victorian House*, nominated for the British Book Awards History Book of the Year. She is a frequent contributor to the *Telegraph*, the *Spectator* and the *Times Literary Supplement*.

From the reviews of *Consuming Passions*:

'Over the course of the nineteenth century, a whole new world opened up to an ever-growing section of the population – a world of retail choice, of travel for pleasure, of cultural and sporting diversion. It is a world explored with much wit and insight by Judith Flanders . . . The subject is a large one. Flanders, however, is excellent at showing the processes by which this general transformation was achieved . . . The themes that lie behind the narrative are interesting, and are well drawn out, but it is the details of the story that engage and entertain. They abound on every page . . . It's a rich mix'
MATTHEW STURGIS, *Sunday Telegraph*

'A panoramic view of a society and economy transformed by retail, travel and the production of inessential goods . . . This excellent study . . . is a major achievement'
JANE STEVENSON, *Observer*

'An absorbing Gladstone bag of a book, from which curious items spill out in delightful profusion, some familiar, some very strange indeed . . . Flanders always leavens her statistics with descriptions and illustrations which bring her material vividly to life . . . [An] absorbing and scholarly study of the inexorable rise of consumerism'
Literary Review

'Illuminating . . . This excellent historical account is written with the sort of gusto that characterizes Cole, Wedgwood and the other heroes of Flanders's book'
TLS

'A deeply satisfying exploration of how the Victorians pursued their leisure time . . . Bursting with original research and statistics, it gives a panoramic view of Victorians at play'
Country Life

By the same author

A Circle of Sisters: Alice Kipling, Georgiana Burne-Jones, Agnes Poynter and Louisa Baldwin

The Victorian House: Domestic Life from Childbirth to Deathbed

CONSUMING PASSIONS

Leisure and Pleasure in Victorian Britain

JUDITH FLANDERS

HARPER PERENNIAL

London, New York, Toronto and Sydney

Harper Perennial
An imprint of HarperCollins*Publishers*
77–85 Fulham Palace Road
Hammersmith
London W6 8JB

www.harperperennial.co.uk

This edition published by Harper Perennial 2007
1

First published in Great Britain by Harper*Press* 2006

Judith Flanders asserts the moral right to
be identified as the author of this work

A catalogue record for this book
is available from the British Library

ISBN-13 978–0-00–717296-2

Set in PostScript Linotype Giovanni Book and
Bauer Bodoni display by
Rowland Phototypesetting Ltd,
Bury St Edmunds, Suffolk

Printed and bound in Great Britain
by Clays Ltd, St Ives plc

For Andy
1945–2006

Wee but mighty

CONTENTS

LIST OF ILLUSTRATIONS

BLACK AND WHITE TEXT ILLUSTRATIONS

COLOUR PLATES

Section I

Section III

ACKNOWLEDGEMENTS

I have incurred many debts of gratitude in the research and writing of this book.

I have previously thanked the members of the Victoria Mailbase for both information and scholarly collegiality, and I would like to do so again: in particular, for information on bicycles, Cathrine Frank, Sheldon Goldfarb, Lesley Hall, Lee Jackson, Ellen Jordan, Andrew Maunder, Terry Meyers, Christopher Pittard, Angela Richardson, Malcolm Shifrin, Madhu Sinha and Beth Sutton-Ramspeck; for coaches and coach-building, Glen Everett, Dino Franco Felluga and Keith Wilson; for the fall of Melbourne's government and the *London Saturday Journal*, Mary Miller; for rhodium pens, Eileen Curran, Sheldon Goldfarb, Michael Hargreave Mawson and Keith Ramsey; for information on photography and prices, Jan Marsh, Julia Momolo and Shannon Smith; and for putting me on the trail of the murderer James Blomfield Rush, Sheldon Goldfarb, Jill Grey and Keith Ramsey. Patrick Leary has been helpful and encouraging far beyond the call of duty: I am most grateful to him.

I would also like to thank the following: Bob Davenport is every author's dream copy-editor, and he also supplied me with information about pneumatic tubes, and Messrs Wickham and Spiegelhalter; Nicholas Dromgoole read the theatre chapter; Hilary Mantel gave me helpful leads on the French Revolution and British art collectors; Jan Morris supplied information about the Craig-y-Don gun. More thanks go to Cathie Arrington, Paul Baggaley, John Bond, Vera Brice, Sarah Christie, Essie Cousins, Helen Ellis, Mally Foster, Robin Gibson, Bill Hamilton, Patrick Hurd, Kate Hyde, Fiona Markham, Alice Massey, Douglas Matthews, David Miller, Arabella Pike, Rama Rahimi, Digby Smith, Fergal Tobin and David Wardle.

As always, the London Library, the Rare Books Room of the British Library, the Bodleian Library, Cambridge University Library and the Guildhall Library, and their helpful staffs, have all provided much needed assistance.

And finally my greatest debt is to Ravi Mirchandani, who has displayed the patience of a saint. He has read sections of the book against completely unreasonable deadlines, given me invaluable advice, and – hardly ever – complained. I owe him a great deal.

PREFACE

In 1775, after a trip to Scotland, Dr Johnson wrote, 'The true state of every nation is the state of common life . . . The great mass of nations is neither rich nor gay: they whose aggregate constitutes the people, are found in the streets, and the villages, in the shops and farms; and from them collectively considered, must the measure of general prosperity be taken.'[1] This seems to be such an unremarkable thought that to us it is scarcely worth saying. But before the nineteenth century it was a radical idea that prosperity, much less the true state of the nation, could be assessed by measuring the quantity and quality of the possessions of the nation's inhabitants. The idea of a quantifiable 'standard of living' was as yet in embryo. By the time of the first ever World's Fair, the Great Exhibition, held in London only seventy-six years later, the idea that one's quality of life could be judged by the number of things one owned or consumed had come to be seen as natural: the consumer society had been born.

One of the ways of measuring the standard of living was by measuring possessions, but possessions did not necessarily have to be expensive or exclusive in order to be valuable to their owners. Dr Johnson's equation of the state of the nation with the state of common life and the 'measure of general prosperity' came towards the start of the era of innovation which today we refer to as the Industrial Revolution, an era that finished towards the end of the nineteenth century, just as the phrase 'standard of living' came into general use. The Industrial Revolution calls to mind images of raw power, of steam engines, of coal and iron. But the first, and for much of the next century the most lucrative and technologically advanced, industry spawned by what we know as that revolution was the manufacturing of textiles – all that iron and steel, to create fashionable fabrics, pretty ribbons, lace and other fripperies that could in many cases be bought for a few pennies.

The Industrial Revolution saw not only the transformation of independent workshops into mammoth factories; it also saw the transformation of small shops into magnificent department stores. The period was one of increased buying and selling generally, and more particularly an increase in the quantity and quality of shops. The expansion of these new stores was frequently driven by new entrepreneurs, who generated previously unimaginable ways to stock them with new goods, new ways of displaying goods – plate-glass windows, gas lighting – and new ways of selling goods – money-back guarantees, advertising, discounts. By the end of the nineteenth century the Crown Princess of Greece was writing to her mother, 'We spent I don't know how many hours at Maple & Liberty! I *screamed* at the things to Tino's horror, but they were too lovely! *No*, these shops I go mad in them! I would be ruined if I lived here longer! – Divine shops!!'[2] Not only were there 'divine shops', but new technologies in transport, from stagecoaches to canals to railways, brought the novelty of newspapers to tens of thousands more people, who could now read about what was available and what could be bought, encouraging them to acquire – or hope to acquire – more and more *things*.

But what the Industrial Revolution, and the new technologies that both drove it and were driven by it, produced was not just things – it was choice. Many items that had been undreamt of luxuries to the grandparents, or even the parents, of the children of the Industrial Revolution became conveniences; less than a generation later they were no longer even conveniences: they had become necessities. Living without sugar, without tea, without cotton, glass or cutlery became unimaginable to much of Britain's population. Over the course of the nineteenth century, mass production of goods, improved distribution of those goods by new and faster forms of transport, promotion by advertising in newspapers and magazines, and new methods of retailing all combined to produce a seemingly endless stream of things that could be acquired by the consumer. It was not expensive rarities that created the new middle-class world of plenty and ease: it was the small comforts of hot, sweet drinks, or cheap and cheerful clothes – perhaps ultimately better symbols of the new world than all the machinery and technical ingenuity that made these items possible. As Gibbon noted in 1781, 'The plenty of glass and linen has diffused more real comforts among the modern nations of Europe, than the senators of Rome could derive from all the refinements of pompous or sensual luxury.'[3]

But the consumer revolution was not only a matter of things. Commercial entertainment – the selling of leisure and pleasure – was also now accessible to the masses, creating myriad business opportunities. Theatre, opera, music-making; pleasure gardens and fairs; newspapers, magazines, books; holidays and tourism, seaside outings and excursion travel; spectator sports such as racing and football – in the nineteenth century these became available to many, who could increasingly afford to pay for their entertainment. No longer was the pub or the annual or monthly fair the prime venue for leisure. The age of mass entertainment had arrived, and the unruly crowd – avidly, enthusiastically – had become eager customers.

In *Consuming Passions* I have chosen to look not at the contents of the world of leisure, but at the containers: not at the literary merits (or otherwise) of books, newspapers and magazines, but at the availability of reading material; not at the subject matter of plays, but at staging and the technological development of theatrical presentation – at lighting, special effects and spectacle; at football and racing not as sporting competitions, but as paying spectator events.

Of course commercial leisure has always existed, in some form or another, but the masses previously had minimal access to much of it. The Industrial Revolution is often represented as having created a new world of commerce and commercialism; of factory routine, endless grind, and dark, Satanic mills. It did that. But it also brought colour, light and entertainment. This new world is the one I want to visit.

To found a great empire for the sole purpose of raising up a people of customers, may at first sight appear a project fit only for a nation of shopkeepers.

Adam Smith, *The Wealth of Nations* (1776), II, iv, vii

CONSUMING
PASSIONS

From Arcadia to Arcade:
The Great Exhibition

THE 1ST OF MAY 1851. Prince Albert is on the dais, welcoming the throng to the Great Exhibition of the Works of Industry of All Nations. Joseph Paxton's extraordinary Crystal Palace, as it has swiftly been nicknamed, throws off sparks of light in the bright sunshine. The choir sings the 'Hallelujah Chorus' from the *Messiah*. It seems that all the doubt, turmoil and trouble of the previous decades has at last been overcome: machinery, technology and science are in the ascendant, and will set the world free. Britain, the world's first industrial society, will lead the way into a glorious future, which can be seen, all mapped out, in the courts and aisles of the Crystal Palace.

The building itself is a triumph of technology: Paxton's great innovation has been to design perhaps the world's first – and definitely the world's largest – prefabricated building, using in his cast-iron and glass structure principles previously applied only to engineering projects. The Crystal Palace, deep in Hyde Park, is a cathedral to the glories of industry, in which power and steam are deified: a twenty-four-ton lump of coal greets visitors at the entrance, a precursor to the steam engines, hydraulic-powered machinery, locomotives, looms, spinning machines, steam hammers and more inside.

Earlier that year *The Times* had reported a speech given by the Prince, in which he had held out an enticing vision of the future: 'The distances which separated the different nations and parts of the globe are rapidly vanishing before the achievements of modern invention . . . The products of all quarters of the globe are placed at our disposal, and we have only to choose which is the best and the cheapest for our purposes, and the powers of production are intrusted to the stimulus of competition and capital.'[1] Others had less exalted ideas. Albert and his supporters and encouragers were concerned with the benefits, both moral and industrial, that were to be found in commercial endeavour, but, in the brave new world of free trade and capitalism, many more were content simply to enjoy, or profit from, the results of those endeavours. The Great Exhibition gave many their first taste of the mass market, a thrilling peek into a future of plenty and consumption. For the Great Exhibition brought with it more than merely machinery. It brought *things* – tens of thousands of things, things piled high in the aisles of the Crystal Palace; things representing the hundreds of thousands more things that were now being manufactured and could be purchased.

The organizers of the Great Exhibition had not meant it to be this way. The origins of the event could be found in many converging trends, but the one that was the most distinctive, the most British, was the club. The Goncourt brothers, those nineteenth-century Parisian novelists and diarists, mocked the national fondness for this institution: if two Englishmen were washed up on a desert island, they said, the first thing they would do would be to form a club.[2] Certainly, by the eighteenth century, clubs were seen as an integral part of the civilizing process in Britain. Joseph Addison, laying down the rules of urbane as well as urban living in the *Spectator*, wrote, 'Man is said to be a Sociable Animal, and, as an Instance of it, we may observe, that we take all Occasions and Pretences of forming our selves into those little Nocturnal Assemblies, which are commonly known by the Name of *Clubs*.'*[3]

Initially informal, sociable outings (the noun probably developed from the verb, from the custom of clubbing together to pay for dinners

---

* Richard Steele had started the *Tatler* in 1709, and it came out three times a week until the beginning of 1711. A single sheet, at first it contained news items, but gradually each number comprised a single long essay, which might be a gentle satire of the social world, or a reflection on the values of the day, mildly attacking the venery and hypocrisy of politics and society. Addison contributed his first essay on 20 May 1709, and in all wrote almost fifty papers, plus another twenty together with Steele.

After the closure of the *Tatler*, Addison and Steele founded the *Spectator*, which has been called 'one of the most triumphant literary projects of the age'.[4] It was published daily for the next twenty-two months, and transformed periodical writing in England. Addison wrote the first number, introducing the 'Spectator' himself – a wry observer of the foibles of polite life – who together with his friends formed a club whose members included the Whig merchant Sir Andrew Freeport, the elderly ladies' man Will Honeycomb, and, ultimately the most famous, the country squire Sir Roger de Coverley.

and drinks), clubs gradually through the eighteenth century developed into a fairly constant form: they were on the whole private groups of men (almost always men), who met on a regular if not necessarily frequent basis, mostly in public places such as coffee houses, taverns, inns or pubs, where their meetings were given point by a focus on one specific aim, whether it was recreation, sociability, education, politics, or a shared profession.*

Soon these clubs expanded further into daily life. Addison wrote approvingly once more: 'When [men] are thus combined for their own Improvement, or for the Good of others, or at least to relax themselves from the Business of the Day ... there may be something very useful in these little Institutions and Establishments.'⁶ By the mid eighteenth century there were possibly as many as 20,000 men meeting every night in London alone in some form of organized group. And it was not just London that had convivial meeting groups: by the early eighteenth century most provincial towns had a range of clubs, whether county societies, military groups, antiquarian or philosophical societies, or simple social clubs. Bristol, with a population of 50,000 in the 1750s, had bell-ringing, clergy, county, floral, political, musical, 'Ancient Britons', Masonic and charitable groups. Norwich, with 36,000 people, had bell-ringing, floral and clergy groups, as well as nine Masonic lodges, a natural-history society, a music society, uncounted sociable clubs, and nearly fifty benefit societies. Oxford had a 'catch' club – for 'all true lovers of good fun, good humour and good music' – Irish clubs, Welsh clubs, a poetry and philosophical club, a bell-ringing club, an anti-quarian society, and a number of Masonic lodges, dining clubs and social clubs – including the Eternal Club, the Jelly Bag Society, and the Town Smarts, whose members appeared in 'white stockings, silver buckles, [with] chitterlings [shirt frills] flying, and hair in kidney'† – as

---

* A very partial round-up of coffee houses that served as meeting points for clubs in London would include Jonathan's Coffee House, Exchange Alley, which formed the basis of the stock market, and Lloyd's Coffee House, Lombard Street, where shipping and insurance brokers met, produced news sheets, then a shipping list (the first in 1734), then a register (in 1760), and finally turned into the insurer Lloyd's. Politics was discussed by Tories at the Cocoa Tree, by Whigs at Arthur's. Booksellers met at the Chapter Coffee House, Paternoster Row; actors at Will's, Wright's or the Bedford, all in Covent Garden, while the Orange, in the Haymarket, was more specialized, and for dancing masters and opera singers. Old Slaughter's, in St Martin's Lane, was the haunt of painters, while the Rainbow, in the same street, and Garraway's in Exchange Alley, not only had artists' clubs, but also mounted exhibitions of prints.⁵
† An eighteenth-century idiom for 'in order'.

well as the more common benefit, political, social, sporting, natural-history and college clubs. Even Northampton, with a population of only 5,000, managed a floral club, a Masonic lodge and a philosophical society.[7] Though most of Scotland had barely any clubs, Glasgow and Aberdeen had a few, while Edinburgh had more than twenty with an occupational or other aim – religious, social, political, musical, anti-quarian – and several that were purely social, like the Easy Club (founded in 1712) for 'mutual improvement in conversation that [members] may be more adapted for fellowship with the politer part of mankind'.[8] It was this thirst for self-improvement that motivated many club-goers.

By the end of the eighteenth century a change had taken place in some clubs. They became more tightly organized, with more rules, more organizers; they began to link themselves to other clubs with similar interests, for a less localized, more national sense of themselves; and many began to look at questions of social cohesion and discipline. Now it was not simply members whose behaviour was to be regulated by the rules of the organization: those members wanted in turn to regulate the behaviour of others. Charitable bodies, religious and civil-reform societies all were set up in the coming years. A number of causes can be attributed to this shift: a series of bad harvests that led to hunger in the country, an influx of jobless immigrants into the cities, and fears of civil unrest; the beginning of the French wars after the fall of the Bastille in 1789; the continued rapid urbanization of society, which brought like-minded men into close proximity with each other, and also with those who were less blessed by worldly goods; the rise of Methodism and Dissenting faiths – all these forces joined together to produce a group of men who thought reform was desirable, and possible.

This may appear to be a long way from the Great Exhibition, but it was in Rawthmell's Coffee House, in Covent Garden, that the first meeting of what ultimately became the Royal Society of Arts, the Exhibition's spiritual parent, took place nearly a hundred years before, in 1754. The minutes of the 'Society for the Encouragement of the Arts, Manufactures and Commerce' preserve the reforming zeal of its founders.[9] The driving force was William Shipley, a drawing master and brother of the Bishop of St Asaph, who had published his intentions in a pamphlet entitled *Proposals for raising by subscription a fund to be distributed in Premiums for the promoting of improvements in the liberal arts and sciences, manufactures,*

&c. At the first meeting of 'noblemen, clergy, gentlemen and merchants', the members considered

> whether a reward should not be given for the finding of Cobalt in this Kingdom . . . It was also proposed to consider whether a Reward should not be given for the Cultivation of Madder in this Kingdom . . . It is likewise proposed, to consider of giving Rewards for the Encouragement of Boys and Girls in the Art of Drawing; And it being the Opinion of all present that ye Art of Drawing is absolutely Necessary in many Employments Trades, & Manufactures, and that the Encouragem' thereof may prove of great Utility to the public . . .

Their brief for prizes for 'improvement' – that is, innovation – included industrial design and technological and scientific discoveries, as well as those things we now consider to fall more naturally into the domain of 'art'. The cash premiums suggested for early prizes were considerable: £30 for the discovery of deposits of ore that contained cobalt (which produced a blue pigment that, before the creation of synthetic dyes in the nineteenth century, was impossible to reproduce), and for the successful cultivation of the *Rubia tinctorum* plant for the production of madder (again for use in dyeing). There were to be two winners of the drawing prize – one for those under fourteen, one for fourteen-to-seventeen-year-olds.* Each was to receive £15. At this time journeymen workers in the arts received weekly wages ranging from 3 to 6 guineas for a drapery-painter, to £1 10s. for an engraver, down to 15s. a week for a gilder, or 10 to 12s. for a colour grinder[10]. By 1758 the RSA was funding further prizes, for designs for weavers, calico printers, cabinet- and coach-makers, as well as workers in iron, brass, china, earthenware or 'any other Mechanic Trade that requires Taste'.

The Society's committee used the burgeoning daily press to promote its premiums, placing an advertisement in the *Daily Advertiser*. The prizes were eagerly competed for, and by 1785 nearly twenty entries had been received for premiums for improving the madder dyeing procedure. There had been a number of attempts to shorten and simplify this complex process. Madder produced a turkey-red colour, but only after the fabric to be coloured had been soaked in successive baths of lye, olive oil, alum and dung, then steeped in a solution of the madder dye,

---

* And the members soon struck lucky: among their earliest prizewinners was the adolescent Richard Cosway, who later became one of London's most fashionable miniaturists.

then taken through a final 'brightening' process. It took weeks to turn out a single batch of dyed fabric. John Wilson, a dyer in Manchester, won a premium in 1761 for producing the best red; then he gained another prize in 1763 for making it even brighter. Others entered with methods to lessen the time the process took, or to lower the cost, or to reduce the number of soakings needed.[11]

The level of interest in 'improvement' throughout society was reflected in the RSA's membership. Within a few years the numbers belonging to this once clubby club had spiralled up to 2,500, mainly composed of the upper reaches of society, as evinced by a minimum subscription of 2 guineas (with a request for 3 if possible, while peers were expected to live up to their station by paying 5 guineas. Life membership was 20 guineas). The club was for the benefit of the lower orders, but they were not expected to be members. Less than a decade after William Shipley's crusading pamphet the club's annual income had risen to more than £4,500, and in that first decade total receipts came to more than £22,000, of which £8,496 had been spent on prizes, £3,507 on special grants, and £291 on art exhibitions. Subcommittees had been set up for agriculture, chemistry and the 'polite arts' (that is, drawing, modelling, etching, medallion- and cameo-making), as well as for manufacturing, technology and for matters relating to the colonies and to trade, and were distributing prizes in their own fields.

But the first run of popularity could not be sustained, and by the 1840s the Society was losing members. It was re-formed first as the Society of Arts, and then, in 1847, as the Royal Society of Arts. It began once more to mount exhibitions, this time as a money-making exercise. In 1844 Prince Albert became the club's president, but when the secretary, Francis Whishaw, attempted to interest him in an annual exhibition, of which he would be patron, he responded in a very non-committal fashion. Whishaw ploughed ahead nonetheless, and put together a committee that included Francis Fuller, Charles W. Dilke and Robert Stephenson. Except for Henry Cole, who was yet to appear on the scene, the men who were to become the prime movers of the Great Exhibition were now all in place.

It was generally agreed by successful middle-class men of taste that the main problem for industry and manufacture in general was the lack of an equivalent level of taste in the consumer to whom the resulting goods were being sold. Rather than producing goods to suit low tastes, they saw it as their job to improve the taste of the common man. The 1847 catalogue for an exhibition held by the Society spelled out their views:

> It is a universal complaint among manufacturers that the taste for good art does not exist in sufficient extent to reward them for the cost of producing superior works; that the public prefers the vulgar, the gaudy, the ugly even, to the beautiful and perfect.
>
> We are persuaded that, if artistic manufactures are not appreciated, it is because they are not widely enough known. We believe that when works of high merit, of British origin, are brought forward they will be thoroughly appreciated and thoroughly enjoyed. We believe that this exhibition, when thrown open gratuitously to all, will tend to improve the public taste.[12]

Even before this catalogue appeared, Henry Cole was on board and was already a prime mover in these improving exhibitions. He had joined the society only two years before, after designing a tea service as a prize submission under the pseudonym Felix Summerly. His submission had received the ultimate accolade: a prize, the commercial manufacture of his design, and, further, the purchase of the original service by Prince Albert. Cole was one of those Victorian powerhouses who produced so much, in so many fields, that it is hard to know when he slept. After a humble beginning as one of several clerks in the Record Commission, a junior civil-service post, he fell out with his superior over his pay. Instead of resigning, he promptly exposed his department as a haven for corruption and sinecures. After a lengthy investigation, Parliament found that he was in the right and in 1838 he was reinstated in the department at a more senior level. That same year he was seconded to help Rowland Hill with the creation of what shortly would become the new penny postage system. In the 1840s Cole became even busier: he designed what was probably the first Christmas card (see pp. 483–7); he wrote guidebooks to various tourist sights, including the National Gallery, Westminster Abbey and Hampton Court; as Felix Summerly he began to design domestic wares for manufacture; he wrote children's books which from 1841 were published as the *Home Treasury* and were illustrated by the leading illustrators of the day; he designed for manufacture children's toys that included building blocks, 'geometrically made, one-eighth of the size of real bricks; with Plans and Elevations', a 'Tessel-ated Pastime' that was 'formed out of Minton's Mosaics with Book of

Patterns', and, what may have been the first paintbox for children, a 'Colour Box for Little Painters', which, it boasted, held 'the ten best colours; Slabs and Brushes; Hints and Directions and Specimens of Mixed Tints'.[13] In his spare moments he contributed regularly to several periodicals, carrying on his various reforming campaigns in the press and by pamphlets.

One of his campaigns was for railway reform, and it was this that moved him into the next great phase of his life. John Scott Russell, his fellow campaigner, a railway engineer and the editor of the *Railway Chronicle*, introduced him to the Society of Arts in 1845. By 1846 he was on the committee, and he and Russell had been asked to mount the next exhibition. Russell had earlier put up £50 'for a series of models and designs for useful objects calculated to improve general taste', but not enough people had entered to permit the entries to be exhibited. Cole's and Russell's 1847 exhibition faced the same problem: manufacturers, fearing piracy of technique and style, did not want to have their products displayed. But Russell and Cole were determined to draw in enough entries for a good exhibition, and when they managed to attract over 20,000 visitors many manufacturers realized that the enormous potential for sales and promotion far outweighed the slight risk that industrial secrets might be stolen. The following year, instead of scratching around for entries, the Society was forced to devise rules that would limit the number of entries flooding in; this time, 70,000 people flocked to see what was new, what was different, what was interesting.

With that success under his belt, Cole moved on to his next campaign: the staging of another improving exhibition, but this time on a national scale. Albert was even less enthusiastic than he had been with Whishaw three years earlier, refusing either to become involved himself or to approach the government for any formal involvement. Cole was not daunted – Cole was *never* daunted. The RSA had highlighted the lack of good industrial and domestic design in the country in general, and from commercial manufacturers in particular. Now Cole became involved with a buoyant and popular campaign to promote new schools of design, to be run under government aegis, founding the *Journal of Design* to promote his cause. A parliamentary commission was set up, loaded with Cole-ites. By the kind of coincidence that Cole was pre-eminent in engineering, its plan – the reform of design and manufacture, and the role of the state in fostering that reform – was exactly what Cole intended his next, national, exhibition should deal with. In the meantime his 1849 RSA exhibition was even more successful than the previous two: Prince Albert agreed to present the prizes, and Queen Victoria gave sovereign approval by loaning an item for display.

For Cole's grander plan, however, the government, in the way of governments in all places and at all times, offered merely lukewarm enthusiasm – and even that only if private sponsors could be found to guarantee that the costs would be covered. But Albert, sensing the momentum, was now ready to come on board. A Royal Commission was established, with Albert as honorary president, and Cole – never one for half measures – widened the Exhibition's scope to include the entire world. Thomas Cubitt, the greatest speculative builder of his age, had given a rough estimate for the cost of realizing Cole's dream: £50,000 for the building costs and £5,000 for administrative costs, with another £20,000 needed for prize money.* A Mr Fuller put up £10,000 for prizes, and the Messrs Munday committed to underwriting the project in return for a percentage of the gate money.

While many discussed the elevating aspects of art, science and education, Cole was promising the businessmen of the City that 'some hundred thousand people [would] come flowing into London from all parts of the world by railways and steamboats to see the great exhibition', and that businesses would feel 'a direct and obvious benefit' from it. The secretary to the executive committee produced a list of those who could expect to profit: the arts, agriculture, manufacture and trade, 'whether as producers, distributors or consumers'. To win over popular opinion, advertising was actively used. The Royal Commission sent out placards reproducing a speech that the Conservative leader Lord Stanley – soon to be prime minister as the Earl of Derby – made in favour of the Exhibition, for public display. Posters were printed to put on railway-station platforms and in trains, and the commissioners arranged for favourable pieces to appear in the papers.[14] The kind of arguments that

---

* Thomas Cubitt (1788–1855) was the son of a carpenter. From small projects, his work expanded to encompass building housing on the Duke of Bedford's land in Bloomsbury, moving on to develop over 8 hectares for Earl Grosvenor in what ultimately became Belgravia, the most fashionable district of London; he also developed much of Pimlico, and more than 100 hectares south of the river, in Clapham. He came to the attention of Prince Albert when Osborne House, the royal family's home on the Isle of Wight, was to be rebuilt, although neither man can have imagined the family connection being sustained nearly two centuries later, when Albert's great-great-great-great-grandson, Prince Charles, the Prince of Wales, married Cubitt's descendant Camilla Parker Bowles.

are now used routinely for the promotion of tourism as an economy-booster were developed for the first time: that visitors would arrive, benefiting everyone from hotelkeepers to omnibus operators to food suppliers; that trade would be advertised both to home consumers and to audiences abroad; that, in effect, Britain would be displayed to the world as 'the emporium of the commercial, and mistress of the entire world', as the under-sheriff for London put it, rather more poetically than one might expect.[15]

Cole's plans for the Exhibition were growing ever larger, and enthusiasm from the public bodies to whom he spoke was increasing too. He soon realized that hundreds of small investors might fund the Exhibition more lavishly, while demanding far less – or no – overall control. He bought Munday's out for just over £5,000, and began to solicit the support of local communities across the nation. Thousands of donations began to flood in, with more than 400 groups of merchants, businessmen and industrialists gathering funds and organizing the exhibits to be sent from their own regions. Before 1849 was over, 3,000 subscribers had been signed up; another 3,000 followed less than two months later. Altogether, £522,179 was raised in this way.[16]

From the first, however, there was a tension over the aims of the Exhibition. There was no question that Albert saw the Exhibition as 'a great collection of works of industry and art', a place to demonstrate how technology had harnessed the natural world to create the Age of the Machine. With this in view, to show how man had become the master of nature, the committee elaborated an initial three-part outline of the subjects to be comprehended by the Exhibition – the raw materials of industry; the products manufactured from them; and the art used to beautify them – into a more formal thirty-section outline:

Sect. I: – Raw Materials and Produce, illustrative of the natural productions on which human industry is employed: – Classes 1 to 4

1. Mining and Quarrying, Metallurgy, and Mineral Products
2. Chemical and Pharmaceutical processes and products generally
3. Substances used as food
4. Vegetable and Animal Substances used in manufactures, implements, or for ornament

Sect. II: – Machinery for Agricultural, Manufacturing, Engineering, and other purposes and Mechanical Inventions, – illustrative of the agents which human ingenuity brings to bear upon the products of nature: – Classes 5 to 10

5. Machines for direct use, including Carriages, Railway and Naval Mechanisms
6. Manufacturing Machines and Tools
7. Mechanical, Civil Engineering, Architectural, and Building Contrivances
8. Naval Architecture, Military Engineering and Structures, Ordnance, Armour and Accoutrements
9. Agricultural and Horticultural Machines and Implements (exceptional)
10. Philosophical Instruments and Miscellaneous Contrivances, including processes depending on their use, Musical, Horological, Acoustical and Surgical Instruments.

Sect. III: – Classes 11–29. – illustrative of the result produced by the operation of human industry upon natural produce

11. Cotton
12 & 15 [*sic*]. Woollen and Worsted
13. Silk and Velvet
14. Flax and Hemp
16. Leather, Saddlery and Harness, Boots and Shoes, Skins, Fur and Hair
17. Paper, Printing and Bookbinding
18. Woven, Felted, and Laid Fabrics, Dyed and Printed (including Designs)
19. Tapestry, Carpets, Floor-cloths, Lace, and Embroidery
20. Articles of Clothing for immediate, personal or domestic use
21. Cutlery, Edge and Hand Tools
22. General Hardware, including Locks and Grates
23. Works in Precious Metals, Jewellery, &c.
24. Glass
25. China, Porcelain, Earthenware, &c.
26. Furniture, Upholstery, Paper Hangings, Decorative Ceilings, Papier Maché, and Japanned Goods
27. Manufactures in Mineral Substances, for Building or Decoration
28. Manufactures from Animal and Vegetable Substances, not being Woven or Felted
29. Miscellaneous Manufactures and Small Wares.

Sect. IV: Fine Arts: – Class 30

30. Sculpture, Models, and Plastic Art, Mosaics, Enamels, &c.
Miscellaneous objects of interest placed in the Main
Avenue of the Building, not classified.[17]

Others, however, saw that there was a danger in this kind of display of pure commodity – a danger that the Prince and many organizers had apparently missed. William Felkin, a hosiery and lace manufacturer, and exactly the kind of man who might have been expected to welcome commercial possibilities, was vehement. In his book *The Exhibition in 1851, of the Products and Industry of All Nations. Its Probable Influence upon Labour and Commerce* he said, 'This collection of objects from all countries, is not intended to be an Emporium for *masses* of raw and manufactured goods. These fill the granaries and factories, the warehouses and shops of the world ... This is not intended to be a place where goods are to be sold, or orders given; not a bazaar, fair, or mart of business; if so, it would be a perfect Babel. No one could possibly thread his way with comfort, through such a mazy labyrinth.'[18]

This was the crux: was the Great Exhibition to be a museum, an exploration of the technology that had created, and been created by, the Industrial Revolution? Or was it to be a supermarket, a display of all the goods, all the commodities, of the age? During the organizational stages the non-commercial, educational aspect seemed to be winning out.

The opening-day ceremonies were not promising to those in the audience who were interested in mercantilism rather than the social whirl. As Horace Greeley, founder and editor of the *New York Tribune*, and a staunch republican, noted:

> To have rendered the pageant expressive, congruous, and really a tribute to Industry, the posts of honor next the Queen's person should have been confided on this occasion to the children of Watt, of Arkwright and their compeers (Napoleon's *real* conquerors;) while instead of Grandees and Foreign Embassadors [*sic*], the heirs of Fitch, of Fulton, of Jacquard, of Whitney, of Daguerre, &c., with the discoverers, inventors, architects and engineers to whom the world is primarily indebted for Canals, Railroads, Steamships, Electric Telegraphs, &c., &c., should have been specially invited to swell the Royal cortege. To pass over all these, and summon instead the descendants of some dozen lucky Norman robbers ... any of whom would feel insulted by a

report that his father or grandfather invented the Steam Engine or Spinning Jenny, is not the fittest way to honor Industry.[19]

Lyon Playfair, one of the commissioners, and a confidant of Prince Albert, agreed with Greeley's views on the virtue of trade, if not with his republican interpretation: he warned that 'Industry, to which this country owes her success among nations, has never been raised to the rank of a profession. For her sons there are no honours, no recognized social position.'[20] He was determined that the Exhibition would alter that.*

This was all part of the series of underlying arguments about the aims of the Exhibition which was still grumbling on. With the arrival of factory production and mass markets, it was no longer clear that labour in itself retained the intrinsic moral value that had previously been attributed to it. Instead, the cheerleaders for the new age saw moral worth as now residing in the creation of goods for the masses. Industriousness and thrift had long been moral values. Now value for money and goods well manufactured joined them. To provide such items for the masses was in itself virtuous, thought Cole and his friends. They were providing the requisites for living a 'decent', a 'respectable' life – a life that, as closely as possible, both in commodities and in ideals, resembled the norms of the middle-class world. Not everyone agreed in the short term. The older view, that imbued labour itself with value, continued to hold sway for many. Hard work itself could still be considered to be worth more than the products that that work created. For example, a cabinet-maker, Charles McLean, had produced a mirror and console table for the Exhibition, but his local committee had rejected them as being of insufficient quality. He appealed, and Matthew Digby Wyatt, secretary to the executive committee, overruled the original decision, because, he thought, the 'getting up . . . was most spirited' – that is, the mirror and table had taken a lot of time and effort to create, and this outweighed the fact that the design and craftsmanship were of indifferent quality.[21] But the new philosophy, with new values – that of supply and demand, and what

* Lyon Playfair is almost as exhausting to contemplate as Cole: a chemist – the discoverer of nitro-prussides, a new class of salts – he was later Professor of Chemistry at Edinburgh University, Postmaster General, an MP, and Deputy Speaker of the House of Commons, interspersed with membership of the Royal Commission on Sanitation, advising on the ventilation of Buckingham Palace (his report was thought too alarming to be shown to Parliament), investigating the Famine in Ireland, producing research for the Geological Survey, advising on the promotion of technical education, sitting on the Royal Commission on cattle plague, and heading the commission inquiring into the civil service that finally replaced patronage with competitive examinations.

the market would bear – was in the ascendant. In the eighteenth century the political economist Adam Smith had seen production as the 'Wealth of Nations'; now the Great Exhibition saw the wealth of nations in 'the produce of all nations'. Product was taking over from process.

The Great Exhibition, 'Wot is to be': a large number of souvenirs were produced to commemorate the Great Exhibition in 1851. This handkerchief satirized visitors and organizers alike. Joseph Paxton, a landscape gardener as well as the architect of the Crystal Palace, is drawn as a watering-can on legs.

The Exhibition revolved entirely around the new industrial world, the possibilities that mass production had created. But the interpretation of that new world was still open. Was the Exhibition, therefore, about the value of work, or about the end result of that work – about how something was made, or about what could be purchased? Was it an ideal version of a museum, or was it a proto-supermarket? Was it education, or was it entertainment? What was it *for*? And for whom?

That the Great Exhibition was, in the widest possible sense, 'for everybody' could not be in doubt by the spring of 1851. There were souvenirs for sale across London: an endless stream of items reproducing images of the wildly popular Crystal Palace – items such as papier-mâché blotters, letter-openers and 'segar' (cigar) boxes. There were mementoes of specific moments, such as 'Lane's Telescopic View of the Opening of the Great Exhibition', a paper cut-out with a perspective view of the main avenue of the Crystal Palace, complete with interior fountain and one of the trees that had been preserved inside the structure (to much admiration from the public for the engineering feat involved). There were handkerchiefs printed with caricatures of the main participants, including 'Prince Allbut'. There were even gloves with maps of London printed on the palms, so that non-English-speaking visitors could have their route to the Crystal Palace traced out for them.[22] But it was far more than the souvenir market that latched on to the commercial possibilities of the Great Exhibition. There were just as many straightforwardly market-driven tie-ins as well, such as that promoted by Mr Folkard, 'Grocer, Tea Dealer and Italian Warehouseman', who advertised his new 'Celebrated Exhibition Coffee', blended from the beans of 'all nations', with labels covered with images of foreigners in national dress visiting the Exhibition.[23] Examples of extreme self-reflexivity included exhibitions inside the Crystal Palace which displayed images of nothing less than the Crystal Palace itself. The 'Cotton' section had a tablecloth 'in the centre [of which] is a view of the "Exhibition Building" . . . from the official design by Paxton, with emblematic borders representing Peace and Commerce with the nations; and a procession displaying the costumes of Europe, Asia, Africa, and America, *en route* to the Exhibition'.[24]

But most exhibits were more concerned to display their manufacturers' technical ingenuity. These were not the type of industrial processes that Albert had put so much faith in. They were not about 'Raw Materials and Produce, illustrative of the natural productions on which human industry is employed'. They were instead 'illustrative of the agents which human ingenuity brings to bear upon the products of nature'. Even here, Albert's interpretation of the word 'ingenuity' and that of the manufacturers were worlds apart. Albert's faith in the benefits conferred by the material world was interwoven with his belief in providence, social welfare and the moral value of labour. The manufacturers were more overtly concerned to show, through their command of technological innovation, how a new ideal domesticity might be formed, what goods were available that might be acquired, or at least aspired to. A 'sportsman's knife' produced by Joseph Rodgers and Sons of Sheffield had a mother-of-pearl handle and eighty blades, on which were etched views of the Crystal Palace, Osborne House, Windsor Castle, a railway bridge designed by George Stephenson, a boar hunt, a stag hunt and more. The same manufacturer also produced a 56-blade knife that was less than 2 centimetres long, a razor with a view of Arundel Castle on the blade, and cutlery with 150 blades and a clock. A vase by Waterston & Brogden showed Britannia flanked by 'Scotia' and 'Hibernia', who were in turn surrounded by four heads representing the four quarters of the globe, while under them diamonds in the shape of a rose, a thistle and a shamrock surrounded images of Britons, Romans, Saxons, Normans and

TRY THE CELEBRATED

EXHIBITION COFFEE,

Consisting of a Combination of the finest Coffees from all Nations.

Price 6d. & 8d. per ½lb. Canister

This beautiful compound of Coffee gives that rich Aroma, so highly appreciated by Continental Travellers, produces a beverage strong, bright, and clear – is rich and mellow in flavor, and must be appreciated by all the **Lovers of a Cup of good Coffee.**

This Coffee, being roasted on the most improved principle, which confines all that fragrance (which evaporates with the common roaster) so delightful and pleasing to the palate, and being packed Hot, both from Roasting and Grinding, in well-seasoned Canisters, which being perfectly air-tight, will keep for any reasonable length of time, or in any climate, without the least injury to its original Flavor; offering at once a Canister of the Finest Compound of Coffees ever imported into Europe.

FOLKARD,
Grocer, Tea Dealer and Italian Warehouseman,
No. 40, DRURY LANE,
OPPOSITE GREAT QUEEN STREET.

'Try the Celebrated Exhibition Coffee'. Many tradesmen linked their products to the Great Exhibition. This grocer and tea-dealer borrowed the Great Exhibition's slogan to promote a coffee made from the beans 'of all Nations'.

a picture of the Battle of Hastings; under these were a range of national heroes – Nelson, Wellington, Milton, Shakespeare, Newton, Watt – all crowned with laurel wreaths, while at the very bottom lurked Truth,

Prudence, Industry and Fortitude.[25] Such items were not goods that anyone needed – or would even think of buying. They were advertisements for the manufacturers, which was not at all what Albert had intended.

Other exhibits concentrated on innovations (many involving clothing) that offered relief from almost unimaginable situations: a safety hat for the prevention of concussion in case of a train crash; yachting outfits that had inbuilt flotation devices; corsets that 'opened instantaneously in case of emergency'; a 'Patent Ventilating Hat ... the principle of ventilating being to admit air through a series of channels cut in thin cork, which is fastened to the leather lining, and a valve fixed to the top of the crown, which may be opened and shut at pleasure to allow perspiration to escape'.* Some promised speed – a doctor's suit had a coat, waistcoat and trousers made in one piece, so in a night-time emergency the doctor might leap into them without any waste of time – while others went for economy – a 'duplexa' jacket reversed so that it could be worn as both a morning and an evening coat.[27] Yet even the most implausible-seeming gimmickry may have had some practical results. Henry Mayhew, the journalist and social reformer, dated the cage crinoline (the metal frame that supported what today are referred to as 'hoop' skirts) to 1851, rather than the more usual 1854–6, and at least one historian of fashion has suggested that it may have developed from a display model at the Great Exhibition.[28]

Further items on display that seemed primarily designed to display the manufacturers' originality included 'harlequin' furniture – furniture that served more than one purpose. One of the exhibits was a couch for a steamship which could be turned into a bed at night, while the base, made of cork, acted as a life raft should the worst came to the worst. Should the worst remain only imaginary, the couch had at one end 'a

---

* Hats throughout the century attracted a range of gimmicks, mostly attempts to keep the head cool while still wearing the de-rigueur heavy felt-fur or silk and plush hats. Among many ideas patented were the 'Bonafide Ventilating Hat' (1849), a hat with an air-flow ventilator, or one with movable shutters (1880s), and the 'Neoteric Ventilating Hat' (1851), which had a woven frame of manila grass or willow. Another group of patents involved pads to keep the hat away from the head, improving ventilation while also preventing the fabric from becoming soiled by contact with the wearer's hair oil: the 'Gutta Percha Hat' (1848) with rubber lining, which protected against both rain and perspiration; the 'Aeolian Hat' (1853), with an air pocket ('In this way a completely encircling air chamber is formed to embrace the head, and making an easy pleasant fit and also preventing the natural grease from the hair penetrating to the exterior of the hat'); and the 'Corrugated Ventilating Hat Antimacassar Pad' (1863).[26]

self-acting washing-stand . . . containing requisites for the dressing room and toilette', while the other end enclosed 'a patent portable water-closet'. Also on show were church pews connected to a pulpit by gutta-percha (rubber) pipes, to allow the hard of hearing to listen to the sermon; an 'expanding hearse'; a silver nose, for those missing a nose of their own; a vase made of mutton fat and lard; an oyster-shucking machine; and a bed which in the morning tilted its occupant straight into a waiting bath.[29]

Even items with more long-standing recognized functions were not necessarily prized primarily for those functions. Of the thirty-eight pianos in the *Official Descriptive and Illustrated Catalogue* to the Exhibition, most were put, logically enough, in the section 'Philosophical, Musical, Horological and Surgical Instruments', but two were listed under 'Furniture, upholstery', because their papier-mâché cases were considered more important than their sound. Even many of the pianos listed under musical instruments had gimmicks, often to do with the problem of finding space for a grand piano in an average-sized house. Some instruments were simply designated 'semi-grand', an acknowledgement that getting a 'real' grand piano into a terraced house was like squeezing a quart into a pint pot. Broadwood's, the most prestigious manufacturer (see pp. 355, 362–3), didn't worry about such matters – the company knew its customers, and it showed four pianos, all grand. But others, with less exalted clients, who therefore had less grand houses which did not permit equivalently grand pianos, could not be so cavalier. Pierre Erard, who listed himself as 'Inventor, Designer and Manufacturer', had a range of sizes to show: 'ornamented extra-grand; extra-grand with pedal keys; small grand . . . grand oblique [which from the picture looks like a decorated upright piano], ornamented in the Elizabethan style . . . grand cottage; reduced cottage . . .'

Others had more elaborate objects to show. George Frederick Greiner had a semi-grand 'constructed on the principle of the speaking-trumpet'; while Smyth and Roberts's piano was 'on the principle of the violincello'. John Brinsmead was far more worried about appearance than sound, and showed a piano whose 'case permits the instrument to be placed in any part of the room. Embroidered device in the central panel.' Another manufacturer enclosed his piano's workings in plate glass instead of wood; yet another highlighted the case's 'paintings of mother-of-pearl on glass'. Richard Hunt meanwhile joined in the general enthusiasm for harlequin furniture. His piano was 'a dining or drawing room table, [which] stands upon a centre block, or pedestal, and contains a piano-forte (opening with spring-bolts) on the grand principle, with a closet containing music composed by the inventor'. William Jenkins and Son had a 'registered expanding and collapsing pianoforte for gentlemen's yachts, the saloons of steam vessels' ladies cabins, &c.; only 13½ inches from front to back when collapsed'.[30] Other manufacturers concentrated on the music student: Robert Allison's piano had keys that 'alternated in colour, to show all the scales, major and minor, according to a single rule for each mood, founded on the place of the semi-tonic interval, which renders the seven notes to be touched for an octave of each of the other eleven scales, as evident as the scale of C'; while Robert Addison showed 'a transposing pianoforte. This piano will transpose music five semitones higher or lower than the written key.'[31]

Even at the time, there was a recognition that gadgetry had got out of hand: the *Illustrated London News* lamented the displays of 'a tissue [fabric] which nobody could wear; a carriage in which nobody could ride; a fireplace which no servant could clean if it were ever guilty of a fire; a musical instrument not fit for one in fifty thousand to play; endless inventions incapable of the duties imputed to them'.[32] This brought to the fore the question: were the exhibits designed to show the inevitable march forward to prosperity for all, or would it be more true to say that many exhibitors – and even more of the public – were seeing the Great Exhibition as an enormous advertising site?

The Official Descriptive and Illustrated Catalogue, reading which was as close as many visitors would get to thinking about the purpose of the fair, claimed in its introduction to be 'a book of reference to the philosopher, merchant and manufacturer'. Thus, in its own view, it was an educational tool – one that would give instruction to those exhibiting, and also to those many manufacturers in the same field who were not providing exhibits. The catalogue would show these people examples of the best work of their competitors, for them to strive towards. Then, for the many visitors, the catalogue would also explain the new world of technology and design, in layman's language, to improve their taste. By this means, the customers would be led to demand more of the manufacturers, and this heightened demand for quality would in turn improve the supply.

That was the idea. Carrying it out was another matter. The planning of the exhibits, both in the catalogue and in the actual display halls, had been a mixture of overlapping responsibilities shared between the centralized and local organizations. The local committees had selected the goods to be displayed from their regions or cities, with the barest guidance, in the form of a preliminary outline, from the commission. Once the items were chosen, how they were laid out, and the organizational structure of the hall, were entirely the province of the central body. The planners had originally wanted the Exhibition to represent a schematic re-creation of their thirty-section outline, laying out the state of industrial knowledge before the visitors in map-like form, walking them through the processes by which goods were transformed from raw material, via labour, to finished products. But both because it was not the commission which was making the initial selections and because of the technical requirements of the building, nothing but lip service could ultimately be paid to this didactic aim. The local committees had not necessarily chosen exhibitions that showed each of the processes, and, even when they had, there were power sources in only one part of the north-west axis of the halls, so all the industrial machinery had to be set up there. Then it was realized that the floor of the upper galleries could not bear the weight of heavy machinery, so they became the logical place for lightweight manufactured goods. The central axis or nave, as the main walkway of the Crystal Palace became known, ended up displaying most of the consumer commodities.

The crowds were required to follow specific routes and not able to wander at will. Rather in the way that out-of-town superstores such as Ikea process their customers past high-priced goods or seasonal overstocks, the route down the nave of the Crystal Palace ensured that all visitors passed by the highly finished consumer goods – the goods that were the most superficially attractive, the most entertaining, and the least educational. While the Exhibition stressed abundance and choice – in Prince Albert's words, 'The products of all quarters of the globe are placed at our disposal, and we have only to choose' – in fact, the choice had been made already, by the selection committee, by the display committee, and by those guardians of public order who decreed which route the consumers were to take. The visitor had only limited choice about where to go, or what to see.

Henry Mayhew's comic novel of the Great Exhibition, *1851: or, The Adventures of Mr and Mrs Sandboys and Family, Who Came Up to London to 'Enjoy Themselves', and to See the Great Exhibition*, opened with a paragraph describing the foreigners going round the Crystal Palace. It began, 'The Esquimaux had just purchased his new "registered paletot" [a loose, coat-like cape] of seal-skin . . . The Hottentot Venus had already added to the graceful ebullitions of nature, the charms of a Parisian *crinoline*.'[33] The humour here is of the simple 'look-at-the-funny-natives-encountering-civilization-for-the-first-time' type, but reading this passage today what is noticeable is Mayhew's unconscious acceptance of the purpose of the Exhibition: the display of fashionable commodities and their subsequent acquisition by the visitors. For it was acquisition that was beginning to hold sway at the Great Exhibition. Horace Greeley had already linked acquisition specifically to an increase in moral good: 'Not until every family shall be provided with a commodious and comfortable habitation, and that habitation amply supplied with Food and Fuel not only, but with Clothing, Furniture, Books, Maps, Charts, Globes, Musical Instruments *and every other auxiliary to Moral and Intellectual growth as well as to physical comfort*, can we rationally talk of excessive Production' (my italics).[34] Now it was not merely food and shelter that were considered necessities, but also education, the arts, and physical comfort more generally. Greeley saw clothes, furniture, books, maps and musical instruments all as necessities, all as 'auxiliaries' to 'Moral and Intellectual growth'.

This was a culmination of a gradual process. Over the previous century and a half there had been an enormous change in the way people lived. The architect John Wood, as early as 1749, had listed a number of improvements that had taken place in domestic interiors over the previous quarter-century – improvements that were taken for granted in homes of moderate prosperity by the time he wrote. Cheap floorboards and doors had been replaced by deal and hardwoods and the bare floors covered with rugs, while mahogany and walnut furniture had replaced the previously more customary oak;* rough plasterwork was now hidden behind elegant wood panelling; stone chimney-pieces were replaced by marble, and iron fixtures by brass; while cane and rush chairs were rejected in favour of upholstered leather and embroidered ones.[36] Yet even the low base of the 1720s that Wood was looking back to had already seen a big step forward to modern notions of comfort. Indeed, the word 'comfort' in the sense of physical and material well-being came

* Mahogany had first been imported from Central America in the 1720s, and Sir Robert Walpole immediately had seats for his commodes made from this new luxury material.[35]

It seemed to many that everyone in the country was planning to travel to London in the summer of 1851 to visit the Great Exhibition. George Cruikshank caricatured the results.

into use only in the last third of the eighteenth century. Previously 'comfort' had a spiritual and emotional meaning – succour, relief or emotional support. It was in the early nineteenth century that 'comfort' in the modern sense became commonplace, and yet only a few decades later Horace Greeley thought it natural to list it as a necessary component of a happy life.

It is hard, in our age of material possessions, and given the stereotypical 'overstuffed' image of the late Victorian period, to appreciate from what a bare minimum the acquisition of possessions began. As late as the 1690s, something as basic to us as a utensil to hold a hot drink – that is, a cup – was 'extremely rare' even in prosperous households. A mere thirty years later, by 1725, 'virtually all' of these households had some.[37] We don't really have any idea of what the poorest in the seventeenth century owned – they died leaving no records. But of those who had enough goods that it was considered worth drawing up an inventory on their deaths, it is illuminating to compare one James Cushman, who died in 1648, with the poorest man listed in the inventories of Sedgley, Staffordshire, ninety years later. Cushman left, in his kitchen, 'one small iron pott', 'a small scillite [skillet]' and 'one small brass scimer [skimmer]'. The deceased in Sedgley in 1739 owned, by contrast, a fire shovel, a coal hammer, a toasting iron, a bellows, a copper can, wooden furniture, a 'tun dish' or funnel, scissors, a warming pan, a brass kettle, bottles, earthenware, two iron pots, a pail, a 'search' or sieve, two old candlesticks, a kneading tub, two barrels, two coffers, a box, some trenchers, pewter, a brass skimmer, a brass basting spoon, an iron meat fork, a tin 'calender' or colander, and more.[38] A similar increase in the quantity of goods can be found among those with more disposable income: in a survey of 3,000 inventories taken on the death of the head of the household in more prosperous homes, in 1675 half owned a clock; by 1715, 90 per cent of households did.[39] This continuous growth in the number of possessions, this concern with the acquisition of goods for the home, was marked enough to be gently satirized in George Colman and David Garrick's 1784 play *The Clandestine Marriage*, in which one character announces, 'The chief pleasure of a country-house is to make improvements.'[40]

These are a few small examples of the marked increase in the number of possessions among all classes, from Garrick and Colman's country-house owners down to those who, in previous ages, would have inherited a few goods, possibly acquired a few more after much struggle, or simply done without. From 1785 to 1800 – a mere fifteen years – the rate of consumption of what had previously been considered luxuries and were now regarded as part of the ordinary necessities of life increased at more than twice the rate of population growth. In those fifteen years the population of England and Wales rose by 14 per cent, while over the same period the demand for candles grew by 33.8 per cent, for tobacco by 58.9 per cent and for spirits by a staggering (literally, perhaps) 79.9 per cent, while demand for tea soared by 97.7 per cent and for printed fabrics by an astonishing 141.9 per cent.[41] (For more on tea, see pp. 56–61.)

By the time of the Great Exhibition it was expected that one's quality of life – one's standard of living – could be judged by the number of possessions one owned, the number of things one consumed. This was an entirely new way of looking at things. The *Oxford English Dictionary*'s first citation for the phrase 'standard of living' dates from 1879. *Punch*, as always quick to spot a novelty, was already making fun of the idea by 1880. In a George du Maurier cartoon, an 'Æsthetic Bridegroom' looks at an oriental teapot, saying to his 'Intense Bride', 'It is quite consummate, is it not?' She responds rapturously, 'It is, indeed! Oh, Algernon, let us live up to it!'[42] Buying goods, owning goods – even living up to goods – were now virtues. Comfort was a moral good. A hundred years after Colman and Garrick wrote of the prosperous and their country houses, the *Illustrated London News* carried an advertisement for a piano, the purchase of which would make the 'home more attractive and save [the family from] more expensive and dangerous amusements'.[43] The advertisement could not be more explicit: buying commercially produced goods, in this case a piano, would make one's family life more entertaining, safer and, somehow, better. This was not simply an advertising conceit. Ford Madox Brown, a founder of the Pre-Raphaelite movement, told one of his patrons that, to be happy, 'much depends upon getting a house and adorning of a beautiful house'.[44] In 1876 the Revd William Loftie, in *A Plea for Art in the House*, expanded on this idea: there 'seems to be something almost paradoxical in talking about the cultivation of taste as a moral duty ... [but] if we look on the home here as the prototype for the home hereafter, we may see reasons for making it a sacred thing, beautiful and pleasant, as, indeed, we have no hesitation about making our churches'.[45] The cultivation of taste had become a 'moral duty', with the 'sacred' space, the shrine, epitomized by Paxton's Crystal Palace, which looked like a great shining box built to hold all the commodities that could ever be produced. All the manufactured items in the world seemed to be collected under its transparent lid. It resembled nothing so much as one of those glass domes that Victorians put on their mantelpieces to protect their most precious objects from dirt and dust.

Looking back, it is possible to see, from the beginning, that the tendency to understand the Great Exhibition as a collection of so many items for sale was constantly being repressed. In 1850 the *Westminster Review*, in one of many press reports about the forthcoming event, warned, 'The object of the Exhibition is the display of articles intended to be exhibited, and not the transaction of commercial business; and the Commissioners can therefore give no facilities for the sale of articles, or for the transaction of business connected therewith.' Yet even the author of this stark caution found it hard to remember, immediately adding approvingly that the Exhibition was a 'gathering together of the commercial travellers [salesmen] of the universal world, side by side with their employers and customers, and with a showroom for their goods that ought to be such as the world has never before beheld'.[46] To attempt to block such commercial thoughts and concentrate visitors' minds on the displays' educational qualities, the organizers forbade the listing of prices, direct advertisements of goods, or any other form of overt selling.*

But, in a way no one could have foreseen, the lack of prices made everything appear much more available. No one looked at a display and thought, 'That is out of my reach.' Instead, everything became acquirable in the imagination, because nothing was for sale in reality. Everything could be dreamed of. At the same time, exhibitors, who had their own agendas, became ingenious in finding ways around the price ban as the fair continued. 'Explanatory' notes were handed out and, just coincidentally, were printed on the back of price lists; trade cards and advertising cards were distributed widely. Others outside the commissioners' control abetted this urge to price the price-less: many press articles speculated on the value of goods when describing them – it seemed to be a reflex

---

* It has been suggested that this lack of pricing was one of the reasons so many exhibits focused on technical ingenuity. If the main selling point of an object was that it was half the price that was usually charged, there was no point in showing it, without a price, at the Crystal Palace.

response to the display. As Walter Benjamin later commented, 'The world exhibitions erected the universe of commodities.'[47]

For the first few weeks of the Great Exhibition, these price-less goods were examined by the prosperous alone. Albert had been insistent that the working class should be able to attend, that it was this group who would benefit in particular. The prices of admission, however, were set at exorbitant levels. Season tickets were £3 3s. for men, £2 2s. for women, and only season-ticket holders could go on the first day; second- and third-day tickets cost £1 each, while day tickets for the rest of the first month were 5s. each. It was not until 26 May, nearly a full month after the opening, that for the first time 'shilling days' came into force, with the following Friday reduced even further, to 6d. But on Saturdays – most workers' half-day off – the price was pushed back up, to 2s. 6d. Many exhibitors wanted this exclusivity extended even further, with shilling days postponed until July – or never. They feared that the middle and upper classes who had thronged the aisles in the first weeks would disappear, not to be seen again, if they were forced to share their viewing space with the lower orders. But Prince Albert and Cole prevailed, and shilling days from the end of May remained.

As the end of the month approached, the big question of the day became, what would happen when the admission charge was lowered to let the working classes in? The gulf between the comfortable middle classes and even the respectable working classes was enormous. In the previous three-quarters of a century the middle class had become increasingly fearful of their social and economic inferiors, a situation brought about by the great political upheavals of the time. The Gordon Riots of 1780, the fall of the Bastille in 1789, the Peterloo Massacre of 1819, the agitations that surrounded the Reform Act of 1832, and the Chartist riots; the failed harvests of the 'hungry forties'; and, only three years in the past, the Europe-wide revolutions of 1848: all had merged to form a nebulous image of the great mass of workers biding their time, waiting to turn into 'King Mob'. This was how *The Times* referred to the working class on 2 May, the day after the opening of the Great Exhibition – the day referred to by Queen Victoria as 'the *greatest* day in our history, the *most beautiful* and imposing and *touching* spectacle ever seen, and the triumph of my beloved Albert'.[48] *The Times* was not so confident. Surely these bogeymen would overrun the grounds, given half a chance? Mayhew despaired of those like *The Times* who were stoking fear: 'For many days before the "shilling people" were admitted to the building, the great topic of conversation was the probable behaviour of the people. Would they come sober? will they destroy things? will they want to cut their initials, or scratch their names on the panes of the glass light-houses?'[49] *Punch*, in 'Open House at the Crystal Palace', also (unusually) championed the workers at the expense of the middle classes, setting up 'Young Mob' as 'the better-behaved son of a wild and ignorant father': 'Am I not seen with my wife and children wondering at MR. LAYARD's Nineveh Marbles [in the British Museum]* – wondering quietly, and I will add, if you please, reverently? Have I, in fact, chipped the nose of any statue? Have I wrenched the little finger from any mummy? Have I pocketed a single medal?'[50] Even those who did not fear that riot and mayhem would arrive with the workers thought that financial ruin certainly would. The *Illustrated London News* warned that 'the gay, glancing, fluttering tide of bonnets and ribbons, and silks, and satins, and velvets', would vanish, with 'the blank . . . filled up by no adequate substitute of meaner, or coarser, or more commonplace material'.[51] These publications were more interested in their thesis than in giving the shilling days a chance: this particular piece was published after only the third shilling day.

It is worth pausing for a moment at the admission charge of 1s. At this price, and with the less expensive catalogue, the *Popular Guide*, priced at 2d., only the upper levels of the working class – the artisans, the master craftsmen, the clerks (who for the most part would have identified themselves with the lower middle classes) – could possibly have afforded to visit the grounds without financial assistance. For most of the rest of the working classes, having 1s. to spend on a day's leisure was unimaginable – and even that price was only for those who lived in walking distance: for the others, transport, accommodation and food would push the day's expenditure to one or two weeks' entire earnings. But the mass of workers was so mysterious to their economic superiors that it was as though the 1s. charge would unleash not just factory operatives and manual labourers, but also the feared 'navvies'† who were building the railroads and, even worse, the masses of the unemployed and the

* For more on Layard, see p. 199.
† Navvies (from 'navigators') were originally the labourers who built the canals. By the 1850s, 'navvy' was shorthand for a labourer on the railways in particular. Navvies had a well-earned reputation for ferocious violence and drunkenness.

unemployable, wild hordes of them sweeping across the plains of Hyde Park. *The Times* warned that 'Summer excursion trains will bring the artisans and mechanics of the north in upon London like an inundation.'[52] The Duke of Wellington thought that at least 15,000 men – he meant soldiers – would be needed to keep order. Members of the Exhibition commission met with the directors of the railway companies to arrange that reduced excursion fares would be restricted to benefit-club subscribers and those belonging to working-class self-improvement clubs such as the Mechanics' Institutes (see below). (However, the agreement did not hold: by February the London and North-Western Railway and the Midland Railway companies had both agreed to supply excursion fares to non-club members, but they took care not to publicize this change – at least at first.)[53] This arrangement, while it stood, had the effect of pushing those who had not previously belonged to such a group into one, in order to be able to have access to railway tickets at affordable prices.

In fact the numbers already belonging to some form of club, whether it was a social group, a benefit club, a sick club or an educational or self-improvement group, were enormously high. Friendly societies or benefit clubs were among the most common clubs for workers. Matthew Boulton, a manufacturer, factory-owner and partner with James Watt in the improvement and manufacturing of the early steam engine, was one of the first to see the value to an employer in setting up an insurance club. From the early 1770s his employees received benefits on illness, accident or death, having made contributions as a percentage of their earnings – from ½d. a week for those earning 2s. 6d. to 4d. for those earning £1. When they were ill they received payments in inverse proportion to their contributions, so that those earning the least received the most financial assistance – about four-fifths of their weekly wage for those employees with the lowest incomes. But if the illness or incapacity stemmed from 'drunkenness, debauchery, quarrelling or fighting', part of the first ten days' payment was withheld. Boulton as well as his workers benefited from this scheme: by having some financial support in hard times, fewer ill or injured workers ended up being supported 'on the parish', which kept the poor rate down, and Boulton's workers were more likely to stay with him, because if they moved on they would lose the benefit of the contributions they had already paid in.[54]

Even without the participation of enlightened employers, mutual-support clubs were becoming common. The 1793 Friendly Societies Act enabled clubs to raise 'separate funds for the mutual relief and maintenance of the ... members in sickness, old age and infirmity'.[55] One estimate suggests that in 1801 there were at the very least 7,200 friendly societies in England and Wales, which together numbered about 648,000 members. In London at least 40 per cent of the working population belonged to a friendly society, while in some new industrial regions the figure was even higher: in Oldham, Lancashire, 50 per cent of all adult males belonged to one of the fifteen societies flourishing there. In Scotland there were nearly 400 friendly societies by 1800. Ireland took longer to develop the concept: in 1800 there were only 7 societies that we know about today, but by 1831 the number had shot up to 281, with half centred in Dublin.[56]

Clubs that were not mainly about financial aid were also popular: working men's libraries, groups to discuss politics or literature, or to buy books. A club in Sunderland met regularly to discuss old English ballads; the members were saving jointly towards the collected volumes of reprints of Early and Middle English texts published by the Early English Text Society. The members consisted of a cork-cutter, two woodcarvers from the docks, a watchmaker, an engine-fitter and 'a painter of photographs'.*[57]

The largest, and most widespread, self-improvement groups were the Mechanics' Institutes. The first one was set up in 1824 in London, with 1,500 members paying 1 guinea each – clearly, a group of high-earning skilled workers and artisans. By 1850 there were 702 Institutes across the country, but by now they had mostly been taken over by the middle classes: the upper middle classes at the administrative end, and the lower middle classes – clerks and shopworkers – as members. The original expectation had been that these institutes would increase the skills and scientific and technical knowledge of manual labourers by offering access to books and pamphlets in reading rooms, and to continuing education via evening lectures. This would produce a more highly skilled and useful workforce, which would be a great benefit to employers. But fairly swiftly it was discovered that the lectures were too theoretical, and the workers found little practical incentive to attend after a long day's work. Instead,

---

* The Early English Text Society's founder, Frederick Furnivall (1825–1910), would have been thrilled. He was closely involved with adult education, teaching evening classes at the Working Men's College when it opened in London in 1854.

lectures that gave some form of recreation were preferred, and were much better attended. In its initial period of worker education, from 1835 to 1842, the Manchester Athenaeum held 352 lectures, of which 173 were on the 'physical and mental sciences'; in 1842–9, out of 394 lectures, science featured in only 81. Nationally, of 1,000 lectures held at 42 institutions in 1851, only 340 were on science, while 572 were classed as literature – although literature here had a fairly broad definition, essentially meaning anything that was not science or music. Included in the list of literature lectures were topics such as 'the funeral rites of various nations, the habits and customs of the Eskimos, the life, death and burial of Mary, Queen of Scots, the games of Greece, the theosophy of India, the sons of Noah, and . . . "Are the Inhabitants of Persia, India, and China of Japhetic or Shemitic [*sic*] Origin?"' There were also twenty-three lectures on Shakespeare, and over the next years many lectures gradually turned into readings from favourite authors, and sometimes simply readings of plays, which was a way of getting around the general disapproval of the theatre by many Dissenters and some Anglicans (see pp. 274–5).[58]

The Institutes began to hold exhibitions and social events more generally. The earliest exhibitions, held by the Manchester Mechanics' Institute from 1837, were in the mould of the lectures on science and technical innovation – exhibitions of 'machinery, industrial products, scientific apparatus and works of art'.[59] Over the next five years, Manchester held four exhibitions, and drew over 200,000 visitors in total.[60] From 1838 to 1840 the various Institutes held at least fifty exhibitions across the country. But almost immediately the emphasis altered, exactly as it had with the lectures. By 1846 the Manchester Institute was showing more than machinery, with exhibitions of paintings by Turner, Benjamin West, Landseer and Charles Eastlake. The urge for entertainment rather than education was nationwide: in 1842 the Institute in York saw working-class membership increase as excursions and social events were added to the calendar; by 1844 the Huddersfield members expected a gala, excursions, exhibitions and tea parties. Most of the other groups had moved in a similar direction, with a general leaning towards culture and recreation. And recreation included travel.

By the time of the Great Exhibition, excursion travel was already a regular feature of the landscape, even if it was the still-exciting exception rather than the run-of-the-mill norm. In 1830 the first passenger railway, the Liverpool and Manchester Railway, had carried sightseers out to the Sankey Viaduct for 5s. (instead of the standard fare of 8s.) only two weeks after the line was opened. A few days later it took Manchester passengers to the Liverpool Charity Festival, and within a year it had made an arrangement with an entrepreneur to carry 150 members of a Sunday-school group from Manchester to Liverpool and back for 40 per cent of the regular fare. The various Mechanics' Institutes quickly saw the benefits of organized cut-rate travel: the Manchester Institute arranged a trip to Liverpool for its members in 1833; in 1840 a group went from Leeds to York; by 1845 the Leeds-to-Hull excursion group was so large that a train with forty carriages was needed, possibly the first of the 'monster' trains that so captured the imagination of the Victorian public.[61] ('Monster' was a favourite Victorian adjective, with monster trains, monster shops and monster exhibitions.) Very swiftly holiday travel took a great share of the excursion market. In 1846 Blackpool got its own railway line; four years later, up to 10,000 visitors a week were pouring into the town. Numbers continued to increase, while fares continued to tumble: in 1844 the London and South Western Railway began to run Easter excursions from Southampton to London at 7s. return; by 1850 the same trip cost 5s.[62]

When it came to the Great Exhibition itself, the railways initially had not been much interested in excursion business – there was a general underestimating of the numbers of the working classes who would wish to attend. As late as January 1851, less than four months before the opening, the trade magazine *Herapath's Railway and Commercial Journal* was warning railway companies against recklessly increasing their rolling stock against a demand it thought could not possibly materialize.[63]

Thomas Cook, whose excursions to the Crystal Palace were later inextricably interwoven into his myth, actually became involved in bringing visitors to London in 1851 by accident. Though subsequently to personify the whole range of possibility that was excursion travel, Cook arrived, surprisingly, rather late in the day. He had entered the field only in 1841, when he arranged with the Midland Counties Railway to have an excursion train put at the disposal of his temperance group. By 1846 he had extended his tours beyond their initial Leicestershire borders, and was organizing excursions to Scotland. So successful were his tours that in 1850 he was thinking of expanding even further, by taking groups to the Holy Land. However, a temperance friend in London advised him against this, warning that there were 'no railways, coaches, or even public roads' there.[64] He suggested that the USA might be better: steamers had been making regular crossings of the Atlantic from 1838, and the east coast of America was now just 12½ days away from Liverpool. So Cook set off for Liverpool to see if he could interest the steamship companies in the same type of arrangement he had been negotiating with the railways, giving him discounted fares in exchange for guaranteed numbers. But he managed to get only as far as Derby. There he met Joseph Paxton, the architect of the Crystal Palace, and his friend John Ellis, who was attempting to stabilize the Midland Railway Company after the crooked dealings of George Hudson, 'the Railway King', had threatened to destroy it and several other companies. Ellis had a vested interest in increased traffic on his railway – especially since he was one of the businessmen about whom *Herapath's* would shortly warn: the Midland had ordered a hundred new third-class carriages to bring working-class passengers to the Exhibition. Paxton also had financial links to the railways. From the other side, Cook approved of the educational aspects of the Great Exhibition, the idea of 'rational recreation' it promoted, and he was further taken by the fact that the Crystal Palace was to be 'dry'.* (There were other aspects that pleased him equally: it was closed on Sundays, religious tracts were distributed throughout the fair, there was a Bible depot, and, at the request of Lord Shaftesbury, all the nude statues were to be respectably covered.)[65]

Cook came to an agreement with the Midland to bring them his excursionists for a fee that he referred to delicately as 'several shillings' per head, instead of his usual percentage of the fare paid. In return for this, the excursionists would get a return ticket, with accommodation in London (including 'a substantial meat breakfast') for another 2s. (plus an extra 1d. if they wanted their boots cleaned); if that was too expensive, accommodation at 1s. could be found in dormitories set up on ships moored at Vauxhall Bridge.[66] Accommodation had been a major preoccupation for the planners. They were uncertain how many working-class visitors would travel to the capital, but, with the fear of the mob that was pervasive, any number seemed to be a threat and was regarded as a public-order concern. A Home Office official had been asked by the

* During the twenty-four weeks of the Exhibition, 1,092,337 bottles of soda water, lemonade and ginger beer were sold.

Royal Commission to look into how best 'respectable and reasonable' lodgings in London could be provided. The Home Office was pleased to comply, because it was anxious that 'arrangements should in themselves conduce to the maintenance of good order and regularity without the appearance of any ostensible precautions, and that they should offer such facilities as will induce the working classes to follow, for their own advantage, the course pointed out'.[67]

Because the success of the Exhibition was still uncertain, not much more than worrying was done by the commission. Others, however, stepped in to the breach, just as Cook and assorted excursion agents were doing despite the unenthusiastic railway companies. The main accommodation organizer became John Cassell, a temperance lecturer and the proprietor of a coffee house in Fenchurch Street. (The provision of tea and coffee was common among those involved in the temperance movement.) Cassell had been the publisher of the *Teetotal Times* from 1846, as well as printing other journals and pamphlets relating to radical politics, Free Trade and universal suffrage, and in 1850 his new periodical the *Working Man's Friend* had been launched. With the coming of the Great Exhibition, Cassell saw a gap in the market that he could fill both to the benefit of the working man and also for the promotion of his journal: the creation of an artisan lodging-house register. He distributed (he claimed) 100,000 forms to lodging houses, had each one that responded inspected, and then charged their owners 2*s*. 6*d*. to register with him (of which 1*s*. 6*d*. was paid as the tax on advertisements). All lodging houses that wanted to be included in the register were required to conform to strict rules: lodging was 2*s*. for a double bed, with boot-cleaning thrown in; a breakfast of tea or coffee and bread and butter had to be available, and could cost no more than 9*d*.; if bacon or ham or a kipper were added, then 1*s*. could be charged. Cassell published a general register that listed the establishments that met his requirements, and a classified register that had the lodging houses listed by religious affiliation. Either could be obtained by sending six penny stamps by post, and both advertised the *Working Man's Friend*.[68]*

---

* Cassell went on to become the publisher of *Cassell's Magazine* and *Cassell's Illustrated Family Paper*, plus many other journals (see p. 157), as well as the first British edition of *Uncle Tom's Cabin*. However he lacked business instincts, and his company was soon taken over by others, although his skills as a publishing entrepreneur were highly regarded, and the house of Cassell's in various guises has survived into the twenty-first century.

It was commercial activities of this nature that made the railways feel that perhaps there *was* money to be made in transporting the working classes to London for the fair. Very swiftly, they went from almost complete apathy to ruthless competition. A price war broke out between the Midland Railway and the Great Northern – at one point the battle became so overheated that a steam engine was hijacked by the opposition. In order to give its new Bradford-and-Leeds-to-London line a boost, the GNR promoted 5s. return fares. The Midland could not match that and still give Cook his 'several shillings'. He agreed to tear up the agreement, which in the long term was very good business on his part, as long afterwards the Midland continued to give him preferential rates when other excursion agents began to set up in his territory.

Cook's son John, aged seventeen, acted as his advance agent. He and others travelled to towns across Yorkshire and the Midlands to publicize the possibilities of travel to London and the Great Exhibition for working people. They distributed handbills, held meetings – often with a band playing outside a mill or factory on pay day, to attract a crowd – and helped to set up savings clubs for the fares and accommodation. These subscription clubs were crucial to the success of the Exhibition. Mayhew's novel *1851* has the villagers of Buttermere paying into the 'Travelling Association for the Great Exhibition of 1851 . . . for months past, subscribing their pennies with the intention of having their share in that general holiday', with the local squire acting as club treasurer.[69] Other groups that came, supported by various savings methods, included parishes led by their clergymen, soldiers brought by their commanding officers, schools and Sunday schools by their teachers, and factory and mill workers by their employers. In Maldon and Braintree, the shops in both towns closed for a day to allow the entire towns' populations to travel en masse to London. And all of them seemed to go by rail. The Great Western increased its passenger numbers by 38.3 per cent over the period; the London and South Western by 29.9 per cent; the London and Blackwall by 28.5 per cent; the South Eastern by 23.8 per cent; and the London and North-Western by 22.6 per cent. The last of these claimed that, for the duration of the fair, it had carried over three-quarters of a million passengers, and that 90,000 of these were excursionists, in 145 special excursion trains, travelling from the north for 5s. return.[70]

While these excursionists were evidently not rich, they brought home to the manufacturers, the industrialists, a new economic truth. It had become increasingly apparent over the previous half-century that there was as much money – if not more – to be made from large numbers of relatively low-income consumers as there was from the tiny numbers of high-earners. The concept of the mass market was taking shape, personified by the Great Exhibition. This was in some ways an oddity, since the fair itself was not a particularly good example of mass production. The 300,000 panes of glass used in the Crystal Palace were not machine made, but instead were each individually hand-blown,[71] although it is true that the very nature of the building, with its innovative prefabricated sections that could be made off-site and then assembled, looked towards the future of mass production. For the moment the mass market centred around the many linked products that were appearing without the formal imprimatur of the Great Exhibition. Cassell produced *The Illustrated Exhibitor*, published at 2*d.* per part, issued weekly, which when completed made up a four-volume illustrated survey of the Exhibition, either as a souvenir of a visit or for those who had not managed to get to London.* Within a month of the first part appearing, Cassell was selling 100,000 copies, giving him a monthly turnover of nearly £3,500.[72] This was only one of many works published to catch on to – and cash in on – the excitement of the fair. There were numerous guides published to coincide with the opening of the Exhibition, by anyone who chose to enter the field. Cassell himself published *The London Conductor*, whose subtitle made it pretty clear at whom it was aimed: *Being a Guide for Visitors to the Great Industrial Exhibition, through the principal portions of the metropolis; including a brief history and description of the palaces, parks, churches; government, legal, and commercial buildings; bridges, statues, museums, hospitals, club-houses, theatres, and streets of London; and the remarkable places in its vicinity* – basically, anyone arriving in London for the first time.† It cost 9*d.*, and went through two editions almost immediately, despite not being particularly accurate. A third edition, without illustrations, came out with corrections and a reduced cover price; a fourth edition, with the pictures reinstated, was needed by September.[73] (Cassell, who rarely missed a trick when it came to marketing,

---

* It was clear from the price that he was aiming at a working-class mass market: the *Illustrated London News*, which featured the Exhibition heavily in its pictures all summer long, sold for 6*d.* an issue.

† Only 200 words were given to the Exhibition itself, and it suggested that four hours would be plenty for the visitor to 'do' the fair.

advertised in the first edition the forthcoming '*Le Conducteur de Londres*, prix 1½ schelling'.)

Far more than just guidebooks found a useful commercial link to the Exhibition. There were comic stories of rustics up from the country, like the, to modern eyes, gloomily unfunny *Jimmy Trebilcock; or, the Humorous Adventures of a Cornish Miner, at the Great Exhibition, What he Saw and What he didn't See*. There were political satires, using the Exhibition for parody purposes, such as *Mr Goggleye's Visit to the Exhibition of National Industry to be Held in London on the 1st of April [sic] 1851*. There were dozens – if not dozens of dozens – of children's books describing the fair, such as *The Crystal Palace: A Little Book for Little Boys*, and *Little Henry's Holiday at the Great Exhibition* (which devoted a remarkable amount of space to the Exhibition's finances, taking an entire page to list ticket prices, and even calculating how much money had been made by the time the book went to press in early June – £137,697 13*s*., the author estimated), and *Fireside Facts from the Great Exhibition* (which appears to have lifted material wholesale from *Little Henry's Holiday*). These were followed by books of educational intent, or instant reminiscence, appearing within months: *Lectures on the Results of the Great Exhibition of 1851; What I Saw in London, or, Men and Things in the Great Metropolis; Frolick & Fun, or What Was Seen and Done in London in 1851; Glimpses and Gatherings during a voyage and visit to London and the Great Exhibition in the summer of 1851*; and many many more.

New forms of advertising also appeared. W. H. Smith, a newspaper distributor, had rented a bookstall at the London and North-Western Railway's Euston station in 1848. In the year of the Great Exhibition he obtained a monopoly of all the London and North-Western's station bookstalls and he also began to rent out space for advertisements on the platforms, which, with the hordes of visitors pouring through the stations heading for Hyde Park, began to seem like a paying proposition.* Soon everyone was advertising individual products through references to the Exhibition. Samuel Brothers' flyer was headed 'The Great Exhibition in London, High Art! High Success!! and High Principle!!!', with, underneath, a list of items of ready-made clothing and their prices, together with an image of the brothers' shopfront, cropped in tightly to make it look like a display case at the fair.[74]

* For more on advertising, see pp. 130–37; for W. H. Smith and newspaper distribution, pp. 145–6; for W. H. Smith and railway bookstalls, pp. 191–2.

The visitors to London were presented with the obvious commercial link between the goods on display at the Great Exhibition and those on display in shop windows. But they were also presented with another link – between the Great Exhibition as a fair, a source of entertainment, and the shows of London. It was not as though there was no other form of entertainment in London, for both rich and poor, for those looking for education and for those out only for amusement. London *always* had entertainment (see Chapter 7), but in the summer of 1851 it particularly revolved around the Great Exhibition. The Zoological Gardens in Regent's Park made sure that its new buildings would be ready in time for the influx of visitors, and highlighted the just finished outdoor tank for its hippopotamus, and two new aviaries. (Attendance soared to a record 677,000 that year.) James Wyld, an MP and map-seller, bought a ten-year lease on the plot of land in the centre of Leicester Square, where he built a rotunda, eighty-five feet in diameter, with a sixty-foot globe on top. A series of staircases led the visitor up to platforms from which illustrations of various geographic phenomena could be viewed – volcanoes, ice floes and so on. The Polytechnic Institute advertised a series of lectures on 'all the MOST INTERESTING DEPOSITS at the GREAT EXHIBITION'.[75]

Theatre did not lag behind in shows that were linked to the Great Exhibition. James Robinson Planché, playwright and creator of theatrical extravaganzas (see pp. 308–9), merged the two most popular shows of the summer, the Exhibition itself and Wyld's Great Globe, to produce *Mr Buckstone's Voyage Round the Globe (in Leicester Square). A Cosmographical, Visionary Extravaganza, and Dramatic Review, in One Act and Four Quarters*. Mr Buckstone was in fact the real-life manager of the Haymarket Theatre, where *Mr Buckstone's Voyage* was being produced; to add further layers of interleaved fantasy and reality, the opening scenes were set, according to the published script, '[In] FRONT OF THE THEATRE ROYAL, HAYMARKET'. The audience then watched as 'Mr Buckstone determines to Circumnavigate the Globe, and gives his reasons for so doing', as the scene shifted to the 'Foot of the Staircase in Wyld's Model of the Earth, Leicester Square. Mr Buckstone, as a preparatory step to a Voyage round the Globe, visits the Model to obtain an insight into the subject and – sleeps upon it.' The viewers then followed the dreaming Mr Buckstone around the world, where he saw many marvellous sights, including 'The "Ripon" steamer, with the Grenadiers on board, on her passage to Malta,

James Wyld, an M.P. and cartographer, opened his Great Globe in the middle of Leicester Square to coincide with the Great Exhibition. Nearly 20 metres high, it displayed a plaster relief of the earth at a scale of half a centimetre to the kilometre, as well as samples of Wyld's own maps and globes.

saluted by a French brig', various battles, 'A GRAND ORIENTAL SPEC-TACLE', which introduced a ballet, a 'WISE ELEPHANT OF THE EAST', 'Chinese Magicians', and an 'Interview with the Esquimaux from Cumberland Straits and the Adelaide Gallery', ending with a cheery scene of a 'violent "Struggle for Gold" by the Theatres in general. Awful Catastrophe. End of Mr Buckstone's Golden Dream'.[76]

With this kind of competition, it was not hard to imagine that the shilling visitors might find better things to spend their money on than a teetotal, didactic piece of rational recreation. But, instead of the *Illustrated London News*'s picture of desolation, to the fair there came hundreds of thousands of the 'respectable' working classes – members of Sunday-school groups, of orderly church and chapel groups, of self-improvement clubs, of Mechanics' Institutes; master craftsmen and artisans and their families – endless streams of all those who could afford to pay the 10s. or so that a 'shilling day' visit entailed (1s. admission, a travel bill of 5s. or more, accommodation at 2s., plus the cost of food for the duration of the trip). Attendance on shilling days averaged between 45,000 and

60,000 people; by the end of the summer, 100,000 were passing through the gates daily. In total, 6 million visitors came to the Crystal Palace; as many as 5 million may have come by train, with 1 million of them on excursion fares. Thomas Cook arranged for the transport of 165,000 excursionists, or nearly 3 per cent of the total, including one single excursion train carrying 3,000 children.[77]

And the fears of the upper classes remained only that – fears. The crowds were in fact orderly, respectful, well-behaved – all that could have been hoped for, but was not remotely expected. *The Times* was forced to eat its words, and after three days acknowledged that, instead of being 'King Mob', the shilling admissions were well dressed and orderly members of society, and a credit to the burgeoning nation of commerce.[78] The volatile mob had become the sedate consumer. The age of the machine had brought with it the triumph of the masses – and the mass market.

2

'A Nation of Shopkeepers': The Eighteenth-Century Shop

NEW SHOPS, BIGGER SHOPS, more heavily stocked shops, speciality sellers, brightly lit windows, fixed prices instead of bargaining, advertisements everywhere – it seemed that the nineteenth century brought nothing but change to how people had shopped for centuries. Yet all these things, and many more, arrived not in the nineteenth century, but in the eighteenth. Shops and shopping had long been undergoing a permanent revolution when the Victorian age had just begun. Dr Johnson had understood this by the 1750s. Shopping was no longer an action rooted in necessity, he wrote, but was now a pastime, a leisure activity: 'He that had resolved to buy no more, feels his constancy subdued . . . He is attracted by rarity, seduced by example and inflamed by competition.'[1] Johnson was talking about fashionable shops in fashionable parts of London. But the daily purchases by the lesser folk were fuelled by the same desires, and it was their mass purchasing power that drove the century-long explosion of shop development.

Much of what we know today about shops in the eighteenth century comes either from the higher strata of life or is sketchy at best. It is, however, becoming increasingly clear that the extent and development of shops across the country has been badly underestimated, owing in the main to poor survival of records. For example, as late as 1822–3 *Pigot's London and Provincial New Commercial Directory* listed no shopkeepers of any sort in Manchester. The obvious reaction, of course, is that this simply could not have been true; but the scale of the directory's oversight was made clear by the historian Roger Scola, who identified 400 small food shops in the city in the 1810s alone – and that takes into account neither the many many more shops for which no evidence has survived, nor any shops that sold non-food items, which were outside the terms of his survey.[2] Furthermore, it is becoming clearer that, just as the number of shops has been underestimated, so too has the sophistication of retail systems been equally misunderstood. In fact the number of shops, the type of shops, and the quantity and quality of goods stocked, as well as the methods used to sell them, all began to develop in the eighteenth century.

Until recently it has been suggested that Britain had about 50,000 shops in the eighteenth century, but, as two recent historians have written, that number has long been accepted not because there was any concrete evidence to back it up, but merely because of a lack of evidence to the contrary.[3] Basically, when trade directories and censuses began to appear in the early 1800s they showed few shops; by the 1850s there were large numbers, so many have assumed a gradually rising curve. Instead, it is now looking more likely that there was a fall in the number of shops in the late 1790s and early 1800s, and that the sharp rise in the next decades was a rebound from a temporary dip, not a stately rising progression.[4] During the Seven Years War (1756–63) the government had considered imposing a tax on shops, and the Excise conducted a survey in order to calculate possible revenue. It identified 141,700 shops in England and Wales with a base income high enough to permit taxation.* This is probably as close as we are ever going to get to an accurate number. If we assume that the survey was, if anything, under-reporting the number of shops of moderate income, and ignoring entirely the smaller shops, it still gives a ratio of 1 shop per 43.3 people throughout the country.

Most of the shops in the survey, however, were located in the more prosperous south, with far fewer shops per head of population north of a line drawn from Lincolnshire to Leicestershire, Warwickshire, Gloucestershire and through to Somerset. South of this line there were 97,890

---

* These did not include bakeries, because the price of bread was controlled by the assizes. Nor did they include many retailers who also produced their own goods. For example, tailors often had a shop, but would have thought of themselves as producers, not retailers. That this 141,700 was a conservative estimate for the number of shops can be seen from various pre-modern court records. As early as 1422, in the town of Ely (with a population of fewer than 4,000), one court session alone had cases that involved 3 bakers, 12 butchers, 37 brewers, 73 ale-sellers, 11 fishmongers and 2 vintners: 138 retailers of one kind or another – and these were only the ones involved in court cases.[5]

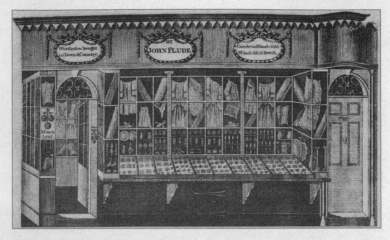

A tradesman's card from the late eighteenth century, showing the elaborate window displays that were becoming common in shops in larger towns.

shops listed by the Excise, in a population of just over 3 million people, or slightly over 34 people per shop. In the remainder of the country each shop served approximately 63.5 people. (It is salutary to compare these numbers to the retail-crazy twentieth century: two hundred years later, in 1950, there was one shop for every 92 people in the country.) According to the 1797 parish returns in London, there was on average 1 shop for ever 21.6 people in the City and Westminster. In fact, while in the first half of the nineteenth century the population grew by 18.2 per cent, the number of shops soared, so far as we can tell, by a dizzying, and almost impossible-seeming, 183.4 per cent – ten times the rate of population growth.[6] This happened before industrialization, before mass urbanization. These figures suggest that it was precisely this retail explosion that created the Industrial Revolution, supply being driven by demand, rather than the more traditional, but less commonsensical, idea that the creation – the supply of goods – came first, and the desire for them followed on afterwards.

In general, it appears unlikely that many people, in England at any rate, were more than a few miles away – a dozen or so at most – from a shop. Most communities, even the most rural, had nearby market towns to which at least some members of the community travelled weekly or fortnightly. Agricultural workers, except in the north of the

Many shops, however, well into the nineteenth century, remained oblivious to display, like this one in Clare Market, in London. Goods were placed on the shelves, and a table for selling was erected daily outside, but no attempt was made to attract passers-by. The overhanging wooden canopy folded down at night and doubled as a shutter.

country, were by the eighteenth century paid mostly in cash, rather than in kind – through food, lodgings, and clothing – as they had been in earlier times. They therefore had money to buy goods, and, equally importantly, the need to do so: they no longer could rely on part-payment either in food or in land to grow or raise their own. For the most part, their wages were 'long pay', that is, paid irregularly, and sometimes for an entire season at once, in arrears. That meant that they needed a local shop, with a shopkeeper who knew both them and their employer, in order to be able to obtain credit until the wage bill was paid.

One of the changes that has affected the way we look at shop numbers is the size of towns. Many towns, even quite major ones, were by our standards almost unbelievably small – Derby in its pre-industrial phase was possibly no more than 500 paces wide. With this kind of size, it mattered little how many shops there were in each town, since all could be reached in a few minutes – there was no need for neighbourhood shops in the more modern sense. What mattered instead was what each shop stocked. The smallest, most basic shops were known as back-street shops. They were the cheapest to stock, required little capital, no training or apprenticeship, and were often set up and run either as a second source of income by the wife of a labourer or as the only way of earning a meagre living by a newly impoverished widow.* In their crudest form, these shops were the front room of a house. Before windows were routinely glazed, the shopkeeper stood at the window and served customers through the hatch. Sometimes the window hatch was enlarged, and sometimes a flap leading from the window down to the pavement was added, to create a small selling area. While London shops began to get glazed windows from the later seventeenth century, many shops in the provinces were still unglazed well into the nineteenth century – a picture of East Street in Chichester in 1815 shows a butcher's display through an unglazed window hatch. In 1827 an onlooker's description of Newcastle upon Tyne noted that many shops had just replaced their shutters with glass.[8] These back-street shops stocked the minimum number of goods. They sold candles, bread, small beer,† and maybe needles, cotton and other small household items.[9] Some might have small hardware goods, or tobacco, and, later in the century, tea, when it replaced small beer as the drink for all ages. Most of the goods were sold wrapped up in paper in minute quantities, a day's supply of tea or sugar at a time. The customers were often nearly as poor as the shopkeeper, and could not afford to buy in bulk at better prices.

The next level of retailing was the village shop. The front room was once again given over to retailing, but now the customers were expected to come into the shop area. William Wood of Didsbury, who also owned the Ring o'Bells inn, sold bacon, 'wheat and barley flour, meal, berm

---

* And meagre meant meagre for many. One surviving shopkeeper's ledger recording the transactions in a back-street shop in Sheffield in the 1840s shows an average of between two and five customers a day.[7]

† In an age when water came from the same rivers that served as sewers, small beer was the standard drink for people of all ages, including children. In traditional beer-making the mash was used three times. Each successive batch of beer was weaker than the one before, as fermentation declined owing to the reduced quantities of sugar in the mash. The third batch, called small beer, had virtually no alcoholic content at all.

[probably barm, a fermenting agent, used instead of yeast], bread, man-chets [small loaves of good-quality wheat bread], tea, coffee, sugar, trea-cle, currants, raisins, figs, salt, pepper, cloves, mustard, rice, candles, soap, starch, blue'.* This was a fairly standard range for most small grocers. In addition, Wood sold some fresh food: 'potatoes, apples, plums, peas, butter, cheese, sometimes eggs, sometimes milk', as well as the much less common 'beef, veal, mutton, lamb and pork', and 'tobacco, snuff, and pipes'.[10] This lack of specialization was found every-where. In Newport, Shropshire, in the middle of the eighteenth century a shopkeeper sold sugar, tobacco, rum and spirits, which he kept in a warehouse space behind his store; the store itself was stocked with small ironmongery goods, 'cartbrushes, wire and cord', and a range of things 'in ye Pedlars Trade' and 'in the Milleners way'. In his inventory he kept another lot of sugar, spices and more ironmongery listed separately; possibly these were goods to be parcelled up and sold through the window in smaller quantities.[11]

These shopkeepers often had three distinct sets of customers: the poor, who bought through the window; the more prosperous, who came into the shop (or sent their servants); and sometimes the wealthy, whom they visited at home. Thomas Turner, a Sussex shopkeeper who supplied some of the needs of the Duke of Newcastle's household when it was resident in Sussex, was summoned to the house by the Duke's steward when he was ready to place an order. The prosperous but non-aristocratic were often waited on in this way too: Turner also called at the houses of 'a substantial tenant farmer' and of Mr French, a landowner.[12] Shop-keepers at this level tended to supply goods in bulk to those who owned back-street shops – it was not until the end of the eighteenth century that separate wholesalers began to emerge, as distinct from large retailers. Many shopkeepers expected to order in whatever was needed for their more prosperous customers, while not stocking these items regularly. A wholesale/retail grocer in a good-sized seaport town in Scotland in the early part of the nineteenth century listed the items that had come through his shop over the course of one year. Tea and sugar were the main items, followed by cheese and butter. Then came various spices – nutmeg, cloves, ginger, cassia, cayenne and pepper – followed by currants,

---

* Laundry blue was a lump of dye used to counteract the yellowing effects of soaps and keep white items white.

raisins and nuts; ham; liquorice; rice; oranges and lemons. It is likely that most of the spices and everything else apart from the tea, sugar, cheese and butter were special orders – the nutmeg, cloves, ginger, cassia and currants appeared only once in his inventory, while the cayenne, raisins, pepper and nuts appeared just twice, with the raisins listed in December, significantly near the new year festivities and Twelfth Night celebrations. Even the rice was noted only three times. He recorded one order of 'aquavita', again in December, and two orders for wine. And, while yellow laundry soap made regular appearances, pearl ash (also for laundry) was bought less often, and starch, blue and soda each only once.[13]

Shopping, for both the prosperous middle classes and the wealthy who lived outside London, was neither entirely local nor entirely London-based. In the first half of the eighteenth century the Purefoy family in Shalstone, Buckinghamshire, bought their wine, sugar, coffee and tea from London, while most of their other groceries came from Brackley, their local market town. But they clearly did not feel restricted to those two places: they bought mushrooms from Deddington; their razors were sharpened in Oxford; their blankets were supplied from Witney; and they bought goods from a clockmaker in Bicester, and more from another one in Helmdon. Their clothes came from London (millinery, mercery and drapery), but Russian leather for a pair of boots was ordered in Buckinghamshire, 'blew Cloath' came from Brackley, while various tailors in Brackley, Tingwick, and Chipping Norton made up their clothes.[14] This pattern of diffuse purchasing was the norm. An advertisement in the *Leeds Mercury* in 1769 can stand as representative for many similar ones: it promised that 'All orders from Gentlemen and tradesmen in the country will be punctually observed.'[15] So many advertisements actively solicited country orders, that these were clearly a large part of any shopkeeper's business.

By the 1770s this kind of – to use a modern term – mail-order business was common throughout England. Midlands manufacturers had long been sending out price lists; now they were also sending illustrated pattern books, for shopkeepers both at home and abroad. In 1773 Josiah Wedgwood was thinking of producing a catalogue in French, to accompany sample boxes of earthenware; by 1787 he had had the catalogue printed in English and French, and then in German and Dutch, and demand was such that it had gone through five editions.[16] Manufacturers in various decorative metal trades – buckle-makers, candlestick-makers, 'toy' manufacturers* – produced illustrated pattern books with goods designed to suit the taste of each particular market. Many manufacturers found it good business to continue to produce old-fashioned lines for export.[18] For example, in the Netherlands the rococo style was popular long after neoclassicism had become all the rage in England. When Wedgwood's revolutionary earthenware, creamware (see below, p. 63), swept coloured ware and 'greengrocery'-shaped novelty items off the shelves, from 1766, his partner Thomas Bentley shipped the old lines to the West Indies, where they remained popular. Even at home, shopkeepers took up the catalogue with enthusiasm: it enabled them to have a wide range of goods available without forcing them to invest too much in stock that might not sell. In 1770 Jackson's Habit-Warehouse boasted that it had many fancy-dress costumes in stock, and it further had 'a book of several hundred prints coloured, which contains the dresses of every nation', which were available to order.[19]

New consumer products made readily available by post or carrier, brought to market by improved transport (see pp. 70–74), advertised and thus made more widely known by a greater range and wider distribution of newspapers (pp. 124ff.): all of this encouraged greater expectations, and even local shops began to have, as a matter of course, higher stock levels, especially in areas serving large populations. In London, Mrs Holt's Italian Warehouse had a tradecard illustrated with a picture by Hogarth (see p. 50).[20]

Greater stock meant that more thought had to go into the display of these goods. For those selling through the window, nothing was required in the way of shopfitting, but, once customers began to come into the shop, the room had to be more than a place where goods were stored. The transformation from storage to selling space began to appear early

---

* In the eighteenth century toys were small items of little intrinsic value, usually decorative ornaments, knick-knacks, or trinkets, for adults rather than children. Until late in the century, children's toys had been distinguished by referring to them as 'playing toys'. Toymakers were categorized by the metal they worked in: gold and silver toy manufacturers produced buttons, watch chains, inkstands, snuffboxes for men and vinaigrettes for women, decoratives scissors and candle-snuffers; tortoiseshell toy manufacturers made combs, buttons and decorative boxes; steel toy manufacturers generally made cheaper versions of many of the same goods as gold or silver toymakers, as well as the small hooks that were used to pin jewellery or flowers on to clothes or hats. Birmingham was the acknowledged centre of toy manufacture, with nearly 20,000 people in the trade in the city and its environs by the middle of the eighteenth century; over 80 per cent of them were in some way involved in exporting their goods abroad.[17]

Mrs Holt's Italian Warehouse is a good example of the range of the luxury market. It offered silk fabrics such as lustring and padesois (or paduasoy), Leghorn straw hats, essences and 'Naple soap', lute and violin strings, and even 'oyl' and 'Bolognia sausidges'. Hogarth drew the illustration on which this engraving was based, and it was used at least twice more by different merchants – once by a wine merchant, once by another grocer.

in the eighteenth century, and an example can be seen in the probate records. In 1719 Thomas Horne, a shopkeeper in Arundel, died; 150 items of stock (drapery and haberdashery) were listed in the inventory made for probate, but there were no goods listed for the use or comfort of his customers. His widow, Susan Horne, who carried on the business, died fifteen years later, in 1734; the inventory then included eight mirrors, counters, shelves and boxes, all illuminated by new sash windows.[21]

By the middle of the eighteenth century, especially in London, and especially in the luxury-goods trades, the decoration of shops developed swiftly. These shops were a big advance on what had been the norm half a century before. Daniel Defoe was contemptuous of those shopkeepers who wanted 'to paint and gild' their shop to make it 'fine and gay': 'Never was such painting and gilding, such sashings and looking-glasses among the shopkeepers as there is now,' he fretted. He also reported a pastrycook who in 1710 spent an astonishing £300 on sash windows, tiles 'finely painted in forest-work and figures', mirrors, a fireplace, candlesticks, a glass lantern, and twenty-five sconces, as well as decoration that involved painting, gilding and carving, and cost another £55.[22]

The pastrycook was not an isolated individual. The booksellers Lackington Allen and Co. had a trade card that promised 'the finest shop in the world being 140 feet in front', with fourteen windows on to the street, and 'Lounging Rooms'.[23] Trade cards showed idealized images, of how shopkeepers wanted their shops to be seen, not necessarily what they were like in reality.* But, at the same time, they cannot have been entire fictions, even if the number of windows was increased a bit, or the perspective from which the interior was drawn was low, in order to make the shop seem bigger. Inventories backed up the impression of luxury that the trade cards worked so hard to project. Many listed mirrors, glass display cases, mouldings on the ceilings, gilt cornices, glass for windows to the street, for display, for internal lighting, screens and skylights – the possibilities seemed endless. Furniture was also abundant: the customer expected to sit while he or she was being waited on, and stools and even upholstered chairs appear regularly in inventories. So do other items that were chosen to suggest that the prosperous customer,

---

* Trade cards were common before the development of newspapers created a new vehicle for advertising. They were given to customers in the shop, receipts or bills were written out on them, they were attached to price lists, handed out in the street, or posted to customers at home.

This is probably New Exchange, one of the fashionable shopping arcades in London in the late eighteenth century. Luxury goods such as the books (at left) and fabrics or lace (right) were commonly sold in these arcades, together with jewellery, musical instruments, millinery, china, lacquerware, fans and other bric-a-brac.

now visiting a shop rather than being called upon by the shopkeeper, was still in some way at home, even if it was not his or her home – there were mirrors, pictures, sconces, curtains, tables, lamps.[24]

By the middle of the eighteenth century successful shops were no longer single rooms, but had expanded either upstairs or by breaking through party walls to take over several ground-floor rooms laterally. In 1774 Wedgwood took a showroom in Greek Street, Soho, at Portland House, the 'grandest and largest house in the street', with a seventeen-metre frontage. It had at one point belonged to a surgeon, whose dissecting room ran the full width of the house. (It was tactfully renamed the 'Great Room'.) Not content with that, Wedgwood immediately began to plan an extension by adding a gallery, linked to the ground floor by a dramatic staircase.[25] In 1794 the bookseller James Lackington moved his shop into a mansion in Finsbury Square, which he named the Temple of the Muses. Inside there was a large circular counter from which to serve customers in a magnificent room – a room so large that, after the first day of trading, as a publicity stunt, a coach and horses were driven right the way around the counter.

Despite such grandeur, Lackington had made his fortune in the mass market. Over the entrance to the Temple of the Muses he had painted, 'Cheapest Bookseller in the World', and on his carriage the motto 'Small profits do great things' reminded passers-by of the source of his wealth.[26] The Industrial Revolution had not yet brought about mass-production techniques – they were to come in the nineteenth century – but there was among some manufacturers the beginning of a very clear idea of the potential of the mass market. Matthew Boulton – originally a steel toy manufacturer, later one of the earliest and most successful proponents of the factory system and, in general, one of the leading innovators and entrepreneurs in an age that was rife with them – grasped the idea of the mass market eagerly. When his London agent suggested that he ought to look more at the upper-class market, he responded, 'We think it of far more consequence to supply the People than the Nobility only; and though you speak contemptuously of Hawkers, Pedlars and those who supply *Petty shops*, yet we must own that we think they will do more towards supporting a great Manufactory, than all the Lords in the Nation.'[27] He returned to this theme frequently: 'I understand my own interest too well to load any articles of my Manufactory with too extravagant a profit, as I rather choose to make great quantities with small profits, than small quantities with large profits.'[28]

This attention to price is an indication that the level of competition was fierce: increased urbanization and improved transport meant that by the second half of the eighteenth century many of merely moderate income had access to a large number of shops selling the same kind of goods. No one could now expect their goods to sell simply because they were the only products available. Early historians of consumerism suggested that fixed-price retailing appeared with the creation of department stores in the mid nineteenth century: that William Whiteley, the 'Universal Provider' (see p. 114), changed the face of shopping by offering lower prices in exchange for fixed prices, instead of haggling, and cash instead of credit. Yet even the most cursory look at the advertisements of the eighteenth century reveals that many of these nineteenth-century 'innovations' were in place in the eighteenth century: newspapers were filled to the brim with advertisements that promised low prices for goods 'charged at ready money prices' – that is, sold for cash. John Hildyard, a York bookseller, advertised 'several libraries and parcels of books . . . [to be] sold cheap, for ready money only'. John Davenport and Co. by 1751 was advertising that wallpaper 'such as is sold by the upholsterer &c. for 3*d*. or 3½*d*. per yard, we sell for 2½*d*. and all other sorts in proportion. The price is printed at the end of each piece without abatement [that is, without discounts] and sold for ready money'.[29]

Nor were the shopkeepers willing to wait for passing trade to come into their expensively fitted-up shops. There is a circular dating from 1778 which is the oldest known example of a shopkeeper soliciting custom by sending a regular client information about his wares. However, the style of the circular, which contains no explanation of its function, suggests that customers would have seen these types of mailing before. It is therefore likely that this chance survival is a remnant of earlier examples that have not been preserved. By the end of the decade, in any case, such items were commonplace: Smith, Nash, Kemble and Travers, 'wholesalers and retailers', in 1779 sent out a circular warning their customers that 'unfortunately we have just received information of the loss of Grenada . . . which has caused an advance in Raw sugar* . . .

---

* As a source of sugar, the island of Grenada was highly valuable. The British had won it from the French in 1762, during the Seven Years War; the French regained control in 1779 and held the prize until 1783, when the island was returned to the British for the rest of its colonial history.

Refined sugars are very scarce and dear, but will be more Plenty [*sic*] in a Month or six Weeks, and hope cheaper . . . We shall be glad to see you in Town if it suits your convenience, but if otherwise, shall endeavour to execute any Orders you may favour us with, on the same terms and with equal Attention.'[30]

This increase in the price of sugar was a cause of anxiety by 1779. Sugar had, for centuries past, been unaffordable for almost everyone. Honey was used by those who had the space and time to cultivate bees; sugar-beet production would not become a practical reality until the nineteenth century. The population for the most part did without sweeteners. Sugar was, in the strictest sense of the word, a luxury – something that provided enjoyment or comfort in addition to what were accounted the necessaries of life. It was a thing that was desirable, but not indispensable. In 1780 Jeremy Bentham, the Utilitarian philosopher, wrote, 'Necessaries come always before luxuries.'[31] But what was a necessity and what was a luxury was more fluid and less absolute than Bentham allowed. In the dedication to *Discourses on Art* in 1778, Sir Joshua Reynolds, the president of the Royal Academy, wrote, 'The regular progress of cultivated life is from necessaries to accommodations, from accommodations to ornaments.'[32] At almost exactly the same date, Anna Larpent, the wife of the Chief Inspector of Plays for the Lord Chamberlain, wrote in her diary, 'I must acquire thought in spending money. An elegant Oeconomy, a proper frugality[;] do nothing from mere spirit of imitation. Every thing with order, nothing giddily – there are: absolute necessities; necessary luxuries.'[33] Necessary luxuries: surely a new concept.*

The president of the Royal Academy and a bourgeois housewife were agreed: necessities were no longer only basic food and shelter, those essentials that kept a person alive and able to function. And a couple of decades later, during the French Revolution, the sans-culottes of Paris showed that this attitude was not solely a middle-class development. In the desperate winter of 1792–3 the starving French workers rioted, demanding what they referred to as 'goods of prime necessity'. These they carefully listed: soap, candles, sugar and coffee – goods their grandparents would have considered unimaginable luxuries. The more

---

* Although it would surely have appalled her, Larpent was precisely articulating the pattern that Karl Marx and Friedrich Engels later noted in *The German Ideology*: 'The satisfaction of the first need . . . leads to new needs.'[34]

prosperous murmured disapprovingly that the rioters had not attacked bakeries, where they would have found bread, for centuries the staple food of Europe. Instead they attacked groceries.[35] What subsistence was, what was 'necessary', had altered for ever.

Part of this elision from luxury to necessity came from the rapid increase in the quantity of goods taxed in the eighteenth century. Numerous wars and the expansion of government saw duties quadruple. A partial list of goods that were taxed in the 1770s includes paper, newspapers, windows, horses, dogs, wagons, leather, printed silk and linen, starch, soap and candles (even soap and candles made from fat from one's own animals), salt, hops, barley for beer, cider, perry, wine, spirits, tea,* coffee, sugar, molasses, spices and chocolate.[36] These were all, therefore, to a degree seen as luxuries, at least by the government. The people who were consuming these items, not unnaturally, felt differently. Luxuries such as soap, candles, salt and tea were in reality by this time clearly necessities to many. It is therefore easy to see how other taxed goods quickly took on a similar aura, and also became assimilated as necessities.

The first advertisement for tea that has survived appeared in the 23–30 September 1658 issue of *Mercurius Politicus*, the official, government-approved political periodical. It notified readers that 'That Excellent, and by all Physicians approved, *China* Drink, called by the *Chineaus* [Chinese], *Tcha*, by other Nations *Tay alias Tee*, is sold at the *Sultaness-head*, a *Cophee-house* in *Sweetings* Rents by the Royal Exchange, *London*.' That same year, Garraway's coffee house in Exchange Alley also advertised tea, which it promised would cure, among other things, headache, stone, gravel, dropsy, 'liptitude distillations', scurvy, sleepiness, loss of memory, looseness of the guts, 'heavy dreams' and colic. Moreover, when 'Taken with Virgin's Honey instead of Sugar, tea cleanses the Kidneys and Ureters, and with *Milk* and water it prevents Consumption.'[37]

It may be that this tea was being sold as a dry leaf, to take away and brew up at home, as medicine – the claims made for it resemble the advertisements for patent medicines over the next two centuries. But from 1660, when the commodity was first taken notice of by the Excise, the tax was levied on the *brewed* item: the initial tax was 8*d.* per gallon – the seller had to make the tea in bulk, have the excisemen check it,

---

* The idea of tea as a luxury persisted – this particular tax was not lifted until 1964.

and then sell it. From 1689, however, the government moved to a tax on the dry leaf, which kept prices high, but did not require an exciseman in every coffee house.[38] From 1664 the East India Company began to import the commodity, but in such small quantities – only 100 pounds to begin with – that it is probable that it was being shipped in for those East India Company employees who had acquired a taste for the drink abroad.

From this small base, consumption rose at astonishing rates. In 1741 Britain imported less than 800,000 pounds a year; by 1746–50 annual home consumption had reached more than 2.5 million pounds. Very swiftly, tea had become a drink that even the working class could afford, at least sometimes. By mid-century the lowest grades cost between 8 and 10s. a pound (the highest grades reached £1 16s.). There were advertisements recommending a certain leaf because it was 'strong, and will endure the Change of Water three or four times' – that is, the thrifty housewife could reuse the leaves and still get – brown liquid? By 1748 John Wesley, the founder of Methodism, saw so many of his flock spending money on tea that he wrote the minatory *A Letter to a Friend Concerning TEA*, while the philanthropist Jonas Hanway warned of the perils of tea and gin in an almost interchangeable vocabulary.[39]

The consumption of tea was very quickly limited only by the high levels of tax. In 1795, during the French wars, tax was raised to a rate of 20 per cent; in 1801 it was 50 per cent for tea costing more than 2s. 6d. a pound, 20 per cent for cheaper leaves; two years later the expensive blends were taxed at 95 per cent, and the nominally cheaper ones at 60 per cent; finally, by 1820, the tax was an eye-watering 100 per cent of the price for all teas costing over 2s. per pound.[40] Even this was not enough to slow the seemingly insatiable demand. Between 1785 and 1800 the population increased by 14 per cent, while tea consumption went up by 97.7 per cent. In 1800 the East India Company's imports stood at 21 million pounds a year; by 1820, 30 million pounds of tea a year were consumed in the United Kingdom; in 1850 it was 44.5 million pounds, or 1.5 pounds of tea for every man, woman and child in the country each year. Still the numbers went on rising – to 3.42 pounds a head in 1866, and 6.3 pounds in 1909.[41]* Given the amount of smuggling that

* This compares interestingly with coffee: in 1821 coffee consumption was less than 1 pound per head per year; in 1909 it was 0.71 pounds, while cocoa consumption was at 1.2 pounds per head per annum. Holland, by comparison, consumed 18 pounds of coffee per head per year.

went on to get around the enormous tax burden, this was one of the earliest indications that the market was not, as economists had thought, a fixed object, but was instead infinitely expandable. As desirable goods appeared, the demand – and the market – would increase.

In the early eighteenth century, for the most part tea was sold by grocers. (Grocers were then at the luxury end of the market.) Then other luxury traders began to carry this new luxury good: china dealers, haberdashers, milliners. Mr Rose, a bookseller in Norwich, sold tea in 1707; Frances Bennett, a Bath draper, did the same in 1744, as did Cornelius Goldberg, a Birmingham toyman, in 1751. But now specialist tea dealers were appearing in large towns. By 1784 there were 32,754 licensed tea dealers, or 1 tea dealer for every 234 customers. Less than a decade later the number had risen by 60 per cent which, with the rise in population, meant that every 150 people were served by a single tea dealer. Even now, though, many tea retailers were performing multiple tasks: as late as 1803 there was Jones's Druggist and Tea Dealer in Birmingham, and Thirsk had Jo. Napier, Milliner and Tea Dealer, in 1804. But this was no longer because tea was a luxury, but because it was a necessity. Once the masses began to drink tea, it had become readily available in all kinds of shops, from the grandest of grocers in London to the back-street shops set up on £10 capital.[42] Even the poorest areas of the East End of London had shops selling tea – the notorious Ratcliff Highway had one, as did Wapping Wall. Another, on the 'foulsome Butcher Row', was a testament to the product's popularity: however impoverished its clientele, at one point the shop held 119 pounds of tea in stock.[43]

Part of the reason that the consumption of tea soared so dramatically was that it was inextricably interwoven with another commodity: sugar. Both had arrived at roughly the same time in Britain, one from India, one from the West Indies. The development of cane sugar in the West Indian plantations had made many British fortunes, through the possibility of sales at dramatically reduced prices.* In 1660, about 1,000

---

* In 1787 Wedgwood produced a range of medallions promoting the abolition of slavery. They were blue on yellow jasper, with the motto 'Am I not a man and a brother?' Men wore them as pins or buttons, or had them set on snuffbox lids; women as brooches or hairpins.[44] It is good to know that Wedgwood, whose fortune in many ways was predicated directly from the import of sugar from the West Indian plantations, contributed his mite to the destruction of slavery. Slavery and abolition is a subject that fits all too well into a book on commodity, but it is one that I have, regretfully, had to leave out.

hogsheads of sugar were consumed in Britain; by 1730 that had risen a hundredfold, to 100,000 hogsheads. By the mid-1770s, sugar imports were valued at £3.3 million. Sugar and tea were now no longer luxuries: they were national characteristics. Consumption was running at 20 pounds of sugar per person per year; and up to 10 per cent of all money spent on food and drink went on sugar and tea.[45]*

Tea had not conquered the market on its intrinsic worth alone. From the late eighteenth century it was heavily advertised, using a range of new methods to entice customers. Many advertisements centred on competitive pricing: one merchant was 'determined to sell teas at such low prices . . . as the public have a right to expect', another, heroically, aimed 'at profits only sufficient to defray expenses, wholesale and retail'. Many claimed to be selling tea more cheaply than anywhere else; others advertised reduced prices for bulk purchases. Many supposedly nineteenth- and even twentieth-century innovations were happily tried out by these eighteenth-century tradesmen: some used the 'loss-leader', selling sugar at below-cost prices with the purchase of full-price tea; others gave the chance of good fortune with a lottery ticket free on purchase of a pound of tea;† some offered customers 'a new treatise on tea', available, not by coincidence, with the purchase of tea; still others advertised money-back guarantees if customers were dissatisfied; some promised to match wholesale prices, or even undercut them[47] – and none of these advertisements suggested that these were new ways of selling.

One shopkeeper who embraced these methods enthusiastically was Edward Eagleton, of the Tea Warehouse in Cheapside. In the *Leeds Mercury* in 1786 he advertised reduced prices, fixed prices for cash, mail-order sales, and money-back guarantees; he offered to post samples, or customers could come into his Tea Warehouse to taste the goods. In other advertisements he promoted his prices, which were, he claimed, 1s. per pound lower than anyone else's. He sold entire chests of East India Company tea to small shopowners with only a 1 per cent mark-up. His

---

* This combination created more than grocery empires: in the 1650s there were 50 sugar refineries in Britain; by 1800 there were 150. These refineries, because of the processing method used, caught fire easily. High insurance premiums made some refiners club together to create their own insurance groups. One of these became the Phoenix Assurance Co. in 1782.[46]

† The expression, still used, if slightly old-fashioned, 'I wouldn't have X if it were given away free with a pound of tea' comes from offers like these, which continued throughout the nineteenth century.

most innovative move, however, was an arrangement with 'outlets' (it is unclear whether he meant shops or simply agents) in twenty-seven towns: he supplied them with packets of tea marked with his own sign, the Grasshopper, and advertised in local newspapers 'fresh . . . teas . . . from Eagleton and Company . . . London . . . wholesale and retail . . . selling from ten to twenty per cent cheaper than [are now] sold . . . and carriage saved . . . [The tea is] packed and marked with the sign of the Grasshopper', with a money-back guarantee and the motto 'Taste, try, compare and judge'.[48]

All of these sales techniques had been tried before, but Eagleton was one of the first to bring them together. The next to take up the retail challenge was a man who had originally been a printer in a firm that produced lottery tickets. When Frederick Gye himself won £30,000 in a lottery, he set himself up as a tea dealer and quickly became one of the most important in the trade, mostly by dint of advertisements. Instead of advertising his tea, he advertised himself as an indissoluble part of his product. First and foremost, he promoted the sale of his packaged tea, which, he promised, would save the 'Tea Trade from the opprobrium attached to it by the late disclosures of adulteration', promising not to 'buy nor sell Bohea tea* . . . so commonly used to adulterate better sorts'. (With this he was in fact blurring the line between blending tea – a legitimate job, and a highly skilled one – and adulterating it, and so attacking other dealers. Attack ads were one of his specialities.) The brand was now all-important: he promised that every order over a quarter of a pound would be sent in a sealed package with a wrapper carrying an engraving of his shop; the quality of the tea, its price and a seal were stamped on it. He used some of Eagleton's other methods as well: free carriage within ten miles of London for cash sales, and agents 'in every principal town in England' – by 1819, four months after his shop opened, he advertised that he had 100 agents; seven months after that he claimed to have 500. Other dealers resented this newcomer, and advertised in return, using his methods, and thus by the early nineteenth century advertisements in local papers, country agents, and prepacked, branded, pre-priced tea were commonplaces.[49]

When tea became fashionable, in the early eighteenth century, it

---

* Confusingly, in the early eighteenth century Bohea was the best grade of black tea; by the time Gye was advertising, 'Bohea' was used for the last, inferior, crop of the season.

naturally became necessary to have the right accoutrements to brew it in and from which to drink it. We have seen that as late as the 1690s hot-drink utensils were rarely to be found domestically, while by 1725 most prosperous households had some.[50] In the early part of the century porcelain had been imported from China, before local production stepped in to capture the market with equipment better suited to British rather than Chinese tea-drinking habits. In China, tea was brewed in a kettle, then cooled before drinking; in Britain, it was brewed in a teapot and poured out while still hot. Therefore the British teapot shape was adapted not from a Chinese tea kettle, but from a wine flask, with a handle added so that the tea could be poured before it was cooled; equally, handles on cups were useful for hot tea.[51] Further, the British drank their tea sweetened, and with milk, so both a sugar bowl and a milk jug needed to be designed, along with a new size of spoon – the teaspoon – and a saucer on which to place the wet spoon, creating by the eighteenth century a British tea set that was considerably different from its Chinese ancestor.

Many manufacturers rushed to fill the void. In 1757 James Watt, soon to be known as the inventor of the steam engine, was working as 'Mathematical Instrument Maker to the University' in Glasgow. Despite living a fairly straitened life, he wrote to his father asking him to send '½ Doz afternoon China tea cups a stone teapot not too small a sugar Box & Slop Bowl as soon as possible'.[52] The use of such precise terms is fascinating – a relatively poor man, Watt still specified 'afternoon' cups, as distinct, one assumes, from breakfast china, and a stoneware teapot, not an earthenware or porcelain one; also, the sugar and slop bowls* were not to be omitted. It is hardly surprising, therefore, that Josiah Wedgwood had such an immediate success when he produced his Queensware in 1765.†

It is almost impossible for us to realize today what a sensation china was when it first appeared. Before the eighteenth century, the rich in

---

* Slops were the leavings in a teacup – the dregs, and any stray tea leaves. They were traditionally emptied into a slop bowl, about the same size as the cup, before a second cup of tea was poured. This letter of Watts's pre-dates the *Oxford English Dictionary*'s first cited use of the word by more than half a century.

† Some specialization seems to us today more outré than most: in 1772, women began to bleach their hands with arsenic; Wedgwood immediately began to promote his black basalt teapots by saying that the colour would make the hand holding the pot seem even whiter.[53]

Josiah Wedgwood's showroom in York Street, St James's Square, in 1809. At the centre of fashionable London, the showroom displayed vases and ornamental goods as they might be shown at home, and the tables were laid with complete breakfast, tea or dinner services, which were regularly changed to encourage repeat visitors.

Britain used silver and pewter; moderately prosperous households used pewter or, sometimes, early forms of earthenware; the poor used wood. European porcelain factories were set up under royal patronage after the secret of hard-paste porcelain was discovered by Meissen in 1709. The hard-paste porcelain from China, however, remained highly prized. The Dutch, who at that time held the monopoly on trade with the Chinese, sent drawings of their pewter and stoneware utensils for the Chinese to copy in porcelain: in this way the goods that arrived in Europe were at once startlingly new in material and reassuringly familiar in shape. A few factories began to produce soft-paste porcelain in Britain – Bow, Derby, Pomona, and Longton Hall in Staffordshire – but the cost of production was staggering: before any work could be carried out, for example, the clay had to be weathered for nearly three years. Without a beneficent monarch to pay the bills, these works had little chance of survival: Longton Hall was bankrupt by 1760, Bow in 1763.[54]

While this was bad news for porcelain manufacturers, it opened up the earthenware market to the manufacturer with an eye to the market. No one would have picked Josiah Wedgwood as that man of destiny at his birth: the twelfth child of a cadet branch of a family of potters in

Burslem,* he started in the general trade, as one of dozens of earthenware potters selling to the local retailers at the cheap end of the market. Earthenware was porous, and chipped and broke easily; stoneware, fired at higher temperatures, was a slightly better product, having a shiny, non-porous surface, but it was still fragile. By the 1760s, however, Wedgwood had produced his first technical breakthrough, which moved him from a local to a national market: creamware, an earthenware that could withstand sudden temperature changes without shattering, had a richly glazed surface, and was still relatively inexpensive. It also had a purer colour than had ever been achieved except with porcelain, and its worth was quickly recognized: in 1765 Queen Charlotte ordered a creamware tea set from him. The technical breakthrough was essential, and through his life Wedgwood continued to work at new methods and processes. Even when he was not the inventor himself, he always recognized important advances and quickly made use of them. In 1750 a mezzotint engraver had developed a way of using transfer printing on earthenware, to decorate it to look like hand-painted porcelain. Wedgwood swooped, and soon creamware was carrying black, rust or purple images of flowers, birds, garlands, genre scenes, classical groups, even Masonic emblems and designs to commemorate people and events – the King and Queen, Frederick the Great, Pitt, Wesley and John Wilkes were all immortalized in earthenware.

These advances would have occurred sooner or later, with or without Wedgwood; it was how he parlayed his successes into an empire that marked out Wedgwood – and his unfairly overlooked partner Thomas Bentley – as unique. Wedgwood saw the route ahead the minute the royal tea set had been ordered. He immediately renamed his creamware Queensware, and asked for the right to call himself 'Potter to Her Majesty'. He wrote to Bentley:

> The demand for this said *Creamcolour*, Alias *Queen's Ware*, Alias *Ivory*, still increases. It is really amazing how rapidly the use of it has spread allmost† over the whole Globe, how universally it is liked. How much of this general use, & estimation, is owing

---

* There had been pottery works for a couple of centuries in Burslem and four neighbouring villages: Tunstall, Hanley, Stoke and Longton. As they grew, they were collectively known as the Five Towns, and now make up Stoke-on-Trent. (Fenton is sometimes included, in which case they became, of course, the Six Towns.)
† Wedgwood's spelling remained individual; I will refrain from noting each non-standard spelling, unless the meaning is unclear.

to the mode of its introduction – & how much to its real utility and beauty? are questions in which we may be a good deal interested for the government of our future Conduct ... For instance, if a Royal, or Noble introduction be as necessary for the sale of an Article of *Luxury*, as real Elegance & beauty, then the Manufacturer, if he consults his own interest will bestow as much pains, & expence too, if necessary, in gaining the former of these advantages, as he would in bestowing the latter.[55]

In 1770 Wedgwood wrote, as always, to Bentley:

Wo^d you *advertise* the next season as the silk mercers in Pell mell do, – Or *deliver cards* at the houses of the Nobility & Gentry, & in the City, – Get leave to *make a shew* of his Majesty's Service for a month, & ornament the Dessert with Ornamental Ewers, flower baskets & Vases – Or have an *Auction* at Cobbs room of Statues, Bassreliefs, Pictures, Tripods, Candelabrias, Lamps, Potpouris, Superb Ewers, Cisterns, Tablets Etruscan, Porphirys & other Articles not yet expos'd to sale. *Make a great route of advertising this Auction*, & at the same time mention our rooms in New-port St – & have another Auction in the full season at Bath of such things as we now have on hand, just sprinkled over with a few new articles *to give them an air of novelty* to any of our customers who may see them there, – Or will you trust to a *new disposition of the Rooms* with the new articles we shall have to put into them & a few modest *puffs in the Papers* from some of our friends such as I am told there has been one lately in Lloyd's Chronicle.[56]

Barely pausing for breath, he had suggested in just a few lines many of the major new selling techniques of the century: advertising in the press – by paid advertisements, by auction announcements and by getting friends to insert 'puff' pieces; delivering trade cards to customers and potential customers; various forms of exhibition – by displaying a service he had made for the King, with its concommitant 'royal' publicity, and more conventionally by auction and in his showrooms; highlighting new goods to attract the fashionable; and redesigning his showrooms, again to attract the fashionable by novelty. And this is a single letter from the hundreds that poured out over the decades.*

Wedgwood understood the benefits of publicity in all its varied forms. His most tried and trusted method was to get nobility (if royalty

---

* Bentley's have unfortunately not survived – perhaps the reason why all the innovation is attributed to Wedgwood.

were not available) to promote his wares for him. In 1776 he had some new bas-relief vases to sell. He fired off yet another missive to Bentley: 'Sir William Hambleton,* our very good Friend is in Town – Suppose you shew him some of the Vases, & a few other Connoisieurs not only to have their advice, but to have the advantage of their puffing them off against the next Spring, as they will, by being consulted, and flatter'd agreeably, as you know how, consider themselves as a sort of parties in the affair, & act accordingly.'[57] To make sure of success, before the vases went on sale Wedgwood and Bentley had private viewings for Mrs Chetwynd (their conduit to Queen Charlotte), the dukes of Northumberland and Marlborough, the earls of Stamford and Dartmouth, Lords Bessborough, Percy, Clanbrazil, Carlisle and Torrington, Sir Watkin Williams Wynn and, by comparison, the rather humble-sounding MP Mr Harbord Harbord (who was, however, later to become the 1st Baron Suffield).[58]

'Fashion,' as Wedgwood recognized, 'is infinitely superior to *merit* in many respects . . . It is plain from a thousand instances that if you have a favourite child you wish the public to fondle & take notice of, you have only to make a choice of proper sponcers. If you are lucky in them no matter what the brat is, black, brown or fair, its fortune is made.'[59] And with his 'sponcers' Wedgwood started at the top, believing that the greatest in the land would influence the lesser: 'Few ladies, you know, dare venture at anything out of the common stile 'till authoris'd by their betters – by the Ladies of superior spirit who set the ton.'[60] Queen Charlotte had started him on his way with Queensware; after a queen, who but an empress? In 1770 Catherine the Great had commissioned a Queensware service decorated with wheat husks. Three years later came a greater challenge: she wanted a service for state occasions: a 680-piece dinner service and a 264-piece dessert service, plus tureens, salvers, fruit baskets, 'glaciers' (ice-cream bowls) etc. to accompany them.† Each piece was to have on it an image of an actual country house, or a park or garden, or a palace, or even industrial 'sights' such as the Plymouth

---

* Sir William Hamilton was minister plenipotentiary to the court of Spain in Naples. A famous collector, he commissioned the enormously influential *Les Antiquités étrusques, grecques et romaines* (4 vols., dated 1766–7, but published 1767–76), which spread the neoclassical style across Europe. A year after publication of the first volume Wedgwood had named his new pottery works 'Etruria', after the Etruscans, and on the opening day he had thrown six black basalt 'first-day vases' based on engravings from the book.
† This service was for the Chesmenski Palace, built on La Grenouillière, or the Frog Marsh. Hence the pieces were decorated with frogs, and the entire service is commonly referred to as 'the frog service'. Some of it is on display today at the Hermitage in St Petersburg.

docks or the Bridgewater Canal. The cost was fantastic – not for the manufacture, but for an artist to be sent around the country to make drawings, and then for the 1,200 drawings to be worked up so they could be transferred to the dishes. But Wedgwood was a born publicist, and he had planned a *coup de théâtre* – he would show the entire service before it was shipped off to Russia, and, whatever he had lost on the manufacture, 'it would bring an immense number of people of fashion into our Rooms – would fully complete our notoriety to the whole Island, & help us greatly, no doubt, in the sale of our goods, both useful & ornamental. It would confirm the consequence we have attain'd, & increase it, by showing that we are employ'd in a much higher scale than other Manufacturers.'[61] His one anxiety was that some of his noble patrons would be offended that their houses were not included, or were put 'upon a small piece, or not flattering it sufficiently'. To make the event even more exclusive, admission to the showroom would be by ticket. It was all a great success, with the King and Queen of Sweden paying a special visit, as well as Queen Charlotte, Prince Ernst of Mecklenberg, and hordes of the aristocracy. No one was aggrieved to find their great houses represented on some of the smaller dishes; on the contrary they came time and again to point their lasting fame out to friends.[62]

The difference between Wedgwood and earlier craftsmen who had relied on the nobility and gentry for their livings was that, as far as Wedgwood and Bentley were concerned, the nobility were a means to an end:

> The Great People have had these Vases in their Palaces long enough for them to be seen and admired by the *Middling Class* of People, which Class we know are vastly, I had almost said, infinitely superior, in number to the great, and though a *great price* was, I believe, at first necessary to make the vases esteemed *Ornament for Palaces*, that reason no longer exists. Their character is established and the middling People would probably buy quantities of them at a reduced price.[63]

Once that principle was established, it was not surprising that Wedgwood thought he could sell anything to anyone. In the 1780s his works could not keep up with the retail demand, and he bought in ware that other manufacturers had been unable to sell. He slapped a higher price on it, together with his name, and everything was snatched off the shelves in a fashionable frenzy. It was the ultimate marketing triumph: to sell goods no one else could shift – and at a higher price.

Wedgwood used every possible route to reach the 'middling People'. There had long been a reluctance for luxury trades in general to advertise in the newspapers, because there was no control over how their advertisements would appear: auctions – of houses, pictures or just household goods – cockfights, draper's shops, patent medicines, bug-killers, carefully worded advertisements for the 'removal of obstructions' (abortifacients), all appeared pell-mell, one after the other, in column after column. The newspapers, meanwhile, were doing their best to make advertisers believe that their pages were the haunts of none but the very finest manufacturers and retailers. In 1757 the *Liverpool Chronicle*, in its first edition, suggested,

> It is not many years since it was thought mean and disreputable, in any tradesmen of worth and credit, to advertise the sales of his commodities in a public Newspaper, but as those apprehensions were founded only on custom, and not on reason, it is become now fashionable for very eminent tradesmen to publish their business, and the peculiar goods wherein they deal, in the News Papers, by way of Advertisement; nor can any one make appear what disgrace there can be in this, for do not the great trading corporations apprize the public of their sales in the public News Papers?[64]

Naturally, the newspapers would say that: they had a vested interest in advertisers believing them. But many manufacturers could not be swayed. For years Wedgwood and Bentley preferred to use 'puffs', articles ostensibly written by the newspaper's own journalists, but in reality supplied to it by the subject of the piece or his friends. Wedgwood complained to Bentley, 'There is a most famous puff for Boulton & Fothergill in the St James's Chronicle of the 9th & for Mr Cox likewise, How the Author could have the assurance to leave us out I cannot conceive. Pray get another article in the next paper to complete the Triumvirate.'[65]

Wedgwood constantly came up with new marketing and publicity ploys. When he was given permission to copy the early-first-century Barberini vase, recently acquired by the Duchess of Portland (and more commonly known today as the Portland Vase), he took orders for a small run of expensive reproductions, promising his customers that if the results were not satisfactory the purchasers would not be required to pay. This was a good marketing ploy, rather than an attack of nerves – the Great Publicist was saying, 'The original is almost unreproducible; when I create a good reproduction, therefore, it makes me a great manufacturer, and the vases more valuable.' This was one small example of his endless marketing ingenuity. He also sent his London agent to collect outstanding payments while carrying new samples, to show rich but dilatory customers what they could have once they had paid up. He made perfectly standard goods seem like limited lines: he warned that his 'serpent handled antique vases' should not 'be seen till the others are all sold, & then raise the price of them 1/ each'; then he countermanded that – instead of just making the price higher, the London showroom should raise the price even further, and 'never mind their being thought dear, [but] do not keep them open in the rooms, shew them only to the People of Fashion'.[66] He pioneered inertia selling, by sending parcels of his goods – some worth as much as £70 – to aristocratic families across Europe, spending £20,000 (altogether the equivalent of several million today), and following up each parcel with a request for payment or the return of the goods. Within a couple of years he had received payment from all but three families.[67] He was an endless fountain of ideas – boxes of samples for distance orders; special terms for a first order; French-, German-, Italian- and Dutch-speaking clerks to deal with export correspondence. By 1777 he had travelling salesmen, and by 1790 he had drawn up a 'Travellers' Book' for them, complete with rules of behaviour and commercial systems.[68] He foresaw self-service, telling his London staff to put the inferior pieces 'in one of the best places of your lower Shop, where people can come at them, & serve themselves'.[69] He had trade cards printed up saying that Wedgwood 'delivers his goods safe and carriage free . . . as he sells for ready money only': he offered free London delivery for goods paid in cash, and promised those outside London that if their orders arrived damaged he would pay for the replacements. Some of this was genuine; much more was perception. The middle classes could buy his goods only for ready money, although the upper classes still received long credit. He had advertised as a novelty that his customers were 'at liberty to return the whole, or any part of the goods they order (paying the carriage back) if they do not find them agreeable to their wishes', but most customers had routinely returned goods to their suppliers if they didn't like them, and they complained vociferously if things arrived broken. Still, the advertisements stood, and drew in new customers by their perceived innovation.

Wedgwood's showrooms, too, were something new. Small producer/retailers had combined workshops and selling areas, but it was unusual for a manufacturer of Wedgwood's size to sell directly to the public. He opened a London showroom in 1768, and he had showrooms in Bath from 1772, and Dublin from 1773.* He saw his showrooms as places of exciting novelty and display, where dinner services were laid out on tables, and

> a much greater variety of setts of vases should decorate the Walls, and both these articles may, every few days, be so alter'd, revers'd & transform'd as to render the whole a new scene, even to the same Company, every time they shall bring their friends to visit us.
>
> I need not tell you the many good effects this must produce, when business & amusement can be made to go hand in hand. Every new show, Exhibition or rarity soon grows stale in London, & is no longer regarded, after the first sight, unless utility, or some such variety as I have hinted at above continues to recommend it to their notice . . .[70]

But perhaps Wedgwood's most astute move had nothing to do with selling goods at all. When Wedgwood first set up in business in Burslem, there were three ways for him to send his goods to market: by road for twenty miles, then along the River Weaver to Liverpool; by road for forty miles, to Bridgnorth, then by the River Severn to Bristol; or by road for forty miles, then via the River Trent to Hull. To get one ton of goods from Burslem to the Weaver cost 18s.; from Burslem to the Trent, 34s. Whatever route was chosen, the goods had to make the initial journey by road – and a 'road' in the eighteenth century was not what we would call a road. The main road out of Burslem was in such poor condition that it was permanently impassable to wheeled vehicles of any kind; everything had to be carried in and out by packhorse. This was not an unusual state for roads across the country. A contemporary described

---

* One incidental feature of the Bath showroom was that the managers, William and Ann Ward, were the parents of Ann Radcliffe, the Gothic novelist and author of *The Mysteries of Udolpho* (1794). Ann Ward was the niece of Thomas Bentley, and Ann Radcliffe had grown up as a close friend of Wedgwood's daughter Susannah, known to posterity as the mother of Charles Darwin.

the road from Knutsford, in Cheshire, to Newcastle under Lyme: 'In general [it was] a paved causeway, as narrow as can be conceived, and cut into perpetual holes, some of them two feet deep measured on the level . . . and wherever the country is the least sandy, the pavement [that is, the road surface] is discontinued, and the ruts and holes most execrable.'[71] And that was a good road: the road between Newcastle and Burslem was worse, partly because until 1720 the freeholders of Burslem had been entitled to dig clay from any unenclosed land, which included the main roads. In the early nineteenth century much of this had still not been filled in.[72] John Ogilby, in his *The Traveller's Guide, or, a Most Exact Description of the Roads of England* (1711), had called Burslem one of the most inaccessible places in England. It was hardly surprising that nearly 30 per cent of Wedgwood's goods were broken in transit.

Wedgwood, as so often, was apparently lucky in being in the right place at the right time. When the novelist and critic Tobias Smollett first travelled to England from Scotland, in 1739, there were no wagons on the roads anywhere between Edinburgh and Newcastle upon Tyne, because there were no roads that were good enough. The roads across the islands were in such a terrible state because their maintenance was still governed by the Highways Act of 1555. This act gave control over the roads to each individual parish, but it did not give parishes the right to levy a rate on residents to pay for professional survey or repair. Instead, those whose land was valued above £50 were required to lend a horse or an ox and a wagon for four days annually, while those householders whose land was rated at a lesser level were required to give four days' labour on the roads a year, unpaid, to be supervised by an unpaid surveyor. It was unrealistic to expect good work or good materials from those supplying them unrecompensed, and now there was the added unfairness that these locally maintained roads were increasingly used for trans-parish transport between towns and cities. The matter of unpaid labour and co-opted transport was not addressed until the Highways Act of 1835, when finally parishes were permitted to use local rates to pay for professional surveyors and paid labourers. In the meantime, turnpike trusts were created, often formed by groups of manufacturers and local merchants who would most benefit from better-maintained roads. From 1706 individual Turnpike Acts were granted by Parliament: in exchange for improvements and maintenance on the roads for a period of (initially) twenty-one years, each trust could set up toll gates and charge for road usage. The tolls in turn were used to pay for the surveyor, treasurer, clerk and labourers to build the road. Between 1750 and 1800, more than 1,600 trusts were formed;* by the mid-1830s, 1,116 turnpike trusts in England and Wales supervised 22,000 miles of roads, out of a total of 126,770 miles of parish highways. Turnpikes now made up nearly 20 per cent of the road system of England and Wales.[74]

From the 1740s, Wedgwood had been at the forefront of a successful campaign by a group of Staffordshire merchants and manufacturers to upgrade the roads into the Potteries; in 1766 alone, six Turnpike Acts affecting the Five Towns were approved by Parliament.[75] The most immediate result of the spread of turnpikes for these businessmen, however, was not only the improvement to the roads – although now, it was true, goods could actually be transported to and from Burslem by wagon – but the speed with which journeys could be made. From the 1750s to the 1830s journey times between major cities fell by 80 per cent; from the 1770s to the 1830s they were halved. An advertisement in 1754 boasted that 'However incredible it may appear this coach will actually arrive in London four days after leaving Manchester'; a mere six years later the same distance took three days; by 1784 the time was down to two days. This improvement was not confined to a single road. The trip from Edinburgh to London had been impossible to undertake by carriage along the entire route in 1739; by the mid-1750s the whole route could be covered in a carriage, taking ten days in summer and twelve in winter; in 1836 a stagecoach travelled the route in 45½ hours.[76] In 1820 for the first time in history it became possible for a person to go faster than a man on a single horse.

Travel had become easier; it had it become speedier; now it was more readily available as well. As the journey times fell, so the number of stagecoaches increased: in 1780 there were approximately 20 stagecoaches leaving Birmingham daily; by 1815 there were over 100; in 1835 the number had risen to 350. Ten major urban centres – Birmingham, Bristol, Exeter, Leeds, Liverpool, Newcastle, Manchester, Sheffield, Glasgow and Edinburgh – saw an eightfold increase in stagecoach

---

* The government had many reasons to approve these trusts, apart from general improvement to trade: after 1745 it was suggested that the Young Pretender, Bonnie Prince Charlie, had managed to get as far as Derby during his unsuccessful attempt to regain the throne for the Stuarts in part because the poor quality of the roads meant that troops could not be dispatched quickly enough.[73]

services in the forty-six years from 1790 to 1836. Even small towns such as Kirkby Stephen, a market town in Westmorland, had regular and plentiful carrier services: from Kirkby Stephen one could travel on scheduled stagecoach services to Newcastle, Stockton, Barnard Castle, Lancaster, Kendal (and from there on to London), Sedbergh and Kirkby Lonsdale. And, apart from the London carriers, eight other carriers travelled regularly from Kirkby Stephen to different parts of England.

Technological developments to stagecoaches also fuelled improved journey times. The coaches were built lower to the ground, so they could be driven more quickly with less fear of being overturned. The invention of the elliptical spring (by the wonderfully named Obadiah Elliot) in 1804 made it possible for carriages to be hung from springs, which made the coaches cheaper to manufacture, enabled them to travel at greater speed and more comfortably – and the increased stability made it possible to have 'outsides', or seats on the roof, without the passengers being tossed overboard. Together with bigger carriages, this meant that by the 1830s stagecoaches carried double the number of passengers they had in 1790. Fifteen times as many people were travelling as had forty years before, in a service that had grown in the number of scheduled routes, and the number of coaches on those routes, by 800 per cent.[77]

It was not merely passenger numbers: the quantity of goods transported by road also increased. In 1823 London had over 700 carriers, twice as many as it had had thirty years before; Exeter had three times as many in 1831 as it had had in 1792, while Sheffield had nearly four times as many; in Birmingham the number soared fivefold in the same period. Overall, across the country, there was a 131 per cent growth in carrier services, which sounds substantial. But, compared to an urban population growth of 120 per cent, it becomes apparent that the number of carriers was barely keeping up with overall growth.[78] The main reason for this lack of expansion was the development of the canal system.

Adam Smith had recognized the importance of transport to the economy, but, while he paid lip service to roads, he was mainly concerned with the benefits brought by water transportation. In 1776, in the middle of this revolution in transport, he wrote in *The Wealth of Nations*, that 'by means of water-carriage, a more extensive market is opened to every sort of industry than what land-carriage alone can afford it, so it is upon the sea-coast, and along the banks of navigable rivers, that industry of every kind naturally begins to subdivide and improve itself.' He returned to this, stressing that 'Good roads, canals, and navigable rivers, by diminishing the expense of carriage, put the remote parts of the country more nearly upon a level with those in the neighbourhood of the town. They are upon that account the greatest of all improvements.'[79] But he was somewhat behind the times in his concentration on rivers. It is true that at the beginning of the eighteenth century most work had been concerned with improving the navigability of rivers. In 1720 the Mersey and Irwell Navigation System had opened; the Weaver Navigation carried traffic from 1720, and improvements to the Wear went on from 1716 to 1759. Yet, despite increasing the extent of the navigable inland waterways of Britain from just over 1,100 kilometres in 1660 to more than 1,800 kilometres in 1720s,[80] this was always going to be a solution limited by geography: the newly industrialized Midlands were over 400 feet above sea level, and in the west the River Severn fluctuated from having a depth of only 16 inches of water in good weather to rising 18 feet in five hours in bad, while in 1796 it remained completely impassable for all but two months of the year. Canals were the logical way forward. Two projects led the way. From 1754 the Liverpool Corporation oversaw the building of the Sankey Brook Navigation system – an entirely new canal along an entirely new route, rather than following an old riverbed. Then in 1757 the Duke of Bridgewater inherited an estate, in Worsley, in Lancashire, and planned immediately to build a canal to link his new coalfields with the urban centres of Manchester and Liverpool. The first ten miles of the Bridgewater Canal were in operation by 1761, and the price of coal in Manchester immediately fell from 7d. to 3½d. per hundredweight.[81] In 1766 James Brindley, the engineer behind the Bridgewater Canal, began work on the Trent and Mersey Canal, which when finished in 1777 linked the Trent near Burton to the Mersey in Lancashire, making the entire breadth of the country from Hull to Liverpool navigable. The canal was 151 kilometres long (225 if you count the bit where it joined the Birmingham Canal and the Severn), and had along its length 75 locks, 5 tunnels, 5 major aqueducts and 155 minor ones – a feat of engineering that ushered in the great age of canal building. By 1830 there were nearly 5,000 kilometres of canals in England and Wales.[82]

Wedgwood and his friends had been enthusiasts from the beginning: Erasmus Darwin had been involved in promoting the Grand Trunk

Canal, which was to link the Trent and the Mersey (1766–77) and the Birmingham Canal (opened 1771), and he and Wedgwood saw the very practical benefits to being able to convey the Potteries' output to the ports of Liverpool and Hull.* Darwin had calculated that the cost of shipping the clay and flint used in Wedgwood's works would drop from 15*s.* per ton to 8*s.* per ton once the canal opened, while the freight charges for the finished earthenware moving in the opposite direction would be 12*s.* instead of the present 28*s.* per ton. (In fact, when the Trent and Mersey Canal was completed, freight prices dropped from 10*d.* to ½*d.* per ton per mile.)[84] Under Wedgwood's watchful eye, the Trent and Mersey had been carefully planned to pass through land he had purchased for his new factory, which in turn was being designed to make loading and unloading from the as yet non-existent canal into the as yet non-existent factory both economical and convenient.

Wedgwood, of course, was not the only manufacturer to benefit in this way. Many of the new factory owners were as successful as they were because they understood that technology and trade went hand in hand. Joseph Wilkes, the child of a Leicestershire farmer, set up as a cheese factor in Burton upon Trent. In 1763 he went into partnership with a Birmingham banker named Sampson Lloyd (whose bank is now known as Lloyds TSB, keeping his name alive into the twenty-first century), buying a lease on nineteen miles of the Trent Navigation; from this he gradually invested in canals, turnpikes (and later railroads), until in 1783 he bought the entire parish of Measham, where he set up a pithead to mine coal, a brickworks, a corn mill, a barge-building company and

---

* Charles Darwin's grandfather Erasmus Darwin (1731–1802) was a doctor by profession and a natural philosopher by inclination. He lived in Lichfield, and was an active member of several provincial scientific societies, including the Botanical Society, the Derby Philosophical Society and the Lunar Society. The latter included among its members the manufacturer Matthew Boulton, his partner James Watt and the scientist Joseph Priestley, as well as Wedgwood and Bentley. Darwin was interested both intellectually and financially in the connection between technology and industry, producing plans for a 'horizontal windmill' to grind pigment for Wedgwood's factory, as well as recommending to Wedgwood the acquisition of Boulton and Watt's steam engine. He was considered expert enough in technical matters to be called as a witness, along with Watt, in one of the many disputes involving the patents of the cotton manufacturer Richard Arkwright's carding and spinning machines.

Wedgwood and Darwin did not, however, confine their canal fever to commerce alone. When fossils were uncovered during the building of the Trent and Mersey, Wedgwood collected them and shared them with Darwin: 'I will in return,' he promised, 'send you some mineral observations of exactly the same value (weighed nicely) for I must inform you I mean to gain *full as much* knowledge, from you who can spare it so well, as I return you in exchange.[83]

a cotton mill. A bigger cotton mill was opened in 1802, which he ran together with several banks in the Burton area.

One final example of these multidisciplinary industrialists was Robert 'Parsley' Peel,* a 'mechanical genius', who was influenced by Lloyd and his partner to set up a cotton mill in Burton upon Trent in the early 1780s, melding two new pieces of innovation and technology: his factory used the new Arkwright cotton-spinning frames, and was located where the Trent and Mersey Canal could handily convey raw materials and finished goods to and from the works. By 1790 his son Robert had 'capital overflowing in his hands', and bought property, including estates from the Marquis of Bath and a parish near Tamworth, which was to be a base to launch his political career. Even though politics was more on his mind than cotton, Tamworth was on the Trent and Mersey too, and soon Peel and his partners owned spinning mills, calico-printing and bleaching works. By the end of the eighteenth century they controlled 20 mills in Lancashire and the Midlands and had 15,000 employees, and Peel, the son of the semi-literate Parsley Peel, was Sir Robert, and considered himself entirely a gentleman, while Parsley's grandson ultimately became prime minister.[85]

Yet it is important to remember that while this modernization – of production, distribution and retailing – was developing at a furious rate, it was not occurring in splendid isolation, but running in tandem with an older system of retail networks. For much of the time the two coexisted quite happily. For those living outside major urban areas – and for many within city limits – there were four ways of buying goods. The first, which remains today and therefore is the one we regard as primary, was the shop. As we have seen, even people in rural areas had regular if not continuous access to shops. But this did not mean that they bought nothing the rest of the time. The most frequent and convenient way of purchasing goods was at daily, weekly, monthly or seasonal markets. From the late eighteenth century, butchers, fruit vendors and greengrocers were the main retailers in markets – corn, flour, cheese, bread and other staples were no longer sold this way, but had moved either into fixed wholesale premises (such as corn halls and cloth halls) or to back-street shops and other fixed retail premises. In 1772 in

---

* 'Parsley' was after a parsley-patterned calico he designed early in his career.

Manchester there were 30 grocers and tea dealers, 3 provision dealers (including cheesemongers and butter, bacon and ham dealers) and 16 flour and corn dealers appearing in the directories listing retail outlets; by 1800 their numbers had risen to 134 grocers and tea dealers, 11 provision dealers, and 262 flour and corn dealers.[86]

While the markets, usually run and operated by local inhabitants, were – just – holding on to the perishable food sales, fairs, which were run for the most part by outsiders, were evolving. Before the eighteenth century an annual fair was for wholesale merchants to conduct business, whether it was in cloth, corn, horses or agricultural material such as feed, animals or machinery. By the 1720s cloth halls and corn halls had appeared – fixed public buildings where trading could go on year round.[87] This trend, from temporary to permanent, from street to shop, continued throughout the century, as fairs lost all their wholesale side, except in a few cases for animals and some food. Instead, the fairs became more and more the haunt of entertainers, pedlars, shows and exhibitions. (For more on fairs in the nineteenth century, see pp. 282–5.)

The final method of purchasing goods in rural areas, and in many urban ones, was via hawkers and pedlars. Most areas were well served by these 'Scotch drapers' and 'Manchester men', whose regular circuits covered most of Britain. These were not the simple men with packs of modern imagining, and they were not selling solely to the poor. The Society of Travelling Scotchmen in Shrewsbury in 1785 had capital of more than £20,000; even the small Bridgnorth society had capital investment of £5,000.[88] The Scotch draper carried a pack 'four feet in length and two or more in depth',[89] and it closely resembled the clown car at the circus, pouring out an endless variety of more goods than logic said it could possibly hold: silks, cotton, calico, linen, hosiery, lace, and ready-made-up women's clothes – petticoats, handkerchiefs, chemises and still more. In 1781 the Revd James Woodforde wrote in his diary that he had bought, from a man 'with a cart with Linens, Cottons, Lace &c. . . . some cotton 6 Yrds for a morning gown for myself at 2s. 6d. per yard, pd. 0.15.0 Some chintz for a gown for Nancy 5 yds and ½ I pd. 1.14.0 . . . Nancy also bought a Linen Handkerchief &c. of him. Mrs How bought a silk handkerchief of him also.'[90] Throughout the nineteenth century, street sellers continued to appear in towns, especially in more suburban areas, carrying more heavy goods than today seems feasible. In his 1851 survey of the working poor, Henry Mayhew listed men who sold 'Door-mats, baskets and "duffer's" packs, wood pails, brushes, brooms, clothes-props, clothes-lines and string, and grid-irons, Dutch-ovens, skewers and fore-shovels' carried across their shoulders.[91]*

Yet these itinerants, as with their equivalent traders in the markets and fairs, were swimming against the tide. As early as the 1730s, Parliament had received more than a hundred petitions from shopkeepers, claiming that pedlars were taking away their livelihood. The pedlars had the manufacturers on their side: they told Parliament that 'the Quantity of goods bought and disposed of by them was considerably more extensive than had been generally conceived, ... great Quantities of goods of almost every description being vended in detail'.[92] In 1785, when Parliament proposed a bill to forbid itinerant traders, manufacturers and wholesale dealers in Liverpool, the 'Linen Committee, Silk Manufacturers and Callico [sic] Printers of Glasgow' all protested that without itinerant traders 'great Quantities of British Manufactures' would remain unsold – in rural areas naturally, but also in the newly industrial heartlands, where mill towns and factories had vast numbers of employees, but, as yet, no fixed retail network.[93]

That was to change in the coming years.

---

* Duffers were people who sold bad-quality goods cheaply, pretending that they had been stolen or smuggled in order to explain their low prices. Dutch ovens were small brick or cast-iron stoves on legs, which were heated by charcoal.

3

The Ladies' (and Gents') Paradise: The Nineteenth-Century Shop

GROCERS HAD ORIGINALLY BEEN wholesalers, those who bought 'in gross'; then they became luxury retailers, purveyors of imported delicacies from abroad – tea, coffee, sugar, spices, dried fruits, 'Italian goods'. As these foods became less expensive, and more readily available to the population at large, the function and trade of the grocer changed. For some time, various food retailers stuck to the old names that indicated high levels of specialization – a grocer was expected to sell the items listed above; a provision dealer to sell butter, cheese, eggs and bacon; then there were flour dealers, butter men, cheese factors and so on. But it appears that the reality, from early in the nineteenth century, was less rigidly structured than the job titles implied: grocers also sold butter, bacon, hams and herrings, oilmen sold cheese, even a butter man might sell pig meat. One flour dealer at the turn of the nineteenth century kept records that reflected this variety: 44 per cent of his spending was on his core trade, the purchase of flour and meal; 18.5 per cent went on butter and cheese, 6.5 per cent on tea, 11 per cent on sugar, while the remaining 20 per cent went on a wide variety of goods: potatoes, bacon, salt, raisins, currants, coffee, treacle, spices, pepper, mustard, rice, sweets, soap, starch, candles, tobacco and snuff. This was not at all unusual: by 1846 the *Grocers' Weekly Circular and Price List*, a trade publication, listed butter, cheese, eggs, pork – all items that, officially, grocers did not sell.[1] Now a grocer was someone who needed to have certain trade skills that other provisioners did not have – he had to know how to blend tea, roast coffee beans, mix herbs and spices, cure bacon, clean dried fruit, and cut sugar.*[3]

* Sugar until well into the nineteenth century was a very intractable object. Sugar was originally processed by boiling the raw cane sugar with lime water and bullock's blood;

For the most part, the staple diet of the working classes and much of the lower middle classes in the mid nineteenth-century consisted of bread or potatoes, a little bit of butter, cheese or bacon, tea with sugar, and a bit of salt. The eighteenth century had shown forward-looking retailers that profits could be made by selling in quantity to the mass market at a small mark-up. The improvements to transport and the consequent development of wholesalers and distribution centres, and the concentration of population in urban centres, soon made the idea of selling a small range of stock items – bought in bulk, for low prices – both practical and astonishingly profitable.

In the early 1790s, before the French wars, wheat had cost between 48s. and 58s. a quarter; by 1795 it was 90s.; and in 1800 it was a shocking 113s. – an increase of 135 per cent in less than a decade. There was an endless succession of food riots: more than twenty between 1756 and 1818, and a dozen of those in the last two decades. There were also attempts throughout this period to find more peaceful ways of dealing with the price escalation. One solution was to turn to the social group that was so familiar – the club. Groups of consumers joined together in flour or bread societies to gain the financial clout to buy these necessities at reduced prices. Many of the societies failed, mostly from inadequate investment or size. But one of the more successful was the Birmingham Flour and Bread Company, set up in 1796 with capital of £6,000 from its members, because 'unless some proper and effectual means are taken, the evil attending the high price of grain and the shameful adulteration of flour will continue'. By 1800 it had 1,360 shareholders (including Matthew Boulton). Others groups followed suit, using what became the standard methods: large-scale orders, paid for in cash, with discounts for bulk.[4] And in the early decades of the nineteenth century there were still other groups, more idealistic in origin, set up in emulation of the principles of the socialist reformer Robert Owen. In 1827 the Brighton Co-operative Benevolent Association and the Co-operative Trading Association were formed, to collect weekly subscriptions which were to

the blood coagulated, absorbing the impurities (and with it sugar's natural brown colour). The remaining liquid was then filtered, concentrated and poured into moulds, where it solidified. The resulting loaves were then broken up and repurified before being formed once more into conical loaves and sold. Grocers broke up the big loaves with hammers, but the smaller loaves bought by housewives still had to be cut into smaller pieces with sugar nippers. Industrial processing, happily, replaced the bullock's blood with centrifugal force.[2]

be used both to educate people in the values of cooperation, and to 'engage in retail trade with the object of accumulating capital from its profits to eventually establish a community' based on cooperative principles.[5] William King, a doctor, was the prime mover, having already set up a Mechanics' Institute in Brighton; he also published *The Co-operator*, a paper with a good circulation in the north and the Midlands, which strongly influenced the later Co-op movement.

An early Co-operative Congress met in Manchester in 1831, to establish the North-West of England United Co-operative Co., to supply a wholesale warehouse in Liverpool for the various societies'. This did not take off, but these early cooperative ventures set an example, and in the 1850s and 1860s a new generation of workers attempted to create similar societies. The town of Rochdale, in Lancashire, was the location. Rochdale had had a thriving flannel industry for centuries, but with the coming of power looms the economic life of the town was no longer so stable. The new industries of coal mining, cotton mills and machine-making were developing, but the 'hungry forties' and reliance in the new factories on hiring 'outsiders' combined to create extreme hardship locally. In 1837, 180 animals a week had been slaughtered for sale in the local market; in 1841 the number was less than 70. So in 1844 the Rochdale Pioneers was formed, a club with thirty members, set up with the intention, in the short term, of selling food and clothing at prices workers could afford; then, when it became possible, the group hoped to move on to building workers' housing, creating their own workshops, and setting up a temperance hotel. The main difference between the Pioneers and other clubs was that profits would no longer simply be divided among the members. Now interest would be paid to each shareholder, and what remained of the profits would be distributed to members in proportion to the amount of money they had spent at the store that year: a dividend on purchases. With capital of £28, the Pioneers began trading with a stock valued at £16 11s. 11d.: 28 pounds of butter, 56 pounds of sugar, 6 hundredweight of flour, 1 sack of oatmeal, and some candles. At the end of its first year, the club's membership had risen to seventy-four, it had increased its working capital to £181, and had made a profit of £22. The trade depression of 1847 only brought in more members: by 1848 there were 140; two years later it was 600.

In 1850 another group of men in Rochdale attempted to start a cooperative corn mill, in imitation of the Pioneers. When they failed to raise the necessary capital, they approached the Pioneers themselves, who invested some of their profits in the mill, creating the Corn Mill Society. By 1852 twenty-two different societies were dealing with the Corn Mill Society, a consumer-initiated, consumer-owned and consumer-controlled group. By 1851 there were perhaps as many as 130 societies working on the principles the Rochdale Pioneers had established, and many realized that cooperation between them was the way forward. In 1862 a conference in Oldham agreed to set up the North of England Co-operative Wholesale Agency and Depot Society; the following year it was formally registered as the North of England Co-operative Wholesale Industrial Provident Society (later thankfully shortened to the Co-operative Wholesale Society, known as the CWS), with forty-three societies owning shares. This was the start of the national cooperative movement: in 1862, branches of the Co-op were opened in Newcastle; in 1874 in London; in 1875 in Liverpool, in 1882 in Leeds, then over the next decade in Birmingham, Blackburn, Bristol, Huddersfield, Longton, Northampton, Nottingham and Cardiff. Furthermore, buying depots were set up across the country, and also outside England: six were opened in Ireland in eight years; then one in New York; followed by, in Europe, Rouen, Dénia, Copenhagen, Aarhus, Odense, Esbjerg, Gothenburg and Hamburg, and, further afield, Montreal and Sydney. As if this unstoppable march were not enough, the Co-op opened its own production sources where necessary: a dairy in Ireland from 1889; pig farms and bacon-curing in Denmark from 1900 and Ireland from 1901; even tea estates in Ceylon from 1913.[6]

By the 1860s the idea of cooperative trading had travelled far from its origins, and various middle-class groups were setting up their own versions. The first was in 1864, when some Post Office clerks in London clubbed together to buy a chest of tea at a wholesale price. They moved on to bulk purchases of coffee and sugar, and in 1865 the Post Office Supply Association was formalized; within six months, it had 700 members, and it had changed its name to the Civil Service Supply Association, whose intention was to supply 'Officers of the Civil Service and their Friends . . . at the lowest possible prices'.[7] In 1866 came the Civil Service Co-operative Society, and in 1872 the Army and Navy Co-operative Society, open to 'officers, their widows, non-commissioned officers, petty officers, secretaries of service clubs, canteen and mess reps', and any friends that they chose to introduce.[8] Both claimed to be offering

Co-operative stores first appeared in the 1840s to supply the working classes with the basics. In the 1860s the middle classes also began to take advantage of lower prices through bulk purchasing. In 1873 *Punch* satirized this trend: this shopper is prosperous enough to have both a coachman and a footman.

a new combination: low prices and reduced service in exchange for cash sales, fixed prices, some goods only in large quantities, others with an extra discount for bulk. It was, perhaps new to them although, as we have seen, none of these notions was innovatory. Soon mail order was added to the list of services, together with expanded ranges: wine, tobacco, baby linen, books, boots and shoes, coal, carpets, drapery, milk and butter, meat, pianos, even surgical instruments – the Civil Service Co-operative Society and the Army and Navy were now a long way from the working-class aims of the originators of the movement, and were heading instead towards the department stores (see below, pp. 110ff.). Those groups formally connected to the CWS stayed true to their origins, selling only groceries, fresh meat, and in some places drapery, tailoring and shoes and clogs.

Despite the financial structure that linked the co-ops to their middle-class brethren, the range of goods available in the co-op shops themselves more closely resembled that in the multiple stores (which today would be called chain stores) that were appearing at a rapid rate in urban centres at the same time. Co-ops and multiples were similar in that they both aimed at the working-class customer; they both relied on their size to achieve price reductions; they both sold a narrow range of goods, primarily food; they sold at fixed prices; they accepted only cash; they reached their customers by branding their outlets with a central name; and they provided a bare minimum of services to keep costs down. They were different, however, in an equally basic way. Co-ops were decentralized groups that shared services, fixed their own prices and shared their profits via membership dividends based on purchases. By contrast, the aim of multiples, first, last and always, was to make profits for their owners.[9] There was no attempt to share the wealth, or form a better society.

The main growth of multiples came in the later part of the nineteenth century, but preliminary stirrings had been there for some time. Williams of Manchester, a typical early example, was created after a Mrs Williams married a miner; she had previously owned a grocery in Didsbury, a prosperous suburb of Manchester. In 1865 she took a double-fronted shop there; in 1888 she opened another shop in Cheadle; in 1891 yet another, this time in West Didsbury; within thirty years Williams of Manchester had five branches, all in prosperous, middle-class suburbs. Eventually it expanded to thirty.[10] Similar in pattern if not in scale was Thomas Lipton. He was born in Glasgow in 1850, the son of an Irish labourer and his wife, who had emigrated during the Famine. At eighteen he joined his parents in the small grocery shop they then ran; with some savings and a year's pay he opened a second shop. By 1880 he had twelve shops in Glasgow, with a turnover of £200,000. His first shop in England was opened the following year, and by 1889 he had 30 shops and a turnover of £1.5 million.[11] Less than a decade later, there were 242 shops in Britain, and a smattering of overseas outlets.[12]

Lipton's shops stocked a limited range of goods – bacon, ham, butter, eggs, cheese – and thus, in order to buy cheaply from wholesalers, he needed to have a large number of shops to supply. He relied heavily on a combination of price-cutting and price promotion. He advertised his cut-rate 'Irish produce' – ham was priced from 5*d.* to 7*d.* per pound, while elsewhere it cost between 7*d.* and 10*d.* In 1877 he famously advertised the 'Lipton Pound Note', which declared, 'I promise to give on demand at any of my establishments ham, butter and eggs as given elsewhere to the value of ONE POUND stg for fifteen shillings.' He made this financially possible – and even profitable – by rapid turnover, low profit margins and low overheads. He aimed relentlessly at the

Advertising appeared widely in a variety of forms: here a Wimbledon grocer printed a picture of his shop on the wrapping paper he used for his customers' purchases.

lower-class market: his shops were either in the high streets or in smaller streets of densely populated working-class neighbourhoods. He sold a strictly limited range of stock in bulk, to vast numbers of customers, from vast shops: in Paisley, a suburb of Glasgow, his shop had a horse-shoe counter so large it was staffed by twelve shop assistants. His Glasgow shops alone, he boasted, daily sold a ton and a half of 'lump' butter, 50 cases of 'roll' butter, a ton of bacon, a ton and a half of ham, half a ton of cheese, and 16,000 eggs.*[14]

Once these huge shops reached a certain level, there were two main ways of expanding: the shops could begin to stock an ever-wider range of goods, while the services for customers were also enlarged; or the goods and services could remain as they were, while the number of customers was increased nationally by opening ever-more branches. The first decision led, essentially, to shops becoming department stores, the

---

* Yet bulk was not absolutely uniform, even for the multiples, and several successful chains had a curious anomaly known as the 'Highland Trade'. As late as the 1910s Cochrane Stores in the west of Scotland were still advertising 'Attention Highest prices given for eggs' – that is, they traded general produce for their customers' eggs. Massey stores went further, bartering goods for eggs and also for Harris tweed. In both cases the eggs were sold in their other branches, while Massey's uncle was a tailor and was happy to accept the tweed.[13]

second to remaining as multiples. Multiples were designed to serve the working classes, and it was judged that essential goods at the lowest prices were what would entice these customers in, while convenience of location and long opening hours were necessary for this market. Department stores catered to the middle classes, with enough cash and enough leisure that price was less important than high levels of service and a wide variety of stock.

The development of department stores in the second half of the nineteenth century was not as sudden, or as radical, as has sometimes been assumed. Instead, two types of older retail style developed and converged to create what seemed like an entirely new phenomenon. The first development was the arrival of new middle-class haberdasheries and drapery shops, larger in size than they had ever been before, and utilizing new technologies such as plate glass for the windows, gas lighting both inside and out, and more (see below, p. 100). The second was the expansion of working-class purchasing power and the concurrent creation of a ready-to-wear market that was encouraging the development of mass-production methods.

It has been said that ready-to-wear clothes were not available in any bulk until the 1860s.[15] For the middle classes in a general way that was so, but even here the evidence must be treated with caution: in 1790 *The Times* carried an advertisement for Ham's Muslin and Linen Warehouse, on the Strand, which was selling ready-made dresses.*[16] It was estimated that no one earning less than £300 a year could afford to buy *The Times* regularly – this was not an advertisement for the working-class purchaser.† Other mentions of ready-made clothes that were probably for the middle classes can be found throughout the eighteenth century: as early as the 1730s, Mary and Ann Hogarth, sisters to the painter, had a shop where, their trade card promised, 'Fashionable Ready Made Frocks' could be bought.[17] In the 1750s in Bath, John Evill advertised that he sold ready-made waistcoats, breeches, gowns, petticoats, stays, cloaks and bonnets.[18] A little book, *A Visit to the Bazaar* (1818), that was more

---

* The prefix 'ready-made' is important, as in contemporary idiom 'a dress' also referred to a length of fabric that was sold to be made up into a dress later.
† A £300 income was earned only by the prosperous middle classes. Yet even this is not the entire picture. Newspapers were regularly taken by coffee houses, where they could be read for the price of a cup of coffee, or rented for 1*d.* an hour. Furthermore, there were often more than a dozen readers per copy of the newspaper even when they had not been ordered for public places. (See p. 126.)

than half an advertisement for the Soho Bazaar, portrayed a middle-aged woman buying a 'beautiful crape dress', which she asked to have delivered immediately as 'I am going out to a ball this evening, and shall want to put it on.'[19]

Apart from these rare middle-class sightings, the working classes and the lower middle classes, especially the more prosperous, had been wearing ready-made clothes in various forms for years. Less exclusive tailors and mercers often had a sideline as 'slop sellers', stocking cheap ready-made clothing. Men's shirts had been some of the earliest ready-made clothes: the garments were of a standard shape, and they were more or less permanently covered by waistcoats and jackets and therefore size and fit were less important than for outerwear. Ready-made shirts had originally been produced for sailors and for manual labourers; then the working classes more widely began to buy them. The next stage in the more general availability of ready-to-wear clothes was the production of uniforms, which were worn by soldiers and sailors, as we would expect today, and also by charity- and other schoolchildren, by servants in livery, by railway workers, by postmen and other low-grade civil-service workers, and by the inhabitants of workhouses and prisons. Sundry small wars had kept the armed-forces market buoyant for a century past, but the beginning of the French wars sharply increased the need for uniforms. With this, and with the working classes buying more ready-to-wear items, came a wider move from skilled tailors creating a garment in its entirety, to vast warehouses farming out jobs to smaller workshops, who in turn hired cheap pieceworkers to produce slops at home – the foundation of the mass-production system that would develop in the nineteenth century.[20]

By the beginning of the nineteenth century many of the working and lower-middle classes bought their clothes (either new or secondhand), both at the cheaper end of the retail market and at weekly or regular fairs, and this increased throughout the century. A large number of police reports throughout the period dealt with the matter of stolen clothes, which showed how strong the secondhand market was: there is no point stealing something that has no resale value. In good times workers bought new suits or dresses; when work disappeared they pawned or sold the items to tide them over. Clothes were not just pleasurable frivolities, but an investment, a protection against hard times. New fashion items could be acquired for relatively little outlay – well within the means of a servant or other member of the working classes paid in cash. In 1871 Daniel Kirwan, an American journalist in London, visited the Rag Fair, held every Sunday morning in Petticoat Lane in the East End. He was told by one customer:

> I had no other togs but them as I was wearing, and they were so wore out I was ashamed to be seen in 'em. So . . . I said to myself, 'Blest if I don't go over to the Fair . . . and moult the mouldys, and buy a tidy suit to wear . . .' I had made up my mind to do the thing to rights while I was about it, and while I had the money in my pocket. I moulted to my very shirt and socks. I gave seven and six for a light suit, and half a dollar for a pot hat, and eighteen pence for a sky blue neckerchief, and likewise bought a shirt with an ironed front to it, and afore I came away I put 'em all on . . . and here I was, all a toff, up'ards and down'ards.[21]

Kirwan was overwhelmed by the sheer size of the market, with its

> hundreds upon hundreds of pairs of trousers – trousers that have been worn by young men of fashion, trousers without a wrinkle or just newly scoured, trousers taken from the reeking hot limbs of navies [navvies], and pot boys, trousers . . . from spruce young shop boys, trousers that have been worn by criminals hung at Newgate, by patients in fever hospitals; waistcoats that were the pride of fast young brokers in the city, waistcoats flashy enough to have been worn by the Marquis of Hastings at a racecourse, or the Count D'Orsay at a literary assemblage; . . . thousands of spencers, highlows,* fustian jackets, some greasy, some unsoiled, shooting coats, short coats and cutaways; coats for the jockey and the dog fighter, for the peer and the pugilist, pilot jackets and sou-westers, drawers and stockings . . .[22]

Fashion was something that everyone could now afford, at least sometimes, and at least for part of their wardrobe. George Augustus Sala, a journalist,† noted the dedication with which, in particular, clerks and other low-income lower-middle-class young men followed the trends:

---

* A spencer was a double-breasted overcoat without tails, well out of fashion by this time. A highlow remains a mystery: the only contemporary sources that list the 'highlow' say it is a boot, whereas from the context here it appears to be a jacket.

† Sala (1828–96) contributed to Dickens's *Household Words* from 1851. At the end of the Crimean War, Dickens asked him to travel to Russia to report on the situation. In 1863 he made his name as a special correspondent covering the American Civil War for the *Daily Telegraph*. He also wrote 'Echoes of the Week', a column for the *Illustrated London News*, for more than twenty-five years.

These are the customers you see at a glance, whom the resplendent wares in the hosiers' shops attract . . . These are the dashing young parties who purchase the pea-green, the orange, and the rose-pink gloves; the crimson braces, the kaleidoscopic shirt-studs, the shirts embroidered with dahlias, deaths' heads, race-horses, sun-flowers, and ballet-girls; the horseshoe, fox-head, pewter-pot-and-crossed-pipes, willow-pattern-plate, and knife-and-fork pins. These are the glasses of city fashion, and the mould of city form, for whom the legions of fourteen, of fifteen, of sixteen, and of seventeen shilling trousers, all unrivalled, patented, and warranted, are made.[23]

By the mid-century, men's clothes in particular had becoming standard, ready-made, and were being heavily advertised. For this to have happened, items we take entirely for granted needed first to be invented. At the Great Exhibition, Charles Cattanach from Aberdeen, who listed himself as 'Inventor', showed an 'apparatus for measuring the human figure, and for transferring the measure to cloth so as to produce an exact fit of garment'[24] – or, as it is known today, a tape measure. He was one of many claiming ownership of this useful invention, which seems to have first appeared around the beginning of the century, and to have been in more general use from around 1825. Once this was available, treatises like Dr Henry Wampen's *The Mathematical Art of Cutting Garments According to the Different Formation of Men's Bodies* (1834) could be written, giving guidance on how to create clothes without an actual, specific body in front of the tailor.[25]

For standardized sizes had not yet arrived. Men's clothes led the way: over the century they moved away from the earlier skintight fitted breeches and jackets, towards the loose, tube-like shape of modern dress. Women's clothes were more difficult to standardize: bodices were expected to fit so tightly to the figure that the stays underneath showed through. By the 1840s shops were advertising 'Sewed' dresses, but they may have been only partly finished, for the purchaser or her dressmaker to alter to fit her own measurements. Challinier of New Bond Street stocked this type of half-and-half item: 'Muslin Bodices . . . can be completed for wearing in a few hours' notice.'[26] Twenty years later Jay's Warehouse was still attempting to find a way to combine the fashion for skintight bodices with a desire for ready-made clothes, coming up with a 'self-expanding' bodice. But the spread of women's ready-made clothing lagged behind men's and children's for some time.

William Keel of Birmingham was one of many who believed that unusually shaped vehicles were useful advertising tools for their businesses. Many others went further, with actual vans shaped like hats, or pyramids, or cheeses, patrolling the streets.

The move towards simplification and standardization created the possibility of major changes in the production, and in the selling, of men's ready-made clothes. Leeds quickly became the centre of mass-produced men's clothes. It had no previous history of tailoring, and therefore no moribund guild system to limit growth; its old linen industry provided the necessary skills, networks and capital bases to new entrepreneurs, while that same industry's collapse meant there was no bar to the shift into new production; and finally the arrival, from the 1860s, of an eastern-European Jewish population well-versed in tailoring skills and closely linked to each other by marriage and trade made possible the formation of an efficient and complex outworking system.* Perhaps most importantly, Leeds also had an established engineering industry, which meant that machinery used in other fields could be retooled for use in the production of mass tailoring.[28]

John Barran, a retail tailor in the local high street in the late 1840s, had sold cheap ready-made clothes for men and children in exactly the

---

* In 1822 there were seventy Jews in Leeds; by 1900 the city had, in proportion to its Gentile inhabitants, the largest Jewish population in the country, at 5 per cent of the population.[27]

pattern we have seen above. In 1856 he set up a manufacturing works; his great innovation was to develop with the engineering firm of Greenwood and Batley the first mechanical cutter, a bandsaw that could cut through several layers of cloth at once. This mass cutting machine forced Barran into further technological and organizational changes, for the bandsaw produced many more cut-out pieces than his tailors could process. So he subcontracted these out to a tailor with a workshop, who in turn passed them on to others as piecework. For the first time in the clothing industry, production was divided into two parts: cutting, via new technology, at the factory, and then a division for the sewing – outwork for the more complicated jackets and coats, while Barran's own sewers dealt with the trousers and waistcoats, which required lesser skills. And for these workers he had equipped the works with the new sewing machines.[29]

These machines had been developed piecemeal, by several different inventors. After the initial crude chain-stitch machine had been invented to sew army uniforms in France in 1829, most of the innovations and improvements occurred in the United States in the 1840s and '50s. In England, Elias Howe Jr had produced a lock-stitch machine in 1846, but, seeing little prospect of financial return, had sold the patent on. In the USA Isaac Singer had seen a similar lock-stitch machine in 1850. It was so complicated that it required special training and then some skill to operate it, and even more technological know-how to service and maintain it. In 1851 Singer's improvements were patented: the new machine now held the needle vertically, was made of iron not wood, and had toothed gears that didn't jam, a spring that permitted variations in the thickness of the fabric without manual adjustment, and a presser foot to hold the fabric in place, which meant the operator could use both hands to control the cloth. The new machine could also, most importantly, sew in curves as well as the straight lines, which had been all the earlier machines had managed. Now an operative could produce 900 stitches a minute, instead of the 40 stitches a quick hand-sewer could make.[30]*

Further improvements followed, but in England any improved

---

* Singer was even better at marketing than he was at inventing: he had been an actor, and he used his selling and promotional skills at first on a circuit of fairs and circuses; he then opened a showroom, a vast hall lined with machines operated by specially trained women – he wanted to show that women at home could use his machines.[31]

machines were blocked by the patent for the earlier – and much inferior – machine. Finally in 1856 Singer opened an agency in Glasgow, to avoid paying English patent fees. Barran swiftly saw how this machine would solve his problem of the imbalance between the speed with which his mechanized bandsaws cut and the appreciably longer time it took his tailors to sew. He had the machines installed in his works, linked to steam-driven shafts instead of the machines' original foot-powered treadle.[32] Soon every Leeds clothing factory was using bandsaws, steam-driven sewing machines, and steam presses and button-holing machines. By the 1880s fifteen sewing-machine-manufacturing firms had set up in the city, and even more engineering works specialized in developing new machinery for this now enormously successful trade.[33]

Technology and technological innovation were changing the entire face of fashion. Waterproof coats and shoes are two examples of this revolution. Before the nineteenth century, when it rained people either stayed inside or they got wet. There was no other possibility. Oiled-silk umbrellas were carried by some, but they were at best water-resistant, not waterproof. In 1823 Charles Macintosh, a Scottish chemist, patented a fabric which had a layer of rubber sealed between two layers of cloth, creating a waterproof material. He was not the first to use rubber to make fabrics waterproof, but his method, which used cheap coal oil, was better suited to large-scale, economical manufacturing than earlier versions had been. Macintosh joined together with a cotton manufacturer, and Charles Macintosh and Co. was set up the following year in Manchester, an ideal location. The city had shipping links with South America for rubber imports; it had a gasworks, for the supply of naphtha, used in softening the rubber; it was the cotton centre of the country, producing an endless supply of material suitable for waterproofing; and, like Leeds, it was also filled with engineering firms eager to work on adapting machinery for this new industry.[34]

At first, waterproofed material found limited numbers of customers, although Captain Parry's expeditionary team heading to the North Pole in 1827 carried waterproof bags. The problem was that the fabric turned brittle in cold weather, sticky in hot; it didn't breathe, and therefore caused the wearer to sweat heavily; and, even worse, the rubberizing process saturated the fabric with a smell that was said to be easily detectable across the road from the coat's wearer. In 1843 the process of vulcanizing rubber was developed: this led to the fabric being treated with sulphur, which kept it stable whatever the weather. Further developments throughout the decade continued to produce improvements, and by the Great Exhibition Bax and Co. showed its 'Aquascutum' cloth, which soon afterwards the army ordered in bulk for its Crimea-bound soldiers. Others benefited too: the India Rubber Waterproof Works in east London was ideally suited to gear up production quickly. By 1844 it already had a site covering 24,000 square metres, and when war was declared it managed to produce 50,000 waterproof suits for the departing soldiers in only forty days.[35]

Civilians were no less slow to adopt the trend. The khaki colour the army used quickly caught on: Bax and Co. was pleased that 'the officers of the guards began to wear light drab cambric capes on their way to field exercises, and the other young men as usual following their example, our material (especially of this drab colour) began to take with the public generally, and more and more as the value of it, and its really waterproof quality, became known.'[36] Then the popular harlequin notion of a garment that performed two jobs at once, was adapted: in 1851 J. Smith advertised a 'reversible waterproof Janus coat . . . two perfect coats in a pocket book'[37] – a coat, a waterproof and, as an extra, so lightweight that the whole thing could be folded up and put into a pocket. This was a popular idea: an advertisement in the *Manchester Post Office Directory* of 1854 promised a '5 oz.' coat that 'can be carried in a coat sleeve or pocket and folded up in the space of a cigar case!'; while an 1855 directory offered a 'pocket siphonia',* which could be put in the said pocket, or even in a hat.[39]

Rubber affected shoe- and boot-making as much as it had overcoats, as did standardization. Shoes went from being personally measured and made to order to being produced in standard sizes fairly early on. From 1848 C. and J. Clark advertised that its lines were available in three widths it called 'fittings', and in seven sizes. In 1875 the company advertising boasted:

> We used to have only three fittings, the N narrow, M medium
> and S scotch. The narrow were seldom called for and we found
> that our range of fittings was not large enough to suit our cus-

---

* A siphonia was a transient name for a waterproof coat, one of the many names that manufacturers came up with to catch the eye in advertisements. Almost exactly contemporaneously with this mention, Sala wrote of clerks in their 'Paletôts . . . Ponchos, Burnouses, Sylphides, Zephyr wrappers, Chesterfields, Llamas, Pilot wrappers, Wrap-rascals, Bis-uniques and a host of other garments, more or less answering the purpose of an overcoat'.[38]

tomers and that ... there was a demand for a fitting wider than N but not so extreme as S. We spent a great deal of pains and labour during two whole years in fixing on the best shape of soles, to cover all parts of the three kingdoms ... and we flattered ourselves at having arrived as nearly at perfection as we could reasonably expect in all three points.[40]

From the 1830s rubber had been used as a cheaper alternative to leather for soles, and from 1837 some boots incorporated another new rubber product – elasticated webbing – as inserts down the sides to replace laces.* Technology then raced ahead, which was welcome for shoe-making, an enormously labour-intensive task: in 1738 one shoe-master in London employed 162 people, each performing a different task.[42] Sewing machines were in use in shoe and boot production by the 1850s; by 1858 American machines were imported to cut out soles in bulk; only a few years later, machine-sewn uppers, and soles attached by a new method of machine riveting, first appeared. By 1883 just 39 per cent of C. and J. Clark's shoes were still hand-sewn.[43]

The new technology changed methods of production, and it also changed what was produced. Once machines for mechanically riveting soles appeared, men's shoes, with their heavier soles, became easier to produce. In 1863 Clark's had had 334 men's lines; in 1896 there were 720. In 1870 the company sold 235 types of boot for women and children; 124 types of slipper, and 36 types of shoe.† By 1883 the price of lighter footwear had been substantially reduced by the introduction of machine-welt sewing. Now there were 246 types of boot, 111 types of slipper, but 153 types of shoe; in 1896 the types of boot were reduced to 223 styles, slippers had only gone up to 144 types, but there were 353 types of shoe listed: ten times as many as twenty-five years before.[44]

While these innovations in production brought new goods to market,

---

* Laces themselves had been revolutionized in 1823, when metal eyelets were patented, making it possible to wear heavier boots and lace them more tightly without tearing the leather.[41]

† Boots were ordinary street-wear for men, women and children, even in cities, since horse dung, alleyway slaughterhouses and overrunning cesspits were common. Given the condition of the streets, once inside the house those who could afford it expected to change into their shoes or, for women, slippers – which were not bedroom wear, but made of silk, satin or other fabrics, or even the more delicate leathers. The primary distinction between slippers and shoes was, not unnaturally, that the slipper was easily slipped on and off, and thus had no fastenings apart from ribbons. For evening wear for more prosperous women, slippers were de rigueur.

an equally important change was occurring at the retail end of things. With mass-produced goods readily available, promotions via the kind of marketing and publicity wizardry seen in the previous century with Wedgwood became more frequent. Innovatory products filled the newly transformed shops and were being sold through the power of the emergent mass-circulation newspapers and periodicals. A leader in the field was Eleazer (later Elias) Moses (1783–1868), the son of a Jewish immigrant from Colmar. With his son Isaac (1809–84) he formed E. Moses and Son, in 1832 setting up a shop in the East End, on the Ratcliff Highway, and then moving into the City, to Aldgate. In their early days they specialized in supplying complete outfits for emigrants, a sadly large market in the hungry forties and for some time afterwards.* In 1845 Moses's Wholesale Clothing Warehouse opened a shop around the corner from the Aldgate shop, in Minories; this increased the selling space fourfold; then the company took over neighbouring premises until the two shops had swallowed all the properties in between, and the Aldgate shop was rebuilt to give a seven-times increase on its original floor space.

Moses and Son represented many of the trends that were to emerge throughout the century: low margins, high turnover and cash sales only were the obvious, and by no means insubstantial, ones. *The Book of Economy: or, How to Live Well in London on £100 per annum*, by 'A Gentleman', said in 1832 that two suits could be bought for 13 guineas; a City tailor advertised two suits in 'extra superfine' wool at £13. Moses and Son, with a less prosperous clientele, arranged 'contracts' with its customers, whereby the purchaser agreed to take two new suits a year, at £8 for two in broadcloth, or £6 10s. for a lesser-quality fabric. This was an extraordinary price, and one Moses and Son made profitable through bulk buying and low margins. But the 'contract' part was a sign of Moses and Son's innovative approach, and shows how it managed to squeeze the last drop of profit out of such small sums. When the

---

* In the 1850s they advertised a £3 10s., a £6 10s., or a 10 guinea outfit for those emigrating. The 10 guinea version comprised: 1 black dress coat, 1 black dress vest, black dress trousers; 1 frock coat, 1 fancy vest, fancy trousers; 1 fishing or shooting coat; 1 hat and 1 cloth cap; 18 shirts; 4 nightshirts; 1 pair Wellington boots, and 1 pair shoes; 6 handkerchiefs; 6 pounds Marine soap; a razor, shaving box, strop and mirror; a fork, a knife, a teaspoon and a tablespoon; a plate and a mug; a bed, a pillow, a pair of blankets, 2 pairs of sheets, 2 pillowcases; a hairbrush and comb; and a strong sea chest to contain everything.[45]

customer returned for his second suit, he handed the first, worn-out, one back to Moses and Son, which then sold it on to the secondhand trade.[46]

The company's marketing genius was every bit as crucial as its prices: the Aldgate shop was designed to reflect the most up-to-date luxury of the expensive shops in the West End, despite prices that were often more than 60 per cent lower. The shop had a three-storey-high classical portico, four-metre display windows, mahogany fittings throughout, and gas lighting (plus royal arms above the door, for which it held no warrant). The not-so-subliminal message was that cheapness did not mean loss of quality. Soon there were branches in Oxford Street and Tottenham Court Road, sitting comfortably beside the new department stores. Moses and Son also produced pamphlets extolling its wares, with titles like 'Habiliment Hall', 'The Pride of London', 'The Dressing-room Companion or Guide to the Looking Glass', 'The Paragon of Excellence' and 'The Exhibition for All Nations'.[47] Many had texts written in rumpty-tump jingles (probably by Isaac Moses), as, for example,

CHRISTMAS EXHIBITIONS

> Once more the glad season of Christmas is here,
> And folks from the country in London appear,
> Some have come to a relative, some to a friend –
> To pass a few days ere the season shall end,
> And visit the fam'd 'exhibitions' of Town,
> Which have ever enjoy'd such a matchless renown,
> Some view the Museum – and others, St Paul's –
> But there's ONE 'Exhibition' where ev'ry one calls
> 'Tis a place to which thousands with eagerness run –
> And that is the warehouse of MOSES and SON . . .[48]

Others were produced in the style of magazine articles:

> Having been given to understand that the Establishment of E. Moses and Son was open to the public for inspection, I thought proper to avail myself of the opportunity, and having arrived at the premises, I entered the private Waiting Hall, where a youth in livery was waiting to attend the door . . .
>
> I . . . was much struck with the beauty and accommodation of the place . . . The Hall has an elegant staircase fronting the street . . . The principal Show Room is certainly an Exhibition. I consider that it has no equal; and if there were 'really and truly'

such a person as Queen Fashion, I think her Majesty could not do better than select this splendid and spacious apartment for the holding of her levees and councils . . .

The Ready-made Clothing department is undoubtedly the most spacious ever before witnessed; and on my asking whether *so much* room were *absolutely necessary* I was informed that the business could not be carried on with any less space . . .[49]

This kind of cod-educational prose, designed to mimic magazines like the *Penny Weekly* and others that were read as much for self-improvement as for entertainment, was in marked contrast to the style of other ready-made-clothing retailers, whose advertising was for the less upwardly earnest. A tailor in Chelsea advertised his shop in 1880 in a mixture of cockney, theatre and sporting slang:

Pay a visit to C. Greenburg, the noted working men's tailor, well known by everybody to be the only genuine clothing manufacturer in Chelsea for flash toggery. The above champion builder begs to thank his customers for their liberal support, and wishes to put them awake to the fact that he has dabbed his fins [put his hands] on a nobby swag of stuff [high-class bag of goods] for his ready brass, consisting of cords, moleskins, doeskin plushes, velveteens, box cloths, pilots, tweeds, &c. . . . A pair of ikey cords, cut slap up with the artful dodge and fakement [trimming] down the sides, from 10 bob. Proper cut togs, lick all comers, for pleasure or business wear, turned out up to the knocker [in fashion, stylishly], from a quid. A pair of kerseymere or fancy doeskin or any other skin kicksies [trousers], any colour, cut peg top, half tights, or to drop down over the trotters [feet], from 10 and a tanner to 25 bob, fit to toe it with any swell. Lavenders [perhaps gaiters or spats], built spanky, with a double fakement down the sides, and artful buttons at the bottom, any price you name, straight. Fancy sleeve vest, cut very saucy, tight cut round the scrag [neck] or made to flash the dicky [show the shirt front], from 9 bob. A discount made to prize fighters, shop lifters, quill drivers [clerks], counter jumpers, bruisers, snobs, scavengers, sparrow starvers [dung-sweepers], and lardy dardy blades on the high fly [foppish swells on a spree] . . .[50]*

---

* This was not a one-off: Harris's, in Whitechapel, used similar theatre and prizefighter slang, mixed in with the vocabulary of the penny-dreadful (see pp. 174–6) and outright thievery: 'Harris . . . The Champion of England, slap-up tog and out-and-out kicksies builder, nabs the chance of putting his customers awake that he has just made his escape from Canada, not forgetting to clap his mawleys [fists] on a rare does of stuff . . .'[51]

Unlike Moses and Son, Greenburg was appealing to the flash Harrys, the music-hall loungers, the street-smart spivs.* Yet Moses and Son's market of upwardly mobile clerks was huge: in 1855 it was estimated that the firm was spending £10,000 a year on advertising (compared to the furniture shop Heal and Son's, which spent £6,000, or Nichol's – later Harvey Nichol's – which had a budget of £4,500).[53]

These figures show how important the retail trade had become to the economy. This was recognized at the time: good, elegant, modern shops were seen as an indicator of national prosperity, of plenty, and of general civilization. Good shops were modern shops: many books of the period made this assumption automatically. *Tallis's Street View* in 1837 praised the completion of Nash's new Regent Street: 'The buildings of this noble street chiefly consist of palace-like shops, in whose broad, shewy windows are displayed articles of the most splendid description, such as the neighbouring world of wealth and fashion are daily in want of.' Even the sweep of Oxford Circus was approved for being 'as elegant in form as useful in application'.[54] (It was 'useful' because carriages could turn easily around its broad curves.) Lincoln in the 1840s was commended for 'several splendid shops, equal to anything of the kind to be found in far larger towns', but condemned for its 'unsightly masses of old buildings which disfigure the principal streets [which, it was hoped, would soon] be supplanted by erections unique with those which modern enterprize has produced'. Chester was similarly approved a decade later for the conversion of its shops 'filled with plate-glass, and with all the brilliancy of the most modern art and taste'.[55]

Stores were developing at the rate they were for a number of reasons: increased demand, new goods from new markets abroad, mass production. But one more immediate reason stands out: it was easier for people to get to and from the shops that held the goods they desired. It is hard to remember just how small most cities were, even in the nineteenth century, well after urbanization had created cities larger than had ever before been known. Central London in the 1830s was 6.5 kilometres across, north to south, and 10 kilometres east to west – its 2 million inhabitants were never more than an hour's walk from the beginnings of more rural countryside. Manchester and Salford taken together were

---

* There was a brisk East End trade in tailors' tabs with the names of West End shops on them,[52] probably for shops like this.

only 1.5 kilometres north to south, and the same east to west. Those who lived in the suburbs walked in to work if they could not afford their own carriage (and most could not), but would not think of coming into the centre specifically to shop. They bought locally, and from itinerant sellers. From the 1760s some of the outer suburbs of London, like Islington or Kensington, had stagecoach services; by 1825 there were 418 routes across London, making 1,190 journeys to the City every day. Their destination shows that these were primarily used to transport people to and from work. It was the omnibus, arriving from Paris in 1829, that made the shopping journey a possibility for many. Within a decade, there were 620 omnibuses and 225 short-stagecoaches licensed in London.

Omnibuses were not cheap to operate – each bus had a driver and a conductor, and was pulled by two horses. To run an omnibus 14 hours a day, 7 days a week, required a complement of 11 horses per bus. A horse cost £20 and the omnibus itself £100, so the start-up fixed capital cost was already £320. Then operating costs included feed, at 15s. per horse per week (or £429 per bus per year); and the costs of stabling, veterinarian bills and shoeing, as well as the maintenance and repair costs for the bus. There was a tax of 3d. per mile per passenger, which on an average route mounted up to 15s. per day, or over £270 a year. The wages of the driver and conductor were another £60 a year each; and, furthermore, many routes from the suburbs were along turnpike roads where tolls were still charged. The original omnibus design had had space for just fifteen passengers in the interior, with another three outside passengers beside the driver. The seemingly extortionate 1s. single fare to the suburbs, or the half-price 6d. fare in the centre of town, no longer looks so unreasonable. Not unreasonable, but affordable only by the prosperous middle classes.

In 1842 the mileage tax was halved (then reduced to 1d. in 1855, ½d. in 1866 and abolished entirely in 1870), and, more importantly, was now levied on the vehicle itself rather than on the number of passengers it could carry. It therefore made sense to reconfigure the buses so that they could carry more people. A 'knifeboard' seat was installed on the roof – a single long bench down the length of the bus, with the men (always men, as the roof was reached by a ladder that was hostile to skirts and petticoats) facing out to the sides, sitting back to back. This increased capacity to 25, and in turn fares were reduced to 3d., or sometimes even 1*d.* for a short 'city' stage as it was known.* Soon the ladders were replaced by a winding spiral stair, and the knifeboard seats with 'garden' seats (the kind of two-by-two backed benches that continue to be used on much public transport today), plate-glass windows were installed downstairs, and the bus was ready to take on its new role as a conveyance for the middle-class female shopper.[56]

Provincial towns and cities differed from London only in size. Otherwise the love of new shops and the means of access to them were all much the same. To get to the shops, similar solutions were adopted to suit the locale: Manchester had a single omnibus in 1835; by 1840 Engels noted that there was one at least every half-hour running from the suburban villas to the centre; by 1850 there were sixty-four services along the main routes. Birmingham had omnibuses running from suburbs like New Hall and Edgbaston in 1834; within the decade Small Heath and Sparkbrook were linked into the system. Glasgow was different from the now increasingly common pattern of a work-dominated centre and suburban housing. Here much of the population still lived in the centre of the city and commuted outwards; many used the Clyde river steamboat service, and it was not until the 1860s that an omnibus service sprang up to reach Kelvinside. Other cities had other solutions: from the early 1870s Edinburgh and Aberdeen (and Glasgow too) had horse trams; by 1890 Liverpool had 225.[57] At the end of the 1870s there were only 321 miles of tramway in Britain, but when the switch to steam power and then electricity began in the 1880s, even towns with populations of 50,000 found it worth their while to lay down tramways. In London in 1896 the trams carried 280 million passengers, while omnibuses carried only 300,000 (a tram ticket cost 1*d.*, and the trams ran every two to three minutes, which might have had something to do with the disparity). By 1914, the number of passenger journeys made by tram throughout the country was 74 times the population of the United Kingdom.[58]

The London figures are the more astonishing given that the capital had yet a further means of mass transportation. In 1863 the Metropolitan Railway, the world's first underground railway, opened, running from Paddington in west London to Farringdon in the City, with an extension to St Pancras in 1868. When the Metropolitan District Railway (a separate

* Note that the fare 'stage' retained its name, and still does, from stagecoach days.

company) began to extend the Underground to Kensington and Victoria, the influx of suburban shoppers to the West End became a reality.[59] In 1864, even on the small bit of route then existing, 6.5 million journeys were taken on the Underground in six months; after the 1868 extension the journeys jumped to 15 million a year.[60]

The various way of reaching the palaces of wonder in that glass-gleaming, gas-hissing West End were new; yet what people were travelling towards was not. It was simply that more of them could now reach it. The sumptuousness, the brightness, the richness – above all, the sheer up-to-dateness – of shops had been commented on by visitors for a hundred years. It was the amount of glass that most forcefully seemed to strike European travellers. A French visitor in 1728 wrote that 'shops are surrounded with [glass], and usually the merchandise [inside the shop] is arranged behind it, which keeps the dust off, while still displaying the goods to passers-by' – clearly something he had never seen at home. The German physicist Georg Christoph Lichtenberg, who kept a diary on his visits to England, also found shopfronts that 'seem to be made entirely of glass' worthy of remark.[61]

Glass was still expensive – both owing to the cost of the glass itself and also because of the glass tax, which was not abolished until 1851. Plate-glass technology made possible larger and larger window panes, which continued to astonish. An American visitor in the early 1830s said that in Regent Street 'many of the bow windows are glazed with panes 24 by 36 inches, 30 by 45, &c. There is a fur shop having a window on each side of the door, the centre pane in each window measuring nine feet by five.' The furrier told him that the centre panes had cost him 50 guineas each.[62] This seems a perhaps pardonable exaggeration. Francis Place had set up a tailor's shop in 1801, and 'I put in a new front as elegant as the place would permit, each of the panes of glass cost me three pounds, and two in the door, four pounds each.'[63] Even allowing for a rise in prices, and the substantial difference in grandeur between Place's small shop and a Regent Street 'emporium', the 50 guineas still sounds like a tall tale. However much it cost, the dazzling plate glass was matched and abetted by developments in lighting: glass and gas together radically changed the look of shops.

The insides of late-eighteenth- and early-nineteenth-century shops had been no less splendid – especially, but not uniquely, in the luxury-goods trades. Many historians have suggested that until the arrival of the department stores the displays in shops were minimal, that everything was kept in boxes, and only grudgingly drawn out piece by piece, with no sense of theatrical display. This cannot have been further from the truth. This misapprehension was set in train by the Victorians themselves, who saw – or wanted to see – what was taking place around them as something unprecedented. Charles Manby Smith, a journalist, described a plate-polisher's shop in about 1810 as 'a dim, dusty-looking house of some thirty feet frontage . . . which you might pass a hundred times, so unpretentious was its aspect, without noticing its existence'. He then took the reader on a tour of the shop's development, as it was renovated by its next incumbent, when it 'displayed . . . a handsome set of new shutters, surmounted by a Corinthian cornice, and a new private door, splendid in imitative walnut and shining varnish. When the shutters came down on Monday morning, they disclosed a handsome mahogany sash, the two lower rows of panes guarded by a stout trellis-work of brass-wire, resting upon a single plate of brass.' Sometime before Manby Smith wrote this in 1857 the shop was pulled down to widen the road, at which point it was rebuilt 'seventy feet high, with a huge semicircular façade, superb in pillars, pilasters, and carved cornices, fronting one of the most imposing approaches to the very centre of the city'.[64]

This may very well have happened to that precise building, but, more to the point, this is what Manby Smith understood to be happening everywhere. To heighten the contrast between past and present, to show how wonderful the mid-century shops were, he needed to believe that the shops of the past had been truly negligible. The trouble was, they simply weren't as insubstantial as he suggested. Visitors to London, who did not have his vested interest in a dull, dark past to hold up against a dazzling, gaslit present, were perhaps more reliable. In 1786 the German diarist Sophie von la Roche went window shopping in London, and was suitably impressed. She visited John Boydell's print shop (for more on Boydell, see pp. 388–91):

> Here again I was struck by the excellent arrangement and system which the love of gain and national good taste have combined in producing, particularly in the elegant dressing of large shop-windows, not merely in order to ornament the streets and lure purchasers, but to make known the thousands of inventions and ideas, and spread good taste about, for the excellent pavements

made for pedestrians enable crowds of people to stop and inspect the new exhibits.[65]

She liked improving things, like prints, but she liked less sober-minded shops too, like the one which had a 'cunning device for showing women's materials. Whether they are silks, chintzes, or muslins, they hang down in folds behind the fine high windows so that the effect of this or that material, as it would be in the ordinary folds of a woman's dress, can be studied. Amongst the muslins all colours are on view, and so one can judge how the frock would look in company with its fellows.'[66]

The lighting was as essential as the windows, and had been even before piped gas arrived. Francis Place had used 'five large Argand lamps* in the shop besides the candles to make the windows and every part of it as nearly equally light as possible'.[67] Johanna Schopenhauer, visiting London in 1803, admired 'the brilliant displays of precious silverware, the beautiful draperies of muslin . . . behind large plate-glass windows, the fairy-tale glitter of the crystal shops'.†[68] That she and Sophie von la Roche both admired hanging fabrics would have won the heart of the 'old draper', the pseudonymous author of a series in *The Warehousemen and Drapers' Trade Journal*. He recalled his early days in the trade at the beginning of the nineteenth century, when 'we made a very large and flaring show of goods upon every possible occasion, piling stacks up outside the door . . . and at times we even had a length of stuff let down from the top storey window to the bottom, so as to attract notice and attention'.[69] Contrary to Manby Smith's and many later historian's view of the period, the 'old draper' knew that presentation was of the essence. He told how, when he first set up on his own, he rented a big shop, which he could not afford to stock properly. So he devised a variety of ruses. He displayed great rolls of 'silks' where only the top layer was an expensive silk, bulked out underneath by cheap fabric he had painted

---

* An Argand lamp burned gas held in a reservoir, with, for the first time, an enclosed flame in a glass chimney; a mechanism allowed the flame to be raised or lowered, regulating brightness, again for the first time.

† Johanna Schopenhauer (1766–1838) was born in Prussia, the daughter of a banker and senator. She married Heinrich Schopenhauer, a merchant, in 1784 or 1785, and travelled widely with him. After his death in 1805 or 1806 she moved to Weimar, where she was the centre of a literary salon, attended by Goethe and Wieland among others. Driven by financial need, she published a number of books, including a biography, travel diaries, novels and short stories. However, her main claim to fame today is as the mother of the philosopher Arthur Schopenhauer.

New Leadenhall Market. The nineteenth century saw the arrival or ornate spaces for selling, filled with light, glass and gas.

to match. He stocked his drawers at the front, putting parcels stuffed with paper in behind, so that when the drawers were opened they appeared reassuringly full to his customers. Without this he would not have been able to persuade his suppliers that he was financially stable and credit-worthy, nor would his customers have been willing to shop somewhere they thought too scantily stocked, and therefore unlikely to carry what they wanted: display was vital.[70]

London had two very distinct streets, or rather sets of streets, which had been dedicated to shopping from the eighteenth century. The first ran from Mile End in the East End to Parliament Street in the West End, taking in Whitechapel, Leadenhall Street, Cornhill, Cheapside, St Paul's Churchyard (famous for books and, later, haberdashery), Ludgate Street, Fleet Street, the Strand and Charing Cross. The other linked chain of streets also began in the eastern end of London, at Shoreditch, and ran westward, taking in Bishopsgate Street, Threadneedle Street, Cheapside, Newgate Street, Holborn, Broad Street, St Giles and Oxford Street.[71] In the eighteenth century, the former streets had the more elegant shops, and were considered to be more fashionable. In 1807 Robert Southey, in the guise of a foreign visitor, described how

> When I reached Cheapside the crowd completely astonished me. On each side of the way were two uninterrupted streams of people, one going east, the other west. At first I thought some extraordinary occasion must have collected such a concourse; but I soon perceived it was only the usual course of business . . . If possible I was still more astonished at the opulence and splendour of the shops, drapers, stationers . . . silversmiths, booksellers, print-sellers . . . one close to another, without inter-mission, a shop to every house, street after street, and mile after mile; the articles themselves so beautiful, and beautifully arranged.[72]

Gradually over the century the fashionable shoppers moved west and north. One of the clearest markers of this westward shift was when the draper's Shoolbred, Cook and Co., which had been in St Paul's Churchyard, moved in 1817 to Tottenham Court Road, which was rapidly gaining a reputation as a middle-class shopping street.* By that year, *Johnstone's London Commercial Guide* listed the following in Oxford

---

* Particularly for furniture: Shoolbred started selling carpets and upholstery not long after the move; John Harris Heal, the son of the owner of a mattress-making company around the corner in Rathbone Place, opened a furniture shop less than a hundred metres away in 1840; Maple's, an enormous furniture shop, set up next door to Shoolbred in 1842. And the tradition is maintained – Heal's, in its early twentieth-century building, proudly takes up nearly an entire block; Maple's closed only a couple of decades ago; and hordes of students looking for sofa-beds and futons today still head for Tottenham Court Road.

Street: 3 linen drapers, 10 straw-hat manufactories [in this context, a manufactory was a place that sold the goods it made in its workrooms on the premises], 6 bonnet warehouses [meaning simply large shops], 5 woollen drapers, 5 lace warehouses, 3 plumassiers [feather merchants, for hat feathers], 24 boot- and shoe-makers, 17 hosiers and glovers, 4 silk mercers, 1 silk weaver, 4 furriers, 12 haberdashers and hosiers, 1 ribbon warehouse, 1 muslin and shawl warehouse, 2 silk and satin dyers, 2 drapers and tailors, 1 India-muslin warehouse, 3 fancy trimmings and fringe manufactories, 1 button manufactory, 2 pressers and dyers, 5 perfumers, 1 patent-thread manufactory, 1 tailor, 3 stay and corset warehouses, 1 stocking warehouse, 1 ready-made linen [that is, underwear] warehouse, and 4 umbrella manufactories.[73]

London was the forerunner, but other towns and cities were coming up hard behind. The developments in London were copied first in the more up-market spa towns, such as Bath (for more on spas, see pp. 231–6), then in the larger cities: Bristol, Liverpool, Manchester and Newcastle. Finally the newer industrial cities followed. The Enabling Act of 1813 had made it possible for businessmen to buy land, develop it, and then make a return by selling long leases to shopkeepers. The act had been passed in order to allow the creation of Regent Street, but many took advantage of the unexpected opportunity to develop other areas in the same way: Dale Street in Liverpool and Market Street in Manchester were both developed for better retail premises, and widened, in the 1820s;* in the 1830s it was the turn of Grey Street in Newcastle. London then developed further shopping areas: New Oxford Street in the 1840s, Victoria in the 1850s, and Shaftesbury Avenue and Charing Cross Road in the 1870s and 1880s. The spirit of emulation then stirred Leeds, Glasgow and Cardiff to follow suit, while Joseph Chamberlain planned Birmingham's Corporation Street to be 'the retail shop of the whole of the Midland counties of England'.[75]

Thus the physical development of shops was one of almost constant change from the eighteenth century onward. Likewise, to match the myth of the dirty, dark, barely stocked eighteenth-century shop, there was also the myth that shopping before the arrival of the department store was a purpose-driven, end-result-based activity: shoppers went in for a specific

* Engels saw this redevelopment as a way of segregating the working classes from the middle classes, to keep these areas free for middle-class consumption. It is an interesting idea, but one I can only briefly mention in this footnote.[74]

item, asked for it, had it handed to them, and immediately left – with absolutely no browsing. There is some evidence that in some places, some of the time, some customers expected to behave in this way. In Fenwick's of Newcastle, as late as 1902, when the owner's sons came back from training in Paris, they advertised what they thought of as new ways of shopping in the *Newcastle Journal*, encouraging customers to come in to browse: 'Assistants are not allowed to speak to visitors. Walk round today, don't buy. There is time for that another day.'[76]* Gordon Selfridge, that arch-myth-maker (see pp. 117–22), was keen to promote the novelty of the idea (mostly so that he could claim to have invented it). He told anyone who would listen that when he had been looking around other shops, planning his own, he was approached by a floor-walker, who asked him what he wanted. Selfridge replied that he was just looking, and was told, ''Op it,' and escorted to the door.[78]

Unfortunately for Selfridge and his charming story, there is a long history of browsing – in manuals for shopkeepers, in novels and plays, and in advertisements. As early as 1726, Daniel Defoe in his *Complete Tradesman* warned shopkeepers that 'ladies . . . divert themselves in going from one mercer's shop to another, to look upon their fine silks, and to rattle and banter the journeymen and shopkeepers, and have not so much as the least occasion, much less intention, to buy anything.'[79] Wedgwood, as we have seen, frequently changed his displays so that customers would come back regularly to look; he also found it worth-while to display commissions for the royal family and for Catherine the Great, which no one could buy even had they wanted to – he was actively courting browsers. At the beginning of the nineteenth century Johanna Schopenhauer described 'going into at least twenty shops, having a thousand things shown to us which we do not wish to buy, in fact turning the whole shop upside down and, in the end, perhaps leaving without purchasing anything',[80] while in Maria Edgeworth's 1809 novel *Ennui* the Earl of Glenthorn describes going to watchmakers' shops 'for a *lounge* . . . to pass an idle hour'.[81]

This was not the case only in luxury shops in London. Fanny Burney's novel *The Wanderer* (1814) portrays a heroine with a mysterious past who works in a millinery shop in a small market town:

---

* There was a mocking response shortly afterwards in the advertisement placed by another shop: 'We have fine displays of fancy goods and toys, including the new non-speaking shop assistants.'[77]

The ladies whose practice it was to frequent the shop, thought
the time and trouble of its mistress, and her assistants, amply
paid by the honour of their presence; and though they tried on
hats and caps, till they put them out of shape; examined and
tossed about the choicest goods . . . still their consciences were
at ease . . . if, after two or three hours of lounging, rummaging,
fault-finding and chaffering, they purchased a yard or two of
ribbon.[82]

(Burney clearly felt strongly about this. Her unperformed play *The Wit-
lings* also revolved around women who spent their time in a milliner's
shop without buying anything.)[83] Yet, while Burney was indignant, many
shopkeepers knew it was good business. The Royal London Bazaar advertised in the *World of Fashion* in 1830, 'You may purchase any of the
thousand and one varieties of fancy and useful articles, or you may
lounge and spend an agreeable hour either in the promenades or in the
exhibitions that are wholly without parallel to the known world.'[84] For
shopping was, and had long been, a branch of entertainment. The Pantheon, in Oxford Street, a concert-hall-cum-social rendezvous, had been
built in 1772 as competition to the pleasure gardens. (For pleasure
gardens, see pp. 276–8.) By 1834 it had become a combination picture
gallery and bazaar – that is, a place where stallholders rented space from
a central landlord.*

Bazaars had developed out of clusters of shopkeepers who had rented
space in large converted buildings in the eighteenth century. Exeter
Change, in the Strand, was the model.† In the eighteenth century the
ground floor had been filled by two rows of forty-eight stalls, initially
rented mostly to haberdashers and milliners. These were soon superseded by toyshops selling bric-à-brac – china, cutlery, lacquerware,
purses, fans, luxury fabrics such as muslins, silks and brocades, watches
and snuff boxes. Above this, on the first floor, was a changing series
of exhibitions, ranging from Mrs Mill's Waxwork Show, to displays of
architectural models, 'an electrifying machine', a Cremona violin, 'a fine
group of heads drawn with a red-hot poker', and Indian bows and

* In between, it had been an opera house and then the home of the National Institute to
Improve the Manufactures of the United Kingdom. Later it became a wine shop, and today,
suitably, a Marks and Spencer's store occupies the site.[85]
† The Change started life where today the Strand Palace Hotel stands. When plans to
widen the Strand were first mooted, in 1828, the Exeter Change moved to King's Mews,
Charing Cross, although this was no more lucky a site – today the mews is underneath
the National Gallery.

arrows. From the 1770s the entertainment side of the Exchange began to predominate, with live entertainments of songs and recitations, puppets, and finally – for which the Exchange was ultimately most famous – a menagerie.[86] (For more on shows in general, see Chapter 7; for the menagerie, see p. 275.)

As the Exeter Change turned into a show, other bazaars were developing in ways which would turn them into department stores. The Pantheon itself, as described by Sala in 1859, had a 'Hampton-court-like maze of stalls, laden with pretty gimcracks, toys, and *papier mâché* trifles for the table, dolls and childrens' [*sic*] dresses, wax flowers and Berlin and crotchet [*sic*] work, prints, and polkas, and women's wares of all sorts'.[87] This was a typical pattern: the Soho Bazaar, which had been set up in the 1810s, had several rooms with counter space 'let on moderate terms to females who can bring forward sufficient testimonies of their moral respectability'.* They paid 3*d.* a day for each foot of counter space they rented, and space could be taken by the day only, which required little or no capital. The Bazaar specialized in 'light goods, works of art, and female ingenuity in general', which meant more or less what was being sold at the Exeter Change and the Pantheon: jewellery, watches, linen, hats, lace, work baskets, 'fancy work', artificial flowers, 'toys', musical instruments and sheet music, prints, books, birds, china, and so on.[88] The Manchester Bazaar had started up on a similar pattern: its initial advertisement in 1821 offered 'to secure to the Public the choicest and most fashionable Articles in every branch of Art and Manufacture, at a reasonable rate'.[89] In 1836 three stallholders bought the company; in 1862 two of them, Thomas Kendal and James Milne, bought out the third and the shop became the draper's Kendal, Milne (although locals knew it as 'The Bazaar' long after). In 1872 the old building was knocked down and the new one emerged, triumphantly, as that thing of the hour – a department store.

Zola wrote the ultimate novel of the department store, *Au Bonheur des Dames* (in its English translation, *The Ladies' Paradise*).† In it, Baudu,

* This appeared in a small book that was published as an advertisement for the Bazaar, so the respectability of the females should perhaps be understood as a selling tool.
† Zola's main source was the Bon Marché in Paris, founded 1852 by a retail revolutionary, Aristide Boucicaut. But Boucicaut's revolutionary ideas – low margins; fast turnover; fixed, ticketed prices; browsing encouraged; the right of exchange or refund; free deliveries – were all, as we have seen, less than revolutionary to nineteenth-century Britain. The argument about who was first, however, is bootless: the department store arrived piecemeal, and early avatars – the Ville de Paris (1844) and the Grands Magasins du Louvre (1855)

who runs a small drapery shop across the road from the 'Ladies' Paradise', sees the link between the bazaar and the coming behemoth. He is incredulous (and afraid): 'Had anyone heard of such a thing? A ladies' shop that sold everything – that made it a bazaar!' Baudu sneers that the staff, 'a fine bunch, a load of popinjays . . . handled everything as though they were in a railway station, treating the goods and customers like parcels'.[90] (It is significant that poor, left-behind Baudu mentions the railways: Boucicaut opened the Bon Marché at exactly the time when Baron Haussmann was carrying out Napoleon III's plans for a new Paris, driving through enormous boulevards that linked the railway stations on the peripheries to the centre of the city. Now trams took the suburban shopper in from the edge of town, down the new boulevards, and straight to the new *grands magasins*.)[91]

Apart from the size, the range and quantities of goods being sold and the sheer abundance of *things* – all of which had so appalled Baudu – service was one of the major changes that customers had to come to terms with. The old system in luxury shops, or shops that served the prosperous more generally, was known as 'shopping through'. The customer was met at the door, preferably by the main floorwalker or by the owner himself (the customer could accurately judge her status by the status of the person who came to meet her). The customer stated what goods she desired; the main floorwalker called over a subordinate, who took her to the right counter, seated her, and called over the shop assistant who specialized in those particular goods. When the customer had made her selection (or not), the shop assistant called over another floorwalker, who escorted her to the next area she wished to visit. If the goods she had purchased at the first counter were small and were to be taken with her rather than delivered later, the floorwalker carried the packages. This was repeated as long as necessary, until the departing customer was escorted out, the floorwalker carrying her purchases out to her carriage.*

This took place in small shops naturally – there were possibly only one or two people to serve the customers anyway. But there were also

---

in Paris; A. T. Stewart's Marble Palace (1848), Lord and Taylor, Arnold, Constable and Co. and Macy's (1850s) in New York; as well as the shops I discuss in this chapter – all contributed.
* In some shops outside London an extremely grand customer expected to remain seated in her carriage while everything was brought out to her for examination. By the nineteenth century in London, this was clearly no longer practicable.

shops that were not yet quite department stores, but were, nonetheless, 'monster' shops. As early as 1799 Glovers of Southampton was advertising 'Ware-Rooms' that were organized into separate departments with a range of stock that would have qualified it as a department store had the name existed: it sold plate, jewellery and musical instruments (including organs 'fit for Churches, Chapels or houses', pianos, harpsichords, harps, clarinets and flutes), as well as an odd mixture of telescopes, microscopes and spectacles, blunderbusses, oyster knives, umbrellas, razors, watches and clocks.[92] By the 1820s drapers' shops in London might employ as many as thirty people; in 1839 several shops in Manchester had turnover exceeding £1 million.[93] Bainbridge's of Newcastle, founded in 1837, was, like its Manchester counterpart that was to become Kendal, Milne, a draper's shop that understood that buying one thing – a dress, say – led to other purchases: gloves, stockings, ribbons and lace. Bainbridge's referred to these goods as 'novelties', and began to stock them early. From trimming for a dress it was a small step to trimming for upholstery, or curtains, which led to rugs, then to soft furnishings, then to furniture and so on. The growth was organic, and it is therefore hard to put a finger on the moment – there – when the department store arrived. By mid-century, however, enough monster shops were in operation that they seemed to have existed for ever.

Department stores were, by definition, middle class. The multiples showed how stores selling the basics – food, tobacco, newspapers – had expanded by increasing the number of their outlets while maintaining their extremely narrow range of stock. This was necessary: where one bought these basics was predicated on convenience. If the quality met an expected standard and the price remained competitive, no one would choose one store over another. For drapery items, for home furnishings, for fashion, customers went to the shop that sold what they wanted: the range of goods and the quality of the goods was now of primary importance, while convenience and location became secondary. When a shopkeeper concentrated on price and location, he was concentrating on customers with little time or money; when another shopkeeper chose to stress the depth and quality of his stock, he was expecting to receive customers who were both cash- and time-rich. Thus department stores stressed the quantity and quality of the goods they stocked, their wide variety, and the level of expertise of their staff in both acquiring these goods and selling them, as well as the design and layout of their shops. One indication of the kind of clientele desired was the proportionately large number of department stores that were to be found in spa and resort towns. Jolly's of Bath hoped to draw the more upmarket elements of the town, advertising itself as a 'Parisian Depot'. Beale's of Bournemouth had opened first as a fancy-goods shop in 1881, when Bournemouth still felt that cheap-day-return excursionists were bringing nothing of economic value to the town (for more on excursion travel and resorts, see pp. 111, 230, 241–44). Beale's turned its back on these visitors, resolutely stocking just the expensive lines, and soon opening a Liberty's franchise, for the clothing of choice of not only the wealthy, but the eccentrically wealthy (for more on Liberty's, see below, pp. 115–17). In general, the south coast had a plethora of department stores – among others, in Brighton, Margate, Plymouth, Torquay, Southsea and Worthing.[94] All saw their role not simply as retailer, but as a participant in the attractions of the resort.

For them, and for department stores more generally, innovation was a matter of pride, as it had been to the smaller shopkeeper. There were two kinds of innovation. The first was the kind of innovation that the customer *saw* – whether it was new buildings, plate-glass windows, customer lifts and escalators,* cash-registers, pneumatic tubes to dispatch orders and payments to a central cash department,† or even Wylie and Lockhead of Glasgow's novel idea of 'flats', where areas were decorated as if they were individual rooms in a private house that customers could

---

* Wylie and Lockhead in Glasgow had the first lift, in 1855. The *Glasgow Herald* reported it as a 'very ingenious hoisting apparatus worked by a neat steam engine, which is intended not only to lift up bales from the Wagon entrance to the upper parts of the building, but to elevate those ladies and gentlemen to the galleries to whom the climbing of successive stairs might be attended with fatigue and annoyance. Parties who are old, fat, feeble, short winded, or simply lazy, or who desire a bit of fun, have only to place themselves on an enclosed platform or flooring when they are elevated by a gentle and pleasing process to a height exceeding that of a country steeple.'[95]

† The old way of taking cash had been for a shop assistant to write out an order, then a floorwalker went with both the order and the payment to the cash department, and waited while a receipt was issued, and brought it back together with any change. As customer numbers – and the amount of floor space to be covered by the floorwalker – increased, this became too cumbersome. In the 1880s a pneumatic tube system was devised: the shop assistant put the money and the order in a capsule, put it in the tube, and it was rushed along to the cash department by vacuum pressure; a receipt and the change were returned in the same way. The method had made something of a comeback, particularly in large superstores: the wholesalers Costco, some Tesco supermarkets and even Ikea empty their tills and send the cash in plastic capsules along exactly these types of pneumatic tube.

walk around to examine the goods displayed, for the first time, as though at home.*[96] The second kind of innovation was those that the customer *felt* rather than saw. These included new ways of organizing space, new service techniques, such as the decline and later abolition of the previously ubiquitous floorwalker; and the creation of service departments such as ladies' lavatories,† hairdressers, reading rooms, restaurants, cleaners and laundry services, carpet-beating, interior decor, estate agents, upholsterers, banks, post offices, smoking rooms and club rooms for men,‡ even undertakers.

Some were better than others at seeing the future. David Lewis, the son of a merchant from London, was first apprenticed to a tailor and outfitter. In 1856 he set up on his own in Liverpool, a town of increasing prosperity – the Crimean War and the development of the American Midwest was bringing big business to the port. At roughly the same time, in the same street, another tailor, named Jacobs, opened his shop. In 1864 Lewis branched out into women's clothes, then in 1874 he added shoes for women and girls; then he started selling perfumery, layettes, umbrellas and patent medicines; in 1879 he added a tobacco department; in 1880 school slates, watches, stationery, books and sheet music. (In that same year he also opened a new store in Manchester and, to advertise it, sold Lewis's Two-shilling Tea, complete with a specially commissioned tea song, 'Lewis's Beautiful Tea', more as a marketing gimmick than with any expectation of finding a market. To his astonishment, by 1883, he was selling 20,000 pounds of tea a year – and all from an attempt to promote clothes.) His neighbour Jacobs had had enough; he advertised, 'Jacobs of Ranelagh Street find it necessary to give notice that it is not their intention to add other departments to their business of clothiers, Bootmakers, Hatters and Outfitters or to enter into any branch of business which they do not thoroughly understand.' It is hardly necessary to tell the rest of the story: Jacobs went out of business, while Lewis became the owner of Lewis's of Liverpool and of the

---

* Wylie and Lockhead remained pioneers: later they were the first in the country to promote art-nouveau furniture.
† A great boon to women, in particular: one early twentieth-century feminist remembered in her childhood being told by her mother that before department stores and coffee shops like the ABC and Lyons Corner House freed women to spend hours out of the house, 'Either ladies didn't go out or ladies didn't go'.[97]
‡ Many shops worked hard to get elusive males through the door: Harrod's advertised a 'Gent's Club Room . . . furnished in the style of the Georgian period', Whiteley's men's hairdresser offered a daily shave for those paying an annual subscription.[98]

Bon Marché, also in Liverpool, one of the biggest and most successful department-store entrepreneurs of the century.[99]

While these department stores increased in size, swallowing up the shops around them, before the late 1870s it was rare that the shops were purpose-built: rather, they extended and extended, but from the front remained visibly separate buildings that had been knocked together. The Bon Marché in Brixton* was, in 1877, the first custom-built department store in Britain (it was said to have cost a staggering £70,000); others followed, sometimes voluntarily, often when street-widening schemes or other civic improvements meant that their original shops would have had to have been rebuilt anyway – Barker's, Derry and Toms, and Pontings, all in Kensington, became monolithic when Kensington High Street was widened from the small country lane it had been.[101] Lewis had with great foresight chosen the location for his Manchester shop with an extension in mind. Starting with six departments in 1877, by 1884 his premises had spread across the entire block, and rebuilding had begun once again.[102]

Messrs Bourne and Hollingsworth in Oxford Street, having had somewhat less foresight, looked about them to see what property they would have to acquire to get their 'island' site (a site that occupied an entire block, bounded by streets on four sides: the retailer's dream). It was a daunting prospect – a pub, a dairy, a barber's, a coffee house, a carpet-layer, a costume manufacturer, two milliners (one wholesale, one retail), a music publisher, a musical-instrument shop, a palmist, a hairdresser, the British headquarters of the New Columbia Gramophone Co., a brothel, a private house, a wholesale lace merchant, a building containing several Polish tailors, a sweet shop, the offices of Doan's Backache Pills, Savory's cigarette factory, a wholesale blouse-maker, a wine merchant's storage cellar, a soda-water manufacturer, a jeweller, a baby-linen manufacturer, a wallpaper merchant, an estate agent, two solicitors and a chapel – but they did it.[103] Others were similarly placed: Peter Robinson, which had opened in 1833, had bought the two adjoining premises in 1854; in 1856 and 1858 two more were bought; in 1860 the final shop, which gave a block of six shops, was acquired. Marshall and Snelgrove had opened as Marshall and Wilson in 1837; just short

---

* No connection to Lewis's Bon Marché: both were linking themselves to Boucicaut's Parisian store; Lewis even borrowed the French shop's stripes for his advertising and packaging.[100]

of forty years later, in 1876, it added the final shop to its, by now, seven shops to complete its own 'island'.[104]*

These shops, like Whiteley's of Paddington, saw themselves as 'Universal Providers'. It was William Whiteley himself who had coined the phrase. He had started as a draper in 1855, and he followed the same path as we have already seen with Kendal, Milne and Bainbridge's: first he opened a drapery, then he expanded to add the goods that might be desired at the same time: ribbons, lace, fancy goods, gloves, jewellery, parasols. By the 1870s he had expanded literally, into the shop next door, and figuratively, into the services market: Whiteley's included an estate agent, a hairdresser, a tea room and a furniture showroom on the Wylie and Lockhead model. What really set him apart, though, was his talent for self-publicity. For example, in 1865 one of his employees, John Barker, a department manager, was earning £300 a year; Whiteley promised to double his salary if Barker doubled his turnover. He did, and by 1870 Barker asked to be taken into partnership. Whiteley refused, but promised him a salary of £1,000 – more than had ever been paid to a draper; more even than the income of many upper-middle-class professionals. Barker declined it, left Whiteley's and started his own department store in Kensington (which closed last year, in 2005).[106] Whiteley, however, more than made up for the loss of his valued employee by ensuring that all the newspapers reported the huge salary Barker had been offered. In the 1870s Whiteley also revived the eighteenth-century custom of the puff, sending the *Bayswater Chronicle* letters ostensibly written by women who shopped at his store.

A completely different route was taken by some other monster shops. Many furniture shops were content to remain furniture shops: Waring and Gillow was proud to announce that it was the 'largest furnishing emporium in the world', but it had no interest in developing other departments; Heal's, in Tottenham Court Road, had picked up the modern department stores' methods of display, but it stuck with furnishings. Even the huge Peter Robinson shop, which employed nearly 2,000 workers across 100 departments, sold nothing but ladies' clothes.[107]

* Such attempts to expand were not always successful: in the Mile End Road 'Messrs Wickham, *circa* 1910, wanted an emporium. Messrs Spiegelhalter, one infers, wouldn't sell out. Messrs Wickham, one infers further, pressed on regardless, thereby putting their Baroque tower badly out of centre. Messrs Spiegelhalter ("The East End Jewellers") remain [in 1966]: two stuccoed storeys surrounded on both sides by giant columns *à la* Selfridges. The result is one of the best visual jokes in London.'[105]

Arthur Liberty, although ultimately diversifying, began by dealing in only a narrow range of merchandise. Liberty had first worked at Farmer and Roger's, a shawl warehouse in Regent Street. In 1862 an international exhibition held in Kensington showed William Morris wallpaper for the first time, next to the first exhibition of Japanese arts and crafts to appear in Europe. (Commodore Perry had sailed into Yedo Bay nine years before, and the first commercial treaty between Japan and Britain had been signed only in 1858.) After the exhibition closed, Farmer and Roger bought some of the displays and set up an Oriental Warehouse in the shop next to their own, with Arthur Liberty as its junior salesman. The Oriental Warehouse became a meeting place for a 'bohemian' set that included the painters Whistler and Rossetti and the actress Ellen Terry – the forerunners of the Aesthetic Movement. As John Barker had done, Liberty asked to be taken into partnership. As with Barker, he was refused, and he too left to start up his own business. (But unlike Whiteley, whose name survives in some form of retailing to this day, Farmer and Roger's went under, while Liberty's continues to flourish.)

Liberty at first specialized in fabrics; in less than a year he had added Japanese goods, as well as fans, wallpapers, fabrics, screens, lacquerware and other exotica from the Far East more generally.* Soon he was arranging for manufacturers to print English fabrics using Japanese techniques and Japanese-y colours, which he dubbed 'Art Colours', but which quickly became known to everyone else as 'Liberty Colours'. *Queen's* magazine had earlier described them: 'There are tints that call to mind French and English mustards, sage-greens, willow-greens, greens that look like curry, and greens that are remarkable on lichen-coloured walls, and also among marshy vegetation.' More memorably, W. S. Gilbert satirized both the fabrics and those who admired them in *Patience*, the operetta he wrote with Arthur Sullivan, in 1881: its protagonist, Bunthorne, is

> A Japanese young man,
> A blue-and-white young man,
> Francesca di Rimini, miminy-piminy
> *Je ne sais quoi* young man!

* This interest in the Far East was catered to by others, just not as successfully, or perhaps as single-mindedly. Zola's department-store proprietor had set up 'a small bargain table' of shop-soiled gewgaws: 'now it was overflowing with old bronzes, old ivories, old lacquer and had a turnover of fifteen thousand francs a year. He scoured the whole of the Far East, getting travellers to rummage for him in palaces and temples.'[108]

> A pallid and thin young man,
> A haggard and lank young man,
> A greenery-yallery, Grosvenor Gallery*
> Foot-in-the-grave young man!

Patience mocked the whole Aesthetic Movement: Bunthorne was an obvious parody of Whistler, while Grosvenor, his rival, was Oscar Wilde.† Yet Liberty's, at the heart of that movement, relished its connection to the parodists Gilbert and Sullivan too, and found it financially rewarding: Liberty's fabrics were used in the production of *Patience*, and credited in the programme beside advertisements for Liberty's 'artistic silks'. When the play moved to the newly built Savoy Theatre, Liberty's decorated a room to receive the Prince of Wales for the opening. The store continued to be linked to Gilbert and Sullivan's works, sending someone to Japan to research clothes and materials before the shop's designers began work on the costumes and sets for *The Mikado* in 1885.

Notwithstanding this interest, Liberty did not neglect his primary business: by 1880 his Regent Street shop had seven departments; in 1883 he bought another shop on the same side of Regent Street, one shop away from his first; he acquired the upper floor of the property in the middle and joined the two by a staircase known as the 'Camel's Back'. Soon he acquired the downstairs of the middle building too, and ultimately he occupied five shops in a row, maintaining the disparate nature of the façades until Regent Street was redeveloped in the 1920s. Although he never went in for 'universality' on Whiteley's scale, by that time he had an Eastern Bazaar basement, which sold Japanese and Chinese antiques, porcelain, bronzes, lacquerware, metalware, brass trays, dolls, fans and other knick-knacks, screens and 'decorative furnishing objects'. There was an Arab Tea Room, and a Curio Department that sold armour, swords, daggers, ivory carvings, bronzes and 'antique metalwork suitable for the decoration of halls'. There were also service departments, includ-

---

* The 'blue-and-white young man' is a reference to the Chinese porcelain beloved by the Aesthetic Movement. The Grosvenor Gallery was also linked to the Aesthetic Movement: in 1877 its first show included work by Burne-Jones, Whistler, Alma-Tadema and others. It was run by Joseph Comyns Carr, an art critic, and C. E. Hallé, the son of the founder of the Hallé Orchestra in Manchester (see pp. 369–72).

† Bunthorne's Aesthetic dress was designed by Georges Pilotelle, whose history was more colourful than the subdued fabrics he used: he had fled France in 1875 after being found guilty of the murder of an unspecified number of people he had taken hostage, most probably during the Commune. His political inclinations were made plain in his collection of relics of the Revolutionary martyr Marat, which was said to be 'the most complete and valuable existing'.[109]

ing a Paper Hanging studio and a Decoration Studio. From 1884 a Costume Department sold dresses designed by Arthur Liberty and made up from his fabrics. Now both a house and its owner could be entirely 'done' by Liberty.[110] Liberty had created a space where – in a very modern fashion – one could acquire a lifestyle.

Yet the idea of the department store as sweeping all before it is a triumph of hype over reality. In 1880 the British department store seemed to have reached its apogee, while other countries were racing ahead: in France, Germany and the United States art colleges taught professional display and design courses for shopfitters. In America, Macy's, Wanamaker's and Marshall Field had stormed ahead in terms of size, display, advertising and organizational structure, while Britain had retreated to older systems, with the floorwalker once more becoming a power – the *Draper's Record* in 1888 noted with distaste that Parisian stores let women walk around unescorted. Anything might happen, was the underlying suggestion: men might make advances to female shop staff, goods might be stolen, or – and this seemed to be the real fear – 'loose women' might invade the premises.[111] The market share reflected the department stores' backward step: in 1900 co-ops held between 6 and 7 per cent of the retail market, while department stores accounted for less than 2 per cent. By 1910 that had crept up to slightly under 3 per cent, but when the increase in population was taken into account the figures showed a fall in real terms.[112]

Gordon Selfridge, an American, smelt opportunity. There were not many opportunities he had missed in his life. In 1879 he had started work as a stock boy at Marshall Field in Chicago; he was promoted to travelling salesmen, then to counter clerk; by 1887, only eight years after his lowly entry, he was the shop's retail general manager, and by 1890 he was a junior partner. His development of Marshall Field followed the now familiar pattern: he opened departments for specialist goods – shoes, children's clothes – and then offered services like glove-cleaning, a tea room, a restaurant. His main contribution, however, was in advertising and promotion: window displays were not simply to convey information about stock to passers-by, he said, but to create desire. He announced the creation of an annual sale – and with typical bombast also announced that he had invented it.[113]

This was demonstrably not true. The 'old draper' in 1872 recounted how in his youth – probably in the 1820s – when some stock accidentally burned, his employer decided to use this as an excuse to clear the over-stock that had accumulated. 'In the first place some large yellow poster bills were struck off, headed, "Fire!!! Fire!!! Fire!!!" which informed the public that in consequence of the fire which took place on Wednesday, the 6th instant, the damaged stock, much of which was only slightly singed, would be cleared out at a great reduction, together with other surplus stock, sale to commence on Monday next.' After closing, the staff quietly singed goods that had remained unharmed. The next morning, 'People bought goods of every description that were at all likely to suit them ... Critical old women, that under ordinary circumstances would have spent a long time ... examining a pair of stockings, bought the same goods, instantly, at full prices, when slightly singed at the tops.' By the end of the day it was found that 'we had actually cleared off whole piles of goods that would have taken us several weeks to have sold under ordinary circumstances, while nearly all the jobbish goods bought for the occasion had been cleared out.' He claimed that it was this fire sale that was 'the commencement of the "selling off" system in London'.[114] That was unlikely too, but it definitely pre-dated Selfridge's 'invention' of the sale by three-quarters of a century.

Selfridge's passion for advertising broke new ground. As with so many innovators, it was not that he did anything particularly novel, but that he took many novel ideas of the period and worked them together, increasing their force by his passion and commitment. Much of his advertising turned on the value of shopping (particularly of shopping at Marshall Field), on shopping as social good, on the benefits shopping conferred on humanity and so on. Marshall Field's restaurant was promoted by the aspiration 'A department store should be a social center, not merely a place for shopping.' He was among the first to hire professional copywriters and set up an 'institutional advertising style', which sold Marshall Field, and shopping at Marshall Field, rather than promoting separate items. He instituted 'free gifts', he mounted special promotions.[115] In 1904 Selfridge suddenly resigned, either because he had been refused a senior partnership or because when the store was incorporated in 1901 he had received what he considered to be an inadequate share allocation. Whatever the reason, by 1906 he was in London. With money from a British shopping magnate, after an abortive start he began to build: Selfridge's was the biggest store ever to be built entirely from scratch, rather than by expansion.

Selfridge had plans for London. He brought over three colleagues from Chicago: one to control the merchandise, one to design the store and its fittings, and one to be in charge of window displays. The buyers were now subordinate to the merchandise manager. No longer were there dozens, if not hundreds, of separate little fiefdoms, each buying to suit itself, with no overall sense of the customer base; nor were buyers any longer entirely responsible for their own staff; nor did they design their own displays, laying out their merchandise as they each thought best. Everything was centralized. Even the flow of information was unified: instead of floorwalkers who led customers to the appropriate departments, based on each individual's opinion of how best to fulfil a customer's request, there was a central information desk. (Marshall Field had had one from early in the 1890s.) Everything was to be coordinated: carpets, wrapping paper, delivery vans, bill heads – even the string used to tie the parcels was in the same colours, with the same design. It was the embodiment of Selfridge's credo: everything and everyone in the store were all working to fulfil a single vision – Selfridge's own.[116]

The opening of the shop, in 1909, was planned as carefully as any theatrical premiere – in fact that was what it most closely resembled, and was clearly intended to resemble. The silk curtains that covered the windows before opening day, said the *Daily Chronicle*, '[suggested] that a wonderful play was being arranged'. When they were drawn back, they revealed a radical departure. Harrod's and Whiteley's both had windows stuffed brimful with as many goods as they could hold. Selfridge's windows were completely different: they displayed unified, thematically coherent images, showing how the consumer might hope to wear a dress or live with the goods on show. The *Retail Trader* understood that this sense of a single vision came from the novelty of having one man solely dedicated to putting goods in the windows. Equally, it understood the theatricality that was aimed at: 'Just as the stage manager of a new play rehearses and tries and retries and fusses until he has exactly the right lights and shades and shadows and appeals to his audience, so the merchant goes to work, analysing his line and his audience, until he hits on the right scheme that brings the public flocking to his doors.'[117]

The public flocked, all right. The shop claimed 1 million visitors in its first week, and, even if the figure needs to be divided in half to allow for pardonable exaggeration, it is a startling number. Other shops became frantic: Waring and Gillow, Swan and Edgar, Peter Robinson,

WE HAVE EVERY PLEASURE IN ANNOUNCING THAT THE FORMAL OPENING OF OUR PREMISES—LONDON'S NEWEST SHOPPING CENTRE—BEGINS TO-DAY AND CONTINUES THROUGHOUT THE WEEK.

WE WISH IT TO BE CLEARLY UNDERSTOOD THAT OUR INVITATION IS TO THE WHOLE BRITISH PUBLIC AND TO VISITORS FROM OVERSEAS —THAT NO CARDS OF ADMISSION ARE REQUIRED—THAT ALL ARE WELCOME—AND THAT THE PLEASURES OF SHOPPING AS WELL AS THOSE OF SIGHT-SEEING BEGIN FROM THE OPENING HOUR

SELFRIDGE & CO.
OXFORD STREET, LONDON. W.

Punch cartoonist Bernard Partridge produced this advertisement for Selfridge's opening, one of thirty-two illustrations that appeared in 104 advertisements commissioned as a preliminary blast of publicity in 1909.

Maple's, Shoolbred, and D. H. Evans all decided to show their new spring lines that same week; Harrod's promoted its diamond jubilee, a mere four years early, with afternoon concerts to be given by the London

Symphony and the band of the Grenadier Guards.[118] But it wasn't enough. The most important thing was advertising, and here Selfridge outshone the others. He was the first to use blanket coverage. He spent £36,000 on press advertising in the run-up to the opening. (Thomas Lipton, as a comparison, was spending between £50,000 and £60,000 a year on advertising – for more than 400 shops.)[119] Selfridge commissioned thirty-two cartoons from artists and caricaturists, including Bernard Partridge, Linley Sambourne, Walter Crane, Lewis Baumer, Leonard Raven-Hill and Fred Pegram, all of whom worked for *Punch* (Crane was a renowned children's illustrator in addition). The resulting 104 full-page advertisements ran for a week in 18 national newspapers.[120] Selfridge's great insight, however, was not simply the motivating power of advertising. It was, more crucially, the weight that advertising carried with newspapers. He was the first to see that if an advertiser was paying thousands of pounds to a newspaper or periodical, and there were likely to be many thousands of pounds more to come, the newspaper would support the advertiser editorially too, if stroked the right way. Selfridge made it his business to cultivate those at the top – in particular, Lord Northcliffe, the owner of the *Daily Mail*, and Ralph D. Blumenfeld, the editor of the *Daily Express* – as well as more humble journalists: he hired one of their own as a publicist; he gave journalists' dinners; he staged a special, pre-opening evening with a private tour of the store; he told them they could always use the telephones in Selfridge's, without charge.[121]

These novelties were matched by novelties in the shop. Again, it was not that no one had thought of such things before – shopping as entertainment had, as we have seen, a 200-year history – it was that no one had pushed them to such extremes. On the opening day, all the customers were given calendars and notebooks listing the 130 departments and emblazoned with the slogan, 'WHY NOT SPEND THE DAY AT SELFRIDGES?'[122] After Louis Blériot became the first person to fly the English Channel in a 'heavier-than-air machine', Selfridge rushed to buy the aircraft, and the day after the flight it was already on display in the store. More than 150,000 people came to see it over the next four days. He held an exhibition of the paintings that were not accepted for the Royal Academy summer show. Soon the shop had a playroom for children, decorated to look like the seaside, with real sand, a pond and a small roller coaster, and the Palm Court had a Punch and Judy show every afternoon. There was a pet shop, a rifle range, a putting green, a skating rink. But, most importantly, Selfridge knew how to convey this information to the general public: through the newspapers.

4

Read All About It:
Buying the News

THE CREATION of the earliest newspapers was a by-product of an event that occurred owing to 'something of a legislative accident', a governmental absence of mind.[1] Government censorship of printed material had collapsed during the Civil War and the Interregnum, but the return of Charles II in 1660, and the Licensing Act of 1662, had reasserted control over the content of all books, pamphlets and other publications, requiring prior consent for each and every publication, and, further, restricting the printing trade to a mere twenty approved printers. In 1695 the act lapsed, with no replacement bill in sight. With it went parliamentary control of the printers and prior consent for printed material. The situation that is now in place more or less began then: anyone could print anything without first gaining legislative permission, although the laws of blasphemy, sedition and libel controlled, post-publication, what could be published.

Within weeks of the disappearance of prior censorship, an unlisted printer set up in Bristol; more soon appeared in other cities. Only six years later, in 1701, what may have been the first newspaper in Britain was published: the *Norwich Post*. The first London paper was not far behind, appearing in 1702. By 1709 there were 19 papers in London alone, between them putting out 55 editions a week; by 1760 there had been at least 150 papers over the intervening 58 years, many of which had survived very briefly. Enough had survived that 35 provincial papers had by that date a combined circulation of 200,000.[2] This sounds like nothing – an average circulation of fewer than 6,000 copies – but by the standards of the day it was considerable: the *Salisbury Journal*, which sold a 'few thousand' copies a week, had the same circulation as a successful newspaper in Paris.[3] The first *daily* paper in France did not appear until the last quarter of the eighteenth century, by which time there were more than 50 papers in England and 9 in Scotland. Wales did not get its first English-language paper until 1804, although there had probably been a Welsh-language paper as early as 1705 or 1706 (of which no copy has survived); by 1785 the population of Ireland (variously suggested at between 2.8 million and 4 million)* was buying 45,000 copies of newspapers a week in Dublin and 2,000 in the provinces.[4]

The pattern was set early in the eighteenth century. The *St Ives Post* was founded in Cambridgeshire in 1717, but failed very quickly. It was then acquired by Robert Raikes, who went into partnership with a printer, William Dicey, and together they set up the *St Ives Mercury*.† Soon after, in 1720, they moved it and themselves to Northampton, where they were the town's first printers, transforming their paper into the *Northampton Mercury*, which flourished by covering far more territory than the name 'Northampton' would suggest. It boasted that it went further in length, than any other country newspaper in England, covering nineteen counties.[5] Newspapers had to appeal to as wide a public as they could reach geographically, because of the small circulation figures: an average provincial newspaper sold 200 copies a week, while by mid-century the larger ones in more urbanized areas might sell 2,000 a week. In 1761, for example, *Aris's Birmingham Gazette* advertised that it had agents in London, Shrewsbury, Wolverhampton, Worcester, Bridgnorth, Newcastle under Lyme, Lichfield, Stafford, Dudley, Walsall and Stratford-upon-Avon; in 1755 the *Bristol Journal*'s agents were as far distant as Liverpool, Sherborne and Gloucester. Agents sent local news to the paper, took in advertisements, and, most importantly, arranged the complicated logistics of moving their paper around the country. The *Cambridge Chronicle and Journal* in 1773 promised:

> This PAPER is dispatched Northwards every Friday Night, by the Caxton Post [i.e. the stagecoach], as far as York, Newcastle and Carlisle; through the Counties of Cambridge, Huntingdon,

---

* Contemporary accounts preferred the lower figure; K. H. Connell in his *The Population of Ireland: 1750–1845* (Oxford, Clarendon Press, 1950), thinks the higher number more likely.

† This Robert Raikes should not be confused with his son Robert (1736–1811), who succeeded him as publisher of a later acquisition, the *Gloucester Journal*, but is better known as the founder of the Sunday-school movement.

Bedford, Buckingham, Rutland, Leicester, Nottingham, Lincoln, Northampton, Norfolk, Hereford, Essex and the Isle of Ely, by the Newsmen; to London the next Morning, by the Coach and Fly; and to several Parts of Suffolk, &c. by other Conveyances. – *Persons living at a Distance from such Places as the newsmen go through, may have the Paper left where they shall please to appoint.*[6]

The small circulations had two causes. First, the population, while rising rapidly, was still low when compared to the nineteenth century; there was nothing to be done about this. The second was a high unit price, and this too was a problem without a solution, because all newspapers were forced into artificially high prices by swingeing newspaper taxes. By the time of the French Revolution there were sixteen daily papers in London, two that came out twice a week, and seven that were issued three times a week, while 8.6 million copies of London papers were dispatched annually to the country.[7] The government taxed newspapers both to raise revenue and as a way of controlling a potentially seditious press. By the end of the century, newspapers carried a tax of 4*d.* a copy: a paper that would otherwise have cost 1*d.* or 2*d.* could not be sold for less than 5*d.* when it was properly stamped to show that the appropriate tax had been paid. This meant that only the prosperous could buy a newspaper regularly. That this was a straightforward targeting of the working classes by rationing their reading matter, and thus the ideas that reached them, is not a retrospective twenty-first-century reading of the situation. The Seditious Societies Act of 1799, passed as an anti-Jacobin act, was reconfirmed in 1811 specifically to stop 'cheap publications adapted to influence and pervert the public mind'. Many outside government saw cheap reading matter for the masses as a real threat – the Society for the Suppression of Vice, run by the Church and the upper classes (with the Duke of Wellington as its patron), paid rewards to members of the public who turned in newspapers, books and pamphlets that had been published in breach of the act. (Even at the time, the more unpleasant aspects of this class- and income-bound separation of access to information were apparent. The Revd Sydney Smith remarked that the Society's proper title should be 'The Society for the Suppressing of the Vices of Persons whose Income does not Exceed £500 per annum'.)[8]

High taxation, however, did not do what the government had intended. Instead of spending – or not spending – 6*d.* on a paper (7*d.*

by 1815), people found various ways of reading communally. By 1789
the Secretary of the Treasury estimated that every paper in London was
read by as many as twenty to thirty people, and then it was sent to the
country, where it was read by even more.[9] In 1799 a surgeon in Devon
had the *London Courier* sent to him regularly; it was then read by a French
émigré, who in turn handed it to a Congregational minister, who passed
it to a druggist, who gave it to an assistant schoolmaster. That was the
first day. On day two the paper went to another resident, who passed it
to a 'sergemaker'; from there it went to unnamed and unnumbered 'common people'. All of these readers would have contributed to the cost of
the paper, in diminishing shares as they reached the bottom of the list.

Other people formed themselves into 'newspaper societies', in which
people clubbed together to buy a regular paper: the *Monthly Magazine* in
1821 said there were 'not less than 5,000' groups of this sort, and thought
that this might mean there were as many 50,000 families who had
contact with a society.[10] Other, more social, clubs started with similar
aims: in Edinburgh, the 'first thing that induced us to join in a society
was the reading of . . . *Spectators*', said one of the founders of the Easy
Club.[11] The simplest and the least restricting way to get the news was to
go into a pub or a coffee house, where the paper could be read for the
price of a cup of coffee and 1*d*. Most coffee houses had reading rooms,
which could be joined for anything from 1*s*. a year upward, and they
kept newspapers and books for their readers – by 1742 booksellers were
already complaining about the 'the scandalous and Low Custom that
has lately prevail'd amongst those who keep *Coffee houses*, of buying one
of any new Book . . . and lending it by Turns to such Gentlemen to read
as frequent their Coffee house'. In 1773 Thomas Campbell went into
the Chapter Coffee House because he heard it 'was remarkable for a
large collection of books, & a reading society . . . I . . . found all the new
publications I sought, & I believe what I am told that all the new books
are laid in.' He later saw a whitesmith, or tin worker, 'in his apron &
[with] some of his saws under his arm, [who] came in, sat down and
called for his glass of punch and the paper, both of which he used with
as much ease as a Lord'.[12] Pubs were equally welcoming, usually just
hanging a sign 'requesting gentlemen not to monopolise the current
day's paper' for more than five minutes at a time.[13]

By this time, coffee houses were part of the landscape. The first coffee
house in England may have appeared in Oxford, but the first of which

we have any concrete information was in London. A merchant who had lived in Smyrna found, on his return in 1657, that

> The Novelty of [the coffee his Greek servant made for him] drew so great Resort to his House, that he lost all the Fore-part of the Day by it; insomuch that he thought it expedient to rid himself of this Trouble, by allowing his Greek servant (in conjunction with his son-in-law's Coachman) to make and sell it publically [*sic*]. They set up their Coffee-House in St Michael's Alley in Cornhill, which was the first in London.[14]

They were on to a winning thing, for over the next five years another 83 coffee houses appeared; by 1801 there were 500 in London alone, and they had developed as places to drink coffee and meet friends, and, equally importantly, as places to conduct business.

Outside London, much social life was maintained in these coffee rooms: they were centres of information and news, and they served a wide range of readers, from the whitesmith to the idle dandy. By 1833 the Manchester Coffee and Newsroom took 96 papers a week, plus several periodicals and reviews; it cost 1*d.* to sit and read, 2*d.* with coffee thrown in. The Exchange Coffee House, also in Manchester, riposted with 130 papers a week, 186 on Saturdays, as well as a range of foreign papers.[15] The upper classes had their own coffee houses, particularly in the spa and resort towns. In 1739 Tunbridge Wells had three coffee houses that we know of, perhaps more, where for 5*s.* visitors could have 'the use of pens, ink, paper &c.' In Bath, the fashionable coffee house was Morgan's, where, jibed one satirist, regular customer

> . . . cannot drink his coffee with a goût,
> 'Till he has read the papers thro and thro . . .

Another visitor

> . . . joined by a whole unthinking crowd,
> At least once ev'ry day calls out, aloud,
> Boy, does the London post go out?[16]

What time the post went out was becoming an increasingly important question for newspapers and their readers. As we saw above, newspapers were transported by an elaborate system of stagecoach routes in the early part of the century. From the beginning of the eighteenth century, newspapers had been carried post-free, as a way of increasing the circulation of pro-government papers around the country. By 1782 the Post

Office was sending 3 million papers a year from London to the country, and in 1788, a parliamentary inquiry recommended that a separate newspaper office be set up by the Post Office to deal with the volume. The Post Office was happy to comply: fraud was keeping its income down. In 1710 the *Flying Post* newspaper had routinely left a section of the page blank, so that people could write a message of some length and then legitimately send the paper on through the post without paying for it.[17] This had been halted, but there was still nothing to stop individuals slipping letters between the pages and posting the newspapers on without charge. It was hoped that a separate department could give better oversight to the problem.

Certainly it could improve the delivery service. The old system of post boys had asked them to travel at a rate of seven miles per hour in summer, five miles per hour in winter, but this was next to impossible to achieve, given the state of the roads. Ralph Allen, from Bath, had done as much as was possible. One of the early eighteenth-century developers of Bath as a leisure town, he had been a shareholder in the Avon Navigation System, and he had furthermore acted as postmaster for the town. By 1719 he had taken charge of all the post roads nationally – that is, the six roads that carried the inter-city posts, which were, in theory, partly maintained by the government. By the time Allen died, in 1764, he had overseen the development of these six roads into a network of nearly twenty main arteries that now reached the new manufacturing towns as well as a number of subsidiary routes. He had also begun to regularize deliveries so that an extensive six-day-a-week service was beginning to emerge.[18]

After his death, however, the system stopped improving and simply stagnated. The post was still being carried by boys on broken-down packhorses, or on small carts. Twenty years later, a letter sent from London to Birmingham on a Monday could not be acknowledged that same week.[19] John Palmer, who held a patent for theatres in Bath and Bristol, grew impatient with the state of communications along the roads and determined to follow in the footsteps of his Bath predecessor. In 1784 he presented to William Pitt, then Chancellor of the Exchequer, a system he had devised to set up contracts with stagecoach owners, who would carry the post in newly designated mailcoaches at between eight and nine miles per hour, providing changes of horse as necessary. They would have an armed guard to sit next to the coachmen, and commit themselves to meeting exact schedules, which would mean that each postmaster would now know exactly what time his post was leaving – and would arrive.* To increase speed still further, these mailcoaches would also be exempt from toll fares along the turnpikes. Pitt agreed to a trial, and the Bristol–London route was chosen. The coach was to leave Bristol at 4 p.m., and was scheduled to arrive in London at 8 a.m. the next morning. It arrived well within that time and, with Pitt's help, by early 1875 mailcoaches were running in Norfolk, Suffolk, Essex, and on the cross roads between Bristol and Portsmouth. By the summer, Leeds, Manchester and Liverpool had their own coaches; by October, mail-coaches had reached Milford Haven and Holyhead, Birmingham, Carlisle, Dover, Gloucester, Nottingham, Shrewsbury and Worcester. (Now that letter from London to Birmingham could be acknowledged in a mere two days.) By the following summer the 400 miles between Edinburgh and London could be traversed in 60 hours, down from the 85 it had taken 25 years before. (Further development in Scotland had to wait because its road improvements lagged behind England's: until 1800 there was only one all-Scottish mailcoach route, Edinburgh to Aberdeen, which after some years was finally extended to Thurso, then to Inverness and on to the Highlands.)[20]

Time, and the spending of it, began to take on more urgency. (It would become a more compelling subject still with the arrival of the railways; see pp. 194–5.) Advertisements for stagecoaches before the turnpike age had said that coaches would arrive 'in about two days', or 'if the roads are good'. Now the Post Office was determined that outside conditions should not interfere. In 1789 snow had caused a driver on the Glasgow route to spend twelve days almost entirely on the road, 'to get the coach through on time'; he was so exhausted by this feat that he had to stay in bed for a week afterwards, but the Post Office paid for his recuperation period in order to encourage others to emulate his dedication.[21] In a similar manner, while newspapers continued to be carried free if they were brought to the post office before 7 p.m., there was a surcharge of ½d. per paper if they came after that hour, to discourage late delivery and permit the eight o'clock mailcoach to depart on schedule.[22] (Although this is not to say that there was not always a way

---

* This was a big step forward. Until these postal reforms, the London post boys were obliged to wait until the government offices chose to deliver their mailbags each day before setting out.

around the schedule: the *General Evening Post* struck a deal with the Post Office, paying a flat fee so that, even if its papers were late, the mail-coaches would wait for them.)[23]

Getting the post to the country was, in many ways, the same thing as getting the news to the country. In the 1810s, some newspapers began to produce boards with breaking news on them, to stand outside the offices of local distributors and to hang on the sides of the mailcoaches as they raced through towns and countryside. In 1837 the *Reading Mercury* had placards on mailcoaches giving the news of William IV's death, and 'in less than an hour . . . there was scarcely a person within the borough' who had not heard: unimaginable speed.[24] In the 1770s, during the American Revolution, and through the late 1780s, with the impeach-ment and trial of Warren Hastings, the concept of parliamentary reporting in the newspapers was created. There were no facilities for writing in the House of Commons, so the *Gazetteer* paid 'impecunious barristers' to sit in relays, listen, then rush across to the newspaper's office and scribble down a précis of what they had heard for publication. Evening newspapers, with the day's news in them, could by 1875 reach some parts of the country by morning: the *Courier* went from selling 1,500 copies to selling 7,000 in four years (it was also the first paper to have a second edition).[25]

All this created a demand for news, and newspapers, but what really drove the engine was advertising. This had been fundamental to local papers from the earliest days: Dicey and Raikes's *Northampton Mercury* had carried advertisements for retailers in Northampton, St Ives, Daventry, Loughborough and Boston.[26] As early as 1750 the advertise-ments in many local papers swallowed up half of the available space (there is a reason, after all, that 'Advertiser' was a popular name for newspapers).

Sophie von la Roche, in 1786, wrote to her family in Germany describing the contents of the daily papers (which she numbered in London at twenty-one). The proportion of news to advertisements and announcements was fairly standard:

> The notices in to-day's paper run: . . .
> (1) Plays produced at the Haymarket theatre; names of actors
>   and actresses . . . followed by the prices of the seats . . .
> (2) Plays at the small Sadler's Wells theatre, where to-day's
>   programme offers a satire on magnetism and

somnambulism in particular, and where tumblers and tight-rope walkers may be seen . . .

(3) At the Royal Bush, Mr Astley's amphitheatre;* men, boys and girls in trick-riding; fireworks; short comedies and ballets . . .

(4) Bermondsey Spa, a place where firework displays are held, announces that the scaffolding has been well and strongly made.

(5) The royal Circus; adults and children in trick-riding, children in comedy and pantomime; Italians in dancing and buffoonery.

(6) Two fine large green tortoises for sale.

(7) A notice against some piratical printer.

(8) Discovery of new pills.

(9) Notice of maritime matters . . .

(10) On the docks at Woolwich all kinds of old ships' timber and nautical instruments to be sold.

(11) Notice that . . . the South Sea Voyagers' company will meet.

(12) Fifty guineas reward for information concerning attack of a customs officer by one or more of the shipping hands . . .

(14) A pleasant villa in Fulham to be sold; with orchards and fish-pond.

(15) Bitter stomach pills . . .

(17) Notice that the king and queen returned here yesterday from Windsor . . . and all the names of the gentlemen presented: further, that the list of criminals committed to die was placed before the king; that yesterday evening in the queen's palace a concert was given for the Archduke and duchess of Milan.

(18) That the East India Company offers several million pounds of tea for sale, terms of disposal consequently much lower.

(19) That on the continent there is a rising against papal power . . .

(20) More congratulations to the king from various cities for having escaped the mad Nicholson woman's attack . . .

(23) Discovery that the bottom of a fishing-smack was exclusively laden with French brandy . . .

(25) That the commercial pact with France would mean permanent peace.

---

* For more about Astley's, see pp. 313ff.

    (26) That all those gentlemen opposed to the minister Pitt are
          gone to the country to increase the number of their
          supporters . . .
    (28) A match [i.e. prize-fight] between a Jew and a
          harness-maker in the Epping Forest . . .
    (32) Miss Farren reprimanded for having been ashamed to
          repeat an epilogue for the fourth time . . .
    (37) A reminder to change the post-time . . .
    (41) News from Paris.
    (42) From Plymouth.
    (43) Horse-racing, breed and virtues of horses.
    (44) Short verses.
    (45) Shipping news – who, where and whither.
    (46) Bills of exchange, per cents, and bank news . . .
    (50) A desirable residence, eighty-four years' lease. In all these
          cases a separate breakfast-room is mentioned . . .
    (52) Several estates, all laying particular stress on the fact that
          fruit-trees are planted there, and are watered by a canal . . .
    (54) In addition several more houses, mills and farms. With
          the houses there is always a note to the effect that they do
          or do not contain many mahogany pieces . . .
    (56) Sixty kinds of coaches for sale.
    (57) Horses of all descriptions.
    (58) All kinds of wines, 110 bottles.
    (59) Inquiry about two missing men . . .[27]

Provincial papers did not have this quantity of notices and advertisements, but in their own markets they satisfied their customer base. Circulations remained small – in 1795 the daily circulation of the *Morning Post* was 350;[28] even multiplied by 30 readers per copy, that was a tiny number. But, properly focused, it was enough. Chester had a population of 10,000 in 1700, and that sustained two newspapers, the *Courant* and the *Chronicle*, which covered, according to their advertisements, the areas across Chester, north Shropshire, north-east Wales, south Lancashire (including Liverpool, Wigan and Manchester) and north Staffordshire. Itinerant sellers found it worth their while to advertise that they would be 'at the Wolf's Head, Watergate Street', to sell 'foreign china', or 'at Mr Maddox's Cork Cutters Shop . . . with great choice of China Ware'. Other retailers advertised their shops selling seeds, bankrupt stock, thread, drapery and alcohol. Many stressed their London connections: those selling fashion items like shoes, fabric, upholstery and furniture all had advertisements suggesting their stock had just been purchased in London, or was 'in the present fashion'.[29]

The advertisements for patent medicine were the mainstay of many newspapers. The *New Bath Guide*, a satire, mocked the fashionable doctor and herbalist John Hill and those who were dosed by him:*

> He gives little Tabby a great many Doses
> For he says the poor creature has got the chlorosis,
> Or a ravenous pica, so brought on the vapours
> By swallowing Stuff she has read in the papers.[31]

Many newspaper owners, or their agents, were heavily involved in the patent-medicine business. By 1730 William Dicey and Robert Raikes were in partnership with Thomas Cobb and Benjamin Okell to sell Dr Bateman's Pectoral Drops. John Newberry, the publisher of the first children's magazine,† had a quarter-share in Dr Hooper's Female Pills, and from 1746 he owned the rights to Dr James's Fever Powders, which he advertised through the newspapers and also in the books he published: *Goody-Two Shoes* – which may very well have been written by Oliver Goldsmith – began, 'CARE and Discontent shortened the Days of Little Margery's Father. – He was forced from his Family, and seized with a violent Fever in a Place where Dr James's Powder was not to be had, and where he died miserably.'[33] At the end of the volume, the child-reader was reminded that the following could be purchased:

> By the King's royal Patent, And Sold by J. NEWBERY, at the
> *Bible* and *Sun* in *St Paul's Church-Yard*.
> 1 Dr *James's Powders* for Fevers, the Small-Pox, Measles, Colds,
> &c., 2s. 6d.
> 2 Dr *Hoope's Female Pills*, 1s.
> 3 Mr *Greenough's Tincture* for Teeth, 1s.
> 4 *Ditto* for the Tooth-Ach [*sic*], 1s.

---

* John Hill (*c.* 1714–75) was a cleric, herbalist, doctor, writer and actor. Dr Johnson praised him with faint damns – 'Dr Hill was . . . a very curious observer; and if he had been contented to tell the world no more than he knew, he might have been a very considerable man.' Hill can, however, be said to have been right in at least one instance: in 1759 his *Cautions Against the Immoderate Use of Snuff* linked tobacco use to cancer.[30]

† His *Lilliputian Magazine: or the Young Gentleman & Lady's Golden Library, being An Attempt to mend the world, to render the Society of Man More Amiable, & to establish the Plainness, Simplicity, Virtue & Wisdom of the Golden Age, so much Celebrated by the Poets and Historians* appeared in 1751 (although it survived for only three issues) and contained rhymes, riddles, the musical score for a country dance, a recipe for mince pie and stories with morals.[32]

    5 *Stomachic Lozenges* for the Heart-burn, Cholic, Indigestion,
      &c, 1s. 6d.

    6 The *Balsam of Health* or (as it is by some called) the Balsam
      of Life, 1s. 6d.

    7 The *Original Daffy's Elixir*, 1s. 3d.

    8 Dr *Anderson's Scots Pills*, 1s.

    9 The *Original British Oil*, 1s.

   10 The *Alternative Pills*, which are a safe, and certain Cure for
      the King's Evil, and all Scrophulous Complaints, 5s. the
      Box, containing 40 Doses. – *See a Dissertation on these
      Disorders sold at the Place above-mentioned.* Price 6d.[34]

Those newspaper proprietors who did not own a medicine could still
help to sell one: 'Dr Benjamin Godfrey's Cordiall' was advertised in the
Leeds Mercury in 1751, and 'for the convenience of those who live in the
country, it will be brought by the men who deliver the News to any place
within the reach of this paper'.[35] Even for those without a newspaper, or
its distribution services, the new Post Office could provide similar
business facilities: 'The True Spirit of Scurvy-Grass' was advertised for
sale

> By the new ingenious Way of the Penny-Post, any Person may
> send for it, from any part of the City or Suburbs, writing plain
> directions where to send it to them: if for half a dozen Glasses,
> they will be brought as safe, as if fetch't by themselves, and as
> cheap as one. But who sends this way, must put a Penny in the
> Letter (besides Six Pence for each Glass) to pay the carriage back;
> for no body can think the profit great: therefore a Penny must
> be sent for every Parcel. None need fear their Money, in sending
> by the Penny-Post, for things of considerable value, are daily
> sent with safety by it, security being given for the Messengers.
> There are Houses appointed in all parts of the Town, to take in
> the Penny-Post Letters.*[37]

It was these advertisements that led, over the next century, to the formation of some of the great drug companies, for there was not much of a

---

* This was not the nineteenth-century penny-post reform of Rowland Hill (for that, see
pp. 484–5), but an earlier attempt, initially confined to London and its suburbs. In 1794
the number of carriers was increased, as were deliveries, to six a day, with the suburbs now
expecting three deliveries a day. Letters were sent, as the name implied, at a cost of 1d.,
although this did not survive long. The 'Houses' referred to 'in all parts of the Town' were
the 125 receiving offices in London and the 135 in the suburbs that were run by the Post
Office. In the 1790s the penny post spread to Manchester, Leeds, Liverpool, Birmingham,
Bristol and Exeter, and then to Glasgow and ultimately Ireland, eventually covering 356
towns and 1,475 villages in England and Wales.[36]

line to be drawn between patent medicines and 'real' medicines, between quacks and doctors. In the eighteenth century the University of Edinburgh's *Pharmacopoeia* listed 'spider's webs, Spanish fly, pigeon's blood, hoofs of elks, eggs of ants, spawn of frogs, dung of horse, pig and peacock, human skulls and mummies' as valid ingredients for medical remedies.[38] Dr Robert James patented an antimonial powder which one historian of medicine thinks probably hastened the death of both Oliver Goldsmith and Laurence Sterne 'among others', while many more promoted things like 'medicinal chocolate', or teething necklaces, or indigestion powders.[39] A Rowlandson cartoon of 1789 shows the draper Isaac Swainson, who owned the rights to Velno's Vegetable Syrup, being attacked by apothecaries and surgeons – not because Velno's harmed people, or because it didn't work, but because Swainson was taking business that they thought was rightfully theirs. (He claimed sales of 20,000 bottles a year, bringing him an income of £5,000.)[40]

It was hard to see the difference between these men and John Hunter, the famous surgeon and anatomist, who in 1984 wrote to Edward Jenner, the pioneer of smallpox inoculation: 'Dear Jenner, – I am puffing off your tartar as the tartar of all tartars, and have given it to several physicians to make trial, but have had no account yet of the success. Had you not better let a bookseller have it to sell, as Glass of Oxford did his magnesia? Let it be called Jenner's Tartar Emetic, or anybody's else that you please. If that mode will do, I will speak to some, viz., Newberry, &c. [to distribute it].'[41]

But while Hunter and Jenner are today considered to have been pioneers of medical science, Dr James Graham was a quack in any period, and he used newspapers and their advertising potential to its full. Born in 1745 in Edinburgh, he was a qualified doctor; by 1775 he had set up in Pall Mall and was advertising that, as a specialist in eye and ear problems, he had 'cured or relieved 281; refused as incurable on their first Application, 317; after a short Trial (by desire) found incurable 47; dismissed for Neglect, &c. 57; country, foreign, and other Patients, events unknown, 381'. Perhaps the honesty of admitting he cured only a quarter of those who applied to him was a legacy of his training. But by 1779 he had opened the Temple of Health, and between 1778 and 1781 he was a regular advertiser in the *Morning Herald*, promoting himself and, more particularly, the 'Temple' with its 'Celestial Bed':

To their Excellencies the Foreign Ambassadors, to the Nobility, Gentry, and to Persons of Learning and of Taste.

THE CELESTIAL BRILLIANCY of the Medico-Electrical Apparatus in all the apartments of the Temple, will be exhibited By Dr GRAHAM himself Who will have the honour of explaining the true Nature and Effects of Electricity, Air, Music, and Magnetism when applied to the Human Body . . . Previous to the display of the Electrical Fire, the Doctor will delicately touch upon the CELESTIAL BEDS which are soon to be opened in the Temple of Hymen, in Pall Mall, for the propagation of Beings, rational and far stronger and more beautiful in mental as well as in bodily Endowments, than the present puny, feeble and nonsensical race of Christians . . .

Admittance to the Temple was 5s., while pamphlets outlining the cures that had already taken place could be bought for a mere 3d. At his lectures, 'Vestina, the Rosy Goddess of Health', stood by in attendance, helping 'at the display of the Celestial Meteors, and of that sacred Vital Fire over which she watches, and whose application in the cure of diseases, she daily has the honour of directing'. (One of Graham's unwitting claims on posterity was that 'Vestina' was none other than the soon-to-be Emma Hamilton, wife to Sir William Hamilton and mistress to Lord Nelson.) Infertile couples hoping to conceive were recommended Graham's *Treatise on Health* (for 10s. 6d.), which gave advice on hygiene, on singing (which 'softens the mind of a happy couple, makes them all love, all harmony'), and on 'drinking of the divine balm, which for the benefit of the human race, I have concocted with my own hand, and which, however, costs only a guinea a bottle'.

If cleanliness, song and the divine balm all failed, then it was on to the Celestial Bed, which was available for rent at £100 (or sometimes £50) a night:

the first, the only one in the world, or that ever existed . . . In a neighbouring closet is placed a cylinder by which I communicate the celestial fire to the bed-chamber, that fluid which animates and vivifies all, and those cherishing vapours and Oriental perfumes, which I convey thither by means of tubes of glass. The celestial bed rests on six massy and transparent columns; coverings of purple, and curtains of celestial blue surround it, and the bed-clothes are perfumed with the most costly essences of Arabia: it is exactly similar to those that adorn the palaces in Persia, and to that of the favourite sultana in the seraglio of the Grand Turk.[42]

In addition, the advertisements promised, 'In the celestial bed no feather is employed . . . springy hair mattresses are used . . . [having] procured at vast expense, the tails of English stallions, which when twisted, baked and then untwisted and properly prepared, is [sic] elastic to the highest degree.[43] And if a celestial bed and the tails of English stallions between them couldn't cure the problem, then clearly nothing would.

It was on the basis of this kind of relentless advertising that newspapers achieved the financial stability that, in the nineteenth century, enabled expansion into ever-growing markets. Very quickly with the new century, circulations skyrocketed beyond anything that had been achieved before. In exactly the same pattern we have seen already, the increase in the number of newspapers and the increase in the number of people who read them were brought about by developments in technology, in this case in printing and papermaking; by developments in transport, for the papers' dissemination; and by the recognition among newspaper proprietors that attention to the vast working-class market could reap equivalently vast rewards.

Before any of this could happen, that vast working-class market, or at least a substantial part of it, needed to be able to read. The figures we have for literacy in the population before the end of the nineteenth century are not terribly reliable – for the most part they come from surveys of signatures on marriage registers, the assumption being that if one could sign one's name, one could both read and write. In fact many who could sign their names could not read, and then a further number who could read could not write. The evangelical writer and educator Hannah More was one of many who thought that it was essential for the working classes to be able to read the Scriptures, but that writing would cause the lower classes to become discontented with their place in the world. At a bare minimum, however, it is estimated that in 1500 only 10 per cent of all men could sign their names, and just 1 per cent of women. By 1750 these figures had risen to 60 per cent of men and 40 per cent of women.[44] Several things went to make this change: urbanization was one, with increased literacy being necessary for a city life; the growth in the numbers of shops and other small trades was another, for it was impossible to sell on credit without being able to write. (It has been suggested that in London and Middlesex perhaps as many as 92 per cent of tradesmen were literate as early as 1730, while even in rural East Anglia the figure approached 70 per cent.)[45] Self-improvement and a desire for education to promote oneself into the ranks of petty traders were great promoters of literacy: Thomas Dyche's *A Guide to the English Tongue* went through thirty-three editions, selling over a quarter of a million copies, in less than fifteen years between 1733 and 1747 (and these figures come from the one printer whose records have survived).*[47] There were numerous other books aimed at the lower middle-class autodidact: G. Bird's *Practical Scrivener* (1733), and Joseph Champion's *Practical Arithmetick* (1733), or even James Dodson's *Antilogarithmic Canon* (1740).[48] An educational framework had also been established for those who wanted to set up in business: by the 1770s and 1780s there were eight schools with a commercial curriculum in Derby alone (which had a population of only 10,000), while *Aris's Birmingham Gazette* contained advertisements for schools in Warwickshire, Worcestershire, Staffordshire and Shropshire with the same sort of syllabus – 70 per cent offered writing; slightly fewer than 60 per cent arithmetic; 40 per cent bookkeeping and accounting; and 30 per cent further mathematics.[49]

Religion was another precipitating factor in the surge in literacy. At the end of the eighteenth century, evangelicalism began its century-long rise, mainly spurred by Anglicans, who soon joined with the Nonconformists to create a nationwide movement whose influence was felt far outside the walls of church and chapel. (For my purposes, I refer generically – and to some degree technically incorrectly – to 'evangelicalism' as it affected society at large, rather than as a form of religious organization.) Evangelical stress on activism and good works led to a society-wide ethos of reform, philanthropy and 'improvement', and much was precipitated by the crusading leaders of the movement – William Wilberforce and the abolition of slavery; Lord Shaftesbury and the Factory Act, as well as numberless voluntary societies, philanthropic organizations and Sunday schools.

By 1800, about 75 per cent of men could read, which opened up opportunities and, to some, increased anxiety. Hannah More, horrified by the threat of atheism as displayed both in the French Revolution

---

* These types of book have a very poor survival rate generally: only five copies of this particular book are extant, and were it not for this one printer's account book noting his print runs we would today have not the faintest idea of its enormous influence.[46]

and in pamphlets like Thomas Paine's *Common Sense* (1792), began to produce tracts, ballads and moral stories for what in 1795 became the Cheap Repository Tract Society. Subsidized by several evangelical societies, these pamphlets were printed to look like the 'old trash' their supporters so despised, and priced similarly, at ½*d.* or 1*d.* In the first six months of 1795, 600,000 copies were sold, and by the end of the year that had mounted to 2 million.[50]

This was a precursor to a new trend in educating the masses. In 1801, only 13.8 per cent of all working-class children attended Sunday school regularly.[51] But after the advent of the French Revolution promoted fears of a similar revolution in Britain, and again after the Peterloo Massacre of 1819, education was seen as a way of socializing the workers, bringing them into the evangelical fold, teaching them to accept their station in life and contribute to the bourgeois civic structure. Adam Smith had seen this – without the evangelical slant – in 1776: 'An instructed and intelligent people . . . are always more decent and orderly than an ignorant and stupid one.'[52] In 1833 the government set aside public funds for education for the first time, and, although its intervention produced very little in comparison to the work of the evangelicals, this was representative of the spirit of the times; by 1851, 75.4 per cent of working-class children attended Sunday school. These Sunday schools, the National Society for Promoting the Education of the Poor in the Principles of the Established Church of England (established 1814), and its non-sectarian counterpart, the British and Foreign School Society, as well as charity schools, tract societies, the Society for the Diffusion of Useful Knowledge (1831), the Mechanics' Institutes, the Methodist reading rooms and many other similar groups and societies all contributed to the creation of a literate working class. Between 1800 and 1830 the sales of stamped newspapers had nearly doubled, from 16 million copies to 30 million copies, while the population had risen only by half, from 10.5 million to 16 million.[53]

What the working classes read, however, was not necessarily what their social superiors thought was good for them. Working hours were long: most shops were open from seven or eight in the morning until ten or eleven at night, while those shopkeepers who were located in streets with a busy nightlife – near theatres, or pubs – expected to stay open until midnight. Artisans and skilled labourers worked equally long hours, while factory shifts could last sixteen hours. These hours were gradually lessened over the century, and from the 1860s increasing numbers of workers had half-days on Saturdays as a holiday (except for the shopkeepers, who worked their longest hours on Saturdays, from seven until midnight). For most workers, however, through much of the century, the expectation was that they would leave home every morning while it was still dark, and return in time only to eat before falling into bed once more, six days a week. Those working in the countryside, even in the old agricultural occupations, also had little time or energy for reading. In Charles Kingsley's novel *Yeast*, which began to appear in *Fraser's Magazine* in 1848, the gamekeeper says, 'Did you ever do a good day's farm-work in your life? If you had, man or boy, you wouldn't have been game for much reading when you got home; you'd do just what these poor fellows do, – tumble into bed at eight o'clock, hardly waiting to take your clothes off, knowing that you must turn up again at five o'clock the next morning to get a breakfast of bread, and, perhaps, a dab of the squire's dripping, and then back to work again; and so on, day after day, sir, week after week, year after year.'[54] (For more on working hours and holidays, see pp. 209–10.) Thus for many the one day on which they had adequate leisure and energy to read was Sunday. And what many chose to read were the newspapers. For them, there was a range of papers which combined short, lurid police-court stories, murder trials and other gore with sensation fiction and a few news snippets.

In 1829 there were seven London morning papers, selling 28,000 copies each on average, while six evening papers sold 11,000 copies each; by 1832 there were a further 130 provincial papers, of which sixty-one had circulations above 1,000, and two above 4,000.[55] Most of these sales, especially in London, were made by the radical press. The Sunday papers in London sold 110,000 copies each week, and there were ten radical Sunday papers to every conservative one. There were some more potentially mainstream papers – the *Observer* (established 1791) and the *Sunday Times* (1822) were both newspapers with a middle-class readership; the *News of the World* (1843) and the *Weekly Times* (1847) were also 'respectable', although radical in political content. But those that sold most to the working classes were the *Weekly Dispatch* (1801), *Lloyd's Weekly Newspaper* (1842) and *Reynolds's Weekly Newspaper* (1850; for more on *Reynolds's* part publications, see Chapter 5), which were 'distinguished chiefly by the violence and even brutality of their tone'.[56] Those papers with the goriest crime and most sensational sensations were those that were the most successful: *Lloyd's*, for example, contained in one issue 'The Emperor Napoleon on Assassination. Fearful stabbing case through jealousy. Terrible scene at an execution. Cannibalism at Liverpool. The Great Seizure of Indecent Prints. A man roasted to death. A cruel husband and an adulterous wife.'[57] In 1886, over half of the space in *Lloyd's* was given over to crime or scandal. Then there were 'specials', editions produced for particular events, such as the execution of a particularly notorious murderer.[58] A summary of *Reynolds's*, *Lloyd's* and the *Weekly Times* shows they were all much of a muchness: except in times of national or international trauma (the Crimean War, the Franco-Prussian War), home and foreign news rarely took up more than 20 per cent of the non-advertising text, while 'sensational' coverage might get as much as 50 per cent of the space. During the Crimean War, *Reynolds's* gave 30 per cent of its space to coverage, *Lloyd's* 32.5 per cent, while the *Weekly Times* gave a grudging 23.5 per cent. After the war was over, however, *Lloyd's* did its best to cater to its market by giving less than 1 per cent of its entire coverage in 1858 to foreign news; even then, it was trumped by the *Weekly Times*, which found space for just three-quarters of 1 per cent.[59] As the century wore on, less and less space was given to news of any sort, while sensation took over.

The *Town*, which started in 1837, was similar, but it was unstamped, and therefore cost only 2*d.*, instead of the 6*d.* that those newspapers which paid tax were forced to charge. Being unstamped, it could not legally carry any news, including any references to politics. But even without news its low price brought it a readership at the bottom end of the middle classes, as can be seen from the large proportion of articles promoting a reduction in working hours, or its several series on different types of workplace, which discussed particularly the head clerks aiming itself at a readership of junior clerks with ambitions. It also published numerous accounts of 'Sketches of courtezans', 'Brothels and Brothel-keepers', 'Cigar shops and pretty women', and articles on 'free and easies' (the precursors to music hall; see pp. 372–4), as well as carrying advertisements for books with titles like *Venus's Album, or, Rosebuds of Love*, which sounds like pornography, but was advertised as a collection of 'the best double-entendre, flash, and comic songs'.[60]

For a couple of decades early in the nineteenth century there was a demand for newspapers that were more concerned with gossip and scandal: *John Bull* (1820), *Paul Pry* (1830/31), the *Satirist* (1831) and the *New Satirist* (1841), and the *Crim.-Con. Gazette* (1840).* Some of these had started off as political journals: *John Bull* was Tory, the *Satirist* an interesting mix of anti-Chartist, anti-abolition, pro-parliamentary-reform, pro-O'Connell views. But ultimately they were – or became – little more than organs of vituperation, as with *John Bull*'s abuse of that 'elderly smug Cockney, William Hazlitt, *alias* Bill Pimple, *alias* the Great Shabberon [a mean, shabby person] . . . an old weather-beaten, pimple-snouted gin-smelling man, like a Pimlico tailor, with ink-dyed hands, a corrugated forehead, and a *spiritous nose'*. The *Satirist* and the *Age* were even worse – they had swiftly degenerated into blackmail sheets: 'If a Reader of the Satirist will furnish us with evidence of the "publication" on the part of the "Gin-and-water Curate residing in the neighbourhood of Dorset-square", we will make the reverend tipler [*sic*] repeat it.' The paper then either received information from disgruntled or vindictive readers, for which it (sometimes) paid, or the person written about got in touch with the editor, and a pay-off guaranteed the rapid insertion of a paragraph countering the original claims.[62]

By the 1840s these frankly vicious papers had more or less run their course, and had either closed or turned respectable. Instead *Reynolds's*, *Lloyd's* and the *News of the World* took over their readerships. There were also, from the 1840s, new penny papers for unskilled workers: the *Penny Times*, which appears, from its pictures, to have expected an audience who read only with difficulty, and centred around episodes of murder, abduction, rape and other violent crimes, and *Bell's Penny Dispatch, and Sporting and Police Gazette, and Newspaper of Romance, and Penny Sunday Chronicle* (all one title), which had 'thrilling tales' every week. These tales took off, and as politics – particularly radical politics – became less of a selling point on the collapse of the Chartist movement, more and more papers joined in: *Clark's Weekly Dispatch* ran 'A Ghost Story' in 1841, *Bell's* began a serial 'The Green Man' in 1842, and in 1843 *Lloyd's Penny Sunday Times and People's Police Gazette* had 'The Waltz of Death' by C. G.

---

* The phrase 'Crim.-con.' immediately conveyed to its readers the primary interest of the newspaper – criminal conversation was the legal phrase for adultery. A wife's lover was, in law, seen to be trespassing on the husband's property, that is, his wife: 'Against an adulterer the husband had an action at common law, commonly known as an action of criminal conversation. In form it was generally trespass . . . on the theory that "a wife is not, as regards her husband, a free agent or separate person." '[61] The creation of the Divorce Court in 1857 made crim.-con. an anachronism.

Ainsworth, with a gory illustration on the front page.*[63] (This paper was made up entirely of fiction and police reports, so it didn't need to be stamped – hence its 1*d*. price, compared to the 7*d*. charged by the *Sunday Times*.) The journalist Henry Vizetelly, looking back at the end of the century, remembered these 'lengthy and exciting stories, telling how rich and poor babies were wickedly changed in their perambulators by conniving nursemaids, how long-lost wills miraculously turned up in the nick of time'. The characters were always of a type: 'The villains were generally of high birth and repulsive presence; the lowly personages were always of ravishing beauty and unsullied virtue. Innocence and loveliness in a gingham gown were perpetually pursued by vice and debauchery in varnished boots and spotless gloves. Life was surrounded by mystery; detectives were ever on the watch, and the most astonishing pitfalls and mantraps were concealed in the path of the unwary and of the innocent.'[64] These tales all had illustrations in keeping with the Gothic sensibilities of their stories. The *British Quarterly Review* in 1859 warned its readers that

> with few exceptions . . . [such stories were] of a violent or sinister character. There is usually either a 'deed of blood' going forward, or preparations for it. If there be not a dishevelled villain in a slouch hat shooting a fair gentleman in lace and tassels, or a brawny savage dragging an unprotected female into a cavern by the hair of her head, we may reckon at least upon a man in a cloak watching from behind a rock, or a 'situation' of thrilling interest, in which the figures look as if they had been taken in a spasm, and were suddenly petrified.[65]

This type of fiction was to prove lucrative for newspapers in general, and for William Frederic Tillotson in particular. He was the proprietor of the *Bolton Evening News*, which he established in 1867. Soon he also owned the *Bolton Journal and Guardian*, and then local editions of this paper (renamed the *Bolton Weekly Journal*), which served a number of towns in Lancashire. In 1872 he published in his Saturday paper a weekly serial called 'Biddy MacCarthy; or, the Murder of the O'Haras'. This was not substantially different from tales published by his many colleagues,

---

* Any newspaper with 'Police Gazette' in its title meant that much of its content was crime reporting. In *Our Mutual Friend*, Dickens had Betty Higden, a pedlar, explain how the boy she looked after read the papers to her, to her great contentment, because 'He do the Police in different voices.' T. S. Eliot used the line in *The Waste Land*, until Ezra Pound advised him to cut it out.

but his next move was. The following year he set up a 'fiction bureau', becoming a broker of fiction, or agent, buying work from authors and selling it on to other newspapers. By the early 1880s he had over sixty established authors on his books for serialized work, including Harrison Ainsworth, R. M. Ballantyne, J. M. Barrie, Mary Elizabeth Braddon, Rhoda Broughton, Wilkie Collins, Conan Doyle, Thomas Hardy, Rudyard Kipling, Eliza Lynn Linton, Captain Marryat, Mrs Oliphant, Trollope, Charles Reade and H. G. Wells. By the 1890s he had agents working for him in the USA, in Europe and in the British colonies.[66] Tillotson's reach meant that authors' work was seen in local papers that, without his centralized selling, would not have had a chance of acquiring the work of such successful writers. For example, in 1900 a short story by Arnold Bennett appeared simultaneously in the *Queen*; the *Evesham Journal*, the *Nottingham Guardian*, the *Manchester Weekly Times*, the *Weston-super-Mare Mercury*, the *Cardiff Times*, the *Newcastle Courant*, the *Carlisle Journal*, the *Sheffield Independent* and the *Huddersfied Chronicle*. But Tillotson's work was not finished, and the story was then reprinted in the *Aberdeen Free Press*, *Irish Society*, the *Blackburn Times*, the *Deal Mercury*, the *Birmingham News*, the *Batley News*, the *Stratford News*, the *Salford Chronicle*, the *Barnsley Independent*, the *Bradford Telegraph*, the *Tiverton Gazette*, the *Portsmouth Telegraph*, the *Hartlepool Mail*, the *Sunderland Echo* and the *Bury Visitor*.[67] The financial stability of many small newspapers now depended on the quality of their fiction.

These papers had survived despite the London – now national – papers being easier to come by than ever throughout the country. The Post Office was still carrying newspapers without charge, but as early as 1827, two years after the opening of the first railway line, a shareholder in the soon-to-be-running Stockton and Darlington Railway wrote to Francis Freeling, the secretary (or administrative head) of the Post Office, notifying him that the railway 'coaches were going as fast as any mail in the Kingdom, with one horse and fifty passengers'. With the opening of the Liverpool and Manchester Railway in 1830, Freeling was in touch with the postmasters in both cities to suggest that they enter into discussions with the railway to carry post; and only months after the line opened, and the first commercial train ran, a contract was agreed.*

---

* Within eight years, it would be a legal obligation for the railways to carry post at the Post Office's request, supplying a mail carriage 'fitted up as the Postmaster-General ... shall direct, for the purpose of sorting letters therein'.[68]

Within a decade, carrying the post by train was the norm: the London to Preston postal route, which had previously taken 24 hours from post office to post office, could now be travelled in 10 hours and 46 minutes.[69]

But long before this, in 1831, the Liverpool and Manchester was carrying newspapers between the two cities – without charge if the printers dropped them off at the station, and the newsagents collected them at the other end. The 'without charge' part didn't last long, but the railways gave greatly reduced rates – up to half the going parcel-post rate – in return for volume and daily orders.[70] A London newsagent, William Henry Smith, saw his chance. He and his brother Henry, 'Newspaper Agents, Booksellers and Binders', ran a business in Little Grosvenor Street that they had inherited from their father. In 1821 they opened a reading room in the Strand, stocking 150 newspapers, journals and reviews, and charging a stiff 1 guinea annual subscription. By 1826 they still had not quite found their niche, and were calling themselves 'Stationers, Travelling-case and Pocket-book Makers, and Newsmen'. (In 1828 Henry left the business.) William understood that getting the news out first was what mattered. When daytime stagecoaches began to replace night coaches, he hired carts to collect the newspapers directly from the printers and deliver them, wrapped and addressed, to the stagecoach offices first thing in the morning. He advertised in *The Times*:

> *The Times*, published on Saturday, the 1st inst., at half-past eight o'clock in the morning, was forwarded, by special express, to Birmingham, where it arrived in time for the inland mails, by which subscribers to the above paper in Birmingham, Liverpool, Chester, Warrington, Manchester, Rochdale, Preston, Lancaster, &c., obtained their papers 14 hours before the arrival of the London mail. The above express was sent by Messrs. H. & W. Smith, newspaper agents, 192, Strand, London, who have sent several expresses since the Parliamentary sessions commenced.

On the death of George IV, in 1830, Smith hired his own boat to carry the news to Dublin, twenty-four hours ahead of the Royal Messenger – or so he boasted.[71]

By 1838 he was deep in negotiations with the Grand Junction Company to carry newspapers by rail between Birmingham, Manchester and Liverpool; by 1847 there were nine special newspaper trains in the region, and soon another ran from Carlisle to London. In 1848 a London train carrying newspapers to Edinburgh had knocked an hour and a half

The newspapers quickly recognized the advertising potential of the omnibuses which thronged the streets of the cities. Here an agent for the London General Omnibus Company uses the *Daily Telegraph* in his own advertisement.

off the regular travelling time between the two cities.[72] Yet, odd as this may at first seem, none of this lessened the sale of local newspapers. By 1847, when W. H. Smith was selling 1,500 copies of the London papers in Manchester every day, the *Manchester Guardian* was happily selling 9,000. The London papers were more expensive, and the local news and advertisements were too important to be missed. With the coming of the telegraph (by 1848 there were over 5,600 kilometres of telegraph wires), the local papers could receive the news from London as quickly

The arrival of improved stagecoach travel and, later, the railways, triggered an expansion to the provincial market for the London papers. W. H. Smith, a newspaper distributor, was one of the first to capitalize on this new market. Here his vans collect *The Times*, before taking the papers to the station for the early-morning newspaper trains.

as the London papers themselves, and they could be out on the streets for sale much more quickly.[73]

After the newspaper tax was abolished in 1855 (during the Crimean War, to allow the nation to follow the news), the *Daily Telegraph* reduced its price to 1*d.* in 1856.* The others followed swiftly: the *Standard* in 1858, then the *Daily News*, the *Daily Chronicle*, the *Pall Mall Gazette*, the *St James's Gazette* and the *Morning Post*. Earlier, when all papers had high cover prices, *The Times* had outsold the next three best-selling papers combined; now it sold between 50,000 and 60,000 copies, while the *Daily News* raced ahead to peak at 150,000 (during the Franco-Prussian War), and the *Telegraph* at 200,000 – which it grandiosely, although probably accurately, claimed as the largest readership in the world.[74]

This increase in circulation was possible because of improved tech-

* Although the tax was abolished, newspapers could choose to continue to pay a lesser sum – usually 1*d.* – for a stamp, which meant that the paper could still be sent post-free. Many newspapers found this worthwhile, and stamped papers appeared until the penny-post reforms of 1840.

nology. The first change came with improvements to paper manufacturing. In the early eighteenth century little paper of sufficient quality to be used for printing was produced in Britain; most paper manufactured in the country was too coarse to be used for anything except wrapping paper. This changed rapidly: in 1763 Edinburgh had three mills, producing 6,000 reams of paper a year; less than three decades later, in Edinburgh alone, twelve mills produced more than 100,000 reams annually.[75] The main change, however, was not in the number of mills, but in the amount they produced. In the 1730s and 1740s Irish paper mills had begun to use water-powered Hollanders, rag-beating machines that dramatically reduced the amount of time it took to transform rags into pulp. With this one innovation, the number of mills doubled between 1738 and 1800, while their output quadrupled. The next big step came via the infant chemical industry. Until this time, paper had been white only if the rags that were used for pulp had also been pale in colour. In 1792 Clement and George Taylor in Kent took out a patent for bleaching rags by 'dephlogisticated marine acid', using sulphuric acid, manganese and salt. The same year Hector Campbell patented a method of bleaching textiles by gaseous chlorine, again using salt, manganese and sulphuric acid, although following a different method. His technique was more commercially viable, and it began to be used more generally. Now rags could be whitened, no matter how dark they had been to begin with, and white paper therefore became less expensive to produce.[76]

During the French wars, various attempts had been made in France to produce a papermaking machine. Eventually, after patents changed hands many times, and improvements were made bit by bit, the Fourdrinier machine was first installed at a paper mill in Britain in 1806. The machine was very much like the spinning jenny or Arkwright's mule, in that it simply replicated in a mechanized form what had previously been done by hand. It created a sheet of paper on a belt of woven wire, whereas previously a sheet had been formed by hand in a separate mould, but the underlying technique and the end result were the same. It took until the 1830s before mechanization really began to take hold in papermaking – more so once it became possible to produce a continuous long roll of paper. Between 1807 and 1822 there were 42 Fourdrinier machines in UK paper mills; by 1837 there were a minimum of 105 machines (and perhaps as many as 279 – the number is disputed).[77]

Further technological advances, including the discovery that permitted expensive rags to be replaced by the previously valueless wood pulp, meant that from 1800 to 1860 there was a sevenfold increase in paper production in Britain.[78]

The next and most dramatic changes to newspaper technology all revolved around printing. Mechanized typecasting had been developed earlier in the century abroad, but was introduced into Britain only in the 1840s. Metal type – the individual letters that were set up in rows to create the words of the printed text – had been cast by hand until this date; at mid-century a good typecaster could produce 4,000 characters a day. Until then, casting had been a slow business. When the newspaper cover prices were reduced after the abolition of the stamp duty, the increased demand for newspapers created a short-term 'type famine'. The long *s*, which had been dropped for clarity earlier in the century, had to make a return until enough new type could be produced to meet the surge in demand.[79] With more and more newspapers being produced faster and faster, existing methods were no longer good enough. Mechanized setting improved the pace of casting, and by 1881 a composing machine powered by electricity cast 6,000 characters every hour. In 1889 the Linotype machine arrived; with it, a complete line of type was cast at once, instead of being set letter by letter. Type was now being cast in a way that would not change for nearly a century.*[80]

Yet, while these changes made a substantial difference to the speed at which newspapers could be produced, the main change to printing came with the new printing presses. The old wooden hand press had been able to make 250 impressions an hour. There had been a small improvement when the Stanhope iron press, imported from the USA, allowed an impression to be made with one pull instead of two, cutting the time and effort in half, but this was still hand printing, something that Caxton – the first Englishman to print books, in the fifteenth century – would just about have recognized. In 1810 the *Annual Register* was printed on an early version of the steam-powered press, which could produce a dizzying 400 impressions an hour. Then the Koenig and Bauer press arrived from Saxony. This could print up to 1,800 impressions an hour, against the old manual's top output of 250. It was the first press to use steam power, and it had first appeared in Britain around 1806,

---

* In the mid-1980s, there were still Linotype machines in daily use.

but it was not used commercially for another four or five years. By 1814 *The Times* had signed a contract with Koenig. There had been much agitation among the printers, who were desperately worried that these new machines would put them all out of work. Fearing violence, *The Times* management had secretly set up a new plant next door to the paper's regular printing works.

> The night on which this curious machine was first brought into use was one of great anxiety and alarm. The suspicious pressmen . . . were directed to wait for expected news from the continent. It was about 6 o'clock in the morning when Mr Walter [the owner of *The Times*] went into the press-room and astonished its occupants by telling them that 'The Times was already printed by steam! That if they attempted violence there was a force ready to suppress it; but that if they were peaceable, their wages should be continued to every one of them till similar employment could be procured.'[81]

By 1828 *The Times* was using Applegarth and Cooper presses, designed by their own chief printer. These machines could produce 4,000 sheets an hour, but even this – more than twice as fast as had been possible fifteen years before – was not the end. The Hoe rotary press, invented in the USA in 1846, was first installed in Britain by *Lloyd's Weekly* in 1855, followed in 1857 by *The Times*, which soon had it printing 20,000 sheets an hour.[82]*

One of the biggest changes that was brought about by the abolition of the newspaper taxes and the development of technology was the spread of newspapers to the provinces. Many local newspapers had long existed, but now, with reduced costs, many more areas began to produce their first papers: Manchester, Sheffield and Liverpool, for example got their own daily papers only in 1855.[84] In other districts it is the number of newspapers per head of population that is so astonishing: by 1878 the Isle of Wight, with a population of 66,000, had ten newspapers; Melton Mowbray, with a population of 6,392, had three; the London suburb of Croydon had nine papers of its own. These papers were local in the truest sense. The *Vale of Evesham News* for one day in 1868 will stand in for the content of most papers for most days. It cost 1½d., and

---

* Not all newspapers needed this level of mechanization, however. The *Middlesex Chronicle*, as late as 1900, had a circulation of only 3,000. It did not trouble to acquire a steam press until 1857, and even then it continued to print flat sheets that it supplied to newsagents for them to fold.[83]

had 8 pages, and 48 columns. Sixteen columns, 33 per cent of the newspaper, were given over to advertisements, mainly for local trades-men and events: blacksmith, a newsagent, a stationer, a bookseller, and sellers of cricket bats, of croquet sets, of China tea, and of insurance all advertised, as did a baker, who was also a 'Dealer in all kind of Pig Food', a wine merchant, a brewer, several surgeon-dentists, a haircutter, who also sold 'Fishing Tackle of Every Description', a seedsman, a builder, a veterinarian, a coach-builder, a chimney-sweep and a pho-tographer ('Under Distinguished Patronage. Animals successfully photo-graphed'), as well as Miss Sprague, who had 'a Good Assortment of Ladies Underclothing' in addition to being the 'Agent for the Celebrated Hair Restorer and Pomade'. This does not include the national advertise-ments, which were mostly for patent medicines, or the personal and small ads, which took up another four columns. The rest of paper included a leader and news reports – local, national (including parlia-mentary) and international – and then what was left of the space was taken up with market information, births, marriages and deaths, fashions, anecdotes, curious facts and jokes, and sport.[85]

Sport and newspapers had long been entwined. In 1729 *An Historical Record of all Horse matches Run* began to appear; in 1751 the *Sporting Kalendar* joined in, and was overtaken in 1761 by the *Racing Calendar* – all issued fortnightly. (For more about racing, and sporting newspapers, see Chapter 11.) Sport was becoming essential for local newspapers, and other general-interest newspapers were more slowly beginning to recognize its value: the *World* in 1787 took great pride in announcing the results of a prizefight only six hours after it finished (it named the wrong man as the winner, but still, it was the speed that counted).[86] Technology soon came to the rescue: in the nineteenth century the telegraph relayed results in a matter of hours, then in minutes. Telegrams were further altering press schedules. In 1889 the *Sheffield Evening Tele-graph* boasted that a quarter-final cup tie had 'finished at six minutes to five, and at two minutes to the hour the result was received in the office. At five o'clock the machines were running and a minute or two later the papers were being eagerly bought up in the street.'*[87]

Sport was now used, especially by the penny weeklies, as a way of

---

* The Press Association continued to keep abreast of changing technology: in 1905 it introduced a telephone football-results service; it added cricket and racing shortly after-wards.

making their readers feel part of the newspaper. Until 1840, postage had been paid by the recipient of a letter, and it was not an insubstantial amount. How much depended on the distance the letter had travelled: in 1801 a letter from Edinburgh to London cost 1*s.*, from Bristol to London 8*d.*; by 1812 the same letter from Edinburgh cost 1*s.* 2*d.*, from Bristol 10*d.*; even a letter carried less than 15 miles cost 5*d.*[88] Newspapers, therefore, not unnaturally discouraged their readers from writing in. It was only in the 1830s, under Rowland Hill, that a wholesale reform of postal charges and how they were levied was undertaken: in January 1840 a flat charge was instituted across the United Kingdom: 1*d.* per ½ oz. letter, from and to anywhere in the country, with postage paid by the sender. With this, the sporting press in particular encouraged their readers to write in – it tied them more closely to the paper, tightening their loyalty to a particular newspaper, it reduced the paper's reliance on paid journalists, and it also marked the papers out as distinct from the mainstream press, who were adamant in their refusal to print any replies to their pronouncements. By the mid-1840s *Bell's Life in London and Sporting Chronicle* was receiving 1,500 letters a week[89] – it claimed a circulation of 20,000 copies, so, if each copy was read by 30 people, 1 out of every 400 readers was writing in weekly.

Bell's was one of a growing trend. There was a range of sporting journals, some of which went back to the eighteenth century, while more began to appear in the mid to late nineteenth century. There was an upper-class magazine, the *Field*, which had started life as the rather less snappily titled *The Field, the Farm, the Garden, the Country Gentleman's Newspaper*. It covered racing, as an upper-class sport, and then subjects of more general interest to the landed proprietor: hunting, shooting, fishing, and stable and dairy management. The second sporting weekly was the *Athletic News*, which was established in 1875 to cover sports 'tending to promote Physical Education'. But very early on it began to cover football, cycling, rugby and athletics; by 1879 it carried football trivia and a gossip column, and it had moved publication to Mondays so that it could bring the results of the Saturday matches. By 1880 it had added a Wednesday edition, sold mainly in the football heartlands: Barnsley, Beverley, Birmingham, Blackburn, Bolton, Bradford, Burslem, Bury, Cheadle Hulme, Chester, Crewe, Derby, Dewsbury, Edinburgh, Fleetwood, Glasgow, Halifax, Hanley, Haslingden, Huddersfield, Keighley, Leeds, Leicester, Liverpool and Manchester. By 1887 it had turned itself into a daily penny paper, and in the mid-1890s it claimed a circulation of 180,000 a week in the football season.[90]

As a penny sporting paper, the *Athletic News* was following a longer tradition. By the time it became a daily, there were already three major papers covering this field. *Bell's Life in London and Sporting Chronicle* was the leader;* it had first appeared in 1822, covering both sports and criminal trials, but over the next few decades it gradually left behind the scandal element and moved more and more to sport, to compete against the *Weekly Dispatch*, which until now had been the leader in the field. The *Dispatch* employed Pierce Egan, who has some claim to being the world's first sports' journalist, and he had an entire page every week to himself. By 1823 or 1824 *Bell's* had begun to employ 'experts' of its own, including Egan, who joined it in 1823. These experts attended matches and reported on them. This was a novelty: previously attendance had not been considered necessary.[92] *Bell's* came out every Sunday until the 1860s, priced at 7*d.* (although this was soon dropped to 6*d.*). By the end of the 1860s it had turned itself into a bi-weekly, with 8 pages and 48 columns on Saturdays, when it was priced at 3*d.*; its Wednesday edition was much smaller and cheaper: 1*d.*, and 4 pages. By 1872, constantly changing to suit the evolving new world of sport, it had returned to a weekly format, appearing on Saturdays, at 5*d.*, and with horse racing and hunting at its heart, plus a few token nods to other sports such as amateur athletics and pedestrianism (foot races).

Its main competition was *Penny Bell's Life and Sporting News*, which was set up in 1859, although *Bell's* immediately went to court to force it to change its name. It became the *Sporting Life* instead, and mostly covered racing, claiming a circulation of 150,000 only two months after it started. Certainly it didn't miss a trick in its battle for circulation: every trainer in the country was sent a copy of the paper twice a week, with a letter stressing that it was 'an excellent medium for the advertisements of Race Programmes which will be placed in a conspicuous position on the first page and inserted at the reduced charge of sixpence a line'.[93] Finally, in 1865 the third sporting paper, the *Sportsman*, began publishing.

All of these papers had great similarities: apart from the stray foray into scandal, or, sometimes, the theatre world, they were entirely

---

* Among other reasons, it bribed newsvendors to sell it ahead of the competition.[91]

dedicated to sport, and of this sporting coverage, most of it revolved around racing. (By 1880 there were few days in the year when there was not some racing taking place somewhere in the country.) After racing news, the papers covered football and cricket, and then, in a less thorough fashion, amateur non-competitive pastimes such as cycling, golf and tennis. Finally, all of them sponsored sports and sporting events themselves: they acted as judges and referees at competitions, many of which they organized and promoted, and they sponsored and awarded trophies. Most importantly, they also priced themselves into the working-class market.[94]

The existence of these exclusively sporting papers did not mean that the regular Sunday newspapers ignored their working-class readers' interests, and from early on sport was a major component of the working-class Sunday paper. It was too important financially to be ignored. Even sports like pugilism, which the middle classes who owned the papers, and who wrote the articles that appeared in them, considered too violent to be acceptable, forced their way into the mainstream. A rise in circulation of 12,000 copies followed a particularly important fight reported by *Bell's*. The other weekly general-interest papers could not ignore that. The *Era* had previously refused to cater to what it referred to in nauseated tones as 'the depraved appetite' that fed on fights. It suffered a disastrous dip in circulation, and rapidly inserted a regular column on pugilism, breathing a sigh of relief as its sales soared by 30 per cent. Unsurprisingly, it then followed up this column with new special pull-out supplements for big fights.[95]

The mainstream daily press was ultimately forced down a similar route. In 1816 *The Times* printed just twenty-four pieces on sport over an entire year – fewer than one piece a fortnight, and the small space it did give was exclusively concerned with upper-class events: the Oxford–Cambridge Boat Race, Ascot, the Eton and Harrow cricket match (from 1880 the paper unbent enough to employ a journalist as a cricket correspondent). The *Daily Telegraph* did a little better: it gave 2 per cent of its paper over to sport, although this was rarely anything other than racing coverage. Even the *Manchester Guardian*, deep in football territory, still gave more space to amateur athletics than to professional sport. Many other local papers, however, understood the link between sport and circulation and followed the example set by the sporting papers in sponsoring events. For twenty years from the 1860s the *Newcastle Daily Chron-*

icle supported rowing and sponsored challenges and cups; the *Midland Sporting News* in Birmingham offered a £70 prize for a 130-yard handicap race, 'in order to give further encouragement to pedestrianism in the Midland district'; the *Dundee Evening Telegraph* gave the trophy for the St Andrews amateur golf championship; and the *Glasgow Evening Times* sponsored an open tournament.[96] Before this, the *Sunday Times* had been the first general-interest national newspaper to think of sport as a major component of its coverage – by 1851 it was promoting itself as a 'literary, dramatic and sporting' newspaper – and it is telling that this develop-ment came in a Sunday paper. The decision to carry sports coverage or not, and then the type of sport each paper reported on, was entirely class-based. The national working-class weeklies, apart from *Bell's* (which, as we saw, soon turned itself into a bi-weekly), barely troubled with sport, and, when they did, sport was interesting only for its potential for gambling. So *Reynolds's* and *Lloyd's* covered racing, pugilism and athletics – all sports where betting was an essential component. The *News of the World* gave sport a single column as late as the 1870s, and it too was interested only in racing, and then only for the possibilities it gave for gambling.[97]

Football, and professional sport more generally, had to await the creation of a new type of newspaper, designed for it alone: the Saturday football special. If Birmingham's *Saturday Night* was not the first football paper, in 1882, it was the first that survived for any length of time. It cost ½d., and was on the streets from 7 p.m. each Saturday, carrying four pages reporting on that day's matches. At the beginning there was no confidence that sport alone could carry an entire newspaper, although it definitely drove the scheduling. So *Saturday Night* advertised itself as 'spicy without being vulgar' and contained 'a first class serial tale, a complete novelette, humorous and spicy paragraphs, three or four col-umns of local chat, the results of scores of athletic events all over the Kingdom, and everything *readable*'. By 1883 Blackburn too had its own football special; by 1884 Wolverhampton had joined in; soon Derby, Glasgow, Sheffield and Manchester had their own Saturday-night specials. In 1884 the *Football Field and Sports Telegram* took the plunge and dropped everything except football, becoming the first sports-only special: it had two pages with the day's results and match reports, and then the remaining pages analysed the previous week's games and had gossip about players and teams, forecasts of their prospects, and so on.

By 1900 there were at least two dozen of these sport-only papers – possibly more. There was now absolutely no question that there was a market for them. When Aston Villa met Queen's Park in the FA Cup final in 1884, copies of the ½d. special – which was produced so quickly after the end of the match that it recorded the result and nothing else – were changing hands on the street for 6d.[98]

By this time, the working population was used to having a number of magazines and newspapers covering a range of subjects all within its financial reach. As early as 1850 there were about a hundred cheap journals published in London alone; it may be that up to 2.9 million copies of periodicals were sold weekly across the country.[99] An early development from the penny newspapers, with the financial and organizational support of the evangelical movement, was the arrival of the educational penny magazines. One of the most successful, as well as the pacesetter, was the *Penny Magazine*, which started publishing in 1832. Its great selling point was its reliance on illustrations. From the 1820s, more expensive books such as annuals had had the new steel engravings, while cheap chapbooks and broadsides had continued to reproduce old-fashioned wood engravings (see Chapter 5). The *Mechanic's Magazine* in 1823 appeared every Saturday for 3d., with many engravings to illustrate its didactic articles on 'new Discoveries, Inventions and Improvements', 'Secret Processes' or 'Practical Applications of Mineralogy and Chemistry'.[100] The *Penny Magazine* fitted exactly in this field of self-improvement, and because it was published under the auspices of the Society for Diffusion of Useful Knowledge it was a third of the price. Within nine months of first publication, circulation had reached 200,000. The magazine covered a range of 'useful' subjects – science, geography, history, biographies of the great and good, with illustrations including diagrams of machinery, pictures of foreign countries, of animals and of famous people, and copies of great works of art. Most of the pictures were intended to inculcate patriotism (particularly the travel images), to promote self-improvement (Benjamin Franklin's portrait showed his 'singular powers . . . of self-control') or to set models of social behaviour (a portrait of the Virgin Mary was an example of maternal devotion, the huntress Diana displayed 'maidenly reserve'; while the Last Supper, rather gloriously, was used as an illustration of 'seemly behaviour in trying circumstances').[101]

The success of the aspirational *Penny Magazine* in the mass market gave impetus to magazine publishing. These broke down into two general types: the inexpensive didactic magazine, of which more below, and the illustrated magazine. In 1842 the *Illustrated London News* began operations, followed the next year by the *Pictorial Times*, and in 1855 by the *Illustrated Times*, as well as the *Illustrated News of the World*. Previously the Sundays had used illustrations to highlight the really big, once-in-a-blue-moon stories – the coronation of Queen Victoria, or a particularly ghastly crime that had caught the popular imagination – or for their serials. The *Illustrated London News* started on a completely new track, establishing itself as a news magazine that showed each and every news event in a graphic as well as a text version. It cost 3*d.* weekly, so it was aimed at the middle- rather than the working-class market. The *Pictorial Times* was careful to make a similar orientation clear to its readers: 'In "THE PICTORIAL TIMES" crime will be chronicled, not illustrated; the assassin will not be masqueraded as a jaunty ruffian, to do a further evil upon the false sensibilities of society . . .'[102] These magazines instead catered to those who would previously have gone to exhibitions of models of the battlefield of Waterloo, or panoramas illustrating Nelson's victory (see Chapter 7). Now world events were reproduced in a form that the middle classes could enjoy at home.

The second group of magazines that rose to prominence in this period, appreciated by the same audience, and also by the aspirant lower middle classes, who might have been stretched to find 3*d.* a week, was the cheap magazines for the self-improver, along the lines of the *Penny Magazine*. There were dozens of these titles, including the *Half-Penny Magazine*, the *Christian's Penny Magazine*, the *London Penny Journal*, the *Girl's* (and the *Boy's*) *Penny Magazine*, the *Penny Illustrated Paper*, the *Penny Illustrated Weekly News*, the *True Half-Penny Magazine*, the *Penny Pictorial and Family Story Paper*, *Dibdin's Penny Trumpet*, the *Penny Comic Magazine*, the *Penny Story Teller* and the *Penny Novelist*.[103] Most of them failed, but one that didn't was *Cassell's Illustrated Family Paper*, which first appeared in 1853, founded by our old temperance lodging-house friend from the Great Exhibition, John Cassell (see p. 35). Cassell had made several attempts at producing an inexpensive magazine for the upwardly mobile, including *John Cassell's Library*, the *Working Man's Friend*, the *Popular Educator* and the *Illustrated Magazine of Art*. But it was the *Illustrated Family Paper* that caught on, combining as it did the threads of both

THE
LONDON SATURDAY JOURNAL.

CONDUCTED BY JAMES GRANT, AUTHOR OF "RANDOM RECOLLECTIONS," "THE GREAT
METROPOLIS," &c. AND FRANCIS ROSS, FORMERLY SOLE EDITOR OF THE JOURNAL.

No. 23. NEW SERIES.]   SATURDAY, JUNE 5, 1841.   [PRICE TWOPENCE.

CONTENTS.

THE "FOURTH ESTATE"—NEWSMEN AND NEWSBOYS.

The London Saturday Journal carried 'improving' pieces for the working classes. Here an article on newsmen and newsboys is illustrated the day after the fall of Lord Melbourne's Whig government by billboards proclaiming a 'Glorious Defeat' – a clear sign that this was a Tory paper.

self-improvement and illustrative material, together with the mid-century swing to the domestic and the familial.

There had been earlier attempts at producing a family magazine – a genre the Victorians took to their heart and developed in the middle of the century. They had had titles like the *Family Herald* (1842), the *Family Friend* (1848), the *Family Economist* (also 1848) and the *Home Circle* (1849). It was Cassell's good fortune – and skill – to latch on to the moment when private domestic life had become a public commodity for sale. Soon the *Family Paper* was selling a quarter of a million copies each week. It contained the same mixture of stories, articles and illustrations that the *Penny Magazine* had produced so brilliantly. Dickens's illustrator, Phiz, contributed, as did Cruikshank; there were newly commissioned engravings of scenes from current plays, portraits of famous people, and fashion drawings. Then, for the 'family' element, instead of articles on inventions, or chemistry, there were riddles, anecdotes, games and needlework, fashion reports and biography, 'queer facts' and 'light verse', as well as an enormously popular 'Notices to Correspondents' section, where readers could write in for advice.[104]

These domestic magazines marked a major shift in emphasis, for, as can be seen from their contents, they were primarily aimed at women. Previously magazines for women had been fashion magazines, rather than magazines with fashions in them. In the early eighteenth century there had been a small number of short-lived miscellanies for women, with verses, riddles, and much moralizing. The first to survive for any length of time was the *Lady's Magazine*, which was issued monthly and contained sheet music, stories, poetry, some news, and correspondence.[105] It had been followed by the *Lady's Monthly Museum*, which merged in 1832 with the *Lady's Magazine*, and then merged again with *La Belle Assemblée* (which had originally appeared in 1806). These were magazines for the upper classes, and *La Belle Assemblée* cost 3s. – about the same as a skilled artisan could expect to be paid for a day's work.[106] *La Belle Assemblée* was the precursor to many fashion magazines, and it will here stand in for them all.

La Belle Assemblée claimed to be interested in more than fashion, but that is a claim that is hard to sustain. The February 1806 issue was typical: it had illustrations of 'her Most Gracious Majesty Queen Charlotte' and of the Marchioness of Townshend 'in her Court Dress', an illustration to go with a song, seven illustrations 'of the London Fashions' and another five for their Parisian equivalents, as well as four needlework patterns for readers to copy. The ten articles included three on fashion (or fashion masquerading as biography and high life), and then the entire second half of the magazine was devoted to a 'Description of the Prints of Fashion, English and French; London Fashions for the Present Month; Parisian Fashions, for February; General Observations on Fashions and Fashionables; and Supplementary Advertisements for the Month', with plates. The plates had 'Explanations' following them, describing, for example, 'a plain muslin gown, with sleeves chequered with pink ribbands, and the gown ornaments in the front also with pink ribbands, the breasts trimmed with puckered net lace, and a pink sash, with short ends hanging behind; an Indian shawl, with Turkish embroidery; white satin shoes, and *peruke* gloves; this half dress has been considered equally simple and elegant.'[107] Each month there was further guidance on sudden changes to the *modes*. One January the reader was notified, 'Fashionable colours are *aventurine* [browny-gold], which has lost nothing of its attraction, crimson, claret-colour, bottle-green, and some dark fancy colours. Cherry-colour, geranium, azure-blue, and pale lemon-colour, are fashionable for evening dress, and for bonnets; but we must observe, that nothing is considered so elegant in evening-dress as white.' By February there was 'the addition of various shades of rose', while in March came a wholesale change to 'cinnamon, fawn, *poussiere de Paris*, claret-colour, beet-red, some shades of violet and of aventurine, rose-colour, and azure blue: the two last, and white, are predominant in evening dress'. By May aventurine was hopelessly out of fashion, and so it went on.[108] Every aspect of personal presentation was given close scrutiny: hairstyles had their own section, and the reader could expect to be updated on 'the style of *coiffures en cheveux*', for which 'there is now more variety ... than we have seen for a considerable time. Those *a la Grecque* are still fashionable, but they are now frequently ornamented with a wreath *a la peruvienne*, composed of an intermixture of *marabouts*, and ears of gold corn. The *coiffure a la Cornelie* differs ... only in the knot of hair behind being brought higher on the head.'[109] (The constant recourse of fashion magazines to half-digested French was happily satirized by *Punch*: 'Gowns should be ... looped with *attachè*. Ladies moving in the highest circles are not unfrequently seen in bonnets of *rechauffé* trimmed with corduroy to match ... Coup d'oeil is not much in vogue for muffs; but those made of *blasé*, are beginning to be the rage. Parasols, to be in the highest fashion, should be of *bombazine a la récherché*, but we have noticed a few of the beautiful fabric *carte blanche*.')[110]

That these magazines were in the selling business was clear. There were few advertisements in *La Belle Assemblée* itself, but instead there was a regularly issued 'Monthly Compendium of Literary, Fashionable, and Domestic Advertisements; Forming the commercial and Supplementary Part of La Belle Assemblee'. This was promoted to retailers as a more enduring form of advertising than magazines that were thrown away after a month.* But the commercial value of the market had not yet been fully understood: by 1846 there were only four magazines solely devoted to women, while forty-eight women's magazines were founded between 1880 and 1900 alone.[111] By this time their commercial value was entirely clear to their proprietors. *Queen's* magazine (1861–1967) had such demand for small ads that in 1868 it had spun off *Exchange and Mart* to cope with the volume – a magazine that dispensed with expensive editorial material, and was instead made up entirely of advertisements (and successful enough that, with a few title changes, it continues today, albeit online). The *Lady* (1885), another magazine that has survived until today (with a few gaps and reorganizations), has done so precisely because its finances are – and always were – based on personal ads.[112]

These were all upper-class magazines. It was the *Englishwoman's Domestic Magazine* that created a new form: a middle-class family magazine that used elements of the upper-class fashion magazine to produce something that was, for the first time, aimed specifically at the middle-class woman of the family. Samuel Beeton, its editor, declared, 'We took the field in the belief that there was room for a cheap serial combining practical utility, instruction and amusement.' He saw it as an instrument of public education, to 'teach women to work much and spend little' and to practise 'wholesome thrift as will disinduce us to spend our time or money without an adequate return either in gain or enjoyment'. It presented itself to its intended market as 'a fund of practical information and advice tending to promote habits of industry and usefulness, without which no home can be rendered virtuous or happy'.[113] Initially it cost 2*d.*, although this was shortly raised to 6*d.* – a sixth of the price of *La Belle Assemblée* – which became the standard price for women's magazines for

---

* In fact, irritatingly for the historian, it is these supplements that were thrown away, and 'complete' runs of the magazine often have few, if any, of the compendiums.

the next few decades. It also had special issues, for which the price was raised again, but it was careful to promise value for money:

> NOTICE, The SHILLING EDITION comprises, besides the content of the magazine, an 8-page Supplement containing illustrations of the CHEMISE RUSSE, New Stitches in Pont Russe, Six engravings of the Newest and most Fashionable Mode of Making Dresses, Hanging Sleeve, Muslin Fichu, Young Lady's Coiffure, Work-Basket Cover, Braiding Patterns, Parasol Cover in Venetian Embroidery, Knitted Square for Counterpanes, Braided Slipper, etc, with full d[i]rections for working and making the same. Also a Fashion Plate of large size and a Photograph of the late Prince Consort.

Now it was presenting itself in a very interesting way, showing what it claimed to be the newest and most fashionable upper-class modes, and yet at the same time telling its middle-class audience that these goods were within their reach, via paper patterns and the new home sewing machines, which made 'dressing in accordance with the latest fashions . . . easy and not too expensive'. The *Englishwoman's Domestic Magazine* ran a whole series of articles on sewing machines, and in other issues it gave away paper patterns that showed how to make 'the original articles furnished by the first Parisian houses'.[114] Such paper patterns were used to promote numerous women's magazines for the rest of the century. Pearson's *Home Notes* in 1895 reminded consumers that 'The price of *Dressmaking at Home* [another Pearson magazine] is only 1*d.* a month, an absurdly low rate when it is remembered that . . . it contains every month a paper pattern of a new and fashionable garment.'[115]

This derisory cover price of 1*d.* at the end of the century shows how the finances of magazines had altered. They were no longer reliant on circulation: it was advertising that made money. The cover price was merely a token contribution, as the *Gentlewoman* was happy to admit: 'Advertisements are indispensable because every copy costs the proprietors nearly double the price for which it is sold.' Nevertheless, magazines told their readers that they should be pleased to see so many advertisements, which now might take up half the available space, as they gave 'a useful directory for ladies'. By the 1870s *The Times* carried approximately 2,500 advertisements in each issue, at an average fee of 8*s.* per ad, clearing a healthy £1,000 a day; the *Telegraph* had fewer advertisements, about 1,500 an issue, and as the second-ranking newspaper it charged less, but they still brought in about £500 a day.[116] The penny weeklies, no matter that their readers often earned less in a day than *The Times* charged in advertising fees, also relied heavily on revenue from advertisements. At mid-century, *Reynolds's* and *Lloyd's* gave about 11 or 12 per cent of their content over to advertisements; by 1870, *Reynolds's* was still at about 14 per cent, while ads in *Lloyd's* had soared to nearly 25 per cent of the overall content. There were two reasons for this: *Reynolds's* radical past still weighed against it with advertisers, and furthermore it gave space to products that other newspapers would not touch – in the 1850s and 1860s over half of the space it sold was for patent medicines that promoted the 'removal of female obstructions', or 'spermatorrhoea' – that is, abortifacients.[117] *Lloyd's*, considered to have a more respectable readership, had more advertisements than any other penny paper; even though it charged more, it was still forced to turn away advertisers for lack of space. By 1886, nearly 37 per cent of its content was entirely devoted to advertisements.[118]

By the turn of the century, *Newspaper Press Directory* was available, an indispensable reference guide for retailers planning to advertise, directing them to, say, *Myra's Journal*, which, it said, had 'a valuable advertising medium . . . a large circulation', while it warned that *Home Notes* had 'crowded advertising columns'.[119] A magazine for brides, *Orange Blossoms*, advertised its own advertising columns in another directory, *The Advertisers Guardian*:

> It is obvious that a Journal of this character, circulating among wealthy people at a time when they are purchasing almost every necessity and luxury of life, must appeal with special force to Advertisers. **Wedding-dresses, breakfasts, cakes, presents, equipages, house-letting, house-furnishing, dressmaking, hotels, tours, and insurance**, as well as all the businesses which deal in personal and domestic comforts and necessities, find in ORANGE BLOSSOMS a *special* as well as a *general* medium.[120]

The commodification of these magazines had become increasingly overt. *Queen's* had for some time run a column called 'The Work-Table' (that is, the sewing table); in the 1890s it renamed it more bluntly 'What to Work and What to Buy'.[121] 'Making' a home had now turned into purchasing a lifestyle.

5

Penny a Line:
Books and the Reading Public

NEWSPAPERS AND MAGAZINES fed an appetite – an appetite that had long been rationed by the price of books. For most of recorded history, books were costly, and were not seen as things that most people owned. In the eighteenth century, however, that began to change. James Lackington, who later made his fortune by selling books inexpensively, had been apprenticed to a shoemaker in 1761. 'My master's whole library consisted of a school-size Bible, Watt's Psalms and Hymns, Foot's Tract on Baptism, Culpeper's Herbal, the History of the Gentle Craft, and an imperfect volume of Receipts in Physic, Surgery, &c., and the Ready Reckoner,'* he recalled. But Lackington's master was old-fashioned. For many, as early as the beginning of the eighteenth century, books had become common enough that they were borrowed and lent freely, and by a wider range of the population than might have been expected. John Cannon, a butcher's son, read a copy of Josephus's *History of the Jewish War* that was owned by a local gardener.[1] Yet others did not find it easy to locate new reading material. In *Northanger Abbey* (begun by Jane Austen in 1798, although not published until 1818), Catherine Morland, the daughter of an upper-class clergyman, says that her mother 'very often reads *Sir Charles Grandison* herself, but new books do not fall in

---

* The 'History of the Gentle Craft' was a chapbook story that was popular from the seventeenth century in various forms; a 1758 edition, attributed to Thomas Deloney, was entitled *The delightful . . . History of the Gentle-Craft . . . Shewing what famous men have been Shoemakers in old time . . . To which is added . . . The Merry Pranks of the Green King of St Martins . . . Concluding with the Shoemakers Glory: being a . . . song, &c.*; 'Ready Reckoners' were printed tables that calculated interest or tax, or other mathematical functions for traders and shopkeepers.

our way'.[2] (Samuel Richardson's *Sir Charles Grandison* was an enormously popular novel, but it had been published half a century before, in 1753–4.)

These two opposing situations existed at the same time: in part the availability of books depended very much on the type of book that was desired. It was possible to buy books cheaply, as the local gardener would have done, either secondhand or as low-priced, mass-produced chapbooks (of which more below, p. 176). But new novels, poetry, travel books – all these were expensive and of the moment. These books were part of the luxury market, catering to the fashionable world. Booksellers were now beginning to move their shops away from specialist areas, such as Paternoster Row and St Paul's Churchyard in London, where they had clustered together for more than a century, to the West End shopping areas where browsers could stop in and 'lounge'. The type of people who were buying these new books were the kind of whom Richardson himself had written when he claimed that a woman had confided to him that 'in this foolish town, we are obliged to read every foolish book that fashion renders prevalent in conversation'.[3]

Because they were fashion items, many if not most books were published in that centre of fashion, London, and then shipped to the country, either to stock shops there or, more often, as special orders. In 1760 Harvey Berrow of Worcester advertised that 'All Sorts of Books, Pamphlets, Acts of Parliament, The several Magazines, And All Other Periodical Publications, Are continued to be sold by H. Berrow, Goose Lane, Worcester; Who procures them from London as soon as possible after they are bespoke, which is the usual Method with Country Booksellers, whose Orders are supply'd Weekly from thence.'[4] In Fanny Burney's novel *Cecilia* (1782), Cecilia visits her London bookseller to 'look over and order into the country such new publications as seemed to promise her any pleasure'.[5]

The publishing industry (although this phrase is an anachronism: publishers were called booksellers well into the nineteenth century)* had expanded greatly after the collapse of the Licensing Act at the end of the seventeenth century. In 1700 there were probably about 200 booksellers operating in 50 of the larger towns.[7] When Samuel Richardson

---

* In 1833 the mathematician Charles Babbage still felt the need to explain, 'The Publisher, is a bookseller; he is, in fact, the author's agent.'[6]

published *Pamela*, in 1740–41, there were double the number of book-sellers' shops, but spread more thinly now, in about 200 towns; by the 1790s, both the number of shops and their geographical reach had risen dramatically, to 1,000 shops in 300 towns.[8] These shops, in general, tended to sell many things besides books: William Owen, a bookseller, advertised on his trade card, 'William Owen, Bookseller, Near Temple Bar, Fleet Street. Imports German Spa Water from ye Pouhon Spring also Seltzer & Pyrmont in their utmost Perfection Bath, Bristol & other English Waters fresh every Week'.[9] The importance of this trade was such that the illustration on his card was of bottles, not books. Fifty years later the commercial inability of booksellers to survive solely by selling books was still the norm: Burgess's Circulating Library in Ramsgate advertised that it had

> all sorts of Books, Stationary [*sic*], Perfumery, and Patent Medi-cines; Maps, Charts, Prints, and Drawing Books; Camel Hair Pencils, and Colours for Drawing; Music, also Musical Instru-ments for Sale or Hire; great Choice of Pocket Books and Etwees; best Plated Goods of the newest Fashion, Jewellery, Cutlery, and Hardware in general; Trinkets and Toys; very neat Tunbridge Ware; an assortment of Ladies and Gentlemens [*sic*] whips, Canes and Sticks, neatly mounted; also Common Walking Sticks, and Cane Strings; Sarsnet, Oiled Silk and Linen Umbrellas and Bath-ing Caps; Silk and other Purses; Purse Runners and Tassels; Hose, Gloves, and Fans; and many other Articles which are sold at reasonable Prices.*[10]

The main problem was the price. Books were still sold on the old system, that it was better to sell a few things at a high profit than many thousands at a lower one. And, unlike many consumer goods at this time, books were becoming more expensive, not less. In the 1770s a complete set of Shakespeare, edited by Samuel Johnson and completed by George Steevens, cost £3, while *Bell's Shakespeare*, which was pub-lished as a 'cheap' edition, cost a still hefty 15s. A new novel at the same period cost 3s.; during the French wars this shot up to 10s. 6d. per volume. As most novels were in two or, more often, three volumes, a new novel might cost as much as a guinea and a half. In the 1810s and

* Historically, a pencil could also mean a fine brush, used for delicate work; an etwee was an ornamental holder for small objects like needles or toothpicks, from the French 'étui', or case; sarsnet, or sarcenet, was a silk fabric, often used for linings.

1820s, prices continued to climb: Byron's *Childe Harold's Pilgrimage* cost from 12s. to as much as £1 16s. 6d.* A teacher earned £12 a year on average; a curate (not, it must be admitted, a particularly remunerative occupation, but a genteel one, nonetheless) might earn £20 a year – the price of twelve novels. Even a 15s. *Bell's Shakespeare* would swallow his entire income for two weeks. It was impossible for anyone earning less than £50 a year to purchase new books, and in 1780 there were only 150,000 families whose income ranged from £50 to £400 – not a large pool of purchasers.[11]

It is not surprising, therefore, that book sales were small. Some members of the upper classes thought that books should remain expensive, not because they wanted to keep these luxury goods for themselves, but to prevent the lower classes from becoming infected with dangerous ideas. William Godwin's *An Enquiry Concerning Political Justice* (1793) was every bit as radical as Thomas Paine's incendiary works, but Paine was prosecuted for his book and Godwin was not. In the 1790s Paine's *The Rights of Man* was sold for 6d., while *Political Justice* cost £1 16s. on first publication, and then appeared in a cheaper 16s. edition – which was still too expensive for most of the population.† The ruling caste felt no need to hide their conviction that ideas which were dangerous for the working class were innocuous when confined to the elite: it was a perfectly conventional assumption of the time. The Attorney General wrote to another author of radical works in the year Godwin's book was published: 'Continue if you please to publish your reply to Mr Burke in an octavo form [a luxury format], so as to confine it probably to that class of readers who may consider it coolly: so soon as it is published cheaply for dissemination among the populace it will be my duty to prosecute.'[13]

The result of this pricing practice meant that even non-seditious

---

* Books were regularly printed in different formats, and sold either bound or unbound, the latter to allow the purchasers to have their books bound up to suit their own taste. Thus the variations in price.

† It is worth looking here at the research William St Clair has done on the sales figures for Paine. It has been repeatedly said that 'many hundreds of thousands' of copies of *The Rights of Man* were sold, or that 200,000 were sold in the first twelve months; or that the pamphlet was available 'in every village on the globe where the English language is spoken'. St Clair produces evidence to show that something over 20,000 copies were printed. Yet the somewhat hysterically inflated figures can be better understood when that 20,000-copy print run is contrasted to the standard print run for a political pamphlet – between 500 and 750 copies.[12]

books were limited in circulation. Henry Fielding's *Amelia* (1752), a great success, sold out its first edition of 5,000 copies in a week; the second edition, however, 'lasted indefinitely'. Thus it appears that there were about 5,000 people in the country who wanted, or could afford, a copy. *Childe Harold* probably sold around 13,000 copies in the first three years, which made it almost unimaginably successful. Most popular novels had print runs of about 4,000 copies, and few sold more than 10,000 copies in total: by contrast, Dr Johnson's periodical the *Rambler* sold about 12,000 copies when it was bound up together.[14]

This was because, apart from the rich and the fashionable, people did not expect to buy new books. Many people bought books from pedlars and itinerants, who sold low-priced, low-production chapbooks; others, who wanted to own either novels or more serious non-fiction, bought from secondhand dealers. James Weatherley in Manchester was a typical example of this type of bookseller. He began in the book trade around 1817, working for a bookseller who had a shop and also a stall or table in the market. Weatherley minded the stall for him while the bookseller worked in his shop. (This having multiple outlets was not uncommon: George Barton, who had had a bookshop in Huntingdon a century before, had what he called 'shops' in Peterborough, St Ives and St Neots, which were clearly stalls: they functioned only on their respective market days.)[15] Weatherley soon set up his own stall, buying stock from auctions and from people who came to his market stall; he also participated in the trade in secondhand copies, where small dealers bought from the bigger, more established booksellers, who had acquired entire libraries, kept the better items, and passed the dross on to the stallholders. Weatherley eventually managed to save enough to rent a cellar in which to store his books; then he rented another cellar, from which he sold directly to passers-by. He was never successful, and sometimes he was barely a bookseller – when business was particularly bad he sold Eccles cakes and what he referred to as 'pop', and, he wrote gloomily, 'if we had kept on in that line it would have paid better than Bookselling.' Yet, while being only one step up from an itinerant seller, he had space to display 2,000 books, and there was no suggestion that his stock was larger than that of any of his fellow sellers.[16]

His customers were those who wanted to own books, but could not afford to buy them new. Many others, like Lackington's shoemaker, had never become book-buyers at all, yet this did not mean that they were not readers. The easiest way to gain access to books was once more via the coffee houses. Some of the stock of the libraries of three London coffee houses – Tom's in Devereux Court and George's in Temple Bar, both near the Inns of Court, and the Bank Coffee House, Threadneedle Street, in the City – was in 1819 acquired by the British Museum. From this small hoard we can obtain a rough outline of the type of books that were bought for coffee-house customers to read. (No other records of coffee-house reading material have survived.) Fifty of the sixty books in the (now) British Library originally belonged to Tom's (probably fifty-three: three books have 'Devereux' written on them); two were marked as belonging to George's, and one to the Bank Coffee House. As well as the books, there are twenty pamphlets in the collection, all of which belonged to Tom's. Another sixty-two titles with 'Tom's' marked on them have been traced in other libraries, and we can thus be sure that Tom's Coffee House had at least 135 books and pamphlets for its customers to read. The range of subjects was not large. Most of the titles were political, some were military, and a few were religious; there was a certain amount of verse, some of that political or satirical too, and a few translations into English – Tasso and Aristotle (and Milton translated into Latin).[17]

What we cannot know from this is whether all these books were owned at one time (although, as they were sold together, it at least seems possible). Nor can we know if Tom's was representative or exceptional in the number and types of book it stocked. There is not even any consensus on how many coffee houses existed across the country and, of those unnumbered coffee houses, how many had substantial libraries. It has been suggested that as many as 500 coffee-house libraries may have existed in London in the late 1840s[18] – a high number, giving good access to reading matter for many.

For those who lived out of reach of a handy coffee house, or for those – like women – who did not expect to enter them, there were several other ways of reading books without buying them. The club, as always in the eighteenth century, was an immediate solution for many. Two kinds of club began to operate as reading groups. The first one, rather less common, was a library: a group of people paid an annual subscription to purchase books which were kept indefinitely. The second type of club, by far the more common, charged members an annual subscription which was used to buy books; then, after they had been read by as many of the club as wanted, either the books were sold off, usually annually, with the proceeds going to buy more books, or they were divided up among the club members, commonly by drawing lots. One club for which good records survive is the Ely Pamphlet Club, which met fortnightly at an inn. This was an average-sized club, made up of twelve members, who paid 10s. a year each. Between 1766 and 1776 they acquired 633 pamphlets, plays, journals and political tracts, as well as a few books. The members could borrow new items every fortnight, with priority for titles wanted by more than one member being decided by lottery; they could visit a 'club room' (probably a room in the inn) to read whenever they liked; and at the end of each year the reading material was distributed among them.[19]

The Luddenden Library in Yorkshire was a hybrid: its members owned shares in the library, which made it a proprietary library,* but they also met regularly for social purposes, which made it a club.[20] (Their meetings, at the Lord Nelson inn, were for a time attended by Branwell Brontë.) The sociability aspect was one that clubs would have said was their *raison d'être*, and Charles Shillito in 1788 gave his jaundiced view of how this might work out in practice in his poem about 'the cottage Book-club, on the village green':

> The Squire calls '*order*' – order soon ensues:
> And the first bus'ness of the club is – news.
>
> Who shines with ill got wealth, who droops with debt;
> Who sleeps on roses, and who treads on thorns,
> Who keeps his hounds, and who retains his *horns* [that is, has been
>   cuckolded];
> What upstart lives in affluence and ease,
> That, t'other day, cried cabbages and pease;
> What noble lord, esteem'd so wise and good,
> Has met a certain lady in the wood . . .

---

* Libraries were divided according to their organizing principles. A proprietary library had a limited number of members, each of whom was required to buy a share on entry; this share could later be sold on to whomever the member chose. A subscription library had its own premises and a membership to which one had to be admitted personally; it bought, for the most part, more serious fiction and a preponderance of non-fiction. A circulating library was run from commercial premises, such as a shop or coffee house, was open to anybody on payment of a fee, and tended to stock more current books, both fiction and non-fiction.

And now the [punch] bowl goes round, with quicken'd speed,
That leaves no vacant time to think or *read*.
While curling clouds are puff'd throughout the room,
Till all are buried in one smoky tomb . . .

Thus, meeting to dispute, to fight, to plead,
To smoke, to drink, – do anything but read –
The club – with stagg'ring steps, yet light of heart,
Their taste for learning shewn, and *punch* – depart.[21]

There is no way of knowing how many of these clubs existed, or how closely they resembled Shillito's version, if at all. The *Monthly Magazine* in 1821 estimated about 600 regular clubs, with another 260 which did not dispose of their purchases at the end of each year. The standard club seems to have averaged around a dozen or so members; this gave, at a rough estimate, about 7,500 subscribers. With families at home sharing their reading, this suggests anything from 15,000 to 25,000 people with access to club books.[22]

Clubs, however, were primarily social institutions, and one had to be on good terms with the other members to join in the first place. More commercial ways of accessing books had been in existence since coffee houses first stocked books to be read on the premises. Soon many coffee houses began to extend their operations, lending out, for a fee, books that previously had been read *in situ*, and becoming in practice circulating libraries. Tom's Coffee House possibly lent out its books – some of the copies in the British Library have lists of names written in them, which suggest they were being lent out in turn. Other shops quickly saw the merit in this system, including most prominently – and sensibly – booksellers themselves. As early as 1718 the *St Ives Post-Boy* had had an advertisement for George Barton, a bookseller in Huntingdon, who offered 'plays, or any other books to be let out to read by the week'. Within a couple of years, these sorts of advertisement were common, showing that circulating libraries were functioning in Bristol, Birmingham and probably Bath and Norwich. By 1770 at least twenty-three towns are known to have had shops where a bookseller or other shopkeeper kept a library of books which, for a fee, were lent out to be read at home.[23] This stock could range from a couple of dozen volumes in villages to several thousand in some cities.

Subscription libraries first began to develop in commercial and industrial towns; the earliest one was in Liverpool, in 1758, then within twenty years Birmingham, Bradford, Bristol, Carlisle, Halifax, Hull, Leeds, Macclesfield, Sheffield, Warrington and Whitby all followed suit.[24] London, by contrast, did not have a single subscription library until 1785. Even then, the London Library Society, according to *The Picture of London, for 1804*, was 'a disgrace to the metropolis' when it was compared to 'those which exist at Liverpool, Bristol, Birmingham, and other places'. It was 'paltry' and 'wretchedly contemptible, and unworthy even of the small degree of patronage' it had managed to obtain.[25] Shortly after this was written that library seems to have folded. Yet at the same time the subscription libraries in the industrial and trading cities were flourishing: a library in Birmingham in 1770 had over 3,000 titles, and 459 members (32 of whom were women); the Bristol Library Society, established in 1773, when it opened held 942 titles for its 137 members (4 of them women), who paid a subscription of 1 guinea a year. Liverpool, which had started everything off, had had 109 members in its first year; by 1760 it had 140 (including 6 women), and by 1800 membership had reached 950, with 'many ladies'. The 1760 catalogue listed occupations next to some members' names, and this gives a rare insight into the type of people who were joining these new institutions. In Liverpool there were 47 merchants of unnamed businesses, as well as a silk merchant, a wine merchant, a sugar merchant, 2 brewers, 2 brokers, 4 attorneys, 4 drapers, a pottery manufacturer, a hosier, a chandler, a grocer, a sail-maker, a rope-maker, a cooper, a cabinet-maker, a painter, a druggist, a mercer, 6 surgeons, 2 doctors, a physician, a customs officer, a teacher, a schoolmaster, a lady innkeeper, 2 clergymen, one 'esquire' and 4 'gentlemen' – a fairly wide social range. The subscribers to the Bristol Library Society were also recorded, although without occupations, and among the names of the members appear the poets Coleridge, Southey, Robert Lovell and, later on, Walter Savage Landor; the politician and writer Edmund Burke; the chemists Thomas Beddoes and Humphry Davy; the educator (and father of the novelist Maria) Richard Edgeworth; and John Hallam, dean of Bristol and grandfather of Tennyson's friend Henry Hallam.[26]

Visitors to seaside and spa towns found circulating libraries particularly useful: these centres of social life lent books, held registers of lodgings for rent or servants for hire, sold tickets for balls, theatres and concerts, and often kept visitors books, which one was expected to sign on arrival.[27] This last was a shrewd commercial move. The visitor went once to the shop to sign the register, and then returned regularly to leaf through the pages and see who else was in town. Many of these seaside and spa shops were small, or open only in the season, but many other towns had circulating libraries that were substantial: John Bell in London had a catalogue with 8,000 titles; Sibbald's, in Edinburgh, had 6,000 titles by 1786; while in Leicester Ann Ireland stocked 2,500.[28]

The cost of an annual subscription to a circulating library depended on the number of books it stocked, its location and the type of reader it was hoping to attract: in the last quarter of the eighteenth century Francis Noble in London charged 12s. a year, which was financially viable for a small shopkeeper, or an artisan in good employment, or for those in poorly paid but genteel occupations – teachers, governesses, clergy.[29] For those below this level, financial or social, there were libraries that charged between 1d. and 3d. per loan, which, said Fanny Burney, meant that 'every butcher and baker, cobler [sic], and tinker, throughout the three kingdoms' could afford to read.[30] The tinkers might have been stretched, but at that price subscribers could include both the petty tradesmen that she named, and even their employees. In 1838 a survey of three Westminster parishes found thirty-eight libraries of this kind, generally operating from tobacconists or stationery shops, or barbers' premises.

The survey categorized the contents of ten of these:

166 volumes of 'Novels by Walter Scott, and Novels in imitation of him; Galt, &c.';
41 volumes of 'Novels by Theodore Hook, Lytton Bulwer [sic] &c.';
115 volumes of 'Novels by Captain Marryat, Cooper, Washington Irving, &c.';
136 volumes of 'Voyages, Travels, History, and Biography';
49 volumes of 'Novels by Miss Edgeworth, and Moral and Religious Novels';
27 'Works of a Good Character, Dr Johnson, Goldsmith, &c.';
76 volumes of 'Romances, Castle of Otranto, &c.';
439 volumes of 'Fashionable Novels, well known';
1,008 volumes of 'Novels of the lowest character, being chiefly imitations of Fashionable Novels, containing no good, although probably nothing decidedly bad';
86 volumes of 'Miscellaneous Old Books, Newgate Calendar, &c.';
39 volumes of 'Lord Byron's Works, Smollett's do., Fielding's do., Gil Blas, &c.';
10 volumes of 'Books decidedly bad'.[31]

Taking as a rough assumption that each book was in three volumes, this meant that these tiny circulating libraries catering to the poor each held perhaps as few as twenty books. It is noticeable that the 'Moral and Religious Novels' and 'Works of a Good Character' formed a distinct minority, while there was a healthy supply of novels 'containing no good'. Many of these books would have been supplied from one place: William Lane's Minerva Press, which specialized in those 'Romances, Castle of Otranto'-type novels, as well as probably many of the 'Novels of the lowest character'.

Lane, the son of a poulterer, had begun as a bookseller, selling books out of his father's shop – yet another example of bookselling as an incidental activity. In about 1784 he struck out on his own, as a producer as well as a seller of books. He set up a press in that year, calling it the Minerva Press, and began to operate what was to modern eyes a chain of circulating libraries (although no one thought of using that term). He arranged for would-be booksellers to receive a small library of his own publications, together with a catalogue and instructions on how to operate. His stock-in-trade as a publisher was romantic fiction which mixed Gothic horror with extreme sentiment – domestic sensationalism perhaps best describes the mood. Later the press moved on to historical fiction, much of it translated from French novels, and 'silverfork' novels – novels depicting the aristocracy and high life. Within a decade of its founding, the Minerva Press was producing about 30 per cent of all the novels published in London, which Lane then sold to other booksellers, as well as supplying the subscription libraries he controlled.[32]

These libraries survived long after Lane himself, who died in 1814, missing out on the newest trend in cheap fiction. From the late 1830s the 'blood-and-thunders' or 'penny-bloods' became staples of the type of shop surveyed above (the phrase 'penny-dreadful' itself became popular only in the 1860s). They were small eight-page booklets with paper covers, which always carried a gory woodcut on the front, and they revolved entirely around violent crime, Gothic horror and sex. The first ones were produced by Edward Lloyd (1815–90), the founder of *Lloyd's Weekly* (see p. 140ff.). Born the son of a farmer, he educated himself via the Mechanics' Institute and began his bookselling career by publishing Dickens plagiarisms: *The Post-Humorous Notes of the Pickwickian Club* (in 112 numbers), and *The Memoirs of Nickelas Nicklebery*.[33] By 1836 he had his first four penny-bloods on sale: *The Lives of the Most Notorious Highwaymen; The Gem of Romance, or Tales of Intense Interest; The History of Pirates of all Nations;* and *The Calendar of Horrors*.[34] Lloyd was based in Salisbury Square in London, and so the 200-odd books he produced, and many others in the same genre, quickly gained the dismissive appellation 'Salisbury Square fiction'.

There was not much merit in the books, even if one ignored the lurid subject matter. Lloyd paid his writers by the page, and it has been suggested that this might be why there was such a heavy reliance on dialogue – short lines filled the pages much more quickly, as did constant repetition. In *Amy: or, Love and Madness*, E. P. Hingston produced the following:

> 'I need no assistance, dear father. But where is Archy gone?'
> 'He has followed your brother Frank.'
> 'And Frank, you said – '
> 'Has gone in pursuit of Ernest.'
> Amy looked at her father inquiringly, and demanded, –
> 'Are you sure that Archy has gone in company with Frank?'
> 'It is my belief that he has,' returned Mr Heyton.
> A smile of satisfaction passed over the face of the maiden, as
>   she ejaculated –
> 'I am glad of that – very glad of that!'
> 'Of what, Amy – of what are you glad?'
> 'That Archy has accompanied Frank; said you not so, dear
>   father?'
> 'He has, child.'
> 'And they have gone to seek Ernest.'
> 'They have.'
> 'That is fortunate; oh! that is very fortunate.'

As one modern historian has noted, such material was cheap and quick to produce, and the readership, many of whom were probably only partly literate, may have found the constant repetition helpful.[35]

There is no question that these books were popular, and that this was a lucrative field. Many other booksellers, not based in the same geographical location, also produced Salisbury Square fiction. T. Paine was one: in 1840 he began to issue *Angela the Orphan: or, the Bandit Monk of Italy*, advertised as 'The most successful Romance every published' and claiming sales of 14,000 copies a week.[36] Other titles in the genre included *Ada, the Betrayed, or, the Murderer at the Old Smithy; The*

Apparition, Crimes of the Aristocracy; The Death Ship, or, The Pirate's Bride; and *Varney, The Vampyre* (this one was also known by the alternative title of *The Feast of Blood*)[37] – and they were fantastically successful. Between 1830 and 1850 there were said to be at least ninety publishers of penny-fiction, which would mean that for every one publisher of 'respectable' works there were ten who published what that Westminster survey had called 'Books decidedly bad'.[38]

These books embraced a wide range of styles. One of the most omni-present throughout the eighteenth and nineteenth centuries was the chapbook. A chapbook was a 24-page booklet, with a paper cover illus-trated with a woodcut. In the eighteenth century many chapbooks had retold traditional or folk stories: Jack the Giant Killer, Tom Thumb, Robin Hood, Jack and the Beanstalk. By the nineteenth century, many of these tales had been displaced into children's books, and chapbooks instead veered towards more sensational stories, together with songs, jokes and retellings of myths and legends, or famous events, such as Dick Turpin's ride, or the lives of criminals like Jack Sheppard, a peren-nial favourite. The cover illustration was generic, and rarely linked to the story – a Turk with a scimitar raised might illustrate the story of Dick Turpin and then pop up again on *The Irish Assassin*, while a Roman centurion graced a medieval story from Italy, the tale of Hero and Leander and the story of Valentine and Orson. At the end of each story the remainder of the space was filled in with similar randomness: a fearsome recounting of the horrors of the Black Hole of Calcutta could be followed by an account of a practical joke, or 'The Comical Sayings of Paddy from Cork, with his Coat Buttoned Behind' might be inserted after the account of a grisly murder.[39] Over the two centuries there were as many as 250 printers of chapbooks in London, and as many again in the provinces. William Dicey, who had founded the *Northampton Mercury* with Robert Raikes, had begun to print chapbooks as well, moving to London around 1730, when he formally joined his business interests with his sister's Bow Printing Office; by 1739 the Diceys were the largest producer of chapbooks in London.[40] These chapbooks were sold by street vendors, who also carried broadsides, single printed sheets with accounts of crimes, deathbed confessions of criminals, patriotic songs, jokes, verses or satirical squibs, which cost only ½d. – half the price of a chapbook. (The vendors also sang through the songs on the broadside for any customers unacquainted with the tunes, and were therefore

A broadside hawker was known as a patterer – a standing patterer had a fixed pitch, while a running patterer roamed the streets. Both sang to their customers, teaching them the tunes to go with the lyrics they were selling.

known as patterers: those who walked the streets were running patterers; those with a fixed pitch were standing patterers.)

Reality, or even accurate reporting, in broadsides was less important than gory details: the crimes of the 'burkers' Williams and Bishop in 1831 were described on a broadside that used the woodblocks illustrating the original burkers, Burke and Hare themselves, whose trial in 1828 had been of all-consuming interest. Another broadside, *The Trial and Execution of the Burkers for Murdering a Poor Italian Boy*, showed three murderers being executed, despite the fact that only two were, while the third was reprieved.[41] This last broadside was published by James Catnach, one of the most successful chapbook and broadside publishers of the century. He employed a stable of writers, known from his location as the Seven Bards of the Seven Dials, who turned out reams of rapes, extortions, murders and deaths. Death was best for business, with highest sales coming from 'public executions . . . to which was usually attached the all-important and necessary "Sorrowful Lamentations", or "Copy of Affectionate Verses", which according to the established custom, the

criminal composed in the condemned cell the night before his execution'. These confessions were in fact usually written by Catnach's
'bards', then rapidly printed up, adorned with a stock image that was
supposed to represent the condemned – and always advertised as 'an
exact likeness of the murderer, taken at the bar of the Old Bailey by an
eminent artist' – and distributed to the patterers.[42]

If there were no really good murders, Catnach and his colleagues
were just as happy to make up the confessions to lesser crimes, and
they even, from time to time, manufactured deaths themselves. In 1828
the Royal Brunswick Theatre, in east London, collapsed. It was during
the day, when a rehearsal was in progress, rather than at night with a
full auditorium, so only fifteen people were killed. One of Catnach's
patterers remembered it well: 'Oh yes sir! . . . It was a rare good thing
for all the running and standing patterers in and about ten miles of
London. Every day we all killed more and more people . . . One day
there was twenty persons killed, the next day thirty or forty, until it got
at last to be worked up to about a hundred, and all killed. Then we
killed all sorts of people, Duke of Wellington, and all the Dukes and
Duchesses, Bishops, swell nobs and snobs we could think of at the
moment.'[43]

In 1821 a new series in monthly parts appeared: Pierce Egan's *Life in
London, or, the Day and Night Scenes of Jerry Hawthorn, Esq., and his elegant
friend Corinthian Tom, accompanied by Bob Logic, the Oxonian, in their
Rambles and Sprees through the Metropolis*, with etchings and woodcuts by
George Cruikshank and his brother Robert. This was the first appearance
of the characters Tom and Jerry (the ancestors of the cartoon animals of
the twentieth century), and each monthly part cost 1s. Within twelve
hours of publication, at least according to Egan himself, Catnach had a
pirate edition printed and out being hawked on the streets, selling for
only 2d.; he quickly followed this with a 'whole sheet', that is, a broadside, called *Life in London*, which had twelve woodcuts that were crude
copies of the original Cruikshank illustrations (but reversed, which
meant that Catnach's cutters simply copied the original illustrations
rapidly, not even taking the time to flip them).

This was the same Pierce Egan who had started the profession of
sporting journalist (p. 152), and it may be that he brought from the
newspapers an audience of admirers. But the success of *Life in London*
cannot be attributed solely to that, for there was very swiftly a vogue for

books on London life, and for all the fashionable accoutrements that Egan's characters wore or mentioned – 'tailors, bootmakers, and hatters, recommended nothing but Corinthian shapes, and Tom and Jerry patterns'. The main popularizer, though, was the theatre: 'Mr Barrymore' produced a play 'in hot haste' at the Royal Amphitheatre a scant four weeks after the first number appeared; the theatre manager Charles Dibdin the younger had his own version on stage at the Olympic Theatre two months later; then the Adelphi advertised 'Mr Moncrieff's* adaptation a fortnight after that:

> On Monday, Nov. 26th, 1821, will be presented for the first time, on a scale of unprecedented extent (having been many weeks in preparation under the superintendence of several of the most celebrated Artists, both in the *Ups and Downs* of Life, who have all kindly come forward to assist the Proprietors in their endeavours to render the Piece a complete out-and-outer), an entirely new Classic, Comic, Operatic, Didactic, Aristophanic, Localic, Analytic, Panoramic, Camera-Obscura-ic Extravaganza Burletta of Fun, Frolic, Fashion and Flash, in three acts, called 'TOM AND JERRY: OR LIFE IN LONDON.' Replete with Prime Chaunts, Rum Glees, and Kiddy Catches, founded on Pierce Egan's well-known and highly popular work of the same name, by a celebrated extravagant erratic Author. The music selected and modified by him from the most eminent composers, ancient and modern, and every Air furnished with an attendant train of Graces. The costumes and scenery supervised by Mr I. R. Cruikshank, from the Drawings by himself and his brother, Mr George Cruikshank, the celebrated Artists of the original Work.[44]

Catnach's speed in cashing in on Egan's success was remarkable, but he was used to producing material quickly: he claimed that his *A Full True and Particular Account of the Murder of Mr Weare by John Thurtell and His Companions* had sold 250,000 copies, which he had managed to print in just one week. This appeared even before the trial itself took place. Afterwards, Catnach needed only another eight days to print 500,000 broadsides reporting on the proceedings. In 1828 he capped

* Barrymore and Moncrieff are playwrights about whom little is known today, but they both wrote many popular plays in the spectacular mode that was to be so successful for much of the century. For more, see pp. 314ff, 330–38.

Pierce Egan's *Life in London* (1820) was wildly popular, and was quickly cannibalized: a pirated edition appeared less than a day after the original, and three theatrical versions were staged in the next two months. Here a broadside shows the mock funeral that was held when the most successful of the stage versions closed in 1823.

even that, claiming to have printed and sold 1,166,000 copies of the *Last Dying Speech and Confession of William Corder.**[46]

It was probably better material than these broadsides that the popular novelist Charles Lever was complaining about when he wrote, 'Our cheap literature and our copious writing – like our low priced cottons and our cheap pen knives – will ultimately disparage our wares, both at home and abroad.'[47] Yet the plenitude of literature of all types came not solely from the discovery of the financial possibilities inherent in the

---

* John Thurtell (1794–1824) was the son of a merchant, a middle-class boy gone to the bad. After probable arson, in an attempt to raise money he lured William Weare, a professional gambler, to Hertfordshire, where he shot him and cut his throat. Weare was memorialized by a play (*The Gamblers*), and by pamphlets, and also in the works of De Quincey, Borrow (in both *Lavengro* and *The Romany Rye*), Bulwer-Lytton, Carlyle and Dickens, as well as by the moving lines 'His throat they cut from ear to ear, / His brains they battered in, / His name was Mr William Weare, / Wot lived in Lyon's Inn.'

William Corder (1804–28) had had an illegitimate child with Maria Marten, his brother's mistress, before he murdered her in what became known as the notorious Red Barn case. He then married an unsuspecting schoolmistress, and when accused of the crime claimed that Marten had shot herself, overlooking the fact that she had also been stabbed and smothered. Corder was, unusually, not only hanged, but drawn and quartered, and then flayed; his skin was used to cover a book about the crime. This grisly relic is today in Moyse's Hall Museum, in Bury St Edmunds, together with Corder's death mask and part of his scalp. His head was on exhibition at Bartholomew Fair in the year of his death, and it was claimed that it earned its owner £100 in the three days of the fair.[45]

mass market: it came, too, from the ability to capture that market by applying innovatory technology to production. Many of the technological developments that were discussed in Chapter 4, from papermaking to typesetting and printing, were easily assimilated into book production. There were also other changes, that were relevant to book production alone. The first of these was the development of the stereotype plate. The first stereotypes, or stereos, had been used in Holland as early as the sixteenth century, but they were not introduced in Britain until 1727. The process was very simple: the text was set in metal type, just as it always had been, then a cast of plaster of Paris (or, later, papier mâché) was made of the entire assembly of pages to be printed in a single impression, after which a metal plate, or stereotype, was made from the cast. Now, instead of thousands of small metal letters held together by metal bars secured with string, a single plate for each side of a sheet could be used for printing. Once the publisher was ready to reprint the book, the plate was taken out of storage and reused: storage itself was much easier, and by keeping the stereos, reprints were produced at a fraction of the cost of resetting type from scratch. However, the Stationers Company, the guild that oversaw book publishing, in overseeing its monopoly cared less about reducing costs and much more about ensuring a constant flow of work for compositors. Thus in the eighteenth century it instituted a rule that only a set number of impressions could be made from any plates before the type had to be destroyed, which defeated the purpose of stereos. By 1840, with the monopoly long gone, print runs had now risen sufficiently that stereos suddenly became a commercial possibility. By 1843, three years after stereos came into general use, Clowes, the largest printer in the country (and one that survives today), was storing stereo plates for 2,500 books.[48]

With papermaking, typesetting and printing to a greater or lesser extent mechanized, the binding of the books, which had to all intents and purposes remained a hand craft, was creating a bottleneck. Unlike printing, binding had numerous small stages, not one big one: the printed pages had to be folded into sections, the folded sections gathered together in the correct order and then sewn into what was called a book-block, which was then trimmed, blocked, pressed and glued; the spine had to be rounded, and the cloth or leather cut and glued on to the boards, which had previously been cut; then head and tail bands might be added, and endpapers had to be pasted down and lettering applied to the spine. In the early days, the only way to keep up with mechanized printing was to hire more people to do each job in the bindery: in 1830 fewer than 600 journeymen bookbinders worked in London; by 1862 that number had more than doubled, to 1,545; and by 1861 it was 7,754 (by which time there was also binding machinery in place).

Most of the developments in the mechanization of binding came in small steps: in the early part of the century a machine for cutting the edges of the gathered sections was developed; then nothing much happened until 1828, when a rolling machine to press the blocks was developed. Then there was another gap until 1843, when machines for embossing the cloth appeared. A flurry of further mechanized processes followed, and by 1851 bookbinding involved so much machinery that it was classed with manufacturing in the catalogue of the Great Exhibition. By the end of the century, a folding machine folded 12,000 sixteen-page sections an hour, a sewing machine sewed 3,600 sections an hour (a skilled woman expected to sew 2,000 or 3,000 sections every day), gathering machines brought together the sections, producing 7,800 book-blocks an hour, and a book-back gluing machine, manned by a single person, did the work that had previously required five people – and, as a final touch, it economized on the glue. All of this meant that more books could now be sold for less money. In 1843 it had cost £180 to produce 6,000 copies of Dickens's *A Christmas Carol*, or just over 7*d.* a copy. In 1852, publishers expected to pay production costs of slightly more than 5*d.* per volume, and by the end of the century that price had fallen further, to 3*d.* per volume.[49]

Even before most of these innovations had filtered through to book production generally, books were becoming more widely available. By the early 1830s it was estimated that there were more than a thousand circulating libraries in the country, although it is likely that this figure excludes those that stocked penny-dreadfuls: probably the lowest level of library that was recognized was the type that catered for those aristocrats of the working classes, the artisans. Libraries for the respectable working classes were being opened with a range of financial support, especially from the various evangelical societies. In 1832 each National School received £5 to spend on books, funded by the Society for the Propagation of Christian Knowledge, which had a Committee of General Literature. The Religious Tract Society also set up library grants, and by 1849 was proud to have supplied between 5,000 and 6,000 libraries with a hundred volumes each, although they were mostly moral tracts. With these libraries, it was possible for much of the working class to turn their backs on the Mechanics' Institutes, which they felt had betrayed them – they were being run by the upper middle classes, and the places were increasingly filled by white-collar workers of the lower middle classes. Instead, artisans turned to libraries like Edwinstowe's Artisans' Library, in Nottingham, which had an enrolment fee of 1*s.*, and a weekly subscription of 1*d.* It had opened in 1838, and by 1846 it held 500 volumes, including works by Scott, Byron, Goldsmith and Shakespeare, as well as the *Penny Cyclopaedia* and a number of periodicals.[50]

For the middle class's own reading, it was Mudie's Circulating Library that represented the ideal. In 1828, in its first editorial, the *Athenaeum* had stated flatly that 'no Englishman in the middle class of life *buys* a book'.[51] G. H. Lewes, George Eliot's long-term companion, wrote of a wealthy friend who had gone to a library to borrow *Romola*, but all the copies were on loan to other members, and, she told Lewes, 'I drove away disappointed.' This was in 1872, when a cheap edition of the book was available for 2s. 6d.; but, to her, novels were not objects to be bought. Many publishers accepted this. *Tinsley's* magazine, which was owned by the publisher Richard Bentley, wrote that it was a 'well-known fact' that no one bought novels.[52]

This was in part because a curious double situation was in operation with regard to book prices. After a drop in prices in the early part of the century, the main publishers formed a Booksellers Committee, which had but one purpose: to control prices. Although it never managed to assert its authority over the cut-price book market, or the railway libraries (see below), for much of the century these publishers had a death-grip on new fiction. So, while the average price of books dropped from 16s. to 8s. 4½d. between 1828 and 1853, the price of a new three-volume novel, which became the standard format for fiction,* remained at 31s. 6d. (1½ guineas) throughout the century.

This was where Charles Edward Mudie came in. Originally he ran a stationery shop, and in 1842, as was common, he began to lend books from it. His subscription rates were, for middle-class borrowers, quite reasonable: 1 guinea a year.† By comparison, Bull's Library charged 6 guineas a year; Saunders and Otley up to 8 guineas; Churton's from 4 to 10. The three-volume novel – or the triple-decker, as it became known – was ideal for this system of borrowing. The subscriber was entitled to borrow a *volume*, not a *novel*, for his or her guinea, which meant that with every novel Mudie could lend out three parts to three paying subscribers simultaneously. But it wasn't only in price that Mudie was ahead of the competition. He also stressed quality, matching the new evangelical mood of much of the middle class. He refused to have any Minerva Press-type books, and instead stocked poetry, history, biography, travel and adventure, religious and moral tracts, scientific works, and, of course,

---

* In the eighteenth century, novels had appeared in anything from two to seven volumes, depending solely on how much the author had to say: Richardson's endless novel *Clarissa* needed seven volumes, Fielding's *Amelia* only four, while Oliver Goldsmith's *The Vicar of Wakefield* had a modest two. Gradually novels of three, four and five volumes became the most commonly produced, and by the nineteenth century three volumes had become the standard: now authors were expected to write to fit the volumes, rather than the volumes being printed to match the length of the novel.

† As with most advertising, this fee was deliberately ambiguous. A 1-guinea subscription gave the borrower the right to take out one volume at a time; for 2 guineas, four volumes could be taken at once; 3 guineas gave eight volumes, and 5 guineas fifteen. For 10 guineas one could take thirty volumes, or for 20 guineas sixty – these subscriptions were mostly for the owners of grand country houses, or for clubs or other organizations.

Mudie's Circulating Library in New Oxford Street: a temple to middle-class taste, the circular desks were consciously designed to evoke the great circular Reading Room at the British Museum.

the latest fiction. He stressed that his 'select' library excluded all immoral books: anything that had Mudie's stamp on the cover was suitable for family reading.

In 1852 Mudie's moved to larger premises, in New Oxford Street, and advertised a 'Constant Succession of the Best New Books'. Soon the operation was so large that simply by buying multiple copies of a new book, and advertising that purchase, Mudie's could frequently create a book's success – as when it ordered 2,500 copies of George Eliot's first full-length novel, *Adam Bede*, in 1859.* By 1858 the library was purchasing 100,000 new books a year; three years later this had nearly doubled, to 180,000.

By 1860 Mudie needed larger premises once more, and, as with Lackington in the previous century, the new building he erected on the

---

* In 1855 Mudie's bulk requirements had created a problem: he had ordered 2,500 copies of Volumes 3 and 4 of Macaulay's *History of England*. Together these copies weighed 8 tons, and the publisher finally threw up his hands and said Mudie would have to arrange collection himself.

same site was designed to reflect both the proprietor's worldly success and his view of a bookshop or library as a 'Temple of the Muses'. The new Mudie's had a classical façade with, inside, semicircular desks for exchanging books set in the middle of a large round hall – not coincidentally, closely resembling the British Museum's famous round Reading Room. Mudie's also had branches in the City, in Birmingham and in Manchester, plus an enormous mail-order business: it supplied book clubs and provincial libraries, although for some reason that has not come down to history it refused to supply Smith's railway bookstalls, which was the reason Smith's started its own library (which survived until 1961). For 2 guineas a year, Mudie's subscribers within twenty miles of London could send in a list and have three volumes a week delivered the same day their orders were received. For those who lived further away, there was a country department that at its peak shipped 1,000 boxes holding up to 100 books each to subscribers anywhere in the world: by 1860 there were regular dispatches to Germany, Russia, China and Egypt, as well as the more expected colonial destinations like India and South Africa.

Mudie's had become a behemoth that swallowed everything in its path, buying up part of Bentley's publishing house, and so overwhelming the market that books had to be produced to suit the company's institutional likes and dislikes. A comparison of orders for one title, *Leah: A Woman of Fashion*, a novel by Mrs Annie Edwards, published in 1875, shows the strength of its buying power. Smith's ordered 25 copies, Day's Library and Cawthorn's each ordered 13 copies, while Mitchell's Library wanted 6; Mudie's asked for 125, or five times as many copies as its nearest competitor. Not surprisingly, the company used this clout to beat down the publishers on price. In 1873 Mudie wrote to Richard Bentley, 'I wish to do what I can for "Burgoyne" [*The Life and Correspondence of Field Marshal Sir John Burgoyne*, who had lost the Battle of Saratoga during the American War of Independence] and if you will let me have 520 as 480 [that is, 520 copies for the price of 480, or a further 77 per cent discount on top of his standard trading terms] in the terms proposed I will place it near the top of my list . . . and give it a leading position in a few special advertisements.' He promised another publisher that he would 'go on *advertising* the book if I can have say *50 or 100 at 18.*' For a book that retailed at 31s. 6d., he expected a 43 per cent reduction.[53]

But by this time Mudie and the publishers who supported him were operating in a curious bubble. While they sailed serenely on with their 31*s*. 6*d*. novels, a major upheaval was taking place. It was triggered, most unexpectedly, by the development of the railway. Today we carry books or magazines to read on all forms of transport, but this was not always the case. Our current assumption that 'travel' means 'reading' arrived only with the railways. Until then, reading while travelling was all but impossible. In the early days, the windows of many conveyances were not glazed, but covered with oiled silk or other fabrics that had been treated to make them water-resistant; not unnaturally, therefore, the apertures were small, to keep out the wind and the rain. When glazed windows arrived, the design was not reconsidered, and coach windows remained small, which made the interiors often gloomy and frequently just dark. The motion of the horses, and the lack of springs and upholstery did not conduce to reading. Nor did the human interaction that was created by a small number of people travelling long distances together, dining in the same inns, sleeping in the same confined space: sociability was impossible to avoid. In trains, by contrast, people travelled together for hours rather than days at a time, and even this was broken up by frequent dispersals at each station; the carriages were lit by oil – and later gas – lamps; and the ride was smooth enough to make it possible to read without becoming ill. In the first-class carriages the seats had fairly large head-rest divisions, behind which one could retreat from one's fellow passengers. The link between railway travel and reading was made from the first; the *Quarterly Review* in 1830, the year of the first scheduled passenger train, in a line intended to stress the smoothness of the journey, noted that train travel was 'so easy that a passenger might read a newspaper with perfect comfort'.[54]

The main change to travel, however, was the number of people now on the move. Even with the difficulties of stagecoach travel, the British had managed to get around their island. Once the railways arrived, numbers soared. In 1838, after the Newcastle and Carlisle Railway opened along its entire length, eleven times as many people travelled by train as had previously used the stagecoach route. Between 1836 and 1848, eight terminuses opened in London alone to handle rising demand. In 1842, with a bit over 3,200 kilometres of rail established, 24.5 million passengers travelled by train; by 1846, by which time there was nearly 16,000 kilometres of track, passenger numbers had reached 43.8 million annually. The rise in the number of travellers seemed unstoppable: numbers breached 250 million in 1865, topped 500 million comfortably in 1875, and by 1890 were around the 900 million mark.[55]

Just before the arrival of the railways, the bookselling business had been convulsed by the collapse of several of the major publishing houses, which led to difficulties in acquiring – or continuing – credit, and a consequent business slump. In order to improve their situation, several publishers hit on the idea of 'libraries', a series of books in uniform bindings that could be purchased slowly over time. From 1827, Constable's Miscellany, the Library of Useful and Entertaining Knowledge, Murray's Family Library and others began to appear. These were wide-ranging in subject matter, educational, practical, and aimed at 'those who think, conduct themselves respectably, and are anxious to improve their circumstances by judicious means' – the expectation was now a readership of artisans, shop assistants and clerks.[56]

Then, simultaneously with the first two decades of railway travel, perhaps as a way of recouping investments more quickly for these financially unsteady booksellers, part-publication of novels became a popular means of reaching readers. Dickens and *The Pickwick Papers* are the heroes of this story, but there had been a few attempts at this method of publication before Dickens: Colburn's Modern Novelists series was published in 1s. parts, with Bulwer-Lytton's *Pelham* appearing as issues 1 to 6. But *Pelham* had been written as a novel, before being taken apart and reissued in parts for serialization; Dickens had planned *Pickwick* specifically to appear in parts, and its episodic nature showed the format to best advantage. After a slow start, about 40,000 copies were sold each month in 1836, creating an entirely new income stream for publishers and authors. First they could part-publish, with income from the sales of each 32-page section, and from the 'Advertiser' supplement that successful part-publication could support: *The Pickwick Advertiser* ran to twenty-four pages per part. This was then followed by publication as a three-volume novel (at the standard price of 31s. 6d., which meant these books were for library sale).[57] Part-publication was not opening up the market to new readers, just making the financial demands on the old middle-class readers slightly easier: after all, twenty-one parts at 1s. apiece meant that readers were paying 1 guinea per book – hardly a bargain, and affordable to many only because payment was spread out over nearly two years. Where new readers were perhaps being gained was at the lower end of the market. There the penny-bloods were issued in a similar fashion to the new middle-class system of part-publication, but these books cost between ½*d.* and 2*d.* a part, instead of 1*s.* The *Romancist* [*sic*] and *Novelist's Library*, from about 1840, issued out-of-copyright novels in 2*d.* weekly parts, and then bound them together for the tobacco-shop libraries. By 1845 as many as half a million part copies may have been sold this way every week.[58] Perhaps the most successful part-publication came originally from the newspapers. *Reynolds's Miscellany* had been started in 1845 by G. W. M. Reynolds, who had edited the *London Journal* previously. He copied Eugène Sue's *Les Mystères de Paris* to produce first *The Mysteries of London* (1845–8); he wrote the first two series, two other writers finished it off, and it was said to have sold 1 million copies in a decade. *The Mysteries of the Courts of London* followed in 1848–56; this was over four series, took 624 numbers to publish and at 4.5 million words is surely worth considering as the longest 'novel' in English.

By the 1840s the 'collected' works of an author or authors joined together with the 'library' style of publishing, and dozens of examples appeared: Pickering's Alden Poets and Diamond Classics, Bentley's Standard Novels, Colburn's Modern Novelists, Blackwood's Standard Novels, Burns's Fireside Library, Hamilton's Biblical Cabinet, Murray's Home and Colonial Library. But the publishers were still not producing inexpensive volumes: in the 1840s most still cost between 6*s.* and 8*s.* each. It was not until 1847 that things suddenly altered: Chapman and Hall produced a 'Cheap Edition' of *Martin Chuzzlewit* (originally published in 1844) in thirty-two weekly parts at 1½*d.* per week; readers thus ended up with a novel that had cost them only 4*s. Oliver Twist*, a shorter book, cost just 2*s.* 6*d.* for its entire run. For those with less patience and more cash the bookseller also produced monthly parts for 7*d.* – that is, for a penny more than the weekly part-issue, readers could find out three weeks early what was going to happen to Oliver next. Cheap editions opened up worlds of possibility to many; how much could be squeezed out of one book was also a revelation to publishers. A book was no longer a one-off event. *Oliver Twist* had appeared in parts in 1837–8; then it had appeared in three volumes in 1838; then it was reissued in ten parts in 1846; then it appeared once more, as a one-volume edition, in 1846. At one point Chapman and Hall had the Library Edition, the People's Edition, the Cheap Edition and the Charles Dickens Edition of Dickens's works all in print simultaneously.[59]

Of course, Dickens was Dickens: most authors could not hope to achieve a hundredth part of his success. But the new formats had given publishers a glimpse of a huge market that was ravenous for books, and the realization, as Wedgwood had had three-quarters of a century before, that very large profits could be made on very small margins. By 1847 Simms, McIntyre was pricing its Parlour Library at 1s. or 1s. 6d. per volume; by the autumn of that year Bentley had produced 109 Standard Novels at the rather higher 5s. per volume. But the real breakthrough came with Routledge's Railway Library, which began to appear in 1848, with its first novel, *The Pilot*, by James Fenimore Cooper, priced, as all the Railway Library volumes were to be, at 1s.[60] (There was no US–UK copyright agreement, and piracy across the Atlantic was rife; in the UK, anyone who wanted could reprint US authors, and vice versa, without paying the author a penny.)

As well as reprinting material not covered by copyright, George Routledge did something that had the other publishers laughing at him: he bought up old copyrights of books that had long been available. This seemed like throwing money away. But these other publishers had not noticed the change in reading habits that was under way. In the first decade of the railways, newspapers had been sold at major railway stations on an ad-hoc basis. For example, at Lime Street station in Liverpool in 1839, the Liverpool and Manchester Railway gave two men and four children the right to patrol the platforms, selling whatever they could carry. In 1841 William Marshall made a deal with the London and Blackwall Railway to open a bookstall at Fenchurch Street station in London; another stall was then opened at Euston station, under the aegis of the London and North-Western Railway. But the railway companies were busy with other things, and did not have time to go into the matter: very soon the stall at Euston, rented for a flat fee of £60 per annum, was making £1,200 a year. At that point the railways sat up and took notice, and the London and North-Western decided to put the contract up for tender. W. H. Smith, the son of the newsagent and distributor of Chapter 4, offered £1,500 for the rights to sell books and newspapers from all the London and North-Western's stations, and he began trading in 1848, the year Routledge gave birth to his Railway

Library. Smith did not have a monopoly – for the next fifteen years the West Midlands and South Wales stations' bookstalls were run by the son of the original lessee of the Fenchurch Street station bookstall – but by 1851 Smith had 35 station bookstalls, and by 1880 that had leapt to 450. In 1902 the company had 777 bookstalls, with another 463 it rather casually referred to as 'sub-stalls'.[61] By 1849, the year after Smith began trading, his Paddington station stall routinely stocked 1,000 books; travellers paid 1*d*. to read them in the shop while they waited for their trains, or for a slightly higher fee they could take the books with them on the train, 'returning' them to the W. H. Smith bookstall at their destinations.[62]

Smith, a devout man (he was known to many as the North-Western Missionary), wanted to run a profitable business, but at the same time he wanted to reform the reading matter of the travelling public, just as Mudie did. Bookstalls had until now mostly carried guidebooks, time-tables and the sort of fiction that the Westminster survey would most probably have called 'Novels of the lowest character'. They also stocked what was later described as pornography, which might have been what we think of as pornography, or might simply have been penny-dreadfuls. Whatever it was, this immoral trash, as Smith saw it, was quickly swept away, and replaced with books from Routledge's Railway Library; soon Smith was ordering 1,000 Railway Library books at a time – and it must be remembered that only twenty years before, total sales of 5,000 copies for a novel was considered a howling success. As *Punch* understood, the North-Western Railway 'promise[d] . . . to become one of the greatest engines of literature', with a train 'decidedly the best vehicle going for circulating a library'.[63] No one was laughing at Routledge any longer. Instead, the other booksellers all jumped aboard: by 1851 Bentley's also had a Railway Library (although it folded after three years), Longman's had a Traveller's Library, while John Murray produced Murray's Railway Reading and Literature for Rail, which consisted of 'cheap and healthy literature . . . containing works of sound information and innocent amusement'. Both Murray's and Longman's libraries were made up entirely of non-fiction works, because, contrary to expectations, W. H. Smith, the North-Western Missionary, had been absolutely right about what his customers desired: nothing less than Murray's 'sound in-formation and innocent amusement', or at least pleasant family fiction. Murray's Railway Reading included *Selections from the Writings of*

Lord Byron (the selections from this worryingly libertine poet rather reassuringly made by 'a Clergyman'), a *History of the Guillotine* (which was lifted from an article in the *Quarterly Review*), Layard's *Popular Account of Discoveries at Nineveh, A Journey to Katmandu (the capital of Nepaul)* [*sic*], and then a few books that were a little less worthy – like *The Chace, the Turf, and the Road* by 'Nimrod' (again lifted from the *Quarterly*) – not to overlook the wonderfully entitled *Stokers and Pokers*, a history of the London and North-Western Railway.[64]

George Routledge took his most famous leap in the dark in 1854: he paid Bulwer-Lytton £20,000 for the rights to nineteen of his old novels for the next ten years. He was warned that the market had been saturated, that everyone who had wanted to read Bulwer-Lytton had done so already. He stubbornly went ahead, producing a 'complete' Bulwer-Lytton Library in twenty volumes for £3 11*s*. 6*d*., or 3*s*. 6*d*. per volume. At first it seemed like the doom-mongers were right: sales were slow. Then, against all expectations, the books began to sell. Routledge then reissued the novels, this time in his Railway Edition format, at 1*s*. 6*d*. each, and sold 46,000 copies. In 1859 yet another format change saw him shift a further 35,000 copies. By 1857 Routledge had made so much money on Bulwer-Lytton that he renewed the agreement annually at £1,000 a year. Bulwer-Lytton was the Railway Library's most successful author for two decades.[65]

The range of subject matter that became available over the next decade was extraordinary: now that the price did not limit the purchase of books to the prosperous classes, the market seemed ever expandable, and people were eager to sample almost any type of book. Cheap literature was suddenly everywhere: an edition of Shakespeare could be bought for 1*s*., an illustrated collected verse of Byron for 7*d*.[66] Matthew Arnold claimed to have seen a copy of his *Empedocles on Etna* on sale at Derby station in 1854;* in 1857 Volumes 3 and 4 of Macaulay's *History of England* were 'cried up and down the platform at York like a second edition of *The Times*'.†[68] As Trollope wrote in

---

* This was a dramatic poem, a study of 'the conflict between sensuous emotion and disciplined thought' – not perhaps what one might immediately think of as railway reading.[67]

† I include this quote from the *Saturday Review* because the idea gives me such pleasure, but it is worth bearing in mind that this fact was reported to the *Saturday Review* by W. H. Smith's itself – which may possibly have had a vested interest in being seen to be purveyors of excellence.

SUNLIGHT SOAP WRAPPER COMPETITION.

BOOK PRIZES during 1895.

Full Particulars round each Tablet of SUNLIGHT SOAP.

A LONG LIST of CHOICE BOOKS to SELECT FROM.

NOTE—IMPORTANT.

Clergymen, Schoolmasters and Schoolmistresses, Sunday-school Superintendents and Teachers, may form "Book Clubs" amongst their Parishioners, Congregations, and Scholars, and by collecting Sunlight Soap Wrappers soon have a valuable Library.

LEVER BROS., Ltd,, Port Sunlight, Nr. Birkenhead.

Cheap books were everywhere by the end of the century. In the 1890s Sunlight Soap, targeting the working- and lower-middle-class market, promoted a scheme to win books by collecting soap wrappers.

1855, 'A man's seat in a railway carriage is now, or may be, his study.'[69]

But more than literature and contemporary fiction were promoted by the railways: all kinds of new books were ushered in by the transport revolution. In 1845 the novelist Charles Lever produced a collection of stories called *Tales of the trains, being some chapters of railroad romance, by Tilbury Tramp, queen's messenger*; four years later Leigh Hunt's *A Book for a Corner, or, Selections in Prose and Verse and Readings for Railways, or Anecdotes and other Short Stories, Reflections, Maxims, Characteristics, Passages of Wit, Humour, and Poetry* (this is one title) appeared; the 'corner' referred to was the corner seat of a railway carriage. Soon after this came *The Railway Anecdote Book*, which first appeared in 1850 and was successful enough to go through at least another two editions, as well as an illustrated version.

Anthologies, however, were hardly a novelty, even if the expected reader was now sitting in the corner of a carriage instead of a corner by the fire. A completely new sort of publication came with the arrival of the timetable. The railway was a contradictory thing: it brought freedom of movement, but, in order to take advantage of that freedom, the traveller had to accept regimentation. In the early days of the railways, many of the upper classes had not recognized this, and instead feared that the new technology would exacerbate an already disturbing tendency towards equality. The Duke of Wellington worried that trains would encourage 'the lower orders to go uselessly wandering about the country', and at first the railway companies behaved as if it were their job to prevent this from happening. The Liverpool and Manchester Railway made would-be travellers order their tickets twenty-four hours in advance, giving name, address, place of birth, age, occupation and reason for travel, so that the 'Station Agent' could be assured that 'the applicant desires to travel for a just and lawful cause'. It quickly became clear that – if for no other reason – sheer volume of traffic rendered this system impracticable. Yet the need for organization, even if one was catching a train to go 'uselessly wandering', was still necessary. Thomas Cook, the great excursion travel agent, put it poetically to his customers: 'Railway time is London time, and London time is the sun's time, and the sun's time is common time; and *Railway time all must keep . . .*' (my italics).[70]

But it was not that simple for those who did not organize travellers for a living to accept 'railway time' over 'God's time', as it was sometimes pointedly known. It had long been understood that, as one moved east or west, the time was different; there was, for example, twelve minutes' difference between London and Liverpool, and thirty minutes between Yarmouth and Penzance. When stagecoaches had been scheduled to take 'about' two days, or were advertised as leaving, 'God willing', before dark, that did not much matter. When railways reduced days of travelling to mere hours, fixed times became essential. In 1840, after a decade of confusion, the South Western and the Great Western railways announced that their stations would synchronize their clocks with London time. Even then, at Rugby station, which was shared between the London and North Western and the Midland railways, the former kept local time, the latter London time. By 1845 it was generally accepted that all railways had to operate on London time, but there remained stubborn holdouts. The Chester and Holyhead Railway insisted on setting its clocks by the Craig-y-Don gun, fired daily on the estate of the local landowners at 'noon', precisely 16½ minutes after the hour according to

Greenwich time.* This was especially annoying to travellers since the line primarily served the Irish Mail, which itself ran on Greenwich time. As late as 1851 there was correspondence in *The Times* debating the merits of a uniform system, and it was only in 1852 that the South Eastern Railway made an arrangement for the Royal Observatory to transmit the Greenwich signal by telegraph to its stations along the line.†[73]

Thus the new leisure and new freedom brought by the railways meant a new regimentation. Thomas Cook, in his *Hand Book* of 1845, which set out the itinerary for his first commercial trip, from Leicester, Nottingham and Derby to Liverpool, felt it necessary to warn his customers, 'Promptitude on the part of the Railway Company, calls for the same from passengers.'[74] Help in achieving this new precision was soon readily available for the anxious traveller. In the 1830s, George Bradshaw, a Quaker map-engraver working in Manchester, had produced *Bradshaw's Maps of Inland Navigation*, showing the various canal routes. From there it was but a short step to producing a printed sheet to go with the maps, to list the times of the few trains that could then be linked to the canals. Bradshaw's *Time Tables* was a small pamphlet costing 6*d.*, supplemented by a *Time Sheet* that was only 3*d.*‡ In 1839 *Bradshaw's Railway Time Tables and assistant to Railway Travelling with Illustrative Maps and Plans* appeared, in the teeth of opposition from the railways, which feared that the timetables 'would make punctuality a sort of obligation'. In some of the more obdurate cases Bradshaw actually had to buy shares in the different railway companies so that as a shareholder he could force them to disclose the information he required. In 1840 his first 1*s.* booklet appeared: *Bradshaw's Railway Companion, containing The Times of Departure, Fares, &c. of the Railways in England*, which included schedules for twelve railway companies.[76] From then on, few prosperous homes were

---

* The Williams family were the owners of this estate near Beaumaris on Anglesey, close to the Menai Bridge. According to local legend the head of the family at the time, Thomas Peers Williams, frequently missed his train because of his stubborn adherence to local time.[71]

† It was not until 1884, however, that there was any formal legislation. That year the Prime Meridian Conference in Washington, attended by representatives of twenty-five countries, agreed that Greenwich would become the 'zero' meridian, and thus British railway time became the starting point from which all other countries took their bearings.[72]

‡ As is so often the case, there was a later claim from another printer, who said *he* was the first to produce a railway timetable, a few months before Bradshaw.[75] Whether or not he was correct, it was *Bradshaw* that became the household bible.

without at least one copy – and often 'the foreign *Bradshaw*', as the schedule of Continental trains was known, as well. By 1885 the *Advertisers Guardian*, used for selling advertising space, listed another six daily, weekly or monthly publications giving schedules.[77]

The Times complained that leisure now meant planning, and organization, which made holidays 'work, and . . . tiring work . . . It entails a perpetual attention to time, and all the anxieties and irritations of that responsibility.'[78] *Punch* could not have agreed more heartily, publishing a squib that could still describe today's frazzled excursionist:

THE WONDERS OF MODERN TRAVEL.

THE STATION.
Wonder if the porter understood what I said to him about the
    luggage.
Wonder if I shall see him again.
Wonder if I shall know him when I *do* see him again.
Wonder if I gave my writing-case to the porter, or left it in the
    cab.
Wonder where I take my ticket.
Wonder in which pocket I put my gold.
Wonder where I got that bad half-crown which the clerk won't
    take.
Wonder if that's another that I've just put down.
Wonder where the porter is who took my luggage.
Wonder where my luggage is.
Wonder again whether I gave my writing-case to the porter, or
    left if in the cab.
Wonder which is my train.
Wonder if the guard knows anything about that porter with the
    writing-case.
Wonder if it *will* be 'all right' as the guard says it will be . . .

THE JOURNEY.
Wonder if my change is all right.
Wonder for the second time in which pocket I put my gold.
Wonder if I gave the cabman a sovereign for a shilling.
Wonder if that was the reason why he grumbled less than
    usual and drove off rapidly.
Wonder if any one objects to smoking.
Wonder that nobody does.
Wonder where I put my lights.

Wonder whether I put them in my writing-case.
Wonder for the third time whether I gave my writing-case to
    the porter or left it in the cab.
Wonder if anybody in the carriage has got any lights.
Wonder that nobody has.
Wonder when we can get some.
Wonder if there's anything in the paper.
Wonder why they don't cut it.*
Wonder if I put my knife in my writing-case.
Wonder for the fourth time whether I gave, &c.
Wonder if I can cut the paper with my ticket.
Wonder where I put my ticket.
Wonder where I *could* have put my ticket.
Wonder where the deuce I put my ticket.[79]

Railways had created new connections to literature, both practical and imaginative; but travel and books had had far older connections too. In the eighteenth century much of travel was undertaken from the comfort of one's own armchair. Travel writing was enormously popular – the more exotic the better. 'Africa', noted Horace Walpole in 1744, 'is indeed coming into fashion.'[80] Half a century later that remained true: Mungo Park's *Travels in the Interior Districts of Africa*, published in 1799, went through four editions in its first year. Even more successful had been the various accounts of the voyages of Captain Cook. These made up some of the volumes most frequently borrowed from libraries, but it was not Cook alone who wrote them, although he produced four volumes. Such was the interest that the Admiralty paid John Hawkesworth £6,000 – more than was earned by almost any author of the time – to write an official account. (This was not a good move: he was a writer, not an explorer, and the results were considered laughable.)† Another account was published by Canon John Douglas. The botanist on the expedition published his version, and his son produced another; there was a pamphlet, *A Catalogue of the Different Specimens of*

---

* Newspapers, magazines and books were all sold with their pages uncut; railway-station bookstalls usually sold special folding paperknives.
† William Combe, the satirist, in his *Tour of Dr Syntax in Search of the Picturesque*, which he produced with Rowlandson's cartoons in 1809, mocked this sort of home-grown travel writing. Dr Syntax's travel journals were rejected by a publisher, who said, 'We can get Tours – don't make wry faces, / From those that never saw the places. / I know a man who has the skill / To make your Books of Tours at will; / And from his garret at Moorfields / Can see what ev'ry country yields.'[81]

Cloth collected in the Three voyages of Cook; and even Cook's alcoholic gunner's mate sold his story to a chapbook publisher.[82] Travel and commerce had merged. Apart from the books published, Omai, the Tahitian who had come back to England with Cook on his second voyage, was painted by Joshua Reynolds; then engravings of the painting made by Francesco Bartolozzi, (the most fashionable engraver of the day – so fashionable that the Royal Academy made an exception to its 'no engravers' rule, and he was a full member from the start) were immensely popular and sold widely in print shops.

With the French wars at the end of the century came a further rash of travel books, as military men fought abroad and then, on their return home, produced their accounts of foreign parts. With the peace of 1815, the Continent was easily accessible for the first time in nearly a quarter of a century, and many rushed abroad. As late as 1800, travellers to Greece had been forced to rely on George Wheler's *Description of a Journey into Greece*, which had first been published in 1682; by 1820, they could choose from more than two dozen new books.[83] The cross-fertilization that had occurred between books and engravings in the case of Cook and Omai only developed: in 1821 Giovanni Battista Belzoni, a strongman who had performed at Sadler's Wells as the 'Patagonian Sampson' (he was actually from Padua), travelled to Egypt to conduct excavations at both Abu Simbel and the Valley of the Kings. He returned with his plunder, and, as well as exhibiting scarabs, papyruses, statues, a scale model of the pyramids, a 'Room of Beauties' with representations of the pharaohs and gods, and galleries of drawings, he also wrote a book, his *Narrative of the Operations and Recent Discoveries within the Pyramids, Temples, Tombs, and Excavations, in Egypt and Nubia; and of a Journey to the Coast of the Red Sea.*[84]*

Austen Henry Layard was neither a military man nor a strongman, but a solicitor. He had been planning to go to Ceylon to practise, but instead in the early 1840s he was paid an advance of £200 from a publisher, which enabled him to travel through Syria, Palestine and Persia, and write about his travels. Once in the Near East he was asked

---

* It was not, of course, necessary to have actually *been* to an exotic locale to feel that one had a vested interest. The poet Thomas Moore wrote to Byron, suggesting that he would gift Byron Turkey for Byron's own literary use if Byron would agree to stay away from Persia, and especially would promise not to write about 'peris' without further discussion. In exchange, Moore dropped a story that seemed too close to Byron's 'Bride of Abydos', despite Byron's assurances that it would not 'trench upon your kingdom in the least'.[85]

by Stratford Canning, then serving as ambassador to Constantinople, to produce a report on a border dispute between Turkey and Persia, using Layard's persona as a writer in search of material to cover what was, in effect, spying. As this was successful, in 1845 he was supplied with funds to excavate near Mosul, which was thought to be the site of Nineveh (in fact it turned out to be Nimrud). Canning wrote to the newly created archaeologist reminding him that 'his professed occupation will be that of a traveller, fond of antiquities, of picturesque scenery, and the manner peculiar to Asia'.

When the excavations were completed, in 1847, Layard took the advice he was given on all sides. The Oriental Secretary at Constantinople told him, 'Write a whopper with lots of plates . . . fish up old legends and anecdotes, and if you can by any means humbug people into the belief that you have established any points in the Bible, you are a made man.' Even his aunt chipped in: 'In this reading age a good book makes a man's fortune here more certainly than by any other means.' John Murray, the publisher who had advanced him £200, agreed to pay the nearly £4,000 that would be necessary to produce engravings, if Layard agreed to write not a scholarly account, but a breathless adventure story. His *Nineveh and its Remains* fitted the bill perfectly, especially with its subtitle, 'With an account of a visit to the Chaldean Christians of Kurdistan, and the Yezidis, or Devil-worshippers . . .' Murray sold 8,000 copies in 1849 alone, and another 12,000 in the following three years.[86]

Murray was one of those who led the way in travel publishing, and accounts of foreign adventures continued to sell in their thousands. But, at the same time, a new kind of book for travel was also appearing. These new books presupposed not dramatic events in exotic locales that readers were happy to read about in the comfort of their home circle, but instead that readers would be visiting the places described, and needed some preliminary advice. Murray was in the forefront here too. In 1854 the playwright and deviser of extravaganzas James Robinson Planché had one of his characters enter holding

> All Murray's Handbooks . . .
> Germany, North and South, France, Holland, Spain,
> Switzerland, up the Rhine, and back again,
> Italy, Russia, Egypt, Turkey, Greece . . .[87]

These guidebooks, even to places that only a generation before had seemed unimaginably exotic, had by the 1870s been domesticated. When the Franco-Prussian War cut English travellers off from their now-familiar travels to Europe (see Cook's tours, pp. 226–8), an avalanche of books appeared as a substitute. Leslie Stephen's *The Playground of Europe*, John Tyndall's *Hours of Exercise in the Alps* and Edward Whymper's *Scrambles amongst the Alps* were all published in 1871, and they notably had similarly tame titles, making the ascent of a glacier seem no more exotic than a day spent walking on the South Downs.

Such guidebooks, though selling better than ever, did have some precedents. In the seventeenth century, local maps had generally shown each county as a separate entity; the towns, villages and natural features were drawn in some detail, but the roads that led into and out of the region were often ignored altogether, or shown only in the most rudimentary form. These were maps designed for the people who lived in the region.[88] By the 1770s Daniel Paterson had developed and published a very different type of map. Paterson was an army officer (he ended up with a sinecure as the Lieutenant Governor of Quebec, although there is no indication that he ever went there), and in 1766 he published *A Scale of Distances of the Principal Cities and Towns of England. Giving in all 4,560 distances in Measured Miles*. This was followed in 1771 by *A New and Accurate Description of all the Direct and Principal Cross Roads in Great Britain*, or, as it became known, *Paterson's Roads* – a series of strip maps showing how best to get from one place to another, designed specifically for travellers who wanted to get from Point A to Point B. So the first entry, for Abergavenny, reads:

ABERGAVENNY,
Monm TU. Angel, Greyhound
146 – *by Ragland*, 141
141 – *by Tregare*, 121
Cross, 350, 486.

Here, in shorthand, the traveller is given all the information needed: Abergavenny is in Monmouthshire, it has a market on Tuesdays, and post horses for the traveller can be found at the Angel and the Greyhound inns. The town has two main roads in, via Ragland and Tregare, which are respectively 146 and 141 miles from London. These roads can themselves be looked up on pages 141 and 121, while the cross roads running through Abergavenny appear on pages 350 and 486. There was obviously a great demand for this type of information; the first edition went through thirteen editions, the second edition eight; by 1811 the fifteenth edition was in print, and *Paterson's Roads* continued to sell right into the railway age, with a nineteenth edition in 1832.[89]

Paterson's Roads also gave information on different sights along the route, and it is interesting to compare the entry on Stonehenge with the entry for a small manor house nearby. 'STONE HENGE', the traveller was informed briefly, 'is a stupendous pile of stones, supposed to have been a temple of the Druids; and is considered as one of the most remarkable remains of antiquity in the kingdom.' So much for Stonehenge. Nearby, Wilbury Park, belonging to 'Sir A. C. St Loo Mallet . . . is a comfortable family mansion, consisting of a centre, with two corresponding wings: the building is of stone, and was erected in the reign of Queen Anne; it is advantageously situated in an extensive well-planted park, whose sylvan beauties form a striking contrast with the bare and open downs around, of which it once formed a part.'[90] This negligible although clearly pretty house received more than double the space allotted to Stonehenge. Yet, remarkably, Paterson had got his emphasis exactly right. Country-house visiting had been the privilege of the mobile upper classes for a century; it was now filtering down to the more prosperous middle classes, who were expecting to learn about the new things they were seeing. They were less interested in ancient history, more concerned with acquiring taste, worldliness, familiarity with the objects that had previously been the province of the rich, and therefore publications were created to meet this demand. (For more on country-house visiting, see pp. 212–15.) Previously, in the eighteenth century, studies of houses had been concerned principally to describe the generations of the family that owned the house, and only tangentially the house itself; sometimes there was a description of the house, but this was not the purpose of the book. By the middle of the century a few books, such as the 1753 publication *A Description of the House and Gardens . . . at Stow* [*sic*], had begun to appear. These did describe to visitors what they were seeing. The Stowe book was extremely successful, going through twenty-two editions in the next sixty years at a cost of 6*d.* for the guide alone, 1*s.* if a map was included, or 5*s.* for a bound edition which also had a series of engravings. It was unsurprising, therefore, that others followed. By the end of the century there were about fifteen or twenty great houses on the tourist trail that had enough visitors who wanted education to warrant catalogues of the contents of the houses and gardens – among them Houghton Hall, Holkham Hall, Stowe, Blenheim Palace and Wilton House.[91]

From these catalogues, it was but a short step to a descriptive guide-book. The *Oxford English Dictionary* dates the first known use of the word 'guide-book', to mean a book used by a traveller, to 1814, but the phenomenon may well have appeared slightly earlier. John Byng, 5th Viscount Torrington, who kept diaries of his travels over nearly fifteen years, had by the end of the eighteenth century seen that 'Tour writing is the very rage of the times.'* At the beginning of the nineteenth century Robert Southey also noted this development: 'Wherever you go, printed information is to be found concerning every thing which deserves a stranger's notice.'[92] By 1810 there was even a guide to Wales, a country that had previously been considered to be a featureless wilderness. *The Cambrian Traveller's Guide* also covered the Marcher counties, and up as far as Birmingham, and it aimed for completeness, for the most studious of travellers: it had twelve indexes, including indexes to geographical features such as 'districts, islets, promontories, peninsulas, vales, valleys, dingles, passes, roads, sands, plains, parks, moors, downs, fields, forests, woods, marches'; physical features such as 'mountains, hills, rocks, cliffs, caverns, caves and clefts' as well as water elements – 'fountains, rivers, estuaries, waterfalls, lakes, wells, bogs, aqueducts, creeks, bays, havens, ports, harbours, moats, ferries' – built-up areas including 'cities, towns, villages, hamlets, solitary inns and houses, bridges'; architectural elements, whether they were 'castles, forts, encampments, walls' or 'palaces, mansions, gentlemen's seats, villas', abbeys, churches or ruins; 'Tumuli, Carneddau or tombs, Cromlechs or monuments, pillars, Druid circles'; mines and potteries; and other miscellaneous man-made objects. (The indexes to the second edition were briefer, but contained the following enticing entries: 'Nails for the shoes in ascending mountains, described; Peasants, diet of; Story, a marvellous; Wreckers, their cruelties; Circumstance, a remarkable one'.) The book did not include a map,

---

* Byng came from a well-known family – his uncle was the Admiral Byng who in 1756 had sailed from Spithead to try to prevent the French from capturing Port Mahon, a mission which was to end in his death by firing squad, as Voltaire put it, *'pour encourager les autres'* – but his travel diaries were unpublished until the twentieth century. Perhaps the only fame of his lifetime was to have had a son who was known to the Regency social world as 'Poodle' Byng.

although it suggested the best one to buy – for 7s. 6d., in addition to the 7s. 6d. charged for the book.[93]

Similarly, the Lake District had been 'discovered' in the late eighteenth century (see pp. 215–8), and a deluge of guidebooks followed. The poet Thomas Gray and the antiquary Thomas West had been the leaders in this field. Gray had travelled through the region in the late 1760s, and in 1775 he published his journal from this time, which popularized both the area and certain spots for which he had a particular affection. In 1778 West laid out these sights and a few others in guidebook form, as *West's Guide to the Lakes*, with each sight marked as a 'station': visitors were told where to stop and what to bypass, as well as what to think at each stop. Each station was highly specific. At Windermere, 'Near the isthmus of the ferry point, observe two small oak trees that inclose the road, these will guide you to this celebrated station. Behind the tree on the western side ascend to the top of the nearest rock, and from thence in two views command all the beauties of this magnificent lake.' By 1799 a small summer house had been built there, with a window designed precisely to encompass this view.[94] A tourist at the time dutifully recorded that 'We remarked most of the stations described in West's *Tour to the Lakes*, a book we had constantly in our hands.'[95] Most tourists seemed to feel the same way: by 1812 the book had been through ten editions.

By the time of the Great Exhibition, guidebooks had become standardized: books like *Knight's Excursion Companion* told the regular railroad traveller about the joys of a seaside town and its environs, or the history of the area, or the sights that could be seen from the train en route. *The Birmingham Saturday Half Holiday-Guide*, one of dozens of books helping the newly liberated clerk and his family amuse themselves on a Saturday, was an encyclopedia of leisure consumption. There was railway information on page 1, then thirty-five pages of walks, sightseeing trips and towns within half a day's distance of Birmingham; a section on the 'Natural history of the District' was followed by five pages on recreational sports – boating, bathing, fishing and cricket. The advertisements covered all the possibilities for the new day-trippers. They were enticed to purchase further publications, such as *Saturday Afternoon Rambles Round London*, and at the same time the Midland Railway also promoted its 'Tourist Tickets', valid for a month for destinations such as 'Scarboro', Windermere, Buxton and others 'as per particulars in the

Tourist Programme, which may be had at Midland Receiving Offices and Stations'. Other advertisements alerted the hungry traveller to cookshops and dining rooms in the vicinity, while E. & F. Bostock, 'Family boot and shoe warehouse', was happy to make sure that ramblers were properly shod. The Birmingham India Rubber Company, 'Manufacturers of VULCANIZED WATERPROOF COATS and CAPES for Walking, Riding, Driving, Hunting, Fishing, &c. CARTRIDGE BAGS, GAME BAGS, FISHING BAGS, COURIER BAGS, TRAVELLING BAGS, HAVERSACKS &C. FISHING STOCKINGS AND BOOTS, SHOOTING BOOTS AND LEGGINGS', was one of many advertisers venturing into an entirely new field of commodity: sport.[96]

As sports themselves developed (see Chapter 11), so did sporting books to be sold to enthusiasts. Racing had led the way, with the various racing calendars discussed on p. 151. By the 1840s, *Ruff's Guide to the Turf*, compiled by *Bell's Life*'s racing correspondent, was issued regularly, listing horses, races, trainers, owners and prize money – all the components for armchair as well as trackside connoisseurship. Other sports did not lag behind. John Wisden, a cricketer, had on his retirement opened a cigar shop, but in 1864 he also began to publish an annual on his first love. His friend and erstwhile business partner Frederick Lillywhite, a sports journalist and the son of a cricketer known as the 'Nonpareil Bowler', produced a *Guide to Cricketers*, a rival to *Wisden*, in 1848 or 1849 (it survived until 1866), and his *Scores and Biographies of Celebrated Cricketers* appeared in 1862. Lillywhite's brother John's *Cricketers' Companion* appeared from 1865 to 1882,* while their cousin James Lillywhite produced *Red Lillywhite*, an annual that appeared from 1872 to 1900. From the 1870s until the First World War, more than a hundred books on cricket appeared; football was almost as popular, spawning about sixty titles – its own almanac, the *Football Annual*, had first appeared in 1868. There were over 250 books on golf, and nearly as many again on guns or shooting. The publishers of these sporting books followed the conventions of the time, producing various matched volumes in 'libraries': the Sportsman's Library, the Sports Library and the Badminton Library, to name a few.[97]

The new worlds that were opening up through books were literal as well as figurative. Books allowed more and more of the population to

---

* Their brother James did not publish, instead opening Lillywhite's, a sporting-goods store that continues to flourish today.

become familiar with places that had previously been unknown, and now the places themselves were fast becoming accessible to the new consumer.

6

To Travel Hopefully:
Holidays and Tourism

WITH THE COMING OF the Industrial Revolution, with increasing urbanization, with the great movement of population from the countryside to the city, with the shift from seasonal to factory work – with all these things, the nature of leisure altered. 'Old' leisure had revolved around community activities, performed by set groups of people at set times of year, whether it was the village men playing a ritual football game every Shrove Tuesday (for more on 'old' sports, and football, see p. 438) or attendance at an annual fair. Now 'new' leisure permitted choices of activities by individuals to suit their own preferences, whether for sport, or the pub, or more professional entertainments such as theatres, shows or music halls. George Eliot, in *Adam Bede* (1859), shook her head sorrowfully over the new times, when 'Even idleness is eager now – eager for amusement: prone to excursion trains, art-museums, periodical literature, and exciting novels . . .'[1]

Eliot was only one of the many to see the change, but while in *Adam Bede* she mourned the new commercial leisure activities, an interesting combination of the upper classes, evangelical reformers, merchants and factory-owners (not necessarily mutually exclusive) was working towards further change in the way the lower classes spent their working – and thus their leisure – hours. There were several intertwined strands to this desire for change. The old social system stood firmly on the notion that the upper classes were defined by their lack of employment – the upper classes *were* the leisured classes. By contrast, a leisured working man was an oxymoron: a leisured working man was merely unemployed, idle. The leisure time of the cultivated was well used; the working classes when idle were probably fomenting disorder, or even crime. It was partly for this reason that there arose a number of societies whose main aim was social control of the lower orders. Even the title of the Society for the Rescue of Boys Not Yet Convicted of Any Criminal Offence was a clear indication that all lower orders were potential law-breakers.[2] The Society for Giving Effect to His Majesty's Proclamation against Vice and Immorality had ceased its activities by the late 1790s, but was re-formed and reappeared in 1802 as the evangelically controlled Society for the Suppression of Vice, which promoted an end to Sabbath-breaking and blasphemy, as well as the suppression of 'licentious' books and prints, fairs, public houses and gambling – to some it seemed to want to suppress every form of commercial leisure for the working classes. In its first two years, 623 of its 678 prosecutions were for Sabbath-breaking,[3] which is surely significant: the main aim was to control the one free day of the workers, the one day when they were not already under the control of someone who was socially their superior.

This was not a view promoted simply by a group of religiously guided, single-issue zealots. It was commonly accepted by the governing classes, and by employers, that idleness in the workforce damaged national prosperity: if a workman was hungry, he would work; if he had enough to eat, he would probably go to the pub. (The rich, however, aided national prosperity by their idleness: by shopping, they were promoting production.) The nature of the agricultural year had traditionally encompassed many regular fairs and wakes.* Now these intermittent eruptions of 'merry-making' were maddening to factory-owners who were trying to maintain steady production. Josiah Wedgwood wrote in endless exasperation on the subject. In 1771, 'I should have sent you some good black [vases] this week, *if it had not been Stoke Wake*'; in 1772, 'the Men have gone madding after these Wakes's so that we could get little done'; and, again the same year, 'We are laying by [laying off men] for Xmass at our works. The men murmer at the thoughts of play these hard times, but they can keep wake after wake in summer.' Nothing much changed, however, for in 1776 he was writing, 'Our men have been at play 4 days this week, it being Burslem Wakes. I have rough'd &

---

* Wakes were originally the celebrations of the feast day of a particular saint, usually the parish church's patron saint, but they had long become local holidays, with village sports, dancing and other communal pastimes taking place on the saint's day and for several days afterwards.

smoothed them over, & promised them a long Xmass, but I know it is all in vain, for Wakes must be observed though the World was to end with them.'[4]

A further irritation for the employer was 'St Monday', the facetious name for the custom of workers taking Monday off after their Saturday payday. This habit was already fading away in the eighteenth century, but in its death throes it showed remarkable tenacity. A survey of witness statements from 8,000 Old Bailey session papers from 1750 to 1800 showed that in 1750 St Monday was almost universally considered a day off; by 1800 it was, for most people, a regular working day. Yet well into the nineteenth century traces of this 'saint' remained: in the 1830s Thomas Cook, a stalwart of the temperance movement, organized his first tours on Mondays (see p. 225). And as late as the 1870s the eminently respectable Hartlepool Temperance Society took its members on an educational excursion to the Middlesbrough Polytechnic on a Monday.[5]

As well as wakes and St Monday, fairs, assize weeks and other local festivals continued to be observed by some through the first half of the nineteenth century. In Warwickshire, many employers expected their hands to stop work about five times each summer, to attend prizefights. A mine in Lancashire gave its workers two weeks' holiday at Christmas, one at Whitsun, three to four days for the Ringley Wakes, and the same again for the Ratcliff Wakes. Others expected their employees to absent themselves for the local race week.[6] (It must be remembered that all holidays were unpaid: much hardship could be suffered by the management 'giving' two weeks' holiday in winter.)* Even when the 1833 Factory Act gave workers eight half-day holidays a year, plus Christmas Day and Good Friday, many workers wanted to keep their traditional holidays, rather than conform to the set days imposed on them by Parliament. In 1840, at Henry Ashworth's mill in Turton, in Lancashire,

---

* By the 1840s some paid holidays were expected, more by clerks in offices than by factory workers. In *A Christmas Carol*, Scrooge tells his clerk, Bob Cratchit, who receives only one day's holiday a year, that paying him for that one day is

> 'not fair. If I was to stop half-a-crown for it, you'd think yourself ill-used, I'll be bound? . . . And yet . . . you don't think *me* ill-used, when I pay a day's wages for no work.'
> The clerk observed that it was only once a year.
> 'A poor excuse for picking a man's pocket every twenty-fifth of December!'[7]

the workers agreed that, as they could not afford to take two holidays in two weeks, they would rather have their traditional day of Easter Monday than Good Friday, which Parliament had nominated as the statutory day; equally, they were not accustomed to stop work on Christmas Day, and asked instead for their traditional day on New Year's Day.[8] In other regions, similar accommodations between government regulations, regional industrial requirements and local customs were made: in the Potteries, the Great Stoke Wakes was instituted as a single surrogate to encompass the many local wakes.

With the gradual habituation to national holidays, even if patchily conformed to, came the closure of fairs, increasingly seen as disruptions to the slowly standardizing calendar. From 1750 to 1850, sixty fairs within a fifteen-mile radius of Charing Cross alone were suppressed. Southwark and May Fair were both shut down in the 1760s; Bow, Brook Green, Stepney, Tothill and Edmonton fairs were ended with the passing of the Metropolitan Police Act of 1822. Bartholomew Fair went in 1854; Greenwich Fair in 1857. More than the working classes saw their leisure curtailed. The Bank of England, with a majority of middle-class employees, can stand for many offices in its contraction of holidays. In the mid eighteenth century the bank had had 47 full days of holiday a year, by 1808 this was down to 44, and by 1825 to 40. Five years later there was an enormous drop, to 18 days a year, and it took just another four years to reduce that by three-quarters: in 1834 the bank closed only on Good Friday, May Day, Christmas Day and All Saints' Day.* This mirrors the rise in working hours across the country. In 1750 the average number of working days each year was between 208 and 255; fifty years later that number had risen to between 306 and 323.[9]

While working days were being increased, working hours followed a contrary path, falling steadily from the eighteenth century onward. There was an unspoken and probably barely noticed trade-off occurring: fewer hours worked daily, in exchange for more regular, more reliable working patterns. As early as the 1720s, many builders had achieved a ten-hour day; by the mid eighteenth century, most artisans in skilled handicraft trades also expected to work 'only' ten hours a day. The fight for further reductions, which was straightforwardly one of employees against

---

* For a table of holidays observed by many civil-service offices in the eighteenth century, see Appendix 3, p. 498.

employers, continued in trade-defined skirmishes through the early part
of the nineteenth century: in the 1830s, the printers managed to win the
right to work from 6 a.m. to 6 p.m. – that is, ten hours' actual work.[10]
(Any time spent not working – eating breakfast or lunch – was unpaid,
as holidays were.)

With the 1867 Factory and Workshops Act, a sixty-hour week was
the norm, but many workers still did not achieve this, because their
workplaces were not covered by the act. In a shipping office in Liverpool
in the 1880s, clerks in the passenger department worked from 9 a.m. to
6 p.m. in theory; in practice they often worked until ten or eleven at
night. Bank clerks, considered 'the aristocracy of the clerical profession'
ostensibly worked from 8.30 in the morning until six in the evening,
but in busy periods they were expected to remain until nine or ten. The
large warehouses in Manchester worked similar hours: as late as the
1900s many opened officially from 8.30 a.m. to 6 p.m., but during any
busy period staff were expected to start work between 6 and 8 a.m., and
go through until 9.30 p.m; on Saturdays they had a 'short' day of 8 a.m.
to 2 p.m. – in all, working nearly eighty hours a week.[11] Shops were the
worst offenders: in the late nineteenth century most shops in the West
End of London closed at six during the week, with a half-day on Saturday,
although Liberty's stayed open until seven on weekdays, and four on
Saturdays until the early 1880s, when the shop closed at two every other
Saturday. (When Arthur Liberty finally announced a regular two o'clock
closing every Saturday, his staff gave him an illuminated address of
thanks.) As late as 1894 Harrod's was still open until seven o'clock two
nights a week. Shops away from the fashionable areas, or shops that
relied on working-class customers, expected to stay open much later on
Saturdays: until midnight, or even later, was common for many types of
shop – one shop assistant in a draper's remembered that on Saturdays
'we never closed at all'.[12]

One of the reasons for shops keeping such long Saturday hours was
because Saturdays more generally were gradually being ceded to workers'
leisure, and workers at leisure meant workers who had time to shop. In
the original Ten Hours' Bill (passed finally in 1847) there had been a
clause asking for a 'short' Saturday, of just eight hours. While the retail
sector ignored this for some time, factories began to see its value, and
by 1850 many textile mills stopped work at two on Saturday afternoons,
reasoning that if early closing helped to kill off the last vestiges of

St Monday then it was well worth doing. For manufacturers who relied on steam power, a partial workforce on a Monday was as much use as none. Many trades soon followed, encouraged by groups like the Early Closing Association, set up by Sabbatarians, who wanted to eradicate Sabbath-breaking by enabling workers to shop on Saturday afternoons.[13] It was becoming a commonplace, not merely among those worried about Sabbath observance, that half-closing on Saturdays would improve both health and morale, and permit employees to work better the rest of the week: workers who enjoyed their leisure on a Saturday 'would thereby become a more healthy, social, and religious people', said one campaigner.[14] Early closing was from the first specifically linked to leisure activities: in 1860 a parliamentary select committee set up to investigate 'promoting the Healthful Recreation and Improvement of the People' recommended that the British Museum and the National Gallery, whose hours seemed to many to be specifically designed to keep out the lower orders (see pp. 397–8), should be made to open 'at Hours on Week Days when, by the ordinary customs of Trade, such persons are free from toil'.[15] Twenty years earlier, mill-owner Henry Ashworth not only kept to the statutory hours, he also gave his workers a week's holiday to 'go to Ireland or London, or Scotland, wherever the coach or steam-boat will carry them, and spend their time rationally'.[16] For him, as for many now, holidays equated to travel.

Travel had been a rarity for all but a minority throughout much of the eighteenth century. Getting around was difficult, and expensive. It was only with the arrival of maps and guidebooks, the creation of the turnpikes and the improvements to the technology of the stagecoach, discussed over the last chapters, that even many of the elite began to travel. For others, even with these developments, any sort of movement away from one's own home was a tremendous upheaval: 'The village of Bridford lay only nine miles south-west of Exeter by road, yet the rector tells us that when Napoleon's invasion of England was considered to be imminent the well-to-do families of Exeter made plans for flight to Bridford as though it were another continent.'[17] Yet, as the wars of the eighteenth century closed off the Continent to those who would previously have gone on the Grand Tour, travel within Britain became more common. In 1771 Sir Watkin Williams Wynn went on a tour of north Wales – with only nine servants, and an artist to record the views.[18]

Yet the idea of recreational travel was spreading, starting with the most prosperous, and then quickly moving down the social scale. In the 1780s and 1890s John Byng referred to himself in his diaries as a 'tourist' (one of the earliest uses of this word), because he was making tours – that is, he was travelling in a circle, beginning and ending at the same point – visiting the great houses of England and Wales every June and July. The eighteenth century had been a great period of country-house improvement, in which the houses in general became larger and more elaborate, particularly in those public areas that were designed not solely for family use, but for status: music rooms, libraries, picture galleries, and even in the 1780s some small theatres. The picture galleries were particularly prominent, as they were designed to hold the art that had been shipped home by the Grand Tourists and now needed to be displayed, for the renown of their owners. (Or to exhibit their gullibility: Horace Walpole, always waspish, made extensive notes of his visits, such as, at Castle Howard, '[Painting of the] Prince of Parma and dwarf, called Correggio, certainly not'.)[19] Until the foundation of the Royal Academy in 1768 and the British Institution in 1805 (see p. 393), there was no other way to see art of any quality, and for the most part the owners of these houses expected visitors: Chatsworth was formally open to the public two days a week from the 1730s, Woburn on Mondays, Fonthill daily and, by the 1780s, Blenheim daily too. In *Pride and Prejudice* (written originally before 1797) Jane Austen had Elizabeth Bennet make a 'Northern Tour' with her aunt and uncle, visiting 'the celebrated beauties' of Chatsworth and Blenheim among others, until Elizabeth became 'tired of great houses; after going over so many, she really had no pleasure in fine carpets or satin curtains'.[20] It was such grandeur that many were looking for, however: Mrs Lybbe Powys, a member of the prosperous gentry class and a formidable tourist, who kept journals of her travels, found in Castle Howard 'the rooms in general too small, though in the wing now building there seems by the plan some fine apartments to be intended'. Furthermore, she disdained Belton House because '"Tis nothing more than a good family house.'[21]*

The system of visiting was informal and the rules unwritten, but there were rules all the same, and those who could afford the time and expense

---

* For changing tastes and values over the years, it is worth noting that, according to the website of the National Trust, which now owns it, Belton is 'one of the finest examples of Restoration country-house architecture', with 'stunning interiors' and 'exceptional plasterwork and wood-carvings'.

implicit in country-house visiting knew how to go about it. The hopeful visitors arrived, and either sent in a servant or went personally to hand in a card and ask if they could see over the house. As long as they looked respectable the answer was usually yes, and they were then escorted around by a servant, often the housekeeper, who expected a tip at the end.* It was quite common to view the entire house: the traveller Arthur Young (who was mainly interested in 'husbandry; but it would have been great stupidity to pass very near a celebrated house without viewing it') said that at Wentworth Castle Lady Strafford 'retired from her apartment' so that he could see it; on another trip he admired 'lady *Townshend's* dressing-room . . . [which] is furnished with prints, stuck with much taste on green [wall]paper'.[23] Mrs Lybbe Powys also thought it a matter of course that she should visit the owner's private rooms at Fonthill, where 'Mrs Beckford's dressing-room has in it numbers of superb and elegant nick-nacks'; she apparently even toured the attics, as she made approving comments about the fireplaces there.[24] But, with the increase in the number of visitors, this informal system was coming under strain. Byng wrote of a trip to Wroxton Abbey, 'I prevail'd upon my party to drive down to it; when unluckily for us Ld G— was just arrived from London, and denied us admittance. Very rude this . . . Let him either forbid his place entirely; open it allways [*sic*]; or else fix a day of admission: but, for shame, don't refuse travellers, who may have come 20 miles out of their way for a sight of the place.'[25] The Earl of Stafford took the first course, refusing access to his fine collection of paintings to any except 'persons of the first rank'.[26]

Gradually, as 'persons of the first rank' became the minority of visitors, Byng's suggestion of more regulation – of fixing a day of admission, or setting down rules for admittance – came to be adopted by many. Horace Walpole began to admit visitors to Strawberry Hill, his house in Twickenham, by ticket as early as 1784. The would-be visitor applied in writing to Walpole in advance, and waited for a letter back which gave the name of the visitor, the date of the visit, and the number of people in the party. This was to be handed to the housekeeper as a token for

* The tip was a not insignificant part of the tour: those lower down the social scale were conducted by lesser servants, and the tip was in keeping with their status; the more elite visitors were shown around by the housekeeper, and were expected to tip lavishly. Mrs Home ferried visitors around Warwick Castle for nearly fifty years, and when she died in 1834 the 'privilege of showing the castle' had enabled her to accumulate £30,000.[22]

entry, but not before the visitor had read the 'rules for admission to see my House' which were printed on the letter:

> Mr Walpole is very ready to oblige any curious persons with the sight of his house and collection; but as it is situated so near to London and in so populous a neighbourhood, and as he refuses a ticket to nobody that sends for one, it is but reasonable that such persons as send, should comply with the rules he has been obliged to lay down for showing it.
>
> Any person, sending a day or two before, may have a ticket for four persons for a certain day . . . If more than four persons come with a ticket, the housekeeper has positive orders to admit none of them . . .
>
> As Mr Walpole has given offence by sometimes enlarging the number of four, and refusing that latitude to others, he flatters himself that for the future nobody will take it ill that he strictly confines the number; as whoever desires him to break his rule, does in effect expect him to disoblige others, which is what nobody has a right to desire him . . . If any person does not make use of the ticket, Mr Walpole hopes he shall have notice; otherwise he is prevented from obliging others on that day, and thence is put to great inconvenience.[27]

This kind of professionalization was noticeable in every aspect of country-house visiting. As we have seen (p. 202), from the mid eighteenth century some houses had begun to provide catalogues of their contents. Mrs Lybbe Powys went to Houghton Hall, the home of Sir Robert Walpole's descendants, in 1756, and promised to bring home 'a catalogue* as I've taken the pains to copy a written one the late Lord [Orford, i.e. Walpole] gave to [her friend] Mr Jackson'.[28] At Houghton, catalogues were thus not generally available, and not for sale to visitors, but given as gifts to friends of a similar rank. Yet these places also expected visitors who were much more humble: Ozias Humphry, later a celebrated miniaturist, but in 1764 simply a hopeful on his way to London, made visits to Hagley Hall, the Leasowes (famous for its gardens), Stratford-upon-Avon (for Shakespearian tourism, see pp. 236–41), Blenheim, Windsor, and Pope's villa in Twickenham, among others.[29]

He was not alone; more and more tourists were about, and many of

---

* The catalogue was not of the entire house, but of the paintings and *objets d'art* that made up Walpole's famous art collection, which was sold by his heirs to Catherine the Great – one of the three great collections she acquired that today form the nucleus of the Hermitage Museum.

the landowners made arrangements to encourage them. In 1776 Mrs Lybbe Powys stayed at an inn near Stourton specifically built 'by Mr Hoare for the company that comes to see his place'. That same year she noted that 2,324 visitors had been to Wilton House that year, which she thought very few.[30] Horace Walpole's Strawberry Hill, so near to London, did not need to provide lodgings, and he did not achieve Wilton's visitor numbers, but, given the house's tiny size, that he received nearly 300 'customers' a year, as he tellingly called them, was impressive. Many of these visitors were no longer solely of the gentry class, or at least they were no longer cognoscenti. By the end of the century Walpole was complaining that 'A party arrived . . . a man and three women in riding-dresses, and they rode post [that is as fast as they could] through the apartments – I could not hurry before them fast enough . . . They come, ask what such a room is called . . . write it down, admire a lobster or a cabbage in a market-piece [still life], dispute whether the last room was green or purple, and then hurry to the inn for fear the fish should be overdressed.'[31] From there it was not far to Dickens's portrayal of the legal clerk Guppy and his friend in *Bleak House* (1852–3), visiting Lord Dedlock's house in Leicestershire: 'As is usually the case with people who go over houses, Mr Guppy and his friend are dead beat before they have well begun. They straggle about in wrong places, look at wrong things, don't care for the right things, gape when more rooms are opened, exhibit profound depression of spirits, and are clearly knocked up . . .'[32]

The difference between these two descriptions was that the great houses were now receiving most of their visitors from the middle and working classes: visiting – travel and tourism – had changed immeasurably in the half-century between Walpole and Dickens. At the beginning of the period, in the late eighteenth century, travel was expensive. In 1800 a trip from London to Scotland cost £14, when a prosperous journeyman earned about £30 or £40 a year.[33] Such a person could not afford to travel for pleasure. And if he had been able to, the next question was, was it worth it? In earlier centuries the answer would have been short and sweet: not really. In the 1630s the Lake District was described as 'a solitary wilderness . . . [with] nothing but hideous, hanging Hills' or, as Defoe saw it on his tour through Great Britain in the 1720s, 'a country eminent only for being the wildest, most barren and frightful of any that I have passed over in England, or even in Wales itself'. Scotland was no better. One visitor in 1754 said the countryside round Inverness was 'of a dismal, gloomy Brown, drawing upon a dirty Purple; and most of all disagreeable, when the Heath is in Bloom'. In 1775 Dr Johnson could not have agreed more, finding that 'An eye accustomed to flowery pastures and waving harvests is astonished and repelled by this wide extent of hopeless sterility.'[34] But, by the time Johnson pronounced, his view had become decidedly old-fashioned. Opinion was slowly moving from the conviction that natural wilderness was barbarous, through to a view that it was still barbarous, but it was also interesting, if not beautiful. Thomas Amory's fictional traveller John Buncle, twenty years before Johnson, had thought that the Lakes had a 'gloomy and tremendous air', but added that this 'strikes the mind with a horror that has something pleasing in it'.[35] This fondness for the 'terrible' was in 1757 given an imprimatur with Edmund Burke's *Enquiry into the Origin of Our Ideas of the Sublime and Beautiful*, which explored the idea that nature in its terrible rawness and vastness was rewarding, producing in the viewer 'a sort of delightful horror, a sort of tranquillity tinged with terror'.[36]

One of the writers who did most to popularize this shift was the Revd William Gilpin (1724–1804), who in 1768 published an *Essay on Prints*, in which he set out 'the Principles of picturesque Beauty'. Picturesqueness, he wrote in an unhelpfully circular fashion, was 'a term expressive of that peculiar kind of beauty, which is agreeable in a picture'.[37] While this may not have been very enlightening, he also toured much of the country and published a series of volumes that identified for his readers a 'new object of pursuit', the picturesque. In 1786 his *Observations on Cumberland and Westmorland relative chiefly to picturesque beauty* appeared, and in 1789 he got around to the Scottish Highlands. These books had enormous influence. What produced picturesqueness, according to Gilpin, could be straightforwardly learned. There was a fixed set of rules, with which either nature conformed – in which case it was admirable in the literal sense – or it did not, in which case it was of lesser value. Addison, in the *Spectator*, had begun to move towards this attitude years before: 'We find the Works of Nature still more pleasant, the more they resemble those of Art.'[38] Now Gilpin codified this, which enabled his followers to turn nature into a commodity that could be valued by comparing how closely it adhered to the rules. The very word 'landscape', which in the seventeenth century had meant a picture of the countryside, by the end of the eighteenth had come to mean the countryside itself, as though its primary function was for it to be viewed.

In *Northanger Abbey* (begun in 1798) Jane Austen gently laughed at Gilpin's followers and their passion for rules over personal observation: the naive Catherine Morland, who had previously thought the country-side around Bath very pretty, went for a walk with her new friends the Tilneys. Henry Tilney 'talked of fore-grounds, distances, and second distances – side-screens and perspectives – lights and shades; – and Catherine was so hopeful a scholar, that when they gained the top of Beechen Cliff, she voluntarily rejected the whole city of Bath, as unworthy to make part of a landscape.' Henry was absolutely 'delighted with her progress'.[39]

Wales, previously an inaccessible wilderness, now had good roads. Earlier generations had not credited its countryside as being worthy of interest: the neoclassical model admired new, well-built houses and formal gardens that imposed order and restraint on untidy, unruly nature. But the fashionable graveyard school of poets, with their reflections on the transitory nature of life, met happily with the vogue for Gothic romances to popularize ruins, in particular, as the ultimate travel accessory. Tintern Abbey became the most famous ruin in the country. In 1766 the *London Magazine* carried advertisements for Llangollen, promising it was in a 'Romantic Country' with 'the most ravishing prospects possible to be conceived'. By the end of the century Wales had become such a magnet for tourists in search of the picturesque that one visitor suggested that the road from Hay-on-Wye to Carmarthen had more gentlemen's carriages on it than did the roads around London.[40]

Cost restricted this hunt for the picturesque to gentlemen and their families, although soon there were complaints about the numbers travelling because it was fashionable to do so, rather than from any real interest. In 1798 James Plumptre, yet another literary clergyman, wrote a comic opera, *The Lakers*, in which 'Sir Incurious Harry' is 'so passionately fond of travelling, and the lakes, that he drives post through the country every year, with his carriage windows up, and never gets out but to eat, drink, and sleep'. Another character, Sir Charles Portinscale, arrives in the Lake District and, as his first action, goes to 'call at Crosthwaite's, and see the list' – that is, as with the circulating libraries of the spa towns, he goes to check the register to see who else of social consequence is in the area.[41] There were certain to be acquaintances, for the Lakes were now big business. Peter Crosthwaite was a former naval commander who kept the register of visitors, acted as a guide to tourists, and from 1783 kept a museum in Keswick. He also produced and sold maps with West's 'stations' marked on them, but by this time visitors wanted more entertainment than the views from 'stations' alone could produce, and this was supplied on the Lakes themselves. There was regular boat hire – if the visitors were 'gentlemen', on Ullswater they could even hire the Earl of Surrey's boat, which had eight rowers, French horns, and twelve brass cannon, which were fired in order to set off the famous echo. A guidebook in 1819 warned visitors against being short-changed: 'It is necessary to see that the full charge of gunpowder is put in, and properly rammed down; otherwise, much of the sublime effect . . . will be lost.' Robert Southey mocked, 'When one buys an echo, who would be content for the sake of saving eighteen pence, to put up with second best instead of ordering at once the super-extra-double-superfine?'[42]*

The development of Scotland as a tourists' paradise followed substantially the same path: from barren wilderness, through curiosity, to the Romantic notions of sublime grandeur. After the 1715 and 1745 rebellions, it became politically expedient for the government to bring the outer districts of Scotland into the mainstream, to dilute their regional self-sufficiency with a greater sense of belonging to the nation as a whole. Roads were improved, the better to move troops around should that again prove necessary, and also incidentally opening up the country to the interested traveller. But visitors were primarily attracted to Scotland by literary associations that could not have been foreseen. James Macpherson, literary forger (or not), did more, perhaps, to lure visitors to Scotland than anyone had ever done.†

Macpherson, born in 1736 in the Highlands, had in 1760 produced *Fragments of Ancient Poetry Collected in the Highlands of Scotland and Translated from the Gaelic or Erse Language*, to modest antiquarian interest. Then, between 1762 and 1765, he published what he claimed were his translations of genuine epic verse. Whether *Fingal, an Ancient Epic Poem* was truly an epic by Ossian, the son of the mythical Finn, dating from

---

* The Lakes were not the only place where this regatta-like air pervaded a beauty spot. In Maria Edgeworth's novel *Ennui* (1809) Lord Glenthorn travels to the Lakes of Killarney, where he finds 'such blowing of horns, such boating, such seeing of prospects, such prosing of guides, all telling us what to admire'.[43]
† Much of Macpherson's life and work is open to diametrically opposed interpretations. I will do my best to look only at the results of the publication of his Ossian poems, rather than exploring what they were, or how they came to be.

an unspecified, misty Celtic past, and translated by Macpherson from oral or written sources, or whether he had edited a more heterogeneous collection to form a coherent whole, supplying his own links as necessary, or whether he had simply made everything up, was (and still is) a matter for heated debate. But for the purposes of the creation of a Scottish tourist industry, what mattered was that the Ossian poems were wildly successful, creating a Romantic vision of Scotland's past that spread like wildfire in Britain and across Europe: in 1802 Napoleon commissioned a painting of *Ossian and his Warriors Receiving the Dead Heroes of the French Army*; by 1806 Ossian was 'almost proverbial in Germany for everything that is wild, romantic, melancholy, pathetic and sublime' – Goethe, Schiller, Mme de Staël, Schubert and Brahms were admirers, as was Thomas Jefferson in America.[44] Ossian was everywhere, and every place in Scotland that could claim the remotest connection with the poems was suffused with his glow: in Smollett's *Humphry Clinker* (1771), Jery feels 'an enthusiastic pleasure when I survey the brown heath that Ossian was wont to tread'. (This was the same brown heath that fifteen years before had been dismissed as 'dismal' and 'gloomy'.) Jery's Uncle Matt agrees: 'Every thing here is romantic beyond imagination.'[45] Because the poems were not strong on specifics, tourists could visit the isle of Rhum and assure themselves it was 'often mentioned in the Poems of Oscian [*sic*], by the name of Tongorma', even though Ossian just said Tongorma is 'probably' 'one' of the Hebrides. Likewise Thomas Gray assured himself that Ben More 'looks down on the tomb of Fingal', despite there being no assurance at all of any such thing in the poems themselves. Even humble oyster shells could be looked on as romantic objects, as they were 'so much signalized in the Poems of Oscian'.[46]

The idea of travel as an end in itself, rather than travelling to go somewhere, was part of a much larger experience, and most of it involved spending money. Travel, and what the places to which one travelled represented, had been neatly packaged, and the experience could be purchased, on location or at home. If one could not manage a trip to Scotland to tread in the footsteps of Ossian, then there were any number of shows that could take its place. William Bullock's London Museum at the Egyptian Hall in Piccadilly (see p. 264) had a model of Fingal's Cave. There were two theatrical productions at Sadler's Wells alone that had Fingal as their subject: a pantomime in 1805 and, in 1810, an 'aquadrama' called *The Spectre Knight*, both featuring the water effects for which the theatre was renowned.[47] For those outside London, or those who did not attend theatre, the Board of Trustees for the Encouragement of Arts and Manufactures in Scotland made collections of Scottish, Irish and Welsh songs, or at least a tidied-up approximation thereof, for publication. The secretary to the Board commissioned famous Scottish writers such as Burns and Scott to write words to traditional melodies, and then further commissioned famous composers – including Beethoven (who was paid £400) and Haydn (£300), as well as Hummel, Pleyel and Kozeluch – to write new arrangements of the melodies for pianoforte, with violin and cello obligato.[48] For the concert hall, there was Mendelssohn's *Hebridean Overture* (also known as *Fingal's Cave*), and his Scottish Symphony, both inspired by a trip to Scotland in 1829. 'Tour' music – music which portrayed the travels of a Romantic wanderer on his travels – was extremely popular. As well as Mendelssohn, Beethoven produced his *Ruins of Athens*, and Schubert his *Wanderer Fantasy*. Liszt made a speciality of the genre: his *Années de pèlerinage* appeared in three sections called 'years', and covered a typical Romantic itinerary – Italy and Switzerland in general, and more particularly the scenery loved by the Romantics, such as mountains ('Valée d'Obermann') and dark woods ('Aux cyprès de la Villa d'Este').*

There was a strong market for books describing travels, too: in the 1760s there were just seven books on tours of Scotland; by the 1820s there were fifty-three.[50] Engravings also brought the foreign into the domestic sphere. By 1752, *Six Select Views in the North of England* was available for 1 guinea, including for the first time topographical views of Windermere, Derwentwater and Ullswater; by the 1760s there were two series of the Lakes, engraved by Thomas Smith of Derby; Joseph

---

* This commodification of the restless Romantic rebel happened repeatedly, and with breathtaking speed. Goethe's *Sorrows of Young Werther*, one of the defining texts of the melancholy artistic temperament, was translated into English in 1779, and eagerly embraced by would-be rebels. But they did not pine after married women and commit suicide, as Goethe's hero Werther had done in the novel. Instead, some bought blue coats and yellow breeches, to dress like him; while others bought tea sets decorated with scenes from the novel, or engravings, or china figurines of the characters; or they went to theatrical versions; or to tableaux of the denouement at Vauxhall Gardens or at Mrs Salmon's Historical Waxworks, where they could see a waxwork scene of Charlotte mourning over Werther's grave. The cult of Byron a few decades later mirrored this closely, when instead of writing, young would-be poets took to wearing their hair brushed back in long curls, and their shirt collars turned down. *The Art of Tying the Cravat* in 1828 had a plate which showed how to create 'the cravat à la Byron'.[49]

Farington's *Views of the Lakes* appeared in 1789, and in 1792 one could also purchase aquatints of the same scenery.[51] In 1832, over a six-month period, *Court Magazine* included pieces on one aspect or another of Scottish tourist life in each of its six issues, including 'A Pleasure Party in the Highlands', 'The Widow's Summer Evening. A Scotch Ballad' and 'Deer Stalking in the Highlands', as well as 'Landscape Illustrations of the Prose and Poetical Works of Sir Walter Scott', which were issued every two weeks for an extra 2s. 6d.[52]

Clothes were very much part of the travel experience. 'Scotch Warehouses' began to sell tweeds, shepherd's check fabrics, and Shetland knits. The Royal Scotch Warehouse in London produced a trade card (unfortunately undated, but probably after 1854), describing itself as 'Scott Adie, Maison Speciale pour la vente des Etoffes et des Châles Ecossais, 115, Regent Street, Au coin de Vigo Street'.[53] This was Scotland not simply for the Londoner, but for the visitor to London: tourism at two removes. By 1840 newly revived – or invented – clan tartans were being sold in Manchester at Kendal, Milne, a full two years before Queen Victoria's first trip to Scotland, often said to be the start of the tartan craze. If she did not begin the craze for all things Scottish, however, she brought it immense exposure: after she had acquired Balmoral, she travelled in a tartan-upholstered barouche, her sons were inserted into kilts at every opportunity, Balmoral was decorated with thistle-embroidered curtains, while Albert produced their own 'Balmoral' tartan. Tartan-fever was a fashion everyone could enjoy, because it did not necessarily require a lot of money. At one end of the scale one could spend less than a shilling on tartan ribbons, or tartan edging for petticoats; at the other the Royal Scotch Jeweller in Regent Street was happy to supply 'national signs and emblems' worked in jewels.[54] At the Great Exhibition, James Locke offered 'Scotch tweeds for deer-stalking, riding, and walking; and for summer and warm climates. Cheviot wool tweeds, for shooting and country wear; specimens of the wool of which they are made in its various stages of manufacture. Regulation tartans, as worn by the Scotch Highland regiments. Scotch mauds [checked blankets or rugs], for riding and travelling. Ladies' clan-tartan shawls. Scotch linsey woolseys, for the sea-side.'[55] Scottish gear was no longer solely for Scotland, or the Scots, but designed for and sold to the stay-at-home.

For the travellers themselves, there were many additional items that were declared absolutely necessary, which had to be purchased before any trip could commence. Perhaps the most essential piece of equipment for tourists in search of the picturesque was a Claude glass, recommended by Thomas West in his *Guide*. This was a hinged case containing a convex piece of glass, about ten centimetres in diameter, placed over black foil to form a mirror. Viewers turned their backs on the landscape they wanted to admire and viewed it instead in the mirror; the glass made the details less distinct, evened out the colours, and thus made a real view into a picturesque one that more closely resembled the landscapes of the neoclassical painter Claude Lorrain. By purchasing glasses with different coloured foil backings, travellers could see what the landscape would have looked like had they been there at different seasons, or at different times of day: no one had any longer to get up early to see the dawn, and difficult winter travel could be replaced by a piece of blue foil. The Revd Joseph Plumptre (the author of *A Narrative of a Pedestrian Journey through some parts of Yorkshire, Durham, and Northumberland, and home by the Lakes and some parts of Wales* (1799), and not to be confused with the Revd James, the comic playwright) thought the traveller should carry a full complement of coloured glasses for best results: 'Though the objects were distant yet they were so large as to be seen with effect in the Gray. The Claude Lorrain gave it a most pleasing moonlight. But seen through the dark red or rather orange it was tremendous, and its burning glow called to mind that day "in which the Heavens shall pass away with a great noise, and being on fire shall be dissolved".'[56]

His namesake the Revd James Plumptre found these short cuts irresistibly comic. In *The Lakers*, Miss Beccabunga Veronica, a formidable traveller, goes into ecstasies over the rapidly altering view: 'Where's my Claude-Lorrain? I must throw a Gilpin tint over these magic scenes of beauty. (*Looks through the glass.*) How gorgeously glowing! Now for the darker. (*Looks through the glass.*) How gloomily glaring! Now the blue. (*Pretends to shiver with fright*). How frigidly frozen!'* Then she moves her companions around: 'Sir Charles, pray come and stand by me for the trunk of an old tree in the foreground. And I beg, Mr Botanist, you and Lydia and Speedwell will form yourselves into a picturesque group.'[57]

But it was more than picturesqueness that the tourist was after. Travellers journeyed encumbered by endless items that were to improve their

---

* Later she looks through her Claude glass at the man she has decided to marry: 'I'll throw a Gilpin tint over him ... Yes, he's gorgeously glowing. I must not view him with the other lights, for a husband should not be either glaringly gloomy, or frigidly frozen ...'

minds on the way. Miss Beccabunga Veronica tells her servant to 'bring my drawing-box instantaneously. I would not lose my sketches and manuscript of my tour for the world'; then he is to 'take my glasses and my drawing-book and my fishing-stool', and another trip is needed for her 'botany-box' of specimens.[58] Plumptre's joking was very close to reality at times. The first thing that the well-equipped traveller required was the new type of guidebook, which gave travellers advice rather than recounting, as Gilpin and his coevals had done, the author's own experiences of travel. By 1851 such books were plentiful. The Great Exhibition catalogue carried advertisements for half a dozen from one publisher alone, at prices ranging from 1s. to 10s. 6d.[59] Once the guidebook had been acquired, it told the travellers what else they needed. In 1779 Joseph Plumptre, on his tour of the Highlands and the north of England, walked 1,774.25 miles precisely – as he knew, because he carried a pedometer, as well as a Claude glass, sketchbooks, notebooks, a watercolour paint set, pens and pencils, a telescope, a barometer, maps, and tour books by Dr Johnson, Thomas Pennant 'and others', as well as a copy of Cowper's *Poems*.[60] He was not particularly unusual. In 1813 *The Cambrian Traveller's Guide* suggested taking 'a change or two of linen or stockings, a small compass, a prospecting glass, *Hull's Pocket Flora*, a portable press for drying plants, this interleaved Guide, a drinking horn', and something to eat.[61] (The 'interleaved' guide was a guidebook with blank pages for travellers to write down their own impressions, opposite the expert's description. Then there were traveller's notebooks which were printed up like account books, with headed columns for places seen, dates, times and the tourists' observations.) Dr William Kitchiner, in *The Traveller's Oracle* (1827), went even further. He recommended that one travel with:

> A portable Case of Instruments for Drawing
> A Sketch and a Note-Book
> Paper, Ink, – and Pins, Needles, and Thread
> A Ruby or Rhodium Pen*
> Pencils
> A folding one Foot Rule

* Rhodium, a reddish metal of the platinum group, had been discovered in 1803. According to an advertisement in *The Times* for Doughty's Perpetual Ruby Pen, which used rhodium in its nibs, 'The nibs of this perfect and permanent Pen are . . . [made from] materials which are neither corroded by ink nor worn by uses.' The pens were priced at 2 guineas, which gives some indication of the income-level of Dr Kitchiner's readers.[62]

OUR ARTIST ENJOYING HIMSELF IN THE HIGHLANDS. * * * *
"ON FINE HOT DAYS, I HAVE THIS TO CARRY ON MY BACK."

"ON WET DAYS, WITH MY WATERPROOF CLOTHING, I AM AS COM-
FORTABLE AS POSSIBLE."—*Extract from a Private Letter.*

The railways made travel cheaper, easier and more accessible to many, but even so, many felt loaded down by the equipment that was advertised. This *Punch* cartoon of 1852 mocks the overburdened holiday artist in the newly tourist-friendly Scotland. The waterproof in the second panel is interesting, because it was only with the Crimean War, the year after this cartoon appeared, that the wearing of waterproofs became widespread.

> A Hunting Watch with Seconds
> A Mariner's Compass
> A Thermometer
> A Barometer for measuring heights
> A One Foot Achromatic Telescope
> Dr Kitchiner's Invisible Opera Glass or Traveller's Vade Mecum
> A Night Lamp
> A Tinder Box
> A Traveller's knife
> Galoshes
> For the Table, Your own Knife, and Fork and Spoon will be no
>   small comfort
> A Welch Wig is a cheap and comfortable Travelling Cap
> No matter what the Weather or the Season, never go a journey
>   without an Umbrella (the stick of which may contain a
>   Telescope or a Sword) and a Great Coat.

He also advised taking, in case of illness, Dr Kitchiner's Peristaltic Persuaders (probably laxatives), a lancet, so that the traveller was never under the necessity of using one that might previously have 'been used in bleeding a person afflicted with an Infectious Disease', and, to prevent further illness, leather sheets for damp beds.[63]

It would have been impossible to imagine, when this list was published in 1827, that a mere four years later no one would ever have to travel with their own leather sheets again. The change came, as it did for so many things, with the railways. Travel had, if slowly, been opening up to a wider class of people for some time. Gilpin's original edition of his *Observations on the River Wye*, published in 1782, had been dotted with Latin epigrams; by the time a second edition appeared, in 1789, these had all been translated – a sign that the less educated were buying his books, and travelling about the country.[64] But it was not until 1830, when the Liverpool and Manchester Railway began to operate, that real change came. Within two weeks of the first scheduled passenger trains, a group of sightseers was carried from Liverpool to the Sankey Viaduct (see p. 32). By 1831 an arrangement had been made to carry 150 members of the Bennett Street Sunday School from Manchester to Liverpool and back again. The age of excursion travel had begun, with trips to a church bazaar, to the seaside, to the races. The trains carried groups of any sort to whatever type of entertainment they wanted. There were no moral values pinned on to the idea of excursion travel: anyone could do it.

Thomas Cook, a temperance campaigner in Market Harborough, Leicestershire, has become the by-word for excursion travel, but he was not the first to organize it – just the first to realize how truly enormous the market was. Initially Cook organized excursions not for profit, but as a way of amusing people while removing them from the temptations of drink. He arranged transport for a large number of people – the exact number is disputed, but it was around 500 – to travel from Leicester to Loughborough, at a cost of 1*s*., or ½*d*. per mile, for a temperance fête. The price included a return ticket, a lunch of bread and ham, a band, a temperance rally, and local dignitaries making speeches.* After this first, successful, expedition, he moved to Leicester, and set up as a retailer of many parts: he continued to publish temperance magazines while working as a bookseller, selling stationery, running a register office for servants and lodgings, and producing an almanac that listed temperance hotels nationwide. In 1843 he took a Sunday-school group to Derby during Leicester's race week, so that the children would not be exposed to pernicious influences (this was a recurring concern: in the late 1840s he

---

* It was this excursion, which travelled on a Monday, that I earlier suggested may have been a late appearance of 'St Monday'.

arranged for 3,000 children to travel to Birmingham to remove them from the proximity of race week in Leicester). Temperance and excursions were by now firmly linked. Chatsworth had been open to the public for the best part of a century, but in the 1840s it closed on Sundays, as many public places were being forced to do at the behest of Sabbatarian campaigners. The immediate rise in the number of people in the local pubs was noticeable, and 'general disturbances' were also reported. The Duke of Devonshire therefore reopened the house, and from then on, said Joseph Paxton – the Duke's agent as well as the designer of the Crystal Palace – 'there has been no difficulty about the public-house nuisance on Sunday in our district.'[65]

Cook's first excursion undertaken for profit rather than for temperance was to Liverpool from Leicester, Nottingham and Derby, taking in Caernarfon and Snowdonia, in the summer of 1845, and with it he established the system he and other excursion agents were to find so profitable. He negotiated with the four railways whose lines his itinerary covered, and the steamer to Wales, agreeing a fare of 14s. return for first-class and 10s. for second-class passengers – most likely taking 5 per cent of that as his own commission. He then travelled the entire route so that he could publish a pamphlet that gave prospective customers enticing details of the itinerary and the places of interest alongside, with hints for the novice traveller. This aroused so much interest that within three weeks he was able to schedule a second tour along the same route. Cook was the guide as well as the agent: he went with his passengers all the way, organizing and giving advice to neophytes.[66]

By late 1846 Cook had decided to branch out. He wrote a *Hand Book of a Trip to Scotland*, along the same lines as his earlier brochure, and arranged to sell the 800-mile round trip for 1 guinea – 93 per cent cheaper than the price for a similar tour in 1800. The 500 tickets went quickly. The first trip had teething troubles – he had not factored in time for rest stops, a tea stop in Preston was without tea, at Fleetwood the food arrived, but there was not enough of it – but these were partly compensated for by the enthusiasm with which the excursionists were greeted: there was a gun salute and a band at Glasgow, more bands again in Edinburgh, and a musical evening was staged to welcome 'English pleasure-money . . . to the heart of the Highlands'.[67] Cook, however, quickly remedied the early deficiencies, and soon he was managing trips to the Lake District, to Blackpool, to the Isle of Man, even to Belfast, where he conveyed 1,200 tourists. By 1860 he had carried over 50,000 excursionists to Scotland, and he was celebrated locally for bringing extraordinary prosperity to the region. Some of this prosperity came more directly than through tourist income. On his first visit to Iona, Cook had been so shocked by the poverty of the region that he began to solicit donations from his tourists, giving impassioned speeches to each group when they reached this island stop. By 1861 he had raised enough to purchase twenty-four fishing-boats for the community (one was named the *Thomas Cook*), as well as nets, tackle and books for the village school.[68] In 1853 he also took thousands of people to Dublin as part of an attempt to bring income into the city after the Famine.[69] But these charitable excursions only helped his business. Within a very short time, he was transporting his excursionists to France, then to Switzerland.*

Excursion travel opened up the world to many more of the middle classes; it also changed the way the world received travellers. Cook negotiated every detail with his foreign hosts: now inns that had a picturesque appearance but less picturesque bedbugs were no longer acceptable. Cook demanded running water, tea and general hygiene for his excursionists, or he would not return. Many hotels advertised that they had a table d'hôte dinner at four or five o'clock – much later than Europeans as a whole tended to eat – to suit the English. In Chamonix there was even a Hotel de Londres et d'Angleterre.[71] In 1906 a traveller looking back to the 1880s wrote that excursion travel had brought to 'foreign places' those 'cardinal British institutions – tea, tubs, sanitary appliances, lawn tennis, and churches'.[72]

Back in Britain, lodgings were changing under the impetus of the railways and excursion travel. The first railway hotel had been built in 1839. This was a station hotel, sited directly next door to Euston station by the railway company, to ease early-morning or late-night travel. In some ways it was simply a development of the inns which had acted as starting and end points for stagecoach travel. By the 1840s, however, the railway companies were buying or building hotels as destinations for

---

* This involved a slightly steeper learning curve than Scotland. On his first trip he had failed to arrange for a translator, although he spoke neither French nor German. Four sisters who were on the trip spoke both, and his constant cry was, 'Where are the ladies who know French and German? Forward, please – and say what this man is jabbering about.'[70]

travellers along their routes. In 1850 Oban, in Scotland, had 'a few' beds for visitors. In 1861 the Great Western Railway began to build its own hotel there. More and more – hotels and visitors – followed the arrival of the railways automatically. By the 1890s, Oban had fifteen fully-fledged hotels, as well as temperance hotels and 'numerous' lodging houses.[73] In 1913 there were ninety-two hotels in Great Britain owned by the railways.[74]

Cook was aided in his promotion of foreign travel by men like Albert Smith. Smith was the first impresario of the Alps. In 1851 he had climbed Mont Blanc, or so he said, and on his return he hired the Egyptian Hall (see p. 264) to put on an illustrated entertainment about the ascent. This entertainment – featuring a cardboard chalet, two chamois (it is unclear whether they were real or cardboard), 'several' St Bernard dogs and water lilies floating in a tub to represent the scenery – was so successful that he continued to present it for nine years, adding new bits all the time. (He was even invited to re-create it privately for the Prince of Wales, and then later for the Queen.) Switzerland became the fashion. 'The Mont Blanc Quadrille' and 'Les Echos du Mont Blanc' appeared as sheet music; children bought the Game of Mont Blanc to play at home.[75]

Yet, however popular Smith's lectures were, however educational Cook's tours, there were many who were appalled by mass tourism. In his essay 'Of Kings' Treasures' in *Sesame and Lilies*, John Ruskin – who was all for humanity as long as it was kept a long way away from him – stormed:

> The French revolutionists made stables of the cathedrals of France; you have made race-courses of the cathedrals of the earth. Your *one* conception of pleasure is to drive in railroad carriages round their aisles, and eat off their altars . . . [There is no] foreign city in which the spread of your presence is not marked among its fair old streets and happy gardens by a consuming white leprosy of new hotels . . . The Alps themselves, which your own poets used to love so reverently, you look upon as soaped poles in a bear garden, which you set yourself to climb and slide down again with 'shrieks of delight'.*

This hysterical dislike, verging on fear, was not peculiar to him alone. The Revd Francis Kilvert in humble Christian charity declared that British

---

* Ruskin wasn't agitated only by tourists defacing the Alps. He also complained of 'the stupid herd of modern tourists [who] let themselves be emptied, like coals from a sack, at Windermere'.[76]

tourists were 'noxious animals . . . vulgar, ill-bred, offensive and loath-some', while the novelist Charles Lever feared that Cook was bringing to Europe 'everything that is low-bred, vulgar and ridiculous'.

That was only the beginning. The *Pall Mall Gazette* was passionately against Cook's travellers, seeing them as doing that fatal thing, attempting to educate themselves out of their class. The tourist showed his 'ignorance, stupidity, and incapacity for enjoyment with the utmost naiveté', thinking 'the grand attraction is that he can qualify himself cheaply and quickly for talking glibly about places and things, familiarity with which he fancies confers some kind of distinction'. Others referred to 'Cook's Hordes', or 'Cook's Vandals' – 'low' and 'vulgar' people, 'an irregular procession of incongruities'.[77]

The level of vitriol is fascinating. It was not as if Cook were bringing parties of hard-drinking navvies or indigent street-sweepers to the boule-vards of Paris. The working classes could not afford these trips, and they could not take enough time off work even had they had the money. Working-class excursionists were content with day trips to a beauty spot, or the seaside. Cook's tours to Europe were made up of doctors, of schoolmasters, of clergymen, lawyers, prosperous merchants and their wives and daughters. Cook himself was under no illusion about how his groups were viewed. He recorded having met a woman in Scotland who suggested to him that 'places of interest should be excluded from the gaze of the common people, and . . . kept only for the interest of the "select" of society'. But, he wrote, 'it is too late in this day of progress to talk such exclusive nonsense; God's earth, with all its fullness and beauty, is for the people; and railroads and steamboats are the result of the common light of science, and are for the people also.'[78]

This was the battleground: exclusivity vs access. The railways had introduced a new phenomenon, the day-tripper. In the 1820s it had taken six hours to get from London to Brighton, at a cost of 12s.; by 1835, 117,000 visitors a year were travelling that way, but they were staying in the town, and spending money in the town – at twelve hours for the round trip, they could hardly do otherwise. In 1841 the Brighton-to-London railway line was opened, with high fares designed to preserve a 'superior traffic'. But then a new chairman – Rowland Hill, of Post Office fame – slashed prices, promoting excursion trains at traditional working-class holiday times, such as Easter, Whitsun, August race week and, especially, Sundays.[79] By 1850, 73,000 passengers arrived at the

Brighton railway station in one week, and in 1862, on Easter Monday, 132,000 arrived in one day, on a trip that took only two hours from London.[80] Now the town's residents and shopkeepers tried to persuade the railway company to raise its day-return fares, so as to 'improve' the class of people venturing down to the seaside. Day-trippers, they warned, brought no money into the town – apart from what was spent on drink. They carried their own food, they didn't shop, but just walked by the sea; few even went to the Chain Pier (opened in 1823 and one of the first pleasure piers), where the right kind of visitors paid their admission, listened to the band, and took a select walk among select people.[*][82]

The seaside population was used to being select. The seaside had been the haunt of the royal and the socially aspirant for a century. For much of the population over the previous centuries, sea bathing had been an aberration. When Brighton was the most supremely fashionable place to be, basking in the patronage of the Prince Regent from his first visits in the 1780s to his death in 1830, the season ran from October to March. Clearly no one was expecting to swim then. Instead, the recommended exercise for health was 'taking the air', either in a 'carriage outing' or by promenading along the front. But sea bathing for health was gradually taking hold. When Smollett went sea bathing in Nice in the 1760s, his English doctor warned him that it would kill him. He was slightly old-fashioned (and Smollett was in very poor health), for at almost the same time George III was encouraged to bathe at Weymouth, for the sake of his health. (A band followed him out to sea in a bathing machine to play 'God Save the King' as he swam.) As late as 1814 Jane Austen had the (old-fashioned, and resolutely hypochondriac) Mr Woodhouse declare that 'the sea is very rarely of use to any body, I am sure it almost killed me once'. If one must go to the seaside, he thought, the best thing was to find a place where one could get 'lodgings . . . quite a way from the sea'.[83] For even then, at the beginning of the nineteenth century, sea bathing was a novelty – although it was becoming a good

---

* A seaside pier was, initially, simply a way of getting steamer passengers from the boat to the shore. In 1814 the first big pier opened at Ryde, on the Isle of Wight; before it was built, passengers had been carried by porters from the beach to the boat and back again. Soon piers were viewed as a logical extension of the promenade, and opened to those who were taking the air or exercise, for a fee. It was only when the railways became a permanent feature, and therefore the piers' primary function vanished, that they became instead places of entertainment.[81]

commercial proposition, replacing the earlier upper-class health craze, the spa.

Bath was the model that every spa aspired to – or, when it became unfashionable, that every spa reacted against. The springs at Bath had been considered medicinal for over a hundred years: Charles II had brought Catherine of Braganza to Bath in the hope that the waters would promote fertility; his brother James repeated the pattern with Mary of Modena. Queen Anne went there looking for a cure for her gout and dropsy. One had to be ill or unhappy to 'take the waters' in the sixteenth and seventeenth centuries, when 'bathing' consisted of sitting in a coarse smock in tubs of heated chalybeate, or iron-rich, spring waters. By the late seventeenth and eighteenth centuries this had been modified, and now drinking a glass or two of the waters was said to produce the same results. As this could be done while fully clothed, and in a social setting, it was a far more attractive proposition. But what made Bath successful was not that its waters were more potent than other chalybeate springs. It was instead that from the eighteenth century canny entrepreneurs (including John Palmer, pp. 128–9) had arranged for the judicious building of public and private spaces, to create an environment in which the pleasures of aristocratic social life could be enjoyed while the medicinal water-drinking was undertaken. This building boom was facilitated by concurrent new transport links. There was the Avon Navigation scheme between Bristol and Bath, which saw the first barge navigate the river in 1727, and, more to the point for the fashionable, which brought Princess Amelia from Bristol to Bath in 1728. By 1740, two daily passenger boats augmented the stagecoach service, which between 1740 and 1777 averaged from 32 to 46 coaches a week along the new turnpike road; by 1800, there were 147 weekly runs scheduled, and the travel time to London had dropped from 36 hours in 1750 to just over 10 in 1790.[84]

Between 1660 and 1750, the population of Bath rose from 1,500 to 6,000 permanent residents; by 1801 there were 33,000 permanent residents, and as early as 1750 another 12,000 visitors crowded into the town during the season.[85]* A leisure town needed visitors, of course, but

* The period that the 'season' encompassed altered over time. In the early part of the eighteenth century there were two seasons, spring and autumn; from mid-century the autumn season of one year began to extend until it reached the opening of the next spring season. By 1780 there was just one season, lasting from September to May.

it also needed a support system to service them. By 1744 there were 120 licensed chairmen to carry visitors about Bath in the then-fashionable sedan chairs; by 1800 there were 340.[86] Inns, shops and coffee houses needed staff to do the heavy work such as carrying coals and water, and mucking out stables, as well as serving staff. The luxury-goods trades needed tailors, seamstresses, jewellers, leather tanners and others to produce their goods, as well as those whose job it was to sell them. The extent of these luxury trades in Bath can be seen from the apprentice records. Within the small permanent population of the 1720s and 1730s there was just one single apprentice who signed his indentures to a cabinet-maker in those decades; fourteen did so between 1741 and 1760. In the same years, the number of apprentice jewellers went from one to six. There were no lacemaker or milliners' apprentices at all in the earlier period, but eleven were indentured in the latter.[87] Between 1724 and 1769 the most common apprenticeships were in shoemaking, carpentry, tailoring, barbering, wig-making, baking, grocery and provisioning, chandlery and similar trades: the service industries. They were there to provide for the visitors, whose business was consumption: consumption of the waters, consumption of entertainment, of leisure, of shopping. Milsom Street, the main fashionable shopping street, supplied 'the real or imaginary wants' of everyone, wrote Pierce Egan.[88] Many shops either started in these spa towns or quickly established branches there. Marshall and Snelgrove, the London draper, opened its second branch in Scarborough, then moved on to a third in Harrogate. Messrs Clark and Debenham, also of London, bought an interest in a shop in Cheltenham, and then opened on their own in Harrogate by 1844. James Jolly, of 'Jolly's of Bath' fame, had opened his shop year round in Milsom Street by 1838. He too saw the retail importance of spa towns, extending shortly thereafter to Margate.[89]

By the early nineteenth century, Bath was double the size it had been in the sixteenth century, and it was, apart from London, the town with the largest commercial entertainment market in the UK. It had the Pump Room, where the waters were dispensed and the elite gently socialized, and it had three assembly rooms, a theatre, and an unknown number of libraries and reading rooms, coffee houses and shops. Its first pleasure gardens were created in 1709. These were a form of entertainment enjoyed throughout the century, providing the middle and upper classes with a place to meet, listen to music and walk in pleasant surroundings, while the working classes could attend too, in unsegregated pleasure. The most famous pleasure gardens in Bath, Spring Gardens, opened in the 1730s, and by the 1760s it routinely staged public and private breakfasts, teas, evening events, concerts and fireworks. Admission was 2s. 6d. for the season, and for that one could walk through the gardens, admiring the artificial cascade and listening to the orchestra. By the 1790s, as private entertainment began to supersede public pleasure (see below), Spring Gardens found itself in a death struggle against strong competition. It joined forces with Grosvenor Gardens, which had added the enticements of a bowling green, archery competitions, a maze, fishponds and pleasure boats. In 1801 Sydney Gardens trumped them both by adding a grotto, winter opening times, horse riding and illuminated walks – and, as a knockout blow, the Prince of Wales had attended a concerts there.[90] (For more on pleasure gardens, see pp. 276–81.)

Concerts had become an important part of Bath life (for concert life in general, see Chapter 9). In 1704 there had been only 'half a dozen' musicians in the town, on temporary contracts with private entrepreneurs and paid by the week; then the Pump Room engaged musicians to play for the season both during the morning promenade at the Pump Room, and in the evenings at the assembly rooms. By 1766 William Herschel had become the organist at the Octagon Chapel, and he soon had so many private pupils among the visitors and residents that more than twenty private concerts a year were necessary to display their abilities – augmented by yet more professional musicians.[91]* Herschel's concerts were rivalled by those of Thomas Linley and his eight musical children. Linley ran the concerts at the New Assembly Rooms from 1766, and made a point of featuring, in particular, his daughter Elizabeth – a soprano of surpassing beauty – until her marriage to the playwright Richard Brinsley Sheridan ended her public performances. Her fame was rivalled by her brother Thomas, a promising composer, who had produced twenty violin concertos, an oratorio, several sonatas and a

---

* This was not, of course, his claim to fame. Herschel (1738–1822) had been a military bandsman in Hanover, and to avoid impressment had fled to England, where first he led the band of the Durham militia. After he settled in Bath his hobbies, astronomy and instrument building, were permitted to come to the fore, especially after 1781, when he became the first person in the modern age to discover a planet, Uranus. In 1782 his increasing astronomical reputation produced a pension from George III, in return for which he left Bath for Windsor, to be on call should a member of the royal family care to examine the skies under his supervision.

comic opera by the time of his early death in a boating accident aged twenty-two.

But the main entertainments of the spas were for the moment the public entertainments, the subscriptions balls and assemblies. These were sponsored either by the civic authorities or by the owners of private assembly rooms, and a seasonal subscription cost enough to exclude all but the 'select'. While the promoters made a nice profit, for much of the eighteenth century a polite fiction was maintained that the subscription was merely a token payment, rather than a fee for a commercial service. *The Original Bath Guide* of 1811 listed a typical week's entertainment for the visitor during the season: on Mondays there was a dress ball, Tuesdays a card assembly, Wednesdays a concert, and Thursdays a fancy-ball. In general, the visitor paid for a series of balls or entertainments. The dress-ball or fancy-ball subscription cost 14*s*. for a man on his own, or 26*s*. for a man who could then escort two women to twenty-eight dress balls. These began at seven, and ended 'precisely at eleven, even in the middle of a dance'. Concerts cost 5½ guineas for tickets to nine concerts, giving entry to one man and two women, or £4 10*s*. for two tickets for nine concerts, 'including two choral nights'. Just as with the entertainment, the card assemblies were on a subscription basis, with men paying 1 guinea for the season, and women 5*s*. for access to the card rooms when one evening a week it was ladies' night.[92]

With the end of the French wars, however, and the revival of travel to the Continent for the wealthy, Bath began to run into trouble. By 1815 the public balls were attracting fewer than 400 'residents and visitors', and the order of those words was important. The residential aspect of Bath was now replacing the seasonal influx. The fashionable were beginning to turn their backs on public leisure, preferring to enjoy their entertainment in private, where they would not have to mix with the newly arriving middle classes. As early as 1779, *The New Prose Bath Guide* had worried that 'the Upper Town [or fashionable] inhabitants seem to have . . . a strong tendency to withdraw themselves', while in 1830 another observer dated this phenomenon even earlier, suggesting that it was from the 1760s that 'Late dinners began, by little and little, to interfere with the regular early attendance at the Upper and Lower Rooms: and fatal "at homes" on the ball nights, to prevent that attendance altogether . . . Taste and fashion . . . chose for solace and display, the private rather than the public arena.'[93] The fashion, from the 1790s, for visitors to take a house rather than simply lodgings added to the opportunities to entertain at home. Bath had become a place where the 'genteel' resided elegantly, and probably rather inexpensively. In *Persuasion*, the Eliot family move to Bath because Sir Walter 'might there be important at comparatively little expense'.[94] By the early nineteenth century the aristocratic level of society was no longer pouring into Bath for a few months at a time, but instead the prosperous middle classes were making it their home. When the Lower Assembly Rooms burned down in 1820, rather than a similar place of public amusement being put up on the site, a scientific and literary institution was built there instead. A decade later, the fashionable shops remained open all year, instead of only in the winter season – a further sign of how the residents had become the primary consumers in the town. But while they were prosperous, they were not necessarily expecting to pass their time in a round of frivolous leisure, as they thought the upper classes whom they had replaced had done: in 1833 the Bath races were reduced from three days to two.[95] In a similar shift, the updated version of *The Original Bath Guide* of 1811, which was published sometime around 1870, had no information at all about balls and only the briefest mention of concerts, and the list of Pump Room activities was replaced by a list of parks. The guide contained pages on schools, on hospitals and on churches – on the civic structure required by residents, not visitors.[96] 'Rational recreation' had taken over from what many now regarded as frivolous idleness.

As early as 1815 a small spa in Wiltshire had tacitly recognized Bath's decline: it hoped, it advertised, to 'vie in every desirable convenience with Cheltenham and Leamington' – it didn't trouble to mention Bath. Cheltenham and Leamington were, in the nineteenth century, the competition. At the height of the spas' reign there had been at one time or another about 175 spas across the country (although not all operating at once). By 1815, with competition from both Continental travel and the seaside, smaller spas with no entertainment began to close; in the early nineteenth century only about forty remained operational.[97] Cheltenham had first promoted its spa waters in the 1730s, but the spa element of the town had not flourished until George III came there to take the waters in 1788; this comparative neglect may have helped in the long term, because in the meantime it had become a prosperous market town. By the early nineteenth century both Cheltenham and

Leamington had assembly rooms, hotels, baths, theatres and inns. Yet, unlike Bath, both towns had other economic activities to rely on, and other pastimes to draw visitors and residents alike. Leamington was helped by its development in the nineteenth century as a hunting town – Lord Middleton installed his hounds there in 1811, and within a year there were another four hunts in the neighbourhood. Cheltenham from 1818 had a race meeting in August which drew thousands – in 1819 as many as 20,000 spectators may have come for the races – and when the flat racing died away, a popular steeplechase event replaced it in 1844.[98]

Robert Elliston, who was one of the main economic movers of Leamington as a spa, demonstrates how, by this time, the spa was a predominantly leisure-based, rather than health-based venue. Elliston, an actor and theatre manager, had started his career performing in Bath. Although he had moved successfully to London by 1804, he knew how profitable entertainment could be in towns where the main occupation was leisure. In 1817 he held the lease to the theatre in Leamington as well as having a circuit of theatres elsewhere. In 1821 he added a ballroom to his Leamington theatre, and downstairs he opened a tea room, a reading room and the rather elaborately entitled 'County Library of Research' (which claimed to have 12,000 volumes), as well as, behind the building, a garden with promenades. Elliston attempted to cover the leisure market in several of the places where he had theatres – he also owned the Ranelagh Pleasure Gardens Exotic Nursery in London, which had walks, a bandstand for military concerts, gala nights, fireworks and fêtes.[99]

The next big change came with the first railway into Leamington, which arrived in 1844, with six trains a day between Coventry and Milverton, a small village halfway between Leamington and Warwick. In its first week of operation it carried 2,500 passengers. There was also a 'Shakespeare Coach' to ferry passengers onward from Milverton to Stratford.

Stratford and Shakespeare tourism had had a long history. New Place, which Shakespeare had bought in 1597, was owned in the middle of the eighteenth century by the Revd Francis Gastrell, an irritable clergyman, who had bought the house in complete ignorance of its history. When he found himself unable to stop tourists penetrating the grounds to search for a mulberry tree Shakespeare was supposed to have planted there, he chopped down the tree; then, after a quarrel with the parish about the rates he owed, he tore down the house itself. The house was gone as a shrine, and so new irons of bardolatry were found. A workman named Thomas Sharp claimed that Gastrell had sold him the wood from the tree. He set up as a manufacturer of Shakespeare relics, and produced an endless supply of boxes, cases, drinking vessels and even furniture. In 1769 one recipient of a wooden inkstand and two small wooden heads of Shakespeare also received an affidavit: 'I have add the pleasure of carving things of one sort or another ever since the Jubilee [see below] . . . and if you should be anyways dubeious as it's not the tree, I will come upon oath that it his of the real tree' (*sic*).[100] Thirty years later, he was still affidaviting away (although his spelling had improved miraculously): 'I do hereby declare, & take my solemn oath, upon the four Evangelists, in the presence of Almighty God, that I never had worked, sold, or substituted any other wood, than what came from, & was part of the said tree, as or for Mulberry-wood.'[101] Attention also turned to Shakespeare's probable birthplace, in Henley Street. In the late eighteenth century half of it was occupied by the Hart family, the descendants of Shakespeare's sister Joan, and run as a butcher's shop, while the other half had become an inn, the Swan and Maidenhead. The actor David Garrick, who was to do so much to promote Shakespeare-worship, said that he just knew, somehow, that the front room over the shop was the room in which Shakespeare had been born.

Garrick had, throughout his career, worked to make theatre-going less of a rowdy entertainment in which the audience expected to contribute as much as the performers to its own amusement, and more of an art form, in which the audience was to be entertained, certainly, but also to be educated.* Part of this education process centred around Shakespeare. In 1769 Garrick was approached by the Corporation of Stratford, who

---

* This audience participation took forms that today seem barely conceivable: orange-sellers threw their wares and caught coins in exchange; whores promenaded through the permanently lighted auditorium looking for customers; even the respectable middle classes sitting quietly in their boxes were not segregated from the hubbub all about them. They had come to be seen and to see their friends, and sometimes they might have more contact with the rest of the audience than they might have wished. *Lloyd's Evening Post* in 1776 reported that 'A fellow who sat on the sixth row of the Upper Gallery threw a Keg (which he had brought full of liquor into the House) over the Gallery front. It fell upon a lady's head, who sat in that part of the Pit which was railed into the Boxes, but the Lady's hair being dress'd in high *ton*, the artificial mountain luckily prevented the mischief that otherwise might have been occasioned.' By comparison, Boswell's story of entertaining 'the audience prodigiously by imitating the lowing of a cow . . . I was so successful in this boyish frolic that the universal cry of the galleries was "*Encore* the cow! *Encore* the cow!"' seems charmingly innocuous.[102]

hoped that he would donate a statue of Shakespeare to their new town hall. He did much better, suggesting for the just-passed bicentenary of Shakespeare's birth a three-day jubilee festival to be held in Stratford. His proposal was very much along the lines of a public entertainment in one of the big London pleasure gardens, or a spa town: there would be balls, public breakfasts, oratorios, fireworks, a masquerade, a horse race and, as the culmination, a great pageant with Garrick at the helm – which last was, however, rained off.

Garrick was a master of presentation. He was a shrewd investor in several newspapers, including the *Public Advertiser*, the *St James's Chronicle*, the *Morning Post* and the *London Packet*, which guaranteed good notices for his work and made it possible for him and his friends to insert editorial puffs as well as advertisements. He was also one of the earliest users of engravings to present the image of himself he wanted the world to celebrate. (A recent biographer thinks that Garrick may have appeared in as many as 450 paintings and engravings.) He was careful always to travel with engravings of himself, which he gave away as film stars now give photographs. When he went to Paris in 1765 he sent home an urgent plea: 'I must desire You to send me by ye first opportunity *six* prints from Reynolds's picture, You may apply to ye Engraver . . . he will give you good ones, if he knows they are for Me.'[103]

A man used to promoting himself in this way was not going to let some rain slow him down. His jubilee pageant may have been washed out, but that would not prevent it from being seen. As manager of the Theatre Royal, Drury Lane, in London, he instead scheduled the pageant at the start of the new season. But Covent Garden, Drury Lane's great rival, had a much better record as producers of spectacle, and it jumped in first, with an adaptation of a play by the French diplomat–playwright Philippe Néricault Destouches called *La Fausse Agnes*, which had been staged posthumously by the Comédie-Française in 1759. George Colman, Covent Garden's manager, simply reset it in Stratford, added an old end-piece of his own called *Man and Wife*, a routine farce for which he wrote a prologue set in Stratford's White Lion inn – mostly because he knew Garrick intended to do the same – and sprinkled in a handful of Stratford references, adding a Shakespeare pageant after Act I, again to copy Garrick, using scenery of Stratford itself. That Colman's was a cynical commercial move he saw no reason to disguise. In *Man and Wife* he had the landlady say that everyone was 'all as busy as bees about the jubalo', although she confessed that she was not quite sure what it is, 'but it is one of the finest things that ever was seen – There is the great little gentleman [i.e. Garrick, only five foot six] from London, and . . . eating and drinking, and processioning, and masquerading, and horse-racing, and fireworks – So gay – and as merry as the day is long.'[104]

Garrick's pageant for Stratford had been a deification of Shakespeare the author – or perhaps it was Shakespeare the man. He had planned tableaux of scenes from the plays, processions of actors dressed in character, music by Thomas Arne and Samuel Arnold (including a song entitled 'Sweet Willy-o'), and at the end Garrick's own 'Ode to Shakespeare' was to be declaimed, but there were no actual performances of, or even recitations from, Shakespeare's plays themselves. Yet Garrick's motives were not cynical, as Colman's had been. Back in London he fought Covent Garden with its own weapons – with spectacular staging and scenery. (For more on theatre as spectacle, see pp. 312ff.) His jubilee pageant opened a week after Covent Garden's, but with a far better production. His scenery painters had produced wondrously realistic perspective views of Stratford sights, including the parish church and the yard of the White Lion inn, and the stage was filled with a dizzying succession of characters. The pageant itself lasted an hour and a half, with 115 extras. Each group of Shakespearean characters was presented as a little dramatic unit, with a banner informing the audience which play the characters were representing. (Garrick had learned from Covent Garden's experience, where the audiences had had some trouble in telling the plays apart.) Each group mimed short scenes from major episodes in nineteen of the plays. There was no shortage of spectacle: *A Midsummer Night's Dream* had sixteen children playing fairies, while Oberon and Titania were brought onstage in a carriage drawn by Cupids and Butterflies. Other characters rode onstage on horseback, and Mrs Abington – 'the unrivalled female ornament of the British stage in Comedy'[105] – was pulled on in a chariot drawn by five satyrs, while Mrs Barry, as the Tragic Muse, was in a chariot pulled by the Demon of Revenge carrying a burning sword, and accompanied by Furies, and Mars with his soldiers. Other special effects included the storm scene from *King Lear*, a cauldron produced by demons for *Macbeth*, and Cleopatra's barge accompanied by Persian guards, Negro slaves and pages with peacock fans (as well as two pages rather mysteriously carrying umbrellas).[106]

Garrick's jubilee pageant was a runaway success, and had to be repeated over the next twenty nights.* His contemporaries saw the irony that Garrick, the promoter of theatre as a serious art form, should find such a triumph in dumbshow spectacle – or, as one wrote,

> Turned useful mirth and salutary woe
> To idle pageantry and empty shew . . .
> To solemn sounds see sordid scene-men stalk
> And the great Shakespeare's vast creation – walk![107]

Dozens of other theatres and playwrights followed this success – some didn't even trouble to wait to see if it *was* a success: George Saville Carey's *Shakespeare's Jubilee* had been published during the jubilee itself, and had Falstaff and the witches from Macbeth on a trip to Stratford. Other blatant thefts of Garrick included Colman (again) with *Scrub's Trip to the Jubilee*, Francis Gentleman's *The Stratford Jubilee*, and many more, right down to an anonymous play entitled *Garrick's Vagary: or, England Run Mad*. (The author was perhaps fortunate it was anonymous. The *Biographia Dramatica*'s entry on this play reads, in its entirety, 'Sad stuff indeed!') By 1770 the concept of the jubilee pageant was so familiar that it had even filtered down to pantomime. *The Harlequin's Jubilee* had a statue of the actor–manager John Rich dressed as Harlequin, surrounded in a final tableau by adoring pantomime characters.[108]

After the jubilee, Stratford was even more a place of pilgrimage than it had been before. Byng visited the town in 1785, and 'pilfer'd (in common with other collectors) from the roman pavement, at the head of Shakesperes grave-stone, a tessellated tile, which I hid in my pocket; and which I should suppose will be honor'd and admired by every spectator'. He was also shown by Mrs Hart what she described as 'Shakespears old chair, and I have been often bid a good some of money for it, It has been carefully handed down on record by our family; but people never thought so much of it till after the jubilee, and now see what pieces they have cut from it, as well as from the old flooring of the bed room!'[109] He bought a small piece of that too, about the size of 'a tobacco stopper', and later went back to buy a crossbar. This was The Chair That Wouldn't Die: however many crossbars were cut off, it continued to renew itself. In 1790 it was sold for 20 guineas to a Polish princess;

---

* It was also a lasting success: in 1775 Garrick was still using it to draw in the crowds. That year the character of Venus was portrayed by a rising young actress named Sarah Siddons, while her Cupid was a four-year-old Thomas Dibdin, the son of the composer, and later to be a playwright and theatrical manager in his own right.

when Washington Irving visited twenty-five years later, it was back in place. Irving was also shown 'the shattered stock of the very matchlock with which Shakespeare shot the deer, on his poaching exploit.* There, too, was his tobacco box ... the sword also with which he played Hamlet; and the identical lanthorn with which Friar Laurence discovered Romeo and Juliet at the tomb!' Irving drily said that he was 'ever willing to be deceived, where the deceit is pleasant, and costs nothing'.[111]

The Stratford Birthplace Committee was formed in the middle of the nineteenth century, when the Henley Street house – together with its neighbours – was put up for sale. The Committee hoped to raise enough money to buy the building and preserve it for the nation. They did manage to buy it, but their method of preservation would not be recognized as such today. Soon after the successful bid, the neighbouring houses in the row were knocked down, and the actual timber of the birthplace itself was replaced, the old wood going the way of the mulberry tree, sold for souvenirs. By 1860 there was a 'new' birthplace on the site, showing how it would have looked if it had not gone through a couple of centuries of wear and tear, and enthusiastic preservation – and if, in fact, it had ever been the site of Shakespeare's birth at all.[112] No one much cared, because it was the business of Shakespeare that was so important, and visitors continued to pour in in ever-increasing numbers to adore at the shrine.

It was iron, however, not poetry, that moved most of the population to what had become by the nineteenth century their favourite holiday destination: the seaside. Earlier, as we saw, the seaside had been a fashionable resort for the few. Mass transport created a new anxiety, as it turned the sea into the destination of choice for the many. Before the railways, steamers had serviced a few sea- and riverside locations. Londoners had frequently travelled down the Thames by steamer. By 1825 Gravesend was a major destination for Londoners out for a pleasant

---

* The hunting expedition had a history that was in many ways representative of the entire Shakespeare industry. In 1709 the poet laureate, Nicholas Rowe, recounted how Shakespeare had once been arrested for poaching deer in Charlecote Park. The revelation that Charlecote had not, in the sixteenth and seventeenth centuries, had a park only saw the story transposed to Fulbrook, a nearby estate. Scott included this legend in *Kenilworth*, and it thereafter became fact. Apart from anything else, it meant that those wishing to follow in Shakespeare's footsteps could visit a charming Tudor mansion rather than a dreary inn-cum-butcher's shop.[110]

Sunday, and most got there by steamer; in 1835 over 670,000 passengers a year arrived in this way. The Margate Steamboat Company, at the same time, was carrying 1,000 passengers every Sunday between London and Margate.[113] Even after the arrival of the railways, steamers remained a useful link: the *London Conductor*, a guide to London for visitors to the Great Exhibition, listed numerous connections and alternative journeys: Gravesend cost 6*d*. by steamer from Blackwall, whereas a third-class rail ticket was 18*d*. For Ramsgate the excursionist was recommended to travel by steamer rather than rail, as it was both cheaper and 'pleasanter'.[114]

Scotland also relied heavily on the steamers: sea-going paddle

Seaside holidays became increasingly popular with the arrival of the railways. In this *Illustrated London News* engraving from 1864, the convenience of a day out in Ramsgate is shown: the Chatham and Dover Railway terminus is virtually on the beach itself.

steamers were used on the firths to connect towns and villages to the big cities: when Felix Mendelssohn was in Glasgow in 1829 he saw seventy steamers, forty of which had daily sailings. In 1810, Walter Scott had been told that only 'half a dozen persons exclusive of yourself' had seen Loch Coruisk.* After Scott had recorded the 'exquisite . . . savage scene' it presented in *The Lord of the Isles* (1815), it became a regular stop on the tourist trail, reached by scheduled steamer.[115] By 1887 Baedeker recommended the weekly steamer for tourist trips to Skye, once one had 'telegraphed the day before to the landlord of the Slighachan Hotel to

---

* And, one assumes, the local inhabitants.

send a guide (and ponies if required; advisable for ladies)' to meet one at the pier.[116]

The railways and the seaside, however, were soon inextricably linked. Sometimes seaside towns developed because of the railways. Morecambe became more than a small village only after the line reached it. Bournemouth had appeared on the map as a small hamlet in 1812; in 1841 there were still fewer than thirty buildings in the village in total, but once the railway extended to the town in 1870 it provoked a sudden surge, and by 1880 the population had reached 16,859.[117] Other towns of some substance already, such as Skegness, later in the century actively sought the railway as a way of encouraging further development. What Brighton, in its mid-century attempts to roll back the railways, had failed to notice was that visitors of any sort created demand and, with it, prosperity in their towns. In the decade before the opening of the Brighton line the population of Brighton had been almost stagnant at about 40,000 people. By 1851 it had grown to 65,000, and the number of lodging-house keepers had leaped from 136 to 573[118] – a very visible sign that Brighton was not being overrun only by day-trippers.

Instead, it was becoming a resort of visitors – by the day, by the week, and for the whole season – and catering to the needs of those visitors was lucrative work. Just as Jolly's of Bath and other shops had discovered the commercial benefits of spa towns, so many more fashion-based shops at the seaside and in big cities began to cater for the visitor, stressing the need for the fashionable to alter their regular city wear to meet new requirements. From the 1840s, London shops advertised special types of clothes for the seaside: 'seaside paletots' were on offer, or 'Scarborough suits'. Clothing for holidays was, in general, cheaper than regular everyday wear, and not expected to last: the salt and sun were said to damage clothes, but in fact, as the goods were less expensive, the use of fugitive dyes and cheaper fabrics probably contributed.[119] By the middle of the century Peter Robinson was advertising in the *Illustrated London News* its stocks of 'Fancy Summer Cloth, and Beach Linseys. Yachting, Seaside, and Summer Jackets in endless variety. The Inverness with cape; the Seacoat with hood and sleeves.'[120]

In the early days of seaside wear, many men had sported an almost fancy-dress element to their clothes, taking in details from sailors' uniforms or wearing 'Turkish' trousers, gathered at the ankle. As days at the seaside became more common, so the clothes began to match those worn for leisure in the rest of the country – except for children, who continued to wear sailor suits throughout the year. Men now expected to wear their ordinary three-piece lounge suit, with rubber-soled canvas shoes, known as plimsolls, as the sole concession to the holiday.* It was not until the 1880s that the blazer – a new piece of informal clothing, often made of striped flannel in lurid colours – appeared. Its attraction was that men could wear linen shirts and ties underneath, leaving off their stiff collars and their woollen waistcoats. Women did not indulge in these whims: until the arrival of sporting clothes at the end of the century (see pp. 460–63), they continued to wear the same fashions that they commonly wore in town.

Their concession to the seaside was in their bathing wear. Before the 1840s, bathing was entirely segregated (as it remained in many places for some decades), and men swam naked, while women wore long flannel shifts. Most people swam from bathing machines, which were first developed around the 1750s in Margate. The machine resembled a horse-drawn caravan. The swimmer walked up the back steps and undressed inside while a horse pulled the machine into the sea. Once the machine was far enough out, a canopy was lowered over the steps and the swimmer entered the sea entirely hidden from view. In the early days the swimmer (who probably could not swim) was led into the sea by a male or female 'dipper'. Later, some resorts alleviated the problems associated with horses by setting up winches which hauled the machines up and down a plank running into the sea.[121]

In the 1840s men's French-style red-and-white striped bathing shorts with a drawstring at the waist began to be worn, and a bathing machine, the shorts and a towel could now be hired for one all-in fee. By the 1860s, up to half the men at resorts had switched to these shorts, while the rest stuck to swimming naked.[122] This was not surprising: without elastic waistbands, a man who began by wearing shorts often discovered suddenly that, embarrassingly, he no longer was. By the 1870s most men found the newer style arriving from France to be more convenient. It was a one-piece knitted jersey suit that looked like a short-sleeved shirt

---

* The Merchant Shipping Act of 1876, sponsored by the MP Samuel Plimsoll, required a line – soon known as the Plimsoll line – to be painted on the hull of all ships, to show at what point they would officially become overloaded. The shoes, which appeared at almost the same date, had a line of rubber running around the canvas, which gave them their topical nickname.

THE LATEST FASHION.

"Now, girls, are you not jealous of my New Bathing Dress!—'Shah Blue,' and White Braid!"

attached to shorts: one stepped into it and buttoned it up securely. This remained the norm for men for the rest of the century. Women's bathing costumes, however, went through a series of small changes instead of a few big ones. By the early 1860s the flannel sacks had been abandoned and many women had taken to wearing 'Mrs Bloomer' suits: a thigh-length jacket was worn above a blouse, and a knee-length skirt went over trousers gathered at the ankle. These suits were trimmed much as day clothes were: when epaulettes became fashionable for dresses in the 1860s, bathing dresses had epaulettes too. By the 1870s advertisements were insisting that 'Bathing costumes . . . are made more stylishly every season: pink, cream and even blue flannel are used . . . loose full trousers to the ankle, and a short blouse fastened at the waist or a long jacket.' In 1880 woollen sashes and straw hats were added as stylish accoutrements, but it was the turn of the century before the vestigial skirt over trousers finally disappeared, as did the jacket over the blouse, and women's bathing costumes were reduced to just two pieces.[123]

What one wore, and how one wore it, depended in great measure on where one was going. The railways had increased the numbers of visitors, and they had also created a hierarchy of resorts, which depended on the ease of travel and the cost of the fares. Thus Margate was inexpensive, and therefore for the lower middle classes, while Ramsgate and Herne Bay, with higher fares, were for the more prosperous, but still middle class. Broadstairs – not easy to get to, and expensive – was for those who liked to consider themselves more 'select'.[124] The types of pastime provided in each town also segregated audiences. Southport, when it built its pleasure pier in 1860, charged 6d. for promenading on it, or sheltering from the wind; then it added a refreshment room for the promenaders; then a tramway out to the head of the pier so that the walkers no longer had to walk at all. In the 1880s and 1890s it acknowledged the new kind of visitor who was using the pier by providing

Opposite:
Bathing machines allowed women to swim while retaining a sense of modesty. The horse-drawn machine was pulled into the sea while bathers changed inside. A canopy could be lowered over the steps, to hide the bathers until they were safely in the water. Female bathers in the 1830s tended to wear plain flannel shifts, as here (above), while men swam naked in a separate area. 'Dippers' attended those who could not swim (here dressed in black, on the left). By the 1870s (below) men were wearing one-piece knitted jersey outfits, while women wore knee-length skirts, with trousers gathered at the ankle underneath; on top they wore blouses and thigh-length jackets.

'pleasure pavilions', concert halls, showrooms and other forms of mass entertainment.[125]

Bournemouth was an interesting example of a resort town that catered efficiently – and creatively – to the need for mass entertainment. More unusually, from the 1870s it began to do so in a centralized fashion: the Corporation had now become the impresario.[126] Seaside towns for the most part made their money by supplying goods and services to visitors, or by supplying goods and services to those who were in turn supplying the visitors. All of these populations, therefore, at first or second remove, were entirely dependent on their town remaining desirable for whatever group of visitors they were appealing to: if better services, better entertainment, better deals appeared elsewhere and drew away their customers, the local inhabitants would lose their livings. The new model that was slowly emerging was for the town as a whole to take a financial stake in the infrastructure of the resort – in the obvious buildings such as theatres, piers and pavilions; in passing regulations to make sure that lodging-house keepers and shopkeepers did not cheat their customers and that standards of hygiene were maintained in hotels and restaurants; and, finally, in ensuring that the customers, wherever they came from, continued to hear about the town via advertising, to keep it a desirable location.

Sometimes a landowner, or a railway company, would try to act as impresario for the town, and might be significant in the investment in infrastructure in watering places in particular. Bath was partially brought to prominence by the financial and commercial acumen of the Duke of Chandos, John Wood and Walter Pultney – an aristocratic investor, an architect and a banker working with a single aim. The Duke of Devonshire put money into Buxton spa, near his Derbyshire home. For the most part, however, few individuals were powerful enough to impose uniform business standards. The civic corporations of towns were, and Bournemouth was a town in which the Corporation fulfilled the expectations of both the residents and the visitors. It aimed at – and achieved – a prosperous clientele, and its methods were novel.

There were two phases to the development of Bournemouth as a resort. In the first phase, from the 1850s to the 1880s, the town mostly drew winter visitors, who were there for the mild air and were often invalids or convalescents. They expected little more entertainment than attractive promenades or carriage drives. In the 1850s no grand plans for the town were in train. The residents and, in particular, the local businessmen looked for a landowner or entrepreneur to invest in the building of a jetty for the steamer. Failing in that, in 1855 they banded together to create a public subscription for that purpose. A jetty was all they wanted: a pier seemed too ambitious a project altogether. Then it was decided that, via the local-government authority, the money could be raised through local rates. The Pier Committee was formed solely to develop the pier, and that is what it did: the first pier, a wooden structure 1,000 feet long, opened in 1861. By the mid-1870s it needed rebuilding, this time in iron, and the Committee organized that too. The new pier opened in 1880, and it was at this point that, having made the investment in the new pier, the local authority recognized that, to maximize returns, it needed to generate business both for the pier in particular and for the town in general.

It set to this new task with a will, forming connections with excursion companies and railways, and coordinating transport with the organizers of fêtes and regattas. It staged free band concerts. It took over the management of the seafront itself, supervising the cleaning and maintenance of the beach, enforcing by-laws, dealing with those who provided catering, huts and deckchairs to visitors, and even initiating the building of a lift to carry visitors up the cliff. Takings rose from £2,000 in 1881 to £10,000 in 1914, owing partly to the growth of the town, but also to the entrepreneurial spirit of the Pier Committee and its success in making the activities on the pier the centre of holiday visits. At the same time as this development was under way, the Corporation took over the lease of the Lower Pleasure Garden from its original proprietor; it then laid out a corresponding Upper Pleasure Garden, and from the 1890s continued to expand its holdings until, at its peak, the town had 620 acres of open grounds for the benefit of the general public, including 33 bowling greens, 20 tennis courts, 10 cricket pitches, 6 football fields, 3 croquet lawns, 2 golf courses, and 2 carriage drives.

The next phase in the entrepreneurial development of the town was to provide more structured forms of indoor entertainment, always under the control of the Corporation. In the 1850s the Belle Vue Assembly Rooms had flourished briefly under private management, but by 1875 the new town hall had become the venue for most entertainment. In 1877 the Winter Garden had opened, to stage concerts and art exhibits, but it had failed within the year; in 1881 a theatre was opened, but it too swiftly failed. So in the early 1880s the Corporation took over the Winter Garden, and allocated £20,000 to be spent on the construction of a pavilion and bandstands. An amendment to the local government act was then passed to permit the rates to be used to pay for a town band – and by this act defined entertainment every bit as much a local amenity as street lighting or rubbish collection. In 1885 regular band concerts were scheduled in the summer; by 1888 the town had two bands, one of which played nightly (except Sundays) from July to September; in 1896 there were, in addition, morning, afternoon and evening variety performances.

With this increasing reliance on musical entertainment, Bournemouth was in harmony with developments elsewhere in the resort world at the end of the century. In Bournemouth in 1893, Dan (later Sir Dan) Godfrey had been appointed to lead a band of wind players on the pier, but he insisted on finding musicians versatile enough to form a string orchestra, also for performances in the Winter Garden; an audience of 5,000 paid 3*d*. each for the first concert, which included Schubert's *Rosamunde* overture and selections from *The Gondoliers*. By 1894 this popular string orchestra had become the country's first permanent municipal orchestra, which three years later had played 100 symphony concerts (and is today still playing, as the Bournemouth Symphony Orchestra). Similarly, Granville Bantock – later Sir Granville, and a respected composer – was employed at New Brighton, Cheshire, a quick ferry ride from Liverpool, to lead the town's military band. The music he was required to play was easily read at sight, so he used his rehearsal time for serious music, and began to stage popular afternoon concerts with some additional string players. Audiences could attend as part of their 6*d*. admission to the grounds (another 6*d*. bought a seat), and by 1898 a typical concert included Tchaikovsky, a bit of Beethoven or Mozart, and some extracts from Wagner and perhaps Liszt.[127] By the time Bantock left, he too had created an orchestra of national importance, which played full orchestral programmes including much new British work.

Even in less distinguished circumstances, music was everywhere at the seaside: at the band concerts, the symphony concerts, the theatres, at the minstrel and pierrot shows. Even teatime was accompanied regularly by 'Viennese' or 'Hungarian' bands. In 1889 in the Isle of Man more than eighty musicians were employed in three entertainment venues: a hall for 2,000 dancers had a band of twenty-six; another band employed twenty-five players, including some from Hallé's and de Jong's Manchester orchestras (see pp. 369–72), who found this a lucrative way of spending their off season; and then there was the enormous Castle Mona Palace, which seated 5,000 for music-hall performances during the week, for which it required a thirty-piece band (whose players performed oratorios on Sundays). By 1892, 530 English towns had 1,300 places of entertainment – 200 theatres, 160 music halls, and 950 halls, galleries and gardens – drawing in 1 million visitors a year, and employing 350,000 workers directly, which was a quarter the number that worked in the textile industry, the largest industry of the Industrial Revolution.[128]

In 1861 in Paris, Benjamin Gastineau, a journalist, had described viewing the passing scenery from a train window as though it were a performance of a theatrical entertainment:

> Devouring distance at the rate of fifteen leagues an hour, the steam engine, that powerful stage manager, throws the switches, changes the décor, and shifts the point of view every moment; in quick succession it presents the astonished traveller with happy scenes, sad scenes, burlesque interludes, brilliant fireworks, all visions that disappear as soon as they are seen; it sets in motion nature clad in all its light and dark costumes, showing us skeletons and lovers, clouds and rays of light, happy vistas and sombre views, nuptials, baptisms, and cemeteries.[129]

This was, to all intents and purposes, a description of that epitome of Victorian entertainment, the panorama. Travel was now a show.

7

The Greatest Shows on Earth?

SEEING THE COUNTRYSIDE from a train window, observing it as if it were a panorama unrolling its scenic views in front of the traveller, was a strange inversion: panoramas were expected to show the world to those who could *not* travel – a sort of static newsreel, they brought to the exhibition halls of Britain a world of 'foreignness'. Yet these panoramas had to jostle for space among a kaleidoscope of entertainments and amusements.[1] It is all too easy, looking back, to think that the entertainments that have survived into our own times – theatre, music, books – were previously the only entertainments, or at least the dominant forces, or at the very very least the only ones that were enjoyed by the middle classes. Some genres have vanished entirely, others have been relegated to amusements for children. But the world of shows was a varied and complex one.

In 1844 James Robinson Planché's Christmas extravaganza – this one called *The Drama at Home* – had a 'Grand Anomalous Procession of the London Exhibitions', in which the 'Puff' asks 'The Drama', 'Will you receive the London Exhibitions?' She replies, 'Yes, for I'm told there are such sights to see / The town has scarcely time to think of me.' The stage directions then instruct: 'Enter in procession, and preceded by Banner-bearers and Boardmen, the Ojibbeway [*sic*] Indians, General Tom Thumb, the Centrifugal Railway [a sort of proto-rollercoaster currently on display] ... the Industrious Fleas, Diver and Diving Bell, and the Chinese Collection.'[2] This list was a random sampling of the current year's hits, but every year had a continually changing panorama of entertainment that unrolled before the eyes of each city's inhabitants. The technology of the nineteenth century had brought new examples, new varieties, but the range of possibilities had been growing over the previous half-century. In *Evelina*, Fanny Burney's novel of 1778, the characters found time to visit seven pleasure gardens, a fireworks display, an auction, a 'ridotto' (a public assembly with music and dancing), three coffee houses or taverns, two spas, five theatres, including the opera and a puppet theatre, and Cox's Museum.

Cox's was one of many entertainments that involved automata and displays of mechanical ingenuity. This particular display was very much the province of the upper classes, if only because of the admission charge of 10s. 6d. – more than anyone had ever charged, or would charge for the next hundred years. Cox, a jeweller by trade, specialized in mechanical items, as did many others, but his were highly decorative, which was much less common. They included a peacock that spread its tail every hour, a swan that 'swam' across a mirror made to look like a pond, and a pineapple that opened to display inside a nest of singing birds.[3]

The love of clockwork mechanisms and automata led very naturally to a desire to set their various movements into a narrative context, to give them their own 'story' and, therefore, a sort of function. One of the most popular of the eighteenth-century shows was Philippe de Loutherbourg's 'Eidophusikon'.* It was also one of the most influential, changing the nature of many shows that followed. De Loutherbourg, born in Germany, had travelled first to Paris, where he was so highly regarded as a painter that membership of the Académie Royale was conferred upon him while he was still three years below the minimum age. He then arrived in London and, despite acceptance by the Royal Academy, went to work for Garrick at Drury Lane. While he was a good painter, as a stage designer and technician he was revolutionary. He was one of the first to integrate theatrical lighting and special effects with the backdrops,

---

* This word was a construction of de Loutherbourg's own, formed from the Greek for 'natural' and 'form'. What it meant was less important than the grand classical sound, which imparted an aura of learning to what was, in fact, a magic-lantern show, if a technologically advanced, thrillingly beautiful and hugely influential magic-lantern show. The fondness for classical names continued with the Holuphusikon, the Eidoranion, the Panoptikon and the Aklouthorama. The panorama ('all-seeing') was another classical creation. Just as the '-gate' ending has been appended to every political scandal since the eruption of Watergate, so in the nineteenth century the success of the panorama meant that '-orama' became the standard suffix for a show that relied on perspectival or *trompe-l'œil* illusions: the aereorama, altchorama, cosmorama, cyclorama, diorama, kineorama, naturorama, padorama, poecilorama and physiorama all advertised their -oramaic charms.

creating atmosphere as well as images. He then used automata and innovative techniques to create remarkable spectacles which made his theatrical productions admired as much for their own sake as for the plays that were performed in front of them: in the 1770s his productions had ships sailing across the back of the stage, or forming naval regattas, or even, in Sheridan's *The Critic*, fighting the Armada battle. *The Wonders of Derbyshire* was barely a play: it was more of an excuse to display his twelve sets, created from sketches he had produced in the Lake District.[4] Before his arrival, stage lighting had been standard, set by a formula that was the same for every production. This one-size-fits-all approach had kept lighting entirely apart from set design. De Loutherbourg merged the two, using a variety of different lights to display different elements of his scenery at different times, experimenting with coloured silks, diffusers and indirect lighting to create novel effects. Now a scene could take place in a fog that was created by light, rather than painted on to a back flat; another scene could display a sunset, or the rising moon, or a fire.

De Loutherbourg was not content to work only in the theatre, however, and the Eidophusikon was his masterwork. This was opened in 1782 in his own house in Lisle Street, in a purpose-built theatre that accommodated 130 people (at 5s. a head) in front of a box stage of the type usually used for marionettes. A series of scenes was programmed, showing the 'Various Imitations of natural Phenomena, represented by Moving Pictures'. The effects were created by many layered elements. A painted back flat with cut-out wings on either side was the basis on which everything else was built; then clouds, the moon or sun and other ephemeral background elements were painted in opaque colours on backing linen and wound across the back flat at varying speeds. Cardboard and three-dimensional wooden models, decreasing in size to create a sense of perspective, were set on a sea- or landscape modelled in clay, or carved out of wood, again sized to suggest a vanishing perspective and painted to match the lighting of each scene: sunlit scenes had brighter colours in front, while objects in the background were painted in darker versions of the same colour, to suggest the hazy distance. Both the models and the land- or seascapes were manipulated by a crank that moved them at varying speeds – the front models moved more quickly, while the rear ones were slower, to imply a greater travelling distance – the lighting was modulated in each scene by stained-glass filters or by fabrics to produce the effects of light and colour playing across the scene. All these ideas were incorporated together for the first time, to produce a scenic effect that looked not like a painting of nature, but like nature itself.

De Loutherbourg also turned his mind to sound effects, which had rarely been attempted. He produced thunder via a copper sheet, rain and hail by yet another crank, which manipulated containers that held seeds, peas, shells or other objects carefully evaluated for their individual noises. He even had a drumhead with the skin stretched so tightly over it that, when rubbed, it produced the sounds of 'souls in torment', which was ideal for his famous finale, a tableau of Milton's 'Satan and his troops with the Raising of Pandaemonium'. This scene, set in a mountain valley, showed the interior of a temple whose colonnades of writhing snakes were consumed by flames while, from the adjacent burning lake, emerged Moloch and Beelzebub, accompanied by demons, to an accompaniment of lightning and thunder.

This was a revelation to a world accustomed to unmoving stage pictures, and, as well as producing a fashionable entertainment that heavily influenced the development of other types of show, these new scenic effects also transformed theatrical practice. By 1820 Edmund Kean's *King Lear* was advertised as having 'A Land Storm. After the manner of *Loutherbourg's Eidophusicon* [*sic*]'. One viewer reported that 'Overhead were revolving prismatic coloured transparencies, to emit a continually changing supernatural tint, and to add to the unearthly character of the scene. King Lear would one instant appear a beautiful pea-green, and the next sky-blue, and, in the event of a momentary cessation of the rotary motion of the magic lantern, his head would be purple and his legs Dutch-pink.' The *Drury Lane Journal* was rather more economical, simply noting, 'King Lear revived with entirely new scenes, particularly the storm scene . . . lighted by a new process from the top of the stage. Very successful.'[5]

After a few years in his home, de Loutherbourg's Eidophusikon was transported by his assistant to the Exeter Change, where many other entertainments regularly found a home. As we saw, the Change had begun life as a bazaar, but very soon the first floor was used exclusively to show a rotating display of exhibitions. The Eidophusikon continued to show many of the favourite old scenes, and it also incorporated new ones, especially of topical events such as the wreck of the *Halsewell*, an East India trading ship, which had occurred only weeks before the exhibition opened. Yet the move to Exeter Change signalled a shift in audience, and perception. The Greek name for the show and the high admission charge, as well as the exclusivity of a private theatre, had given a magic-lantern show an air of artistry. At the Exeter Change, appearing alongside a menagerie, waxworks, automata and musical instruments, by the end of the 1790s the Eidophusikon had become just another amusement-arcade show: at one performance Count Boruwlaski, a dwarf who exhibited himself, accompanied de Loutherbourg's scenes of Miltonic grandeur with guitar music; at other times George Saville Carey performed 'Comic Songs, Readings and Imitations . . . of many characters of the past and present age', or 'the Sieur Comus' displayed 'his astonishing performance on Cards, Caskets, Rings, Watches, Medals, Sympathetick Clocks, and many Magical Deceptions'. (However, it is true that one series had 'Master Hummell singing', and the foremost historian of Victorian shows and entertainments has suggested that this was the composer Johann Nepomuk Hummel, who at the time was studying in London with Clementi.)

Exeter Change may have signalled the descent of the Eidophusikon, but the location of shows was not necessarily a defining factor in how the exhibit itself was viewed. Displays of 'natives' from various far-away countries were often held in taverns – in 1772 two Mohawks were to be seen in the Sun tavern, the Strand, while the same year two 'esquimaux' were at Little Castle Street, Oxford Market (although there had been Inuit in Britain for more than 250 years: the first three had settled in Bristol as early as 1501). For the most part, though, the popular way to learn about foreign customs or episodes in history was at waxworks exhibitions. Mrs Salmon's was the most famous in the eighteenth century. A handbill described her wares:

> The Royal Off Spring: Or, the Maid's Tragedy Represented in Wax Work, with many Moving Figures and these Histories Following. King Charles the First upon the Fatal Scaffold, attended by Dr Juxon the Bishop of London, and the Lieutenant of the Tower, with the Executioner and Guards waiting upon our Royal Martyr. The Royal Seraglio, or the Life and Death of Mahomet the Third, with the Death of Ireniae Princess of Persia, and the fair Sultaness Urania. The Overthrow of Queen Voaditia [Boudicca] and the Tragical Death of her two Princely Daughters . . . Margaret Countess of Heningbergh, Lying on a Bed of State, with

her Three hundred and Sixty-Five Children, all born at one Birth, and baptized by the Names of Johns and Elizabeths, occasioned by the rash Wish of a poor beggar woman . . . Old Mother Ship-ton* . . . All richly dress'd and composed with so much variety of Invention, that it is wonderfully Diverting to all Lovers of Art and Ingenuity.

By the time Boswell visited, in 1763, there were representations of royal christenings and a 'Cherokee king with his two chiefs, in their Country Dress, and Habiliments', as well as Antony and Cleopatra surrounded by their children.

Mme Tussaud, who in Paris had made death masks of many of the decapitated aristocrats fresh from the guillotine, and then of the revolutionaries Marat and Robespierre as well, arrived in England in 1802 and toured with her own waxworks for nearly thirty years before setting up in the Baker Street Bazaar in 1835. Her 'Adjoining Room' (not yet dubbed the Chamber of Horrors) had death masks, the blade and lunette from the guillotine, and several bloodstained relics. By 1844 her exhibition was famous enough for Planché to memorialize her:

> To see you in clover, comes Mme Tussaud,
> Your model in wax-work she wishes to shew,
> The King of the French and Fieschi the traitor
> Commissioner Lin and the Great Agitator,†
> Kings, Princes and Ministers, all of them go,
> To sit for their portraits to Mme Tussaud.[7]

Another form of show also presented itself as a way of seeing the world: the architectural model. Such models were designed to show visitors famous sights, to allow them to travel the world without travel-ling, or to see re-creations of times past – such as Solomon's Temple, or the Holy Sepulchre. Some of these models were notable for being constructed out of strange materials, be it paper, playing cards or beef bones carved by French prisoners of war – one model was even made

---

* Mother Shipton, a stock figure of legend for hundreds of years, has recently vanished from popular consciousness. Her origins can possibly be found in a real woman living in Yorkshire early in the sixteenth century, who was said to be a witch, or a seer, or a prophetess. A raft of prophecies attributed to her was published and treated seriously by many – including Pepys, who in 1666, after the Great Fire of London, heard a member of the royal family saying that 'now Shipton's prophecy was out [had come true]'.[6]
† Fieschi had attempted to assassinate the emperor Louis Philippe, while Lin was a Chinese official who became famous in Britain during the Opium Wars; the Great Agitator was of course Daniel O'Connell.

from 'Baccopipe Clay'. But many more were straightforwardly obsessive attempts to reproduce places of interest. In James Street a 5 metre square model of Paris boasted that it had 50,000 individual houses; another of the same city claimed that it was reproduced at a scale of about 1:750. Then there were models of the Alps, of Rome, or of Venice. Others were more local, depicting Lord Burleigh's house at Chiswick, or the city of Bath, or the Radcliffe Camera in Oxford. Most of these displays were temporary, exciting transitory interest (and admission fees) and then vanishing. The only permanent exhibition in eighteenth-century London was the Classical Exhibition, in Pall Mall, which was built of cork and reproduced places mentioned in Greek and Roman literature. (However, in 1785 'Vesuvius' set fire to the rest of the display, and this model vanished too, this time literally in a puff of smoke.)

These educational models gave viewers the sight of great buildings, past or present, across the globe (or at least across Europe). Many people also visited their own great buildings and monuments nearer at hand, for sightseeing and exhibitions and shows were tightly linked together. In 1711 Addison had visited Westminster Abbey, and 'in the poetical Quarter, I found there were Poets who had no Monuments, and Monuments which had no Poets.' The general gloominess of the place, its air of shabbiness, was, he thought, not altogether out of keeping with the intimations of mortality that were appropriate to tombs and memorials. This was soon to change, and by the middle of the eighteenth century there had been an active campaign to clean the place up, with the monument to Shakespeare by the sculptor Scheemakers being erected in 1741. By 1760 the name 'Poets' Corner' was in use, and Westminster Abbey had become just one of the many tourist sights that visitors were now expected to see. By 1801 there was an entrance fee charged (and worshippers at services were asked to leave promptly, to make sure no one got a free look around). Different areas were blocked off, and charged for separately, so that to see the whole Abbey cost nearly 4s. In 1835 a visitor described the church as 'a labyrinth of wooden partitions, doors, screens, railings and corners . . . It seemed as if all these nooks and swallows' nests were contrived merely to increase the number of showmen and key-bearers who lurk in them.' It was not until the mid-1840s that Poets' Corner was freely opened, and even then other parts of the building retained an entrance fee (albeit much reduced).

St Paul's, previously barely on the tourist itinerary, was given a boost into the big leagues when Lord Nelson was buried there in 1805. (Westminster Abbey, annoyed at the competition, commissioned a wax model of the dead hero.) As with the Abbey, there was a general low-level controversy over admission charges, and, again as with the Abbey, various parts of the building were off-limits without extra payments: 2s. 6d. to go up to the dome, 1s. to see Nelson's tomb. James Fenimore Cooper reported that his party's guide finished her tour by reciting, 'By the rules of the church I am entitled to only twopence for showing you this, and we are strictly prohibited from asking any more, but gentlefolks commonly give me a shilling.'[8]

Sightseeing in general, and in London in particular, for the middle and lower classes was given an enormous boost by the Great Exhibition. A comparative table of attendance for some of the London entertainments shows the growth through the period:[9]

	Armoury, Tower of London	National Gallery	British Museum	Westminster Abbey
1827–8	[no figs.]	—	81,000	[no figs.]
1837–8	11,104	397,649*	266,000	[no figs.]
1850	32,313	519,745	720,643	'no account'
1851	233,561	1,109,364	2,230,242	6,000 a day

Hampton Court, now on the South Western Railway's line from London, could be reached very quickly, and for very little money, by Londoners on a day out. Before 1838 the palace had been shown in the same way that country houses were: those who knew enough to ask were taken around by a housekeeper, who expected a tip for her trouble. A few hundred people a year had visited. In 1839, after free admission was put into place, with no housekeeper and no regimented tours, 115,971 made the journey.[10] Yet it was more than historical places, or churches, that drew the crowds. Technology, or just novelty, made many things worth a visit. In 1841 the Armoury at the Tower of London was reopened after a terrible fire. It was not the new Armoury that was on display, but instead, for 6d., a view of the fire damage together with a trip to the specially erected marquees that were selling 'various specimens saved

* This was its first year in Trafalgar Square; see p. 401.

from the ruins, showing the effects of fire on the different metals, and other substances destroyed by it'. For an additional 6*d.* one could leave with some fire-damaged flints from a gun; larger items, or ones more badly burned, were available for £1. Nearly 2,500 visitors a week descended on the site over the next two months.[11]

Another site of devastation that drew the crowds was the Thames Tunnel. The tunnel was an engineering marvel, the first ever to be constructed under a navigable river. Work had begun in 1825, and up to 700 visitors paid 1*s.* each to watch the progress. But in 1827 the river broke through the tunnel walls and flooded a tower at the entrance. Within a month of the accident, the German traveller Prince Pückler-Muskau was one of the sightseers who went down to the riverbed in an early version of a diving bell and, 'for half an hour, watched the stopping of the breach with sacks of clay'.[12] By 1828 the investors had got cold feet, and work stopped and the tunnelling shield was bricked up, but a mirror was installed at the entrance so that visitors could continue to examine the work as far as it had got. In 1836 tunnelling began once more, and advertisements in the entertainment columns of the newspapers notified the public that visitors could walk down to where the navvies were excavating at Rotherhithe. In 1843 the tunnel was finished, and 2 million people paid the penny toll for the novelty of walking underneath a river, while hucksters sold refreshments, engravings, cardboard cut-outs and other representations of the tunnel, including paper panoramas and a cosmorama (see below).

Industrial sites and new technology more generally were also considered to be well worth a visit, and were very much part of any sightseeing trip. One traveller listed touring 'the new turnpike road, the Leeds cloth hall, the new locks on the Leeds to Liverpool canal at Bingley' and poor children winding silk; another a cotton printing factory; a third 'the Preston and Liverpool docks, a paper factory, a coal pit, a picture gallery, a china auction, an army exercise and the opening of the Lancaster assizes'. Other visitors recommended the Bridgewater Canal and mines, silver-plating works in Sheffield, and iron-smelting at Rotherham. Mrs Lybbe Powys visited the carpet factory at Axminster, which she judged 'indeed well worth the while', as well as a china factory in Worcester and a coalfield in Westerton, in the Midlands, where 'many ladies even venture down the pits to see the entire manner of it'.[13]

Mrs Lybbe Powys did not herself descend down the mine: that was

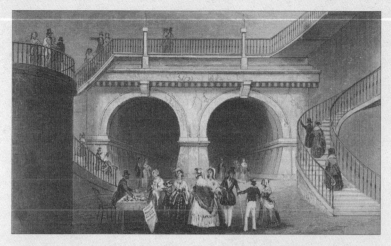

Industrial sightseeing remained popular for much of the century. The Thames Tunnel was completed in 1843 and, despite the penny charge, hordes of visitors descended: it was the first time a tunnel had been built under a navigable river. Hawkers sold souvenirs of their visits – engravings, cardboard cut-outs and other representations of the tunnel.

too much for her. For many like her, the desire to see the huge possibilities in the world could be met in a variety of ways. For those who could not travel to see the sights, theatres were popular for their representations of famous places, or topical events (see p. 338), and they also satisfied the desire for travel on a more informal basis. The comedian Charles Mathews became famous for monologues which he called 'At Homes'. These were so successful that he performed a new one every year from 1824 for a decade. His first one was 'A Trip to America', and in it he told stories, anecdotes, jokes and sang songs to give the flavour of his voyage; another was 'Country Cousins and the Sights of London', encompassing word pictures of St Paul's, the Royal Academy exhibition, Westminster Abbey and a panorama of the North Pole.*

It was hardly surprising that a panorama was evoked by Mathews as an essential tourist sight, since panoramas were to become one of the

---

* This panorama had been produced following John Franklin's return from his first trip to the Arctic in 1822, when he was hailed as 'the man who ate his boots'. His *Narrative of a Journey to the Shores of the Polar Sea* was published in 1823, and the audience for the panorama was promised 'a scene of awful grandeur and sublimity beyond description – Music, Savage Dance, composed on purpose'.[14]

most popular entertainments of the century. In *The Prelude* Wordsworth slipped naturally into the vocabulary of the shows, evoking a panorama, as well as a show that appeared to be similar to the Eidophusikon, and even architectural models:

> At leisure, then, I viewed, from day to day,
> The spectacles within doors, – birds and beasts
> Of every nature, and strange plants convened
> From every clime; and, next, those sights that ape
> The absolute presence of reality,
> Expressing, as in mirror, sea and land,
> And what earth is, and what she has to shew.
> I do not here allude to subtlest craft,
> By means refined attaining purest ends,
> But imitations, fondly made in plain
> Confession of man's weakness and his loves.
> Whether the Painter, whose ambitious skill
> Submits to nothing less than taking in
> A whole horizon's circuit, do with power,
> Like that of angels or commissioned spirits,
> Fix us upon some lofty pinnacle,
> Or in a ship on waters, with a world
> Of life, and life-like mockery beneath,
> Above, behind, far stretching and before;
> Or more mechanic artist represent
> By scale exact, in model, wood or clay,
> From blended colours also borrowing help,
> Some miniature of famous spots or things, –
> St Peter's Church; or, more aspiring aim,
> In microscopic vision, Rome herself;
> Or, haply, some choice rural haunt, – the Falls
> Of Tivoli; and, high upon that steep,
> The Sibyl's mouldering Temple! every tree,
> Villa, or cottage, lurking among rocks
> Throughout the landscape; tuft, stone scratch minute –
> All that the traveller sees when he is there.[15]

When Wordsworth wrote this, between 1799 and 1805, he was, in theory, looking back to 1791. But in that year only the first, the original, panorama was in existence. This was the brainchild of Robert Barker, an Irishman living in Edinburgh, who, as a 'portrait painter and teacher of perspective', developed the old tradition of long views of cities and landscapes, which easily went back to Wenceslaus Hollar in the seventeenth century. His improvement was to work out how to curve the lines of a perspective drawing to minimize the distortion created by showing a 360-degree painting – Wordsworth's 'whole horizon's circuit'. That was clever. His genius came in recognizing the commercial application of his technique. His first panorama, a 360-degree view of the hills above Edinburgh, was displayed to great acclaim locally. He and his son, Henry Aston Barker, who had done much of the actual painting, then travelled to the mecca of showmen, London. First they set up a temporary exhibition of their original panorama, but popular acclaim was so great that in 1793 they opened a purpose-built exhibition space just off Leicester Square, which they called the Panorama, and where two panoramas could be mounted at once over two floors. The panoramas were lit from above, and guard rails kept audiences at the correct distance to create the appropriate *trompe-l'œil* effects. The stairs were in the middle of the floor, so that the two images entirely encircled the viewers, drawing them into this new world.

From the 1800s, panoramas became popular across the country, despite the necessity of purpose-built rotundas to achieve the perfect circumstances for a *trompe-l'œil* effect. In 1802 Barker opened a rotunda in Birmingham, and a second one was built there in 1817, but even in more temporary accommodations the excitement of the form was enough to override the lack of perfect verisimilitude that occurred outside the controlled conditions of the rotundas. In 1816 Lillyman's Hotel in Liverpool managed to show a panorama of the battles of Ligny and Waterloo without a rotunda, and others followed this example: in no time at all there were panorama showings in Leeds, Norwich, Exeter, even in smaller towns such as Teignmouth.[16]

Soon Henry Aston Barker was travelling the world to record new views – Constantinople, Paris, Mont Blanc, the Alps, Vienna, Pompeii, Florence, Milan, Lake Maggiore, Messina, Lisbon, Badajoz – he even went to Niagara Falls. Sometimes the resulting panoramas were just views of famous cities or majestic scenery; others depended for their success on their depictions of historical or contemporary events. After Napoleon's first abdication, in 1814, Barker went to Elba to sketch the Emperor for a panorama; in 1815 he went to Waterloo to see the battlefield, and he interviewed veterans for further details. His resulting Waterloo panorama was particularly successful: it was said to have earned him £10,000.

This was only one contribution to the craze for all things Napoleonic after 1815, and for many years afterwards. The Duke of Wellington himself visited Barker's Waterloo panorama, and approved it. The Duke was an assiduous visitor to exhibitions, an enthusiast of every kind of entertainment, many of which included his own impersonators. He even posed for a portrait standing in front of Napoleon's wax effigy at Mme Tussaud's. (Mme Tussaud's was a favourite of his – he asked for special notification if any new exhibits were added to the 'Adjoining Room'.) He also attended J. H. Amherst's *The Battle of Waterloo* at Astley's Amphitheatre, the second most successful 'hippodrama' ever staged. (For more on Astley and the hippodrama, as well as his Napoleon plays, see pp. 313ff.) When the Duke was present at a reconstruction of the Battle of Waterloo at Vauxhall Gardens (see below), he was said to have 'laughed heartily at his representative'.[17] Indeed, for such a grim-visaged man, he seems to have laughed heartily quite frequently. Tom Thumb's impersonation of Napoleon at the Egyptian Hall also amused him, especially when the mini-emperor told him that during the show, 'I was thinking of the loss of the battle of Waterloo.'

The Egyptian Hall had a history of successful displays linked to the Emperor. William Bullock, a jeweller-turned-traveller-turned-showman, had opened a small museum in Liverpool in the 1790s, showing his collection of curiosities, natural-history specimens, and weapons and armour. In 1809 he moved to London, setting up his newly named London Museum in Piccadilly in 1812. He continued to add to his collections in what became known as the Egyptian Hall, from its dramatic façade, mounting a display of Roman objects and, soon, Napoleonic memorabilia.* In 1816 Bullock bought Napoleon's travelling carriage, in which the Emperor had ridden to Waterloo: the original coachman was part of the display, as were two of Napoleon's horses, his camp bed, and the contents of his travelling case, which included 'close on a hundred pieces . . . nearly all in solid gold, two leather bottles, one of rum and the other of fine old Malaga, a million francs-worth of diamonds and a cake of Windsor soap'.† Nearly a quarter of a million

---

* Bullock sold off most of his collection in 1819, but the hall continued to be a popular exhibition space, let out to artists or entrepreneurs until it was demolished in 1904.
† It has frequently been repeated that Byron too was the owner of Napoleon's travelling carriage. In fact he had Bullock's carriage copied, except that he replaced the Emperor's specially designed map chest with bookshelves and a dining table. Mme Tussaud later acquired the actual carriage and camp bed and carriage, along with another hundred odd items associated with Napoleon.

visitors queued to see Bullock's hoard, and even more when he travelled around Britain with it. With the proceeds – said to be £35,000 – he opened a 'Museum Napoleon, or Collection of Productions of the Fine Arts executed for and connected with the History of the ex-Emperor of the French, collected at Considerable Expence [*sic*] from the Louvre and Other Places &c.'

Bullock did not have a monopoly on the craze. A Waterloo Museum was set up in Pall Mall, a Waterloo Exhibition in St James's Street; by 1824 these were joined by Waterloo Rooms, almost next door to the Waterloo Museum (the Rooms had the Emperor's horse, Marengo: a big draw). At the Egyptian Hall again, long after Bullock had sold his lease, a display of a model of the Battle of Waterloo was popular. The army had commissioned it from an ex-officer, who went to enormous lengths to produce a minutely accurate representation, including living for some time near the battlefield itself, and interviewing officers repeatedly for information on troop movements. In 1838 his model was unveiled: it covered 40 square metres, and was scaled at about 1:600 with 190 minute figures of soldiers and horses, which could be examined with the magnifying glasses carefully chained to the display table – even the different types of crops in the fields were indicated by different coloured silks and wools.

Napoleana cropped up in the most peculiar places, in 'high' as well as 'low' art forms. A serious collector like Sir John Soane had Napoleonic bits and pieces on display in his museum, mixed in with his classical statues, Flaxman neoclassical drawings, Chinese ceramics and Hogarth pictures.[18] Johann Maelzel, a German automata-maker, worked with Beethoven in 1813 to produce music for his 'Panharmonicon', which mimicked the sounds of various orchestral instruments. The resulting piece was entitled *Wellington's Victory* (it was later renamed the 'Battle' Symphony), but the two men fell out before it could be performed. In 1818 Maelzel and the Panharmonicon – now called the Orchestrion – arrived for several years' successful touring in Britain.* In 1815 a production of *Richard III* advertised that in Act V, at Bosworth Field, 'Mr Cooke will (accoutred in a real) French cuirass, stripped from a cuirassier, on the field of battle at Waterloo, and which bears the indenture of

* The 'Battle' Symphony was in fact premiered in Vienna with a real orchestra, but the Panharmonicon played some marches by Dussek and Pleyel on the same programme. Maelzel's more lasting fame is as the inventor of the metronome.

several musket shots and sabre cuts go thro' the evolutions of the attack and defence, with a sword in each hand!'[19] Many theatres staged more straightforward representations of some aspect of Napoleon's career: in 1831 at the Surrey Theatre there was *Napoleon, or, The Victim of Ambition*, and in the same week Covent Garden produced a 'Grand Historical and Military Spectacle' entitled *Napoleon Buonaparte, Captain of Artillery, General and First Consul, Emperor and Exile*. In the first six months of that year alone there were at least five versions of Napoleon's life story on stage, most of them showing Napoleon as the hero.[20]

The Surrey production of *Napoleon; or, The Victim of Ambition* accommodated the Napoleon craze and added in the new fad for dioramas, with depictions of the retreat from Moscow and Waterloo. Panoramas were still drawing the crowds, but they were last week's novelty. The dioramas at the Surrey were probably not real dioramas (see below), but only moving panoramas, which had begun to appear in theatres in the 1820s, and consisted of a panorama that was unrolled across the back of the stage to give the illusion of actors moving through a constantly changing landscape.* The first moving panorama appeared in 1820 in the pantomime *Harlequin and Friar Bacon, or, The Brazen Head*, at Covent Garden, where the lovers 'crossed' to Ireland in a model boat while behind them a panorama was unrolled in the opposite direction, showing a variety of seascapes that culminated in a view of Dublin harbour. Drury Lane fought back with *Giovanni in Ireland* the following year, advertising a 'moving Panoramic view of the coast of Milford Haven'. In 1822 another pantomime, *Harlequin and the Ogress*, had a royal party embarking for Scotland while behind them the panorama scrolled along the banks of the Thames from Greenwich to the Nore.[22]

Away from the theatre, panoramas were being merged with lighting and movement to create dioramas. The diorama had been invented in Paris by Louis Daguerre, an assistant to a panorama painter, and later the inventor of the daguerreotype, one of the earliest photographic processes. The diorama gave a new three-dimensionality to a previously flat image, and with rapid changes of lighting created an illusion of move-

---

* Ballet-goers today still see a moving panorama in traditional productions of *The Sleeping Beauty*. The scene in which the Prince travels to find Aurora is known as the 'panorama scene', and Tchaikovsky's music was commissioned specifically for (in the choreographer Petipa's notes of the production scenario), a 'Panorama . . . As the boat advances, the banks of the river change; villages, countryside, forests, mountains are seen, and finally, the castle of the sleeping beauty comes into view.'[21]

ment. In the early days audiences had to sit in a purpose-built theatre, facing an opening that looked like a picture frame. Behind this frame there was in fact a perspective tunnel, although the audience could not see it. The picture at the far end of the tunnel was painted in translucent and opaque paints, which were lit by different light sources; a system of pulleys opened and closed screens, curtains and shutters to modify the light on the image and produce a short (quarter-hour) 'performance'. The entire room was then rotated on its axis (hence the need for the purpose-built theatre) to face a second tunnel and set of frames, and a new image replaced the first for a second quarter of an hour. The images were mostly landscapes, cathedrals, ruins and so on – like the panoramas, but initially without the historical and topical images to which the public had grown accustomed.

The Diorama, near Regent's Park, opened in 1823,* and within a very short period of time dioramas could be found around the country. In 1825 the annual fair at Bristol advertised a diorama 'for a short time in a spacious building purposely erected in St James's Church Yards . . . with a turning saloon as at the Regent's Park, London'. In the same year, further dioramas opened in Liverpool and in Manchester.[23] These last two were possibly licensed by the patent-holder (the one at Bristol almost certainly was not), but very swiftly a diorama simply came to mean a *trompe-l'œil* picture that was altered by dramatic lighting; within a decade the word was used in advertisements to mean any panoramic view.

The most popular dioramas and panoramas were topical, and it became a race to 'capture' a big event before the competition. The Battle of Navarino, fought on 20 October 1827, was recreated in a panorama the following month. When the Houses of Parliament burned down on 16 October 1834, one panorama of the fire was painted and open to the public a week later; a second one appeared only six weeks after that, and within two months of the fire the Cosmorama Rooms in Regent Street advertised a diorama of a 'Grand Tableaux, of the Interiors of the Houses of Lords & Commons, As They Appeared Previous to Their Destruction

* The architect of the original Diorama theatre was Auguste Pugin, father of the architect who worked on the Houses of Parliament. The building was sold in 1848. In 1853 it was turned into a Baptist chapel, which survived until the 1970s, and was then converted into a mosque. The façade of the original building survives today, with the word 'Diorama' appearing on the frieze. It is now the site of the Prince's Trust charity, and its theatrical beginnings explain that building's peculiar layout.

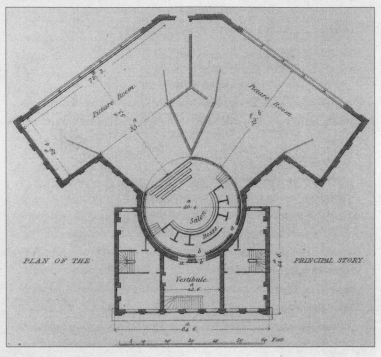

A floor plan of the Diorama in 1838. The audience sat in the central circular salon, looking through a perspective tunnel into the picture room where the diorama screens were positioned. After the first scene had been viewed, the central hall swung on its axis and the second diorama was appeared in the second picture room.

by Fire, with a Correct Moonlight View, of the Exteriors ... from the River Thames, And a Splendid Representation of the Conflagration with Dioramic & Mechanical Effect. Also a View of the Ruins, as Visited by their Majesties.'

News events and catastrophes were popular in various genres. In 1820 Géricault's 1819 painting of dead and dying shipwreck survivors, *The Raft of the Medusa*, was exhibited at the Egyptian Hall, to great success. (For more on art exhibitions, see Chapter 10.) It was followed shortly by a panorama entitled 'Marine Peristrephic Panorama of the Wreck of the Medusa French Frigate and the Fatal Raft', which was shown first in Edinburgh, and then in Dublin when Géricault's painting was exhibited there.* Dublin spurned the painting for the panorama, however: admission charges for the painting had to be dropped from 1s. 8d. to 10d., and even then few visitors bothered to attend, while the Marine Peristrephic Panorama packed them in three times a day.

Another type of novelty appeared in 1834, when the Baker Street Bazaar advertised its 'Padorama': just under 1,000 square metres of that technological marvel, the railway. The image depicted was 'the most interesting parts of the country traversed by the Liverpool and Manchester Railway ... [Mechanical scale-models of the] Locomotive Engines [will run in front of the panorama and] ... give a more correct idea of the mode of transit on this great work of art and science than can be conveyed by any description, however elaborate. Every one of our juvenile friends ought in particular to see it, as it is very instructive for youth.'† The Baker Street Bazaar, in its passion for instruction, was not breaking new ground. The hero in *Evelina* in 1778 had condemned Cox's Museum because, although the mechanical ability behind the displays was remarkable, 'I am sorry it is turned to no better account; but its purport is so frivolous, so very remote from all aim at instruction or utility, that the sight of so fine a shew only leaves a regret on the mind, that so much work, and so much ingenuity, should not be better bestowed.'[25] Many agreed with this desire for 'instruction or utility', and a great many shows therefore slanted their promotion away from the presentation of spectacle.

One way of making entertainments acceptable to the more serious-minded was to claim a scientific basis for them, as did Dr Katterfelto, who lectured at Spring Gardens, in the same place as Cox's. (Spring Gardens was where Admiralty Arch, in London, has since been built,

---

* This was a particularly felicitous meshing of various forms of entertainment: the newspapers had carried accounts of the shipwreck, particularly dwelling on the episodes of murder and cannibalism; two books by survivors were quickly translated into English; a week after the opening at the Egyptian Hall the Coburg Theatre staged *The Shipwreck of the Medusa, or, The Fatal Raft*. A decade later the playwright William Moncrieff found that the subject still had some mileage in it, using the same title – with only an exclamation mark to distinguish it.

† This was only one of the dozens of spin-offs that emerged from the excitement of the early passenger train. There were also commemorative coins, ceramics and pottery, printed handkerchiefs, jigsaw puzzles, peep shows and engravings, including in 1831 six aquatints, which were so popular they were expanded to a series of thirteen and reprinted the same year; they had to be reissued again in the three following years, before they were issued separately as lithographs. Ackermann, the bookseller, also produced two long aquatints, *Travelling on the Liverpool and Manchester Railway*, which also went through two editions.[24]

but a small pedestrian turning carries the name still.) Dr Katterfelto, advertising himself as 'the greatest philosopher in this kingdom since Sir Isaac Newton', lectured on 'mathematics, optics, magnetism, electricity, chemistry, pneumatics, hydraulics, hydrostatics', as well as, more mysteriously, 'proetics', 'stynacraphy' and 'caprimancy'. Despite the latter subjects, his lectures were not entirely bogus. He exhibited a solar microscope, although he could not resist claiming the invention as his own (in fact an early model had been presented to the Royal Society over forty years before), or selling Dr Bato's Remedy to destroy the 'insects' that could be seen through it. Other lecturers presented 'Philosophical Recreations', which were in reality conjuring tricks, or optical illusions, or performances of mind-reading; there were even demonstrations of 'Philosophical Fireworks', which were fireworks displays that were prefaced by short lectures on chemistry, or the history of gunpowder. Magic lanterns, which otherwise would be classed as entertainment, were educational if they explained 'all the Phenomena of the heavenly bodies, and give the most interesting and comprehensive View of the sublime works of the Creator'.

Some of these lectures were of real technological import: in 1804 an enterprise that was to change the entire nation was presented as an entertainment at the Lyceum Theatre, when Friedrich Albert Winsor gave lectures on the power of gas to illuminate. In 1808 Richard Trevithick, the engineer who produced the first steam locomotive, attempted to publicize his new locomotive, the Catch-me-who-can, by staging a 'Steam Circus' in front of what is now Euston station and giving rides to passers-by.[26] At the Egyptian Hall in 1824 'The Egg in Labour', which sounded like a magic act, was in fact a 'steam egg-hatchery', or incubator for chicks: 'Cantelo's Patent Hydro-Incubator … Chickens Always Hatching! Machines and Chickens Constantly on Sale!' They were also constantly on view – between 10 a.m. and 10 p.m. visitors could watch the chicks hatch, and examine bottles that held specimens of chickens at various stages in their development.

In 1832 the Adelaide Gallery – or, to give it its formal title, the National Gallery of Practical Science, Blending Instruction with Amusement – opened in the Lowther Arcade, a passage off the Strand that was well known for shopping and other entertainment. In 1839 it was the first place to display a photograph, illegally to begin with, but then with the permission of Louis Daguerre, who licensed a photographer to set

ILLUSTRATED

ONE PENNY WEEKLY

Paris Fashions
— The Very Latest —

Office : Granville House, Arundel Street, **LONDON** W. C.

Illustrated Paris Fashions was one of dozens of magazines that used new printing technology to make shopping for clothes ever more alluring to its women readers. This illustration is ostensibly promoting millinery, but the large, well-lit shop, the method of display of goods, the large mirror and the up-to-the-minute Japanese-style vase all give a subliminal message about the modernity and thus the desirability of shopping itself.

The Great Exhibition, in Joseph Paxton's Crystal Palace in Hyde Park, displayed 'the goods of all nations', including furs, as in this illustration (above) from *Dickinson's Comprehensive Pictures of the Great Exhibition of 1851*. At the right of the picture is a telescope, and, in front of that, the edge of a display of textiles. Many books of this type found a ready market, including *Recollections of the Great Exhibition*, which reproduced original drawings that had been made for Prince Albert, including this one (below) of farm machinery from the Agricultural Court.

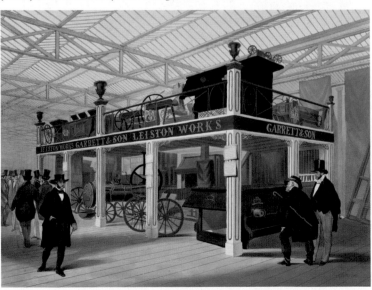

Left Thousands of souvenirs of the Great Exhibition were produced. This 'expanding view' used new colour lithography, printed over six sheets, and unfolded to present the viewer with a panoramic depiction of the opening ceremony.

Below The Great Exhibition entered literally into people's homes. This wallpaper, manufactured in Manchester *c*.1853–5, gave the middle-class home a lasting souvenir of the Crystal Palace. The fashionable chinoiserie bridge is an imaginative addition.

Harding and Howell were drapers in Pall Mall, and this 1810 illustration of their shop contradicts the notion that pre-Victorian shops were gloomy, with all the goods tucked away in drawers. Hanging swathes of fabrics seems to have been a common method of display among drapers; the skylight and big glass doors and windows meant that customers could see the goods at their best. By contrast, as late as 1880 some shops remained little better than single dark rooms (below). Here a tea-dealer's shop is carved out of a cellar in Whitby. Only the sign and a small window with a few items on display alert the passer-by to its existence.

Above Newspapers were increasingly available to all in the nineteenth century. Benjamin Robert Haydon's *Waiting for the Times* (1831) represented an everyday scene. Many coffee houses and clubs subscribed to a range of papers and magazines, which were available for the price of a cup of coffee, or to the members of the club. Pubs often had a sign asking gentlemen not to monopolize the current day's paper for more than five minutes at a time.

Right Books became cheaper early in the nineteenth century, and stalls like this, selling second-hand books, made them accessible to many of the working classes. As well as their own premises, some booksellers had 'shops' – that is, stalls – on market days in various towns.

Vauxhall Pleasure Gardens was, in the eighteenth century, the most fashionable place for all classes to go to dance, eat, drink, listen to music or simply walk in the grounds. This aquatint of 1808 shows the gardens just as they were beginning to decline in popularity. With rural walks beginning to seem dull, the gardens began to concentrate more on display – fireworks, lighting and theatrical extravaganzas, including using the banks of the Thames to stage 'naumachia', or sea battles.

The 'Eidophusikon', an elaborate miniature theatre that opened in the home of its creator, the painter Philippe de Loutherbourg, in 1782. De Loutherbourg had worked at Drury Lane with Garrick and Sheridan, and had created revolutionary stage effects, pioneering the use of lighting to indicate mood as well as simply to illuminate. The Eidophusikon showed scenes from Milton, including 'Satan and his troops with the Raising of Pandaemonium', which is depicted in this painting by Edward Francisco Burney.

Giovanni Battista Belzoni, 'the Patagonian Sampson' (he was actually from Padua), was a strong man who performed at Sadler's Wells from 1803. He is a good example of how 'entertainment' covered a multitude of disciplines: he was also an archaeologist, digging at Abu Simbel and the Valley of the Kings, and he later exhibited the material he found, and wrote a book on the subject.

Left Theatrical special effects became more and more elaborate throughout the nineteenth century. In 1862 John Henry Pepper, lecturer on chemistry at the London Polytechnic, staged a Christmas Eve production of Dickens's 'The Haunted Man' in a lecture hall. It had been planned as a prelude to a lecture on optics, but the tumultuous reception when a glowing skeleton appeared and disappeared before the audience's amazed eyes persuaded him to keep the 'ghost' a theatrical secret. 'Pepper's Ghost' in various guises drew a quarter of a million visitors in fifteen months.

Right The more old fashioned entertainments were still popular, however. This street peep show, illustrated in a magazine of 1894, showed the continuing attractions of a murder committed nearly three-quarters of a century earlier. The murder of Maria Marten at the Red Barn was enacted in song, at fairs, and in perspective boxes like this one.

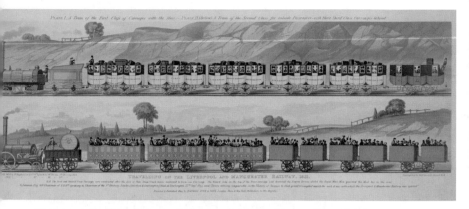

The greatest development in tourism came, of course, with the railways. The first passenger railway, the Liverpool and Manchester, is shown in this illustration of 1831. At the top are the first-class carriages, designed to look like the more familiar stagecoaches (together with a mail van at the rear); on the lower level are second-class (the first three on the left) and third-class (the remaining six) carriages. Both second and third class were open to the elements until the early 1840s.

Where travellers went, commercial opportunity was sure to follow. Handcrafted goods had long been available to the wealthy, but by the end of the nineteenth century there was also a substantial market for luxury items for the middle classes, as this 1890s advertisement for fitted travelling bags shows.

Steamers also began to be used by excursion travellers, especially in Scotland. In 1829 in Glasgow, the composer Felix Mendelssohn counted seventy steamers, forty of which had daily sailings. This steamer, in an engraving of 1825, took tourists around Loch Lomond, already a popular day trip.

Other tourists were heading to more exotic locales. By the middle of the century, Thomas Cook was taking excursionists to France and Switzerland. Here the Mer de Glace in Chamonix, in about 1880, looks somewhat like Hyde Park with its row of smartly dressed pleasure-seekers. (Note the parasols carried by two of the women.)

Left Thomas Cook produced booklets that were part promotional material, part guidebook. This 1865 booklet (left) gives details of his tours to Paris (inaugurated in 1855), Switzerland (1863) and Italy (1864). This opened a new market, with many of the middle classes now travelling abroad.

Below By mid-century, day excursions were becoming more common for the workers, too. The employees of Eno's Fruit Salt Works went to Eastbourne for their annual outing in 1886.

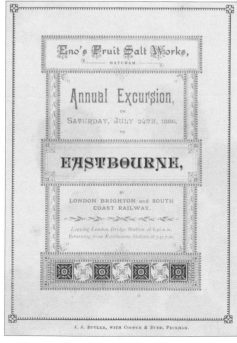

The Gallery of Antiquities in the British Museum, in about 1857. Art students were allowed to set up their easels in the galleries to copy the classical sculptures. The photographer, Roger Fenton, had been a founder member of the Photographic Society of London, the earliest group to promote photography as an art, and he was the official photographer to the British Museum.

Opposite A coloured aquatint (above) showing Christie's Auction Rooms, *c.*1808. Auctions were fashionable social occasions by this time, and were satirized in prints which were in turn sold themselves. By 1881, the Royal Academy's annual exhibition (below) was treated with greater respect. Here W. P. Frith shows a group of well-known faces: Oscar Wilde is the tall man on the centre right, next to the woman in the red dress.

Dion Boucicault's enormously popular play *The Corsican Brothers* (1852) relied for much of its appeal on the ingenuity of its staging. The first act (above) ends with Fabien dei Franchi at his desk, writing to his brother Louis (both played in the original by Kean), whose ghost appears behind him, gliding across the stage, ascending gradually through the floor before passing through the wall and disappearing. At the same moment the back of the stage opens to show a glade in the Forest of Fontainebleau (below). Louis dei Franchi lies dead, and the audience understands what has happened when Fabien says, 'Pray for Louis, dearest mother. I go to avenge him.'

It was bridges like this one that made the staging of *The Corsican Brothers* possible.
Originally winched by hand, this bridge at Drury Lane, photographed in 1894,
permitted appearances from under the stage, creating the effects for ghosts, vampires,
or simply star entrances. Louis dei Franchi stood on a platform that was rolled along
an incline on top of a similar bridge; as it rose it gave the appearance of his ghost
rising and gliding across the stage.

Astley's Amphitheatre, c.1790, when it consisted of a ring where the horses performed, and a stage, separated by the orchestra pit, where burlettas, ballets and pantomimes were produced. In 1800 the two spaces were integrated, to allow the horses to become part of the dramatic action. Astley's staged the two most successful hippodramas in the nineteenth century: *The Battle of Waterloo*, which played for fifty years, and *Mazeppa*, with its famous scene of the hero tied to a wild, runaway stallion.

Extravagant staging was also very much a part of legitimate drama. Charles Kean's production of *Henry V* in 1872 had a scene interpolated into the original, in which the King returned to London in triumph, to be met by hundreds of extras playing his cheering citizens. It became known as the 'shower of gold' scene, for the gold dust that was sprinkled down over the conquering heroes.

In 1821 a new series was published in monthly parts: Pierce Egan's *Life in London; or, the Day and Night Scenes of Jerry Hawthorn, Esq., and his elegant friend Corinthian Tom* . . . with etchings and woodcuts by George Cruikshank. Here Tom and Jerry enjoy a Cock and Hen Club evening. These clubs were the predecessor of music hall. They were held in a saloon or tavern, where a chairman (on the left, with the gavel) presided, and all who cared to sang, told jokes or otherwise entertained their friends.

The earliest purpose-built music hall did not appear until 1851, but before that many saloons and taverns held evenings where the programme was indistinguishable from music hall. The Rodney Inn and Concert Hall, Birmingham, photographed in 1846 (above), was one such. Later, extraordinary palaces of entertainment were built, such as the Alhambra Palace (below), in London, which became a music hall in 1860.

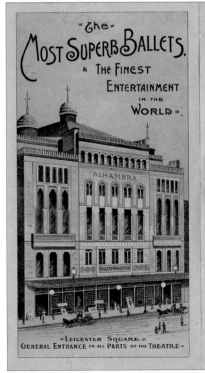

Popular songs in the music hall were sold as sheet music by the tens of thousands. George Leybourne, performing at the Canterbury Music Hall, made a hit with the song 'Champagne Charlie', and soon he was under contract to appear dressed as a 'swell' offstage too, and drink champagne copiously in public – all paid for by a wine merchant, to advertise his wares.

A decorative screen of 1815 shows racing in its eighteenth-century state. There is no grandstand: spectators either stand and watch (at the front) or follow the race on horseback or by carriage (at the rear).

Opposite Sports for the amateur produced a wide range of commercial opportunities. *The Modern Bicycle* (above) was one of hundreds of books on sport that appeared at the end of the century. Other manufacturers found scope in equipment: this advertisement for tennis equipment (below) does not stop with racquets and shoes, but has court markers, a tent for spectators, belts for players, and a boxed set that includes all the equipment required.

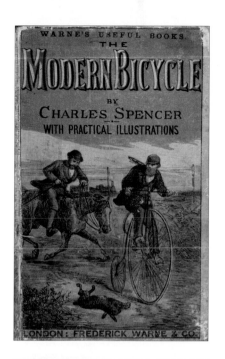

The first known Christmas card was commissioned in 1843 by Henry Cole, one of the moving forces behind both the Great Exhibition and the Victoria & Albert Museum. In the centre a family at Christmas dinner toasts absent friends, while at the sides charity is dispensed to the poor. About a thousand of these cards were printed, but there was no great demand. It was not until the 1870s that cheaper colour printing and the new penny post, combined with the increased emphasis laid on the holiday, made them as popular as Valentine's Day cards had long been.

Above Sheet music with Christmas carols and songs was increasingly popular as pianos were found in more and more homes. The cover of the 'Mistletoe Galop' shows a scene of the type of home entertainment which Christmas was now supposed to embody.

Left The railways made it likely that families no longer lived near each other; they also made it possible to have a family reunion at Christmas relatively cheaply. Even if people could not travel, the new parcel post meant that presents could be sent at a cost that most could afford. Here, on the Eastern Counties Railway, *c.*1865, parcels are being loaded into the luggage van, while travellers crowd the platforms.

When your friends arrive
give them a bright reception
By Using **HEARN'S LAMPS**

By the end of the nineteenth century, Christmas was used to sell all sorts of unrelated products. Here Hearn's Lamps are given a Christmas theme to promote a year-round product. Many manufacturers followed suit. One of the most famous and long-running advertisements was for Pear's soap, which had a picture of a small child under an over-turned bathtub, with the caption 'Oh! Here's a Merry Christmas'.

up a studio on the premises. This was so popular that in 1844 he expanded into the next-door building. In 1847 he had a second branch in Regent's Park, tellingly at the Colosseum, which housed panoramas, and by the mid-1850s his 'Temple of Photography' was established on Regent Street, the home of upper-class shopping, making the perfect link between education, technology and entertainment.

Photographs could be taken away and studied at leisure.* This was another way of taking entertainment and taming it, moving it from the street into the home and therefore domesticating it. Many children's toys followed this pattern, being based on public entertainments, but enjoyed safely away from the crowds. The Panorama of Europe: A New Game appeared in 1815, and had a map of Europe on which various routes had to be traced out. Other toys relied on public entertainments that were less educational, less satisfactory to the more serious, evangelical middle classes in particular. But by domesticating the public element, and disguising its origins with references to other, more educational, shows, the toys became welcome in many homes where theatre and magic displays were frowned on. A Geographical Panorama was not actually a panorama at all, but a toy theatre; another toy theatre claimed its educational credentials by calling itself a diorama. Home 'panoramas' were really magic-lantern versions of images taken from current panoramas, but they were even better, because 'by the magical power of this little instrument, [they are] brought in all their reality and beauty, to our own homes and firesides', said the *Art-Journal*. The privatization of the show was important in the success of these toys.

Separate lectures in new locations away from the shows and exhibition halls were similarly aimed at those who were inclined to distrust 'entertainment' alone. One of the founders of the Adelaide Gallery helped to set up the Polytechnic Institution, which was dedicated to the encouragement of invention and technology, and the education of the working classes. Yet soon after it opened in 1838, its educational and scientific demonstrations and lectures had been diluted and were in practice already indistinguishable from the entertainments of the town – 'Dissolving Views' were dioramas by another name, and its science

---

* At mid-century they cost anything from 10s. 6d. to 1 guinea for a whole-plate portrait, although two people could be photographed together for 15s. After 1860 the price for good studio photographs dropped to about 1s., but other photographers specialized in working-class sitters for far less.

lectures were equally reliant on popular entertainment. Yet the Polytechnic's reputation for rational recreation kept it secure. In Thackeray's 1853–5 novel *The Newcomes* (with its careful subtitle, 'Memoirs of a Most Respectable Family'), Lady Newcome says that when her children are home from school, 'I send them to the Polytechnic with Professor Hickson, who kindly explains to them some of the marvels of science and the wonders of machinery. I send them to the picture galleries and the British Museum. I go with them myself to the delightful lectures at the [Royal] Institution in Albemarle Street. I do not desire that they should attend theatrical exhibitions.'[27]* But they would really be attending 'theatrical exhibitions' in all but name. John Henry Pepper, 'chemical professor to the establishment' from 1848, lectured on chemical reactions by using as an example the case of Dr William Palmer, the Rugeley Poisoner.† He was soon even more famous as the creator of 'Pepper's Ghost', a theatrical effect that produced the illusion of ghostly transparent figures moving onstage. In 1862 he staged a Christmas Eve production of Dickens's 'The Haunted Man' in a lecture hall at the Polytechnic. A student at his desk was suddenly transfixed by the vision of a glowing skeleton which appeared and disappeared before the audience's amazed eyes. Pepper had planned this as a prelude to a lecture on optics, but the tumultuous applause persuaded him to keep the 'ghost' a theatrical secret, and Pepper's Ghost drew a quarter of a million visitors to the Polytechnic in the next fifteen months, as well as making spectral appearances in theatres across the country, suitably licensed by Pepper.[29]

Given the success of this type of razzmatazz, the value of stressing education did not go unremarked by members of the show community. Some simply commented on various world and current events in their own entertainments: Planché's *The New Planet; or, Harlequin out of Place*, his Christmas pantomime of 1847, revolved around the recent discovery of the planet Neptune: Neptune descends to earth and makes solemn

* When Colonel Newcome asks for his son to attend some Shakespeare, Lady Newcome graciously sends the child with their footman.
† Dr Palmer (1824–56) was convicted of murdering a friend who had just won heavily at the Shrewsbury races. However, in Rugeley he had long been suspected of murdering his children (five of his six legitimate children died of convulsions; as did two of his illegitimate ones, soon after visiting him), his mother-in-law (who died two weeks after coming to live with him), his wife (after he insured her life for £13,000) and his brother, all between 1849 and 1855. The drinker's query 'What's your poison?' first appeared in popular speech during his trial.[28]

visits to many 'educational' spots, including the Colosseum in Regent's Park, the Egyptian Hall and the Polytechnic, where the 'lecturers' sing of new scientific and technological discoveries, such as the telegraph, ending with a tableau of Shakespeare, Wellington and Britannia.[30] But other entertainers dedicated themselves more seriously to highlighting the educational sides to their shows. Mme Tussaud printed 'a general outline of the history of each character', which would 'not only greatly increase the pleasure to be derived from a mere view of the Figure, but [would] also convey to the minds of young Persons much biographical knowledge – a branch of education universally allowed to be of the highest importance'.[31] For an extra 6*d*. Robert Barker had, with his earliest panoramas, provided booklets that had outlines of the pictures, then summaries of the history and geography of the regions shown. And panoramas were sometimes regarded as tedious precisely because of their educational reputation. Charles Lamb painted a sad picture of a poor schoolmaster who in his holidays had 'some intrusive upper-boy fastened upon him . . . that he must drag after him to the play, to the Panorama, to Mr Bartley's Orrery, to the Panopticon'.[32] Dickens tried to make his example sound more enticing, promoting a moving panorama of the Mississippi and Missouri Rivers as 'a picture three miles long,* which occupies two hours in its passage . . . It is an easy means of travelling, night and day, without any inconvenience from climate, steamboat company, or fatigue.'[33]

The Mississippi panorama was gigantic, but its success may have come from a new element: it had, for the first time, a narrator – the artist himself, who stood beside the panorama and lectured on his voyage as the view unrolled. Soon narrators were regularly employed to provide historical and geographical information as the audience watched. Other panoramas straining for educational content incorporated images of engineering works into their scenes – engineering was always educational – and this made a success of 'A Trip from Primrose Hill, via the London and North Western and Chester and Holyhead Railways to Holyhead', which included depictions of railway bridges and the industrial sights of Wolverhampton and Coventry. Some panoramas added music: the

---

* This measurement was given not only by Dickens but also in advertisements, but it has been pointed out that, if the show lasted two hours, then the scenes would have had to zip past the audience at 132 feet per minute, which seems improbable; 1,200 yards has been suggested as a less hyperbolic possibility.

cyclorama showing Lisbon after the earthquake of 1755 was unfurled 'to the sound of congenial music',[34] although how Beethoven's Pastoral Symphony in a version for organ, and extracts from operas that included *Don Giovanni*, *Masaniello* and *Mosè in Egitto* were 'congenial' with the devastation wrought by an earthquake was left unexplored. Panoramas of the Holy Land were accompanied by 'Grand Sacred Vocal Music by the Great Masters' at St George's Gallery, and by 'Hebrew Melodies' at the Egyptian Hall. Sheet music was sold to link up with the panorama of the moment – after the Mississippi panorama's success, it was possible to buy what in today's terms would be understood to be the official tie-in, a piano score of 'Mississippi Waltzes, Played during the Moving of Banvard's Three Mile Picture of the Mississippi River'. There were more opportunistic offerings, too: 'Nelly was a Lady (Down on the Mississippi)', 'I was raised in Mississippi' and 'By de Mississippi Ribber' (*sic*) all appeared within two years of the panorama. Other panoramas produced similar pieces for home entertainment from sheet-music publishers with an eye for the topic of the moment. There was 'The Pyramid Galop', 'The Niagara Falls Galop', 'The Lago Maggiore Galop', even 'The Holborn Viaduct Galop' – not to mention polkas, mazurkas and schottisches.[35]

While this was music to be played at home, *en famille*, musical accompaniments to the panoramas themselves were a way to circumvent another problem: the attitude towards theatre in its various forms as it developed over the eighteenth and nineteenth centuries. For some, theatre had always been an abomination. But for most people through the previous centuries theatre had simply been an upper-class pastime. Now, as it became more accessible to the middle and working classes, those presenting theatrical entertainments needed to find a way of not entirely losing the great mass of the bourgeoisie who were, from the end of the eighteenth century, turning ever more to evangelical values. In the evangelicals' view, the theatre was a place of falsehood, where the credulous were duped by illusions and deceit. Theatre, like novels, was too much concerned with the passions, and too little with morality; both genres fed the imagination, which if anything needed to be quelled. The Nonconformist *Evangelical Magazine* published a 'Spiritual Barometer' which went from +70 ('Glory; dismission from the body') to 0 ('Indifference') and then down through −30 ('The theatre, Vauxhall, Ranelagh, &c'), to −40 ('private prayer totally neglected . . .'), −50 ('parties of pleasure on the Lord's day, masquerades; drunkenness; adultery; profaneness; lewd songs'), and finally −70 ('Death, perdition').[36] It should be remembered, warned the *Christian Observer* in 1815, that 'The last age in France was characterized by the number of profligate novels, and behold the consequences in the total corruption of the present.'[37] This was a perfectly mainstream view: *The Times* warned in 1809 that 'The stage has proved, and will ever prove, subversive of the order, peace, and purity of morals, and consequently, of Christianity itself.'[38]

Thus a range of entertainments was carefully staged in neutral surroundings that enabled those to whom theatre was barred still to partake of some of the associated pleasures. In 1838 the Adelphi Theatre had a troupe of dancing 'Bayadères', who also performed at the Egyptian Hall 'at the solicitation of many Families and Individuals who are not in the habit of visiting Theatres'. This was fairly overt. Thiodon's Grand Original Mechanical and Picturesque Theatre of Arts in Spring Gardens was more circumspect, promising that 'The Entertainments offered at this Theatre are quite distinct from that of a Theatrical Description, and on this Account, together with its surprising Ingenuity, and harmless Tendency, is peculiarly calculated to attract the Notice and Support of those, whose Religious Tenets forbid their Participation in Amusements of a more marked and decisive Character.' The Gallery of Illustration in Regent Street was suitably innocuously named, and from 1850 held 'one-man entertainments' which were in fact if not in name play-readings. Sometimes the neutral locale was not necessary, and a playbill that promoted a lavish spectacle as educational was all that was necessary. Astley's Amphitheatre staged a version of St George and the Dragon in which, it was promised, the dragon's 'Mechanism and Automatous Serpentine Movements [were] so ably calculated and put into play, as to stamp the Action-Scene with the character of TRUTH throughout its progress, and thereby constitution the principal merit of the whole Performance.'[39]

Even more than mechanical animals, real animals were educational – no evangelical could 'behold the works of Nature without [also] admiring Nature's God', while the scientifically minded were reassured to be told that the descriptions in the guidebook supplied by the most famous turn-of-the-century menagerie, in Exeter Change, were 'chiefly extracted from the works of Buffon and Goldsmith'. Yet even in such a respectable environment the link with theatre was there for those who wanted to see it: Exeter Change's elephant, Chunee, was loaned out to appear in a Covent Garden pantomime in 1811, and when she was killed in 1826

The Exeter Change, on the Strand, from the 1770s had a menagerie, including a unicorn (in reality a rhinoceros), a zebra, a kangaroo, a 'fiery lynx', 'a ravenous wolf from Algiers' and, most famously, in the early nineteenth century, Chunee the elephant.

(by a firing squad, after running amok on her daily walk down the Strand and killing her keeper) Sadler's Wells quickly staged a production of *Chuneelah; or, The Death of the Elephant at Exeter 'Change*. So, for those who found the Exeter Change too much the showplace, in 1828 the Royal Zoological Society opened a menagerie in Regent's Park in a form that was more calculated to appeal to supporters of 'rational recreation'. For the first time animals were housed more or less in a manner that imitated their original habitats (except for the llamas, who for some reason were housed in a Gothic pavilion). At first, entrance was restricted to those who could obtain a letter of introduction from a member of the RZS, and even then admission was 1s. From 1847 those worries about the working classes and how they were spending their leisure that were to surface in so many different areas of life – in the planning of the Great Exhibition, in the parliamentary select committee looking into museum access for the working classes, in concern about lack of open spaces for healthy games-playing – brought a change of policy. The RZS's new director believed strongly in the power of rational recreation to educate and 'improve' the working classes, and admission was consequently lowered to 6*d.* on Mondays and holidays, creating an entirely new audience for the zoo.

In many ways the zoo was the end of a much-loved but by now almost extinct species of leisure, the pleasure garden. London had been famous for its pleasure gardens for much of the eighteenth century. Vauxhall Gardens, the best known, had opened just after the Restoration, under the name Spring Gardens (or Faux, or Fox, Hall Gardens). Pepys had visited in 1667, and put his finger on the attractions: 'It is very pleasant and cheap going thither, for a man may go to spend what he will, or nothing, all as one – but to hear the nightingale and other birds, and here fiddles, and there a harp . . . and here laughing, and there fine people walking, is mighty divertising [*sic*]. Among others, there were two pretty women alone . . .'[40] That, in sum, was what people enjoyed for the next 150 years: pleasant walks in beautiful grounds, for only a small fee, music, and – for the men – women. Over time the entertainments became more elaborate, moving inexorably from simple rural pleasures to the presentation of spectacle. In 1728 Jonathan Tyers bought the lease, and it was under his direction that paintings by Francis Hayman and Hogarth, and a bust of Handel as Apollo by Roubilliac, were commissioned, and that dances, ridottos, masquerades and balls were held. By the 1760s buildings were dotted about the grounds, designed in an eclectic range of fashionable styles – 'a noble Turkish Tent', a Gothic pavilion with a 'painting in the Chinese taste, representing Vulcan catching Mars and Venus in a net',[41] a neoclassical rotunda with supper boxes, a Gothic obelisk. Every night at nine o'clock the crowd was entertained by the Cascade, where

> by drawing up a curtain is shewn a most beautiful landscape in perspective of a fine hilly country with a miller's house and a water mill, all illuminated by concealed lights; but the principal object that strikes the eye is a cascade or water fall. The exact appearance of water is seen flowing down a declivity, and turning the weel [*sic*] of the mill, it rises up in a foam at the bottom, and then glides aways. This moving picture attended with the noise of the cascade has a very pleasing and surprising effect on both the eye and ear.[42]

This was not a panorama, despite the use of the words 'moving picture': it was a three-dimensional representation, with the noise produced by strips of tin that were dropped with a clatter, and the water effect achieved via the shimmering of dozens of lamps.

By the middle of the eighteenth century, admission was 1s., and Vauxhall was drawing 1,000 people a night in a summer season that lasted somewhat over three months. In 1749 the rehearsal for Handel's *Music for the Royal Fireworks* had an audience of 12,000;* simply because the Duke of Cumberland was planning to attend, another evening, in 1781, saw the presence of 'more than eleven thousand persons' according to the management of the Gardens, who estimated they had served food to 7,000 of them.[43] Food and drink were a large part of the business of Vauxhall, and they were notorious for their extortionate expense: in 1796 a plate of ham cost 2s., a slice of bread 1d. – at a time when an entire loaf could be bought for that in the shops – and a single biscuit was the same price.[44] By 1817 things had reached the height of absurdity, when a plate of lettuce cost 18d. But gradually, as Vauxhall fell in people's estimations, so did the prices; by 1833 ham was 'only' 1s., while a plate of salad plus 'the use of the cruet' was now 6d. less than it had been fifteen years before.[45] The prices had dropped, but the hoped-for surge in popularity did not follow. Vauxhall was no longer the fashion, and it was forced to compete with the other entertainments of the town on their terms.

The proprietors were aware they had an advantage in the Gardens' size, and they began to stage extravaganzas to compete with the theatres. With space for huge crowd scenes, with the sky above for fireworks, and, as a supreme advantage, with the River Thames for 'naumachia', or re-creations of naval engagements, Vauxhall held on to some of its many visitors for a while. In 1827 Prince Pückler-Muskau attended an evening performance of its Battle of Waterloo re-creation (this was the one the Duke of Wellington also attended):

> An open part of the garden surrounded by ancient chestnut trees serves as the stage. Between four of these trees a 'tribune' had been erected with benches for twelve hundred or so people which was at least 40 feet high . . . The moon shone brightly and showed between two gigantic trees a great red curtain, painted with the combined arms of Great Britain.
>
> After a moment's silence, a cannon shot thundered through the wood and at the same time the fine military music of the

---

* For more on this episode, see pp. 349–50.

2nd Regiment of Guards rang out in the distance . . . Out of the wood advanced the French Guards with the bearded Sapeurs at their head. They formed themselves into ranks and Napoleon, on his white horse and in his grey overcoat, accompanied by several marshals, rode past them *en revue*. From a thousand throats echoed '*Vive l'Empereur!*' The emperor touched his hat and went off at a gallop, while the troops bivouacked in closely packed groups, and marched off. Soon afterwards Wellington appeared with his general staff, all very good copies of the originals. He harangued his troops and slowly rode off. The great original himself was in the audience and laughed loudly at his representation.

Now the fight begins with skirmishes; then whole columns rush at each other and attack with the bayonet, while the French cuirassiers charge the Scottish squares. Since there were about a thousand men and two hundred horses in the action, and no lack of gunpowder, at moments it was just like a real engagement. The thick smoke of a real fire enveloped the combatants who, for a time, could be seen only by the lightning flash of the artillery, whilst the foreground was occupied by the dead and dying. As the smoke cleared away Houguemont was seen in flames, surrounded by the English as victors and the French as prisoners, and in the distance was Napoleon on horseback, with his carriage and four horses behind him, fleeing across the stage. Wellington the victor was greeted under the roar of the cannon with shouts of 'Hurrah, hurrah, hurrah!'[46]

Vauxhall made more and more of the firework displays as time went on. In 1823 it produced a 24-metre-high fireworks Bay of Naples with an erupting Mount Vesuvius, later there were fireworks of Fingal's Cave, Gothic abbeys, the burning of York Minster – in fact the same subjects that were popular for panoramas. In 1833 it staged a Jubilee Centenary Week (despite the fact that it was not its centenary, or anything like it), with a portrait of the master of ceremonies, Mr Simpson, 'in Fire Works, [which] will bow to the Company, soon as ignited'.[47] Marylebone Gardens, a less fashionable pleasure garden, which covered about 30,000 square metres north of Oxford Street, had started to produce firework displays in the 1740s.* In 1763 it had 'an illuminated Steeple forty feet high', and by 1772 the fireworks were the main purpose of a trip to Marylebone. 'Signor Torre', who had produced firework displays at

---

* Another aspect of these gardens – concerts – will be discussed in Chapter 9.

Versailles for the wedding of the Dauphin and Marie Antoinette in 1770, was under contract, and in his first season he produced 'Transparencies of Their Majesties', followed by depictions of Vulcan leading the Cyclops – who lit a fire and forged arrows for Cupid and Venus – and Mount Etna. Mount Etna then erupted, with glowing lava rolling down its sides.[48]

Instead of the great gardens – Vauxhall, Cremorne, Marylebone, Ranelagh – it was the smaller inns and taverns that called themselves pleasure gardens, or wells, that prospered into the nineteenth century. For one thing, they charged less for admission: Vauxhall had alternated between 1s. and 2s. for most of its existence, while Ranelagh, determined to keep out the middle classes, much less the working classes, charged 2s. 6d., and the Pantheon even more.[49] These places did keep out the middle and working classes, but when their fashionable patrons deserted them, they were financially doomed. Marylebone Gardens charged a modest 6d., but many spas combined admission and a drink of their waters for only 3d., while an entire breakfast could be purchased at Islington Spa for 9d.[50] These spas were for the newly prosperous, and for the working classes. When Evelina, in Fanny Burney's novel of 1778, went to stay with her embarrassingly lower-middle-class cousins the Branghtons, she was asked if she had enjoyed George's, a pleasure garden in Hampstead; she was forced to admit to not having been there – or to Marylebone, or to Vauxhall Gardens, or to Don Saltero's in Chelsea (see p. 396), or to Sadler's Wells, St Paul's or the Tower of London. Her cousin exclaimed, 'Why then you might as well not have come to London for aught I see, for you've been no where.'[51] The point was that, having been living with gentry families, her entertainment had taken place in private – or, if in public, at Ranelagh, the most exclusive of the pleasure gardens.

London had many pleasure gardens, but it also had a number of so-called spas, which were mainly for the lower middle classes and below, or for middle- and upper-class men when not accompanied by their families. These were not actually spas at all, except that they had originally been established because there was a chalybeate spring on the site. For the most part, water-drinking and health had little to do with their visitors' enjoyment. Many London spas were in fact if not in name inns, or taverns, with a bit of a garden in which perhaps a sporting area or tea garden could be found. In Marylebone, the main pleasure garden was surrounded by satellite pleasure gardens, so called, such as the

Queen's Head and Artichoke, which was an inn with a skittle ground, and the Jew's Harp house, another inn, with 'bowery tea-gardens, skittle grounds, trap-ball grounds' and a real-tennis court (all of which were destroyed when Regent's Park was laid out). The Bayswater tea gardens barely mentioned their waters, preferring to advertise Mrs Graham, who made an ascent in a balloon every day at five, accompanied by fireworks. Hampstead, as Evelina's cousins knew, had many tea gardens, including Hampstead Wells and Wells Walk, which had a coffee house and a bowling green, and held concerts and dances. Kilburn Wells, near Belsize Park, also had a small spring, as closer in towards the City did Pancras Wells and Adam and Eve Tea-Gardens (both now underneath St Pancras station). This was fertile territory for springs: Islington Spa had existed from the early eighteenth century, and was not to be confused with Sadler's Wells, now a theatre, but then a spring, as its name suggests. This spa's abiding claim to fame was that the princesses Amelia and Catherine had visited to drink the waters there in 1733, but by the end of the century it was a tea garden in all but name. Many others were similar: spas by name, pleasure gardens in reality – Spa Fields Pantheon, London Spa, New Wells, English Grotto, Bagnigge Wells, Lord Cobham's Head in Cold Bath Fields, St Chad's Well, Spring Gardens. When one looks at the names of London, it is clear how many springs have been tarmacked over in the last century and a half.[52]

The focus thus far has been mainly on middle-class entertainment, or on entertainments that encompassed within their middle-class audience a certain number of the high-earning, industrious working classes. Many of the shows just described claimed to attract audiences from every walk of life, but there was also a set of entertainments that were the province of the working classes entirely. Many of these working-class entertainments were similar in kind to middle-class entertainments – peep shows, wax-works, music and animals. It was the attitudes behind them that made them so different. Working-class animal shows, for instance, did not worry about providing extracts from Buffon in guidebooks – they did not in fact produce guidebooks at all. Instead, these shows were part of the older fair traditions, and specialized in deformed animals, dancing animals, animals that played an instrument, or 'learned' animals, which tapped out the time with their paws, or hoofs, or pecked at correct letters or numbers in answer to their owners' questions. There were 'Industrious

Fleas', and trained bees, and Breslaw's birds, which, in the first half of
the nineteenth century,

> formed themselves into ranks like a company of soldiers; small
> cones of paper bearing some resemblance to grenadiers' caps
> were put upon their heads, and diminutive imitations of muskets
> made with wood, secured under their left wings. Thus equipped,
> they marched to and fro several times; when a single bird was
> brought forward, supposed to be a deserter, and set between six
> of the musketeers, three in a row, who conducted him from the
> top to the bottom of the table, on the middle of which a small
> brass cannon charged with a little gunpowder had been pre-
> viously placed, and the deserter was situated in the front part of
> the cannon; his guards then divided, three retiring on one side,
> and three on the other, and he was left standing by himself.
> Another bird was immediately produced; and a lighted match
> being put into one of his claws; he hopped boldly on the other
> to the tail of the cannon, and, applying the match to the priming,
> discharged the piece . . . The moment the explosion took place,
> the deserter fell down, and lay . . . like a dead bird; but, at the
> command of his tutor, he rose again; and the cages being
> brought, the feathered soldiers were stripped of their ornaments,
> and returned into them in perfect order.[53]

Many of these shows had no single home, but travelled around the
country, or the cities, from yard to yard, inn to inn, fair to fair. The fairs
were dying out in the nineteenth century, but until the 1850s they were
still a major force: from 1750 to 1850 there were sixty fairs within fifteen
miles of Charing Cross alone, and as late as 1843 200,000 people were
said to have attended the Easter fair in Stepney, claimed by 'Lord' George
Sanger, of Sanger's Circus (see below), to be 'the biggest gathering of its
kind in Europe'. Some fairs which had been more rural events came to
life again in the nineteenth century, in part because of improved transport links. These fairs were no longer only for locals, but instead were
destinations for a much larger population intent on enjoying a day out.
Greenwich Fair in the 1820s and 1830s was attended by thousands who
travelled to the fair by steamer; in the 1840s even more came by the
London and Greenwich Railway.[54] Transport links worked both ways:
visitors could attend fairs that might previously have been too far away,
and showmen, conjurors, tumblers and rope dancers could all travel
more easily around a wider circuit of fairs, while those who had larger

exhibits to transport – those with peep shows, panoramas, puppet shows or waxworks – could move about the country economically by train. It is notable that only after the emergence of the railways were major centres of entertainment built in the suburbs – after the Great Exhibition closed, the Crystal Palace was moved not to another central location, but to the southern suburb of Sydenham, while Alexandra Palace was built in Muswell Hill, and Sanger's Circus had a permanent base at the Agricultural Hall in Islington.

For many years the circuses were just one element of the fairs: Wombwell's and Atkins's circuses were prominent at Bartholomew Fair, and both in London and in the provinces these were two of the largest circuses, together with Sanger's. It was Lord George Sanger (and his wife, 'Mme Pauline de Vere', a lion-tamer) who transformed this form of livelihood from a temporary travelling show into a mass-entertainment business. By the 1850s Sanger had a permanent base in Liverpool, and in 1860 he also had a three-ring circus in Plymouth. Soon there were permanent sites in Aberdeen, Bath, Birmingham, Bristol, Dundee, Exeter, Liverpool, Manchester and Plymouth, as well as at the Agricultural Hall in Islington and in such seaside towns as Ramsgate and Margate (where his 'Hall by the Sea' acted as his headquarters). When Sanger's Circus toured Europe in the 1870s it needed 46 carriages to transport 160 horses, 11 elephants, 12 camels – and 230 employees.[55]

Many of the fairs that prospered in the nineteenth century were held each spring, around Easter and Whitsun, when workers traditionally had holidays, while two of the largest fairs, Southwark and Bartholomew, which were held later in the year, suffered precipitous declines. At the beginning of the century Bartholomew Fair had been a byword for entertainment fairs in general. Wordsworth in *The Prelude* set his reader 'Above the press and danger of the crowd / Upon some showman's platform', to see:

> . . . chattering monkeys dangling from their poles,
> And children whirling in their roundabouts;
> With those that stretch the neck and strain the eyes,
> And crack the voice in rivalship, the crowd
> Inviting; with buffoons against buffoons
> Grimacing, writhing, screaming, – him who grinds
> The hurdy-gurdy, at the fiddle weaves,
> Rattles the salt-box, thumps the kettle-drum,

And him who at the trumpet puffs his cheeks,
The silver-collared Negro with his timbrel,
Equestrians, tumblers, women, girls, and boys,
Blue-breeched, pink-vested, with high-towering plumes. –
All moveables of wonder, from all parts,
Are here – Albinos, painted Indians, Dwarfs,
The Horse of knowledge, and the learned Pig,
The Stone-eater, the man that swallows fire,
Giants, Ventriloquists, the Invisible Girl,
The Bust that speaks and moves its goggling eyes,
The Wax-work, Clock-work, all the marvellous craft
Of modern Merlins, Wild Beasts, Puppet-shows,
All out-o'-the-way, far-fetched, perverted things,
All freaks of nature, all Promethean thoughts
Of man, his dullness, madness, and their feats
All jumbled up together, to compose
A Parliament of Monsters. Tents and Booths
Meanwhile, as if the whole were one vast mill,
Are vomiting, receiving on all sides,
Men, Women, three-years' Children, Babes in arms.[56]

As Wordsworth described it, so it was: these fairs were now almost entirely entertainment. The retail element of country fairs was dying, and in the cities it was already dead. As early as 1748 Bartholomew Fair had consisted entirely of entertainments, including a play of *The Bloody Contest between Charles the Twelfth and Peter the Great, Czar of Muscovy*; plays made up of snippets from chapbook stories such as *The Blind Beggar of Bethnal Green* and *The Adventures of Roderick Random and his Friend Strap*; a farce (possibly performed by puppets) called *The Constant Quaker, or, The Humours of Wapping*; a pantomime, *Harlequin's Frolics*; a waxwork show entitled The Court of the Queen of Hungary; freaks both human and animal, including 'The Young Oronatu Savage', a 12-foot long, 120-stone hog and a dwarf billed as 'Maria Theresa, the Amazing Corsican Fairy'. There were fireworks, Italian sword dances, hornpipes, folk dances, puppet shows and menageries. In 1752 there were also a learned horse and a learned pig, an American dwarf, 'the tall lady from Norfolk, and the short one from Durham', ribbon- and breeches-sellers (the only retailers at the fair, apart from those who sold food), a Punch and Judy show, fire-eaters, rope dancers, wire dancers and conjurors. By 1825 the fair had twenty-two large-scale shows, including Wombwell's Circus and Atkins's Menagerie; eight shows with human 'curiosities' such as dwarves, giants or 'natives'; and another five shows displaying performers with various skills, such as jugglers, tumblers, rope dancers, clowns or equestrians. Then there were secondary shows including a mare with seven feet, a learned horse, and a pig billed as 'Toby the Swinish Philosopher', who counted, knew the alphabet, drew up accounts, and told the time.

Highlights were a peep show of the murder of William Weare (see p. 181) and waxworks of the royal family, Mother Shipton, an Irish giant and the acquitted murderer Abraham Thornton.* Murder had already become big business as the Sunday newspapers and the penny-bloods spread the taste for police reports and accounts of trials. They also moved crime from a local onto a national scale: in 1834, seven years after the murder, there were five panoramas or other representations of Maria Marten at the Red Barn, and a peep-show proprietor later told Mayhew, 'There was more [money] took with [James Blomfield] Rush's murder than there ever has been by the battle of Waterloo itself.'†[59]

Retrospectively it is possible to classify each show, but in reality the various types of entertainments all merged. Peep shows, which were more or less elaborate perspective boxes, gradually took in elements from automata and, later, photography. Waxworks used clockwork mechanisms so that previously stationary 'processions' of figures now moved across a room or a stage. Puppets were mixed together with clockwork figures, or placed in front of panoramas. Equally, places like the Egyptian Hall, or Savile House near Leicester Square, let out exhibition space as individual rooms, so instead of visitors seeing just a panorama, or a set of waxworks, a kaleidoscope of shows passed before them:

> Serpents both of land and sea; – panoramas of all the rivers of
> the known world; jugglers; ventriloquists; imitators of the noises

---

* Abraham Thornton (c.1793–1860) was accused of raping and murdering a woman he met at a dance in 1817. It became a case of national interest when Thornton demanded 'ordeal by battle', which he was entitled to by law, but which had not been used since the early seventeenth century. It was finally agreed that he did have the right (abolished in 1819), but he dropped the attempt.[57]

† In 1848 Rush, a bailiff, murdered the recorder of Norwich and his son, and wounded his daughter, in a case that revolved around a disputed will. It was a popular sensation, and special excursion trains were run for spectators wishing to attend the execution, one of the last public executions outside London. Rush was a popular subject not only for peep shows but also for Staffordshire potters, who produced models of Rush, the property under dispute and of Rush's own farm.[58]

of animals; dioramas of the North pole, and the gold-diggings
of California; somnambulists (very lucid); ladies who have
cheerfully submitted to have their heads cut off nightly at sixpence per head admission; giants; dwarfs; sheep with six legs;
calves born inside out; marionettes; living marionettes; lectures
on Bloomerism; expositors of orrery – all of these have by turns
found a home in Savile House.[60]

And all could be viewed in one day.

The shows were advertised in a similar melange, with strident messages bombarding the public daily. The press had been carrying advertisements for entertainments since the first daily newspaper appeared, and
now magazines like *Punch* (founded 1841) and, especially, the *Illustrated
London News* (founded 1842) also carried notices. Journalists were
regaled with oyster-and-champagne suppers (courtesy of Albert Smith
before his 'Ascent of Mont Blanc' lectures), or special viewings, or free
passes for their families. Out on the streets, advertising was livelier still.
The very first omnibus in 1829 had carried an advertisement for the
Regent's Park Diorama, but that was the very least of it. Carts pulling
oversized models of the object to be sold had long been one of the
major causes of congestion in the streets, as huge umbrellas, hats or
cheeses fought it out with private carriages, hackneys, delivery carts and
omnibuses. The entertainment business was not behindhand, and as so
often was the case, it was a visitor to the country who recorded the
extraordinary sight:

> Behold, rolling down from Oxford Street, three immense
> wooden pyramids – their outsides are painted all over with hiero-
> glyphics and with monumental letters in the English language.
> These pyramids display faithful portraits of Isis and Osiris, of
> cats, storks, and of the apis; and amidst these old-curiosity shop
> gods, any Englishman may read an inscription, printed in letters
> not much longer than a yard, from which it appears that there
> is now on view a panorama of Egypt . . . This panorama shows
> the flux and reflux of the Nile, with its hippopotamuses and
> crocodiles, and a section of the Red Sea . . . [And] here is another
> monstrous shape – a mosque, with its cupola and blue and white
> surmounted by a crescent. The driver is a light-haired boy, with
> a white turban and a sooty face . . . The Panorama of the Nile,
> the Overland Route, the Colosseum, Madame Tussaud's Exhi-
> bition of Waxworks, and other sights, are indeed wonder-works
> of human industry, skill, and invention; and, in every respect,

Street advertising was common: carts with large panels advertising shops, manufacturers or, as in this 1830s cartoon, entertainment, crowded the streets, as did men with sandwich boards (the ones on the right advertising a Napoleon-themed product).

> are they superior to the usual productions of the same kind. But,
> for all that, they must send their advertising vans into the streets;
> necessity compels them to strike the gong and blow the trumpet;
> choice there is none. They must either advertise or perish.[61]

That was what many believed.

In the first half of the nineteenth century, many forms of advertising were so ephemeral that we know only that they once existed. There were sandwich men, there were men who carried placards, or models of the item being advertised. There were also handbills, passed out on the street or, as time went on, delivered door to door. After the arrival of the penny post, handbills were mailed, just as direct mail is now. For all of these, few examples have survived.

Bill-posters or bill-stickers were another group of whom little is known. By the nature of their displays – posters glued to the walls of buildings – survival of their handiwork from one week to the next was

Overleaf:
In 1887 *Punch* summarized the various forms of street advertising. Much remained the same as it had been for half a century, but now the bills posted on walls were highly illustrated rather than typographical.

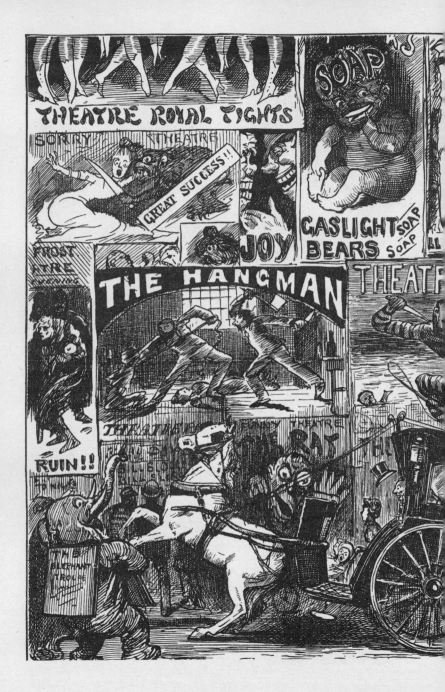

minimal. And yet they were in the forefront of advertising: posters could be stuck up on walls and fences without permission, there was no tax to pay on them, as there was on newspaper advertising and, unlike in newspapers, the advertisements were not confined to a single set column width. Dickens interviewed a man he named 'The King of the Bill-Stickers', who claimed his father had been 'Engineer, Beadle, and Bill-Sticker to the Parish of St Andrews Holborn' in 1780, which if true is as far back as this practice can be traced. By 1851, claimed 'The King', there were 150 stickers in London, and he estimated that each man could post 100 bills a day.[62] This gives a total of 15,000 bills a day in London alone. If this could indeed have been the case, it is not a surprise that bill-sticking died out: the risk – pretty well the certainty – that any bill would be overstuck within days, if not hours of its being posted made it futile.

Bill-stickers paid little if any attention to who owned the walls they stuck their bills on. By-laws and pressure on the police to monitor their activities changed the situation slightly, but it was the Great Exhibition and the railways, those two catalysts, that made the next stage in advertising possible. In 1851 the *Illustrated London News* carried the following advertisement:

> NOTICE TO ADVERTISERS – LONDON and NORTH-WESTERN RAILWAY STATIONS. Messrs. W. H. SMITH and SON are prepared to receive Bills and Advertisements for putting on the Walls and Platforms, and in the Booking-offices of these Stations, 188 in number, including London, Liverpool, Manchester, Leeds, and Birmingham. The number of Passengers travelling over the line was about 6,000,000 in 1850, and will probably greatly exceed that number in the present year. Advertisements will be received for one or more Stations, or for the whole Line, for periods of one, three, six or twelve months.
>
> Persons contracting for space for hanging Advertisements, may change them not oftener than once a week. Further particulars and copies of Rules and rates of charge may be obtained from Messrs. W. H. SMITH and SON, 138 Strand, London; or at the Book Stands and of the Booking-clerks at all the Stations of the Line.[63]

W. H. Smith had reinvented itself once more, becoming a new thing, an advertising agency, a broker that negotiated between the retailer with goods or services to sell and the owner of the space on which those goods or services could be promoted. By the 1870s 'advertising contractors' were employed to 'purchase the rights, exclusive and absolute' to particular spaces; these spaces were then 'sublet' to companies who wanted to advertise.[64] The new techniques in reproducing engravings and the possibilities that would soon come for printing cheaply in colour added still more to the enticements of railway and poster advertising.

Spectacle was now becoming the important element, and size mattered. In 1867 the Adelphi Theatre advertised its play *The Dead Heart* to such an extent that it used (and advertised the use of)

> 10,000,000 adhesive labels . . . 30,000 small cuts [that is, illustrations] of the guillotine scene, 5000 reams of note-paper, 110,000 business envelopes, 60,000 stamped envelopes, 2000 six-sheet cuts of the Bastile [*sic*] scene, 5,000,000 handbills, 1000 six-sheet posters, 500 slips, 1,000,000 cards heartshaped, 100 twentyeight sheet posters,* and 20,000 folio cards for shop windows. This was quite exclusive of newspaper wrappers and various other ingenious means of attracting attention.[65]

Theatre was selling itself as *the* spectacle. And perhaps it was.

* Posters were made by sticking standard-sized pages together: thirty-two seems to have been the maximum that was technically manageable.

8

Penny Plain, Tuppence Coloured: The Theatrical Spectacular

THEATRE WAS RADICAL. Theatre was dangerous. Theatre needed to be contained. This was the message that was reiterated over and over from the Restoration of Charles II until – well, in some ways until prior censorship of plays was finally removed in 1968. In fact, if theatre had not been so much fun for the very people who feared its influence on others, it probably would have been banned entirely. But, as it was not banned, it needed to be fiercely regulated. Theatrical performances since 1662 had been controlled by giving royal patents, or permission to perform, the possession of which was necessary before a theatre could function. This requirement for a patent to perform legitimate drama remained in place until the Theatre Regulations Act of 1843. In addition, from 1737 all plays, even those performed by the companies holding patents, were also required by a new Licensing Act to be submitted for prior censorship to the office of the Lord Chamberlain.* The collapse of the Licensing Act of 1695 at the end of the seventeenth century had freed other writers to write and publish as they pleased; after publication they could be prosecuted for libel, sedition or blasphemy, but playwrights were not even given the freedom to run that risk. It was a sign of how fearful the government was – or, at the least, of how very cross it was about being ridiculed onstage.

The government was right, because theatre represented anarchy,

---

* This 1737 Act was passed after details of a particularly scabrous play about the private life of the King and Queen, *The Festival of the Golden Rump*, were made known by the Prime Minister, Sir Robert Walpole, who read the dialogue concerning George II's haemorrhoids out loud in parliament.[1]

and control of its exuberant, riotous heart was never entirely achieved. Even with these draconian laws, there were constant attempts to circumvent the legislation. Repression was equally constant, but only intermittently successful. The 1737 Licensing Act had restricted public performances of straight drama or comedies, known as 'legitimate' theatre, but had not included musical forms such as burletta (comic opera), melodrama, pantomime, and other types of what now became known as 'illegitimate' theatre. Theatrical managers therefore set up private theatre clubs, saying they were not subject to the legislation, which referred to public performances; or they claimed to be presenting musical performances, with a play thrown in to add sufficient length to the programme; or they charged for refreshments, or even snuff, and said the play was free; or claimed that the entertainment was a lecture, or a rehearsal, or a demonstration. These theatres were repressed time and again, but they kept popping up. Charles Macklin, the great dramatic actor, offered a School of Oratory in rented rooms in 1754; in 1764–79 George Alexander Stevens gave 'Lectures on Heads', which were disguised satires on the political events of the day; in 1748 Henry Fielding's feud with fellow playwright Samuel Foote was conducted on his part by a vicious puppet show called *Madam de la Nash's Breakfasting Room.*

Foote himself, who had played many comic parts for the patent theatres, leased the Haymarket Theatre from 1746. There he staged *The Diversions of the Morning, or, A Dish of Chocolate*, which he claimed was permissible because the satirical revue itself was free, although the audience had to pay for a concert afterwards. He continued with further revues, and with puppets, and finally, in 1766, managed legally to breach the duopoly of the two patent theatres – Drury Lane and Covent Garden (Covent Garden did not switch entirely to opera until 1847) – when he was given a patent to perform in the Haymarket during the summer months. This was an act of royal atonement rather than an indication that the government's grip was weakening. At a party given by the Earl of Mexborough, Foote had been challenged to demonstrate his riding skills on the Duke of York's horse. He was, predictably enough, thrown, and, rather less predictably, his leg had to be amputated. The patent followed by way of apology, and Foote cheerfully promoted what he called 'His Majesty's Company of Comedians'. Apart from Foote, others managed to perform in that blurred area somewhere between 'theatre' and 'entertainment', often by using non-conventional theatre spaces. Pleasure gardens and fairs were common locations for plays. Even the legitimate theatre companies often performed at the fairs during their off season – Charles Macklin made his London debut at a fair, and many Drury Lane comedians played Smithfield without any sense of incongruity. The pleasure gardens found burlettas one of their most successful forms of entertainment.

Outside London, many places had to rely on the plays produced at fairs, both because their smaller populations could not sustain a full-time theatre and because the 1737 act, by making London patents the pre-requisite for legal productions, had thereby made all provincial theatres illegal. Yet theatres continued, even if precariously. Provincial magistrates were no more going to forbid their own entertainment than the London-based government was, and in 1788 an Enabling Act conceded a compromise: local magistrates could now license theatres for up to a year at a time. Even so, many places had to make do with touring companies for most of the eighteenth century. Wilkinson Tate's touring company was a fairly typical example, operating from 1769 to 1830 on a regular circuit: York for the spring assizes, Leeds in June and July, Pontefract in August, back to York again for August race week, to Wakefield for September race week, to Doncaster for the race week in October, and finally to Hull in November and December.[2]

As time went on and increased urbanization produced populations large enough to sustain them, permanent companies were set up in the more prosperous towns, even before the enactment of the 1788 legislation. By the late 1720s three English towns outside London had permanent companies: York, Bath and Norwich. The latter's resident company by mid-century performed in the city for six months of the year, and then toured the smaller towns in Norfolk. By the 1750s there was also a company in Birmingham and another in Plymouth, and in 1765 there was one in Salisbury.[3] These companies performed in the towns themselves, and then made regular circuits of the locality, thus bringing theatre to a much wider audience. Eventually there were eleven Theatres Royal outside London (in Bath, Brighton, Bristol, Dublin, Edinburgh, Hull, Liverpool, Manchester, Newcastle, Norwich and York). These theatres – which named themselves 'Royal', although, licensed by the magistrates, they in fact had no formal warrant from the crown – all had semi-permanent companies, touring set circuits annually, often to coincide with race meetings or assize-week festivities.[4] By 1770, twenty-six towns had their own theatres; soon afterwards Lincolnshire alone had fourteen theatres, while by the 1820s there were over forty regular ircuits across the country.[5] Spa towns were particularly welcoming for semi-permanent theatre companies. In the 1770s the Orchard Street Theatre in Bath was managed jointly with a theatre in Bristol, sharing the costs and employing nearly thirty people permanently.* (Sarah Siddons performed there early in her career, from 1778 to 1782.)[6] By 1815 six further spas – Buxton, Cheltenham, Harrogate, Leamington, Scarborough and Tunbridge Wells – all had purpose-built theatres, even if they were open only for the season, and not every night then.[7]

There were more theatres, and the theatres that already existed were growing larger. In the late seventeenth century Drury Lane had seated 400; by the 1730s Covent Garden and the King's Theatre in the Haymarket (which was solely for opera) seated 1,400 each. After Covent Garden and Drury Lane were rebuilt over the course of the century, they held, 2,500 and 3,600 respectively.[8] (Covent Garden today, when at capacity, and including standing room, holds 2,253, Drury Lane 2,237, and these are two of the largest theatres in London.) It was not London alone where this expansion occurred, however: the Birmingham Theatre burned down in 1791, and was rebuilt to seat 2,000.[9] Before the second half of the nineteenth century, when iron was first used in the structure of buildings, it was impossible to create overhanging balconies without stout supporting pillars beneath, and the only way to increase the size of a theatre was to expand it ever outward. By the end of the eighteenth century the playwright Richard Cumberland was complaining,

> The splendour of the scene, the ingenuity of the machinist and the rich display of dresses, aided by the captivating charms of the music, now in great degree supersede the labours of the poet. There can be nothing very gratifying in watching the movement of an actor's lips when we cannot hear the words that proceed from them, but when the animating march strikes up, and the stage lays open its recesses to the depth of a hundred feet for the procession to advance, even the most distant spectator can enjoy his shilling's worth of show.[10]

* The Orchard Street Theatre secured a patent in 1768 – becoming the only patent theatre outside London – by the intervention of its proprietor, John Palmer, of postal-reform fame (pp. 128–9).

Theatres had become so large that not much could be heard; and so large that they needed to appeal to the masses to fill the huge auditoriums. The age of spectacle was beginning.

The nineteenth century saw a further liberalizing of the licensing situation, in the short term as a pragmatic response to a short-term situation. In 1808 and 1809 both Drury Lane and Covent Garden were badly damaged in fires. The pressure created by the lack of more than 6,000 seats every night forced the Lord Chamberlain to license new theatres, and the Lyceum, the Olympic and the Adelphi in the West End gained legal status to produce burlettas, music, dancing and 'the entertainments of the stage', but not legitimate theatre in the form of Shakespeare, drama or comedy. By the 1830s there were another thirty theatres operating under annual licences, or simply with illegal impunity. This growth was equally matched in the new industrial cities. Liverpool, to take one example, by 1830 had six theatres – the Theatre Royal, the Liver, the Royal Amphitheatre, the Sanpareil, the Rotunda and the Diorama.[11] At the same time, the pleasure gardens and taverns were moving enthusiastically into staged theatre: in 1832 alone there were fifty-four applications at the Middlesex sessions for entertainment licences for public houses and pleasure gardens. Vauxhall Gardens in its death throes staged burlettas and other musically-based performances; Astley's had entered the most thrilling stage of its career (see below). So in 1843 the Theatre Regulations Act gave legal acknowledgement to what had previously been tacit: it was no longer possible to privilege the patent theatres alone, and all theatres could now apply for a licence and perform legitimate drama.

As one set of theatres was swept into the mainstream, another series of small theatres – many in working-class areas outside the West End, some licensed by the Lord Chamberlain, some by local magistrates – took over their function. Known as the 'minor' theatres, they performed the old melange of songs, burlettas, melodramas and illegitimate drama.[12] These entertainments were also held in taverns and supper clubs. Taverns and clubs also held 'free and easies' and 'cock and hen clubs' (both evenings of singing, the difference being that the former were men-only events) and 'judge and jury' entertainments (in which the notorious crim.-con. cases of the day were staged), forming a precursor to what would shortly become the music-hall world (see pp. 372–4). Some tavern theatres were already well established: the Royal Albert Saloon and Standard Tavern and Tea Gardens, in Shoreditch, had an extension built which housed two stages, where pantomimes, tumbling, songs, comic ballets and melodramas took place.[13] Then there were the penny gaffs, which, like the taverns and supper clubs, had mixed entertainments and were again one of the precursors of the music hall. By the 1830s there were probably around a hundred of these in London, and they held up to nine shows a night, for 150 or so spectators, usually boys aged under sixteen. Some of the largest gaffs may have held as many as 2,000, which meant audiences every night larger than all but the largest West End theatres could hold. The gaffs had a similar mix of entertainment to the taverns, as reported by one shocked (middle-class and eminently respectable) journalist. After a comedian and a dancer,

> a fool comes upon the stage, and keeps the pit in a roar, especially when he directs his wit to the three musicians who form the orchestra, and says ironically to one of them, 'You could not drink a quartern of gin, could you?' and the way in which the allusion was received evidently implied that the enlightened but juvenile audience around me evidently had a very low opinion of a man who could not toss off his quartern of gin . . . But the treat of the evening was a screaming farce, in one act, in which the old tale of 'Taming the Shrew' was set forth in the most approved Shoreditch fashion. A husband comes upon the stage, whose wife . . . is an unmitigated shrew. She lords it over her husband as no good woman ever did or wishes to do. The poor man obeys till he can stand it no longer. At length all his manhood is aroused. Armed with what he calls a persuader – a cudgel of most formidable pretensions – he astonishes his wife with his unexpected resistance. She tries to regain the mastery, but in vain; and great is the delight of all as the husband, holding his formidable instrument over his cowed and trembling wife, compels her to obey his every word. All the unwashed little urchins around me were furious with delight . . . and I fear, as they passed out to the number of about 200, few of them did not resolve, as soon as they had the chance, to drink their quartern of gin and to whop their wives.

He attended another penny gaff south of the river, which shocked him even more, but all he would say about it was that 'A great part of the proceedings were indecent and disgusting, yet very satisfactory to the half grown girls and boys present.'[14]

Other theatres called themselves 'private', but were really just minor theatres, operating in the grey area between public and private, minor and illicit. The Strand Theatre was one of these: the building had originally held a panorama; it was then taken over by Benjamin Rayner, who called it the New Strand Subscription Theatre, which allowed it to operate under the pretence of private membership.[15] Its location, near the Olympic, the Lyceum and the Adelphi, soon pushed it into licensing and legitimacy. It was theatres like these that were to form the basis of the newly emerging West End.

The Olympic had been licensed to Mme Vestris in 1831. Lucia Vestris (1797–1856) had an impeccably artistic family tree: she was the granddaughter of Francesco Bartolozzi, considered by many to be the greatest engraver ever to have worked in Britain (see p. 198). Her mother, a pianist, had studied with Clementi, and was the dedicatee of five works by Haydn. The young Lucia married Armand Vestris, a dancer at the King's Theatre, and also the son of Auguste Vestris, one of the finest dancers of the century.* After a successful performing career, particularly in breeches roles, Mme Vestris acquired the lease of the Olympic, and managed to create one of the first theatres that had visibly modern elements. As a minor theatre, the Olympic was not officially entitled to perform straight drama. However, Mme Vestris had it redecorated to look like a fashionable drawing room; she kept the various areas of the auditorium rigidly segregated, so the middle classes could feel comfortable in their surroundings, without worrying about the 'loose women' that prowled so many theatres.† She managed to turn the restrictions on programming to her advantage, scheduling light comedy, a lot of music, and a lot of pretty dresses, with the whole thing winding up by eleven o'clock. The upper classes dropped in before moving on to more aristocratic haunts later; the middle classes attended and took part in a fashionable event, and they could still be home and tucked up in bed in good time for an early start at the office the next morning.

Now the majority of the audience was no longer the sort who had

---

* Napoleon refused him permission to travel, saying 'Foreigners must come to Paris to see Vestris dance.' (After Napoleon's abdication, he travelled to great acclaim.) He was also renowned as a teacher, listing Fanny Elssler, August Bournonville and Marie Taglioni among his pupils.

† Until the end of the eighteenth century the green room at Covent Garden was known as the 'Flesh Market'; throughout the nineteenth century the Empires promenade was a haunt of prostitutes, while its gallery was a gay cruising spot. As late as 1902 'this exchange, this traffic, this Flesh Fair' continued to take place nightly.[16]

attended the theatre when it was mocked by Maria Edgeworth in *The Absentee* in 1812. Then Lady Dashfort was mortified by the behaviour of her daughter Isabel: 'Isabel! Isabel! lord D— bowing to you . . . Isabel, child, with your eyes on the stage? Did you never see a play before? . . . Major P— waiting to catch your eye this quarter of an hour; and now her eyes gone down to her play-bill!'[17] Clearly this is satire, but satire works only if it is based on some element of truth, and through to the end of the nineteenth century sociability was a major component of theatre-going. In 1882, for the British premiere of Wagner's *Ring* cycle, the auditorium was darkened for the first time, and one historian has suggested that the icy response to this work had more to do with the fact that the inhabitants of the newly named 'dress circle' had dressed to be seen, not to sit in the dark.[18]* By the end of the century, lighting was lowered intermittently in the auditorium, depending on the action on stage. For Herbert Beerbohm Tree's production of *Hamlet* in 1894, the production notes read:

> Act 1, sc. 1: house dark
> 2: house ½ up
> 3: house ½ up
> 4: house dark†
> Act 2: house ½ up
> Act 3 house ½ up
> Act 4 house ½ up
> Act 5, sc. 1: house ½ up then general check
> 2: gradual check.[19]

Gilbert and Sullivan, and the D'Oyly Carte company, knew their market better than the Wagnerians. Although their Savoy Theatre was the first theatre to be lit entirely by electricity, the auditorium lights were left up during the performances. The audiences preferred it, and so did the theatres – many did a nice little trade in librettos, which they feared

---

* The boxes in the first balcony began to be removed over the course of the century, and the new open seating area became known as the dress circle. The boxes that survived were those nearest the stage – that is, the worst place in the theatre from which to see the performance, but the one where the audience can most easily see the box's inhabitants. The royal box at Covent Garden to this day is virtually on top of the stage, and requires a mirror on one wall to give some of the box's rear inhabitants any idea of what is taking place onstage.

† As there is no Act I, scene v listed, it must be assumed that scenes iv and v were run together, and thus the two scenes with Hamlet's father's ghost are the two that have the house lights down.

would vanish if the audience could not read them alongside the action. In 1882, after a performance of *Iolanthe*,* a reviewer in the *Illustrated London News* confessed, 'I was so interested in the book that I could scarcely attend to the stage, except with my ears, and this feeling was general, for the whole audience was plunged into the mysteries of the libretto, and when the time came for turning over the leaves of the book there was such a rustling as is only equalled when musicians are following a score at an oratorio.'[20] (For more on theatre lighting, see pp. 310–12.)

This audience with its eyes down, reading, was a far cry from Lady Dashfort and her friends. Most of this new audience had appeared in the theatres during the half-century since Maria Edgeworth's parody appeared, and they had arrived not merely because they wanted to see plays, but because theatre had become accessible for the reasons that we can now recognize: new methods of transport, improved roads, and increasing urbanization. As early as 1816, the theatres of London had begun to draw larger audiences as new bridges were built across the Thames: Vauxhall Bridge was opened in 1816, Waterloo Bridge in 1817, Southwark Bridge in 1819. Coaches brought spectators to the Surrey Theatre by 1819, and in 1821 an advertisement for the same theatre advised its customers that there was now a hackney-coach stand in St George's Fields, for their convenience. By the early 1830s the Red Rover Omnibus ran a special shuttle from Gracechurch Street, on the north side of London Bridge, to the Coburg Theatre in Waterloo before and after performances.[21]

This south- and eastward expansion of the theatres was a replication of the southern and eastern expansion of the city. The spreading dockyards along the Thames had created good job opportunities, and the population followed the work until, in 1901, the East End of London had the largest working-class population in the world – possibly as high as 2 million.[22] With that expansion in population came an expansion in entertainment locally: from the 1828 opening of the East London Theatre (later the Royalty, and then the Brunswick; this was the theatre that collapsed on p. 177), a stream of theatres followed – the City Theatre in Cripplegate and the Garrick in Leman Street (both 1831), the Standard in Shoreditch (1835), the City of London in Norton Folgate (1837),

---

* With this appearing soon after the *Ring* cycle, Gilbert had the Queen of the Fairies topically costumed with breastplate, winged helmet and spear.

and the Grecian and the Britannia in Hoxton and the Effingham in Whitechapel (1830s and 1840s, all saloon theatres, see pp. 372–4). By 1866 six East End theatres accounted for 34 per cent of the total theatre audience in London, while more than 63 per cent of the capital's theatre capacity was found outside the West End.[23]

The East End audience for the most part lived and worked near the theatres. But fewer and fewer of the audiences of the West End lived in that part of town. There was a general consensus by mid-century that most members of the audience travelled in to London, or at least in to central London, to attend the theatre. In 1855 John Hollingshead, later manager of the Gaiety Theatre, told a parliamentary select committee that 'the old metropolitan playgoer lives out of town, and does not go so much to the theatre as he used to do; the provincial people come to town, and fresh audiences are created every night.' Horace Wigan, the manager of the Olympic, agreed with him, saying that theatres were 'in very great proportion' supported by the non-London resident.[24] This had been made possible by the railways and, from 1863, by the new Underground system, which was expanding to meet demand. Those living in the suburbs or even further away could travel in to see a play without having to have their own transport to get home. By the 1880s and 1890s, in addition, the new streets of Charing Cross Road and Shaftesbury Avenue with their stylish theatres had been bulldozed through the old slum areas, creating middle-class entertainment locations where previously had been Dickensian rookeries. To add further to a suburban audience's sense of safety in foreign territory, these streets were now well lit with gas lights. Winsor's gas-light demonstration of 1804 had led to the creation of the first company to supply gas lighting, in 1814; within eight years 200 miles of gas mains had been laid.[25] G. A. Sala wrote for many in London when he said that 'He who will bend himself to listen to, and avail himself of, the secrets of the gas, may walk through London streets proud in the consciousness of being an Inspector – in the great police force of philosophy – and of carrying a perpetual bull's-eye [lantern] in his belt.'[26] Gas meant light, and light meant safety.

The railways brought in new audiences to London; they also transported London theatre to the provinces. Previously, as we have seen, touring companies consisted of local theatrical troupes on annual circuits performing a repertory of plays. Now two new forms of touring were made possible by the ease and economies of the railway. A West End hit, a single play, could be toured throughout the country by a company that was created by the play's London management solely for that purpose, and that disbanded at the end of the tour. The second type of touring company was closer to the old provincial tour: this was a first-rate company which had a repertory of pieces ranging from melodrama to farce to Shakespeare, which toured continually, but, unlike the old provincial companies, was formed by top-class performers with West End-standard productions. These companies could be very successful: the Compton Comedy Company toured for thirty-five years. (Both kinds of tour eventually killed off the provincial theatre company, if very slowly – it survived in a ghostly form into the 1950s.) Audiences everywhere expected first-rate actors in first-rate productions, and the number of people prepared to attend a performance could now support several touring companies of a single successful play from London, all out on the road simultaneously. Gilbert and Sullivan's operettas were particularly suited to this system; in 1879 there were a 1st and 2nd *Pinafore* company; by 1880, there were A, B and D companies touring the same, plus a C, or Children's, company. In 1881 the D'Oyly Carte company had five touring companies; in 1884 there were seven, as well as the London company, *the* D'Oyly Carte company.[27] While Gilbert and Sullivan had a number of hits to tour, there was enormous potential even for one-off successes: *Charley's Aunt*, in 1893, had seven touring companies criss-crossing Britain.[28]

The continued growth of the cities was changing access to theatre. It was also changing the way plays were produced. Previously, when populations were small, and the number of regular theatregoers smaller still, a run of a few weeks was considered perfectly successful for any show – Garrick's Jubilee pageant had been a great success, running as it did for twenty nights in a row, and then another fifty-one performances after that. Until the catchment area for theatres had become large enough to be able to draw on audiences for months at a time, the repertory system, which relied on a small group of very regular customers, of necessity had to prevail. Once the population passed a certain level (it appeared to be about 3 million in London), then a long run could be sustained, with an audience that constantly renewed itself. Long runs were naturally more economical, as the investment in rehearsal time, in costumes and in scenery became a smaller proportion of the whole.

In the 1840s only four plays ran for more than 100 nights, and they were not consecutive. In the 1850s sixteen managed that feat, and Charles Kean's 1857 production of *The Winter's Tale* ran for 102 consecutive nights, then the longest run ever. By the 1860s eleven plays had achieved 200 nights, while six had reached 300. Tom Taylor's *Ticket-of-Leave Man* (1863) ran for 407 performances.* In 1875 Henry James Byron's *Our Boys* began its record-shattering run of 1,362 performances.† In the 1890s, 169 plays made it past their hundredth performance, another 73 reached 200, and 39 passed 300.[30] Now, instead of small productions, economically staged, for a finite audience that returned time and again, the theatre world revolved around plays with large casts and even larger technical support teams to produce elaborate scenery and special effects for audiences that were constantly renewed.[31]

The new long run contributed in part to a drop in the price of admission. In the eighteenth century the pit, which was the location for 'honest citizens', cost 3s.; the first gallery, for the upper working classes, cost 2s. This was a high sum, but the production costs were equally high – at Drury Lane 150 people worked in the theatre (just over half of them actors), with annual running costs of approximately £40,000.[32] By 1842, prices for seats in the pit ranged from 1s. (for the Queen's and the Surrey), to 1s. 6d. (Sadler's Wells), 2s. (the Adelphi, the Olympic and the Strand), and up to 3s. for theatres that considered the appeal to exclusivity worth the reduction in audience size – Drury Lane, Covent Garden, the English Opera, and the St James's and Haymarket theatres.‡ The first gallery at the Queen's or the Surrey, could be gained for a mere 6d., however, and most others settled at 1 or 2s.[33] East End theatres charged even less: the Britannia had gallery seats at 3d. or 4d., and the pit was 1s. 6d.[34] Yet it was not as if the number of people employed in

---

* Tom Taylor (1817–80) was another of those exhaustingly busy Victorians. He was, in turn, a professor of English at the University of London, a barrister, a journalist and the editor of *Punch*. He was also secretary to the Board of Health and an art critic for *The Times* and the *Graphic* (although one very much of his time and place: he appeared as an expert witness for Ruskin in the notorious Whistler libel trial, testifying that Whistler's paintings were really no more than wallpaper – although very nicely coloured wallpaper). In between times he managed to write nearly forty plays. *Our American Cousin*, his most famous play, is however known today simply as the play at which Abraham Lincoln was assassinated.

† Byron's reputation has not lasted, and the two most interesting facts about him may well be that he was Lord Byron's second cousin, and that he named his daughter Crede, after the Byron family motto, 'Crede Byron'.[29]

‡ The Italian Opera at the Haymarket outdid even Covent Garden – it charged 10s. 6d. for a pit seat, while boxes, which were privately owned, could be rented for a mere 2 or 3 guineas, compared to other theatres' 2 to 5s.

the theatres had dropped commensurately with the prices (and neither had the wage bill: wages rose steadily through most of the nineteenth century). In 1832 Covent Garden had 1,000 employees, and spent over £60,000 annually.[35]

Instead, money was being made in part from non-theatre revenue: from refreshments, either directly or from selling licences to serve food and drink to an outside contractor. There was also a small income from playbills, which were sold in the auditorium until the 1870s, when they were replaced with programmes. Librettos were sold too, and many theatres had annual sales of their props and costumes. But the main increase in revenue came from increasing audiences, and increasing professionalization of the box office.* Until the 1880s, tickets were written out by hand, which was a slow, laborious process and one that was open to fraud – a dishonest booking agent could sell many more places than the theatre held, or claim to have sold far fewer and hang on to the cash. Possibly as a result of this, in the late 1860s a large number of patents were filed for various methods of checking admissions, or producing printed consecutive tickets, and by the 1880s the modern system of pre-printed tickets with counterfoils, which had a date, price and seat number on both halves, was in place.[36] From the 1860s to the end of the century many bent their minds to finding ways to fit more and more people into the same-sized theatres: in 1860 a patent was filed 'for the purpose of facilitating the passage of spectators between the rows of seats in the pits of theatres or in other places where long rows of benches are used'; another proposed a seat that is 'raised, and the occupiers of the seats can then stand close to the projecting parts'; in 1873 there was yet another, this one for the first time proposing something similar to the modern tip-up seat that makes it possible to set rows of seats tightly together while still giving access to late-comers.[37]

All these things made theatres more comfortable, as well as easier to get to, and theatres in the West End and the provinces were attended by the most respectably bourgeois in the land (apart from an evangelical minority). Queen Victoria adored the theatre: in 1838 alone she went to Covent Garden for Bulwer-Lytton's *The Lady of Lyons*, James Kenny's farce *The Irish Ambassador*, and another farce, *The Omnibus*, by Isaac

---

* In the eighteenth century, only boxes could be bought in advance; all other seats were sold on a first-come, first-served basis. The boxes were sold from an office near the stage door: hence 'box office'.

Pocock, as well as his melodrama *Rob Roy McGregor*; she also attended a pantomime and the opera there (but didn't trouble to write down the titles of the shows she saw). At Drury Lane that year she saw *Harlequin and Jack Frost*, plus a 'lion drama', *The Lions of Mysore* (see below).[38] Apart from the lack of Shakespeare, it was a fairly standard – and wide – range: farce, pantomime, melodrama, drama and animal shows.

Pantomime was a new genre, having developed only in the eighteenth century, and its novelty encompassed its spectacular form, the use of new technology to achieve it, and also the length of its run. By the middle of the nineteenth century, pantomime took up an ever larger proportion of many theatres' calendars: the investment in the spectacle was huge, and the audience to witness it equally huge. In Leeds in 1885 the Grand Theatre made an annual profit of £2,067, of which £1,766, or 85 per cent, came from its ten-and-a-half-week run of *Sinbad the Sailor*, which was popular with the Leeds audiences, and further drew in nearly a quarter of a million visitors from the surrounding regions, who arrived in specially organized excursion trains. Many other theatres devoted similar periods of time to such lucrative business. As Charles Kean said pragmatically, 'There is a certain sum to be got in a certain time . . . The case reduces itself to a matter of arithmetic. So many holiday visitors for a given number of weeks, give so much and no more.'[39]

On its first appearance pantomime was not considered to be primarily for children. It was Joseph Grimaldi, almost single-handedly, who took the genre to the forefront of theatrical entertainment. It had already been popular; now it was fashionable. Grimaldi had been born into the trade: his grandfather (nicknamed 'Iron Legs' Grimaldi) had been a pantomime performer, as had his father; Grimaldi made his first appearance, aged three or four, as an 'Evil' that popped out of Pandora's box in a 1781 pantomime of the same name. His great achievements were first at Sadler's Wells and then at Covent Garden, where he transformed the role of the Clown from a rustic booby into a mischievous, vengeful sprite, gleefully spreading havoc as he lightly danced his way through the evening.

At the beginning of the century, pantomime appeared at four set times in the year: from Christmas Day to mid-February, at Easter, in early July, and from the Lord Mayor's Show in November for a few weeks. (Provincial theatres also used this November date, even without the street pageant.) Gradually, the dates began to spread, with the weeks after the Lord Mayor's Show trickling on until they met the performances that started on Christmas Day. The original form developed too over the same period.

At the beginning of the century the formula was fairly rigid: there were a couple of scenes where a standard fairy-tale story was set up, usually involving a wicked father refusing his daughter's wish to marry. These straightforwardly dramatic scenes, told in verse, ended with a spirit of some sort descending and turning the lovers into Harlequin and Columbine, and the father and his approved suitor (or perhaps his servant) into Pantaloon and the Clown (always Grimaldi's role). A harlequinade followed, taking up the rest of the performance, as Pantaloon and the Clown chased Harlequin and Columbine through a variety of settings, which ranged from the purely imaginative to scenes of contemporary life with satirical or political undertones. In the last scene the spirit descended once more and blessèd the happy couple, and a rousing finale finished off the evening.

By the 1830s the harlequinade began to atrophy, and the earlier scenes, inflated into major spectacles, took over, followed by a transformation scene that could last up to half an hour. These early scenes used stock fairy-tale characters – Cinderella, the Babes in the Wood, Dick Whittington – and set them in an imaginary fairy realm.* In 1827 Prince

* The nineteenth-century obsession with fairies really needs a chapter to itself, but this brief footnote summarizing some of the places where they turned up will at least highlight their extraordinary omnipresence. In 1840 *A Midsummer Night's Dream* had its first grand nineteenth-century staging, at Covent Garden, which included an Act V that was more or less a pantomime transformation scene. The 1853 Sadler's Wells production carried this even further, with green and blue gauze drops in the earlier acts, and gas jets covered with gauze inside the columns of Theseus's palace in the last act. When the lights dimmed, the columns glittered brilliantly in the darkness. But fairies were not only a pantomime theme: ballet treated fairies in Henry's *La Silfide* (1828) and Taglioni's and Bournonville's *La Sylphide* in 1832 and 1836; in Coralli and Perrot's *Giselle* (1841), which had a libretto by Théophile Gautier, based on a legend described by Heine. Opera found the subject as rewarding, with Carl Maria von Weber's *Oberon* (1826), a fairy ballet (also choreographed by Taglioni) in Meyerbeer's *Robert le Diable* (1831), Wagner's *Die Feen* (1834), Lortzing's *Undine* (1845) and Puccini's famous debut opera, *Le Villi* (1884); even W. S. Gilbert planned for 'Self-lighting fairies, with electricity stored somewhere about the small of their backs in *Iolanthe* (1882). Offstage, fairies were everywhere: Richard Dadd's fairy paintings were painted throughout the 1850s and 1860s; and fairy-tale books poured off the presses: the collections made by the brothers Grimm were first translated into English in the 1820s, T. Crofton Croker's *Fairy Legends and Traditions of the South of Ireland* was published between 1825 and 1828, followed by Andersen's fairy tales in English from 1846, in dozens of editions, Ruskin's *The King of the Golden River* (1851), Cruikshank's *Fairy Library* (1853–4), Thackeray's *The Rose and the Ring* (1855), Charles Kingsley's *The Water Babies* (1863), Andrew Lang's thirteen 'coloured' fairy books (1889–1910) and, finally, on to J. M. Barrie's *Peter Pan* in the new century.[40]

Pückler-Muskau went to see *Mother Goose*, and described it in some detail:

> At the rising of the curtain a thick mist covers the stage and gradually rolls off. This is remarkably well managed by means of fine gauze. In the dim light you distinguish a little cottage, the dwelling of a sorceress; in the background a lake surrounded by mountains, some of whose peaks are clothed with snow. All as yet is misty and indistinct; – the sun then rises triumphantly, chases the morning dews, and the hut, with the village in the distance, now appears in perfect outline. And now you behold upon the roof a large cock, who flaps his wings, plumes himself, stretches his neck, and greets the sun with several very natural Kikerikis. A magpie near him begins to chatter and to strut about, and to peck at a gigantic tom-cat . . . this tom-cat is acted with great 'virtuosité' by an actor who is afterwards transformed into harlequin . . . Meanwhile the door opens, and Mother Skipton [Shipton], a frightful old witch, enters with a son very like herself. The household animals, to whom is added an enormous duck, pay their morning court to the best of their ability. But the witch is in a bad humour, utters a curse upon them all, and changes them upon the spot into persons of the Italian commedia dell'arte, Pantaloon, Harlequin, Columbine and the rest, who then persecute each other without rest, till at last the most cunning conquers.
>
> In the next scene we are transported to a village street, the centre of which is occupied by a tailor's workshop. In the open front of this sit several apprentices stitching industriously. A gigantic pair of shears is fastened above the lintel as a shop sign. Harlequin races in and, with a gigantic spring and a somersault, crashes through the first-floor window. Pantaloon and his friends now rush in in pursuit, gesticulating to each other, and one of them points to the broken window. Pantaloon enters the shop but, as he is rushing up the stairs, Harlequin emerges from the chimney and escapes over the rooftops. Pantaloon then enters the upper room, puts his head out through the broken window and turns this way and that in search of Harlequin; unfortunately at that moment the great blades of the shears close and cut his head off. Not in the least discouraged, Pantaloon withdraws from the window, comes downstairs and begins to look about the street for his head. At this moment a poodle comes on, sees the head and runs off with it, with Pantaloon in hot pursuit. Before Pantaloon gets off the stage, he is met by

Harlequin who is now disguised as a doctor. He explains his plight (by gestures), and Harlequin takes from his pocket a jar of ointment with which he rubs the stump of Pantaloon's neck. This causes the head to reappear out of the neck. Pantaloon recognizes Harlequin and sets off after him. His followers cannon into each other and fall on top of one another on their way off the stage . . .

The scene now changes to the path, which winds up a mountain-side towards a lofty castle in perfect perspective scale, so that everyone who is climbing up it diminishes in size proportionately. Gradually they all disappear, and finally [a] colossal pie, which is being carried by [an] assistant, goes down like the setting moon.

We now find ourselves in the great hall of the castle, which belongs to a beneficent magician who banishes Mother Shipton and her son to the centre of the earth and restores all the characters to their proper human form. Harlequin is recognized as the rightful prince and marries Columbine.

Clouds now cover the stage, and from the midst of them rises a balloon in which there is a pretty little boy. This ascends to the roof of the theatre and, as it is circling round the chandelier, the whole stage scene disappears through the floor and stars shine through the clouds – a very pretty illusion. The balloon now descends, the earthly scene rises again, and the whole spectacle ends with tightrope artists and acrobats.[41]

The harlequinade still survived in Pückler-Muskau's account, but within four years it would be banished almost entirely. By then many of the pantomimes had ceased to be pantomimes, even in name, and had become simply extravaganzas. The hero of the extravaganza was James Robinson Planché (1796–1880), a descendant of Huguenot refugees. His first play, 'a Serio-Comick, Bombastick, Operatick Interlude', had been staged at Drury Lane in 1818, but it was in 1831, with his *Olympic Revels, or, Prometheus and Pandora*, the opening production at Mme Vestris's Olympic Theatre, that he created a new genre. *Olympic Revels* was the first of thirty-six pieces he was to write in the next seven years (his total output numbered at least 180, and included the libretto for Weber's opera *Oberon*). Its tone can be judged from the opening scene. Jupiter, Neptune, Hercules and Plutus, the god of wealth, are playing whist, but Jupiter has lost his temper over their chattering and refuses to play any more:

JUPITER:	I will not, I say.
	Turn up the table; take the cards away.
	Let's have some music. Hermes, where's Apollo?
MERCURY:	Gone to the Glee-club at the Cat and Swallow.
JUPITER:	Deuce take the fellow; where is Bacchus now?
MERCURY:	He's at the Punch Bowl, drunk as David's sow.
JUPITER:	Where's Mars?
MERCURY:	He's gone to drill.
JUPITER:	Where's Juno, pray?
MERCURY:	She's in the laundry, sir; it's washing day.[42]

A summary of Planché's *The Island of Jewels* (1849) can stand as representative of the type of production that was to prove so popular. Princess Laidronetta is rejected by her family because she is saddled with the curse of ugliness by the malevolent Fairy Magotine. When a green serpent begs her for help, she is magically transported by a fairy boat to a rocky cavern with her friend Fidelia (played by Mme Vestris). The cavern is then transformed into a palace made of jewels, and jewel soldiers appear bearing Emerald inside a litter. From inside, Emerald asks Laidronetta to marry him, warning her that she must not look at him before the wedding in order to break Magotine's spells over them both. She agrees, and a 'crystal proscenium' appears for the ballet of Cupid and Psyche. But, as in all the best fairy tales, Laidronetta succumbs to temptation and takes a peek at Emerald, who, she discovers to her horror, is the green serpent. The entire set vanishes in a violent storm, out of which Magotine appears, to take Laidronetta prisoner for seven years. After much backing and forthing over a series of impossible tasks, the good fairy Benevolentia finally appears, helps Laidronetta perform the tasks, and transforms Emerald back into the prince he had been before Magotine cast her evil spell. The scene is equally transformed, to a Fairy Garden, where Emerald is once again surrounded by his court. Magotine is banished to hell, Laidronetta's family are remorseful (especially as she is no longer ugly), and the great transformation scene, 'The Brilliant Discovery of the Crown Jewels in the Palm of Success', takes place. All this is interspersed with songs, dances, jokes about current concerns, including the 'Railway King' and card sharps, and sideswipes at other plays being performed in London.[43]

It is scarcely surprising from the above two long descriptions that when David Copperfield first went to the theatre, a pantomime at Covent Garden, he came away overwhelmed by the 'mingled reality and mystery of the whole show, the influence upon me of the poetry, the lights, the music, the company, the smooth stupendous changes of glittering and brilliant scenery, [which] were so dazzling, and opened up such illimitable regions of delight, that when I came out into the rainy street, at twelve o'clock at night, I felt as if I had come from the clouds'.[44] This 'glittering and brilliant scenery' that Dickens wrote so feelingly about had long been overseen by artists of some substantial reputation, such as David Roberts and Clarkson Stanfield, or was the work of theatrical set-painting dynasties like the Grieve family, who designed for Charles Kemble, Charles Kean, W. C. Macready, Grimaldi, Mme Vestris and more, over careers that spanned many of the innovations of the nineteenth century.[45]

For new technology was changing the appearance of the theatrical flat, making stage design one of the most quickly evolving developments in theatre. The magic lantern had been in use in the theatre since the beginning of the century, but until the 1830s the oil lamps produced only a weakish light, and it was hard to create images that could be seen clearly, with enough definition, at a distance. On p. 255 we saw how Kean had used de Loutherbourg's innovations to create light-enhanced scenes in his *King Lear* in 1820. By 1827, images as well as colour were being used: a production of *The Flying Dutchman* had managed to focus the lights sharply enough that a 'ship' could be projected successfully. But it was limelight that brought about the next phase of stage effects, allowing the creation of complex projected images. It may have been at a production of Balfe's opera *Joan of Arc* at Drury Lane in 1837 that limelight first appeared in a theatre. (If it was not then, it was at the Christmas pantomime staged by Macready at Covent Garden that same year.) Drury Lane advertised that 'a new and extraordinary Light will be introduced, called PHOSHELIOULAMPROTERON', and this was probably limelight. Limelight was produced when a bag was filled with oxygen by heating manganese dioxide; another bag was filled with hydrogen. The hydrogen was expelled and lit, to warm the lime. When the calcium in the lime began to be consumed, the flame turned from pale yellow to red. At this point the oxygen was added, and the mixed gases gave an incandescent light. To produce an even light, the gases had to be expelled from the bags evenly and continuously. To do this, each bag was put between two pressure boards, and the light was produced by an operator pressing down on the boards. When *Faust* was mounted at the Lyceum there were twenty-five limelights; therefore twenty-five

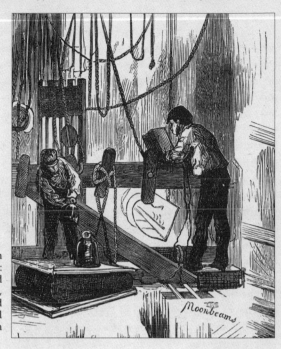

A limelight man operates his boards: the bag is inserted between the wedge, and a weight pressed down on it to expel the gas in an even flow.

limelight operators were needed. By 1881, wrote one journalist, in the Strand every evening one is 'certain to encounter men carrying on their shoulders enormously inflated bags, much as the "sandwich men" carry their boards. These are now found necessary at every theatre, and contain the gases for supplying the fiercely-glowing limelight lanterns.'[46] The high level of manpower was more than compensated for by the elaborate effects that could be created.

With limelight, dissolving views had become possible, created by two magic lanterns focused on the one spot: one lantern was then slowly extinguished, while the light in the second was similarly brought up. 'Snow' could be produced by making pinholes in a strip of black fabric and fixing it on to rollers; a crank unrolled the fabric across the light of another magic lantern. If all three images were used together, a stage picture of some complexity could be built up: for example, magic lantern 1 projected an autumn scene with a windmill; magic lantern 2 superimposed a 'snowfall' over this; a dissolve took the audience to magic lantern 3's view of the same windmill, now covered with snow.

Limelight was particularly useful for the transformation scenes of pantomimes and extravaganzas; when electricity arrived, in the early 1880s, it was enthusiastically adopted to be used for stage effects, well before its use to light the auditorium. In Gilbert and Sullivan's *Iolanthe* the fairy queen and her attendants wore electric stars in their hair, and by 1883 the Princess' Theatre in Manchester had staged a ballet for twenty-six women who 'danced nightly by the light of small Swan lamps placed in a flower on each lady's head'.* In an 1895 production of *Cinderella* at Drury Lane there was a rotating wheel in the background lit by electricity. The 'electric ballet' became a feature of many extravaganzas, and as late as 1897 the Alhambra, a music hall, had a Grand Electrical Finale.[48] A version of *Cinderella* at the Hippodrome had lamps on the dancers' headdresses, Cinderella's ball gown was covered with 'diamonds' that were lit electrically, and her coach, wheels and spokes included, was outlined by 1,000 bulbs. The final scene, the Palace of Lustres, had 10,000 electric lights.[49]

These giant productions required giant resources: Macready's production of *Coriolanus* in 1838 had somewhere between 100 and 200 'senators' in the crowd scenes; Charles Kean required 250 'citizens' for Bolingbroke's entry into London in *Richard II* in 1857; by the time Irving came to produce *The Corsican Brothers* in 1881, with its relatively small cast (for more on that production, see pp. 333–4), he still needed 30 gasmen and 90 stage carpenters backstage to produce the effects he wanted. Pantomime required even more: *Little King Pipkin* at Drury Lane in 1865 employed 48 seamstresses and wardrobe mistresses, 45 dressers and 17 gasmen, while 200 children and 60 ballet dancers appeared onstage. In 1866 Augustus Harris at Drury Lane marshalled nearly 500 'thieves' to accompany *The Forty Thieves* of the pantomime's title.[50]

And that was without the animals. Animals were an essential component of spectacular theatre throughout the nineteenth century.

---

* *Iolanthe* set off a craze for 'electric jewellery', the most famous example of which was Mrs Cornelius Vanderbilt having Worth make her an 'Electric Light' ball gown in 1883 (although it is not clear from the description if the whole dress lit up, or only the lamp she carried with it). In 1888, Woodhouse and Rawson, 'manufacturers of incandescent lamps', produced a 'Complete set [of jewellery], superior, for Ball-Room purposes' for the Princess of Wales. But the connection with the stage meant that electric clothing and jewellery were at best seen as fit only for fancy-dress parties. However, a book on the subject, *Decorative Electricity with a Chapter on Fire Risks*, was written by Mrs J. E. H. Gordon, the wife of a director of an electricity company.[47]

Where circuses ended and drama began was not a question that troubled the times much. At the Royal Circus, St George's Fields, in 1806 *The Cloud King; or, Magic Rose*, 'A New Splendid Melo Dramatic Tale of ENCHANTMENT', was staged, with a set that combined much of the new lighting and special effects that were developing, together with animals brought on as part of the drama:

> *A dark Wood, through which, from the situation of the Trees, appear a variety of intricate avenues, backed by a mazey labyrinth – a most tremendous storm, intermingled with cries of distress, vivid flashes of lightning, and tremendous peals of thunder, &c. &c.*

> In the intervals of the storm Scander is seen on his Horse, which attacked by an angry Lion, as it crosses the stage, emits fire from his nostrils, followed by Cymballo on foot in the greatest agitation . . . They are attacked by an immense Serpent, which they at length destroy; and, the atmosphere appearing lighter, thanking Heaven for their deliverance, the Travellers, by the light of the Moon, prepare to renew their journey, but are suddenly prevented by a torrent of rain – in vain they endeavour to shelter themselves, the trees they select for that purpose being struck by thunderbolts, and torn asunder – at length a chasm suddenly appears, discovering a distant illuminated portal, leading to a splendid Palace, richly adorned with festal lamps . . .[51]

The following year, the success of shows similar to this was such that the patent theatres began to feel the financial loss. Philip Astley (1742–1814) had been in the 15th Light Dragoons during the Seven Years War, and afterwards he had opened a small show where he did trick riding. In about 1770 this was expanded into Astley's Amphitheatre, at the southern end of Westminster Bridge. Astley's presented horsemanship, acrobatics, acrobatics on horses, strongmen, juggling and other similar feats of dexterity, combined with little sketches or character scenes. By 1786 the Amphitheatre consisted of a ring (where in a theatre the stalls seats would be), where the horses performed, separated from the stage by an orchestra pit. Onstage Astley produced burlettas, ballets and pantomimes and, as with panoramas later, it was commercially expedient to get the latest world events dramatized quickly. Astley had a staged representation of the fall of the Bastille open to the public six days after the event had taken place. He had already produced *Paris in Uproar* in 1789, and followed this up with *The Champ de Mars* (1790) and

Bagshot-Heath Camp (1792). In 1801 *The British Glory in Egypt*, with the defeat of the French by the Highlanders, with 'REAL CAVALRY and INFANTRY' was proudly announced.[52] He was up against competition from Sadler's Wells, which used the nearby New River to mount aquatic battle scenes, including in 1804 *The Siege of Gibraltar*, for which Woolwich Arsenal workers provided the model ships.

Astley had a summer licence, and he and his competitors at the Royal Circus were constantly in danger of losing even that, owing to such stagings, which came perilously close to legitimate drama. Astley was once prosecuted for venturing into legitimate theatre, but popular resentment prevented his conviction. In general, to get around the ban on dramatic dialogue, the illegitimate theatres tended to use scrolls, banners and pennants with text on them. During the French wars patriotism was literally visible. In the Royal Circus's *Blackbeard*, the villain carried a scroll that announced 'THE ENEMY IS BRITISH AND WILL DIE OR CONQUER.'[53] Patriotism was a large part of the Amphitheatre's output – and of Astley's own life. After the fall of the Bastille, he re-enlisted as a soldier, aged fifty. When his Amphitheatre burned down in 1794, however, he was given a discharge. As with most theatres in the nineteenth century, fire was a constant hazard, and the Amphitheatre burned down and was rebuilt with variations to its shape in 1794, 1803 and 1841.

It was 1800 when for the first time the horses moved from the ring to the stage. John Conway Philip Astley (1768–1821), Astley's son, produced *Quixote and Sancho; or, Harlequin Warrior* with 'mechanical tricks and . . . on the Stage, TWO SQUADRONS OF HORSE, mounted by Warriors clad in Gold and Silver Armour'.[54] The Royal Circus (from 1806 renamed the Surrey Theatre) countered by staging a pantomime of *The Magic Flute; or, Harlequin's Champion*, set during the reign of Charlemagne and with 'an appropriate and splendid Procession on the Stage of Equestrian Knights, on real Chargers, caparisoned in the Housings, Trappings, and variegated Armour, of the Times; the Stage representing the Amphitheatre of Renown'.[55] But Astley *fils* produced a knockout blow that established his Amphitheatre firmly in the hearts of spectacle-hungry crowds. *The Blood Red Knight*,* produced in 1801, ran for 175 perform-

---

* No one is quite sure who wrote this early hippodrama. The names that have been put forward include William Barrymore, J. H. Amherst and George Male. A. H. Saxon, the leading expert on hippodrama, thinks it was probably by Male, and later claimed by Barrymore (whom we met on p. 179 as author of a knock-off version of Pierce Egan's *Life in London*).[56] This was a pattern that was to recur with many theatrical productions later

ances and was said to have netted him £18,000. It was later revived over and over for the next quarter-century and more. The stage directions for the last scene show how far Astley had already developed his genre: 'Horse and foot are seen in action on the bridge. The Castle being forced, the action becomes general on the Stage, ramparts, water, and bridge. Some of the Guards are immersed in water, surrounded by friends and foes. The Castle is at length seen on fire in several places . . .' In 1807 further rebuilding gave Astley, as he promised enticingly in an advertisement in *The Times*, 'Stage Elevations, Platform Work, Devil's Bridges, &c. of New Invention'.[57]

This was too much for the legitimate theatres to bear. In 1811 Covent Garden had its cake and ate it too. While producing a new staging of George Colman the Younger's *Blue Beard; or, Female Curiosity* (which had had a production at Drury Lane in 1798), complete with horses from Astley, the manager, John Philip Kemble, wrung his hands about having 'with strong reluctance to innovate upon the usual entertainment of a theatre royal', sacrificing the 'scruples of exact taste' and stooping to such gutter tactics as animals onstage. Yet it was *Blue Beard* and its horses that produced the single most profitable season Covent Garden had ever had. Annual receipts were usually in the region of £80,000; in the 1810–11 season the theatre cleared £100,000, of which the first forty-one nights of *Blue Beard* alone contributed £21,000, or a fifth of the theatre's turnover.

The success was unsurprising: Astley and Colman between them had filled the stage with wonderfully exciting scenes. Early on came a procession of animals, including a mechanical elephant and wooden camels. But then the real animals appeared. Fatima had been married off to Bluebeard (for some reason also known in this production as Abomelique) against her will. Selim, her true love, came to the rescue, accompanied by a troop of soldiers on horseback, who drew up in formation across the stage before galloping off over a bridge and then across the hills and into the distance. In the finale Abomelique's and Selim's forces rode towards each other, as the *Examiner* breathlessly described to its readers:

> Firstly, the aforesaid gallopings are repeated over mound and bridge, till every steed has reappeared often enough to represent ten or a dozen others; then one or two of them get interestingly

___
in the century, especially melodramas, where the staging of the spectacle was considered far more important than the mere words.

entangled in a crowd; then a drawbridge, breaking down, is scaled by three or four at full gallop, which calls down the thunder of the galleries; – then a duel ensues between a couple of the horsemen . . . Lastly, comes the grand display, the dying scene; and here it is difficult to say which is more worthy of admiration, the sensibility or science of these accomplished quadrupeds . . . [One of the horses] entered the stage with as much indifference as if nothing had happened, though it was soon evident that he had received his mortal wound, for after a little meditation he began to die, bending his knees one after the other . . . and then turning upon his side and becoming motionless, just as a human actor does upon his back . . .[58]

Blue Beard was programmed with *The Comedy of Errors*, and it continued to appear together with legitimate drama over the next half-century, as Covent Garden realized it was stuck with staging spectacle for its financial well-being. (In 1816 Macready's London debut at Covent Garden, as Iago, was on the same bill as an 'equestrianized musical romance' called *Lodoiska*.)[59] There was a lot of press comment along the lines of the most un-British suggestion in the *Satirist, or Monthly Meteor*, that 'It were better to poison the manager's horses, than that he should poison the national taste.'[60] But in fact the legitimate theatres had been producing this sort of thing for some time, both in pantomimes and in new plays, if on a smaller scale. Prince Pückler-Muskau had seen Kemble play Falstaff, followed on the bill by a melodrama in which a Newfoundland dog 'really acted admirably; he defended a banner for a long time, pursued the enemy, and afterwards came on the stage wounded, lame, and bleeding, and died in the most masterly manner, with a last wag of the tail that was really full of genius'.[61]

Other theatres, which did not have Covent Garden or Astley's resources, got in on the craze for horses via satire – satire always being a sure indicator of success. In 1811 the Drury Lane company (at the Lyceum, as Drury Lane had once more burned down) revived an old Samuel Foote comedy about a tailor, which was quickly retitled *The Quadrupeds; or, The Manager's Last Kick*, with a finale of tailors and apprentices staging a cavalry charge on donkeys. At the Haymarket, Colman produced a parody of his own play with what he called a 'Tragico-Comic-Anglo-Germanico-Hippo-Ono-Dramatico Romance', *The Quadrupeds of Quedlingburgh; or, The Rovers of Weimar*, with soldiers on wickerwork horses this time.[62]

Parody was easy; developing the original form required more skill.

Out of the general run of hippodramas came the 'lion dramas' of the 1830s. The first, and principal, venture in this genre was by Henri Martin, a French equestrian, initially in France and in 1831 at Drury Lane, with *Hyder Ali; or, The Lions of Mysore*. In this lion drama Martin himself played the nabob Sadhusing, who is hiding in the forest of Mysore to escape the angry sultan Hyder Ali, who is in love with Delhi, Sadhusing's daughter. As the piece opens, Sadhusing wakes up in the forest and rescues his sons from a pair of boa constrictors (pausing only for the three of them to reproduce a tableau of the Greek sculpture the *Laocoön*). Then the sultan's troops attack, but Sadhusing is protected by two lions. Act II opens with a comedy scene, with a pelican stealing the sultan's jester's dinner; then it is back to the forest, with Sadhusing now sur-rounded by llamas, a buffalo, a monkey and a kangaroo. The sultan enters on a tiger hunt, seated on an elephant, and Sadhusing attacks him, but is captured. Given the chance of freedom by agreeing to fight a lion, this Sadhusing does, and the final tableau is of Sadhusing in a triumphal procession with the lion, the sultan and Delhi on an elephant, followed by dancing girls, bands and happy crowds. The story was of course irrelevant: it was the wild beasts roaming loose onstage that were so exciting. In fact wire netting was concealed in the scenery, so that, while it looked as if the animals were wandering about at will, they were in reality penned into a small area with Martin, while all the other performers remained safely on the other side of the net.[63] The playbill for this production announced a performance of *Macbeth* in the same evening, but it was *Hyder Ali* – 'the Most Gorgeous Spectacle ever pro-duced' – that was given the most space. Two sure signs of its success: Queen Victoria attended, and the Adelphi produced a spoof version, with popular actors playing the different animals.[64]

But there was a very limited number of animal-tamers. In 1823 Covent Garden staged its next big hippodrama. Astley *père et fils* were now both dead, but their Amphitheatre had been taken over by a worthy successor, Andrew Ducrow. Ducrow (1793–1842) was the child of circus performers,* who trained him as an equestrian from his earliest days.

---

* Ducrow's background, according to journalists, gave him an attractively 'creative' way with language. His completely filthy vocabulary apparently came as a shock to the refined souls at the legitimate theatres, but he has come down to us as the man who said, apropos of his belief in the merits of as little dialogue and as many cavalry charges as possible, 'Cut the cackle and come to the 'osses.'

('Trained' is a euphemism: he was once beaten by his father for breaking his leg during a performance.) After travelling through Europe with his equestrian act in the post-Waterloo period, he returned to London and appeared in an extravaganza mounted by Planché at Covent Garden in 1823, *Cortez; or, The Conquest of Mexico*. This was full of dramatic incident, including Cortez quelling a mutiny in which his ships were set on fire, and his entry into Mexico at the head of an army, with both horses and men in full armour appearing at full gallop. But the big scene was in Act II, when Cortez and his men were attacked by the 'natives'. *The Times* was admiring:

> A steep ascent runs from the floor of the house up the side of a cataract; over which a bridge is thrown at a considerable height from right to left; and again, at a very sharp angle, from right to left. Up this steep the horses pass – rising from below the level of the stage, as though they sprang from some defile by the bed of the waterfall – they cross the line of bridges, thus making two turns within the view of the audience – and return . . . descending dexterously by the same pass which they ascended.

Then a 'native' manages to unseat one of the Spaniards, wrestles his horse away from him, and mounts. But he has never ridden before, and 'the steed darts up the precipice by the cascade in pursuit of his companions; crossing the first bridge over the waterfall, [the rider] is laid hold of by some tree or projections; he falls from the saddle, over the bridge, and sinks in the gulf below.'[65] This astonishing stunt was performed by Ducrow himself.

But Ducrow was not content simply to perform. In the following year he moved on to the next great stage in his career, when his production of J. H. Amherst's *The Battle of Waterloo* opened at Astley's. This was the second-most successful hippodrama ever staged (for the most successful, see below); it received the traditional approval of the Duke of Wellington, and ran for 144 nights, before being revived endlessly over the next fifty years.* It was in three acts, each act ending with a battle: Act I had the battle at Marchienne; Act II the battle of Quatre Bras, and Act III Waterloo itself, with scenic extras including a baggage wagon set on fire, frightened horses bolting, the Black Brunswickers forming squares to

---

* By the 1860s, even when Astley's was virtually defunct, and no longer staged hippodrama, *The Battle of Waterloo* limped on, with a production that was reduced to a single horse, ridden in turn by all the commanders of the various forces.

repel the cuirassiers, and, the popular finale, the flight of Napoleon. Napoleon was played by Edward Gomersal, who spent most of his career as the French emperor, also appearing in *Bonaparte's Passage of the Great St Bernard*, *Bonaparte's Invasion of Russia; or, The conflagration of Moscow* and *The Life and Death of Napoleon.*[66] In 1831 the Surrey staged *Napoleon; or, The Victim of Ambition*, with moving dioramas, and in the same week Covent Garden staged a 'Grand Historical and Military Spectacle', *Napoleon Buonaparte, Captain of Artillery, General and First Consul, Emperor and Exile.*[67]

But Covent Garden was competing that year with a hippodrama that was more successful than even *The Battle of Waterloo*. This was Ducrow's *Mazeppa*. In 1819 Byron had published his poem *Mazeppa*, in which an officer in the army of Charles XII of Sweden recounts how, in his youth, he had been caught in a scandalous liaison, and as punishment was tied naked to the back of a wild stallion that was whipped into madness and released to gallop off with him. The stallion stopped only when, at the point of death, it reached the Ukraine. There Mazeppa was found and rescued by Cossacks. Henry Milner produced a version of this piece of exoticism for the Coburg Theatre in 1823, and when he became the house playwright for Astley's in 1831 he reworked it as a hippodrama.* John Cartlitch, who played the hero, became as closely linked with Mazeppa as Gomersal had been with Napoleon: he played it over 1,500 times (and when he was demoted in old age to playing the Tatar khan, he wept).

The play had everything: troops in procession, troops in cavalry charge, troops in hand-to-hand combat. While the production throughout was up to Ducrow's high standard, it was the wild ride of the stallion carrying Mazeppa across the steppes of Russia that created the frenzy. The stage directions for the end of Act I and the opening of Act II read:

> The horse is brought forward by three or four grooms, who with difficulty restrain him. He is led to the centre . . . Music. Cassimir [another name for Mazeppa] is now bound to the horse's back . . . Music. The horse is released, and immediately rushes off with Cassimir. He presently re-appears on the first range of hills from L. to R., all the spectators rushing to the L., and as he crosses

---

* Given *Mazeppa*'s long-term fame, it is extraordinary how little is known about Milner. He flourished from the 1820s to the 1840s in the minor theatres, adapting plays from other sources for the most part, but never again with the success of *Mazeppa*.

Astley's 1833 publicity woodcut showing Mazeppa's wild ride, lashed to the back of a stallion.

Punch, twenty years later, showing perhaps more accurately how *Mazeppa* was staged. Note the vulture hovering overhead, and the wolves entering to the right.

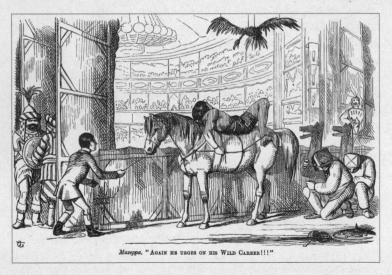

Mazeppa, "AGAIN HE URGES ON HIS WILD CAREER!!!"

again from R. to L., they take the opposite side. When he has reached the third range of hills, they commence pursuing him up the hills, and as he progresses, they follow. When he has disappeared in the extensive distance, the whole range of hills is covered by the servants, females, guards, and attendants, shouting, waving their arms and torches, forming an animated tableau. Olinska [the woman with whom Mazeppa had the affair], who has fainted, is supported . . . in the front, while the Castellan [her father] expresses exultation, completing the picture, lighted by the glare of torches and red beacon-flares, on which the drop falls. [End of Act I]

[Act II] Moving panorama of the course of the Dnieper River, running from L. to R. On the flat is seen its bank, with a tract of wild country. A tremendous storm of thunder and lightning, hail and rain . . . Music. Mazeppa discovered on the wild horse, stopping a few moments, apparently from exhaustion . . . The wild horse gallops off with Mazeppa, R. Music. The storm abates, the sun rises, and the panorama begins to move. The horse, still bearing Mazeppa fastened to his back, is seen wading up the stream from R. to L. . . . Music. A group of wolves is seen on the opposite bank, as if watching and pursuing the horse and Mazeppa . . . Music. An enormous vulture is seen hovering above him.[68]

In fact the horse galloped across the stage three times, in zigzags, with Cartlitch tied to its back; then another horse, with a dummy on it, continued the ascent up the bridges at the back.[69] The horse was then placed on a treadmill in front of a moving panorama of the banks of the Dnieper, to continue its wild ride to the accompaniment of music, thunder and lightning.[70]

Mazeppa continued its unabated popularity for more than half a century: in the 1830s in America alone there were two productions running simultaneously in New York, two in Philadelphia and one in St Louis. Sanger's Circus toured with another version throughout Britain. The money it brought Ducrow was phenomenal. In 1841 Astley's burned down yet again, and Ducrow suffered a stroke, dying the following year. Even when the depreciation in value from the fire was taken into account, Ducrow left £60,000 in his will – the same sum that Prince Augustus Frederick, Duke of Sussex and a son of George III, left when he died the following year.

In 1861 Adah Isaacs Menken, an American actress, debuted in the role of Mazeppa in Albany, New York (her ride made even more exotic by the fact that she wore nothing but skin-coloured 'fleshings' – quite a different thing from when Cartlitch had done so). This quickly became her most famous role, and she was soon playing Mazeppa on Broadway, in San Francisco, in Baltimore and in other cities in America, as well as in London and Paris.* With this, *Mazeppa* had become nothing more than an opportunity to look at women's legs: its glory days were over. But it was not that Menken finished off hippodrama; instead, it was the fact that hippodrama was dying which made it possible for Menken to appear at all. What was killing off the genre was an alternative type of reality that was appearing onstage – a reality that made horses seem un-modern, and a relic of the old century.

Now real animals onstage were no longer exciting in and of themselves. Instead it was a separate strand of stage effects, which had been developing since de Loutherbourg's sets had been so well received in the 1770s, that was coming to the fore. By the 1820s, many reviewers saw it as part of their brief to review the scenery – sometimes to the detriment of the play. *Arnold's Library of Fine Arts* warned theatregoers that 'The only thing at present worth entering a theatre for is the scenery', while Henry Crabb Robinson wrote in his diary that the pantomime at Covent Garden in 1825 was dull, 'but the scenery beautiful; and this is one of the attractions of the theatre for me'. Spectacle was expected in the provinces no less than the metropolis. The *North Shields Dramatic Censor* told its readers that for one play the designer had created 'several exquisitely painted scenes'; the *Norwich Theatrical Observer* reported that in the production of *Macbeth* under review, 'The Banquet scene was finely displayed; the Gothic screen behind the throne, executed by that ingenious artist, Mr Thorne . . . was truly magnificent.'[72]

Some designers began to take umbrage at their traditional lowly place in the hierarchy of theatre. In 1834 Clarkson Stanfield, known as the heir of de Loutherbourg, was aggrieved when his sumptuous backdrop for *King Arthur and the Knights of the Round Table* at Drury Lane was constantly hidden from the audience by a milling retinue of actors and

---

* Menken (c. 1835–68) was a much-married (and possibly rather less often divorced or widowed) actress, who, were it not for *Mazeppa* and a scandalous private life, would barely be remembered. In Paris she had a notorious affair with Alexandre Dumas *père*, and in London a slightly more peculiar one with Swinburne, who is said to have immortalized her in his 'Dolorida'. She died in Paris, and was buried at Montparnasse under a tombstone that mysteriously informed the viewer, 'Thou knowest.'[71]

supers, not to mention horses. He demanded that the curtain should go up first on a stage empty but for his set, 'for the audience to gaze on and admire, and the multitude sent on afterwards'. When he was refused, he quit.[73] Stanfield was right; the Drury Lane management was wrong. Percy Fitzgerald, a journalist and protégé of Dickens, made the situation explicit: 'We go to the theatre not so much to hear as to look. It is like one gigantic peep-show and we pay the showman, and put our eyes to the glass and stare.'[74]

There were two paths that were followed, both developing from this urge for scenic effects, one 'high', one 'low'. The high was interesting, and – as is often not the case – also successful. The low was not only interesting, it radically altered the direction of drama for half a century. For those who believed theatre to be an art form, not mere entertainment, it was simple, perhaps even natural, to see a link between theatre and painting. This connection had been made before. As early as 1733 Drury Lane had mounted *The Harlot's Progress; or, the Ridotto al'Fresco*, written by Theophilus Cibber and dedicated 'to the ingenious Mr Hogarth, (On Whose Celebrated Designs it is Plann'd)'. Cibber had attempted to produce an animated version of the first four engravings in Hogarth's series, creating stories for the dramas they depicted, using both traditional narrative and *tableaux vivants*, in which the actors struck poses when they reached the point that Hogarth had shown. Hogarth's episodic narratives made an easy transition to drama: seventy years later the Coburg advertised 'a New Interesting, Local and Moral Drama, replete with Splendid Pageantry, founded partly on Hogarth's celebrated series of Engravings, and partly on a Drama which has recently acquired great popularity in Paris, called, THE LONDON APPRENTICES; OR, INDUSTRY AND IDLENESS'.[75]

By 1800, tableaux were common enough that the theatrical versions were integrated into other art forms. In Maria Edgeworth's novel *Belinda* (1801), the novel's happy ending parodied the form. Lady Delacour was in charge: 'Let me place you all in proper attitudes for stage effect . . . Captain Sunderland – kneeling with Virginia, if you please, sir, at her father's feet – You in the act of giving them your blessing, Mr Hartley – Mrs Ormond clasps her hands with joy . . . Clarence, you have a right to Belinda's hand, and may kiss it too – Nay, miss Portman, it is the rule of the stage . . . There! quite pretty and natural!'[76] This took for granted that the novel's audience would understand precisely the theatrical references. It was also an early precursor of the 'picture plays' which became increasingly popular from about 1830 for the following half-century. In Planché's *The Brigand* in 1829, the stage directions read, 'The distance is shrouded in mist at the rising of the curtain and becomes clear during the execution of the following Round[,] the Symphony to which must be sufficiently long to allow the contemplation of the picture formed from the 1st of the popular series of Mezzotinto Engravings after Eastlake – "an Italian brigand chief reposing &c.".' Later in the stage directions the brigand's wife is instructed to leap up on a rock so that she can be seen 'looking anxiously down the mountain. – Forming the second picture from Eastlake's Series, "The Wife of a Brigand Chief watching the result of a Battle".' The scene ends with the characters grouped to resemble the last picture in the series, 'The Dying Brigand'.[77] Eastlake's engravings had just been published, and could be seen in print-shop windows, enabling all in the audience to make direct comparisons.

The most famous realization of a painting was probably in Douglas Jerrold's play *The Rent Day* (1832), which was written specifically to produce a scene that mirrored Sir David Wilkie's painting of 1815, *Distraining for Rent*, as Jerrold's stage directions made clear: 'The Interior of Heywood's Farm. The Scene, Furniture, &c., as in Wilkie's Picture of "Distraining for Rent".' At the end of the play, Heywood cries, 'God Help us! God help us!' and 'buries his face in his hands. The other Characters so arrange themselves as to represent WILKIE'S Picture of "DISTRAINING FOR RENT".' A reviewer reported that 'The arrangement of the various persons, as the drop fell, was so striking that the audience testified their approbation by three rounds of applause.' But Jerrold did not have a monopoly on a popular image, and within a couple of months another two plays based on the same painting had opened. In addition the *Examiner* praised the 'Domestic Burletta' at the Adelphi, which had not one but two realizations, reproducing Wilkie's *Village Politicians* as well as his *Reading of the Will*: 'Both were very good . . . the characters exactly filled the scene in most perfect grouping . . . The artist has reason to be satisfied with the arrangement of the manager, he has done ample justice to his original.'[78] Other popular images that were reproduced in this way included Cruikshank's *The Bottle*, Abraham Solomon's *Waiting for the Verdict* and Frith's *Railway Station* and *Derby Day*. A slight variant on this sort of representation was to be found in the reproduction of the *Laocoön* already noted in *Hyder Ali*. Ducrow was admired for his imitations of classical statues, as well as for hippodramas: his *Raphael's Dream, or, The Mummy and Study of Living Pictures* (1830) was an entire series of references to classical statuary, produced while standing on the back of his horse as it galloped around the arena.

This idea that theatre and paintings were in some way interchangeable was perhaps reinforced in the 1880s when the managers of the Haymarket Theatre produced a new design for the proscenium arch, 'set all around in an immense gilded frame, like that of some magnificent picture', wrote Henry James, understanding immediately its function.[79] From the early part of the century, stage designers had used painterly elements specifically to be recognized as restatements of themes and images found in old-master paintings. Equally, contemporary artists incorporated elements from stage design into their own work. John Martin's wild imaginings of chaos could perhaps not have been painted without his having seen many scenes of stage destruction, and his paintings in turn fed back into stage design. In 1834 *Sardanapalus*, based on Byron's poem of a dramatic revolt against the Assyrian king Sardanapalus, was presented at Drury Lane, and the *Athenaeum* commended it highly – especially the last scene, when the vanquished king and his favourite slave immolated themselves on a blazing funeral pyre: 'The burning itself, and the disappearance of *Sardanapalus* and *Myrrha* were capitally managed, and drew shouts of applause . . . We believe we need not inform our readers, that the last scene is a copy by Mr Stanfield, from Mr Martin's picture, "The Fall of Nineveh".'[80]

In 1853 Charles Kean also produced a version of *Sardanapalus*, and now the threads of influences were so tightly interwoven that it is difficult to see where each began and ended. A. H. Layard had encouraged the British government to purchase the 'winged bulls' from his Assyrian excavations, and in 1847 they arrived to be displayed at the British Museum to great fanfare, the *Illustrated London News* having recorded their journey as they made their way to Britain. There was also Layard's own book, *Nineveh and its Remains*, with the winged bulls as a frontispiece, which appeared the following year; by 1851 it had been abridged as a popular railway-library book. The possibilities for paying entertainment did not end there: there was a panorama of Nimrud and a diorama of Nineveh, complete with a simultaneous lecture by the artist, who had been at the excavations with Layard. So by the time Kean began work on his production the public was familiar with the accepted view of what Assyrian art looked like. Kean thought that *Sardanapalus* could not have been produced successfully earlier, because 'until now we have known nothing of Assyrian architecture and costume'.[81] For him, and for many of his audience, the 'reality' of pictorial imagery was a mark of the success or failure of serious drama. Not everyone agreed. The essayist G. H. Lewes heavily criticized Kean's production, and by extension the growing reliance on stage effects more generally: 'Is the Drama nothing more than a Magic Lantern on a large scale? Was Byron only a pretext for a panorama? It is a strange state of Art when the mere *accessories* become the aim and purpose of representation – when truth of archaeology supplants truth of human passion – when "winged bulls" dwarf heroic natures!'[82]

Yet when it came to Shakespeare Lewes felt exactly the opposite: 'We must have some accessory attraction to replace that literary and historical interest which originally made Shakespeare's historical plays acceptable . . . Scenery, dresses, groupings, archaeological research, and pictorial splendour, can replace for moderns the poetic and historic interest which our forefathers felt in these plays.' Many in the theatre felt the same. By 1873, in a production of *Antony and Cleopatra*, half the text was cut – twenty-eight complete scenes vanished, as well as chunks of dialogue from the remaining text. This was to make way for a scene in which Cleopatra's entire barge was brought onstage, while perfume was wafted across the audience 'by means of Rimmel's Persian Ribbon'.* There was also the insertion of a Grand Roman Festival with 'a Path of Flowers', ballets, songs, and processions for Venus, Juno, Diana and Flora.[83] Charles Calvert at the Princess' Theatre, Manchester, travelled to Venice to bring back a gondola to copy for *The Merchant of Venice* in 1871; in 1872 he interpolated a scene into *Henry V* so that the king could return in triumph to London:

> Those who saw the scene will not have forgotten the crowds of citizens, artizans, youths, maidens and nobles of the land who filled the streets and temporary balconies hung with tapestries . . . One remembers the distant hum of voices, and how the volume of sound swelled as the little army approached on its

---

* This was one of several attempts to add to the sensory assault on the audience: scented programmes, perfume fountains, vaporizers and other mechanisms were all used briefly in theatres.

march from Blackheath; how the sound burst into a mighty
shout as the hero of Agincourt rode through the triumphal arch-
way . . . Showers of gold dust fell from the turrets, red roses of
Lancaster covered the rude pavements, the bells clashed out, and
a great thanksgiving went up to heaven for the preservation of
the gallant King and his little army of heroes. The curtain
descended on a perfect picture of mediaeval England.[84]

These crowd scenes were popular – as popular as the variations on
Shakespeare that the illegitimate theatre had been producing from the
early part of the century. In the eighteenth century Garrick had promoted
Shakespeare tirelessly; in 1740 Shakespeare had made up only 25 per
cent of London theatre productions; under Garrick at Drury Lane alone,
25 per cent of all tragedies and 16 per cent of all comedies were Shakespeare.[85] In 1809 the patent theatres lost their monopoly on Shakespeare,
unofficially if not officially, when the Surrey Theatre came up with a way
of doing Shakespeare while staying on the right side of the Licensing
Act. It advertised 'a Grand Ballet of Action, with recitative, founded
on Macbeth' – a musical version, with whatever dialogue was necessary
communicated by banners and scrolls, while a chorus of sprites sang
Macbeth's thoughts to the audience. For example:

Is this a dagger which I see before me?
My brains are scatter'd in whirlwind stormy.

Similar productions quickly followed. The Coburg produced a version
of *The Merchant of Venice* entitled *The Three Caskets*, a 'New Tragic Comic
Melo-Drama', as well as a *Hamlet, Prince of Denmark* that was based on
a French neoclassical rewriting, complete with serio-pantomime in the
French style and Gothic scenes of the 'Cemetery of the Kings of Denmark,
by Moonlight' and the 'Royal Museum, with the Sarcophaguses and Urn
of the Late King'. At the Surrey, Hamlet was put on trial for his father's
murder, and the attempted murder of his mother, and was saved at the
last moment by Gertrude's confession, whereupon he was proclaimed
king.[86]

By the end of the 1820s the Pavilion Theatre, in Whitechapel, was
staging more Shakespeare than Covent Garden and Drury Lane combined, including productions (always in song or dumbshow, it must be
remembered) of *Richard III*, *Macbeth*, *Othello*, *Hamlet*, *Cymbeline*, *Henry
IV*, *Romeo and Juliet*, *The Merchant of Venice* and *Coriolanus*.[87] A good

indication of how well known these plays had become was the sudden eruption of burlesques on Shakespeare. The first appeared in 1810: *Hamlet Travestie* by John Poole, which was staged at the Regency Theatre. Its success on stage can be measured today by the fact that it went through at least six printed editions before 1817. In 1813 it was staged at Covent Garden itself, making the circle complete: now the legitimate theatre was relying on the illegitimate theatre for nourishment. These burlesques grew ever more numerous by mid-century. Most relied for their comedy on inserted business – Juliet's dog barking throughout the balcony scene, or *Hamlet*'s graveyard scene sung to the tune of the popular song 'Dorothy Dumps' – or they reset the drama in contemporary situations – Othello as a street-sweeper. There were also topical allusions, political satire, interpolated songs, references to prizefighters or magic shows or legitimate productions of the plays, or even just out-and-out silliness – when Hamlet tries to embrace his father in *Hamlet according to an Act of Parliament* (1853) he is rejected by the ghost, who says, 'Spectres ain't allowed to cuddle.' Yet many of the jokes showed that the audiences possessed a formidable range of theatrical references. In *Masaniello; or, The Fish o'Man of Naples* [*sic*] at the Olympic in 1857, the lead opened with:

> My Lord, the Earl of Hammersmith is taken!
> Stop! That's in *Hamlet*. I'm Masaniello!
> To be or not to be was – that's in *Othello*,
> Translated into Irish – for Ristori.
> Pop goes the Weasel – that's from *Trovatore*! *[88]

Planché had been expecting his audience to be well versed in Shakespeare for years, and he was adept at mingling Shakespearean references with the contemporary and the commercial in his extravaganzas. In *The Good Woman in the Wood*, King Bruin mixed Hamlet and shopping:

> Though yet of our late brother, who has been
> So long defunct, the memory's so green
> That we have subjects who dare still look blue
> When that grave subject is alluded to;

---

* A quick untangling: 'The Duke of Buckingham is taken' is from *Richard III*, with a glancing reference to Dennis Lawler's *The Earls of Hammersmith*, a spoof Gothic melodrama; 'To be or not to be' is of course *Hamlet*, while Adelaide Ristori had performed not in Irish, but in Italian, and in *Macbeth*, not *Othello*; 'Pop goes the Weasel' is, unsurprisingly, not to be found anywhere in *Trovatore*.

> This is to give you all a gentle hint
> Not to presume at acts of ours to squint
> Through spectacles of any hue but those
> Made by our order of 'Couleur de Rose',
> And sold, to suit all ages and conditions,
> By Wink and Company, the Court opticians . . .
> But now, our cousin Sylvan, and step-son.
>
> PRINCE (*aside*): A little more than *cozened*, I am done
> Unutterably brown, if all be true . . .

And the references went beyond theatre. At the Olympic, in Francis Talfourd's *Atalanta, or, The Three Golden Apples*, an extravaganza staged in 1857, King Schoeneus of Scyros appeared in a chariot loaded down with a picnic basket which was labelled 'FOPTNYM ANΔ ΜΑΣΟΝ'.[89] In *The Sleeping Beauty*, Planché had Beauty comment on 'The lock upon the door at the first landing, / The only Locke upon my understanding.'[90] It is hard to imagine today straight theatre, much less pantomime, expecting its audiences to read Greek characters, or appreciate jokes about political philosophers.

While some audiences enjoyed these knowing winks and nods, others wanted more visceral amusement. The Coburg managed to win over working-class audiences with blood and guts – this was in the period when the theatre was nicknamed the Blood Tub or the Bleedin' Vic for its fondness for staging melodramas* – while it reassured its middle-class customers that all was done in the name of historical accuracy. Milner's *Lucius Catiline, the Roman Traitor* (1827) was advertised as 'a faithful picture of the Manners, Warfare, Religious and Civil Ceremonies, &c., of the Ancient Romans'. This followed the line Thomas Dibdin had taken when he ran the Royal Circus after 1819, staging versions of *The Bride of Lammermoor; or, The Spectre at the Fountain* and *Ivanhoe; or, The Jew's Daughter* which amused the lower classes with strong melodramatic elements, and reassured the more serious by being adaptations of Sir Walter Scott.[91]

As well as an assurance of taste, an adaptation, a well-known plot, also gave the audience a head start in the huge theatres where audibility

---

* It was renamed the Royal Victoria in 1833; by 1871 it was the New Victoria; less than ten years later it had metamorphosed into the Royal Victoria Coffee and Music Hall, a temperance music hall, with the word 'theatre' removed to dissociate the venue from the stage's notoriously dubious standards. In 1898 Lilian Baylis took over, and gradually the colloquial name for the theatre became its formal title: the Old Vic.

was often a problem. Really popular works were adapted over and over, and the characters of novels and poems achieved afterlives their authors could never have imagined: Byron's *The Corsair* was adapted for the stage, and was then followed by a new theatrical 'family' with *The Corsair's Bride* and *The Corsair's Son*.[92] Within a single month of publication of Dickens's Christmas story 'The Cricket on the Hearth', seventeen adaptations had been staged. Earlier, Moncrieff, who had adapted *Life in London*, was one of many who produced a version of Mary Shelley's Gothic novel *Frankenstein*. The first version of this amazingly popular story appeared in Birmingham in 1824 as *Presumption; or, The Fate of Frankenstein*, and it was helped along by a vociferous campaign mounted by those shocked at the immoral life of the novel's author. The Coburg produced *Frankenstein; or, The Demon of Switzerland* in the same year, and managed to fill its nearly 4,000 seats every night. Other versions reset the novel in Venice, or Sicily; some gave the characters 'comic' foreign names such as Ratzbaen or Tiddliwincz.[93]* There were pantomime *Frankenstein*s, and musical ones; there were burlesques, there were parodies, and there were straightforward melodramas.

It was melodrama that was best suited to the dramatic stage effects that had been in vogue since de Loutherbourg. Melodrama had been developing over the century, from the Gothic effusions of the eighteenth century, through military dramas like *Mazeppa*, to plays that explored the social world of their own audiences. Jerrold's *The Rent Day*, which was superficially about a rural world of oppressed peasants and wicked squires that few of his audience now knew at first hand, was in reality very close to home: it was about being turned out of one's home for lack of money to pay the rent. After its success, a series of factory- or work-related plays followed, with titles like *The Factory Strike; or, Want, Crime, and Retribution* (1838), and *Mary of Manchester; or, The Spirit of the Loom* (1847), and *The Foreman of the Works* (1886).[94] And melodrama appealed to more than a taste for stories of good triumphing over evil: its reliance on spectacle was a great selling point. In its early days in the illegitimate theatres, spectacle had been necessary owing to the ban on dialogue. Later, in the mega-theatres, the visual could make clear what was lost through inaudibility. The manager of Astley's in the 1860s testified to a

---

* It was these productions that created the slippage that shifted the name 'Frankenstein' from the scientist to the monster, and it happened within the first year of these many stage versions.

parliamentary select committee, 'For a person to bring out a merely talking drama, without any action in it, or sensational effects, is useless; the people will not go to that theatre; they will go where there is scenic effect, and mechanical effects to please the eye.' This had nothing to do with class any more. The *Theatre*, an upmarket arts journal, in 1882 thought that

> The great success achieved at Drury Lane . . . certainly justifies Mr Harris [the manager] in his strong opinion that at a theatre so large his action is vastly more important than dialogue, and situation infinitely preferable to sentiment . . . As a rule the play-goers of to-day want to see and not to think. A facile stage workman who understands dramatic effect is nowadays of far greater value to a manager than a man of letters who has a capacity of writing for the stage.[95]

The early-nineteenth-century melodramas were frequently set in the rural world. Isaac Pocock's *The Miller and his Men* (1813 at Covent Garden, by 1814 in the provinces) had, according to the *Norwich Mercury*, 'a variety of spectacular scenic effects – a windmill working, a boat passing, a cottage room with a fire, a dark forest, a bandits' cavern, an inn, and a celebrated finale involving a bridge from a high rock to the ground and an explosion' involving a drawbridge 'which passes to the Rocky Prominontory [*sic*] across the Ravine; from whence Lothair fires . . . a dreadful Explosion ensues, the Mill and Millers are blown into the air, &c. &c.'.[96] From the late 1830s a number of melodramas revolved around the railways, as the biggest, most dramatic new topic that could be portrayed. The very first, in 1836, was Edward Stirling's *The Lucky Hit; or, Railroads for Ever!*, a drama about railway speculation, but while there was emotional turmoil aplenty, there was little of scenic excitement in it. It was *The Scamps of London* (1843), based on Eugène Sue's French melodrama *Les Mystères de Paris*, and set in Waterloo station, that really began to take the measure of what could be achieved scenically. In 1863 a 'real' train was brought onstage, in *The Engineer*, at the Royal Victoria: 'In the thunderous finale, young George Stephenson mounts the footplates, shunts the heroine to safety in a ballast truck, and crushes her prostrate seducer beneath his cardboard wheels.'[97] And in *London by Night* (1868) came the apotheosis of the railway melodrama. The opening scene was set in 'A London railway terminus, exterior, The stage filled with passengers, newspaper boys call-

ing out the names of their papers, shoeblacks following their occupation, vendors of fruit and cigar-lights, porters with luggage. Railway
and engine heard without; the scene, in fact, to realise the arrival of a
train.' The final scene took the audience to 'The brick-fields at Battersea.
Lone house, L. The river in the distance. Night, and moonlight. A railroad
track runs at back from L. to R.' Our hero, the rather wonderfully named
Dognose, has been knocked unconscious and left on the railroad track;
Louisa, the heroine, can see him from the house where she has been
locked in. 'Locks and bars alike defy me,' she wails. She finds an axe.
'Heaven has not deserted me. Courage! (Strikes gate) Courage! (The
steam whistle is heard again nearer, and rumble of train on the track) It
must give! (Noise of train increases. A last blow. Gate flies open and
Louisa rushes to Dognose. Just as his head is removed from the track,
the train passes with a roar and a whistle.)' The hero declares of his
arch-enemy, 'Let the law punish him', and heads into his golden future
with Louisa.[98]

Who wrote this deathless narrative it is difficult to say. One historian
of Victorian melodrama has suggested that it was a combination of
Moncrieff, Sue, and Dion Boucicault, who was to do so much for the
genre, with perhaps others all adding bits and pieces as it was re-staged
in different theatres, and all claiming it as their own.[99] But, whoever
wrote it, it was Boucicault (1820–90) who became for ever connected
with 'sensation scenes'. Alfred Thompson's *Linda of Chamouni, or, Not
Formosa, An Operatic Incongruity, in Three Scenes and a Sensation* (1869)
was happy to acknowledge Boucicault's primacy even as it derided it:

> I'll sing you the tragic story
> Of a young man of our days,
> Who gained not tin, but glory,
> By writing five act plays.
> He soon found plays legitimate
> Could never boil the pot;
> He voted Byron second-rate
> And Shakespeare awful rot.
> All this was laid to the fault,
> Of one whose name was *Boocicault*,
> Of one whose name was Boo bar sic was salt,
> Was *Boocicault*.
>
> Chorus. All this, &c.

He did away the cupboards old,
The screen that used to fall,
The folding doors which would unfold,
With 'Heaven bless ye all.'
And to his aid sensation calls,
Real cabs, real turning tides,
Real railway trains, real music halls,
Real plunging suicides.

All this, &c. . . .[100]

Boucicault's first play, *London Assurance*, a tidied-up version of a Restoration comedy, had been produced by Mme Vestris and her husband at the Olympic in 1841, to enormous success. But it was with his adaptation of *The Corsican Brothers* in 1852 that he achieved the impossible: he tamed the melodrama, domesticated it, and made it safe for the middle classes – and thereby hugely increased its audience numbers.* *The Corsican Brothers* was taken from a French play that was in turn adapted from a story by Dumas *père*, and it opened at the Princess's Theatre, which, like the Olympic, was one of a handful of theatres that were attempting to lure in the respectable middle classes by stressing their gentlemanly elements, both onstage and off. These were in general smallish theatres, with foyers decorated in a style that mirrored the homes of their desired patrons. The dramas they mounted also revolved around scenes of domestic life that their audiences would recognize, or, as in the case of *The Corsican Brothers*, a historical setting that could be considered educational.

The plot itself was very simple: the story of a murdered man and his brother's revenge. But there were two elements, one of plot construction, one of staging, that took the audiences of the day by surprise, and lifted the piece out of its genre category. First, Boucicault set Acts I and II so that they had to be understood to have taken place simultaneously. This novel approach gave the illusion of depth to a straightforward narrative. Taken together with the innovative technology and staging, many thought they were seeing far more than was in fact the case: the plot had been raked over a hundred times before. What was shatteringly original was the staging. At the end of Act I, Fabien dei Franchi sits at his desk,

* And Boucicault's family went on entertaining the middle classes: his son Dion Boucicault Jr directed the first production of *Peter Pan* in 1904, while his daughter Nina played Peter.

writing to his brother Louis (both played in the original by Kean), with his mother nearby.

> At the same time Louis dei Franchi appears, without his coat or waistcoat, as his brother is, but with a blood stain upon his breast; he glides across the stage, ascending gradually through the floor at the same time, and lays his hand on Fabien's left shoulder ... Louis dei Franchi waves his arm, passes through the wall, and disappears; at the same moment the scene at the back opens and discloses a glade in the Forest of Fontainebleau. On the side, a young man who is wiping the blood from his sword with a handkerchief; two seconds are near him. On the other side, Louis dei Franchi, stretched upon the ground, supported by his two seconds and a surgeon. Picture.

Act II opens in Paris, with the events that are to lead up to this duel, and then 'A glade in the Forest of Fontainebleau ...', and the duel takes place, an exact replica of the conclusion of the previous act, except that, as the scene ends, '[Louis] sinks back exhausted and dies ... The back of the scene opens slowly and discovers the chamber of the first act, the clock marking the hour ... Mme dei Franchi and Fabien, looking exactly as they did before. Fabien: "Pray for Louis, dearest mother. I go to avenge him."' The third act concerns Fabien's pursuit of his brother's murderer. He finally avenges Louis's death and, at the end of the act, 'He passes behind a tree up stage; then advances, with face covered by his hands, and sinks weeping upon the fallen tree. A pause. Louis dei Franchi appears, rising gradually through the earth and placing his hand on the shoulder of his brother. Louis: "Mourn not, my brother. We shall meet again." Curtain.'[101]

This ran for sixty-six nights consecutively, and within a year there were seven adaptations onstage in London alone. G. H. Lewes thought it 'the most daring, ingenious and exciting melodrama I remember having seen'.[102] Partly its success was due to the clever mix of melodrama with chivalric morality that gave sober audiences who did not normally attend melodrama permission to be stirred. But what was really exciting was not the rather moth-eaten story, but the technology that produced the ghostly double.

Stage machinery had undergone a transformation during the century. Earlier, scenery was painted on to flats that were set in grooves on the floor; each successive scene slid into place in front of or behind the current scene. Now some scenery was flown down from newly developed fly-towers high above the stage, while other sets were built as free-standing boxes, creating a sense of three-dimensional reality. These three-sided sets, which we take for granted, were completely revolutionary, a newly created reality appearing in front of the audience. To change them from one scene to the next, a front cloth was dropped down before all but a thin strip at the front of the stage, music was played to drown out the noise, and playwrights were asked to provide 'carpenters' scenes' that could be staged on the narrow front stage while the set was wheeled into place behind. To produce special effects within the box, planks were removed from the floor, and scenery was raised from underneath. The most advanced stages had four bridges built under the stage, set between the grooves for the scenery; these wooden platforms were then raised by ropes to the level of the stage, while the orchestra once more produced extra-loud music to cover the noise. Specialized 'grave', 'star' and 'vampire' traps were set, each opening at a different place on the stage, with different types of hidden door, to permit ghosts, demons, vampires – or simply the star of the show – to appear suddenly, and ostensibly out of thin air. The Corsican trap, devised for Boucicault's show, was different: the performer stood on a wheeled platform that moved slowly and silently up an incline built into the understage bridge: the ghost of Louis dei Franchi floated ominously across the stage, rising ever upward behind his oblivious brother.*

This was a sensation, and created the now almost obligatory parodies. The Strand Theatre produced a burlesque of both *The Corsican Brothers* and Kean's recent production of *Hamlet*: both, after all, were in essence plays about taking revenge for the murder of a family member. So the ghost of Hamlet's father appeared through a Corsican trap, and the playbill also mocked Boucicault's novel dramatic structure, promising that 'The Action of the Second Scene is supposed to take place immediately after the First, and not before, as many, perhaps, will be inclined to suppose. Scene the Second will be followed in regular succession by Scene the Third; the Action of which is supposed to Occur after Scene

---

* Nowhere in the surviving script, however, is it explained how the two brothers appear simultaneously onstage in the first scene, played as they are by the same actor. It is noticeable that in all the other scenes where they appear together the stage directions have one brother's face partially hidden, but in the first scene the opposite is clearly stated. One must assume, perhaps, that the technology behind the ghost's appearance was so overwhelming that a double playing the ghost could creditably pass.

the Fourth, before Scene the First, and simultaneously with the Second, Fifth, and Seventh Scenes.' Another parody, Planché's *The Discreet Princess* of 1855, had one brother who was Hamlet and one who was Louis dei Franchi. *Masaniello; or, the Fish o'Man of Naples* took this idea even further: at one point the audience was watching the comedian Frederick Robson play Masaniello, who was impersonating Prince Richecraft from *The Discreet Princess*, who was in turn playing Louis dei Franchi. This may have been an audience who loved stage gimmicks, but it was hardly an unsophisticated one.[103]

With *The Poor of New York*, staged in that city in 1857, Boucicault harnessed the power of the sensation scene; now the grand spectacle was intended from the first to be more important than the story. The stage directions stress the importance of this scene, by their minutely detailed instructions:

> The house is gradually enveloped in fire; a cry outside is heard. 'Fi-er!' 'Fi-er!' It is taken up by other voices more distant. The tocsin sounds – other churches take up the alarm – bells of engines are heard. Enter a crowd of persons. Enter BADGER, without coat or hat – he tries the door – finds it fast; seizes a bar of iron and dashes in the ground-floor window; the interior is seen in flames. [he climbs in through the window, followed by Dan] . . . Another shout. DAN leaps out again, black and burned, staggers forward and seems overcome by the heat and smoke. The shutters of the garret fall and discover BADGER in the upper floor. Another cry from the crowd, a loud crash is heard, BADGER disappears as if falling with the inside of the building. The shutters of the windows fall away, and the inside of the house is seen . . .

And at this point, on to the stage rolled a real fire engine.[104]

The formula was set: Boucicault's *Pauvrette* (1858) had an avalanche; his 1859 play, *The Octoroon*, had the firing of a Mississippi riverboat;* in *London by Night* (1868) a life-sized express train roared across the stage; this was the progenitor of so many later train melodramas, with the hero tied to the railway track while the express rushed onwards.

Boucicault was not alone in his love of sensation. *Uncle Tom's Cabin* was published in Britain in 1852, and by early 1853 there were eleven versions competing onstage, many with a sensation scene of Eliza escap-

* And also a villain unmasked through photography: the first time a camera appeared onstage.[105]

ing over the ice, pursued by the evil slaver and his dogs. (Astley's version had a runaway horse, which 'loved freedom' too.)[106] The Standard Theatre, in the East End, in the 1880s specialized in sensation scenes: *The Ruling Passion* (1882) had a real balloon in which the heroine, an escaped lunatic and his keeper all rose from the Crystal Palace and landed in the Channel in a storm, to be rescued by a lifeboat. *Glad Tidings* (1883) was set in Rotten Row, with a full complement of riders on horseback. *Daybreak* (1884) staged the Derby with real horses (this was two years before the same thing appeared at Drury Lane, but, to make up for coming second, from 1886 Drury Lane set plays at Goodwood, the Derby, Newmarket, the Grand National and Longchamp). The Standard did not have Drury Lane's facilities, but nevertheless managed to create the necessary racetrack drama by taking over some of the street outside. The scene docks with their ramps leading down to the street were opened on both sides of the stage. The horses gathered at the bottom of one ramp, cantered out into the street, then raced around the building to the other side, up the opposite ramp, and at full gallop tore across the stage, out the other side and down the first ramp, to be pulled up in the street. This arrangement also provided essential working space to gather the crowds used in pageant and processional scenes: *Our Silver Wedding* (1886) had 250 children on a Sunday-school excursion to Epping, in 12 horse-drawn wagons.

For some, one sensation scene per play was no longer enough. At Drury Lane in 1882, in *Pluck*, there was a burning house, a blizzard in Piccadilly Circus, an angry mob breaking the windows of a bank, and an express train ploughing into the wreckage of another, already derailed, train. There were plays with scenes of an underwater fight with the heroes in diving suits, or an avalanche, or the Royal Academy summer exhibition, or the entire stage and auditorium of a music hall.[107] The Lyceum even had a version of *The Bride of Lammermoor* with 'accommodating quicksand that allowed Edgar to stand on it with Lucy in his arms till he had quite finished his theatrical business, and then let him go suddenly down, together with the curtain'.[108]

These spectacles were astonishingly transportable. Boucicault's *The Colleen Bawn*, a huge success in 1860, had a sensation scene where the villain's servant Danny went rowing with the heroine, Eily, on a lake in Killarney. When she refused to give up the marriage certificate that proved she was the legal wife of the villain, and not a fallen woman,

Danny pushed her overboard, but Myles (played by Boucicault himself in the first London performance) appeared in the nick of time, shot Danny, dived into the lake, and saved Eily from drowning.* The journalist Henry Morley, in *The Journal of a London Playgoer*, commended the 'incidents of plunging, swimming, drowning and fishing up, of which the illusion provokes rounds of applause'.[110] Boucicault initially granted licences to provincial theatres to produce versions, but he quickly realized that if he ran his own touring companies he would do better financially. In 1861 the Theatre Royal, Sunderland, became the first to receive *The Colleen Bawn*, with Brighton following later that same week; soon Boucicault was earning £500 a week from touring productions alone – the first West End productions on tour.[111] And his *The Poor of New York*, which he had written for the New York stage in 1857, was equally innovatory: in 1863 Boucicault rewrote the play as *The Poor of Liverpool*, and opened it in the port city, clearing £1,000 in the first nine weeks. Over the succeeding years he created individual productions of *The Poor of* —— for Birmingham, Leeds, Manchester, Glasgow and Dublin, and even *The Poor of Islington* for Sadler's Wells. Finally *The Streets of London* opened in the West End, with a set that replicated Charing Cross station and Trafalgar Square, just outside.[112]

This was another trend that was popular: theatrical re-creations of domestic or local settings, which succeeded or failed by virtue of their similarity to the originals. Boucicault's *Janet Pride* in 1855 had called for an exact replica of the Old Bailey; Tom Taylor's *The Overland Route* was set on a replica of a P&O steamer, and the manager of the theatre boasted, 'We were also fortunate in securing some real . . . lascars, and ayahs, who lent great reality to the picture.'[113] Other plays set in hotels hired waiters from the actual hotels. *Human Nature*, about the fall of Khartoum, advertised that it had 'real police officers' to control the stage crowds which gave the returning troops a hero's welcome, while in the Grand Saloon of the theatre were displayed 'interesting articles illustrative of African life and warfare', together with maps and 'a recreation of Ahmad Urabi's Cairo cell, designed from on-the-spot sketches and featuring the actual carpet and furniture used by the Egyptian nationalist leader during his confinement'.[114]

---

* 'The Colleen Bawn Galop', 'The Colleen Bawn Waltz' and 'The Colleen Bawn Quadrille' were all shortly available as sheet music, and they all had the picture of Eily's near-drowning on their cover page.[109]

Theatre was a sort of newsreel, but it was also a magazine, and by the 1880s the links between theatre and display, display and fashion, fashion and shopping were being thoroughly exploited. Theatres had long carried advertisements: in 1855 Henry Morley had commented on the 'bad taste of the curtain [at Covent Garden] which ... is a mass of advertisements collected from Moses and Son and other well-known advertisers'.[115] But this simple appeal to those waiting for the play to begin soon became a more complex interaction. Gilbert and Sullivan's *Utopia (Limited)* in 1893 had a drawing-room scene that was advertised to be an exact replica of one of Queen Victoria's receptions. George Bernard Shaw wrote, 'I cannot vouch for its verisimilitude, as I have never, strange as it may appear, been present at a Drawing-Room; but that is exactly why I enjoyed it, and why the majority of the [audience] will share my appreciation of it.'[116] It was the aspirational nature of voyeurism that was being played on, posing and answering the question: how do the rich live?

The magazines that reviewed plays carried long, detailed descriptions of the sets and, especially, the costumes. Retailers and dressmakers now supplied props and dresses to the theatres, seeing them as an advertisement for their wares. *Youth*, at Drury Lane in 1881, had its set dressed with furniture from Gillows. B. J. Simmons and Co. advised the public that it had created the 'costumes for the Blue Moon Scene, the Irish Girls, and the Moonbeam Dance in "Our Miss Gibbs"'.[117] In 1892 the *Lady* began a column called 'Dress on the London Stage', written by 'Thespis', who was confident that no play could be considered a failure if from it the audience could 'get a new idea for a bonnet, hat, or other feminine trifle'.[118] Dozens of magazines listed details of all the best stage costumes throughout the decade, and often reproduced fashion plates as well, while for the first time theatre programmes began to give the names of the dressmakers who had made the costumes. *Black and White* magazine sold paper patterns for the costumes described in its pages, while the *Lady* described the eponymous fan in *Lady Windermere's Fan* (1892) in great detail – it had, the fascinated reader was informed, sixteen ostrich feathers fixed to a handle of yellow tortoiseshell, with the name 'Margaret' picked out in diamonds, and there was also an illustration, for those who wanted more. *Queen's* simply advised its readers to visit Duvelleroy's in Regent Street, where they would be able to buy a similar item.[119]

Many department stores sold theatre tickets from special booths, and 'going to the West End' was no longer a geographical description, but meant spending the day either shopping or at the theatre, or both. From the 1860s the Gaiety Theatre had been a place for the man about town, but in the mid-1880s it was taken over by a new manager, who produced a series of musical comedies, many set in fashionable commercial locations – at the milliner's or the dressmaker's, or, best of all, in a department store. H. J. W. Dam, the author of *The Shop Girl* (which ran for two years from 1894) said, 'As many thousands of people do business at the large shops and stores in London . . . [it was clear to me that] the stores formed an excellent sphere to make the basis of a musical piece.' The first act was a conflation of the interiors of Whiteley's and the Army and Navy Stores, and singing shoppers compared 'the loyal, royal stores' to 'a daily dress rehearsal'. The even more successful *Our Miss Gibbs* (1909) was set in 'Garrod's' department store, and its song lyrics linked, completely naturally, clothes, shopping and desirability:

> Some people say success is won by dresses,
> Fancy that!
> But what are dresses without a Hat?
> If you would set men talking when you're walking out to shop,
> You'll be all right if you're all right on top!
>
> That's the last Parisian hat,
> So buy it,
> And try it!
> Keep your head up steady and straight,
> Though you're fainting under the weight!
> We'll declare that you are sweet,
> Men will wait outside on the street,
> If you have that hat![120]

In the 1870s a number of department stores had added their restaurants at more or less exactly the time that theatres had stopped using afternoon performances as try-outs for new playwrights, and instead established regular matinee performances of whatever was running in the evening.* The stores, the restaurants and the theatres were now all

---

* However, in 1880 the journalist and theatre critic William Archer could still get the Gaiety Theatre for a matinee to stage his translation of Ibsen's *The Pillars of the Community*, the first time Ibsen was performed in Britain. Ten years later Gaiety would appear to be a strange place for Ibsen.

HOME CHAT. 93

MISS JULIA NEILSON.

Miss Julia Neilson—or rather Mrs. Fred Terry—for that is the celebrated actress's name in real life—was not quite ready to see me when I called on her the other day; so I had some leisure moments, whilst waiting for her, in which to glance round the pretty drawing-room.

A woman's tastes can generally be judged from the things with which she surrounds herself, and Miss Neilson's certainly lie in the direction of a love of beautiful things. The room was full of them—quaint pieces of Chippendale furniture, pretty old miniature frames, palms, old silver, and, above all, heaps of photographs; in one corner of the room hangs the life-size portrait, painted by Collier for the Academy of the year before last, and on a table close by stood a beautiful photograph of her in her new part.

Further investigation, however, was cut short by the appearance of Miss Neilson herself.

"I am so sorry I am late," she said, "but you know I am very busy just now—we have three *matinées* this week and four next, so as you can imagine I have not much spare time. Now what is it you want to know? I feel I really haven't much to tell you.

MY FIRST REGULAR APPEARANCE

was in *Brantingham Hall*, at the St. James's Theatre, though before that I had acted in *Pygmalion and Galatea*, at a *matinée* at the Lyceum. Mary Anderson was playing the leading part.

"Then after *Brantingham Hall*, I went to Mr. Tree at the Haymarket—*A Man's Shadow* was on

at that time—and—well, I've stopped at the Haymarket ever since."

"What made you first think of taking to the stage?" I asked.

"Oh! well, you know, I didn't originally intend to go on to the stage at all. In fact I was studying music, with a view to concert singing and that sort of thing; then someone recommended me to go on the stage for a time to gain experience, and I gradually drifted into it."

"Now when you are learning up a part have you got any special method? I mean do you work at regular fixed hours?"

"Oh no! I STUDY AT ALL SORTS OF ODD-AND-END TIMES. While I am walking up and down the room, or in a cab; anywhere and everywhere in fact. I am fairly quick, it never takes me long to learn a part."

"What do you mean by long?"

"Well, supposing I had to take a new part to-morrow night, I should set to work on it now at once, and I should be fairly word perfect in time for the performance to-morrow. Of course, I don't mean to say I could get along entirely without prompting, but I should know it well enough to scrape through."

"Which do I think is my favourite part? Well, really I hardly know. I like my present one very much; it's rather a tiring one though."

"Do you design your own dresses?" I asked, thinking of the beautiful gowns she wears in *The Ideal Husband.*

"Well, I always choose them myself, of course, and

MISS JULIA NEILSON.
From photo by Alfred Ellis, Baker Street, W.

Home Chat was just one of many women's magazines which reproduced photographs of actresses in their stage costumes. Here, Julia Neilson poses in her costume for *The Ideal Husband* in 1895.

working in concert. The idea was to get women to spend an entire day between these various places of commodified leisure: to come in from the suburbs by train or Underground, shop, have lunch in a department-store restaurant, attend a matinee, and take tea – from 1913, possibly at the Queen's Theatre, which advertised that women could there 'meet one's friends, write letters, read all the papers and magazines, use the telephones, send messages . . . take tea and generally make themselves at home, *as at Selfridges'* (my italics).[121] They could do all this and still be home to greet their husbands as they returned from their offices.

9

Going for a Song:
The Music Market

IN 1904 A GERMAN JOURNALIST produced a polemic entitled 'Das Land ohne Musik' – 'The Country without Music', the country being Britain. While he was actually discussing the lack of indigenous composers, had he been discussing concert life in Britain for much of its history he might very well have had a point, because until the late seventeenth century there were simply no public concerts at all as we understand them, and little court-based music-making such as could be found in the palaces of many of Europe's rulers and aristocracy. Instead, music was a side effect of theatre, or of sociability, of clubs and taverns.

In Britain, the earliest concert that charged for admission probably dates to 1672, when a man named John Banister 'opened an obscure room in a publick house in White fryars; filled it with tables and seats, and made a side box with curtaines for the musick, 1 shilling a piece . . . Here came . . . much company to hear; and divers musicall curiositys were presented.'[1] Soon after that Tom Britton, the 'Musical Small Coal Man', began to hold popular and successful concerts in a room above his coal store.* Not much is known of Britton's concerts, although Handel may once have played there, and the harpsichordist J. C. Pepusch probably did: the British Library holds a copy of a 'Sonata by Mr Pepusch, called Small coal'.[2] It is likely that the concerts were staged as part of a club gathering. The only other venues in which to hear music were at concerts performed by groups such as the Musical Society, who from 1683 had given an annual public concert at Stationers' Hall, for which

---

* Britton was not small himself, but sold 'small coal', which was either charcoal or small pieces of coal, also known as slack.

an ode in praise of music was commissioned; these concerts ended in 1703, but not before Purcell had written St Cecilia's Day pieces in 1683 and 1692, and Dryden had written two odes, 'An Ode for St Cecilia's Day' in 1687, and 'Alexander's Feast' in 1697. (Handel set both to music, in 1739 and 1687 respectively.)* There was also the Corporation of the Sons of the Clergy, which had since 1655 annually staged a St Cecilia's Day concert (and continues to do so today), and the Foundling Hospital, which staged an annual performance of the *Messiah* from 1750. There were St Cecilia's Day concerts in Norwich, Oxford, Salisbury, Winchester and Wells in the first part of the century; the Three Choirs Festival was set up in 1718 to raise money for the clergy, alternating (as it still does) between the cathedrals cities of Gloucester, Worcester and Hereford. Towns began to hold annual music festivals as well, and concerts were scheduled during assize and race weeks. By the second half of the century there were festivals of different sorts in Birmingham, Bristol, Norwich, and Winchester.[3]

A music festival occurred once a year for two or three days. For those who wanted more, a club was the obvious answer, for men at least. As was usual, clubs met on fixed nights, in a tavern, an inn or some other place where refreshments could be served; the members played, then ate and drank, and then often sang as well, especially glees and catches. (Glees are for three or more unaccompanied voices, in two or more contrasted movements; catches, or rounds, are for three or more singers, all singing the same melody and words, with the second singer joining in with the first line as the first singer is beginning the second.) The Castle Society, at the Castle tavern, in Paternoster Row, ran what it considered to be a very exclusive music club, banning as it did 'vintners, victuallers, keepers of coffee-houses, tailors, peruke makers, barbers, journeymen and apprentices'.[4]

The more exclusive clubs were made up of groups of friends who played for their own pleasure either in their own houses or in a room taken in a tavern and closed to the general public. Advertisements inviting new members to apply for these groups appeared regularly in the newspapers in the 1750s and 1760s. One of the prime functions of any music club was to share the costs of sheet music, for in the 1760s a

---

* St Cecilia, the mythical inventor of the organ, is the patron saint of music, and by the sixteenth century many societies celebrated the day of her martyrdom in musical form with St Cecilia's Day concerts and specially commissioned odes.

Handel oratorio could cost as much as 2 guineas. For upper-class amateurs, sheet music could be obtained from London; for those with less
money, a single copy was copied by hand as many times as necessary.
Clubs grouped together to fund their purchase, just as they did for
reading matter. Other purchases could similarly be subsidized in this
way. From the beginning of the century there had been a sudden increase
in primers and other instruction books for different instruments, to
match the increase in the number of instrument-makers.[5] Dance music
and songs were also published in general-interest magazines, which
groups subscribed to.

Whatever the level of ability or social status, the members of all these
clubs wanted to perform, wanted an audience. One of the earliest music
clubs, the Society of Lovers of Music, in Salisbury, was giving St Cecilia
Day concerts by 1700. The Anacreontic Society, founded in 1766 as a
dining club, with singing afterwards, by the 1780s was giving fortnightly
concerts 'during the season', and soon had audiences of 400 or more.[6]
The grandest of the music clubs, the Concert of Antient Music, was set
up in 1776, with the Earl of Sandwich at its head, and from the 1780s
it had George III as a supporter. The club played only music that was at
least a quarter of a century old, and it had the backing of clerics who
appreciated its desire to promote music as something more than an
evening's entertainment: 'Music is not an amusement of the careless or
idle vulgar; the musician is somewhat more than a Mountebank or
Rope-Dancer; he should preserve his dignity, he must not trifle and play
tricks, he must not be gay, he must be serious.'[7] The seriousness of the
club's members, and their irreproachable social status, meant that the
fact that they played at the Crown and Anchor tavern was immaterial.
(By the 1790s they were ensconced in their own club rooms behind
Oxford Street.)

The Concert of Antient Music gave very select public concerts – tickets
were available to those who had personal acquaintance with a club
member, and up to half the audience consisted of the aristocracy and
gentry. But the audience for music was much wider than this. In 1784 the
Concert of Antient Music outlined a celebration to mark the centenary of
Handel's birth, planning to give three concerts: two at Westminster
Abbey – one a selection of sacred works, the second a complete performance of the *Messiah* – and a third at the Pantheon, of operatic highlights.
Even the rehearsals were oversubscribed, and the Abbey concerts had to

be repeated by popular demand. The Royal Society of Musicians' fund for 'decayed musicians', a charity Handel had been involved with from its inception, was the recipient of all the revenue raised during the centenary, amounting to more than £7,500.

Before this popular celebration, music had for the most part been something that was played either ceremoniously at a set time of year – odes to St Cecilia on St Cecilia's Day, oratorios on the relevant religious festivals – or by the composer and his students in private groups, to be overtaken by new composers and new compositions as the old ones died or became unfashionable. One of the unexpected side effects of the Handel celebration was the acceleration of the creation of a formal canon: music was becoming a commodity, a package of culture to be acquired through sheet music, and concert-going.[8] Until the 1770s, concerts advertised in the newspapers usually stated only the name of the performer; from the 1770s an outline of the programme was given, with perhaps the name of the 'director' (conductor), or the patron of the evening. By the 1790s a complete programme was the norm, with songs given individually by title, instrumental pieces carefully described ('the New Overture, as performed last Friday'), and the director and the performers named.[9] Audiences were no longer purchasing an evening of general musical entertainment, but an evening of *this* specific music, played by *that* particular group of performers.

This new market for music in all forms created a niche for the professional musician. Many clubs played as amateur groups among themselves, but needed support from professionals for their concerts. The growing number of professional musicians was startling: between 1675 and 1750 there were more Italian composers in London than in any other city in Europe apart from Vienna.[10] William Herschel, whom we met in Bath (p. 233), was one of the many German and Italian musicians who had made their way from the courts of Europe to the musical 'free market' of Britain. By the 1760s, over twenty towns in England alone had public concert series. Generally a church organist was the prime mover of the town's concert life, and in many places the local military band filled in on those instruments that amateurs did not play, or did not play well enough.

For the difficulty of contemporary music was one of the reasons for the slow development of orchestral music. Composers were catering for the amateur market – in 1782 and 1783 Mozart produced piano quintets of his piano concertos nos. 6, 12 and 13 for home music-making – but for the most part they were thinking of upper-class amateurs, with copious time for daily practice and money for instructors. In Britain the members of the middle classes did not have the time, even if they had the money, and therefore lacked the requisite skill. In 1799 one club had bought the music for six Mozart quartets, 'but we found them so very difficult, that (except for [the one professional musician in the group]) none of us could do them anything like justice'.[11] In the 1780s there was an amateur group that met on Fridays to play concerti grossi by Corelli, Geminiani and Handel among themselves, but when they gave monthly public concerts in the winter season they hired a leader from Portsmouth, and two horn-players from Sussex. In 1785 in Leicester a series of subscription concerts was set up for an orchestra consisting of a vicar, his son, seven amateurs, and 'five professors of music' who were paid 2*s*. 6*d*. per performance.[12] When festivals increased in size after the success of the Handel Centennial, they also increased in professionalism. By 1799 the festival in Salisbury was hiring professional singers and musicians from London: Johann Christian Bach and the sopranos Nancy Storace (see below, p. 352) and Sarah Harrop all appeared. Harrop was paid £100 to sing in a performance of the *Messiah* and join in some glee-singing.[13]*

In London, opera had been established at the beginning of the century. Unlike in most of the European states, there was no court culture to support this very expensive art form. Many capitals in Europe were small, and when they were not, the court had deliberately been moved away – to Versailles in the case of Paris – in order to ensure that court life dominated everything. In London, however, court life was one of many possibilities for the upper classes. It did not even dominate the lives of the members of the aristocracy. The households of George I and his son never consisted of more than 1,500 people, who came and went from their estates in the country; Versailles in 1740 had 10,000 courtiers permanently based in the palace.[14] The first British performance of an Italian opera was not court-sponsored, but was a commercial venture, at the King's Theatre, the Haymarket, in 1711. Only in 1719 was the Royal Academy of Music set up, under royal charter, to produce opera – the

---

* She later married Joah Bates, one of the organizers of the Handel Centennial, and it was rumoured that she had brought a dowry of £7,000 into the marriage, earned in just four years on the professional circuit.

closest the House of Hanover ever got to subsidizing the art. But, while it was a commercial undertaking, opera was still very much an upper-class concern, both in the management of the Academy and in the audience of the King's Theatre (although not in the theatre management itself). By 1728 there was already an English-language backlash among some audiences. Gay's *The Beggar's Opera*, which rejected the notion that 'art' had to be performed in a foreign language, and therefore remain inaccessible to the bulk of the population, was wildly popular. But it added to the possibilities for the viewing audience, it didn't replace other forms. Nevertheless, opera remained largely the province of the aristocracy. A seat in the gallery at the King's Theatre cost 10s. 6d., compared to Drury Lane's 1 or 2s. For the first fifty nights of the season, boxes went solely to subscribers; for the next set of nights a second subscription was in operation, for those of a slightly lower social eminence. And even then only a few boxes were available for a single performance.[15]

Orchestral concerts were becoming somewhat more accessible, if slowly. From the 1760s they were scheduled more regularly when Teresa Cornelys, a singer and professional society hostess, produced evenings of subscription concerts as well as assemblies at her house in Soho Square. (She also tried to produce semi-staged opera performances, but was charged with breaching the 1737 Licensing Act.) However, just as with the Concert of Antient Music, these concerts were limited to the aristocracy, with no tickets sold openly. In 1763–4 the concerts in Soho Square were supervised by Johann Christian Bach and Carl Friedrich Abel, from Dresden. From 1775 these two set up on their own, building, together with a partner, the Hanover Square Concert Rooms, which seated 900, and from which they ran subscription concerts open to any of the general public who could afford to buy tickets to a series which cost from 5 or 6 guineas for twelve concerts. After Bach's death in 1782, Wilhelm Cramer created an orchestra known as the Professional Concert, which charged 6 guineas for twelve concerts and was run as a cooperative by the musicians, who hired their own soloists – a sort of professional club.

London was a magnet for musicians from Europe who at home were constrained to perform as servants in the household of the court, or of a great nobleman. Johann Peter Salomon (c.1745–1815), the son of a violinist at the court of the Elector of Cologne, fitted this profile exactly.

He had joined the Cologne court orchestra at thirteen (his fellow musicians had included Beethoven's father and grandfather), before moving to Prussia to become music director to the court of Prince Heinrich. In 1780 he moved to London, where he became a popular concertmaster, performing also in Dublin, Oxford and Winchester. In the 1790s he twice enticed Haydn to London. Over fifty concerts of Haydn's music, including twelve new symphonies written for the occasion (nos. 93–104, the 'London' or 'Salomon' symphonies), were given in the Hanover Square Rooms, with the composer directing from the pianoforte. On his 1794 visit Haydn made £800 from his concerts alone, not including any income from the sale of his sheet music.

He incidentally by his success contributed substantially to the collapse of the Professional Concert: there was not yet a sufficient-sized audience for music to sustain two orchestral groups in the same rooms in the same season. Yet there were enough paying customers that, for the previous decade, the newspapers had reviewed London concerts as a matter of course. At the same time the growing number of concerts, and the consequent competition for this same small audience, had created a need to advertise. For now there was sufficient musical activity that audiences were able to pick and choose: in the season, especially in April and May, there were two subscription concerts series, two oratorio seasons, and concerts at two pleasure gardens. Even when the pleasure gardens were closed, and it was not the oratorio season, by the end of the century London concert life was still active: the *Public Advertiser* for 7 January 1791 listed opera performances for the coming week on the Tuesday and Saturday; the Professional Concert at the Hanover Square Rooms on Monday; the Concert of Antient Music at its own Rooms in Tottenham Street on Wednesday; the Pantheon (see below) on Thursday, and a performance by Haydn, again at the Hanover Square Rooms, on Friday. There were in addition private subscription concerts on Sundays, when public performances were forbidden.[16]

Concerts in general were seasonal: the winter saw the bulk of the performances in concert halls, while in the summer the professional musicians moved from the theatres and concert halls to the pleasure gardens. Businessmen and their families, rather than the aristocracy or the court, had rapidly become the main audience for music. Via their entrepreneurial skills, businessmen were also the prime movers of concert life. In 1749 George II wanted to stage a celebration to mark the

An overview of Vauxhall Gardens in the mid eighteenth century. The Gothic pavilion is in the centre, while the supper rooms line the arcades on the right and left.

Peace of Aix-la-Chapelle, for which Handel agreed to write what became the *Music for the Royal Fireworks*. The royal household lacked the technical expertise to mount a display, however, and was forced to call on Jonathan Tyers, the lessee of Vauxhall Gardens, to provide the stands, the decorations and the material for the fireworks, as well as the equipment and staff needed for the event. He agreed on the condition that he could stage a preliminary rehearsal at Vauxhall, for which he charged admission. He later claimed that 12,000 people had attended, at 2*s*. 6*d*. a head. The actual event in Green Park was literally a damp squib, when rain prevented the fireworks from igniting, although one of the stagehands did manage to set a pavilion on fire.[17] That was by the by. What it showed was that public entertainment, even in the name of the King, was to be found not via the court, but by courtesy of the business world.

The most select place for public concerts was only nominally a pleasure garden, in that it was not outdoors at all. But the Pantheon was classed by its audience as similar in kind to Vauxhall and Marylebone Gardens. The Pantheon had been built by James Wyatt in 1772, modelled on the Hagia Sophia in Constantinople, with additional Adam-style flourishes unaccountably overlooked by the Byzantines. It had been planned specifically as competition to the gardens, with the same programme of balls, masques, suppers and concerts as its outdoor competition. Fanny Burney's *Evelina* attended a concert there, and 'was extremely struck with the beauty of the building, which greatly surpassed whatever I could have expected or imagined. Yet, it has more the appearance of a chapel, than of a place of diversion; and, though I was quite charmed with the magnificence of the room, I felt that I could not be as gay and thoughtless there as at Ranelagh.'[18] (Fanny Burney probably felt the need to mention the Pantheon as often as she did – it appeared in *Cecilia* too – as her father, Charles Burney, was a shareholder.)[19]* The tickets were the upper-class standard price of 6 guineas for twelve concerts. The building, so ingenious and original on its opening, burned down only twenty years later, and, although it shortly reopened, it was never as fashionable again.

Much more accessible to the public were the concerts in the pleasure gardens themselves. Vauxhall had been staging concerts from the 1730s, and was swiftly joined by Marylebone Gardens, which in 1738 advertised concerts from six to ten every evening, with 'Eighteen of the most celebrated Concerto's, Ouvertures, and Airs'. Soon both had concerts six evenings a week in the season. (Ranelagh, more select, limited itself to three evenings.) Vauxhall particularly enjoyed galas presented for the birthdays of various members of the royal family, with specially commissioned music. Extraordinary events got their own musical accompaniment, such as the death of Frederick, Prince of Wales, which produced a solemn dirge, George III's marriage, which was commemorated by Arne's 'Beauty and Virtue', and George III's escape from an attempted assassination in 1786, which was marked by a song by James Hook, Vauxhall's music director.

---

* Charles Burney's life was a good example of the broad range of tasks expected of the professional musician. In 1749 he became organist of St Dionis Backchurch in Fenchurch Street, London, which gave him an income of £30 a year, as well as access to pupils for private tuition. He also performed at concerts held at the King's Arms tavern. As a composer, he published intermittently until the 1760s, especially songs for the stage. Illness forced him to move to King's Lynn, where he became organist of St Margaret's in 1751, again with the opportunity of obtaining private pupils. In the meantime he was writing *A General History of Music* (4 vols., 1776–89), the first part of which appeared in 1771 as *The Present State of Music in France and Italy*. To find the time for this work he had to write in his carriage as he was driven from one pupil to the next: he saw his first pupil at seven in the morning. It has been estimated that these various tasks provided him with an income of between £30 and £100 a month in the London season.[20]

From 1752 all places of public entertainment needed a licence for concerts and other public entertainments, and Marylebone took the opportunity of this formalization of its music to enlarge its premises. Now it covered nearly 35,000 square metres. Thomas Arne, whose opera *Henry and Emma* was running at Covent Garden in 1750, became closely involved. Arias from his operas were sung at Marylebone that summer, and the following year his son, aged ten, appeared to sing 'The Highland Lassie' and 'The Bonny Broom', after which Arne's overture to *The Judgement of Paris* was played, as was his new organ concerto, Handel's overture to *Samson* and the Coronation Anthem – 'Tickets 3s., and purchasable at Mr Arne's House in Beaufort Buildings, Strand'.[21]

Both Vauxhall and Marylebone made a point of performing patriotic songs about military and naval battles, such as a patriotic piece at Vauxhall in 1739, said to be by Handel, celebrating Admiral Vernon's famous taking of Portobello in the West Indies from the Spanish, François-Hippolyte Barthélémon's *Victory*, marking the acquittal of Lord Keppel after a court martial in 1779, and Carl Stamitz's chorus to mark Rodney's relief of Gibraltar in 1780. After the French Revolution broke out there was further subject matter: songs like Stephen Storace's 'Captivity', about Marie Antoinette, and Arne's 'Naval Ode' entitled 'When Britain' (which included what is today entitled 'Rule, Britannia'), were performed to great acclaim in 1794.[22]

From 1756 the lessee of Marylebone Gardens, Stephen Storace, joined with his uncle, the Revd John Trusler, to produce a series of burlettas translated from Italian. (John Trusler was the son of Marylebone Gardens' landlord; the younger Stephen Storace and his soprano sister, Nancy, were the grandchildren.) The Storace family connection shed great lustre on the gardens: Nancy joined the Emperor Josef II's opera buffa company in Vienna, and premiered works by Salieri and Paisiello, as well as Mozart's *The Marriage of Figaro*, in which she created the role of Susanna. She later returned to London, where she sang in the Italian Opera company in the Haymarket, and later at Drury Lane. (She was the highest paid singer at Drury Lane, earning 10 guineas per performance.) But by the summer of 1760, the Truslers and the Storaces had fallen out, and in 1760 the *Public Advertiser* ran a notice that

> Whereas the Master of Marylebone Gardens has thought proper to publish the following Paragraph: . . .
> This is to assure the Public that the books of the several

Burlettas sold at the Door are the same Books that have been performed there, and those sold at the Bar are Copies pirated from me, which (contrary to Agreement) have been re-printed in order to deprive me of the Advantage which (by Contract) I was to have, I being the Author and Inventor of all the Burlettas there performed.

STEPHEN STORACE[23]

This was not the only quarrel over publication of words and music. The pleasure-garden songs were big business at the gardens themselves – and outside. In 1741 Thomas Arne brought a suit against two book-sellers who were printing his songs from *Comus* and *As You Like It*. These continued to bring him in money for decades: in the 1750s, advertisements appeared for 'New Musick. *This Day is Published*, VOCAL MELODY. BOOK IV. A favourite Collection of English Sngs [*sic*], sung at the Publick Gardens. Composed by Mr Arne.'[24] Songs from the pleasure gardens appeared in book form, as sheet music, and in more general publications, and this became one of the easiest ways to get to know new music, without even attending the gardens. Over a single year, in 1750, the *Gentleman's Magazine* published a dozen songs, including a Handel aria, an aria from Boyce's *The Chaplet*, and 'The Highland Laddie Written long since by Alan Ramsay, and now sung at Ranelagh and all the other gardens; often fondly encor'd, and sometimes ridiculously hiss'd'.[25] As Marylebone Gardens was sliding inexorably towards closure, a ladies' pocket diary for 1776 contained 'Favourite New Songs sung at the Public Gardens', together with a 'Poetical Address to the Ladies' and 'Rates of Coachmen, Chairmen, &c., &c., Compiled at the Request of several Ladies of Quality'.[26] The pleasure-garden songs had become ubiquitous. Goldsmith's *Vicar of Wakefield* joked that they are 'all cast in the same mold: Colin meets Dolly, and they hold a dialogue together; he gives her a fairing to put in her hair, and she presents him with a nosegay; and then they go to church together, where they give good advice to young nymphs and swains to get married as fast as they can.'[27]

Thomas Lowe took over the running of Marylebone Gardens in 1763, and Stephen Storace continued to be allied with him, while Thomas Arne remained the principal composer. Over £2,000 was taken in 1768 for concerts, but by the 1770s the concert schedule had become erratic and music was beginning to be crowded out by fireworks, lectures, magic-lantern shows and the like.[28] Orchestral concerts and musical theatre in purpose-built halls and theatres had begun to take over from the gardens in this respect, but by the 1790s they too were suffering: poor harvests, the French wars, and the consequent lack of touring virtuosi from Europe all contributed to a drop in the number of concert performances that can be seen in the advertisements in the newspapers. In 1792 thirty benefit concerts were advertised for various artists; in 1798 there were only eleven.[29]* Another reason for the dip can be traced to the rising evangelical beliefs of many of the middle classes. Music with no religious overtones, music in public, began to appear as an undesirable thing for more and more of the population. And, just as these beliefs were becoming prevalent among society at large, two technological changes made it possible for many to give up public music-making, without giving up music itself. The first was the development of the piano; the second innovations in the printing of sheet music.

In the middle of the eighteenth century, musical instruments were, naturally, played, but they were also objects that showed off the prosperity of a household. Many group portraits of family members in domestic settings (known as conversation pieces) revolved around new objects of consumption: some showed the family at tea, so that their new bone china could be displayed; others had women holding guitars, or standing by a harpsichord, not because they were musical, but because the instruments were expensive. In Nollekens' painting *The Conversation Piece* (1740), the harpsichord was actually moved outside, where it was set in front of the majestic façade of the house, both equal signifiers of the wealth of the family depicted with them.[30]

The first pianos were made by a harpsichord-maker named Johannes Zumpe. Zumpe's piano was in essence a box about 1.25 metres long, with a compact action and no escapement.† It was possibly a Zumpe piano that was played in 1766 at the first public performance on a piano in Britain, when, according to the playbill of Covent Garden, 'At the end of Act I., Miss Brickler will sing a favourite song from "Judith",

---

* A benefit was a concert or a theatrical performance where the receipts for the evening were given to a particular performer. Many professional singers had benefits regularly, usually staged or promoted in some way by their supporters.

† The action is the mechanism by which the movements of the pianist in striking the keys are transmitted to the hammers which hit the strings to produce the notes. The escapement is the mechanism that causes the hammer to fall back into the rest position immediately after striking the string; thus on Zumpe's piano the hammer continued to rest against the string, damping the sound, until the key was released.

accompanied by Mr Dibdin, on a new instrument, called Piano Forte.'[31] It was a Zumpe on which Johann Christian Bach played the first pianoforte solo in a concert, during one of the Bach–Abel concerts two years later. He had paid £50 for his instrument, and from now on his keyboard music was published 'for the harpsichord or pianoforte'. In 1773 the first set of six sonatas, Op. 1, by the keyboard virtuoso Muzio Clementi were also published in the same way: 'for the harpsichord or pianoforte'; they became one of the foundations of the later piano literature.[32]

Meanwhile, the young John Broadwood, a Scottish cabinet-maker, had been apprenticed to Zumpe's old master, Burkat Shudi (a corruption of his Swiss-German name, Burkhardt Tschudi). In 1769 Broadwood married his master's daughter, and in 1771 he was taken into partnership. As well as producing harpsichords, he began to develop the Zumpe pianoforte: he found a way to improve the resonance of the sound, and he created pedals to raise and lower the dampers. In 1773 he hit on the idea of the sustaining pedal, and later he added the soft pedal. In 1777 he filed for a patent for a new action, applying the word 'grand' to a piano for the first time; the result became known as the 'English action'. He also worked on expanding the range of the piano: the long strings needed for the bass gave a weak sound, so he made a separate bridge for them, with greater tension, which meant that shorter, thicker strings could be used; then he built the treble half an octave higher. Soon he extended the bass, until in 1794 he had a six-octave keyboard. He promoted his new piano among the fashionable musicians: he sent one to Hummel and one to Dussek, who gave the first public concert on a six-octave piano, the new concert grand.[33]* Beethoven received one too, and immediately began to compose music that took advantage of the new range.

Other firms began to move in on the territory Broadwood looked to be conquering. Longman and Broderip were music publishers who by the 1780s were making both harpsichords and technologically advanced pianos. In 1789 they advertised a new action, which 'can never fail in the operation . . . Soon as the Hammer strikes the String it immediately falls back; whereas in other Instruments, the Hammer dances on the jack, and occasions jarring noise in the Tone.' They also produced

---

* Jan Ladislav Dussek was the first concert pianist to turn the piano sideways to the audience. He was known as 'le beau Dussek', and it has been suggested that he thought his profile was his best feature.

One of the many decorative pianos on display at the Great Exhibition. This one is made out of papier mâché, as are the stool and canterbury to hold the sheet music beside it.

'portable' grands, and small pianos that 'could be conveyed, and even played on in a coach'. (This was not an advertising fantasy. When in 1784 Dr Johnson's friend Mrs Thrale married the music-master Gabriel Piozzi and went abroad, they travelled in a coach which had a fitted portable pianoforte, and Mrs Thrale reported that Piozzi played it regularly.)[34]

Home music was becoming more popular than ever before. No longer was it just the man at his club, or the enthusiastic amateur, who played: now women were also learning, as it was seen as a new domestic skill – they could accompany others and amuse their families. Sheet music was now also aimed at the growing army of amateurs, and many publishers began to produce music to sell in monthly instalments, by subscription. This was particularly successful for music from current shows, or for the newest dance tunes.[35] Much of the expansion in the market came from a decrease in the price of the music, which had been made possible by a technological development in the way music was printed. Until this time, music had been printed by punching pewter plates, rather than using movable type. The plates produced only about 2,000 impressions before they had to be renewed.[36] In 1768 Henry Fougt filed to patent a system for printing music from type. Now sheets of music could be set as easily as a book, and Fougt began to sell single-sheet ballads for 1*d.*, or eighteen sheets for 1*s.* – a third of the price most music publishers were charging.[37]

Then came another innovation: lithography was first invented in 1798, and, although it did not become popular immediately for books, the possibilities for music printing were grasped at once. To produce a lithographic image, a drawing was made on a stone with 'fat ink', which adhered to the stone. Water was then poured over the stone; it was absorbed by the blank areas, but rejected by those that had been inked. A roller with printing ink was run over the stone, and the dry area – the drawing – trapped the ink. A sheet of paper was then placed on the stone and both were put in a press; the printer's ink transferred itself to the paper, while the 'fat ink' remained behind. Music printing, even with Fougt's improvements, had been a slow and expensive business. Now music could be quickly and cheaply reproduced as a lithograph, which was either sold in this form or used as a basis for an engraving, which was then sold as a more elegant (and expensive) version.[38]

The amount of sheet music published kept rising: in 1766 the Scottish music publisher Bremner listed 120 works in his catalogue; in 1773 Weicker had 500; Longman and Broderip's music catalogue of 1789 had 1,664 separate pieces of music for sale; and in 1824 Boosey's had 280 pages listing 10,000 foreign publications alone; D'Almaine and Co. claimed in 1838 to have 200,000 engraved plates in stock. To return to the end of the century, at that time Longman and Broderip's catalogue had 565 pieces for the piano, 333 for the voice with harpsichord, and 90 pieces of dance music to be played on any keyboard instrument. Of the complete listing, 60 per cent were for the keyboard, and 300 of these pieces were listed as 'sonatas or lessons'. The range was tremendous. There were works by (among others) J. C. Bach, Boccherini, Cherubini, Clementi, Corelli, Giordani, Haydn, Kozeluch, Mozart, Pergolesi, Pleyel, Scarlatti, Schroeter and more. These were sold in sets at 7*s.* 6*d.* the set or 10*s.* 6*d.* for a bound volume. They could also be purchased as single sonatas or lessons for 1 or 2*s.* each. Then 'Single Italian Songs', that is, arias, were available: extracts from *Iffigenia*, *Alessandro nel Indie*, *Alceste* and *Armida*, or from light operas like *La Cosa Rara* or *Il Contadino in Corte*. Overtures could also be bought on their own, and while some were from Italian opera, for the most part it was musical comedies in English that were listed: Dibdin's *The Blackamoor*, Samuel Arnold's *Inkle* *and Yarico*, William Shield's *The Choleric Fathers* and *The Farmer*. These mostly cost 6*d*. or 1*s*., while complete piano and vocal scores for the shows from which these pieces had been extracted were available at between 3*s*. to 10*s*. 6*d*. The catalogue then listed 'favourite airs with variations', which had titles like 'Black Joke' (with variations by Clementi), 'Jack's Return from Dover', 'Sow's Tail to Geordie' and 'Twiggle and a Friz'. These were very likely pleasure-garden songs. Then there were traditional airs: 'Allan a Roon', 'Auld Robin Gray', 'Highland Laddie' and 'Over the Muir among the Heather', many of which were also performed in the pleasure gardens.[39] These could be bought in a variety of formats: as vocal scores for male or female voices, or arranged for different instruments or different combinations of instruments.

As in all new markets, many schemes were advertised and promoted. James Harrison, a music publisher, saw, as Wedgwood had seen, that the middle classes, if they were charged less, would actually return a larger profit to the entrepreneur. Handel's works had previously been published by subscription, at 2 guineas. Harrison produced a vocal score of the *Messiah* for just 7*s*. – a sixth of the price. He also began to publish the *New Musical Magazine*, which provided sheet music for oratorios, operas and other vocal music adapted to be sung at home. His new *Piano-Forte Magazine* began to appear in 1797, at 2*s*. 6*d*. weekly. It survived only until 1802, and perhaps some of Harrison's marketing schemes were to blame. An advertisement in *The Times* promoted the *Piano-Forte Magazine* by saying that each issue would contain a promissory note signed by Harrison. When 250 notes had been collected, they could be exchanged for 'a Brilliant and elegant Pianoforte, far superior to many instruments sold for 25 guineas each'.[40] The magazine went under before anyone could have saved up for a piano, but the scheme made no sense anyway. To get a piano, readers needed to purchase nearly five years' worth of sheet music first. If they already had a piano, they didn't need a second one, and if they didn't have a piano, what were they going to do with five years' worth of sheet music in the meantime? Finally, over the period of the offer, £31 5*s*. would have to be spent buying the magazine – £5 more than the value of the 'free' piano.

Other music publishers were more pragmatic. With increasing numbers of amateur performers, publishers saw a market for popular music such as traditional folk songs, especially if they were arranged by famous composers, like the Scottish songs on p. 220. Music commemorating battles or marking public events had long been popular at the pleasure gardens. With the advent of the French wars, similar songs as well as piano solos and duets also became available as sheet music: compositions marking the battles of Jemappes, Neewinden, Marengo, Austerlitz, Jena, Leipzig and Waterloo were all published. Stephen Francis Rimbault, the organist of St Giles-in-the-Fields, wrote a fantasia entitled *The Battle of Navarino*, which gave guidance to the pianist (and audience): one section was a depiction of 'Turkish and Egyptian ships blown up', another 'The Asia loses her Mizzen Mast'. Dussek composed *The Naval Battle and Total Destruction of the Dutch Fleet by Admiral Duncan, Oct. 11, 1797*, to mark the British victory at Camperdown; he also wrote *Le Combat naval*, which had no direct references to a specific fleet or country, and could therefore have a wide appeal, for the supporters of any side in any naval battle. Other pieces were opportune in different ways: *The Battle of Copenhagen . . . Dedicated to Lord Cathcart* was in fact a piece that had earlier been published as *La Bataille d'Austerlitz*.[41]

By 1805 the music market was booming. Such was the call for sheet music that the composer and pianist Josef Wolfl wrote from London to his music publisher in Leipzig:

> Since I have been here, my works have had astonishing sales and I already get sixty guineas for three sonatas; but along with all this I must write in a very easy, and sometimes a very vulgar style . . . in case it should occur to one of your critics to make fun of me on account of any of my things that have appeared here. You won't believe how backward music still is here, and how one has to hold oneself back in order to bring forth such shallow compositions, which do a terrific business here.

The business *was* terrific. In 1750 there had been about a dozen music shops in London; in 1794 one directory alone listed thirty; by 1824 there were at least fifty.[42]

This amount of music publishing depended entirely on a large number of people who could play the piano in the first place, and thus it was that, as well as sheet music for the already proficient, from 1800 the range of books of piano tuition and exercises was growing rapidly. In 1798 the piano virtuoso Clementi took over the firm of Longman and Broderip, and three years later his *Introduction to the Art of Piano Playing* appeared, which contained a selection of 'lessons' by a variety of composers. This was followed in 1804 by J. B. Cramer's book of forty-two études. If Clementi's publication was the culmination of one style of tuition book, Cramer's was the introduction of the next. Earlier manuals had been compilations of pieces of more or less the same level of difficulty. Cramer's études set out, for the first time, pieces that each contained a technical difficulty, or a series of technical difficulties, which had to be mastered and which then incorporated into the next étude in the series, on an ascending scale of difficulty. These études were so successful that in 1805 another publisher produced a similar *Study for the Piano-Forte, Containing 500 Exercises*, and in 1810 Cramer published a second set of forty-two. In 1817 Clementi returned with the first part of his great masterwork, the *Gradus ad Parnassum*, which, as well as distilling the many years of his own teaching, was also heavily influenced by his discussions with perhaps the best-known of all piano-exercise composers, Karl Czerny (a pupil of Beethoven and the teacher of Liszt).

The audience for these books, a market of amateur piano-players, was now more than large enough to support an industry: the development of the piano had made home performance a possibility for many. In the middle of the eighteenth century a harpsichord had cost between 35 and 50 guineas at the lower end of the price spectrum; a decorated, ornate instrument cost much more. Zumpe, in 1768, had charged J. C. Bach £50 for his primitive piano. By the end of the eighteenth century a grand piano was priced at 70 guineas, while an inexpensive, space-saving upright might cost only 20 guineas. The prices had continued to fall: in 1815 a large, decorated grand from Broadwood's was £46, while the company's square piano, with the new action, cost £18 3s.[43] It was large-scale production that enabled manufacturers to lower their prices. Burkat Shudi and his son had, in their sixty-four joint years of harpsichord-making, produced somewhat under 1,200 harpsichords, or fewer than nineteen a year, which appears to have been more or less the norm. In Vienna at the beginning of the nineteenth century one of the premier piano manufacturers was making about fifty pianos a year using the English innovations – the pedals, the extended keyboards and (later) the metal bracing. By contrast, John Broadwood had, by 1802, made 8,000 pianos in his twenty years of piano-production – or 400 a year, eight times the number of his Viennese rival. In the next twenty-two years, his company produced another 45,000, an average production of 2,045 a year, or over five a day: every four days, Broadwood replicated Shudi's entire annual output.[44]

One of the greatest motivators to get pianos into the middle-class home was the arrival of the upright. Many had wanted a piano; many could even afford a piano; but they simply had no space for one. Then, in 1795, William Stodart, the younger brother of Robert Stodart, who had developed the English action and pedals together with Broadwood, took a grand piano, set it upright on a stand, and put it inside what was effectively a cupboard. Although Stodart's upright saved space, it was not yet an item for the average home – his instruments measured about 2.6 metres high. But even at this size, when Broadwood's began to produce them it sold more of these than it did grand pianos: the market for a smaller piano was already making itself felt. Gradually these vast uprights, or 'cabinet' pianos, were reduced to a height of 'only' 1.8 metres. The hammers of a grand fall back through gravity, so, once they were set side-on in an upright, a mechanism was needed to replicate what had previously occurred naturally. In 1802 experiments were made with the strings, and it was found possible to stretch them obliquely, which further reduced the height of the entire structure.* This smaller instrument became known as a cottage piano, and it was one of the most popular domestic pianos throughout the century.[45] Further improvements were mostly made for sound rather than space reasons – by the 1820s Broadwood's was using iron resistance bars against the soundboard, which allowed the hammer heads to strike the strings more heavily, giving a better sound, and one that made possible the development of the new, Romantic style of playing.

It was not until the middle of the century that any form of mass production entered the manufacturing process, and for this reason, until instruments at substantially lower prices created a new bottom end of the market, pianos had remained firmly in the luxury class, even if they were now an affordable luxury for the prosperous middle classes. In 1850 about 83,000 families had an annual income of between £150 and £400, while a lower-middle-class family's average income was £90.[46] Broadwood's sold its grand pianos for £135, while its uprights ranged from 80 guineas down to 45 guineas. Even manufacturers with lesser reputations charged high prices: a six-octave 'piccolo' (that is, a small upright) cost from 60 to 40 guineas, and cottage pianos were about the same. In 1851 the manufacturer Collard showed two small 'semi-cottages' in plain

---

* Stodart's first upright had kept the long stringing of the grand piano, with the case curving in at the treble end. He suggested that bookshelves might nicely fill the gap.

deal wood, undecorated, at what was described as the very low price of 30 guineas. These prices limited good new pianos to the homes of the prosperous. However, there was already a strong secondary market, with substantially less expensive pianos available outside London or from second-rate manufacturers. An 'artisan' piano could be bought for as little as £10, a quarter of the generally accepted price for a good piano.[47] Furthermore, there was also a brisk trade in secondhand pianos, as this new luxury began to seem more like a necessity. This, combined with a rise in wages that began in 1857, brought pianos, whose prices were falling, ever closer to the reach of the majority of the middle-class population.[48]

Many of the manufacturers who produced pianos at the lower end of the market were not in fact manufacturers at all: they bought instruments from more established firms, who didn't want to sully their names with cheap pianos, and stencilled their names above the keyboards. In 1851 200 manufacturers were listed in the trade directories, of whom some were stencillers and about 50 only made parts (they were fret-cutters, or they manufactured the hammer rails, or the felt for the hammers and dampers; some even simply produced the shirred silk for the front of uprights, yet they still called themselves piano manufacturers). Of the factories who did manufacture pianos, nearly 90 per cent were companies employing fewer than ten men. In 1854 T. & H. Brooks became the first company to often complete actions for sale, making it possible for smaller companies to buy partly processed goods and lower their overheads. And the overheads for piano manufacturing were enormous. For a start, the wood needed to be seasoned for at least two years before it could be used, and a grand piano then took a minimum of six months to produce: thirty months' investment before any return was possible. The better the piano, too, the heavier the investment of time and resources. A Broadwood piano did not have a ready-purchased action; Broadwood actions each had 3,800 separate pieces: ivory, several different types of wood and metal, cloth, felt, leather and vellum, all of which were assembled by a minimum of forty different workmen – key-makers, hammer-makers, damper-makers, damper-lifter-makers, notch-makers, hammer-leatherers, beam-makers, brass-stud-makers, brass-bridge-makers, and so on.[49] It was not perhaps surprising that at the Great Exhibition, Broadwood's, confident in the supremacy of its instruments, disdained the gimmickry of fellow manufacturers (see

p. 20), and simply showed its four best grand pianos. William Rolfe and Sons, from Cheapside, at the opposite end of the scale, also showed just its best: a cottage piano, 'in which stability, economy, and excellence are the objects aimed at'.[50]

Broadwood had revolutionized piano manufacture in the eighteenth century, but by the middle of the nineteenth it was the American manufacturers who were ushering in the next big changes. America had long had a shortage of skilled manpower, and therefore labour was costly and industry as a whole worked hard towards mechanization; Britain had a plentiful, thus cheap, labour force, and saw much less need to mechanize. By the 1800s American manufacturers were exploring the use of machinery for preparing wood for a variety of uses – sawing, planing and other basics. Half a century later Broadwood's and its competitors were using almost no machinery at all, not even to prepare the wood. As late as 1857 a paper on 'The Conversion of Wood by Machinery' read to the Institution of Civil Engineers was considered an astonishing innovation.[51]

But it was more than production methods that were being overhauled in America: it was the entire construction of the pianos. Beneath the traditional grand piano (or at the back of an upright) was a wooden bracing, which held a plank that in turn held the tuning pins for the strings. As the range expanded higher and higher, the pitch was raised, and with it the string tension had to be increased, exerting more and more pressure on the wooden frame, which was just not strong enough to bear it. With a metal frame, the force on a concert grand could be increased, and it went from about 16 tons in 1860 to 30 tons in the next three-quarters of a century. Even before the force increased, the wooden frames had been annoyingly susceptible to climate changes, which made the wood expand and contract, destroying the tuning of the instrument. The overall cast-iron frame from America produced a better sound, and it guaranteed that that improved sound would not fluctuate seasonally. The first iron-framed piano to be shown in Britain, at the Great Exhibition, was a Chickering, a grand piano with 'the whole framing consisting of string plate, longitudinal bars, wrest block and drilled bridge . . . of iron cast in one piece'.[52]

The next innovation was also American, and it was particularly relevant to the domestic instrument. In 1863 an upright with bass strings that crossed the treble was built, producing the first upright to have a sound that even remotely matched that of a grand. As well as improved sound, it had a one-piece iron frame, which made possible greater tension of the strings, and, following on from that, heavier hammers, thicker felt and a better action.[53] Almost all uprights from now on were built on this model.

For some time, the fact that the British were dropping behind in both technology and price went unnoticed, for pianos were increasingly available to the general public. The new 'three-year system', or hire purchase as it later became known, made it possible to obtain a new piano for as little as £6 a year. In 1864 an advertisement offered a piano 'Let on Hire for 3 Years, after which the instrument becomes the hirer's property'. A 28-guinea 'pianette' could be acquired for 10 guineas a year; a 40-guinea cottage piano for 15 guineas, and a '60 guineas semi-oblique' for only 20 guineas a year. The *Bethnal Green Times*, a local paper in respectable suburbia, in 1867 advertised, 'Let or hire. 3 years system. Pianettes 2½ guineas per quarter. Piccolos 3 guineas. Cottage pianos £3.10.0. Drawing-room model cottage £3.18.0.'[54] Even this quarterly payment could be further broken down into manageable monthly payments: Molsom and Son's Piano-Forte Saloon in Bath advertised pianos for 10s. a month in 1866 – a stretch, but no longer impossible for that respectable family on £150 a year.[55]

Even as this new accessibility arrived, the British pre-eminence was over. In 1861 there had been fewer than 8,000 workers producing musical instruments in Germany; by 1875 that number had doubled; and by 1882 there were at least 25,000 working in the piano trade, and they were producing up to 70,000 pianos a year, of which nearly 25 per cent were shipped to England. This was a victory of modern mass production over hand craftsmanship, because the German manufacturers were not producing better pianos, they were producing cheaper pianos. By the 1880s their mass-produced uprights were being sold at half the price of English pianos. This was done by economizing on materials that did not affect the quality of the sound, and by leaving unfinished those parts that could not be seen without taking the piano apart. By 1914 one out of every five pianos bought in England was of German manufacture.[56] The English piano-manufacturing industry was not dead – far from it. But it was facing extraordinary competition at the cheap end of the market from Germany, and at the concert grand end from America. For the moment, however, the market was large enough for everyone. By the early twentieth century, 1 person in every 360 people in the country bought a new piano, compared to the 1 in approximately 1,100 that had bought one in 1851. By 1910 there were perhaps between 2 and 4 million pianos in Britain – one for every 10 to 20 people.[57]

So once more there was a surge in sheet music, and a subsequent drop in price. In 1837 that score of the *Messiah* that had cost 2 guineas in the 1760s now sold for 1 guinea; by 1887 it was just 1*s*., and could be found in stationers' shops as well as in specialist music stores. Alfred Novello, a music publisher and the producer of the shilling edition, pushed through another technological change, moving from engraved sheet music to new mechanized typesetting, which did not have the built-in obsolescence of engravings, the plates of which could make only a limited number of impressions. This new technology became essential for a sheet-music industry that was seeing enormous growth. Arthur Sullivan's drawing-room ballad 'The Lost Chord' (1877) sold half a million copies in twenty-five years; singer and composer Michael Maybrick's sea song 'Nancy Lee' sold over 100,000 copies in two years, and his 'Holy City' was still selling 50,000 copies a year in the 1890s.[58]

Novello saw that new printing methods were cheaper and thus increased his profits. More than that, though, he saw that if new technology could be combined with the amateur music market there were fortunes to be made. In 1842 he published *Singing for the Million*, a tuition manual for amateur choirs. He then began to publish *Mainzer's Musical Times and Singing-Class Circular*, a weekly music magazine (it later changed its name to the *Musical Times*) that reached out to the amateur rather than the professional. To teach the many millions of piano-owners and singers to play and sing their new songs, there were so many music teachers that, for the first time, they were separated out from the professional musicians. By 1900, in London, a directory listed 2,533 'orchestral instrumentalists', but 4,823 'professors of the pianoforte, organ, singing, etc.'.[59]

Professional musicians had been the beneficiaries, and also the driving force, of the piano mania that had overtaken Britain. No longer a mere adjunct to the amateur, the professional was now an autonomous performer in his (it tended, apart from singers, to be 'his') own right. Amateurs were relegated to their own homes, and rarely played in public as they had in the past. At the turn of the nineteenth century, an astonishing range of keyboard virtuosi had displayed their talents in London –

Clementi, Dussek, Field, Hummel, Steibelt and Wölfl among them. But concert halls outside London also had an active concert life and visiting virtuosi: when Paganini toured in the 1830s, he performed in Edinburgh, Glasgow, Perth, Cheltenham, Chester, Leeds, Sheffield, Southampton, Yarmouth and York.[60] This was part of a revival of concert life, after the trough of the 1790s and through to the end of the French wars. By the mid-1820s there was already a rise in the number of concerts performed: to over 100 in the 1826–7 season in London alone.

There were more concerts, and the concerts were also more accessible to more of the population. The Philharmonia Society had been founded in 1813 as a counter to the ideas of the Concert of Antient Music and its like. It was established by a group of middle-class patrons – upper middle class, it is true, and prosperous, but no longer aristocracy, or even the gentry. Instead the founders, and the audiences, were solicitors, doctors, journalists, architects and the like, who wanted to take their families to concerts of contemporary music, performed by professionals.[61] Even so, in the early part of the century concerts were still essentially a class-based activity, and tickets were limited both by price and by subscriptions. The upper-class subscription concerts, well into the 1830s, cost between 10s. 6d. and 1 guinea per ticket, if tickets were available on the open market at all; concerts for the middle classes cost between 5s. and 10s., while working-class concerts were between 1s. and 5s. This segregation by price was clear to those attending, and was seen by many as a desirable situation. A journalist from the magazine *Musical World* said that tickets for less than 10s. 6d. were to be recommended, to increase the numbers attending, but that tickets priced at less than 5s. were unthinkable: 'The art must not be degraded . . . To play the finest music to an audience which has been admitted for a shilling apiece, is what I can never give my consent to.'[62]

By the mid-1840s there had been an increase of over 300 per cent in the number of concerts given in London – a growth that far outstripped the growth of theatre and opera or musical theatre.[63] Yet this surge came from exactly the same developments that changed so much else in the leisure world: increased leisure time; improved public transport with an equivalent decrease in its cost, which made it possible for audiences to travel from further afield; improved lighting and safer streets, which made an evening out seem less daunting; and increase in the number of magazines and newspapers that carried advertisements and reviews, and an equivalent reduction in their cover price. As with theatre, the extension of transport links worked in both directions. Audiences found it easier to travel to concerts, and musicians could travel more easily to towns that did not yet have the population to sustain their own orchestra or musical life. In the 1830s a sextet had had to hire two carriages to transport itself and its instruments; after the railways had arrived an entire opera company could perform in London, complete with sets and costumes, get on a train, and perform the next day in Manchester, or Bolton, or Glasgow. Not merely the trains, but Bradshaw's timetable, the telegraph, ticket agents who arranged advance publicity – all these things made touring possible, and profitable.

In 1865 J. H. Mapleson set up a series of touring companies for opera. In his first full year of business two of his companies toured a circuit of 70 towns in 60 days, performing 120 concerts, with, as a finale, joint performances of the two companies in Edinburgh and Glasgow. Mapleson was a pioneer, and others soon rushed in. By 1893 the field was so well established that the newly created *Dramatic and Musical Directory* listed four set rail itineraries that it recommended as suitable for touring theatre, concert and opera companies, taking in thirty towns that could be booked all together, in sequence, at a cost of less than £8 for the whole tour. Eighty-nine towns were listed that had at least one theatre, and the directory ranked them by size: Hull and Glasgow led the fourteen 'first-class towns'; while Bournemouth and Torquay were fourth class. By 1900 there were 142 special Sunday trains in England and Wales that were scheduled specifically for the convenience of theatrical and musical touring companies: a company could now do a week in a town, finish on a Saturday night, travel on the Sunday, and be ready to open on Monday night in the next town.[64]

The audiences for music were ready and waiting for them, increasing throughout the nineteenth century. Mme Tussaud had in 1833 imported the French custom of promenade concerts, where, as in the pleasure gardens, the audience listened to music while walking and taking refreshment. But it was with Louis Jullien that these promenade concerts became overwhelmingly popular, expanding ever further the audience for concert-going. The son of a French bandmaster, Jullien by 1845 was conducting at the Surrey Zoological Gardens, which had many of the features of the pleasure garden – fireworks, garden walks, music – together with the animals and conservatories. Jullien rapidly became known for his 1s. 'monster' concerts. At the first one an audience of 12,000 listened to extracts from Bellini's *I Puritani* played on 20 cornets, 20 trumpets, 20 trombones, 20 ophicleides and 20 serpents,* with 'God Save the Queen' punctuated by cannonfire as a finale. In 1849 another concert had an orchestra made up of 400 musicians, supplemented by 3 military bands, 3 choirs and soloists. Despite his love of gigantism, it was not size alone that motivated Jullien. He was passionate about bringing the best of classical music to the masses. He scheduled all the Beethoven symphonies (with sound effects, it must be admitted: during the Pastoral Symphony peas were rattled in a tin to imitate hailstones), and Mozart and Mendelssohn could be heard regularly, between feeding time at the zoo at 5.30 and the fireworks display which began every evening at 9.30.[65]

Other large concert halls were also supplying the demand for popular classical music: the St James's Hall, which seated 2,000, opened in London in 1858, financed by two music publishers. Their series of Monday and Saturday Pops were held regularly over the next forty years. Other music publishers also saw concerts as a shrewd investment: Boosey and Co. established a series of ballad concerts in 1867, while Novello, which had a large back-catalogue of ecclesiastical music, promoted oratorios, including the famous 1854 performance of the *St Matthew Passion*, which introduced Bach to many for the first time, perhaps even more than Mendelssohn's celebrated championing of him had done in 1829.[66] The Crystal Palace, newly relocated to the suburb of Sydenham, staged orchestral concerts from 1855 for nearly half a century. The original band of the Crystal Palace consisted almost entirely of brass and wind instruments, and played mostly popular tunes. August Manns, a German ex-military bandleader, took over and transformed it into a symphony orchestra, although for some time he had to hire better string players for the Saturday-afternoon classical concerts.

Outside London, Liverpool's Philharmonic Hall opened in 1849, and Manchester's Free Trade Hall was not far behind, in 1856. Both these towns had large populations of German immigrants who were regular concert-goers.[67] Manchester was a model of what could be achieved by

---

* An ophicleide is a wind instrument with a U-shaped brass tube with keys, similar to a bass version of the keyed bugle or cornet; a serpent is another deep-toned bass instrument, made of leather-covered wood, about 3.5 metres long, and with three U-shaped turns. Once almost vanished, it has reappeared with the emergence of period-instrument groups.

a professional middle class eager to take part in a cultivated leisure industry. In 1848 Carl Halle, a German conductor and pianist who had fled the revolution in Paris, was performing as a soloist in London. A German calico-printer in Manchester wrote to him to suggest that, should he chose to come to Manchester, there was an audience ready and waiting. Halle (by now Frenchified for the English to Charles Hallé) arrived and conducted a single performance of the Gentlemen's Concert Society orchestra. The Gentlemen's Concert Society was a music club that had been running since the eighteenth century on the old model of amateurs bolstered by professionals for the tricky passages. The experience so appalled him that 'I seriously thought of packing up and leaving . . . so that I might not have to endure a second of these wretched performances,' he later wrote.[68] He was, however, persuaded to stay by the music-hungry bourgeoisie, who told him they had invited him to Manchester specifically to improve standards. He agreed to stay on condition that he might weed out the poor players at will, and that the concerts would be opened to the general public. The burghers of Manchester were happy to accept his terms: they knew the audiences were there. In Hallé's first year he also began a chamber music series, which had 67 subscribers; two years later there were more than 200.

The orchestra's – and Hallé's – big opportunity came with the Manchester Art Treasures Exhibition of 1857 (see pp. 407–9). It had been decided by the exhibition committee that daily concerts would add to the public's appreciation of the pictures, and Hallé tendered for, and won, the job. Over the period of the exhibition, 1.5 million people listened to Hallé and his orchestra, many hearing symphonic music for the first time. Hallé used this success as a basis for enlarging his orchestra, and in 1858 he launched the Hallé Orchestral Concerts (making, in his first year, 2*s*. 6*d*. profit). He hired his musicians for four or five months of the year on permanent contracts, forbidding them to take work elsewhere during those months. It was the first symphony orchestra in Britain that did not have a constantly changing roster of musicians. In addition, Hallé encouraged local talent. Until now, although there had been many concerts in Manchester, the city had relied on London for many of its performers: in 1836 a music festival had hired forty-six musicians, including virtually all the soloists, from London, using just nineteen local musicians. By 1881, 70 per cent of Hallé's musicians were resident, and only four came from London. Soon 'Hallé trains' were running every

In the early part of the nineteenth century, music festivals were one of the best ways to hear classical music. In 1846 the *Illustrated London News* shows off Birmingham's new Great Music Hall during its annual festival.

Thursday, to and from the suburbs, and from as far as Cheshire, to bring the orchestra's regular audiences to weekly concerts.[69] In 1891, in one month alone, there were eighteen concerts in Manchester, in five fortnightly series. Most involved popular classics, choral works and drawing-room songs, but the pianist Ignacy Paderewski and the violinist Eugène Ysaÿe had both appeared onstage in the city that month.[70] In 1896 the leader of the Hallé, Adolph Brodsky, and three other members of the orchestra founded the Brodsky Quartet.

Liverpool was in a similar situation, although for lack of a Hallé it developed somewhat more slowly. It too had a semi-amateur group left over from the days of amateur music clubs: the Philharmonic Society. The Society gave public performances, with the gallery seats alone available for the general public – the rest belonged to the members of the clubs and their friends. Until 1909 the rules in force included:

> No Gentleman above twenty-one years of age residing or carrying on business in Liverpool or within ten miles thereof, and not being an Officer of the Army or Navy, or Minister of Religion, is admissible to the Boxes or Stalls at the Philharmonic Society's concerts unless he be a Proprietor, or member of the family residing at the house of a Proprietor, or has his name upon the list of Gentlemen having the *Entrée* exhibited in the Corridors.[71]

When Hallé first brought his chamber group to Liverpool, in the 1848–9 season, the audience numbered eleven – including the four reporters sent to cover the event.[72] But Liverpool's concert scene soon caught up with Manchester's. Leeds too was developing quickly, staging nine concerts in one month in 1891.[73]

In fact throughout Britain the number of professional musicians increased by a factor of seven between 1840 and 1930, from 7,000 to 50,000, while the population itself only doubled, from 27 million to 50 million.[74] There were jobs for more than orchestral musicians, more than theatrical or even seaside musicians. Professional musicians were now needed by taverns and music halls, in ever-larger numbers. Before wholesale urbanization had taken place, pubs had simply been the front rooms or kitchens of private houses, but from the 1830s purpose-built pubs began to appear – as did the 'gin palace', the highly decorated serious drinking den. Within these pubs, new forms of musical entertainment quickly developed. Free and easies were communal amateur sing-songs involving all the regular customers. In the 1830s and 1840s these began

Evans's Supper Rooms marked a transition from the more informal atmosphere of the free and easies to the professional music hall. The performers are now separated from their audience. Note the number indicating who is performing on the sign behind the singer. The chairman, a vestige of the club days, sits facing the audience just beneath the performer.

to develop into 'singing saloon' concerts or 'open harmonic meetings', which were held at a specific time and in a space specially cleared by the publican. The old core group of the free and easy, which may originally have been a formal club, was still present, but now strangers could join in too. The token nod towards professionalism was that there was often a piano to aid the singing. Gradually, however, a shift could be perceived. The same people continued to attend, but the singing was supplemented by professional 'room singers'. They were still mixed with the amateur singers who had always performed, and there were still group renditions of glees and catches, but the notion of a private entertainment organized around a group of people who knew each other was beginning to fade away.

Some of the saloons even referred to themselves at this early stage as music halls: the Star Music Hall, in Bolton, had nightly musical shows from 1840. Thomas Youdan owned Youdan's Royal Casino, which had nightly musical performances, as well as 'Sacred Music on

Sunday Evenings, with an Efficient Band', and which ultimately became the Surrey Music Hall.[75] But before that there were a number of saloon theatres which did not yet use the term music hall but were nonetheless music halls in prototype, like the Rodney in Birmingham. There were also many saloon theatres in the East End of London: the Eagle or Grecian Saloon in the City Road; the Union Saloon and the Albert Saloon both in Shoreditch; the Britannia Saloon, in Hoxton; the Bower Saloon in Lambeth; the Effingham Saloon, in Whitechapel. A few, like the Apollo Saloon in Marylebone, were geographically separate, but catered to similar working-class or lower-middle-class customers. The programmes at these saloons were a mixture of opera, drama, farce, songs, music and dance. From 1831 the Royal Albert Saloon and Standard Tavern and Tea Gardens, to give it its full title, had two small stages in an extension built beside the original pub building. An evening at the Royal Albert might include a concert of popular songs, a melodrama, a fire-eater, a ballet and a pantomime, complete with harlequinade, and all for 6d. – or 1s. to have a good seat and a drink included.[76] The Eagle or Grecian Saloon, in the City Road, had developed out of the London tradition of working-class pleasure gardens. From 1832 it advertised a garden, an orchestra and dancing; inside the saloon there were concerts and vaudevilles every evening (with sacred music during Lent). By 1837 the Eagle had been remodelled, with a pit and boxes, and performed mixed programmes of concerts which in one evening might include a Weber overture, a Rossini aria and 'It's all very well, Mr Ferguson', a comic song. This range, from opera to pantomime, continued, with productions of both *The Barber of Seville* and a burlesque called *Nobody in Town*.[77]*

The Theatres Act of 1843 loosened the restrictions on spoken drama outside legitimate theatre, but in exchange set down that theatres could no longer serve alcohol. Many saloons had to decide what they were. A few, like the Britannia, chose to become theatres, but the bulk moved to what would shortly be known as music hall. Now many concert rooms were erected in what had previously been gardens, with professional singers engaged for 'parlour concerts', and sometimes a speciality act or

---

* By 1882 the mix of open-air dancing, pantomime and melodrama had come to seem old-fashioned, and the tavern was sold to General Booth, to become the headquarters of the Salvation Army. A massive tent was erected over the open-air stage for religious revival meetings. The entire building was demolished in 1899.

two. Admission tickets were required, and a 'chairman', a vestige of the old club days, introduced the acts. In 1851 Charles Morton opened the Canterbury Arms tavern in Lambeth, staging these parlour concerts. In the following year he built out into the tavern's skittle alley, and renamed the building the Canterbury Music Hall. This is generally accepted as the first purpose-built music hall. It seated 700, with an admission charge of 6d. and a refreshment stall inside; for a further 6d. seats could be obtained in the balcony, and for 1d. a pamphlet with the lyrics to the songs could be purchased.[78] In 1860 Morton leased the Boar and Castle tavern in Oxford Street, and on its site built the Oxford Music Hall, ushering in the era of the grand music hall, with vast purpose-built spaces. In most cases, although the concert areas were far larger than the pubs to which they were nominally extensions, access was still through the pub, as though in homage to their origins. But once through the small opening the customers found themselves in a room of up to twenty-five metres long, with chandeliers, gilt decorations, mahogany bars, and a host of supper tables spread across the floor. Wilton's, built in 1856, was a prime example of this type of hall.

By the 1850s most Midland and industrial northern towns had some form of music hall, even if the buildings were not yet as elaborate as in London. In Manchester in the early 1850s 25,000 millhands divided their favours among three large saloons and beer halls, where they could watch programmes not dissimilar to much early music hall: 'singing in character, dancing of various kinds, clog and grotesque dancing, juggling and tumbling'. The price of entrance was the purchase of a 2d. refreshment ticket. By 1866 there were three or four specially built halls, and many smaller ones which had licences for drink, if not for professional singing and dancing. In Liverpool by this date there were no halls that had been purpose-built, but 33 pubs held up to 100 customers each, and, while 70 per cent of them still relied on the amateur free and easies for entertainment, 30 per cent were hiring professional entertainers.[79]

By the 1860s the Alhambra, with a capacity of 3,500, had opened in London; the Oxford Music Hall seated 1,200. There were over thirty of these large halls in London, including Wilton's, Weston's Music Hall, Holborn (1857), the South London Palace (1860), the London Pavilion, the Bedford, Camden Town, and Deacon's, Clerkenwell (all 1861), and Collins', Islington (1862).[80] There were also at least 300 more purpose-built halls in the provinces, and in the 1870s nearly 400 halls that had some sort of formal, professional form of entertainment.[81]

By the 1870s there was yet another shift to the shape of an evening at the halls. The supper tables were pushed aside, now only taking up half the floor space, while a theatre pit was built over the remainder. The old-fashioned group singing with the audience, the glees and catches, was finally phased out, and instead headliners and serios (singers who performed comic songs in mock-serious form) – professionals all – appeared. A proscenium arch was added around the stage, to further indicate the division between the audience and the professionals. The halls were becoming in form, if not entirely in content, theatres, with a static audience who were no longer expected to socialize with each other in groups, or to join in the performance, but only to be entertained as individuals, segregated by the price of their tickets.[82]

The professionalization of the performers was also complete: they were rarely local, but did their turns at several halls each night, on prearranged circuits, both in London and in the provinces. The first agency for music-hall artistes had opened in 1858. Vacancies were advertised in the theatrical newspapers, which were beginning to emerge. The first, the *Era*, had originally been a trade journal for the licensed victuallers' trade. It was not unnatural that the brewers who had financial interests in taverns and saloons should also choose to include information for performers in their trade paper. Then the performers took over the content completely, and it became a theatre paper only. In 1856 the *Magnet*, devoted solely to music hall, began publication in Leeds, and in 1859 the *Entr'acte* followed.* In 1865 the Music Hall Provident Society was founded, to act as a pension and benefit society for music-hall employees.[83]

The 1870s were a turning point for music hall. In the previous ten years the cost of setting up of a hall in London had reached nearly £10,000 on average, and more for a particularly large or lavish establishment. Morton had spent £40,000 on the Canterbury as early as 1854, and with a partner another £35,000 on the Oxford in 1861.[84] Many proprietors could no longer rely on their takings to fund the huge and costly architectural changes, but had to sell shares to brewers, or form themselves into syndicates. In 1864 the Alhambra had been funded by

---

* The *Magnet* survived until 1926, but the *Entr'acte* had a rather bumpier ride, opening and folding three times in the first thirteen years. Once established, it lasted until 1907.

a limited-liability company, and in 1893 the London Syndicate was formed, with three large West End halls; soon Edward Moss, Oswald Stoll, Frank Allen and Richard Thornton were all building regional chains of halls, moving quickly across the country.[85]* The turns they could finance were now more elaborate and sensational – and were also more standardized. In many ways, by the time music hall had reached this period it had virtually become 'variety', a more homogenous, more refined, less raucous style of performance, which was better suited to suburban audiences.

What these audiences loved was that an image of the upper-class world was being conveyed to the workers, in the same way that film would convey an image of the life of the rich to those suffering through the Depression. In 1890 Percy Fitzgerald commented that 'The East Ender has created his idea from a gentleman or "gent" of which he has had glimpses at the "bars" and finds it in perfection at his music-hall. At the music-hall everything is tinselled over, and we find a kind of racy, gin-borne affection to be the mode; everyone being "dear boy" or a "pal" . . . a suggestion of perpetual dress suit, with deep side pockets, in which the hands are ever plunged.'[86] The descendant of the 'gent' was the 'lion comique', the leading comic singer, who performed 'swell' songs such as 'Champagne Charlie' (1866) by George Leybourne. Leybourne, who performed under the sobriquet 'the Original Champagne Charlie', 'flaunted the broad check suits, the puce jackets, widely striped trousers and lurid vests of his so-called swells'.[87] The song, and the persona, celebrated the things that cash could bring – flashy clothes, flashy women and, of course, plenty of champagne to splash around. Leybourne was appearing at the Canterbury when this song became a hit, and for an astonishing £1,500 a year he was contractually obliged to dress as a 'swell' offstage as well as on, driving around in a carriage, very publicly drinking champagne that had been specially provided by a wine merchant.[88] As with the 'young Werther' outfits of the Romantics a hundred years before, now the 'Champagne Charlie' hat was popular among lower-middle-class young men, who idolized their hero and his glamorous life.

Then the 'masher' took over from the 'swell'. Younger, even more gaudily dressed, many of the stage mashers were in fact male imperson-

* The Stoll Moss group, only recently amalgamated with Andrew Lloyd Webber's Really Useful Theatre company, was a descendant of two of these chains.

ators, the most famous of whom was perhaps Vesta Tilley. On a tour of America, she noted that 'the dudes of Broadway were intrigued with my costume, a pearl grey frock coat suit and silk hat and a vest of delicately flowered silk – one of the dozens which I had bought at the sale of the effects of the late Marquis of Anglesey. Grey frock coats and fancy vests became very popular in New York.'[89] One night when she forgot her cufflinks, she tied her cuffs together with black ribbons: there was a stampede in the direction of the ribbon counters, and haberdashers began to sell cufflinks made to look like her improvisation.

Although the songs of the music halls, and the personalities of the singers, were the highlights for many, much of the success of music hall came from its variety of genres. In 1896 the first moving picture was shown at the Regent Street Polytechnic. So successful was it that it was quickly transferred to the Empire Music Hall, Leicester Square, where it ran for eighteen months. But as yet it was only an interlude in music hall's domination. The programme at the Empire consisted of an over-ture, Tyrolean singers and dancers, a ballet, a trio, some Russian dancers, Cinquevalli (a famous juggler), the films – which were four in number: the arrival of the Paris express; a practical joke played on a governess; the collapse of a wall; and boating in the Mediterranean – followed by acrobats, a singer, a performance of *Faust* lasting an hour, and a pair of 'eccentrics'. Such a mix of 'high' and 'low' culture under one roof was not to disappear until the twentieth century.

10

Going, Going:
Art and the Market

IN 1764 DR JOHNSON SET UP a literary club, to meet at the Turk's Head tavern, in Gerrard Street. Soon members included the artist Joshua Reynolds, the writer Oliver Goldsmith, the historian Edward Gibbon, the naturalist Joseph Banks, the musicologists Charles Burney and John Hawkins, the political economist Adam Smith, the politicians Edmund Burke and Charles James Fox, and the men of the theatre David Garrick, Richard Brinsley Sheridan and George Colman.

Part – much – of their renown rests on their achievements. Some, however, is the result of their mutual support system, their 'clubbability' (a word coined by Johnson). They wrote about each other's work, they reviewed each other's plays, they promoted each other's books; Johnson wrote the dedication to Burney's *History of Music*; Boswell dedicated his *Life of Johnson* to Reynolds. And Reynolds gave to posterity the faces of his fellow club members, in nearly two dozen portraits. These portraits in turn were engraved, printed, sold and displayed, disseminating the fame of Reynolds's friends, and of Reynolds himself, far and wide.

That decade, the 1760s, marked an astonishing new phase in the history of the art market in Britain: the first national academy was founded; the first annual art exhibitions were held; the first serious competition with European art markets was mounted – and the first real alternative to aristocratic patronage was stirring. Until this point, art in Britain had been a private matter. There were no royal palaces open to the public; there were no churches where great paintings could regularly be seen by any congregant. Artists who wanted the public to see their work used their own studios: Hogarth showed his *Harlot's Progress* and

Mariage à la Mode at home in the Piazza, Covent Garden, in 1730–32, and later in his Leicester Square house. In 1749 and again in 1751 Canaletto took advertisements in the newspapers to notify potential buyers that his work was on display at his lodgings in Golden Square.[1] Angelica Kauffmann had her studio on Suffolk Street, 'one [room] in which I paint, the other where I set up my finished paintings as is here the custom . . . The people come into the house to sit – to visit me – or to see my work.'[2]

Sometimes the houses of the great were open to the 'respectable' public, but more often a painting was enjoyed only by its owner and his family and friends. Their own first exposure to art may have been in the houses of their social equals, but for many it was on the Grand Tour that great art was first studied. The tour was commonly the province of young men of money and birth, sent to Europe to imbibe a classical education. There were plenty, naturally, who simply imbibed, but there were others who saw Italy, in particular, as the place to 'not only improve my taste, but my judgement, by the fine originals I expect to see there', as Lord Nuneham wrote in 1755.[3]

Many of these men expected, and were expected by their families at home, to bring back spoils, either antiquities or old masters: the 1st Marquis of Rockingham instructed his son to buy antique statues for the rebuilding of Wentworth Woodhouse (although he actually ended up with copies); William Weddell, of the Dilettanti club, sent back nineteen cases of classical sculptures for Newby Hall in Yorkshire, while William Locke purchased Claude's *St Ursula*.[4] Others commissioned paintings from artists who lived very nicely off this up-market tourist trail: Pompeo Batoni had a profitable sideline in portraits of British tourists, painting over 150, while Canaletto produced 'several hundred' paintings of Venice specifically for the British market.

The Dilettanti had been formed in 1734, a club for connoisseurship, for which the primary qualification for membership was to have made the Grand Tour. (Horace Walpole said that 'the nominal qualification for membership is having been in Italy, and the real one, [is] being drunk'.)[5] In the late 1740s there were discussions among its members about setting up an academy, but nothing came of it. In 1755 they met once more with a group of artists – including Hayman, Reynolds and Roubilliac – to discuss an academy, but the artists and the Dilettanti had different aims. The artists hoped for financial support; the Dilettanti wanted a stable of craftsmen to produce work under their direction, and, the artists 'finding that they were to be allowed no share in the government of the academy . . . the negotiations ended.'[6] For many Dilettanti, the concepts behind the art were what was important, while the artists, for the most part, they considered to be mechanics, tradesmen. They were useful to have in one's entourage, to produce images on request, but it was the theory of aesthetics and a knowledge of the classics, rather than mere technical ability, that was valued. The Earl of Shaftesbury gave instructions to the painters he commissioned concerning the structure of the composition, what symbols should be used, and how. Richard Payne Knight, one of the Dilettanti, although he admired Reynolds greatly, admired him as an artisan: he thought that the artist's lack of classical education meant he was incapable of judging art himself.

The idea of patronage and of the superiority of the patron over 'his' artist was not confined to painting. When Pope had first read his translation of Homer to an audience, the Earl of Halifax 'in four or five places . . . stopped me very civilly, and with a speech each time much of the same kind: "I beg your pardon, Mr Pope, but there is something in that passage that does not quite please me. Be so good as to mark the place and consider it a little at your leisure. I'm sure you can give it a better turn."' As Pope told the story, he later reread the passages exactly as they had been before, while giving Halifax to understand that they had been amended following his advice. Each time Halifax said approvingly how much better he now thought them. In Pope, the neoclassical courtier, one can see the beginning of the change that would flower in the Romantic movement of the following generation, when the artist promoted himself, and was accepted, as a creator of originality and imagination, rather than a servant producing work to order, as a carpenter makes chairs.* But while Pope was certain that he, the artist, was superior to his patron, in the middle of the century this was still a vexed question. He returned to this theme more than two decades later, in 1741, when he and Dr Arbuthnot produced *The Memoirs*

---

* One present-day writer has suggested that the question of the attribution of Shakespeare's works continues endlessly because Shakespeare fits in with none of our ideas of authorship, which are an entirely Romantic construct. Shakespeare wrote for money, he invested that money with care, and he was apparently concerned more about that money than about the afterlife of his plays via corrupt or pirated texts. Not only that, but he used others' work as the basis for his own, directly countering our notions of genius, which, in its Romantic guise, is indivisible from originality.[7]

of the *Extraordinary Life, Works, and Discoveries of Martinus Scriblerus*.
Scriblerus, their fictional hack, spends his entire inheritance on a 'Roman
shield' which, once it is cleaned, is clearly only a broken candle sconce.
Scriblerus sells it on to Dr Woodward, who 'incrust[s] it with new Rust'
and 'exhibit[s] [it] to the great Contentation of the learned'.[8]

Reynolds, in the *Universal Chronicle* in 1759, was equally vehement
regarding the ignorance of the 'learned', and no more polite: 'To those
who are resolved to be criticks in spite of nature, and at the same
time have no great disposition to much reading and study, I would
recommend to them to assume the character of connoisseur . . . The
remembrance of a few names of painters, with their general characters,
with a few rules . . . which they may pick up among the painters, will go
a great way towards making a very notable connoisseur.'[9] That both Pope
and Reynolds – neither of them a rebel; both of them criticized in their
lifetimes for their flattery and even servility to the great – were willing
to attack some of the wealthiest and most influential men in the art
world this overtly might indicate that the day of the connoisseur was
waning.

While the Dilettanti and their descendants were to rule for some time
to come, another part of the art world was developing – one that in the
next century would become economically and socially dominant. Public
art exhibitions had begun with an act of charity, when Thomas Coram's
Foundling Hospital, built in 1742, received a portrait of Captain Coram
from Hogarth as a gift on its foundation. Within five years, fifteen of
Hogarth's friends had also donated works of their own, and by 1760 the
Foundling Hospital collection included paintings by Reynolds, Gainsborough, Ramsay and Benjamin West. In 1759 they planned an annual
exhibition, and the Society of Arts (see pp. 6ff.) agreed to let them use
its rooms in the Strand. This was to be the first ever public exhibition of
paintings in Britain.

The Society had insisted that the exhibition have no admission
charge, but 6,582 catalogues were sold, at 6*d.* each, suggesting that as
many as 15,000 or 20,000 people may have attended. However, some
of the artists, including Reynolds, felt that more could be achieved with
an admission charge, and they formed a breakaway group to exhibit
at James Cocks's auction rooms in Spring Street the following year.
Notwithstanding a 1*s.* admission charge, they sold over 13,000 catalogues, and in their best year they claimed nearly 23,000 visitors. They

called themselves the Society of Artists of Great Britain (and later the Incorporated Society of Artists), while the Free Society of Artists was those who continued to show at the Strand.[10]

In 1768 the architect William Chambers, who had seen with dismay the squabbling and the factionalism between the two groups, went to George III with a petition, signed by twenty-two of the Incorporated Artists, asking for a royal charter to set up a school of art, to be funded by an annual exhibition.* Chambers was the obvious man to head the delegation, as he had been in charge of architectural work at Kew for Princess Augusta, and had also been the architectural tutor to George III himself when he was still the Prince of Wales. By December of the same year, everything was arranged: Reynolds had been, reluctantly and to his surprise, persuaded first to attend a meeting of the petitioners, then to become the nascent Royal Academy's first president. (He did get a knighthood out of it, so it probably ultimately seemed worthwhile.) The Royal Academy school was to be free to promising students, their tuition to be paid for out of the proceeds of the annual exhibition, as were mooted prizes and scholarships to study abroad. By the end of the first year, seventy-seven students were already enrolled, including among the first intake Thomas Banks, Richard Cosway and John Flaxman.[11]

Until 1779 the annual exhibition was held every year in Pall Mall, in what had been Dalton's Print Warehouse but was then occupied by the auctioneer James Christie. There was, at this stage, nowhere except auction rooms and shops for the public display of art. The line between exhibition and sale was blurred anyway – the art at the Royal Academy's annual exhibition was, after all, for sale, and many auctioneers and dealers charged for pre-auction viewings. Christie was not an art specialist. In 1767 he had held, to choose randomly, sales of 'The real genuine Household Furniture, China, Linnen [*sic*], a gold repeating Watch by *Tompion*, a plain ditto, 2 Brilliant Rings, and other effects, of a Gentleman, retired into the country . . .' and also of works by Italian, French and Flemish painters, consigned from abroad.[12] In this he was not alone. Other auctioneers sold paintings with catalogue entries that read 'A landscape Italian' or 'A scene with peasants', with no other description,

---

* The signatories included the portraitists/history painters Nathaniel Dance, Benjamin West and Angelica Kauffmann, the landscape painter Richard Wilson, the sculptor Joseph Wilton, the engraver Francesco Bartolozzi, and the painter and engraver Francis Hayman, but not Joshua Reynolds.

no artist's name, or date.[13] Auctions were auctions; selling was selling; art was a commodity like any other.

This was what the Royal Academy now worked very hard to disguise. That art should be openly linked to commerce was not desirable at all. Art as commerce lowered the occupation – now designated a 'profession', or 'calling' – of the artist, reaffirming his hated position as a craftsman. If art, instead of being a trade, was a moral good, worthy of study for the improvement it worked on the beholder, then the artist was in a position of strength, as an instructor and preceptor even to the upper classes. Many of the prominent painters of the day came from distinctly humble backgrounds – Hogarth's father had been a schoolmaster, and the painter's sisters ran a shop; Benjamin West's father was an innkeeper, Gainsborough's a publican, Wilton's a plasterer – although some came from more elevated backgrounds. Reynolds, while his father had been 'only' a schoolmaster, boasted two uncles who were fellows of Oxford and Cambridge colleges, and a grandfather who had been prebendary of Exeter.

Reynolds understood that, for the taint of 'artisan', of 'mechanic', to be removed from the role of the painter, those who influenced opinion would have to be convinced that artists had as much learning and taste as the people who bought the pictures. He worked for this in two ways. In 1771 he established the annual Royal Academy dinner, which placed artists and connoisseurs together in a social setting, with the artists acting as the hosts. (It was held with some emphasis on 23 April, St George's Day, celebrating the patron saint of England, and it continues to this day.) His second chosen battleground was a series of lectures. He gave the first at the opening of the Royal Academy, and it was published in 1778 as *A Discourse, Delivered at the Opening of the Royal Academy*, to be followed by another fourteen discourses between 1769 and 1790. Publication was crucial, taking the skirmish into the enemy's own territory, proving that theory was not the exclusive province of the connoisseur. Reynolds made sure to present a copy to each member of the Academy, and also to each member of his club. (Johnson and Goldsmith had both at separate times confessed – boasted? – that they knew nothing of art: they admired Reynolds not for his painterly skills, but for his personal charm and his literary abilities.) The first seven discourses were republished in a single volume in 1778, and then in Italian, French and German editions, further ramming home the point that the president of the Royal Academy – and by extension its members – was part of the civilized community of the Grand Tourists.

Reynolds's first Discourse looked primarily at art education, but then he spread his wings, incorporating a wide range of aesthetic ideas, references to Renaissance artists, and citations from classical authors and French seventeenth-century theorists, as well as more recent authors such as Johann Winckelmann, Edmund Burke and Adam Smith. His constant theme was that the 'great style' of painting – history painting – had an 'intellectual dignity' that 'ennobles the painter's art; that lays the line between himself and the mere mechanick; and produces those great effects in an instant, which eloquence and poetry, by slow and repeated efforts, are scarcely able to attain'.[14] He was saying that painting in the grand manner relied on the classics and theories of aesthetics that formed the basis of an upper-class education every bit as much as connoisseurship did.

Yet, while this may very well have been the case, the purpose of the Royal Academy was to display the works of its members in order for the public to buy them. Financially it was managing very well, with Chambers as its extremely astute treasurer. Chambers had been commissioned to redesign Somerset House, which was to provide a permanent home for the Royal Academy, as well as for the Royal Society and the Society of Antiquaries. The function of the Royal Academy as a conduit to commissions could be seen even here, however: Royal Academicians supplied £600-worth of work to decorate their own premises, in contrast to the Royal Society artists, who received a mere £63-worth of commissions for the same building.[15]

In 1780 the first exhibition at Somerset House drew 61,381 visitors – more than twice as many as any previous exhibition had seen. But first the Academy had to deal with the muddle caused by Reynolds's extremely effective propaganda, which promoted the Royal Academy as a bastion of intellectual creative effort rather than a selling mechanism, and in addition had produced the general perception that it was under the patronage of George III. It was, if 'patronage' can be understood to mean 'approval', or 'liking'; but not if it suggests sustained financial support. While George III used art intermittently to promote his reign – he had copies of a portrait of himself by Ramsay sent to every British embassy abroad, he commissioned Benjamin West to produce paintings for Windsor Castle portraying great moments in British history – he did not have any plans to use British art to promote the glory of the state of which he was head, as many European rulers did, nor did he see the Royal Academy as a tool to provide propaganda for his reign.[16]

Thus the notice in the first catalogue of the Royal Academy exhibition was a tad disingenuous:

> As the present Exhibition is a part of the Institution of an Academy supported by Royal Munificence, the Public may naturally expect the liberty of being admitted without any Expence.
>
> The Academicians therefore think it necessary to declare that this was very much their desire but that they have not been able to suggest any other Means than that of receiving Money for Admittance to prevent the Room from being fill'd by improper Persons, to the entire exclusion of those for whom the Exhibition is apparently intended.[17]

The 'Munificence' extended by royal approval consisted of covering the losses that the Academy had made until it moved into Somerset House in 1780 – a total of £5,116 over eleven years. Any money in future was all to come from the income from admission charges and catalogues, not the royal coffers.

The exhibitions showed pictures for sale, but the Academy did not act as a picture dealer, and charged no commission. Its sole contribution was to display the works of its members, and to indicate what was for sale by asterisks in the catalogues. But the huge crowds, particularly after 1780, guaranteed wide publicity, and therefore sales. By the middle of the nineteenth century the sale of pictures had topped £7,345; in the 1870s and 1880s the annual sales were around the £15,000 mark, and by 1888 they came to £21,594. Yet even without sharing in this income stream with its artists, five years after the Academy moved into Somerset House it had £6,000 invested in consols (government stock) and a charity fund that was worth £2,100; by 1796 its stock holdings were valued at £16,000. In the first half-century of its existence, the Royal Academy had made nearly £40,000 of pure profit, after the outgoings were taken into account.[18]*

However, Reynolds and the Royal Academy were concerned that it should be seen not as a commercial enterprise, but as one of education,

---

* By 1879, when Sir Frederic Leighton was first made president of the Royal Academy, attendance at the annual exhibition was over 400,000, 115,000 catalogues were sold, and profits for that year alone were more than £20,000.[19]

and moral value. One of the most important arguments they mustered involved the importance of history painting. History painting presented not what had been, but what ought to have been – it idealized the world, and created 'great truths', relying on episodes often derived from epic poetry or classical literature. The problem was, history paintings were enormously expensive to produce – they might take years to complete, and the artists needed cash up front for models, for research into the historical period and costume, and for space to work on a large scale, as well as the basic costs of paint and canvas. And then, once the pictures were finished, for all the acclaim they might receive, only the very largest rooms could house a history painting comfortably, and even then the subject matter often made a work un-domestic. The rape of the Sabine women might be a perfectly good classical subject, but did one want to look at it over the breakfast cups? Even subjects that started out as marketable might not be by the time the pictures were finished. John Singleton Copley, one of the few artists who made history painting pay (although even he had to take on other work at times), had started work on *Charles I Requesting from Parliament the Five Impeached Members* in 1782, right after he completed his hugely successful *Death of Chatham*. In the thirteen years it took him to finish it, political realities had altered, and after the French Revolution scenes even tangentially connected to regicide were not particularly commercial. Other artists simply found that they worked too slowly for there to be any way of making history painting profitable: James Barry spent seven years on *The Progress of Human Culture* for the walls of the Society of Arts, and never earned more than enough to cover his expenses. Given that it was a mural, he could not even exhibit it elsewhere, and, worse, no commissions followed from it.[20]

Some artists, including Reynolds, found solutions that broadened out the meaning of the words 'history painting' until more commercial genres could fit comfortably under their umbrella. When Reynolds returned from his travels in Italy, he let it be understood that he was painting in the grand manner of the old masters. All his work, including his lucrative portrait commissions, should therefore be considered a species of history painting. Copley's *The Death of Chatham*, however, showed what could be achieved in the market, and its success probably kept the genre alive far longer than would otherwise have been the case. In 1781 Copley hired a room in Spring Gardens to display his canvas, and sold tickets at 1s. each to over 20,000 visitors. (It was said that the success of this show reduced the attendance at the Royal Academy exhibition that year by 30 per cent.) In 1791 he once more hired a space, this time a tent in Green Park, to show *The Floating Batteries at Gibraltar*, which had been commissioned by the Corporation of London. When the neighbours complained about the crowds, he moved the picture to a site even nearer to Buckingham Palace, and scored a coup when the royal family visited, along with 60,000 paying visitors.* Copley had been paid £1,000 by the Corporation for the picture; it was recognized that, given the amount of time it would take him to paint, this was not a very substantial fee, but 'the advantages of an Exhibition of the Picture and the publication of a Print from it will compensate him for the time and study requisite for completing so large a work,' they reasoned.[21] It probably would have, had he not then become embroiled in a three-way lawsuit between the Corporation, himself and the print-seller John Boydell.

It was the print-sellers who were the biggest commissioners of history paintings, and it was they who kept the genre afloat. In the 1770s John Boydell, one of the most successful print-sellers of the day, had an arrangement to commission engravings of the history paintings which were shown each year at the Royal Academy, scoring a great success with Benjamin West's *Death of General Wolfe*, which West had painted without a commission, and sold to Lord Grosvenor for between £400 and £600. He may have sold the copyright to the image separately to Boydell, or Boydell may have bought it from Lord Grosvenor, but one thing is certain: it was Boydell who earned the £15,000 that came from sales of this phenomenally successful engraving.

Boydell had arrived from Shropshire in 1740, and apprenticed himself to a landscape engraver, setting up on his own in 1746 and specializing in cheap topographical prints. By 1760 he had almost entirely stopped engraving himself, and instead moved into print-selling, commissioning others to produce works he thought he could sell. He had clearly understood his market. As well as the upper classes, who had always bought prints, collecting images of art they had seen on the Grand Tour, now the newly cash-rich middle classes were also buying. Collecting prints had become a fashionable pastime, even for those with

---

* It is not hard to connect the popularity of these history paintings with the success of panoramas of current events in the next decade. (See pp. 267–8.)

only a moderate disposable income, encouraged by that arbiter of taste William Gilpin, whose *Essay upon Prints* (1768) had levelled the playing field: 'A Painting, or Picture, is distinguished from a print only by the Colouring, and the manner of execution. In other respects, the foundation of beauty is the same in both; and we consider a print, as we do a picture, in a double light, with regard to a whole, and with regard to its parts.'[22] People collected prints of certain places or of certain subjects, or prints by certain artists. They framed them and hung them, as paintings, or they put them in albums and scrapbooks. Auctions featuring prints became increasingly common, newspapers advertised the upcoming sales, and then reported on the results.

Prints became more affordable to more of the population as the century progressed. Earlier in the century, Hogarth had charged as little as 6*d.* for some of his prints, and by his depictions of daily life in London he attracted many who had never before thought of acquiring 'art'. Gradually, different subjects became available at different price levels. At mid-century a set of engravings of the Raphael cartoons at Hampton Court were sold for a 5-guinea subscription; cheaper versions were then produced by lesser engravers for 1 guinea per set, and then single engravings went on sale for 1*s.* 6*d.* each. In 1785 *Pendred's Directory of the Book Trade* listed sixty-one engravers and printers in London, with another twenty-four print-sellers. By 1800, London was the centre for prints in Britain – and also for all Europe.[23]

Now print-sellers like Boydell commissioned, or at least encouraged, artists to produce paintings not for the saleability of the painting itself, but for its commercial engraving potential. Landscapes sold well; portraits, which were the most commercially successful types of painting, sold poorly as engravings – no one wanted to buy a portrait of Mr and Mrs Smith, except Mr and Mrs Smith themselves. Historical, mythical and allegorical subjects were infinitely reproducible, as were the more humble genre scenes. Francis Wheatley, a modestly successful painter, had exhibited a series of paintings entitled *Street Cries of London* at the Royal Academy between 1792 and 1795. His real success came only a couple of years later, when sets of engravings after these paintings were among the most popular ever produced, finding a place in thousands of middle-class homes.

By this time, Boydell had set up his Shakespeare Gallery. Just as history painters in general, under the influence of Copley, had begun to choose popular moments in British history – great military victories, the climactic moment in the life of a national hero – so Boydell saw that Shakespeare could be equally commercial, as *the* national poet. His plan was to commission the most popular artists of the day to paint various scenes from the plays, which would first be displayed in his new gallery and then be reproduced as engravings in a nine-volume edition of the plays. The artists he ultimately used were the portraitists and history painters Hoppner, Romney, Kauffmann, Opie, Rigaud and West and the landscape painter Ibbetson, as well as Henry Fuseli and Robert Smirke, who specialized in literary illustrations.* The two most popular artists who were not included were Copley – with whom Boydell had quarrelled over money – and Gainsborough, because he too wanted more than Boydell was willing to pay, and died before a compromise could be effected. Boydell was not to be swayed when it came to money: he understood that the market ruled. He had also wanted to commission a work from Joseph Wright of Derby, who refused, claiming that Boydell was offering other artists more money, while slighting him. Boydell responded, 'You begin your letter by telling me that you understood that I had classed the Painters according to their rank, and you gave me a list of the first class, in which you place your own name. Now, Sir, I never presumed to class the Painters. I leave that to the public, to whose opinion and judgement I bow with great reverence and respect.'[24]

Boydell was bringing together all the elements of the Shakespeare market: the theatrical revival spearheaded by Garrick, the concurrent increase in the number of images depicting actors in scenes from the plays, and the publishers' new interest in producing editions of canonical authors – to edit the volumes Boydell hired George Steevens, who had revised Johnson's edition of Shakespeare. The Shakespeare Gallery opened in a building specially designed by George Dance the Younger, in Pall Mall, in 1789. Its first exhibition showed thirty-four paintings, its second, the following year, expanded into another three rooms, with another twenty-four. Every year until 1805 more pictures were added, to produce a panoply of the greatest, or just the most popular, scenes from Shakespeare.

* Smirke was also the father of the architects Sir Robert and Sydney Smirke, who built much of the British Museum: Robert started on the east wing, and produced the King's Library; Sydney completed many of Robert's plans after his death, and designed the great round Reading Room.

Unfortunately for Boydell, while he understood the print market perfectly, this understanding did not extend to publishing, and the financial outlay for a multi-year, multi-volume publication was more than he had expected. Then his financial situation more generally was fatally undermined when the outbreak of the French Revolution closed off his main export market overnight. By 1805 he was bankrupt. This should not overshadow his achievements. First, entirely on his own, as a commercial enterprise, he had shifted the balance of the print market: by 1786 Britain exported more prints than it imported.[25] Then, his Shakespeare Gallery had encouraged the idea, also promoted by the Royal Academy, that the dissemination of art to the masses was a patriotic act. When Boydell's bankruptcy became inevitable, he circulated a pamphlet calling for the establishment of a national museum like his own Shakespeare Gallery, of the Royal Academy. By this he actually meant a commercial gallery, as he expected it, like the Royal Academy, to sell the pictures it displayed. But instead a European-wide movement was forcing an alteration, rather late in the day, to the way the British viewed their art.

In 1794 some students at the Royal Academy had paid for a newspaper advertisement to thank Boydell and his rival print-seller Thomas Macklin 'for the privilege granted them to go into the picture Galleries without expence'.[26] The lack of access to original artworks was becoming a national embarrassment. Apart from the print shops, there was nowhere in Britain for everyone to be able to look at art without charge. Instead, many art-lovers ended up going to shows like the one attended by Mrs Lybbe Powys in 1798, when she went to see 'Miss Linwood's worsted work' at the Hanover Square Concert Rooms, where famous paintings were re-created in embroidery panels: 'It is beyond description. They are chiefly taken from the most celebrated artists, such as Raphael, Guido, Rubens, Sir Joshua Reynolds, Stubbs, Opie, &c., thirty-four pieces, beside the cave with a lion and tigress . . . In the inner apartment is a fine whole-length [copy in worsted of] Salvator Mundi, by Carlo Dolci.'[27] This situation was compared by many to that in Vienna, which had set up a publicly funded national gallery in 1781. And in 1793, soon after the revolution began, the Louvre had been thrown open so that France's new citizens could enjoy its now national, rather than royal, art treasures. This latter might have been brushed aside as an ugly symptom of revolutionary fervour – the general opinion of the British ruling class was that the opening of the Louvre was an indecent display of war plunder[28] –

but then monarchical Sweden also opened a national gallery the following year. It was impossible to avoid the comparisons. A French journalist sneered at those across the Channel, 'That country has no centralized, dominant collection, despite all the acquisitions made by its private citizens who have *naturally* retained them for their private collection.'[29]

Even if only in terms of public opinion, discomfort was clearly felt, and some thought that access to art ought to be improved – or, if not access, the *appearance* of access ought to be improved. The embarrassment of the art-owning upper classes increased when John Julius Angerstein, the chairman of Lloyd's in the City, set up a fund for the families of those who had died fighting the French, publishing a list of donors and the precise amount of each donation. The predominance of City financiers and the mercantile middle class made the upper classes, notable by their absence, feel that they had been put at a disadvantage. Angerstein was also known for opening his collection of paintings to artists and writers, and several of the aristocracy decided that they could, and should, compete on these grounds.

Great country houses had been open to the public for some time; now some of their owners felt that it would be a face-saving exercise to open their London houses as well, which was where for the most part their art collections were held. In 1797 the Duke of Bridgewater built a gallery next door to his London house to display his old masters. It was open every Wednesday to the holders of tickets which had been obtained in advance by writing to the Duke; the visitor was then attended in the gallery by twelve liveried footmen as well as an additional two dozen servants.[30] Much of Bridgewater's collection was newly purchased, a recent acquisition from the collection of Philippe d'Orléans, which had been broken up after the Revolution had put an end to the luxurious lifestyle of Philippe Égalité. The pictures were exhibited before they were auctioned off, and this viewing constituted the first old-master exhibition to be held in Britain. At the sale, the Duke of Bridgewater, the Earl of Carlisle and Earl Gower formed a syndicate to buy the bulk of the lots, choosing what they wanted and selling off the remainder. It does not appear that the government contemplated making a bid for the Orléans collection on behalf of the nation.

Instead of the government, it was the upper classes, perhaps in an attempt to hold on to their deteriorating positions as arbiters of artistic merit, who made the next move. By 1800 there were twenty-one private collections open to the public intermittently, with entry to them for the most part dependent on class.[31] More importantly in the long run, in 1805 a group of gentry and aristocrats produced a prospectus for the formation of the British Institution for Promoting the Fine Arts in the United Kingdom. Its sole aim, the pamphlet humbly suggested, was 'to encourage and reward the talents of the Artists of the United Kingdom, so as to improve and extend our manufactures, by that degree of taste and excellence which are to be exclusively derived from the cultivation of the Fine Arts; and thereby to increase the general prosperity and resources of the Empire'.[32] This was to be achieved by establishing a public gallery for the display of a permanent collection of contemporary British paintings, to be bought by funds raised by the Institution, as well as mounting a series of temporary exhibitions showing contemporary art that would then be sold. This was to be an entirely ruling-class operation. George III, in a pointed snub to the Royal Academy, which was run by artists for artists, supported the new Institution on the condition that artists 'should not have any concern with the management'. This was scarcely a worry, as only two artists were given membership: one was to be the keeper; the other was the president of the Royal Academy – and he was invited, one feels, with only a disdainful sense of *noblesse oblige*. The majority of the founders were peers, or had substantial old-master collections, or, of course, both.

The Institution's first exhibition was held in February 1806, and more than 10,000 members of the public attended. It was also financially successful: £11,000-worth of paintings were sold. (Unlike the Royal Academy, from 1809 the Institution was to take a 20 per cent commission on sales.) In 1813 the Institution held a summer exhibition, which previously only the Royal Academy had done; in the same year it mounted an exhibition of Reynolds's work – the first one-man exhibition of a British painter. (Not quite 'contemporary' art, but awfully close: Reynolds had died in 1792.) Exhibitions the following year, showing works by Richard Wilson, Gainsborough, Hogarth and Zoffany, were promoted as exhibitions that would 'teach the Collector what to value, and the Artist what to follow'. Thomas Lawrence understood the subtext, and warned that the members of the British Institution 'had departed from the original objects . . . and were becoming *Preceptors of Artists*',[33] or, in today's terms, they were attempting to keep alive the idea of the aristocratic patron.

After 1813 contemporary British paintings took a back seat, and the members of the Institution instead began to lend their own old masters, which became the essential portions of the shows. Because of the stated aims of the Institution, because of the social position of its members, and because this was, still, the only way possible to study old-master paintings in depth in Britain, the private wealth of private individuals somehow became transformed into a public good. 'The British Institution', remarks one present-day historian,

> allowed patricians to influence the development of British art without conceding a national gallery, which might seem to challenge the principles of private ownership . . . In virtually every Continental state at this time, aristocracies had to live with the risk that their property might be pillaged or confiscated. Only in Great Britain did it prove possible to float the idea that aristocratic property was in some magical and strictly intangible way *the people's property also*.[34]*

The single national museum in Britain was the British Museum, which had been in existence for half a century, but it was not a museum of art. By the beginning of the nineteenth century, in fact, its critics – who were almost everyone – were wondering exactly what its purpose was. It had been founded in 1753, in a rather half-hearted manner, set up on an ad-hoc basis to enable the government to purchase two large private collections that had suddenly appeared on the market. (The plan for a national museum was so much in its infancy that when the Cotton Collection of manuscripts had been bought by the government in 1722 it was simply stored for the next three decades at Westminster School. No one had any idea what to do with it.) When the Harleian Collection of manuscripts and Sir Hans Sloane's collections were both put up for sale in 1753, a public lottery was established to raise the money to enable the government to acquire them without having to allocate government funds. Horace Walpole, an old-fashioned virtuoso and a keeper of curi-

---

* She also shrewdly notes, 'The British Institution helped to forge a set of cultural assumptions that remain enormously influential today: namely, the quite extraordinary idea that even if an art object comes from abroad, and even if it remains securely in private ownership, as long as it resides in a country house it must somehow belong to the nation and enhance it . . . The fact that hundreds of thousands of men and women today are willing to accept that privately owned country houses and their contents are part of Britain's *national* heritage is one more proof of how successfully the British elite reconstructed its cultural image in an age of revolutions.'[35]

osities, was by a quirk of circumstance destined to usher in the modern world of museum-keeping. 'Sir Hans Sloane is dead, and has made me one of the trustees to his museum, which is to be offered for twenty thousand pounds to the King, the Parliament, the royal academies of Petersburg, Berlin, Paris and Madrid. He valued it at four-score thousand, and so would anybody who loves hippopotamuses, sharks with one ear, and spiders as big as geese! It is a rent charge to keep the foetuses in spirits!'[36] The lottery fund had also raised sufficient cash to purchase Montagu House, a seventeenth-century nobleman's mansion in Blooms-bury, which was in the wrong area of town, in a terribly run-down condition and in any case completely unsuitable for public displays. (The purchase price was £10,250; it then cost another £12,000 to turn it into something that could begin to house the collections adequately.)[37] The trustees were named, among them the Archbishop of Canterbury, the Lord Chancellor and the Speaker of the House of Commons. In this first public museum in Europe, it was as yet unclear that an administrative structure would have to be put in place. Instead, jobs were allocated as sinecures to dependants of the trustees. The Museum would not manage to open to the public for another six years. (Compare that to the Royal Academy, nine years later, which was up and running within months of receiving its charter.)

When it finally did open, in 1759, the 'Statutes and Rules relating to the inspection and use of the British Museum' confirmed suspicions that its aim was to do everything within its power to bar public access. These statutes limited entry to 'such studious and curious persons' as were willing to submit a written application, giving name, address, occupation and character references. The tickets were then allocated after the references had been fully checked (a lengthy business: in August 1776 there were complaints that the April applicants were still waiting), and even then entry was for the day *after* the ticket was collected, necessitating three trips for every one visit. The museum was open on Mondays, Tuesdays and Wednesdays, and 120 people were given entry on each of these days, in groups of 15. Once inside, the visitor was escorted around by a warder, who moved his group on when he was ready by ringing a bell.[38] In 1784 William Hutton, an earnest visitor from Birmingham, had jumped through all the hoops necessary to get a ticket and described his visit:

[My group] began to move pretty fast, when I asked with some surprize, whether there were none to inform us what the curiosities were as we went on? A tall genteel young man ... who seemed to be our conductor, replied with some warmth, 'What! Would you have me tell you everything in the Museum? How is it possible? Besides, are not the names written upon many of them?' I was too much humbled by this reply to utter another word. The company seemed influenced; they made haste, and were silent. No voice was heard but in whispers.

If a man pass two minutes in a room, in which are a thousand things to demand his attention, he cannot find time to bestow on them a glance each ...

In about thirty minutes we finished our silent journey through this princely mansion, which would well have taken thirty days. I went out much about as wise as I went in ...

I had laid more stress on the British Museum, than any thing I should see in London. It was the only sight that disgusted me ...

In my visit to Don Saltero's curiosities, at Chelsea, they furnished me with a book, explaining every article in the collection. Here I could take my own time, and entertain myself.[39]

Don Saltero had been Sir Hans Sloane's servant (as well as a barber), and in 1695 had gone into business running a coffee house in Chelsea, which he filled with cast-offs from Sloane's collection, creating an old-fashioned 'cabinet of curiosities'. He had died in 1728, decades before Hutton's visit, but the coffee house continued to be run by his children. Some of the exhibits (listed from the catalogue Hutton was so impressed by) included a 'lignifed hog' (a piece of petrified wood in the shape of a pig), 'A piece of Solomon's temple. Job's tears that grew on a tree. A curious piece of metal found in the ruins of Troy ... A curious flea-trap. A piece of Queen Catherine's skin. Pontius Pilate's wife's great-grandmother's hat.'[40] Another private museum that competed happily on more than equal terms with the British Museum at this time was the East India Company's rooms in the City, where an Oriental Repository displayed a jumble of objects collected by the Company's many employees, including by 1808 Tippoo Sahib's Tiger (1793), a clockwork painted wooden tiger, nearly two metres long, that, when wound up, mauled a prostrate Redcoat. (It is now in the Victoria & Albert, but sadly it is too fragile for the machinery to be operated any more.) The Oriental Repository was only a few rooms, badly lit, poorly arranged, but in default of anything better at the British Museum it welcomed tens of thousands of visitors every year. By contrast, in 1805 the British Museum managed to admit 2,500 people.[41]

The British Museum, by the start of the nineteenth century, was labouring under two serious problems: one was money, the second was its understanding of its purpose, and it was hard to say which of the two was the more pressing. The building itself was costing thousands: seven years after it opened, dry rot had appeared; in 1767 a weight fell off the clock and through the roof; in 1780 a vase fell off the colonnade and damaged a passing carriage, mercifully failing to kill or maim anyone inside. During its first fifty years, £50,000 of good money was thrown after bad in trying to keep Montagu House from falling apart. And yet the Museum was supposed to be self-sufficient financially. After the purchase of the collections and the building, there was still £30,000 left from the funds raised by the lottery, and the interest on this had been allocated to the costs of running of the institution. But by 1760, the year after the Museum opened, the interest, some £900 a year, already covered only half of the outgoings. In 1762 a one-off grant was made by Parliament, for £2,000, which carried the Museum through for another year or so. Yet it was not until 1816 that an annual grant was established.[42] In the interim, any money that the Museum received was all set aside for the purchase of further collections, and none for its running or maintenance. Between its opening in 1759 and 1816, £120,000 was spent on books for the library, the Townley Collection of classical sculptures, Sir William Hamilton's collection of vases, a vast collection of antiquities from Egypt (including the Rosetta Stone) and the Elgin marbles.[43] There was nothing to spend on cataloguing; nothing to spend on what today would be called curating; nothing for conservation; nothing for administration.

In 1807, as a gesture towards the Museum's remit as a public institution, there was an attempt at liberalizing the ticketing system, allowing 'any person of decent appearance' to enter on four days a week, but still limiting the daily attendance to 120. Even this little helped: in the following year, 13,000 managed to see the collection. This invasion was obviously unacceptable, and in 1810 the opening hours were returned to just three days a week. There was no question: those with snug, comfortable jobs inside wanted to keep the great unwashed out. This sounds like a retrospectively harsh judgement, but in fact it was the opinion of many of those observing at the time, while those who ran the Museum did nothing to help their case. Before the opening in 1759, one of the trustees warned that any attempt to admit the wider public would produce

> many irregularities . . . [which] cannot be prevented by a few librarians who will soon be insulted by such people, if they offer to control or contradict them . . . A great concourse of ordinary people will never be kept in order . . . If public days should be allowed, then it will be necessary for the Trustees to have the presence of a Committee of themselves attending, with at least two Justices of the Peace and the constables of the division of Bloomsbury . . . supported by a guard such a one as usually attends at the Play-House, and even after all this, Accidents must and will happen.[44]

This was very much of a pattern with public exhibitions for the rest of the century. When the Society of Arts lent its rooms for the first exhibition of art from the Foundling Hospital, it warned that it would 'exclude all persons whom [it] shall think improper to be admitted, such as livery servants, foot soldiers, porters, women with children, &c.'.[45] As we saw on p. 382, the first show at the Royal Academy had insisted that it was necessary to charge an admission fee so that 'improper persons' could be kept out, and in 1807 a visitor to the summer exhibition still shuddered at 'the Canaille . . . a fry of wretches who have shoaled in (after dinner!) [that is, they ate their main meal in the middle of the day, unlike the upper classes] from all the unheard of holes in the City and suburbs'.[46] This was in a reference to people who had paid a shilling entrance fee.*

There were only two art galleries in Britain that were in any real way accessible to all the public in the first part of the nineteenth century. In 1811 Sir Peter Francis Bourgeois had died and left his collection to Dulwich College, which in 1814 opened the Dulwich Gallery, the first major art gallery in London. In 1816 the 7th Viscount Fitzwilliam had bequeathed his collection to Cambridge University, the basis of the

---

* At the beginning of the century a retired senior commander in the navy with 'a reasonable but not extravagant income for members of the upper- or upper-middle-class' received a pension of £5 a week, while Hazlitt briefly married a widow with £300 a year, or just under £6 a week, which financially transformed his life. Letitia Landon, 'one of the most famous and prolific authors of the later romantic period', had an income of £120 a year, or less than £2 10s. a week.[47] Thus a 1s. admission charge guaranteed that these visitors were all not only middle class, they were from the prosperous middle classes and above.

Fitzwilliam Museum. Although more accessible, both of these were still privately owned, and run by academic institutions. Neither was bringing any closer the creation of a national collection – a national gallery. Two separate ideas about the purpose of art, and therefore what a collection was for, were battling for supremacy, and it was not at all clear which would win. First there was a group – which included most of the members of the British Institution – which saw exhibitions and museums as temples of the muses, places for the elite to enjoy themselves surrounded by their social equals, with some access for those beneath them who showed promise. A second group, which was slowly gaining ground, wanted art and museums to serve a utilitarian and educational purpose. This group of reformers saw museums as places where the working classes could be educated, where they could be socialized, where they could learn how to be a middle-class-in-waiting, first by mixing on an equal footing with their social superiors, and then also by being in the same room with great art. This sense of the improving value of art remained a constant throughout the century. In 1808 John Landseer, an engraver and the father of the painter, in his preface to *The Review of Publications of Art* reminded his readers that the fine arts were 'copious fountains both of commercial prosperity and public happiness'.[48] Eighty years later, Ruskin was certain about the influence of art on man: 'The first function of a Museum . . . is to give example of perfect order and perfect elegance, in the true sense of that test word, to the disorderly and rude populace.'[49]

Then there was the utilitarians' final argument: that access to art would improve standards of design and production in industry. In 1821 the founders of the Birmingham Society of Arts set out their stall: 'The due cultivation of the Fine Arts is essential to the Prosperity of the Manufactures of this Town and Neighbourhood.' This was not an idea that was specific to any one group; the Bristol Institution likewise promoted art exhibitions, because the arts 'supply the manufacture with those tasteful models without which even the Steam-Engine with all its powers would only produce hideous forms and grotesque combinations.'[50] A national gallery, moreover, would do all this, but somehow, in an intangible manner, because it was 'national' it would also do more. Landseer had continued that the fine arts 'not only irrigate and enrich the fields of national opulence, but fertilize the still fairer fields – the paradise of national value'.[51] The collector Sir George Beaumont agreed, and added that the goal had to be free access for any of the public to a gallery owned and run by and for the nation, because, 'By easy access to such works of art the public taste must improve . . . Works of high excellence pay ample interest for the money they cost. My belief is that the "Apollo", the "Venus", the "Laocoön", &c. are worth thousands a year to the country which possesses them.'[52]

Others, more simply, felt that a national gallery, that art in general, was a pleasant recreation, a place of retreat from industrialization, and this was an important thread in the argument at a time when many of the working class could expect never to leave their smoky, grimy cities. Charles Kingsley wrote of how 'the townsman may take his country-walk . . . and his hard-worn heart wanders out free, beyond the grim city-world of stone and iron, smoky chimneys, and roaring wheels, into the world of beautiful things'.[53] All these motives drew together and became more urgent in 1823, when, after Angerstein's death, Beaumont promised to donate the sixteen choicest paintings in his collection if the government would purchase Angerstein's collection for the nation. As Beaumont's collection included three Claudes, a Poussin, a Rubens and a Constable (and a Michelangelo tondo, which, unfortunately for the nascent National Gallery, Lady Beaumont bequeathed to the Royal Academy), and Angerstein's included Raphael's portrait of Julius II, Rembrandt's *Woman Taken in Adultery*, a Sebastiano del Piombo and some more Claudes, Lord Liverpool, the prime minister, swiftly opened negotiations on behalf of the government. The collection was purchased for £57,000, with a further sum of money going to buy the lease of Angerstein's house, in which the pictures would be shown.[54]

Its trustees had fully expected that the British Museum, as the sole national museum, would soon become the 'National Gallery' too, and for some time it appeared that this might be the case. The government had put the new National Gallery under the control of the Treasury, to be run by a 'Committee of Gentlemen for the Superintendence of the National Gallery in Pall Mall'. That committee, however, was made up of exactly the men who were already serving as the trustees of the British Museum, and so for some time the Department of Prints and Drawings at the British Museum acted as if it were in charge of the Angerstein and Beaumont paintings, even though these were in Pall Mall rather than Bloomsbury. It was only in 1827, with a change of government, that two non-British Museum trustees were appointed to the Committee of Gentlemen, and the two institutions could no longer be treated as one.[55]*

A similar raft of issues to those that vexed the British Museum continued to keep the new National Gallery's trustees' meetings ticking over nicely. Who was running the Gallery? was one question. For whom? and Why? were others. The first meeting of the trustees had referred to the 'Royal National Gallery', despite the fact that royalty had given no pictures, no money, not even the blanket aura of its approval by a royal charter. In 1834 a lack of space forced the Gallery to move further down the road until William Wilkins's new National Gallery, begun in 1832, was completed on the north side of Trafalgar Square. This opened in 1838 – already short of space on its first day, since the government had seen the new building as the ideal opportunity to clear the Royal Academy out of Somerset House, which it wanted for its own offices. (The government gave up some of its hard-won space in Somerset House in 2001, and claims to be in the process of vacating the rest.)

As part of this move to permanent quarters, a parliamentary select committee was set up in 1835 to find 'the best means of extending a knowledge of the Arts and of the Principles of Design among the People . . . [and] also to inquire into the Constitution, Management, and Effects of Institutions connected with the Arts'.[56] The committee was chaired by the MP William Ewart, who was closely linked to the Benthamites and other utilitarian-minded politicians. Of the fifteen members, only three plus Ewart actually managed to attend all the meetings – many members attended none.[57] Thus it was these radicals and utilitarians who ran the proceedings, and whose views were therefore to predominate. Their aims were twofold: first, to improve the taste of working classes, and by so doing, to improve the levels of design and the overall competitiveness of industry, and then 'to look into the alleged malfeasance, corruption, and antidemocratic management of the noncommercial institutions', unmasking the men who, as they saw it, ran the nation's cultural institutions for their own benefits and interests, instead of for the promotion of the greater good of the majority of the population. It was, they stated, their duty to remove the 'spirit of exclusion in this country'.[58] As a result of this select committee, the British Museum was forced to open at Easter

---

* They were in theory separated at this point, except that nothing was set down in writing; it took another thirty years before the Treasury could bring itself to formalize what had happened.

and Whitsun – the people's holidays, and, not coincidentally, until then the days that the Museum had chosen to close for 'cleaning'. The librarian (the British Museum's title for its director) Sir Henry Ellis warned, somewhat hysterically, that this would open the gates to a flood of 'sailors from the dock-yards and girls whom they might bring with them', but the committee was adamant, and in 1837 Easter Monday saw 23,000 visitors promenading peacefully through the galleries.[59]

The committee then looked at the management of the National Gallery, which in its few years of operation had not seemed to be able to make the shift from being a 'gentleman's collection' to an institution that was designed to provide an education for the masses. For the first time there was a discussion of the purposes of – and the differences between – public and private collections. The keeper, William Seguier, was interviewed, and it was found that he had never been to Italy (the *ne plus ultra* of pictorial life); he had no plans to hang along historical lines, according to the new museological theories coming from Germany – indeed, he had never heard of such things – he had never thought of attaching a descriptive label beside each painting to tell the viewer the name of the artist; and he had no purchasing policy for further acquisitions to balance the collection. In contrast was a range of experts invited to appear by the select committee, who reported on the new ideas in Germany, Vienna and Paris. Baron von Klenze, from Munich, explained to the committee about the new ways of hanging pictures in groups according to the schools of art and their dates, rather than by subject or just aesthetic whim. He then spoke about labelling, fireproofing, heating and 'scientifically researched lighting and colour schemes'. Gustav Friedrich Waagen, the director of the Royal Gallery in Berlin, gave similar testimony, and further suggested that, while the 'Renaissance art from the time of Raphael' so beloved of the British Institution and its followers 'would form the best taste', at the same time 'Raphael's fifteenth-century Italian predecessors were also necessary, as were representative works from earlier times'.[60] In other words, an educational and art-historical programme needed to be established, instead of purchasing more paintings simply because they were pretty.

The old guard fought back: in 1845 the board of trustees unilaterally took the responsibility for purchasing new works away from the keeper; they were, they felt, much better qualified. In a select committee in 1853,

Lord Aberdeen, a trustee, warned once more against the purchase of 'antiquarian and medieval pictures' (that is, anything that pre-dated Raphael), and vehemently rejected setting up a purchase fund, which might lead to what he darkly referred to as 'rash' acquisitions.[61] Then Charles Eastlake appeared to testify before the committee. He had been the National Gallery's keeper for four years from 1841, but had been so constantly overruled by the trustees, and rendered as powerless as every other keeper, that he had left in despair. Now he heroically faced a total of 1,156 questions from the committee, and in answering set out a plan for the professionalization of the Gallery. This included the allocation of an annual Treasury grant for purchases, together with the appointment of a director, a keeper and an agent to scout for pictures abroad. His advice was not accepted by the trustees. But in 1854 the truly amateur nature of the board became apparent when so few trustees troubled to attend that several times meetings were cancelled for lack of a quorum. This is how Gladstone, in his position as Chancellor of the Exchequer, came to supervise the purchase of sixty-four pictures from a collection in Germany. When they arrived, three-quarters of them were of such terrible quality they could not be displayed. It was rumoured that Waagen, who had testified in 1835, was to be invited to take charge. Instead, Eastlake was appointed as the first director of the National Gallery.[62]

That this was occurring in the years immediately following the Great Exhibition was natural. Attendance had risen from 397,649 in the Gallery's first year in Trafalgar Square to 519,745 in 1850; in the year of the Great Exhibition it reached an extraordinary 1,109,364. Even after the visitors had returned home, attendance held up, at 700,000 in 1861.[63] These numbers were increasingly being seen as a way of assessing the success or failure of any arts institution. Sir Henry Cole, after his labours at the Great Exhibition, had moved swiftly on to the founding of the South Kensington Museum, a museum of arts and design (now the Victoria & Albert), which opened in 1857. His ambition was similarly educational. He wanted to welcome as many of the working classes as he could, in whatever leisure hours they could find, and he was determined that his museum was going to be open for their convenience, not for the convenience of the staff. To teach consumers and producers to differentiate between good and bad design, to teach the masses the norms of 'decent' behaviour, one had first to get them there, and this could not be done by opening only for a few hours during the working week:

> If you wish to vanquish Drunkenness and the Devil, make God's day of rest elevating and refreshing to the working man; don't leave him to find his recreation in bed first, and in the public house afterwards; . . . give him music in which he may take his part; show him pictures of beauty on the walls of churches and chapels; [and then], as we cannot live in church or chapel all Sunday, give him his park to walk in, with music in the air; give him that cricket ground . . . open all museums of Science and Art after the hours of Divine service; let the working man get his refreshment there in company with his wife and children, rather than leave him to booze away from them in the Public House and Gin Palace. The Museum will certainly lead him to wisdom and gentleness, and to Heaven, whilst the latter will lead him to brutality and perditions.[64]

Cole was proud that his museum had the first refreshment room in any museum, for he saw a museum as a place for a family to spend the day, and a family needed to be able to eat and drink. He said that, if the hours were right, and admission free (or at any rate low), then even having alcohol on the premises would not disturb the air of quiet industry and education. He boasted in 1860 that the total sale of alcohol in the refreshment rooms over the previous two years had averaged out at 'two and a half drops of wine, fourteen-fifteenths of a drop of brandy, and ten and a half drops of bottled ale per capita'.[65]

Certainly something was drawing the working classes to South Kensington. In 1858 the cost of gas for lighting the galleries was £780; in 1864 it had risen to more than £3,600 – not because the price of gas had shot up, but because of the increased number of hours the galleries were open in the evening. In 1865 entrance was free on Mondays, Tuesdays and Saturdays, and the galleries were open from 10 a.m. to 10 p.m. On Wednesdays, Thursday and Fridays admission was 6*d.*, and the galleries were open from 10 a.m. to 4, 5 or 6 p.m., depending on the time of year (that is, until dusk). The art school, which was of equal importance to the museum for Cole, was open until nine every evening, so that artisans could attend lectures there after their day's work. In the first three months of the South Kensington Museum's life, admissions were more than 330,000, Cole boasted 'three fold the numbers at Marble House' – his name for the British Museum, which he despised for its exclusionary tactics.* In the first complete year, attendance reached '456,288 persons. It was not until 1841 after 70 years from its foundation and an expenditure of about a million of pounds sterling that the annual visitors at the British Museum reached even 319,374 persons a year,' he crowed.[67] Between 1857 and 1883 the South Kensington Museum saw more than 15 million visitors pass through its galleries, over 6.5 million of whom came in the evening, which suggests that they were not of the leisured classes.

As well as the South Kensington Museum itself, a branch was opened in the working-class suburb of Bethnal Green; by 1872 it was getting nearly a million visitors a year, although this did drop as the century progressed, by 1887 to less than half, at 409,929.† In addition, the South Kensington Museum had been planned as a 'circulating' museum, with one of its primary aims the lending of works from its collection to areas where art exhibitions were scarce. Between 1854 (three years before it had officially opened) and 1870 it sent ten loan exhibitions to Birmingham, seven to Leeds, eight to Liverpool, five to Manchester, eight to Nottingham and fourteen to Sheffield.[68]

The provincial cities were not sitting meekly by, however, waiting for culture to drop down on them like manna from the capital. Outside London, from 1800 onward public art exhibitions were increasing, becoming more and more an integral part of the civic amenities of the cities and towns. In 1800, despite active social calendars in many cities – calendars that included lectures and theatres, concerts and dances – there had been just two art institutes in Britain: one in London and one in Dublin. It was Norwich, with its Society of Artists, that first filled this gap, with plans for annual exhibitions, the first of which was held in 1805.‡ In 1807 and 1808 Bath also had annual exhibitions (about which almost nothing is known); then in 1809 the Bath Institution for

* It would not be too strong to say that Cole *hated* the British Museum and all it stood for. In 1859 a parliamentary select committee was appointed to look into the 'Hopeless confusion, valuable collections being wholly hidden from the public, and great portions of others in danger of being destroyed by damp and neglect' at the British Museum. Cole did not neglect to quote this in an article he wrote for the *Edinburgh Review*, nor, he added on his own, should the 'air of sleepy slatternly shabbiness' which he thought made its trustees entirely unfit to run their museum be overlooked.[66]

† But still, more than the 1990s, which saw an average of 236,000 at the Bethnal Green site.

‡ Liverpool had had two art exhibitions in the 1780s, but until the Liverpool Academy was formed in 1810, and the Liverpool Institution in 1814, exhibitions did not become a regular feature.

Promoting the Fine Arts was set up, under the patronage of the local gentry, and two annual exhibitions were held before the Institution faded away. That same year in Leeds the Northern Society, modelled on the British Institution, was formed, again planning an annual exhibition to be held in its Music Hall. The first one was very successful, running for two months, and although there was later a hiatus from 1812 to 1822, regular exhibitions resumed again, including two loan exhibitions of old masters. In 1825 the sales and admission charges together cleared £2,000 for the organizers and artists. By 1830 art exhibitions had been held in Birmingham, Bradford, Brighton, Bristol, Carlisle, Exeter, Gloucester, Hull, Manchester, Newcastle upon Tyne, Plymouth and Southampton; in Aberdeen, Dumfries, Edinburgh and Glasgow; and in Cork. Even small towns like Ross-on-Wye and Greenock managed exhibitions. Some of these centred around famous London artists – the Leeds exhibition in 1809 had shown two pictures by Benjamin West – but many more consisted of work by local artists, almost all of them professionals. Birmingham's first exhibition, in 1827, had sixty-one local artists, among them drawing masters, portraitists, miniaturists, engravers and sculptors.[69]

Manchester was a good example of the way in which artistic life in a large industrial city developed. Over the eighteenth century, the prerequisites fell into place: Manchester had a good-sized mercantile community, with leisure time and disposable income; it had good roads and – later – rail links; the professional middle classes and the roads together combined to produce local prosperity, which led to a wide variety of shops and services. And thus concerts were followed by two theatres, a library, and a literary and philosophical society. In 1772 there was one print-seller in the local directory, and one artist, a 'Miniature-painter, and Musick-maker'. By the end of the century there were a couple of local collectors, but no public artistic displays were held. Then in 1823 the Royal Manchester Institution was formed, initially by a group of artists who wanted to show their art regularly, although it was quickly taken over by the professional middle classes to be run as a cultural institution.[70] Now the gentry were no longer assuming leadership automatically; more, in this case they actively refused it. Sir John Leicester, the last of the landed class still to live in Manchester, and an early collector of contemporary British art, solicited the support of several aristocrats who themselves bought British art: the Duke of Bedford, the Earl of

Egremont, Robert Peel.* None of them was interested in supporting the Institution, as the chairman wrote in exasperation: 'Would you believe it? that tho' Mr Peel purchases Paintings of the Old Masters at very high Prices and that his immense fortune, his Fathers and his Uncles, were all acquired by cotton spinning at Manchester, and altho' they have had at least 40 guineas worth of *compliments* paid them by their Friends, upon this occasion, yet not one of them have had the good sense to support us.'[72]

The cholera epidemic of 1832 changed the focus of the Institution somewhat, as did the furore around the Reform Bill of 1832, and the subsequent development of the Chartist movement: now education and reform seemed more important than a leisured environment for the middle classes, and culture was linked to education and improvement, both in exhibitions and in newspapers and magazines. From 1832 the *Penny Magazine*, promoted by the Society for the Diffusion of Useful Knowledge, stressed self-education and, to help supply what every working man should know, printed engravings of famous paintings. The Mechanics' Institute from 1837 began to mount exhibitions, of scientific displays and new machinery as well as paintings loaned by local owners. The Royal Manchester Institution began to worry about its perceived middle-class exclusivity. In 1845 its annual exhibition stayed open on Saturdays in the evenings, and charged 6*d.* instead of the standard 1*s.*; in 1847, in the year of the Ten-Hour Factory Act, admission was further reduced to 2*d.* for the final two weeks of the exhibition: 11,000 people attended. By 1849 the entire final month was given over to 2*d.* admissions.[73]

By this time, Manchester had a Natural History Society, a Botanical Society, a Statistical Society, a Medical Society and a Geological Society, for the most part run by the new professional classes. After the success of the Institution's shows in the 1840s, a group of local worthies began to plan their own fine-arts exhibition. Thomas Fairbairn, the chairman, was a Unitarian who saw art as a moral force for good (he was also a remarkably prescient collector, buying Holman Hunt's *The Awakening Conscience* among other works). He was a commissioner for the Great Exhibition, helping to raise £60,000 to send as Manchester's contribution. In 1857 the Manchester Art Treasures Exhibition, the largest fine-arts

---

* Sir John was the second aristocrat, after the Duke of Bridgewater in 1797, to open his collection to the public, from 1818, and he was also one of the founders of the British Institution, together with the Marquis of Stafford.[71]

In 1857 the Manchester Art Treasures exhibition was the largest art exhibition ever to be held in Britain. The style of the building, not unnaturally, harked back to the great success of the Crystal Palace only six years earlier.

exhibition ever to be held in Britain, opened its doors. Attendance was low. The commissioners approached Thomas Cook, and he advertised 'Moonlight Trips' to bring workers from Newcastle, so that all could 'feast in the glorious noon day of Art's finest representations and richest treasures'. Ultimately Cook transported about 26,000 tourists from the north and east, but this was the least of it.[74] The public's imagination had been captured, and up to 1.5 million visitors poured through the doors. Many employers now arranged for their workers to visit, as they had for the Great Exhibition. Sir Titus Salt brought 2,500 employees from Salt and Co. textile works (which had been designed, incidentally, by William Fairbairn, Thomas Fairbairn's father). The *Art Treasures Examiner*, a special weekly journal published during the run of the exhibition, saw them arrive,

> all dressed in their Sunday best . . . in three special trains . . . The fine brass band belonging to the establishment accompanied the first two trains, and the Saltaire drum-and-fife band the last . . . They were accompanied by their generous employer, Mr Titus Salt, who paid all the expenses connected with the trip, and remained with his interested charges during the time they were in the palace. The 2,500 partook of dinner in the large refreshment tent adjoining the second-class room.[75]

That 1.5 million people thought it worth travelling to see a collection of paintings marked a very pronounced shift, from even a hundred years before. Two things had happened over the course of the late eighteenth and early nineteenth centuries to make art a natural leisure activity for many in the population: the arrival of so many works of art from Europe, latterly driven by political upheaval, and the creation of an internal print market, through the development of retail networks and technological innovation. These two things were not isolated, but fed off each other. When the French Revolution brought a large number of European collections on to the market, and the end of the French wars even more, many rich men seized the opportunities to buy paintings and sculpture. Dealers sold at auction, and dealers sold privately, on commission. And even before that, in the half-century between 1720 and 1770, around half a million prints had been imported from Italy, France and Holland, priming a market where even those at the low end of the middle class could afford to buy prints now and again.[76]

Arthur Pond (*c.*1701–1758) was an example of an old-fashioned eighteenth-century print dealer. Originally he produced engravings after drawings he owned, or drawings that were owned by his patrons. From that he moved on to commission others to engrave works for him, producing first a series of Italian landscapes, and later Roman antiquities, Dutch landscapes and a second series of Italian landscapes. These were sold in sets of four uniform prints for 5*s.*, which were published at three-month intervals. The uniformity made them suitable for framing, and they could even be hand-coloured first. Despite the success of these prints, and the increase in the size of the print market, from 1745 onward only about 12 per cent of Pond's income came from this part of his business. The rest was earned in the way artists had always earned money in the past, via patronage. For much of his life Pond worked as a drawing master to upper-class women, who would in turn introduce him to others, who might commission portraits from him. At the same time he acted as agent and general factotum to their husbands, supervising the reception of pictures sent from abroad, cleaning them, arranging for them to be framed; Pond also painted his patron's families, attended auctions as his representative, and copied old masters.[77] The value placed on these services by society can perhaps best be seen in Oliver Goldsmith's *Vicar of Wakefield*, when a relative of the eponymous vicar

> informed me of his own business there [in Paris], which was to collect pictures, medals, intaglios, and antiques of all kinds, for

a gentleman in London, who had just stept into taste and a large fortune. I was the more surprised at seeing our cousin pitched upon for this office, as he himself had often assured me he knew nothing of the matter. Upon my asking how he had been taught the art of a connòscento [*sic*] so very suddenly, he assured me nothing was more easy. The whole secret consisted in a strict adherence to two rules: the one always to observe, that the picture might have been better if the painter had taken more pains; and the other, to praise the works of Pietro Perugino.[78]

But this was the past, not the future. The future lay with the middle classes, who were by the turn of the century already finding art ever more accessible. In two auctions, in 1798 and 1800, the main purchasers included two dukes, four earls, five lords, a lady, six 'gentlemen amateurs', four painters, six art dealers, three bankers and ten merchants (four of whom were also MPs). The MPs seem to have been buying for profit rather than pleasure, so altogether there were fourteen upper-class or leisured collectors, against twenty-three buying for trade purposes.[79] Even then, this may be an underestimate: many who described themselves as – and understood themselves to be – collectors would today be considered to be dealers. For example, the collector Benjamin Godfrey Windus cornered the market in drawings by David Wilkie, holding on to 650 works until Wilkie's death raised their price, when he sold them at a good profit. He put two paintings by Turner into sales at Christie's twice, buying them back both times until he could bid them up to the prices he wanted.[80] Then there was William Quilter, who in 1875 claimed to be selling his collection of watercolours because he was moving house. David Cox's *The Hayfield* was sold for £2,950, bid up by a collector and Agnew's; equally, Copley Fielding's *The Mull of Galloway* reached £1,732 after a tussle between Quilter's son-in-law and Agnew's. Altogether Quilter was said to have made £80,000 at the sale, and was regarded as nothing more than a clever collector until his death in 1889, when many of the pictures that had been sold appeared still to be in his possession. Gradually it emerged that he had arranged for some lots to be bid for, ostensibly by others, in fact on his own behalf, to raise the prices of the other items in the sale.[81]

Prints, meanwhile, were continuing as a lucrative market in their own right, and print-sellers like Boydell were able to make a living from their professional activities, in a way that Pond had not. In 1800 the directories listed one specialist art shop in Manchester, which sold prints and framed pictures (there were probably several others we cannot know about today, because they listed themselves as booksellers). In 1804 Vittore Zanetti had a framing shop, and gradually moved into cleaning pictures and selling prints and *objets d'art* – coins, clocks, medals and figurines. This kind of mixture was becoming the norm. *The Stranger's Guide to Modern Birmingham* in 1825 boasted of the city's showrooms, which included 'Eginton's Painted Glass Manufactory, Thomason's showrooms . . . displaying medals, jewellery, plate, cutlery, and bronze facsimiles of the Warwick Vase . . . and Jones's Pantechne-theca [*sic*] . . . otherwise known as the General Repository of Art, New Street', which had a picture gallery in the back.[82] After the creation of the Royal Manchester Institution, by 1825 there were ten art dealers listed in Manchester, which had expanded to fifteen by 1836 (again, probably an underestimate). In 1817 Thomas Agnew, Zanetti's appren-tice, became his partner, and Zanetti and Agnew moved increasingly into works of art and print-selling. By 1823 their business was doing well enough that the marriage of Agnew to the daughter of the mayor of Salford could take place; by then the firm had an annual turnover of £8,000, of which £2,000 was profit. Agnew's at mid-century was showing works by Constable, Frith, Turner, Etty, Landseer, Maclise, Martin and Clarkson Stanfield.[83] In 1860 Agnew's (now officially Thos. Agnew and Sons) had branches in Liverpool and London, with a showroom in Waterloo Place, just off Pall Mall, the traditional site of auction rooms. By 1875 the firm had built a new gallery in an old coaching yard in Old Bond Street, complete with sofas, tables, and the odd discreet picture on display, but no counters, no glazed windows.[84] The Agnews, the message was clear, were not 'trade': they were gentlemen who happened to sell pictures.

Another dealer who began as a print-seller was Ernest Gambart, although his career took a more individual route. He was born in Bel-gium, the son of a bookseller, and he had arrived in London in the early 1830s as a representative of the French dealer Goupil. He set up on his own, although how, and with what capital, is unknown. Whatever the route, by 1846 he was one of the leading print-sellers in the country, and he also had a branch in Paris.[85] He had linked up with Fox Talbot, the pioneer of photography, who had set up Talbot's Reading Establishment, where Talbotypes of landscapes and genre subjects were produced in

Rudolph Ackermann opened the 'Repository of Arts' in 1798, selling prints, old masters and artists' supplies. In 1809 he began to publish *The Repository of Arts* every month, which contained both fashion plates and social and literary news. Here his trade card from 1809 shows the interior of a prosperous printshop.

bulk.* Gambart purchased 219 prints, and then another 123 only a few weeks later. Although Talbot's establishment closed the following year, Gambart had seen the potential of mass-produced art. He moved swiftly to form an association of print-sellers which would be able to control the number of proofs and prints being sold, to protect the dealers.[86]

In 1849 Gambart held his first art exhibition, and he quickly became associated with many group shows. He began to deal with Charles Morton, who ran the Canterbury Music Hall. In 1856 Morton had built an extension to house a picture gallery, and Gambart supplied him with pictures on a sale-or-return basis. A painting at this time had three values: the price it could be sold for; the price that could be charged for viewing it in an exhibition; and the engraving and reproduction rights. Gambart took full advantage of all these income streams. In 1853 Holman Hunt's *The Light of the World* was sold for 400 guineas; in 1854 Gambart approached him about the rights to reproduce it in an engraving. Hunt had, unusually, not already sold these rights, because he was worried

---

* Talbotypes were produced by the first widely used photographic process in which multiple copies of the same image could be printed on sensitized paper; daguerreotypes, which had appeared two years earlier, were unique images, fixed on to a coppered plate, with no possibility of duplication.

about the quality of the engravers being mooted. Gambart reassured him, and purchased the rights for 200 guineas. The engraving was published in 1858, and it was the single most successful print Gambart was ever to produce, and one of the most successful of the century, earning him enough to live on 'for many years'. But Gambart had no intention of sitting back. Jacob Bell, the founder of the Pharmaceutical Society, had purchased William Powell Frith's panoramic painting *Derby Day* for £1,500; Gambart offered the same amount again for the copyright together with the right to exhibit the picture while it was being engraved – a new idea. Before the painting was even exhibited, he had puff pieces inserted in the *Athenaeum* and the *Art-Journal*. Once the picture went on show, he made sure that the world knew of its success by pressing the Royal Academy to install a rail and a policeman, to keep the crowds away.[87] Once more his engraving was phenomenally successful.

Frith was himself already an old hand at this sort of thing. His first great panoramic picture had been a bit of a gamble, but it had succeeded: engraving rights to *Life at the Seaside* (more generally known today as *Ramsgate Sands*) had been bought by a print-seller for 1,000 guineas, and the engraving and the purchase of the painting itself by Queen Victoria made him a popular as well as a financial success. Frith's final picture in his trilogy of Victorian leisure pursuits, *The Railway Station* (1860–62), was sold not by Gambart but by Louis Flatow, a dealer who was reputed to be illiterate. Under Flatow's management 80,000 people were said to have paid 1s. to see it, and many of those, and many more across the country, bought the subsequent engraving. Flatow was reputed to have made about £30,000 from his part in the transaction.[88]

Flatow may have made more on this one deal, but Gambart was the more innovative, with a view of the wider potential of the market, pioneering a complex interrelationship between art, the market and the dissemination of images and information. He commissioned F. G. Stephens, just before Stephens went to work for the *Athenaeum*, where for the next forty years he would reign as one of London's pre-eminent art critics, to write a monograph on Holman Hunt. Stephens was well suited to the task. He had, together with Hunt, been a founder member of the Pre-Raphaelite Brotherhood (before deciding that he would never make a good painter, and destroying all of his work that he could get his hands on). The formal monograph he produced had several beneficiaries: Hunt himself, of course; Gambart, as Hunt's dealer, who could now point would-be collectors to this work of scholarship; and Stephens, who raised his own profile and bolstered his status as an expert.[89] (Stephens would go on to write monographs on Mulready (1867), Landseer (1869) and Alma-Tadema (1895), as well as catalogues for the Grosvenor Gallery and the Fine Arts Society.) It is hard, looking back, to realize quite how innovative this symbiosis was, but its very naturalness to us is in fact an indicator of the great prescience of Gambart.

In addition, these monographs were useful in an additional, unexpected, way. Dealers and their profits were beginning to worry both the artists and their collectors: art was beginning once more to look too much like 'trade'. The monographs were a way of subduing overt commercialism, taming it, making it appear as scholarship. In a similar manner, although many dealers worked successfully and openly – like Agnew's, or Sir Coutts Lindsay and Joseph Comyns Carr at the innovative Grosvenor Gallery – others did not call themselves dealers at all, even though they acted for collectors and artists exactly as any dealer would. The Pre-Raphaelite collector Constantine Ionides relied on the artist Alphonse Legros to advise him; the painters Frederick Shields in Manchester and William Bell Scott in Newcastle were both active in the promotion of Dante Gabriel Rossetti to local collectors.[90] That this was an ambiguous profession, however, can best be illustrated by the career of Charles Augustus Howell (1840?–1890), dealer and con man – it is hard to say which aspect was more important, although Dante Gabriel Rossetti was sure he knew the answer:

> A Portuguese person called Howell
> Who lays on his lies with a trowel
>   Should he give over lying,
>   'Twill be when he's dying
> For living is lying with Howell.

Howell's career is interesting because in many ways it resembled Pond's, except that now the factotum was at the service of the artist, not the collector. Howell began as he meant to go on. He had fled England before he was twenty because of a mysterious involvement in the Orsini conspiracy to assassinate Napoleon III. He claimed to have spent the next decade diving for treasure off the coast of Portugal and living in Morocco as a sheikh – or sometimes it was in Rome as the Portuguese ambassador. Whatever the case, in 1865 the sheikh–ambassador returned to London, to the rather less glamorous locale of his aunt's villa in Brixton, until he became Ruskin's secretary. Despite his ability to produce wonderful reproductions of Ruskin's drawings – or perhaps because of it – that ended unhappily. Then he helped Rossetti in a slightly unusual undertaking for a dealer. Rossetti's wife, Lizzie Siddal, had died in 1862 of a laudanum overdose, and Rossetti, overwrought and guilt-stricken, put the manuscript copy of his new poems in her coffin to be buried with her. By 1869 he was ready to publish them, and Howell arranged for their exhumation. He also worked for Whistler, helping him make prints of his etchings, and acting as his secretary during his suit for libel against Ruskin in 1879. He dealt in Japanese prints and the newly fashionable blue-and-white porcelain from China, he negotiated sales for a number of artists, including Watts, Sandys and Burne-Jones. He may in between projects have turned his hand to blackmail, and it is thought that by the end of his life the 'Rossettis' he sold would not always have been recognized as such by their notional creator.[91] Apart from his sidelines in blackmail and forgery, Howell had taken on many of the attributes of the modern dealer more completely than many of the more respectable had done. No longer an agent of a patron, nor a shopkeeper, Howell served no one except himself: a businessman.

As with the agent, so with the artist: from craftsman to Romantic genius was a long, hard haul, as we have seen. From genius to social equal of the patron was a much smaller step. *Punch*, as so often, spotted the trend quickly. (There were always lots of cartoons about artists in *Punch*; after all, most cartoonists either were or aspired to be one.) In 1888 'Studies in Evolution. – The Artist' (see next page) showed the 'Old Style' artist, a bearded, pipe-smoking bohemian chatting up the barmaid of the Pig and Whistle, next to a sign that advertised a goose club, a free and easy, and a harmonic meeting – sure signs of lower-middle- or working-class status every one. The 'New Style' artist, by contrast, was shown as a handsome, well-dressed, moustachioed gentleman kissing the hand of an elegant woman 'At Her Grace's Garden Party'.[92]

The full professionalization of the art market was perhaps epitomized by Marion Harry Spielmann (1858–1948). He was not an artist, nor was he a dealer, but from 1887 to 1904 he edited the *Magazine of Art*, and he was an art critic for half a dozen more magazines and newspapers.

STUDIES IN EVOLUTION.—THE ARTIST.

OLD STYLE.
At the "Pig and Whistle."

NEW STYLE.
At Her Grace's Garden Party.

The main thread running through his writings was not the artists' skill. Instead he was concerned that artists were trained properly, that they were supported by professional bodies, and that they learned how to benefit from advertising and the increasingly lucrative market. In 1886 his article 'The Costs of Painting a Picture' treated art like any other business; other articles looked at the economic aspects of production, at the print market and photography, and at copyright of the artist's work. What interested him was not art, and not commerce, but the place where the two met. To promote the artist as a professional, he stressed over and over that the artist was a hard-working businessman. When he praised the Newlyn school of *plein-air* painters, he did not analyse their pictures, or discuss their technique, but commended them for living 'a life of economy undisturbed by modern Bohemianism'. Another artist was presented as a model for others to follow because of his 'pleasant, gentlemanly tone'.

Spielmann recognized that 'patronage has gone from the Church and taken refuge with the middle-class collector and the advertising tradesman. The transition is fairly complete: from the Cathedral to the Stock Exchange; from Godliness to cleanliness; from the altar and the cabinet to candles, screws and soap.'[93] He was referring here to John

An poster designed by the Beggarstaff Brothers in the 1890s, showing the new emphasis of graphic design over typographical content for advertisements.

Everett Millais's painting of his grandson. Entitled *Bubbles*, it had been purchased by A. and F. Pears to advertise their soap. It was used for decades, and may be one of the most famous advertising images of all times.

In 1894 the artists William Nicholson and James Ferrier Pryde joined together under the name the Beggarstaff Brothers. They called themselves (and were seen as) artists, producing highly innovative, influential designs, with clean, clear outlines, flat colours and stark lettering. That they were advertising Rowntree's Elect Cocoa and Kassama Corn Flour was beside the point. Artists were no longer expected to starve in garrets; they were professional men.

The transformation of the art market into a market pure and simple was complete.

11

Sporting Life

IN THE NINETEENTH CENTURY, many looked backwards to an ideal, to a vision of the real, rural England that was rapidly vanishing. In 1836 Peter Gaskell, in his *Artisans and Machinery: The Moral and Physical Condition of the Manufacturing Population*, described 'the days of quoit and cricket-playing – wakes – May-day revels – Christmas firesides, and a host of other *memorabilia*, now ranked but as things that were', but which no longer existed in the new industrial world, where instead the working man now expected to find his amusement in 'the pursuit of debasing pleasures . . . viz. in the beer-shop, the gin-vault, or the political club'.[1]

Had happy, apple-cheeked rustics truly spent misty summer afternoons tossing quoits? Had such a time ever really existed? Only in part. Sport had, for many rural communities, been a ritual event, specific sports taking place on specific days in the year, and requiring the participation of specific sections of the community. Samuel Bamford, a radical weaver, remembered the community festivities of his Lancashire childhood at the turn of the century. Although he had lived in a town of some 3,000 people, many traditional events were still marked in the old ways. On Easter Wednesday the young women, both those who were just married and those still courting, dressed up in their best clothes and promenaded out with their men; then all went to the pub, where there was dancing for all and prizefights for the men. At wakes week at the end of August, each parish or hamlet in the area decorated a special rush cart. The women dressed up once more, everyone went to church, then to a dance, and there were again fights for the men.[2] Thus tradition contained the violence, turning it into an annual ritual.

Many of the sports that were in decline by the end of the eighteenth century would be seen by future generations as cruel beyond imagining. Cock-throwing, which took place on Shrove Tuesday, Good Friday, Easter Monday or Whitsun, depending on the village, was still occurring at the end of the century; bull-baiting took place at some fairs – every Monday and Thursday at Hockley Hole until the 1750s, for example – and even frequently under the patronage of the church: in Staffordshire, the Feast of St Michael and All Angels was firmly linked to bull-baiting, bear-baiting, dogfighting and cockfighting into the nineteenth century. The Sabbatarians who protested against bull-baiting did so not because it was cruel, but because it took place on Sundays.[3]

Gradually, with the increase in urbanization, sports began to be class-oriented, rather than community oriented. Shooting became a pastime of the moneyed. By the mid eighteenth century the new game laws and increasing enclosure (see pp. 436–7) meant that access to what had previously been common land was all but barred to the working classes. In 1751 a prosecution for poaching took into account as an exacerbating factor the fact that the defendant was 'not the son and heir of an esquire or a person of higher degree'. The difference in attitudes to cockfighting and dogfighting show this class separation. Dogfights were for the working class, and were improvised, impromptu affairs. Cockfighting, in contrast, drew many of the upper classes, and was highly formalized, with rules laid down, and model agreements for the participants printed in the *Racing Calendar* every year. The fights were often scheduled to take place during race week in towns, and the towns might even have permanent cockpits. There was little opposition to cockfighting, whereas dogfighting was more frequently condemned.[4]

It was condemned not on the grounds of cruelty – that came later – but because it promoted 'lawlessness', unruliness. Such working-class sports drew large crowds, which appeared threatening to onlookers. Sometimes working-class sports were suppressed for what today seems almost no reason at all. Bamford reported that the bowling green next to the church was dug up, to stop the locals playing, 'chiefly, it was said, because the late steward under the [local landowners] could not, when he resorted to the place, overawe, or keep the rustic frequenters in such respectful bounds as he wished to do'.[5] Possibly – although it must be borne in mind that Bamford had a highly politicized view. (In fact his reforming vigour had twice seen him arrested for treason. He was once acquitted and once, unjustly, after the Peterloo Massacre, convicted.) The core difference between gentry- and middle-class leisure pastimes and those of the working classes was that, by the nineteenth century, many if not most of the leisure activities of the prosperous had moved away from the areas where the social classes might mingle, to take place in private spaces – in zoos, in pleasure gardens, in circulating libraries, in art galleries and museums – all of which excluded many of the working classes by charging admission. One of the few places where the classes still met and mixed was at the racecourse, but even here – especially here – great changes were under way.

In the seventeenth century, most horse races were what were known as 'matches' – that is, they were races run between two horses, head to head. For the most part, the horses were ridden by their owners, and if there was a trainer it was the horse's groom. The purpose of the race was the wagers placed by the owners and their friends. Racing was a betting sport for the most part, not a spectator sport. Newmarket was the single exception to this. Nominally, it was the centre of racing, an aristocratic redoubt established by James I, who had spent £20,000 setting it up. By 1718, according to the listing in Muir's *The Old New-Markitt Calendar* (*sic*), only two owners were not aristocrats.[6] As yet there were no general rules, no overall government of the sport, no central hub for the racing year. By the 1770s Newmarket had more racing than anywhere else: three weeks in the spring, one week in July, another three in the autumn. Yet, because of its exclusivity, its separation from the rest of the world of racing, it remained old-fashioned: much of the racing there even as late as the mid eighteenth century was between two horses; there was little provision for spectators, as the owners and their friends were expected to follow on horseback or in carriages; the course was not fixed, but was marked out on the heath by stakes, which were often rearranged.[7]

Newmarket saw huge sums poured into racing – in the 1730s, up to 30 per cent of all the money going through the sport probably passed through Newmarket, and by 1750 it may have been as much as 50 per cent.[8] In the 1770s some races were run for prizes that reached 300 guineas, and up to 1,000 guineas was not unknown. Yet its very exclusivity worked against it, and it was in the county towns that racing changed and developed. Racing was ultimately an expression of urban development, not rural. Towns had the adjuncts that were necessary for the sport

– the stables, saddlers and blacksmiths – as well as the facilities for the spectators – food, drink, accommodation and entertainment. Racing was a great enhancement to a town's economic prosperity, and the development of municipal interest in racing began early. In 1708 the Corporation of the city of York donated £15 annually 'towards a plate to encourage and bring about a horse-race . . . and to invite the gentry to run their horses for the same', and the following year a collection was made for the purchase of five further plates. That year there were three days of racing in York; by 1712 there were five days, by 1713 six; and in 1721 the King's Gold Cup was run every year, worth 100 guineas, together with the Ladies' Gold Cup with a 6-guinea purse and a silver cup worth £20.[9] York had become the most prominent race meeting of the northern circuit, and there were dozens of meetings that were pressing hard behind in terms of quality and quantity: in Yorkshire alone there was also racing in Beverley and Doncaster, and across the country a further 109 towns had race meets.

The money that came with racing was there for everyone to see, and race meetings had quickly become essential for a town's leisure development. During race week, the working-class residents were catered to with stands selling refreshments, as well as fair-like entertainments, such as sideshows and strolling players, and a number of other local sports and their associated gambling – 'cudgel play' in the swathe of country from the Cotswolds down as far as Devon, wrestling in the north and the West Country, cockfighting pretty well everywhere.[10] There was money to be earned from this working-class market, but for the moment far more came from providing services to the gentry. The local innkeepers understood how closely entwined racing was with their own financial well-being, and acted to promote the events in their areas from the first. In Yarmouth at the beginning of the eighteenth century a group of inn- and tavern-keepers jointly leased land from the Corporation to build a racecourse; in Yorkshire other innkeepers saw acting as clerks of the course as part of their business. In some places, to enter the race, the horse had to be stabled at the inn that was putting up the prize money; in others, refreshment stands were allocated on the basis of the amount of prize money the stallholders had put up.[11]

All this was worthwhile, as the gentry and their friends descended on the town for the week. There were balls, dinners, breakfasts, assemblies – many taking place in the towns' inns – while theatres frequently had their only regular performances scheduled for these weeks. In 1732 York race week included daily concerts given by visiting musicians, as well as other concerts performed by the city waits; 'private' dinners and break-fasts at the local inns; and grand public assemblies, with up to 300 subscribers for each.[12] Mrs Lybbe Powys was a good representative of the type of people the towns hoped to draw. In 1757 she went to Chester-field, Derbyshire, for race week. On the first day, she and her friends attended the races and got home about eight in the evening, then 'about ten we went to the Assembly Room, where the Duke of Devonshire always presided as master of the ceremonies, and after the ball gave an elegant cold supper . . . We got home about five. The next evening were at the concert . . . and on the third day again went to the [race]course . . . That evening's ball was equally brilliant as the first night, and both gave us as strangers a high idea of these annual assemblies at Chester-field.'[13] In the 1770s at the Ludlow races she was told that ''tis the custom of the place' for everyone to attend theatre in race week, and then for the men to lunch 'at the ordinary' while the ladies were given a lunch by a local 'gentleman of large fortune', finishing off the day with more racing and an assembly.[14] The hopes of the towns' merchants were that the gentry would come for the week itself, and then the delights of the town would keep the spending public there for a longer season. York scheduled Friday concerts for the winter season from mid-October to mid-March, and when the new racecourse was planned (the old being too near the Ouse, and prone to flooding) it seemed sensible that new assembly rooms should be built at the same time: the new course created a need for new places of entertainment. The course itself was a fully professional affair, laid out by a landscape designer, John Telford, and when it opened in 1754 the stands for the spectators were among the earliest permanent structures erected for the convenience of the public: 'The form of the race being like a horseshoe, the company in the midst and on the scaffolds, can never lose sight of the horses,' wrote Francis Drake, an eighteenth-century historian of the city of York.[15]

In the 1730s, the intermingling of classes caused a certain amount of hand-wringing, not only with reference to the races themselves, but concerning all leisure activities. A number of pieces of legislation were passed that, in retrospect, can be interpreted as sharing a common pur-pose: that of keeping some leisure activities exclusively the province of the more prosperous. In no cases were these activities banned: they were just hedged about with enough restrictions to make it difficult for the common people to be present. The 1737 Licensing Act restricted some types of theatre performance; there was another act in 1739 which attempted to ban some popular card and dice games, and to segregate gamblers into certain (upper-class) locations. In 1740 it was the turn of racing. The sport was overhauled, and races with prize money under £50 were banned entirely. This completely wiped out smaller, more localized, and less elite race meets. An unintended result was that when the more working-class meets vanished, instead of not going to the races, the working-class spectators simply began to attend race meetings that had previously been the exclusive province of the upper classes. To reduce this 'promiscuous' mixing of the classes that the law had inadvertently brought about, grandstands were created at several courses – places where the upper classes could pay to be separated from the people. As well as York's new racecourse, Doncaster (1751), York (again, in 1754), Manchester and Newmarket (early 1760s), Stamford (1766) and Beverley (1767) all built stands.[16]

The 1740 legislation caused a sudden, precipitous decline in the number of racecourses, and also in the number of days given over to racing, the number of prizes and the amount of money that was up for grabs. In 1739 there had been 138 courses, with 406 prizes and a total of £13,496 in prize money; only a year later there were 84 courses, 227 prizes, and the prize money was a mere £9,279. Yet, while this was obviously a step backwards for those with financial interests in the sport, there were other developments that were more encouraging, showing, at least in retrospect, the beginning of a commercial underpinning to racing. In 1726 John Cheny of Arundel had announced his seven-year plan to list retrospectively all the races that had been run in the country. The following year his first volume, *An Historical list of all Horse-Matches Run, And of all Plates and Prizes Run for in England (of the value of Ten Pounds or upwards)* appeared.[17] In the same year the *Racing Calendar* began publication, listing the dates of future meetings. This notification increased the numbers of entries into a race, and also the numbers of spectators who attended, and it survived to be replaced in 1751 by a fortnightly *Sporting Kalendar*, which in turn was superseded in 1761 by a new *Racing Calendar*. Newspapers soon joined in. By 1731 *Read's Weekly Journal* was carrying a 'List of the Horse Matches to be run at Newmarket in March, April and May'; other papers also listed races, with the names of the horses, the owners, the weights, the number of miles to be run, the wagers laid and the forfeits offered, as well as, later, the results.[18] All this greatly increased the number of people interested in racing.

In 1752 the Jockey Club was formed. There is little information about the early intentions of the Club, although its location was originally London, not Newmarket, and it was most probably a straightforward social club for owners. That year an advertisement in the *Sporting Kalendar* announced that 'A Contribution Free Plate [will be held, to be run] by Horses the Property of the Noblemen and Gentlemen belonging to the JOCKEY CLUB at the *Star and Garter* in *Pall Mall*, one heat on the Round Course, weight eight Stone, seven Pound' would be run. Even while based in London, the connection with Newmarket was paramount: in that same year the *Kalendar* published the Club's 'Newmarket Rules' – half of which set down conditions for racing, half for betting – and in the following year the Club seems to have migrated to Newmarket.

By 1757 it had already begun its expansion from a social group into a group that systematized and regularized the sport outside its Newmarket home. That year a dispute at the Curragh racecourse in Ireland was referred to the Jockey Club for resolution, and the next year the club gave its first 'general order', setting out how much weight could be carried. Soon the Club had set down rules for what to do if a horse was entered for two races, and how the weight–age allowances were to be determined. Within the next five years, nineteen owners had registered their colours, which had previously been altered at will, with the Jockey Club, and a list of owners and their colours was published, formalizing the system – and by extension the Club's rights to supervise it.[19] By 1770 it was generally accepted that this was the body that could permit, or forbid, access to any racecourse in the country. That year the *Racing Calendar* published the following notice, without feeling any need to state on what authority it was made: 'Chester Races. In order to save Mr Quick, Mr Castle, or any of the Ascott [*sic*] confederacy the trouble and expense of training, they are desired to take notice that none of their horses will be allowed to run for any of the above plates, neither will they be suffered to run for any of the plates at Conway, Nantwich, or Holywell; nor will Thomas Dunn be permitted to ride.' The Club shortly took on the further responsibility of resolving disputes on any racecourse in the country.[20]

Yet, while the socially exclusive Jockey Club represented the face of the great to the world, many of the changes that occurred in racing were actually planned and executed not by these aristocrat owners and their friends at Newmarket, but by the middle-class administrators at the courses across the country. In 1770, 70 per cent of all races were held in market towns, being organized and attended by the local middle classes. Even at Newmarket, things were changing. James Weatherby was the son of a solicitor in Newcastle. In 1771 he was named Keeper of the Matchbook, Stakeholder and Secretary to the Jockey Club, and from 1773 he began to issue a *Racing Calendar* that quickly became the standard publication, superseding the various rival journals that had been appearing from John Cheny's onward. Weatherby's *Calendar* set out the Jockey Club rules, and listed the results of races throughout Britain, as well as the 'Colours worn by the Riders of the following Noblemen and Gentlemen'. By choosing which race meets to include in his *Calendar*, Weatherby gave status and authority to those selected. He also was the conduit for permission to enter horses to race at Newmarket, Epsom and other elite courses. His position as both Keeper of the Matchbook and publisher of the *Racing Calendar* was later inherited by his nephew, also named James Weatherby, and then in succession by a series of descendants who, through the nineteenth century, came to control the structure and development of racing as a commercial enterprise, via their long-term professional training, whatever the amateur and more informal members of the Jockey Club may have thought.

In 1791 James Weatherby II produced *An Introduction to the General Stud Book*, followed in 1793 by *The General Stud Book*, which laid out the pedigree of every recognized thoroughbred in Britain.* The *Stud* was updated five times over the next half-century, and then began to appear regularly every four years. Inclusion (or exclusion) from the *Stud* meant the possibility or prohibition of running a horse in any given race. As well as giving formal access to the races, the *Stud* was the written expression of the changes that had been taking place in husbandry for much of the century. In the early part of the century, horse breeds in Britain had been improved by the introduction of Arabian bloodstock, in particular via the Darley Arabian, which was brought from Syria to Thomas Darley, in Yorkshire, and the Godolphin Arabian, which was sold by Louis XV and

---

* Weatherby's continues to operate today as racing's administrator, under contract to the British Horseracing Board, and also remains the publisher of *The General Stud Book*.

eventually ended up in Britain.* But the changes in selective breeding were not developing from horse racing; instead, horse racing was picking up on innovations first explored among farm animals, and which can be epitomized by Robert Bakewell, a Leicestershire stockbreeder.

Previously, environment had been considered to have as much effect on animal breeding as inheritance; diet and weather were thought to be as crucial as any genetic contribution (to use an anachronistic term). The quality of a farm animal was judged solely on the quantity of offspring it produced, rather than on the quality of those offspring. Bakewell, however, concentrated on selective breeding of his sheep, and, instead of trying just to increase the number of offspring born to each animal, he was more interested in how reliable the offspring were as breeders in their turn. In 1760 Bakewell began to supply his animals for stud to other farmers, and that year he charged 17s. 6d. per animal per season; by 1784 he was asking £100 per animal per season, and by 1789 his rates had gone up to £400 – a more than 450-fold increase over three decades. This indicates that there was something going on beyond the quality of Bakewell's animals. There had also been a perceptual shift by the purchasers: they were looking at what they were buying in a different way. Nothing else can explain this extraordinary rise. The *quantity* of offspring cannot have increased 450-fold. Therefore the buyers must have understood that they were purchasing, at great price, an extremely valuable intangible. They were buying potential: the potential inherent in Bakewell's breeding animals, the potential that these animals had to improve the quality of the future flock.[21] There is an obvious connection between this and *The General Stud Book*, which promised 'to correct the . . . increasing evil of false and inaccurate Pedigrees'. By the 1760s, in the racing community the money to be made in breeding and stud fees was equal to – and a good deal more certain than – the prize money to be won. In 1768 the great racehorse Eclipse, a great-grandson of the Darley Arabian, was sold for 1,750 guineas, and was claimed to have earned £25,000 in stud fees.[22] Similarly, in 1779 Richard Tattersall bought Highflyer, Lord Bolingbroke's unbeaten racehorse, descended from the Godolphin Arabian, for £2,500, and comfortably saw a good return on that initial outlay from stud fees and the sale of Highflyer's offspring (which included twelve champions).[23]

---

* It has been suggested that as much as 90 per cent of the world's bloodstock today can be traced back to the Darley Arabian.

The Tattersalls were another family, like the Weatherbys, which infused professional entrepreneurial skills into a sport that preferred to portray itself as run entirely by and for gilded amateurs. Richard Tattersall (*c.*1725–95) was the son of a farmer. In his youth he had been apprenticed to a wool-stapler, but he soon found his way into the horse world, and by 1756 he had already done well enough that he was able to marry a granddaughter of the Earl of Somerville.[24] By 1766 he had enough money to open an auctioneer's room for horseflesh at Hyde Park Corner. Cleverly, he set aside a private room (and a cook) for the members of the Jockey Club: by providing for their creature comforts, he guaranteed that the Club members would also bring their horses to him for sale. Tattersall's quickly became the leading saleroom for horses of all types: racehorses, hunters, hacks, and coach and carriage horses. Previously sales had been private arrangements between social equals; under Tattersall, selling a horse became an impersonal business transaction, where the market price ruled. His professionalization of the saleroom changed horse racing permanently.

Soon Tattersall's had cornered and likewise professionalized a large part of the betting market. In the 1790s the London saleroom boasted a Subscription Room, where members met to make and pay gambling debts. Membership was talked of as though Tattersall's were a socially select club, but it was in fact open to anyone who paid an annual subscription. Soon owners and gamblers knew that this was where bookmakers, horse dealers and jockeys were all to be found. Now betting, like the sales, was market-driven rather than a social arrangement. Tattersall had managed to create an impersonal betting mechanism, a business, open to every class and type. By 1843 Tattersall's Rules and Regulations were accepted for all matters pertaining to gambling on the course. The Rules said that they were 'under the sanction of the stewards of the Jockey Club', but it was Tattersall's that was producing the odds for bookmakers. It became known as the Turf Exchange, the Lloyd's of gambling.[25]

Thus, despite the setback after the 1740 legislation, racing was quickly back to where it had been in 1739, and, further, through the winnowing out of the minor – and therefore more amateur – meetings, the sport in general had become even larger, better organized and more lucrative for everyone involved. The racing world had been rationalized, and commercialized, by its enforced diminution. A sample comparison of meetings in Blandford, in Dorset, in 1737 and in 1773 is instructive. In 1737 the race meet was held over three days in May, with one race a day (plus preliminary heats), for purses of 30, 20 and 10 guineas. On the first day, racehorses ran; on the second day the race was for ponies, on the third day for hunters. In 1773 the meeting took place over three days in July, when an average of six racehorses competed in each race (a good field for the time), for three purses of £40 each, one sweepstake of 110 guineas, and two matches (head to heads) for wagers of 100 and 200 guineas.* Furthermore, the meeting was scheduled right after the Winchester races, and just before the Stockbridge and Exeter meetings, all of which were within striking distance for both the horses and the spectators.[26]

That the towns were relatively proximate and the meetings one after the other was essential, for a simple reason that is rarely considered today: before the railways, the horses had to be walked from one race to the next. For the most part, either horses raced on small local circuits or their energy was saved for the few big races of national importance. The arrival of the turnpike roads increased the size of each of the circuits. Many of the important races began to be established only after the development of the turnpikes: the St Leger in 1776; the Oaks in 1779; the Derby in 1780; the 2,000 Guineas in 1809.

With the arrival of the railways, horses could more easily be entered for more races across the country. But this was not the only change. With rail transport, the age at which horses could be raced was substantially reduced. Previously a horse had had to be at least four years old to have the stamina to race, then walk to the next meeting, then race again. Goodwood to Epsom was a four-day walk; on to Newmarket was another seven days; while to Doncaster took two solid weeks.[27] Now, with a heavy schedule of races, but no intervals of long-distance walking, two-year-olds were strong enough to race. This made a great difference to the owners and trainers, who saw financial returns on their animals much sooner and, perhaps as importantly, could stop investing in horses that were evidently not going to pay off. As the horses grew younger, the races got shorter to accommodate their lesser stamina. The administrators and racecourse managements liked this reduction: more races could be

---

* A sweepstake was a race where there was no purse provided by a third party; instead, each owner paid an entry fee, and the total of the fees was raced for.

scheduled each day, and the more races there were, the longer the crowds stayed, spending their money.

The advent of the railways had also changed the type and frequency of the crowds. Before railways, most race meetings were attended by locals and by the wealthy, who could ride or drive to the meetings and could afford to pay for accommodation. A few of the big races drew crowds from further away – for the St Leger, working-class spectators from Sheffield walked the eighteen miles to Doncaster, and then walked home again the next day.[28] But it was the opportunities created by the railways that propelled racing into a new league, creating the possibility of ever-larger crowds. These opportunities were recognized from the very first days of passenger trains. In 1831, the year after it opened, the Liverpool and Manchester Railway carried racegoers to Newton-le-Willows and Liverpool.[29] Sir John Easthope, the chairman of the London and Southampton Railway, was a keen follower of horses, and within a week of the opening of the line from London to Kingston, in 1833, the company had scheduled eight special trains to take spectators to the Derby. At Kingston, there was a long walk from the station to the racecourse, but such was the enthusiasm that, after the seventh train had left Nine Elms station in south London, 5,000 would-be spectators were still waiting to board the final train. (When they realized that most of them were not going to reach Kingston, they staged a riot.) Undeterred, a few weeks later the company ran excursion trains to Ascot, and by 1841 the mainline railways were regularly carrying racegoers to Surbiton for Epsom and both Woking and Slough for Ascot.[30] In 1840 more than 25,000 passengers were transported by train to a race meeting in Paisley.[31] After the Great Northern Railway began to carry passengers, employers hundreds of miles outside Doncaster learned to accept that the day of the St Leger was a de-facto local holiday. Ultimately the Great Northern had to remove all freight trains from its schedules on the day of the race, and clear its sidings for excursion trains to wait for their return passengers. In 1888 nearly 100,000 racegoers travelled to the St Leger by train.[32]

Newmarket was the only holdout. The Jockey Club disapproved of the type of people travelling on the excursion trains, and considered that preserving Newmarket's socially exclusive air was essential for the course's continued pre-eminence. Unlike other racecourses, which were enthusiastically negotiating with the railways for links to major stations, and the scheduling of more and more excursion trains, the Jockey Club scorned the railways. When the Great Eastern Railway scheduled excursion trains to a station near Newmarket, the Club arranged the races to begin and end miles apart, so that the only spectators who could watch the entire race were those who rode or drove along the course beside the horses, in eighteenth-century fashion. This attitude did not last for long, however. The Club was forced to change its stance not because it suddenly welcomed the proletarian masses, but because the cash benefits brought by the transport of horses outweighed the social demerits of working-class attendance. If Newmarket wanted to remain the country's most prestigious racecourse, it needed to have the best horses entered for its races, and the owners had already begun to withdraw their horses from any meetings that were unreachable by train. By 1847 the Club was actively supporting the creation of a rail link to its once sacrosanct grounds.[33]

As the railways became an important part of racegoing, the carnival element of the race meetings began to fade away. Spectators could now come by train, spend a day watching the races, and go home again. They no longer needed to be entertained over a two- or three-day period. The socially eminent also arrived for the racing alone, which meant that the theatres, concerts and assemblies that had been laid on to amuse them in the past were no longer as important. The money was vanishing from the social events, but it was not vanishing from racing. As the extraneous elements began to wither away, the number of race meetings and the number of days per meeting were both increasing. In the 1850s there were 62 new events in the calendar; in the 1860s another 99; then 54 more appeared between 1870 and 1875 alone. In 1848 there had been 13 courses that held more than one meeting a year; by 1870 there were 32.[34] The major requirement for a successful meet was a large population that could be reached by rail. Thus the courses that were accessible by train from London – Lingfield, Sandown, Windsor, Kempton Park and Hurst Park – each had five flat meetings a year, and more under National Hunt rules (over jumps). Only Newmarket staged more days of racing at a single course. And these race meets were, for the most part, held on weekends: Hurst Park's meetings were on Whit Monday and the August Bank Holiday – the two 'people's holidays' – which made it abundantly clear where they thought their income was coming from.[35]

The railways brought prosperity, and the lack of railways could quickly destroy a racecourse. The Blandford racecourse that was discussed above, pp. 428-9, had held race meetings since the 1660s. Then in 1840 the South Western Railway routed its new line through Salisbury, twenty miles away, bypassing Blandford. Within two years, the Blandford meeting had entirely vanished from the racing calendar. Instead, the South Western Railway was sponsoring its own, new, meetings in towns along its line, offering prizes in the 'Railway Stakes'.[36]

By this date there were 202,137 guineas available to be won as prize money annually.[37] This does not take into account the money spent on gambling on the sport, which was a separate matter. Yet gambling too was changing because of technology. Bookmakers' lists with odds were as readily available for working-class gamblers away from the racecourses as they were for those betting in the more rarefied atmosphere of Tattersall's: by the 1850s there were 150 betting shops in London alone. While betting by the working classes was frowned on, betting had become a modern, efficient, commercial enterprise, driven to increasing expansion by the use of the telegraph and the press. The telegraph disseminated an almost instantaneous knowledge of the race results to the public, and, linked with new sporting newspapers, so created a widening public interest in the sport.

In 1851 the *Racing Times* had begun to appear, following in the steps of the earlier 6d. papers such as *Bell's Life*. It was in 1859 that the penny press entered the racing world, and found a ready market: the *Sporting Life* (1859), the *Sporting Telegraph* (1860), the *Sporting Gazette* (1862), *Sporting Opinion* (1864), the *Sportsman* and (known universally as the 'Pink 'Un') the *Sporting Times* (both in 1865). *Sporting Life*, published twice a week, was selling 150,000 copies in its first year, and 300,000 copies in the 1880s.[38] All these sporting papers relied on the telegraph for their content, their air of omniscience, their crucial 'insider' status: they supplied hot gossip from the stables, betting advice and starting prices, and then, finally, the results. In 1868 the telegraph companies sent news to 144 towns and to 173 newspapers; by 1870 the Post Office (which had taken over as the sole administrator of the telegraph system) was sending news to 365 towns and 467 newspapers, and charging each one less for doing so. Racecourses themselves increasingly saw the value of the telegraph: Newmarket had sent 30,168 messages in 1870; five years later that number had more than doubled, to 71,716. Other courses increased their usage even more sharply, indicating a rising arc of professionalism: Epsom went from 5,600 telegrams a year in 1870 to 17,081 in 1875, Ascot moved from 3,700 to 12,812, while Goodwood went from a very modest 2,632 to even more than Ascot, at 14,432.[39] And it was not simply the racecourses, the sporting papers or even the spectators who benefited. The Post Office itself found racing a very steady earner. By the end of the century the racecourses were valuable enough to the Post Office that it was worth setting up a department dedicated to 'turf telegraphists'; in 1901 the St Leger alone required the services of eighty-two telegraph operators.[40]

In 1875 the next development in race meetings took place: the enclosed racecourse. The first grandstands had appeared over a century before. These early structures had enabled paying spectators to sit in comfort, to obtain a better view, or more select company, but most racegoers had attended without expecting – or being expected – to pay. The course owners were happy enough with the money visitors spent on incidentals and betting. But now Sandown Park was designed from the first to be a course that was completely enclosed by its grandstands, and suddenly an entirely new source of income had appeared. At Sandown, no one could watch a race without paying.

As was so frequently the case, this novelty actually had a long and varied history. Some smaller courses had earlier charged all their visitors, but these were racecourses that were owned and run by the upper classes, and the purpose of the admission fee was to keep a certain class out, not to make money from the gate: if spectators were content to watch at a distance, from the neighbouring fields, they were perfectly at liberty to do so. Haigh Park, in Leeds, had attempted to charge in 1823, and managed to survive for about a decade, but there were never enough admissions to be able to increase the prize money as was hoped, let alone make any profits. In 1837 the Hippodrome in central London was enclosed, but it too failed, and rapidly. From 1847 a racecourse near Manchester had charged a 1*d*. admission. In 1868 it became the first racecourse to attempt to stop the non-paying spectator from seeing any part of the race: its new course included a four-metre ditch and a stockade to block the view of those outside.[41] But it was Sandown, completely enclosed, that showed the way forward.

Sandown, Kempton Park and Lingfield Park were created by newly formed companies which had bought land, enclosed it, laid out the courses and built grandstands to surround each course completely.

This illustration of the Derby by Gustave Doré in 1872 shows how the select watched the race from the grandstand (rear, left), while most spectators expected to crowd along the course without any bar to admission. In 1875, the days of free attendance would vanish with the enclosure of many racecourses.

Sandown further ushered in the 'club' system, whereby a members' enclosure was set aside for those who had been proposed and seconded along club lines, creating a secure social environment for women – and doubling the prospective audience at a stroke. There was not a single racecourse that failed to copy Sandown's extraordinarily successful example if it was at all financially possible. The companies that had formed some of these new racecourses had had to raise huge sums – £34,000 in the case of Haydock Park, ultimately £80,000 for Newbury in 1906[42] – but the returns were equally huge, and the older courses were forced to imitate. Just as Newmarket had been forced to accept the railways, because owners would not otherwise enter their horses, so now owners showed a preference for the enclosed racecourses, which offered more prize money, funded as it was by the takings at the gate. To survive, therefore, enclosure became virtually compulsory. Sandown had started in 1875 with two meetings a year; within two years, it held four, by 1880 it was five. Others rushed to copy this formula, and, aside from the London-circuit racecourses, in the Midlands alone Derby enclosed in 1880, Leicester in 1884 and Colwick Park (Nottingham) in 1892; in the north, Gosforth Park and Haydock Park in the 1890s both joined in. In Scotland, Hamilton Park in Glasgow was the only enclosed course before the turn of the century. It had opened as a fully enclosed course in 1887, but as it drew a mere 12,000 spectators for its biggest day, from a population of over 1 million, it was unsurprising that few others followed for some time.[43] The only courses that managed to survive without enclosure were those that were important for social reasons – Ascot, Epsom, Doncaster and York – or were owned by a single individual, like Goodwood.[44]

With enclosure, with limited liability companies owning racecourses, with increased prize money, many courses were also simultaneously entering into financial arrangements with the railways. No longer were the railway companies simply sponsoring Railway Stakes at courses along their lines. Instead they were building lines that decanted passengers just outside the gate of the racecourse (or, sometimes, a racecourse was built beside an already existing line; the result was the same). From the 1880s, falling real prices and rising wages brought an increase in prosperity to the working classes, and the racecourses worked on ways of luring spectators by improving their facilities: railways with better links, or stations that were closer to the course, or, at the course itself, better clubhouses. Some stations even built covered passageways to take their passengers directly from the station to inside the enclosure.[45] The money that was washing about the sport was no longer in doubt: jockeys earned up to £1,000 a year (the salary of a distinguished surgeon), champion stallions were charged at 600 guineas per cover.[46] Up to 70,000 or 80,000 people were expected at the larger races near the big metropolitan centres. In 1896 the income earned by the racecourse at Doncaster was as follows:

Grandstand tickets: £9,415 10s.
Stand and second-class stand tickets: £1,195
Private stand: £55
Lincolnshire stand: £400
County stand: £868
Private boxes: £220 10s.
Paddock: £1,939
Tattersall's enclosure: £1,160
Carriage stands: £577 7s. 6d.
Publican's booths: £414 6s.
Temporary booths, tents, carts, wagons: £1,612 18s. 6d.
Refreshment rooms: £800
Race cards: £325
Fruit stalls: £25[47]

This came to nearly £20,000 – and the income from the rental of the refreshment booths alone was more than the total earned by most meetings just fifty years earlier.

The enclosed racecourses exacerbated what had been, for the working classes, a growing problem throughout the nineteenth century. Increasing industrialization and urbanization meant that open spaces were at a premium, as the continuing enclosure of public spaces removed what was left from common use. George Offer, a London magistrate, testified to the 1833 Select Committee on Public Walks that he 'often regretted [that] the places, when I was a boy, where I used to play and amuse myself, are now entirely shut up, and devoted either to buildings or to places of promenade for the higher classes'.[48] That a select committee was looking into the problem at all was an indication of how acute the situation had become. The committee was, at the end of its hearings, 'convinced that some Open Places reserved for the amusement (under due regulations to preserve order) of the humbler classes, would assist to wean them from low and debasing pleasures. Great complaint is made of drinking-houses, dog fights, and boxing matches, yet, unless some opportunity for other recreation is afforded to workmen, they are driven to such pursuits.' Public provision of free leisure spaces might stop the trespassing on private property (which, the committee pointed out hopefully, would also mean a drop in the costs of policing), and would improve the general health of the workers, stop them from drinking, and more generally 'promot[e] Civilisation, and excit[e] Industry'.[49]

Momentum to prevent common ground from being enclosed picked up. The General Enclosure Act of 1836 forbade enclosure of common land near big urban centres; in 1837 it was agreed that 'in all Inclosure Bills provision [should] be made for leaving an open space sufficient for the purposes of exercise and recreation of the neighbouring population.' Yet, as is the way with all governments, at the same time as these steps were being taken to provide more free leisure ground, the General Enclosure Act of 1845 produced the exact opposite result, making it easier to alter the designated usage of land from public to private by holding local inquiries rather than parliamentary ones. Communities could ask for a different piece of land to be allocated to common use for 'Exercise and Recreation', but no one was obliged to take their wishes into consideration. In fact, between 1845 and 1869, nearly 250,000 hectares of common land were enclosed, while only 1,600 hectares were set aside for the general public, and of those 1,600, only 705 were specifically designated for recreation. (The rest were given over to allotments.)[50]

This did not mean that the idea of fully accessible open spaces for the masses had entirely vanished. London led the way by setting aside money to purchase lands for public parks: the land for Primrose Hill park was bought from its ground landlords, Eton College, for £20,236 in 1846; Victoria Park was laid out in east London in 1849; Battersea Park was purchased for more than £100,000 in the 1850s. But little happened outside London at first. In 1844, Preston was the one town in Lancashire to have a public park. Though in 1840, £10,000 had been set aside in a general fund for the provision of public parks, nearly twenty years later, only Manchester and Bradford had come forward, Manchester requesting £3,000, and Bradford £1,500.[51] Instead, many parks outside London were bought and laid out by charitable institutions or private philanthropists: the Duke of Norfolk gave Sheffield its first park in 1847; Sir Titus Salt created a park in Saltaire; both Hull and Halifax had parks donated by private benefactors; Middlesbrough's Albert Park was funded by a local ironworks.[52] Although the creation of public parks was a slow change, and for the most part funded by private enterprise, still by the second half of the century it was accepted that some public land must be kept for the working classes' use. There had been riots when Epping Forest was threatened with enclosure and deforestation in 1849, and when in 1882 it was finally opened to the public it was Queen Victoria herself who performed the opening ceremony.[53]

Many of these parks, however, were for families, for decorous walks, for listening to the music played in the bandstands, for socializing in general. They were not for games-playing. Games instead still tended to be played on land owned by pubs, as had been the case from the sixteenth century. Publicans and innkeepers arranged the matches and held both the prize money the gambling stakes for a variety of games: skittles, bowls, wrestling, cricket, pedestrianism (foot races). Football was not originally a pub sport.

The origins of football are wreathed in myth – partly because 'football' was a generic term for various sorts of throwing, carrying and kicking ball games. One kind of football, and possibly the earliest, took the form of one of those ritual games that were played in each locality by a certain group of people (for football it was the young men of the community) at a certain time, usually Shrove Tuesday. This was not absolute – in Devonshire the annual football game was on Good Friday, in parts of Nottinghamshire it was on Easter Tuesday, in Kirkham, Lancashire, on Christmas Day[54] – but in general village football was a Shrovetide game. Some parishes played the game over an entire village – between the east and west districts of a parish, perhaps; some played ten or fifteen a side; some restricted the players to parish residents, others welcomed anyone who wanted to join in. Derby can provide one example of the form the annual village game could take. The Derby match was, in theory, played between two parishes, St Peter's and All Saints, but in practice anyone in the area could take part, and many travelled to Derby every year just to play. The match started at two o'clock on Shrove Tuesday in the town marketplace, with, by the very early nineteenth century, between 500 and 1,000 a side, such was its fame. The aim was to get the ball to a goal a mile outside the town – to the gate of a field on one side, and to the wheel of a watermill on the other. The side that was aiming for the field found it helpful to head for the River Derwent and then swam with the ball if they could manage it: there was a good landing place fairly near the goal. Their rivals, on the other hand, tried to start up the watermill to prevent a goal being scored. A frequent tactic by both teams, if they saw no way through their rivals' defence, was to hide the ball until dusk, or remove its stuffing and smuggle it out under someone's shirt.[55]

Yet while this type of game certainly existed – and today continues to be played at Shrovetide in a few communities, such as Ashbourne, in Derbyshire – it was not the direct ancestor of football as the sport is known today. This type of football most likely developed out of a more impromptu game, a kickabout, that was played on rough ground, or during fairs and on market days. This football had none of the ritual elements of the annual game, and was played in an informal manner by anyone who wanted to in the villages, and, later, when enclosure and industrialization put common land at a premium, in the same pub grounds as other sports. By the 1830s and 1840s pub football teams were issuing challenges in *Bell's Life*, just as other pub teams did. There were announcements made by football teams from the Grapes and the White Lion pubs near Dudley, the Bee Hive in Rugby, the Hole in the Wall in Blackburn, the Horns in Penistone, the Blue Ball at Thurslestone – and many more.[56] In 1865 the local postal directory for Sheffield listed thirteen clubs, of which eleven had their addresses at pubs. Other pub teams included Newton Heath, based at the Three Crowns, Oldham Road, Manchester (later it changed its name to Manchester United). Everton was based in its early days at the Queen's Head pub, in Everton village; West Bromwich Albion in 1879 used the White Hart inn and the Roebuck for changing. As late as 1894 three professional clubs – Gainsborough Trinity, Nottingham Forest and Manchester City – were still using pubs as changing areas, and then walking to their grounds.[57]

Some teams did not even have the organization that pub support provided: they were established simply by groups who played in the street together, and they tended to take their names from their neighbourhoods: in Blackburn there were the Red Row Stars, the Gibraltar Street Rovers, the Cleaver Street Rovers and the George Street West Rovers. In Stirling, of the sixty-eight teams known to have existed between 1876 and 1895, forty-two had neighbourhood or street names.[58] Many of those who supported football came from Methodist or other Nonconformist backgrounds: they saw football as a substitute for attending sports such as racing and pugilism, where there was a heavy betting and drinking element. Other teams were therefore formed by schools, churches or chapels, as a way of keeping the local boys occupied and out of trouble: the Droop Street Board School, in Kentish Town in

London, was the starting point for Queen's Park Rangers.[59] Yet even these teams often had links with groups like pubs or clubs. A Church of England school team from Wolverhampton (later the Wolverhampton Wanderers) was based only geographically in a church group: its financial support came not from the school itself, but from the father of one of the players, who was a publican, and a local businessman. The Christ Church Football Club, in Bolton, was established by the Revd J. F. Wright, but after four years the team gave up his schoolroom as their meeting place and moved to the Gladstone Hotel, renaming themselves the Bolton Wanderers.

Aston Villa's beginnings show how complex the 'origins' of a team could be. Aston Villa is usually referred to as a church team, and it did have links to the Bible class of the Aston Villa Wesleyan Chapel in Lozells, Birmingham, but the field the team played on belonged to a butcher, and the changing-room facilities were provided courtesy of a publican. Furthermore, in 1870 Aston Villa was still functioning as much as a social club as as a football team: it held regular meetings on Monday evenings at a coffee house in Aston High Street, and in 1883 the members continued to enjoy music on 'quiet social evening[s]'. Equally, Tottenham Hotspur could be said to have had pub origins, as it was supported by the brewery that owned the White Hart pub, which gave it access to the land near the lane the pub was situated on. Yet the team also received support from the local YMCA.[60]

Other teams were more straightforwardly formed in the workplace, either by a group of like-minded men (such as the employees of the Woolwich Arsenal) or with the encouragement of their employers, who thought team sports were character-forming. West Ham was originally named Thames Ironworks, drawing its men from the A. F. Hills shipyard; West Bromwich Albion was the team from Salter's Spring Works; Stoke City was a railway team (as late as 1912 twenty-seven out of the thirty-eight clubs in the Crewe and District League were railway sponsored).[61] In Birmingham, of the 218 teams mentioned in the local press between 1876 and 1884, 84 were linked in some way to religious groups, 13 were named after pubs, and 20 were formed at or by local works or factories.[62]

Sporting clubs in general did much to make football a coherent force, and it was often at a cricket club, whose members wanted some winter sport, that football began to raise its profile beyond the working classes and schoolboys. Between 1840 and 1850 two county cricket clubs,

Leicestershire and Surrey, had football matches in the winter, with Leicestershire changing its name as early as 1840 to the Leicestershire Cricket and Football Club. In 1849 the Surrey Football Club was formed within the Surrey County Cricket Club, which had been set up at Kennington Oval in 1845. Football teams that grew out of cricket clubs included Sheffield, Sheffield Wednesday, Accrington, Darwen, Preston North End and Sheffield United.[63]

Other clubs were formed when former schoolboys met to continue playing the game they had enjoyed at school. The Sheffield club, founded in 1857 and possibly the first purely football club to be established, was set up by ex-students of the Sheffield Collegiate School. It was, noted the *Sheffield Daily Telegraph* in 1867, a more prestigious club than many, 'due to the character of the members . . . [who] are almost exclusively of the middle class'.[64] The Forest Club was started *c.*1859 by a group of boys who had played together at Harrow, and in Scotland the Edinburgh Academicals was founded in 1857–8 by members of the Edinburgh Academy.

The main impediment to football being played throughout the country was the lack of a single set of rules. Racing had had rules imposed on it from the top by the Jockey Club, but there was no overall body to do the same for this more working- and middle-class game. Football was played at many schools, but each school had its own version of the game, with its own rules. When the various clubs played, be they pub, works, church or socially based, for the most part the rules had to be agreed between the teams before each match, including establishing how many would play on each side. In the early days of the game, that number was part of the announced challenge that appeared in the newspaper. In 1838, in one of the many advertisements of this type, *Bell's Life* printed the challenge: 'A match at football will be played at the cricket ground, Leicester, on Good Friday next, between eleven (principally printers) from Derby and the same number from Leicester. The winners to challenge an equal number from any town in England, for a purse not exceeding £25.' As time went on, there was no more consistency in the numbers playing, and the teams usually ranged from twelve, to eleven, down to six a side. In 1844 *Bell's* reported, 'A football match took place on Hampton Court Green on Tuesday last between 12 men of the F and 12 men of the D troop of the 13th Light Dragoons for a supper, which, after a severe struggle, was won by the D troop. Between

30 and 40 sat down to an excellent "spread" at the Toy Tap.' Even as late as 1859, at Lord's, the 3rd Battalion the Grenadier Guards beat the 2nd with twenty-five on each side, led by Captains Jarratt and Coulson (the rest of the teams were made up from the ranks). A week later there was a rematch, this time fifteen a side, with six officers taking part.[65]

In 1858 a letter was published in *Bell's Life* putting forward the suggestion that schools should all adopt the same rules, so that they could compete against each other. This engendered a lively, opinionated correspondence, all contributors highly partisan, all refusing to accept any rules except the writer's own. Frederick Lillywhite (see p. 204) wrote to concur with the original suggestion. He thought it would be highly advantageous if his next *Guide to Cricketers* could include the 'rules of all the sports and athletic games which are enjoyed in this country'. In part, he no doubt genuinely wished for standardization, but as a businessman he saw that it would bring commercial opportunities. The following year, no more conformity had been reached, so his *Guide* published the Eton laws; and by 1862 his brother, John Lillywhite, was selling at his Cricket Warehouse 'FOOT BALLS and the LAWS, as played at Eton, Harrow, and Rugby; boxing gloves, quoits, hockey sticks and balls, and all articles for winter sports'. In 1863 'the laws now in use at all the schools' were available alongside 'Boxing gloves, footballs . . . rackets, hockey-sticks and balls, dumb-bells, &c.,' at his newly expanded and renamed Cricket and British Sports Warehouse.[66]

The question of standardization was becoming urgent, and in 1863 a dozen clubs and groups of old boys, mostly from the south-east and London, met to attempt to agree 'some set of rules which the metropolitan clubs should adopt among themselves'. They called themselves the Football Association, and they were pleased to discover that Cambridge had codified a set of rules which included regulations on the offside rule, permissible forms of tackling, goals and goal kicks. Hands, these rules warned, 'may be used only to stop a ball and place it on the ground before the feet'.[67] Two months after this announcement, Lillywhite was announcing, 'The FOOTBALL ASSOCIATION – The POCKET LAWS of the above are now ready, price 6*d*., per post 7*d*., and in a few days will be ready, the Laws on sheet varnished, with rollers for the Club Room, price 1*s*., per post 1*s*. 2*d*. Published only (by authority) by JOHN LILLYWHITE, Cricket, Football, and British Sport Warehouse'[68] (and yet again the name of the shop had changed to reflect the popularity of the new sport).

In 1868 another association of clubs was formed, this time in Sheffield, and this group also established its own code, although it soon liaised with its southern counterpart to attempt to merge the rules of the two regions.* Inter-association competition began – in 1871 Charles Alcock, the new secretary of the Football Association, took a team to Sheffield for a game – but it was not until 1877 that the two sets of rules were finally merged into one that was acceptable to most of the teams. (Most: the miners in east Northumberland agreed finally to accept these rules only in 1882.)[69] This codification went some way towards making the Football Association an arbiter of all football disputes, but it was by no means the only association: the Birmingham Football Association had been established in 1875, Staffordshire and Surrey each had their own association in 1877; Lancashire, Berkshire, Buckinghamshire and Cheshire followed in 1878; Durham and Northumberland in 1879; Cleveland, Lincolnshire and Norfolk in 1881; London, Liverpool, Shropshire, Northamptonshire, Nottinghamshire, Sussex, Walsall and Scarborough and the East Riding in 1882; Derbyshire, Essex, Kent and Middlesex in 1883; Cambridgeshire, South Hampshire and Dorset in 1884; and Somerset and Suffolk brought up the rear in 1885.[70] Only towards the end of this period of development did the FA become an association of county and district associations, rather than an association of clubs. Thereafter the local FAs ran their own competitions and supervised their teams; the FA itself arbitrated disputes brought by members or associations, monitored the rules of the game, and organized the FA Cup.

In 1886 the International Football Association Board was established, with two representatives each from the English FA and from the parallel FAs that had been set up in Scotland, Ireland and Wales. It aimed to bring national coherence to the governing bodies. It was this group which agreed across all four countries such standards as ball size, how the ball could be thrown in from touch, how to mark touchlines, that crossbars had to be used instead of tapes – all the details that made inter-association competition possible.[71]

But by the time the International Football Association Board was formed there was a whole new lot of questions to be resolved – ones

---

* In line with the northern bias in the development of the game, perhaps it was natural that Sheffield's code was for the most part adopted, and thus the rules of the current game more closely resemble Sheffield's code than the FA's.

that were a great deal more fundamental than crossbars and tape. In the early 1870s county cups had been established in Lancashire, Birmingham and Staffordshire, while in 1871 the English FA Cup competition was started, based on Alcock's idea of a knockout competition; the Scottish Cup competition followed in 1873, and the Welsh in 1877, with the aim of providing inter-school competition. These competitions were held in front of large (although today unquantifiable) numbers of spectators. At exactly the same time as happened in racing, the mid-1870s, it was discovered that football spectators were happy to pay to watch their sport. So, was football pleasant exercise for its participants, or was it a lucrative business opportunity? If the former, how to justify charging spectators; if the latter, where was this income to be directed?

Up until 1881, most of the football clubs from the south had been made up of former public-schoolboys or other members of the metropolitan-based middle classes. Of the 158 players from southern clubs who participated in the FA Cup finals up to this date, 39 had a legal background, 38 were army officers, 16 clergymen, 14 teachers (this category overlapped with the clergy, some being both teachers and clergymen), 11 in banking, 8 brewery directors or managers or wine merchants, 6 civil servants, 2 doctors and 2 professors, the rest listing themselves as company directors or simply 'gentlemen'.[72] By the end of the 1870s, northern clubs were already semi-professional, made up of working men who needed to be recompensed for giving up a day's pay to play. The aims of these two groups could not have been further apart, and the vexed question of whether it was acceptable for players to be paid for their performances was a constant irritation – in the background to begin with, but soon, bitterly, in the open.

In fact by the late 1870s some players were fully professional. In 1878 the *Darwen News* reported with perfect equanimity that Blackburn Rovers had been 'well marshalled by McIntyre, who, we believe is engaged as professional to the Rovers'. McIntyre was an upholsterer from Glasgow, and had played for Glasgow Rangers before he moved to Lancashire to find work. In 1881 the *Midland Athlete* reported carefully that 'at present we know of no GLARING case wherein men have been paid to play football . . . [but] we do know of cases where men have received more than their legitimate expenses to play for a club.' Others were more concerned about importation, the practice of bringing players into the team just for important matches. This appeared to be on the increase from the late 1870s, when some particularly talented players appeared for several clubs in the same competition in the same season. In 1883 Nottingham Forest placarded the streets of Sheffield with offers of a £20 reward to anyone who provided proof that Sheffield Wednesday was fielding three imported players in a cup tie against Forest. The problem was patched over in different ways in different places. In Lancashire from 1882 two years' residency was required before those born outside the county could play in cup ties, and it was generally agreed that no one could play for more than one club in the same season in competitions. Other teams established rules that forced players to prove that their expenses were used solely for travel and accommodation.[73]

Many of the southern teams complained that the northerners were cheating, and the FA, a southern organization, now banned any payments. In 1883 Accrington was expelled from the FA, with Preston excluded from the Cup the following year, both for the sin of professionalism. This was the tipping point. Many in the north saw the FA's ruling as based on anti-north, anti-working-class prejudice, and there were mutterings that the southern clubs had not objected to northern professionalism until the southerners began to be beaten. And beaten – even humbled – they were. In 1882 Blackburn Rovers had become the first northern team to reach the FA Cup final; in 1883 Blackburn Olympic, a team made up of 3 weavers, 1 loomer, 1 gilder, 2 ironfoundry workers, 1 clerk, 1 master plumber, 1 licensed victualler and 1 dental assistant, beat the Old Etonian team in the final of the FA Cup – the first northern industrial team to win the Cup.[74] Previously, these teams had been at enormous economic disadvantage. In 1879 when Darwen was drawn against the Old Etonians in the FA Cup it had to appeal for funds 'to enable the working lads of our town to compete against government inspectors, university professors, [and] noblemen's sons', as the *Darwen News* put it. A collection in the mills and works raised £175 to compensate for loss of earnings. By the time Blackburn Rovers was preparing for its FA Cup appearance, before both the semifinal and the final it received financial aid from a local industrialist, who paid for the players to stay in a Blackpool hotel for a week before the competition. Here the team trained together, and also received a special diet: a glass of port wine and two raw eggs at six a.m., before a walk on the beach, porridge and haddock for breakfast; a leg of mutton for dinner; porridge and a pint of milk for tea; and half a dozen oysters per man for supper.[75]* Without their benefactor, the public-school grip on the finals might have taken several more years to dislodge. Instead, Rovers reinforced the northern supremacy by winning the Cup in both 1884 and 1885.

Payments were illegal, but most people understood that they happened. It was very hard to prove, and supporters on both sides pointed to contributions such as those raised by Darwen's fans, or the provision of food, lodgings and training time to Blackburn Olympic. These were all indirect payments, regularly and openly made. At the heart of the matter was a difficulty in accepting the changing nature of the game. A pastime had become a business; maximizing profits meant playing to win; better, richer clubs would corner the market in the best players, and smaller clubs would go to the wall. This was directly contrary to the ethos of local competition on which the game had hitherto been based.

Charles Alcock was the highly influential secretary of the FA for twenty-five years. Educated at Harrow, he was a founder member of the Forest Club, and then helped that develop into the Wanderers in 1864. First elected to the FA committee in 1866, he became secretary in 1870 (and from 1886–7 he began to receive a salary for the job).† Although an amateur himself, Alcock saw that, if the FA was to survive, it would have to accept professionalism. He agreed with *Sporting Life* when it wrote that 'there can be no possible objection to the recognised payment of men who cannot afford to play for amusement, and we can see no reason why the principle which exists in almost every sport should be considered detrimental to football.'[77] Alcock thought that the amateur opposition to payment was wrong, suggesting as it did that it was 'immoral to work for a living'. The *Bolton Chronicle* was blunt: 'In the South the players are mainly of the "upper ten" [per cent]. They can afford time and money for training, and travelling, and playing. In the North the devotees of the game are mainly working men. They cannot play the game on strictly amateur lines . . . They cannot afford to train,

---

* It is worth remembering the diet of the average millhand in the nineteenth century: bread or potatoes, a little butter and cheese or bacon, and sugared tea.[76] The increase in protein alone, even for a week, must have made an astonishing difference.
† He was also, in his spare time, a journalist, and president of Surrey FA, vice-president of London FA, secretary of the Surrey County Cricket Club, chairman of the Richmond Athletic Association and vice-president of the Royal Mid-Surrey Golf Course.

or to "get in form" ... Besides, they command big "gates" and they naturally think they have a right to a trifle from it.'[78]

In 1884 thirty-six northern teams threatened to leave the FA and form a new British Association, which would be professionally based. The Lancashire FA immediately agreed that it would leave, and the Midlands FA was wavering. Not all the teams were divided on strict north–south, professional–amateur lines, however. It was not until 1890 that the final purely amateur team in the north, Middlesbrough, turned professional, after it failed consistently when competing against the new professionals.[79] But the threat of secession of the north looked solid enough to scare the FA, and it took a small step forward, suggesting a compromise: that clubs would be able to reimburse players for any wages they lost by playing. But then it scampered backwards again, adding that all financial details would have to be revealed by the clubs, including wages for every player. At that point Sunderland and Aston Villa threatened to leave. Finally, on his second attempt, in 1885, Alcock coaxed the FA into agreeing to accept professionalism under strict rules: any player who received more than accommodation and travel expenses was a professional; professionals had to live within six miles of the club (this was to foil importations); they could play for just one club; they could not sit on FA committees, or represent their own or any other club at FA meetings; eligibility for cup matches was birth or two years' residency.[80]

The FA bias towards amateurs had formally been overcome, but tacitly it continued to operate: in the first year that a professional played openly, he was forced to wear a different-coloured shirt from his team-mates. As late as 1888 *Punch* remained exercised by northern and Midland supremacy and professionalism, as its heavy-handed piece entitled 'Midland Yahoos v. North Country Savages' made clear: 'Under the Thugby Association Rules', it smirkingly informed its readers, 'the takings for gate-money were enormous.' Many southern clubs and some FAs remained amateur as long as they could. In 1891 the Woolwich Arsenal began to pay its players, followed by Millwall and Southampton. When the London FA, still resolutely amateur, threatened to ban them, Arsenal simply turned its back on its own association and began to play the northern and Midlands teams. Yet, wherever it could exert control, the FA remained stubbornly committed to the superiority of amateurism. The selection for the England team, entirely in the hands of the FA, was notably tilted towards the amateurs, even when, as in 1894–5, only one amateur player made the team – by the most amazing coincidence, the FA named him captain.[81]

In 1889 a further large step was taken away from football as a recreation, and towards football as commerce. The Football League was formed, with the stated aim of promoting the benefits of professionalism. William MacGregor, of Aston Villa, the prime mover of the League, was a shopkeeper; his co-promoter John Davies, who later rescued a Manchester United sliding towards bankruptcy, was the chairman of Manchester Breweries. In 1893 Arsenal joined the Football League, and with another six clubs in 1894 it formed a new Southern League for professional clubs. Amateurism had had its day.[82]

Arsenal is an interesting example of how a team came to terms with professionalism. The club was formed in 1886 by workers at the Woolwich Arsenal, and, although early records are not clear, it is likely that it was entirely run by working men elected from the membership. Long before the club turned professional, in 1891, potential players were recruited to work for the Arsenal and were given well-paid jobs supervised by foremen sympathetic to their training needs. When professionalization had become inevitable, the club initially rejected the idea of a limited-liability company. John Humble, an engineer at the Arsenal who sat on the club committee (and later became a director), said that the club had been formed and run by working men, and he hoped to see it carried on by them, whereas if it became a limited-liability company Arsenal would degenerate 'into a proprietary or capitalist club'. Despite these aspirations, limited liability had to be accepted: in 1893 the owner of Arsenal's ground demanded a rent increase of £150, 'the transfer of rate payments from him to the club, and [the right to appoint] a nominee on the committee'. He was firmly rejected, but it was decided that the best way to protect the club in future was to form a limited-liability company to raise the money to buy its own ground. The company was floated with nominal capital of 4,000 £1 shares, of which 1,552 were allotted to 860 shareholders, the majority of whom were manual workers in the Plumstead and Woolwich districts, probably mostly employees at the Arsenal. Money problems swiftly arrived anyway: the club was burdened by large mortgage repayments, while attendances were not as high as they might otherwise have been because the area had poor public transport; also, the team's travel costs had soared after professionalization, when they began to play the northern and Midlands clubs. The Boer War of 1899–1902 finished off the ideal of a club owned by working men. The war brought a large increase in the number of employees at the Arsenal, but it also brought a large increase in compulsory overtime and a consequent decrease in leisure time for both the players and their paying fans. In 1900 the club made a loss of £3,400, and control passed to local businessmen and professionals.[83]

In the early days of the sport, brewers had patronized the clubs, lending support and facilities to working men. With the commercial possibilities of the game seemingly infinite, instead of football being played where the drink was, the drink followed the game. The teams no longer – at least in the short term – needed the financial backing of the publicans. Sunderland had used a field owned by the Blue House inn, but the £10 rent was steep, so the club simply moved, no longer dependent on the backing of the pub. Wolves quarrelled with its pub landlord and also moved to a new ground. Arsenal was different in that its move, from Woolwich to Highbury, was based not on a dispute, but on demographics: it suspected (correctly, as it turned out) that north London, with better transport links, would provide more spectators and therefore more gate money for the club. Everton's story was more typical. John Houlding, a brewer, part-owned the Anfield ground, conveniently located next door to his Sandon Hotel, which had the sole right to sell refreshments at the matches. In 1890–91 Everton won the League Championship, making over £1,700, and Houlding wanted some of it. He raised the rent on the ground, and then he and the team fell out noisily. When no resolution seemed possible, Everton picked up and moved to Goodison Park (whereupon Houlding started a new club, Liverpool FC, on the old site). In the opposite direction, Spurs moved its pitch to the White Hart inn when the inn gave the club good terms.

That the White Hart inn enticed a club to play nearby showed good business sense: the pubs recognized the commercial importance of football. The size of the crowds kept on growing: there seemed no limit to the number of people who wanted to watch the game. Between the 1889–90 and 1913–14 seasons, the crowds at First Division English League matches rose from an average of 4,600 per match to an average of 23,100. In 1892 there were 32,810 spectators at the FA Cup final – and there would have been more had Kennington Oval had larger capacity. In 1893 the final was played at the Fallowfield Athletics Ground in

Manchester, and 45,000 paid to watch (several thousand more broke down the barriers to watch without paying). In the 1890s the final moved back to London, and in 1895 45,000 went to Sydenham to watch Aston Villa play Wolverhampton Wanderers. (In 1905 Sydenham would get its own team, Crystal Palace, named for Paxton's building, located in the suburb for half a century.) Even more telling than these one-off events, it was estimated that by 1909, on any Saturday afternoon across England alone, around 1 million people were attending football matches, and once more it was the railways that had made this possible.[84]

This transport element, the football excursion train, was essential for the players as well as the spectators, making out-of-town fixtures feasible even for those men in full-time employment. In 1879 Glasgow Rangers' players left Glasgow after work on a Friday evening, arrived in Manchester at 4 a.m., played a match on Saturday afternoon, and returned to Glasgow that night. The train companies, understandably, were even more interested in the spectators. In the 1880s the North Greenwich line admitted that it no longer had the capacity to transport all of Millwall Rovers' fans; the Great Eastern had to install extra-wide doors at White Hart Lane to allow the speedy dispersal of Tottenham Hotspur fans, arriving as they were at five-minute intervals before each match; by 1901, at the Crystal Palace, half of the 110,000 fans were carried to the match by train. Many fans belonged to Final Clubs, in which up to 10,000 members paid a weekly subscription that was then used to buy bulk excursion fares to transport fans to the Cup final.[85]

More and more breweries saw the proximity of a football ground as a major commercial asset for a pub. Pubs were key places where the Saturday-night football specials were hawked, and in turn these newspapers carried heavy advertising for pubs in general and different brewers in particular. In Portsmouth the magistrates were unwilling to license a new pub for Brickwood's brewery as the company had four beer-houses in the city already; Brickwood's found it commercially expedient to close these four beer-houses down in order to obtain a licence for the one football pub. Likewise Whitbread thought it worth giving up one pub in order to open another next to the White Hart inn. And the breweries did more than just link themselves by location: many invested in the clubs as shareholders. Overall by 1911 14.9 per cent of shareholders in Association clubs were in the drinks trade, holding 6.9 per cent of all shares; in Scottish football, the 11.3 per cent of drinks-industry shareholders owned 31.2 per cent of shares. Breweries also found alternative means of financial investment: some lent clubs money to buy or improve their grounds; others bought the grounds themselves and leased them back to the clubs. Watford was rescued by Benskins, a local brewer; Manchester United became entirely dependent on Manchester Breweries' chairman John Davies, while Liverpool was in the same financial situation with John Houlding.[86] Very soon the clubs were as heavily dependent on the great brewers as they had once been on individual publicans.

For, as teams became more successful, they became harder to manage by part-time administrators, who could not give them their full attention. In the 1881–82 season alone, the administration of Blackburn Rovers required fifty-seven committee meetings to be held, not including meetings of the various subcommittees. The Lancashire FA's secretary sent 4,000 letters in 1882–83. These jobs were full-time, beyond any doubt. What businessmen had that working men did not were the two things that all administrators needed: time and money. In 1884–5, the year before Bolton Wanderers became fully professional, its balance sheet showed entries for financial outlay on new stands and on the ground, and payments for 'Rent, rates, ground and gatekeeping, police, accounts'; uniforms; 'Printing, posting, advertising'; 'medical attendance on players'; 'Players' insurance' and half a dozen other categories of a similar nature.[87] Some teams raised funds through lotteries, bazaars, raffles and prize draws. But, like Arsenal, most found limited-liability companies the way forward, and most of their shares were bought by professional men. Blackburn Rovers had 93 shareholders in 1897, mostly cotton manufacturers, mill managers and publicans; by 1914 there were 241 shareholders, with one brewer owning 150 shares and two cotton manufacturers owning another 150 between them. Bolton Wanderers listed journalists, jewellers, publicans, brewers and bleachers as shareholders in 1895; by 1914 one brewer had 400 shares. Preston North End was also owned mostly by the drinks trade: twenty-six publicans or licensed victuallers, six brewers. Manchester City in 1894 had as shareholders two brewers with 50 and 100 shares, an innkeeper and a secretary with 20 shares each, and a publican and a brewer with 10 shares each; the other 209 shareholders had just one or two shares each.

The future was visible in the finances of Manchester United, which had been formed from the defunct Newton Heath club, which had gone into bankruptcy in 1902, when most of its shares were owned by working-class men. By 1908 John Davies, the managing director of Manchester Breweries, held 100 shares – 40 more than the next six directors put together. Of those six, he employed three directly, while two more had commercial links to his brewery. By 1913 the new ground at Old Trafford had been opened, and the club was on its way to a century of pre-eminence. The connections between football and the drinks industry went on and on: in 1897 15 per cent of Blackburn Rovers' shares were owned by the drinks trade; by 1909 West Bromwich Albion had £700 in debentures with Mitchells and Butlers brewery, while two other breweries had £500 and £100 worth. Wolverhampton Wanderers' new ground, dressing rooms, offices and covered stands in Molyneux had been laid out by Northampton Brewery Co., which charged a rent of only £50 a year.[88] No one was in any doubt by now that football was business – big business, just as racing was.

After looking at these two professional sports, one upper class in origins, one working class, both developing out of older forms of sport, of gambling, and of ritual community life, it is time to turn to another sport, one that was created in the late nineteenth century entirely from scratch. This was a sport that relied for its existence on new technology, that found its early popularity exclusively in the middle classes, and that had gained its adherents with barely any competitive elements: cycling.

At the end of the eighteenth century, for many of the middle class sport was considered either a working-class pastime, and therefore almost indistinguishable from riots, or an upper-class one, in which case many thought it closely resembled dissipation. In the nineteenth century that began to change, as the middle classes started to appropriate elements of sports for their own purposes, facilitated by the spread of public-school educations to a wider tranche of the prosperous and professional. At the beginning of the century these schools had themselves for the most part regarded sport as nothing but a necessary evil. Samuel Butler, the bishop of Coventry and Lichfield, was the headmaster of Shrewsbury School from 1798 to 1836. In those thirty-eight years he had moved the school from a dying institution to an educational powerhouse (his most famous pupil was Charles Darwin). But he thought games were beneath contempt – football, he sniffed, was 'only fit for butcher boys'.[89] A few decades on, another reformer, Thomas Arnold, the famous headmaster of Rugby School from 1828 to 1842, also had little or no interest in organized games, but now he recognized them as useful, serving as an outlet for boyish aggression. Other schools increasingly saw sports as a way of inculcating Arnold's educational and moral reforms: games gave boys the illusion of self-management while fostering teamwork and discipline. In the 1840s Charles Kingsley wrote that 'There has always seemed to me something impious in the neglect of perfect health, strength and beauty . . . I could not do half the little good I do do . . . if it were not for that strength and activity which some consider coarse and degrading.'[90] Here was a combination to suit the middle-class palate – sport mixed with both piety and self-improvement. Games had become health-giving, they were 'manly', and they were improving.

All this long preceded the arrival of the first two-wheeled object with a mechanical crank operated by pedals, not yet named the bicycle. The earliest ancestor, usually known as a velocipede, appeared in Paris in 1867. Previous prototypes had been, rather than forms of self-propulsion, no more than aids to walking (the way a scooter still is). In 1868 a young man, Rowley Turner, visited his uncle Josiah Turner in Coventry. Josiah Turner was an engineer who ran the Coventry Sewing Machine Co. With the sewing-machine business in a slump, he was persuaded by his nephew's enthusiasm to switch production over to manufacturing these novelties – for which, by happy coincidence, his nephew had an order for 400 for a Parisian firm. The company was quickly renamed the Coventry Machinists Co., and began to turn out velocipedes. These machines had a vogue in France, and a – very brief – moment in the USA. But it was in Britain, with its highly developed metalworking trade, its good selection of newspapers that were interested in sport, and its elaborate road network, that bicycling took off. By 1869 a Liverpool agent was importing cycles from the USA; a local club had been established, and had sponsored a race between Chester and Rock Ferry. Further races were staged at the Crystal Palace, while the Agricultural Hall in Islington had trick-cyclists. In this first wave of interest, cycles were seen as objects to be ridden by professionals for the spectators' amusement: a crowd of 4,000 was claimed for road races in Birmingham.[91]

But that same year a technical improvement began to move the bicycle towards recreational status. In 1869 James Starley, the foreman of the Coventry Machinists Co., produced an improved model, known as the Ordinary. Starley had made steering easier by getting rid of the tiller which had previously manipulated the front wheel, and replacing it with handlebars. He reduced the driving wheel to 122 centimetres and encased it in rubber to cushion the ride – previous models had been known as 'boneshakers' for a reason. Finally he perched the cyclist high above the dust kicked up by horses and carriages. Enthusiasm was spread by the club, still in the late nineteenth century the most common social grouping. In 1870 the Pickwick Bicycle Club and the Amateur Bicycle Club were formed in London, and over the next decade were soon joined by at least a dozen more clubs. Young men, clerks and shop assistants, particularly enjoyed the spice of danger in cycling: it gave them an aura of masculinity, of virility, which they appreciated. Lower-middle-class white-collar work was popularly supposed to be the province of weaklings, and cycles and cycling clubs were a very visible counter to this image.

By 1875 further modifications to the Ordinary made the front wheel larger once more, at about 152 centimetres, while the back wheel was only 40 centimetres, the two radically different sized wheels giving the machine the nickname the penny-farthing. In 1880 springs were added to the seat, and the frame was hollowed out to lessen the weight of the machine. The next two important technological advances, which took the bicycle away from the hobbyist and gave it to the world, followed swiftly. In 1876 Starley produced the Safety Bicycle. The rider was now no longer perched high above the road, in danger of a headlong fall. Instead, both wheels had been made almost the same size, and the rider could touch the ground while seated. It was easier to respond to untoward circumstances, especially now the cyclist could mount from a standstill, rather than the running start that had been necessary before, and could stop merely by putting his feet down. The Safety Bicycle 'set the fashion to the world' (Starley's motto), but what spread that fashion and made the cycle a routine means of transportation rather than an odd hobby was an invention that came entirely separately. In 1888 the Dunlop pneumatic tyre appeared on the market and was immediately fitted to the bicycle, giving a smoother ride and increasing the machine's possible speed by 30 per cent. In 1891 Edouard Michelin refined this innovation by producing a tyre that, in case of a puncture, could be mended by removing its inner tube alone.[92] This meant that punctures could be dealt with by a single cyclist by the side of the road, rather than needing a mechanic with specialized tools. It also reduced costs by a large margin.

The pieces were all in place for an industrial boom, much like the railway mania of the 1830s and 1840s. Ernest Terah Holley appeared in 1895 with £100,000 and a good reputation. He purchased the Dunlop works for £3 million and floated the company for £5 million just a year later. In the next few years he promoted two dozen companies with, between them, nominal capital of £18.6 million. Fifteen of these companies were cycle manufacturers, including Raleigh, which was floated for £200,000, and the Singer Cycle Co., floated for £80,000.* The bubble soon burst, as it was bound to, and Holley was bankrupted and jailed for fraud.[93] With this sort of volatile market, it is hard to say how many cycles were produced, but it is suggested that, by the 1890s, on average 750,000 a year were being manufactured. Whatever the actual figure, cycles had become part of everyday life. In the twenty years that cycles had been manufactured in Britain, *Punch* artists had mentioned or drawn them in their cartoons just over once a year. Even in 1894 there were only two cartoons. Then in 1895, the boom year, there were twenty-three, in 1896 thirty-five. Cycles were now part of the vocabulary of cartoons just as omnibuses and hansom cabs were: vehicles for a joke, not joke vehicles.

In the first year of the decade there were 300 cycling clubs in London alone. Cycling was no longer just for hobbyists: it was for delivery boys, for postmen, for policemen, for poor curates and for teachers. Cycles were rather like pianos: the best ones were expensive, at up to £30 when bought new in 1895, but many could be found of a lesser quality for about £10, and secondhand ones were even cheaper. Those that did not have the latest tyres, or seats with springs, could be acquired for as little as £2. When the first boom period was over in 1897, even the expensive models became affordable to more of the population: a Rudge-Whitworth Special, one of the best cycles on the market, dropped in price from £30 to 16 guineas, while the company's standard model was priced at 12 guineas, down from £20.[94]

Many took advantage, because, while the initial commercial manufacturing boom might be over, there was no diminution in the number of enthusiasts. If anything, as the industrial depression deepened and

---

* Holley was also involved with both Schweppes and Bovril: for cycling and refreshments, see below, p. 459.

prices dropped, more and more of the population became cyclists. In 1878 the Bicycle Touring Club (shortly the Cyclists Touring Club, the CTC, as it remains today) had been set up to help its members who wanted to tour through the countryside on their cycles. The CTC negotiated with the railways to reduce the charges for carrying its members' cycles – in the summer of 1898 the Great Eastern carried 60,000 cycles in and out of Liverpool Street station alone.[95]* Once members reached the town of their choice, they could consult the CTC publication which listed all the inns and hotels in the country, dividing them into 'Headquarters' or 'Quarters', depending on price and quality. On showing their club badges, members received a discount of between 1½*d.* and 3*d.* in the shilling at any of the hotels or inns listed.[97] These hotels also had set prices for tea and dinner for club members – between 1*s.* 6*d.* and 2*s.* 6*d.* (an extra 3*d.* if attendance at meals was required, and 6*d.* for the maid).[98] By the 1890s the publishing industry had joined the tourist market, and the dedicated touring cyclist could purchase 'Safety' cycling maps, with different roads marked in different colours, indicating difficulty of ascent, the speeds that could be achieved, and unrideable roads. The *Contour Road Books* at the end of the century showed all this plus elevations, gradients, lighting-up times, railway rates for cycles, maps of the main towns, and blank 'summary' pages to be filled in by the cyclist.[99]

It was the quality of the roads that formed one of the CTC's most sustained – and successful – campaigns. As early as 1874 the *Book for Riders* was a litany of roads that were impassable to cyclists: 'Liverpool to Prescott, 8 miles of good road, then within 6 miles of Newcastle-under-Lyne [*sic*] a very bad bit full of holes ... From Mansfield to Doncaster stiff clay, very rutty and uneven. Tadcaster to York is quite impassable ... from Rivesby to Horncastle nearly all loose flint: after this the road degenerates into two wheel ruts and a horse track, driving [i.e. riding a cycle] being sometimes impossible.' 'The road between Birmingham and Wolverhampton is very bad and wearying: in fact it is full of holes and tramway ruts. The bicyclist had better train this bit.' Except for the reference to trains, this sounds much like Josiah Wedgwood and his friends campaigning for the arrival of the turnpikes a century before. In the mid-1880s a meeting of the National Cyclists

---

* Most lines charged 5*s.* for cycles to be carried for up to 400 miles, or 7*s.* 6*d.* if they were classed as parcels; tricycles were between 10 and 20*s.*, tandems 50 per cent more per additional seat.[96]

Union was held in Birmingham to attempt to find a solution to poorly maintained roads. The Union funded test cases in which road surveyors were brought before local magistrates for failing to keep the roads passable. Ultimately the NCU and the CTC formed a Roads Improvement Association 'to circulate popular and technical road literature in order to enlighten ratepayers ... and to guide county councillors, highway boards and their employees about proper road repair and maintenance; to remonstrate with responsible authorities where neglect of roads became a public scandal, and take legal action where necessary; to watch or introduce fresh legislation to remove anomalies; and to take up the question of fingerposts and milestones and their erection and maintenance.'[100] In 1896, as a result of the Association's campaigning, the Locomotive Highways Act was passed, which raised the speed limit to twenty miles per hour (from twelve).[101] This was swiftly satirized by W. S. Gilbert in his 'Bab Ballads':

> The idiot who praises, with enthusiastic tone,
> All centuries but this, and every country but his own;
> And the lady from the provinces, who dresses like a guy,
> And who 'doesn't think she waltzes, but would rather like to try';
> And that singular anomaly, the scorching bicyclist –
> I don't think he'll be missed – I'm sure he'd not be missed!

The results of these campaigns – for improved roads, for better signage, for good roadside food, drink and accommodation – helped create the environment in which shortly the motor-car industry found it possible to flourish.

By this time cycling was no longer just for men. Women had joined in with great enthusiasm. In 1894 Constance Everett-Green, soon to become the leading female cycling journalist, had written that it was 'still more or less of an open question in England whether ladies can with propriety ride the bicycle'. The following year she commented, 'It would hardly be too much to say that in April of 1895 one was considered eccentric for riding a bicycle, whilst by the end of June eccentricity rested with those who did not ride.' And in March 1896 it was reported that, on a pleasant morning, between 2,000 and 3,000 cyclists could be seen daily beside the Serpentine in Hyde Park.[102] Cycling was the done thing, and it gained the overtones of conspicuous consumption that many pastimes had tried to do, so that the wealthy might take it up, and the less wealthy would desire to emulate them. The *Illustrated Sporting and*

Dramatic News started a 'Sportswoman's Page' in the 1890s. Describing a new cycle, the page's correspondent declared, 'I . . . fell violently in love with it. It had nickel rims, and the handles of ivory are cased at the end in caps of pieced gold.'[103]

Writers of all stripes found a new subject in the bicycle. First there was a deluge of travel books: *From the Clyde to the Jordan: Narrative of a Bicycle Journey*, *In Jutland with a Cycle*, *Awheel to Moscow and Back*, *Sketches Awheel in Iberia*, *A New Ride to Khiva*, *Across Siberia on a Bicycle*. The first novel to feature a bicycle (or at least the *Athenaeum* reviewed it as such) was Ben Hayward's *All Else of No Avail* in 1888. Perhaps of more lasting value was George Gissing's 1901 short story, 'A Daughter of the Lodge', in which cycling is portrayed as a rich New Woman's indulgence. E. Nesbit's *Five Children and It* (1902) includes an episode where a baby is magically turned into a young man; being grown up, he automatically owns a bicycle. Perhaps the most enjoyable of these ephemeral cycling tales are Grant Allen's detective stories featuring the female detective Lois Cayley. In 'The Typewriter Girl' (two New Women symbols in one!) she frantically cycles away from an anarchist community at top speed, only to crash into another (woman) cyclist. In 1899 Allen's *Hilda Wade: A Woman with Tenacity of Purpose*, set in Rhodesia, had a heroine who escapes the assegais of the ferocious Matabele by 'vaulting lightly on to the seat of her bicycle and pedalling for dear life', while the 'savages' draw back, superstitiously afraid of a woman on an 'iron horse'. She is somewhat hampered by the baby she is carrying, so the hero leaps to the rescue – literally, as he jumps on to her cycle, steering with one hand, while firing a gun with the other, as she swaps her cycle for his pony.[104]

But short stories filled a small niche market. The real publishing money in cycling was in the new specialist journals. In 1896 *Cycling Magazine* claimed to be selling over 41,000 copies every week. This was one among many, though: *Wheel Life* (founded in 1876, and soon incorporated with *Bicycling News*), the *CTC Gazette* and the *Cyclist* (both 1879), *Wheeling* (1884), the *Cycling Budget* (1886), *Cycling* (1891, and surviving until 1957), the *Lady Cyclist* (1895) and *Wheelwoman and Society Cycling News* (1896) all found an audience. The *Boy's Own Paper*, which had been founded in 1879, was selling 1 million copies per issue by 1900, giving middle-class boys school stories, sports stories and adventure stories, interleaved with advertisements for bicycles and other sporting equipment.[105]

More than just advertisements for the cycles themselves appeared. Now bicycling was popular enough to be referred to as a socially desirable pastime in advertisements for entirely unrelated products. Elliman's Universal Embrocation, 'for stiffness, aches, sprains, bruises', promised that its product was so splendid that 'Boys Race for It!', with an illustration of boys on cycles speeding towards the prize, the embrocation, under glass. Advertisements for prepared foods also often featured cycles: both the foods and the cycles were presented as ideal for the woman who was not always stuck at home. Meredith and Drew merged these two ideas in its 'cycle biscuit', heavily marketed for a while. Advertisements for Stower's Lime Cordial assured readers that it was 'the only healthy beverage that can be safely taken after cycling or other exercise'. It showed a woman in fashionable dress and hat (although not cycling clothes, see below), sitting down beside a cycle. Another advertisement for Elliman's was more daring, with a woman in bloomers (although chaperoned by an old man on a tricycle).[106]

Specialized clothes for sport had been good business for some time. In 1851 at the Great Exhibition one merchant had promoted his specialized wear for 'deer-stalking, riding, and walking'.[107] In Chapter 6 we saw how seaside fashions had altered over the century. Team sports, too, had specialized clothing. By the 1840s the boys playing football at Harrow were wearing different coloured jerseys to identify the two teams, although at Rugby in *Tom Brown's Schooldays* (1856) the concession to sporting wear was that the boys removed their hats, jackets, waistcoats, braces and 'neck-handkerchiefs'. In 1867 *Routledge's Handbook of Football* described players wearing broad leather belts and their oldest and dirtiest trousers, with 'tight' jerseys, although it suggested that 'the prettiest costume . . . [should include] a coloured velvet cap with a tassell'. It also suggested that 'if it can previously be so arranged . . . one side [should wear] striped jerseys of one colour, say red; and the other . . . another, say blue. This prevents confusion and wild attempts to . . . wrest the ball from your neighbour. I have often seen this done, and heard the invariable apology – "I beg your pardon, I thought you were on the opposite side."' By the 1880s the FA was recommending striped jerseys and below-the-knee-length shorts, with plain or striped stockings.[108] As always, however, the larger market was not the players, but the amateurs and the fans. No one was yet buying replica team-wear, but cotton handkerchiefs with a picture of the England team printed on them could be bought in 1886.[109] For the weekend players themselves, in 1880 Lewis's in Manchester was selling football jerseys for 3s. 11d., knicker-bockers at 6s. 9d., and stockings at 1s. 9d.[110]

Tennis, a sport of the middle classes, had even more possibilities for fashionable playing wear. Men wore the same sort of clothes as they did at the seaside: flannels, striped blazers, open-necked shirts. Women, again as they did at the seaside, wore their everyday clothes, barely modified at all. When tennis was first played, in the 1870s and 1880s, this meant corsets, petticoats and trimmed, decorated frocks that were cut narrowly down to the knee and of course included a dress-improver (bustle), with the entire outfit finished off with a hat. A lady's magazine in 1879 suggested that 'a cream merino bodice with long sleeves edged with embroidery; skirt with deep kilting, over it an old-gold silk blouse-tunic with short wide sleeves and square neck', together with 'a large straw hat of the coal-scuttle type', was an eminently suitable outfit for the game.[111] The only specialist accompaniments were the new rubber-soled shoes, although for women until the 1880s these continued to have leather uppers, and even heels.[112]

England vs. Scotland in 1872. The two teams are now differ-entiated by different-coloured jerseys, with badges: a leopard for England and a lion for Scotland. Head-gear appears to be optional. The player in front has elastic-sided boots instead of laces (see p. 93).

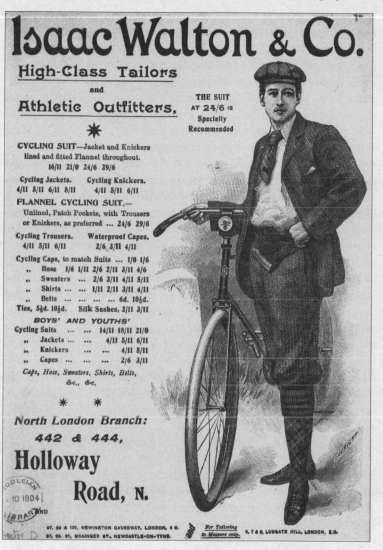

By 1900, cycling clothes were part of the huge market in sports clothes and equipment for the amateur.

The upper classes also had specialized gear for hunting, shooting, riding in town and country – each had its own required dress. But for the middle classes and below it was really with the arrival of the Ordinary, and then the Safety Bicycle, that first clothes for men, then for women, saw great changes. For cycling, men began by wearing close-fitting suits, usually made of flannel. In the 1880s Lewis's of Liverpool was advertising 'Lewis's splendid bicycle suits'. When women began to cycle in the parks, appropriate wear was a skirt that could be turned up at the ankle and fastened, to give the freedom to pedal without the fabric becoming enmeshed in the wheels. But by the late 1880s more was considered necessary. Professor Hoffmann's 1887 *Tips for Tricyclists* insisted that 'the only truly hygienic system of dress is the "all woollen",' and promoted for both men and women the clothes advertised by the CTC as 'at once neat, sanitary and durable'. Tweed was best for the outer garments, with flannel underneath. Men might wear a jacket, knicker-bockers or trousers, a waistcoat or a sweater, a flannel shirt, suspenders, gaiters, a helmet or a straw hat (with club ribbon), stockings, a handker-chief and a scarf. The Professor did worry that an 'ordinary linen collar . . . usually becomes a limp and flabby rag before the rider has passed his fifth milestone', while a flannel collar 'has a rather slovenly appearance in the coffee room of a hotel afterwards. The wheelman may meet both conditions by wearing a woollen collar to match his shirt while actually riding and carrying in his bag a celluloid collar for evening use.' For women cyclists, he suggested a 'coat bodice' or Norfolk jacket and a skirt, with knickerbockers or trousers to be worn underneath, wool combi-nations (all-in-one underwear), gloves, stockings, a hat or helmet, a handkerchief and that finishing touch, a 76-centimetre muffler.[113]

By the 1890s, tailor-made suits for women were replacing dresses for everyday wear as well as for sport. These consisted of a shirt with a stiff collar and tie, a heavy leather belt, a long skirt, and an underskirt finished with leather to protect against the mud. In 1887 *Woman's World* recom-mended something similar for cyclists:

> Practical experience has taught that the prettiest and most suit-able dress is a skirt of tweed or flannel of some dark shade, made ordinary walking length and width, with a deep kilting, well taped down, and drapery stitched down to prevent its blowing into the wheels. This skirt should be worn with neither steels [stays] nor dress-improver [bustle], but be well tied back with

elastic, and fastened with buttons to the round bodice, to throw all the weight upon the shoulders. Shoes must be worn, not boots; and the hat should be a plain sailor straw, or a felt hat, without more adornment than a wing or a club ribbon ... A plain Norfolk jacket for cold weather completes the whole. A linen collar, or tiny frill, fastened by a plain brooch, finishes this pretty and trim costume.[114]

By 1894 *Punch* was mocking that fearsome thing, the lady in bloomers: she wore knickerbockers, a Norfolk jacket, a trilby, black stockings, and a shirt and tie. All very worrying for those who wanted ladies to be ladies. But fashionable shops were not going to lose potential customers, and by the turn of the century Burberry was promoting a coat and skirt which 'unites the freedom in the upper part of a Norfolk jacket with expanding pleats, and the smartness below the waist of a skirted coat', while Harrod's sold cycling and golf knickers, with a band below the knee and a back opening, lined in pink flannelette, calico, nainsook or 'nun's-veiling'. Cyclists were also offered black serge knickers with a chamois-leather seat, or the 'Rideasy Skirt', which was divided at the back, to hang down modestly when cycling.[115] (Hilda Wade was wearing something similar on her wild Rhodesian ride.) The market was large enough that shopfitting companies found it profitable to sell 'position' mannequins to display various types of sporting wear, or more specialized Cycle Figures, which could be mounted on a real bicycle in a shop window.[116]

For it was now clear to everyone that the real money was not in professional sports. The great commercial market for sporting goods lay with the amateurs, the hundreds of thousands of consumers who were happy to purchase their leisure from the tens of thousands of manufacturers who were equally happy to supply them. Many sporting goods had been manufactured for decades, or even centuries, but almost all of them were improved by new technology, and were being made more cheaply by a shift to mass production. Others, like the bicycle, had emerged out of nowhere, and created an industry. Even the most cursory summary of the development of sports equipment gives an indication of the vast changes that had taken place and transformed the market over the last half-century. Gutta-percha balls, with better distance and more reliable flight, replaced feather-packed balls and altered golf out of all recognition, as did iron- and steel-working improvements for the

NECESSITIES OF LIFE.

By 1895 the enormous amount of sporting equipment owned by the amateur was satirized in *Punch*.

clubs. Tennis, a sport that, like cycling, had been created from scratch in the 1870s, benefited from vulcanized rubber balls. Football used the new inner tube for its balls.[117] All three of these sports, and a dozen others besides, were transformed by improved rollers and lawnmowers, which produced even surfaces to play on. The breech-loading gun, copper percussion caps and self-contained, central-fire cartridges made guns more reliable, and shooting less dangerous.[118] Cyclists enjoyed innovations in metalworking that gave them stronger, lighter bicycles, and dozens of accessories of greater or lesser necessity: cycle lamps, cyclometers, bells, pumps, mudguards, gear-cases, brake sets, adjustable wrenches, tool bags, carriers, baskets. By the end of the century, 1 million cycles had been built; by the early twentieth century, golfers were spending £4.7 million a year on their sport. William Shillcock, whose company sold 40,000 to 50,000 footballs a year, said that football outfitting was 'a great and profitable industry'.[119] Not a sport. An industry.

12

Visions of Sugar Plums:
A Christmas Coda

THE CHRISTMAS FAMILY-PARTY that we mean, is not a mere assemblage of relations, got up at a week or two's notice, originating this year, having no family precedent in the last, and not likely to be repeated in the next. No. It is an annual gathering of all the accessible members of the family, young or old, rich or poor; and all the children look forward to it, for two months beforehand, in a fever of anticipation. Formerly, it was held at grandpapa's; but grandpapa getting old, and grandmamma getting old too, and rather infirm, they have given up house-keeping, and domesticated themselves with uncle George; so, the party always takes place at uncle George's house, but grandmamma sends in most of the good things, and grandpapa always *will* toddle down, all the way to Newgate-market, to buy the turkey, which he engages a porter to bring home behind him in triumph, always insisting on the man's being rewarded with a glass of spirits, over and above his hire, to drink 'a merry Christmas and a happy new year' to aunt George. As to grandmamma, she is very secret and mysterious for two or three days beforehand, but not sufficiently so, to prevent rumours getting afloat that she has purchased a beautiful new cap with pink ribbons for each of the servants, together with sundry books, and pen-knives, and pencil-cases, for the younger branches; to say nothing of divers secret additions to the order originally given by aunt George at the pastry-cook's, such as another dozen of mince-pies for the dinner, and a large plum-cake for the children.

On Christmas-eve, grandmamma is always in excellent spirits, and after employing all the children, during the day, in stoning the plums, and all that, insists, regularly every year, on uncle George coming down into the kitchen, taking off his coat, and stirring the pudding for half an hour or so, which uncle George good-humouredly does, to the vociferous delight of the children and servants. The evening concludes with a glorious game of blind-man's-buff, in an early stage of which grandpapa takes great care to be caught, in order that he may have an opportunity of displaying his dexterity.

On the following morning, the old couple, with as many of the children as the pew will hold, go to church in great state . . . When the church-party return to lunch, grandpapa produces a small sprig of mistletoe from his pocket, and tempts the boys to kiss their little cousins under it – a proceeding which affords both the boys and the old gentleman unlimited satisfaction, but which rather outrages grandmamma's ideas of decorum, until grandpapa says, that when he was just thirteen years and three months old, *he* kissed grandmamma under a mistletoe too, on which the children clap their hands, and laugh very heartily, as do aunt George and uncle George; and grandmamma looks pleased, and says, with a benevolent smile, that grandpapa was an impudent young dog, on which the children laugh very heartily again, and grandpapa more heartily than any of them.

. . . A hesitating double knock at the street-door, heard during a momentary pause in the conversation, excites a general inquiry of 'Who's that?' and two or three children, who have been standing at the window, announce in a low voice, that it's 'poor aunt Margaret'. Upon which, aunt George leaves the room to welcome the new-comer; and grandmamma draws herself up, rather stiff and stately; for Margaret married a poor man without her consent, and poverty not being a sufficiently weighty punishment for her offence, has been discarded by her friends, and debarred the society of her dearest relatives. But Christmas has come round, and the unkind feelings that have struggled against better dispositions during the year, have melted away before its genial influence, like half-formed ice beneath the morning sun . . .

As to the dinner, it's perfectly delightful – nothing goes wrong, and everybody is in the very best of spirits, and disposed to please and be pleased. Grandpapa relates a circumstantial account of the purchase of the turkey, with a slight digression relative to the purchase of previous turkeys, on former Christmas-days, which grandmamma corroborates in the minutest particular. Uncle George tells stories, and carves poultry, and takes wine, and jokes with the children at the side-table, and winks at the cousins that are making love, or being made love to, and exhilarates everybody with his good humour and hospitality; and when, at last, a stout servant staggers in with a gigantic pudding, with a sprig of holly in the top, there is such a laughing, and shouting, and clapping of little chubby hands, and kicking up of fat dumpy legs, as can only be equalled by the applause with which the astonishing feat of pouring lighted brandy into mince-pies, is received by the younger visitors. Then the dessert! – and the wine! – and the fun! Such beautiful speeches, and *such* songs, from aunt Margaret's husband, who turns out to be such a nice man, and *so* attentive to grand-mamma! Even grandpapa not only sings his annual song with unprecedented vigour, but on being honoured with an unani-mous *encore*, according to annual custom, actually comes out with a new one which nobody but grandmamma ever heard before; and a young scapegrace of a cousin, who has been in some disgrace with the old people, for certain heinous sins of omission and commission – neglecting to call, and persisting in drinking Burton Ale – astonishes everybody into convulsions of laughter by volunteering the most extraordinary comic songs that ever were heard. And thus the evening passes, in a strain of rational good-will and cheerfulness, doing more to awaken the sympathies of every member of the party in behalf of his neigh-bour, and to perpetuate their good feeling during the ensuing year, than half the homilies that have ever been written, by half the Divines that have ever lived.[1]

Should one want to find the ultimate Christmas celebration, the oldest traditions, the most cherished customs, surely Dickens is the author to turn to. The problem is that when Dickens described Uncle and Aunt George's Christmas in 1837–8, most of these traditions were barely traditions at all. Dickens described a festival of continuity (it was 'an annual gathering') even as he noted the newness of his traditions (the celebration had only recently moved to Uncle George's, which had immediately become the place where it 'always' is). Some of the standard markers of the festival were already in place: family parties, mistletoe and holly, churchgoing and benevolence to poor relations, entertain-ment, and food – turkey, plum pudding and mince pies. Yet just as many traditional Christmas symbols were missing: there was no tree, no carols, no cards, no stockings, no crackers, no Father Christmas and, perhaps most surprisingly, no presents, apart from those given to ser-vants, and tokens to the children.

Dickens was, in fact, on the cusp of the great changes that were coming, and when he began to write (and the above extract is from one of his very earliest works) the 'traditions' for this 'traditional' festival were still in the process of being created. From the seventeenth century, Christmas had been in hibernation. A few magazines and journals had references to the festivity in the eighteenth century, but the holiday was of little importance in the secular calendar. Between 1790 and 1836 *The Times* made no mention of Christmas at all in twenty of those forty-seven years, and in the other twenty-seven the references were cursory.[2] In 1824 the *Gentleman's Magazine* dismissed Christmas as for the 'middling ranks' alone.[3] Certainly the upper class seemed to disregard the importance of the day. In 1833 a routine meeting of the Committee of the Carlton Club was scheduled for Christmas Day: only three members attended, it is true, but the absences were not marked down as the result of the day. In 1837 the Court Circular listed a meeting between the Commander of the Forces and the Colonial Secretary on 25 December – once more, an entirely routine engagement, not an emergency session.[4]

Until the mid-1830s Christmas had not taken hold of the popular imagination. When it did, it was rather like those mythic sports of the rural past. The holiday was presented as a re-creation of what in fact had never existed: an idealized, prettified past was summoned up for nostalgic appreciation. Some of this was an attempt – perhaps not entirely conscious – to eradicate a few of the rougher elements of Twelfth Night, the Feast of Epiphany on 6 January, which had previously been the winter festival that was more commonly celebrated. Twelfth Night was for many a family feast, when all gathered to eat together. A bean and a pea were traditionally baked into the Twelfth Night cake, and the lucky recipients of the tokens became the King and Queen of Twelfth Night, harking back to the earlier custom of choosing a seasonal Lord of Misrule for the winter festival. Some remnant of that idea was still, occasionally, to be found on the streets. As late as the 1820s one writer warned:

> Let all idle gazers in the streets of London, beware Twelfth Night! There is then, that spirit of mischief abroad which carried on without the superintending power of the Lord of Misrule, exhibits itself in the catching of the coat tails, of the unsuspecting passer-by, and fixing them to a nail, or such like as may be available on the frame of a door or window ... [with] some

other part of the garment of a person of the opposite sex, so neither can be freed.[5]

But, while a few may have enjoyed these pastimes, the population at large no longer participated.

For many, much of the increasing fondness for Christmas as a holiday depended on an equivalent increase in leisure time. As was discussed in Chapter 6, the early part of the nineteenth century at first saw a contraction of the number of days given over to religious festivals. By 1871 the Bank Holiday Act gave bank employees Boxing Day off; the Holiday Extension Act of 1875 extended bank holidays from bank employees alone to many government offices. Much of the population happily followed suit. Until then, Christmas was largely still a festival for those who controlled their own working hours. Even so, the upper classes were slower to take this festival to their hearts. Through the diary entries of Lady Amberley for 25 December one can track the gradual creeping of Christmas upwards long after it had become the central family festival for much of the population.* In 1868 Lady Amberley recorded, 'the same as usual, a rainy afternoon so we did our work first till 5 and then had a nice long talk the whole evening.' In 1870 things were 'just the same as any other day; except that we had a plum-pudding'; yet by the following year Lord Amberley was 'dressed up as Knicht [*sic*] Ruprecht in an Inverness coat, conical hat and long grey beard, birch rod and green . . . bag full of toys on his shoulder'.[6]† Quite a journey in three years.

Although Knecht Ruprecht was an unusual representation of Christmas, it was perhaps significant that the Amberleys chose a German custom to mark the festival, because the most important, and most long-lasting, representation of Christmas was also German: the decorated pine tree. Possibly the first surviving reference to a Christmas tree in the British Isles appears in *Court and Private Life in the Time of Queen Charlotte, being the Journals of Mrs Papendieck*, published in 1789. Mrs Papendieck, the wife of a minor court official, mentioned that there had been a

---

* Lord Amberley was at the heart of the British Establishment, although of heterodox views. He was the son of the prime minister Lord John Russell, and the father of the philosopher Bertrand Russell.
† Knecht ['Servant'] Ruprecht was, in the German Christmas tradition, one of St Nicholas's helpers – sometimes a demon who punished bad children, sometimes just a more general attendant.

discussion about having a lighted tree, 'according to the German fashion'. Given the still strongly German atmosphere of the Hanoverian court, this is perhaps not a surprising place for the custom to bob up, but for the next forty-two years nothing more was heard of decorated trees. Then there was a mention in 1831 that a Swiss governess had introduced the custom into the house of her employers in Durham. And around the same time the German merchants in Manchester (whose descendants would later in the century hire Charles Hallé to conduct for them) were becoming famous for putting up trees in their own houses. One observer mentioned 'pine tops being brought to market for the purpose, which are generally illuminated with a paper for every day in the year'. By 1840 the Regius Professor of Medicine at Oxford told a friend that he knew of someone who was 'going to have a Christmas tree at Roehampton tonight', and he did not feel any need to explain what a 'Christmas tree' was: he expected his correspondent to be familiar with the custom.[7]

By 1844 a pamphlet called *The Christmas Tree* was promoting 'the great event celebrated in the cheerful festival of the Christmas Tree . . . The German form of celebrating Christmas Even [*sic*], by an illuminated tree, has long been well known to a few in England; especially to persons in any way connected with the old court. It now seems likely to become a naturalised plant.'[8] This blithe reference to the custom having 'long been well known' was, nonetheless, still fairly wide of the mark. Victoria and Albert, who were to push the Christmas tree into the forefront of seasonal celebrations – to the point where Albert is often mistakenly assumed to be the man who introduced the tree into Britain – had their own tree for the first time in 1840. In 1845 the *Illustrated London News*, very *au courant* with the fashions of the world, thought it necessary to explain the custom: a party at the London Mission Hall was

> crowned by the exhibition of a German Christmas Tree or Tree of Love . . . This is the usual mode of celebrating the Eve of the birth of Christ, in Germany and on the Continent. In almost every family is set up this pleasing figure, having the resemblance of a growing tree, loaded with a profusion of fruits and flowers; and upon its branches, the different members of the family suspend the little presents which they intend for those they love best; and on the Exhibition of the Tree, the presents are claimed by the donors, and handed, with compliments, to their friends.[9]

Three years later, the magazine printed an illustration of Queen Victoria and her family grouped around their own tree.[10]

Now everyone knew what a Christmas tree was, and shops in particular seemed to have picked up on the possibilities. Charles Manby Smith noticed the custom, in 1853, of Christmas trees 'loaded with fruit, oranges, lemons, and clustered grapes, and liberally adorned with imitative flowers and wreaths. The confectioners purchase these trees, and load the branches with choice delicacies . . . and will present each member of a customer's family with an appropriate token of affectionate remembrance.'[11] The tree as a source of presents spread quickly by these commercial displays. Dickens – who else? – turned this 'pretty German toy' into a full-fledged English institution in 1854:

> I have been looking on this evening at a merry company of children assembled around that pretty German toy, a Christmas Tree. The tree was planted in the middle of a great round table, and towered high above their heads. It was brilliantly lighted by a multitude of little tapers; and everywhere sparkled and glittered with bright objects. There were rosy cheeked dolls, hiding behind the green leaves; and there were real watches (with movable hands at least, and an endless capacity of being wound up) dangling from innumerable twigs; there were French polished tables, chairs, bedsteads, wardrobes, eight day clocks, and various other articles of domestic furniture (wonderfully made, in tin, at Wolverhampton), perched among the boughs, as if in preparation for some fairy housekeeping; there were jolly, broad faced little men . . . [whose] heads took off, and showed them to be full of sugar plums; there were fiddles and drums . . . there were teetotums, humming tops, needle-cases, pen-wipers, smelling-bottles, conversation cards, bouquet-holders, real fruits, made artificially dazzling with goldleaf; imitation apples, pears and walnuts, crammed with surprise; in short, as a pretty child before me, delightedly whispered to another pretty child . . . 'There was everything, and more.'[12]

Or, as a modern observer might note, the tree had become a commercial opportunity.

Dickens had mentioned few presents seventeen years before. Now his tree was just a background and foil to the sweets, toys, flowers, fruit, jewellery and elaborate knick-knacks which hung on its branches or were placed underneath. Trees, which had to be bought, replaced in importance earlier festive decorations such as holly and ivy and other greenery, which could be gathered without payment in the rural communities of pre-industrial times. Then the central decoration was the 'kissing bough', a number of branches bundled together, adorned with mistletoe, tinsel, and maybe nuts and fruit, and perhaps lighted candles.[13] This was a country custom, and often considered suitable only for rustics and servants in the early part of the nineteenth century, but by the 1850s *Punch* signalled its entry into the middle-class consciousness with regular cartoons about mistletoe capers. The primacy of the tree, and its naturalization, was so complete that by 1860 one writer on Christmas customs simply thought that mistletoe, because of its pagan origin, was a strange thing to find 'as a Christmas tree'.[14] Yet, while the tree was new, mistletoe, and carols about holly and ivy, could be traced back to the thirteenth century.

These carols were yet another tradition that had not featured in Dickens's 1837 Christmas party: Grandpapa sang his annual song, and a cousin sang a comic number, but these were not mentioned as having any seasonal content. Six years later, not only was Dickens's (perhaps) most famous story entitled 'A Christmas *Carol*', but carol singers were mentioned in it in passing, as though they had always existed.* Most carols had been written between 1400 and the 1640s, dying out as the Puritan attitude to Christmas saw them fade from common knowledge. There was a partial revival at the Restoration, although most of the carols that were printed in the seventeenth and eighteenth centuries were about feasting, rather than Christmas. Two of the very few 'real' carols that were written in that period were 'While Shepherds Watched their Flocks', written in 1698 by Nahum Tate, the poet laureate (whose claim to fame will probably always be his rewriting of *King Lear* to give it a happy ending) and 'Hark! the herald-angels sing', based on a poem by Charles Wesley which appeared in 1782, although our current melody is nineteenth century, by Mendelssohn.

In the early nineteenth century the antiquarians began to search out the old carols, and in 1822 the first modern collection of traditional carols, *Christmas Carols Ancient and Modern*, was put together by Davies

---

* Which surely helped to spread the notion even further: the story sold 15,000 copies in its first year, and it went on selling throughout the century. Even those who did not necessarily read would have known of it: forty years after it was first published, nine stage versions appeared in London alone in one single year.[15]

Gilbert, an MP of antiquarian bent.* It was popular enough that a second edition was published the following year, but Gilbert's presentation of the carols did not alter: he thought that, apart from antiquarian research, carols were entirely dead, and all that could be done now was to collect and preserve the remnants. Singing was not part of his programme. William Sandys, a solicitor, had collaborated with him on this book, and in 1833 he produced his own collection; he too thought carols survived in just a few remote locations, and were 'more neglected every year'.[17] However, had they looked to the urban working classes, instead of to the shrinking agricultural communities, they would have found that one redoubt against complete extinction was holding firm. Carols appeared without intermission in the broadsides printed by men like James Catnach (p. 177). The Christmas broadsides were routinely printed on double-sized sheets, with three or four carols, a scriptural episode, a few highly coloured woodcuts, possibly with some Twelfth Night characters, and a title like 'Faith, Hope and Charity'.[18] The patterers sang the carols through for their customers, handing on the traditional tunes in this way.

Outside this working-class oral tradition, by the time *A Christmas Carol* appeared, the word 'carol' had come to mean hymns more generally. Others used 'carols' to mean any writings with a Christmas theme: *Christmas Carols: A Sacred Gift* (1848) was a collection of poems about the Nativity, with no music at all. It was only in the 1850s that musicians joined together with the antiquarians and the revival of carol singing really took off. William Chappell published two volumes of carols with their traditional tunes in 1855–9, and in the 1860s Chappell's co-founder of the Musical Antiquity Society, E. F. Rimbault, also produced further collections.[19] These publications meshed very neatly with the arrival of the piano in more middle-class houses: families could now gather around the piano and carol away together.

The togetherness was important. As public-school education spread

---

* Calling him just this does his reputation a great disservice. Davies Gilbert (1767–1839) was an extraordinary character, a facilitator and administrator who influenced much behind the scenes. Born to a clergyman in Cornwall, Gilbert took a degree in mathematics and astronomy at Oxford, offering encouragement to a young scientist from Cornwall named Humphry Davy. His mathematical skills were used to look at the efficiency of the compound steam engine, the design of the rotary engine, and even Richard Trevithick's high-pressure steam engine. Thomas Telford's design for the Menai suspension bridge was adapted after Gilbert published his calculations on the relationship between the maximum tension in the chains and the depth of curvature of the suspension; his methods of calculating strength remained the norm for suspension bridges for the next hundred years.[16]

to more of the middle classes during the century, as industrialization and the railways made working hundreds of miles away from home more likely for the working classes, family reunions became increasingly valued. In 1843 in *A Christmas Carol*, Dickens superimposed contemporary feelings on the childhood of Scrooge, who was taken by the Ghost of Christmas Past to see himself, small, unloved and friendless, left all alone at school during the Christmas holidays. This was much more of a reality from the middle of the nineteenth century, but by then the railways had also brought the possibility of travelling home for the holidays, whether from school or from work. Servants were the least likely to travel home: increased home-based festivities for their employers made their presence on Christmas Day a necessity. Hannah Cullwick, a maid-of-all-work, wrote in 1872, after more than a quarter of a century in service, 'I often think what a most delightful pleasure that must be, going home for Christmas, but I've never once had it.'[20] For other workers, the speed of the trains made a short visit feasible, and the cost of an excursion ticket ensured it was economically within reach. By 1900 almost all shops and offices were shut on Boxing Day as well as Christmas Day, to allow workers to spend time with their families.[21] (Unlike today, they could travel on Christmas Day: throughout the nineteenth century the trains ran on 25 December.) In 1912 *Railway Magazine* calculated that between 1861 and 1912 during Christmas week some companies saw five times the level of regular traffic.[22]

While many travelled home for the holidays, one Christmas visitor was still absent. Father Christmas had yet to arrive on the scene. After the Reformation, St Nicholas, who had been a popular saint – over four hundred churches were dedicated to his name in England – vanished from the calendar, and instead Old Christmas, or Sir Christmas, was invoked as a spirit of the season. Pictures in the *Illustrated London News* in the late 1840s showed a thin old man, bearded and a bit droopy, more like our notions of Father Time. In 1868 Planché published three Christmas plays for 'Amateurs who were desirous of varying the usual character of Christmas Entertainments'.* The three plays were entitled

---

* Even at this date, there was not a carol in sight. Planché chose songs that were 'principally old national melodies or ballads, and snatches from operas equally familiar to the general ear', including 'Se vuol ballare' from *The Marriage of Figaro* and 'Va, pensiero, sull' ali dorate' from *Nabucco*; the traditional songs 'Begone Dull Care' and 'Cheer, Boys, Cheer'; and a 'Gavotte de Vestris', which was most probably, given Planché's working relationship with her, a song from a show in which Mme Vestris was currently appearing.

'Stirring the Pudding (a Mirthful Morality for Christmas Eve)', 'The Compliments of the Season (a Fancy-ful Interlude for New Year's Eve)' and 'The King of the Bean (A Mediaeval Masque for Twelfth Night)'. In 'The Compliments of the Season' the character of Christmas is given a 'Long white robe, trimmed with white fur, and bordered with holly, ivy, and mistletoe; a broad belt over right shoulder, studded with mince pies; shoulder knots made of sausages; cap in the shape and painted like a plum pudding with a twig of holly stuck in the top, and a garland of holly round the base of it; a bough of holly in his hand; face highly coloured; with ample white beard': he is a mixture of symbols of feasting, of plenty and of seasonal greenery.[23]

It was not until the late 1880s that the American Santa Claus was imported, to be melded with Old Christmas and transformed into Father Christmas, the jolly, red-robed figure of much of the twentieth century. In the USA the 1800s had seen the Dutch Sinterklaas become the American Santa Claus, who travelled the world on Christmas Eve instead of 6 December (the original saint's day of St Nicholas); by the 1820s he had picked up a sleigh and reindeer, and by 1870 he was wearing the red hooded robes of a bishop. These were soon turned into a red jumpsuit in America, but Father Christmas remained more traditionally dressed in Britain for some time. Part of his appeal, part of the reason this symbol was so quickly adopted, was that he fed into two streams that were running increasingly strongly in the nineteenth century: Father Christmas was part of the home-based, domestic holiday (Father Christmas came to each house, he was not visited elsewhere), and he was a symbol of giving, of rewards for doing (and being) good. The Victorian world of public philanthropy was wonderfully quick at assimilating this representation into its own work. By the 1890s charity ladies were dressing up as Father Christmas to hand out Christmas gifts to 'deserving' children, and the *Santa Claus Gazette* appeared, 'The Official Organ of the "Santa Claus" Christmas Distribution Fund', while every New Year's Eve the Fund's charitable workers dressed up as Santas to give gifts to the poor. This was no small group of eccentrics: In 1910 they handed out 10,000 parcels.[24]

For charity had become a major component of the middle-class Christmas. It almost seemed as if, as middle-class homes became more filled with Christmas goods, there was an equivalent need to look outward to those who had less. In 1837 *The Times* noted that the 'Houses

Old Christmas, in 1848, has a yule log on his back, and is wearing a crown of holly. His punch-bowl is a sign of the celebratory nature of the season, but he has not yet begun to have the jovial appearance that, as Father Christmas, he would develop in the 1870s and 1880s.

of Correction' were making 'not the slightest relaxation in discipline or addition of diet' for Christmas Day, although as a concession the treadmill had been stopped.[25] Only a few years later, in 1842, an overall instruction was given by the Poor Law Board that on Christmas Day (and Good Friday) workhouses must expect no work except housework to be performed by the paupers. In 1847 the Board also added a rider that the local guardians were now at liberty to dole out extra food to the workhouse inmates if they so desired, to be paid for by the ratepayers; in 1864 in Chepstow this seasonal cheer consisted of 'a modicum of tea and sugar wherewith to regale themselves'.[26] But by this time the expectation of providing Christmas cheer to the inmates was regarded as natural, and sometimes took elaborate forms. In January 1862 the *Illustrated London News* ran an article on the treats the Greenwich workhouse had provided. Some of the traditions continued to hark back to previous times – the celebration, despite being called 'Christmas', was

STRANGERS.

FATHER CHRISTMAS. "WHAT! NOT KNOW *ME!*—OH, THIS MUST BE ALTERED!"

By 1883 Father Christmas has definitely arrived, wearing his bishop's robes and holding a staff topped by a Christmas tree. This illustration from *Punch* stresses his charitable function, as he brings food (there are two birds in his basket) for the poor.

actually held on Twelfth Night, and the presents the paupers received were called 'New Year's gifts'. Some traditions, however, were new – the room was decorated with Christmas trees.[27]

If the inmates of the workhouses were given parties, it is unsurprising that working men earning decent livings also wanted to celebrate. In Manchester, at the Mechanics' Institute, from the 1830s Christmas parties were staged by and for the members, and over the next quarter of a century they became more and more elaborate. They had begun humbly enough. In 1832 it was suggested that 'a mutual improvement society' might be set up to encourage members to attend more classes, and in 1833 'Christmas and its Customs' was one of the talks given by the society, followed by a party with a 'substantial repast'.* In 1838 a miracle play was staged, then a lecture 'On Christmas in the Olden Time' was given, and supper followed. This was only the beginning: in 1840, 600 guests attended the lecture, given by Benjamin Heywood, a philanthropist and chairman of the Institute, then everyone moved across to the town hall for 'festivities'. In 1844 Old Christmas made his first appearance, and a procession of 'ambassadors of various ages and nations' was staged. At the 1847 party there were 3,100 guests, including the mayor. A medieval banquet was served, complete with boar's head, and costumes courtesy of a local theatre company (except the 'helmets, partizans and halberds', which curiously enough were loaned by the police force). Both Old Christmas and a Christmas Prince were represented, together with a number of now-traditional symbols: mistletoe, a burning Christmas pudding, and a tree (this might even have been its first appearance at the Institute). In 1851 the plays added yet more nostalgia to the running medieval theme, with 'a scene of village life' showing 'old-time' sports. But suddenly the party began to decline in popularity. It may not be coincidental that it was in this decade that more emphasis was being laid on celebrating within the family circle. The masques were discontinued, and the event became a small social event in a calendar that was more concerned with other forms of charitable giving.[28]

Throughout these mid-century decades, newspapers printed Christmas appeals for donations, for the deserving poor, for the sick, for the elderly. In 1868 the *Baptist Magazine* approached Christmas as an entirely charitable time, and advertised that it had 10,000 gifts available to give

* As with the workhouse parties, these celebrations were generally held in January of the following year.

to the needy – many Nonconformists rejected all Christmas celebrations, and the magazine found that stressing charitable giving as the centrepiece of Christmas was a good way of helping its readers to avoid the 'Popish' superstitions the holiday represented.[29] Other magazines similarly became conduits for charitable Christmas campaigns. The *Children's League of Pity Paper* and the *Band of Mercy Advocate* had a number of year-round fund-raising projects – for a cot in a hospital, a lifeboat, or other worthwhile causes – but they always mounted special Christmas campaigns. *Young Man* had a fund for Christmas dinners for hungry children, while girls' magazines ran competitions for home-sewn donations of warm clothing.[30] These were matched by articles in the mainstream press that depicted the poor dining sumptuously, courtesy of this or that benevolent society. *The Times*, in 1877, told how

> Cow Cross Mission collected one hundred and fifty little mud-larks to act as beefeaters on Christmas day. They were arranged according to sex at two long tables on which were knives and forks, water cups, and hunks of bread. In less than a couple of minutes the whole of the bread was eaten. Immediately after-wards large joints of beef and pork were brought in and great sieves of potatoes. These were soon cut up by half a dozen carvers, with numbers of ladies and gentlemen acting as waiters. There was no stint of either meat or plum pudding, everyone being allowed to come as often as he or she liked, and many sly bits of meat and pudding were slipped into pinafores and caps to take home.[31]

Such meals were an attempt to create for the paupers a semblance of the domestic felicity now found at a family Christmas dinner, which for many was the centrepiece of the festivities. In 1853 Charles Manby Smith wrote about Christmas presents, and then immediately dismissed them: 'But . . . these are very minor and subordinate preparations. Eating and drinking, after all, are the chief and paramount obligations of the Christ-mas season.'[32] Obligations, mind. He was using the word with a journal-istic flourish, but he didn't think it was too overstated. As with every other tradition, the Christmas dinner had also mutated over the century. Plum pudding had at some stage replaced the earlier plum porridge, a beef broth thickened with bread and enriched with dried fruit, wine and spices. This had been a staple in the eighteenth century – 'Everyone', wrote a French visitor at the time, 'from the King to the artisan eats soup

Phiz, Dickens' illustrator, depicts a typical scene in 1850: the Goose Club, commonly organized by a publican. Customers paid in to a fund all year, in order that at Christmas each might take home a bird.

and Christmas pies. The soup is called Christmas-porridge, and is a dish few foreigners find to their taste.'[33] Twelfth Night cakes with their bean and pea tokens had long been traditional, and continued to appear well into the nineteenth century, when the bean, the pea and the iced fruitcake were seamlessly transferred into the new Christmas cake. By 1840 the Twelfth Night cake was no more.

Both the cakes and the mince pies depended on the richness of dried fruits, which until the steamships and railways of the nineteenth century had been both rare and expensive – prime luxury goods. Railways also brought down the price of the main course, which traditionally had been goose. Many of the working classes belonged to paying-in clubs, usually run out of their local pubs. At the end of the year a lottery was held, and all received the goose they had paid for, with the holder of the winning ticket given the fattest bird. Turkeys were only slowly becoming more common: for many purchasers they were still far too expensive, as the birds did not travel well. In the early nineteenth century turkeys were reared for the most part in East Anglia, and were driven down to London in August, wearing little leather boots to protect their feet. They started their trek in August because they lost so much weight on their forced march that much of the fattening-up process had to be recommenced once they arrived at their destination. Some were transported by stagecoach, but this meant Norfolk was three days' journey from London. Only with the arrival of the railways did it become feasible to slaughter the birds where they were reared.[34] Goose may have had a better flavour, but the size of the turkeys made them more desirable for the large mid-Victorian family. In *A Christmas Carol* the goose that the Cratchits eat on Christmas Day has to be eked out among the seven of them; when Scrooge becomes a reformed character, he sends a boy to buy them a turkey, an animal that more than goes around.

With the great stress laid on the Christmas feast came additional items for the table. In 1847 a London confectioner, Tom Smith, attempting to create a novelty to distinguish his imported sweets, produced a wrapping that made a small explosion when it was opened. The result, first sold as 'fire-cracker sweets', then as 'Bangs of Expectation', harked back to the Lord of Misrule elements of the old holiday, but soon the sweet vanished and the (fire)cracker took on the form we know, complete with paper hats and trinkets.[35] These tamer, more domesticated objects chimed better with the tone of the sedate, multi-generational gathering that was now looked on with approval, and they became enormously successful: in the 1880s Tom Smith's, now a dedicated cracker manufacturer, had 170 types of cracker for sale, and in the 1890s it was producing 13 million crackers a year.

The type of decorations recommended by women's magazines in the second half of the century completed the bourgeois, domesticated picture: hanging banners that said things like 'A Hundred Thousand Welcomes' or, more straightforwardly, 'Happy Christmas', with the mottoes picked out in cotton wool or tinfoil, or embroidery, or shells or evergreens shaped in the form of letters. By the middle of the century 'fairy lights' were in use: small candles in jars, placed decoratively on the mantelpiece or the dinner table. (By the 1890s electric fairy lights were on show in some of the more advanced houses.) Many of the magazine suggestions at the end of the century were unfeasible for all but the very wealthy, and were probably more the product of a journalist's fevered imagination than a reality. Nevertheless, they do show how the holiday had become a festival of display, of artifice, with the expectation that this would be supplied by bought-in goods. The *Lady* in 1896 suggested that the dinner table might have pieces of mirror laid down the centre, surrounded by scraps of moss, branches of holly and mistletoe, 'and sprays of red-veined tree ivy, in which some electric lamps, or, failing these, fairy lights are half hid', to resemble a 'mimic lake' with illuminated bushes. Out of the greenery 'rise other little trees, and here and there are placed birch-bark canoes, painted with silver paint, and each apparently guided by a "Father Christmas", bright with silver drapery, the boats being freighted with glittering white bon-bons', while the four corners of the table hold four miniature trees – 'in reality the top of a seedling fir gleaming with frostine powder'.[36] Should one choose to take this as having the slightest connection to any arrangement that might in reality appear, the question must arise, where to put the food?

However, the message of these magazines was that theirs was a vision of what Christmas *should* be like: how, if everyone had endless disposable income, things *ought* to look. And the way it ought to look was, apparently, shop-bought. While stories and songs centred on the bliss of domesticity, on how happy families entertained themselves, in fact Christmas was becoming the most commodity-based time of the year. All the games and indoor pastimes that were mentioned were promoted and marketed by magazines; their rules were laid out in magazines, pamphlets and books; riddles, puzzles and charades were not home-created, but published and purchased. Music was played at home, carols were sung at home and in the streets, but the sheet music for carols was now a commercial enterprise, and fashionable seasonal songs were all the rage: 'The Christmas Bazaar Gallopade', 'The Christmas Tree Polka', 'The Christmas Tree Quadrille', 'The Christmas Quadrille for 1865', 'The Christmas Echoes Quadrille', 'The Christmas Box Quadrille', 'King Christmas Quadrille', 'Around the Christmas Tree Quadrille' and 'A Merry Christmas and a Happy New Year Quadrille' were a few out of hundreds that poured off the presses to be purchased.[37]

These seasonal purchases provided pleasant hours for the families at home; they also provided work for the needy, as the increase in business meant a seasonal rise in casual labour. One of the main beneficiaries of the latest Christmas tradition to develop was the Post Office, with the arrival of the Christmas card. These cards and the Post Office were symbiotic developments: until the arrival of the penny post in 1840, sending and receiving Christmas greetings was too expensive to become a mass preoccupation; with the arrival of the seasonal missive, by 1878 the Post Office was seeing a December increase to its income of £20,000 every year – and rising.

A number of different precursors all exerted an influence on the creation of the Christmas card. Firstly, in the eighteenth century, children at school were often required to produce 'writing sheets' or 'Christmas pieces' to show their parents their new handwriting skills. On specially decorated paper bought from printers and stationers, they drew pretty borders and wrote greetings, proverbs and mottoes. The second influence was the Christmas broadside market (above). The final eighteenth-century ancestor was the vogue that sprang up at the end of the century for sentimental cards with lettering and a verse, and perhaps a scrap of cheap lace or ribbon attached, with a message of affection hidden inside: Valentine's Day cards. These were widely available. In *The Pickwick Papers* Sam Weller stops at a stationer's window:

> The particular picture on which Sam Weller's eyes were fixed . . . was a highly coloured representation of a couple of human hearts skewered together with an arrow, cooking before a cheerful fire, while a male and female cannibal in modern attire, the gentle-man being clad in a blue coat and white trousers, and the lady in a deep red pelisse with a parasol of the same, were approaching the meal with hungry eyes, up a serpentine gravel path leading thereunto. A decidedly indelicate young gentleman, in a pair of wings and nothing else, was depicted as superintending the cooking; a representation of the spire of the church in Langham Place, appeared in the distance; and the whole formed a 'valentine', of which, as a written inscription in the window testified, there was a large assortment within, which the shopkeeper pledged himself to dispose of to his countrymen generally, at the reduced rate of one and sixpence each.[39]*

These cards were no passing fad. They grew in popularity until, by 1820, the Post Office estimated that as many as 200,000 cards were being dispatched in February in London alone.[40] Given that valentines were expressions of love, not friendship, it must be assumed that each sender sent only one (or perhaps two, if one is being cynical) each year, so 200,000 cards meant that a lot of people were participating in this custom. The market was certainly large enough to sustain the publication

---

* Sam Weller was looking at a middling kind of card. The price could be as little as ½*d.*, or as much as 5*s.*[38]

of a number of small booklets that appeared in the 1820s, supplying quantities of verses for the unimaginative to inscribe in their cards. They were carefully focused: some for women, such as *Cupid's Garland, or, Love's Annual Resource, A Collection of Original Valentine Verses . . . for Ladies to Declare their Sentiments to Gentlemen*, and some for men, such as *Hymen's Rhapsodies, or Lover's Themes . . . Written expressly for this Work, for Gentlemen to Address Ladies in Sonnets, Superior to any other*. By the 1830s most of the books with valentine verses were now, instead of romance, producing 'Amusing' offerings, or ones 'Calculated to Excite Risibility in all Countenances'. These may have represented a more profitable trend for the card manufacturers – a decent person could send an expression of love to only one person, but comic verses could go to many.

The first Christmas card was produced under the aegis of Henry Cole. In the early 1830s Cole had been given leave from his clerkship at the Record Commission to help Rowland Hill in his campaign for postal reform. Cole, rather brilliantly, came up with the idea of producing a weekly newspaper with news about the campaign: because this was a newspaper, the Post Office was forced to carry without charge propaganda for its own reorganization. Until the reforms were implemented, however, the sender paid a heavy price for the receipt of each letter. An expression of love from a swain in Birmingham might be worth the 9*d.* charge levied by the Post Office on his heart's desire in London, but would Christmas greetings from a friend? The penny post arrived in 1840, and in 1843 Cole commissioned a drawing for a card. The picture was probably produced by the artist and illustrator J. C. Horsley: it showed a family at Christmas dinner toasting 'absent friends', while, in a panel, charity was being administered to the poor.[41] Cole had about a thousand of these cards printed and hand-coloured by a professional colourer; they went on sale at 1*s.* each, but there was no great demand. Instead, printers began to pick up on the older example of the children's Christmas pieces, producing packs of notepaper printed with engravings, with twelve different engravings per set – one for each month of the year. Each sheet had the month engraved along with the picture, but the image with the December sheet did not usually have a Christmas-theme. One that has survived, from 1853, had a seaside picture for December, with a naked child refusing to go into the water and his mother saying, 'Go in, do, you naughty boy.' Others had mottoes like 'Grand-Mothers [*sic*] Love to all the little Children that are good'.[42] These were all-purpose greeting cards, now made viable by the penny post.

In the 1850s a printer in London began to produce cards that were specifically for Christmas, and their design was so similar to the card that Horsley had designed for Cole that this must have been the inspiration. But, again, this was only a small ripple. It was not until printing technology had moved on that cards became more popular. In the 1860s, die-sinking arrived, which meant that decorative embossing could be added to the cards as well as a printed image. Most importantly, in the 1870s it became possible to use chromolithography, first invented in the 1830s, on a large scale to produce mass-coloured prints. Cole and Horsley's original Christmas card, which had sold for 1s. in 1843, was reprinted in 1881 by chromolithography and sold at 3d.

One final factor was necessary before Christmas cards were ready to spread into the mass market, and it occurred at exactly the same time as chromolithography was taken up by most printing firms. This was the arrival of the postcard. To begin with, postcards were small blank cards that could be sent through the post without envelopes, with the address on one side and a space for a brief message on the other. The important point was that they cost half the price of a letter to post, and they were seized on gladly as the perfect way to send brief messages. With multiple postal deliveries each day, for just ½d. a husband could send his wife a postcard at lunchtime to tell her he would be home late that evening. Soon people were sending postcards with Christmas messages on them, and the phrase 'Christmas card' appeared in common speech for the first time.* In 1871 the Christmas Letter Mission was set up by a church group in Brighton, with the aim of sending a Christmas card to every hospital patient in Sussex. By 1881, as a great number of people began to send cards to their nearest and dearest, the sending of charitable cards had increased in a similar fashion. The Christmas Letter Mission became a national charity, posting cards to every hospital patient in the country, and then, in a further expansion of ambition, to every prison and workhouse inmate.[43]

To meet this extraordinary demand, a huge variety of cards appeared for sale. Some had fairy-tale characters like Little Red Riding Hood, or traditional folk characters like Robin Hood; others were humorous –

---

* In the 1880s picture postcards were first produced and if the pictures were seasonal these too became 'Christmas cards'.

'Christmas with Punch and Judy'. Still others were elaborate paper con-structions, some created concertina-style, in which the card came in sections; each page could be bought separately, or as part of a set. There were also 'Rough Rustics', which were illustrations of village children; 'Humorous Gatherings from the Animal World', with 'Three clever sketches – "The Puppy and the Chicken", "The Kitten and the Crab" and "A Very Strange Bird"'; and 'Fairy Glimpses. Highly attractive and pleasing delineations of fairy gambols in sea and air, from original water-colour drawings, by Miss E. G. THOMSON.'[44] In 1884 the first art-reproduction card appeared, with an engraving after Raphael.[45] Few of the cards had religious imagery: most had what were by now the traditional Christmas symbols – plum puddings, holly, mistletoe and Christmas trees. There were a large number of cards – probably even the majority – that were neither seasonal nor religious, showing animals, flowers, seaside pictures and comic images. Other styles of card were not illustrated at all, but instead were heavily decorated, with embossed or lace-bordered paper, or with silk fringes, or tassels, or silk cords. Still others had perfumed strips of cotton wool glued into sachets and sealed inside a doubled card.[46]

In 1883 *The Times* was pleased that this 'new trade' had 'opened up a new field of labour for artists, lithographers, engravers, printers, ink and pasteboard makers'. Even more trades and professions than this benefited. Many book illustrators, including such luminaries as Marcus Ward, Kate Greenaway, Walter Crane and Randolph Caldecott, found in Christmas cards a lucrative new market. Postal workers, too, had a seasonal rise in employment. In 1878, 4.5 million cards were being sent every December – about the same number as went through the system on 14 February.[47] And the Post Office processed far more than mere cards and letters, finding it expedient in 1883 to establish a parcel-post department. When private carriers had been the only way to send parcels, it had been too expensive for many to send tokens home at the end of the year. In the first year of the parcel post, a package weighing 7 pounds cost 1*s*. to dispatch; seven years later, 11 pounds could be sent for 11*d*. – a penny a pound.[48]

There were similar seasonal increases in other businesses, and the need for seasonal labour was felt throughout the large industry that had built up to service the Christmas market. The railways required additional porters as people began to travel for the holidays. Theatres put on special Christmas shows, and more performances meant more backstage crews, more extras onstage. Theatres and shops hired sandwich-board men and bill-stickers to advertise their seasonal products. Some street hawkers came in from the country with seasonal goods – holly, ivy and mistletoe – although it is possible that there was no change to their actual numbers: street sellers were accustomed to rotate their goods seasonally throughout the year. Even if there were no additional sellers, many tradesmen by the end of the century fully expected an increase in their sales in December. In 1895 a Christmas-tree vendor in Covent Garden claimed that he sold 30,000 trees a year.[49] Even if the number was closer to half that amount, it still meant a tidy sum to set aside for his own Christmas presents.

For, by the middle of the century, Christmas shopping had already begun its long march to seasonal domination. In 1856 Nathaniel Hawthorne had noticed that on 20 December a few shops were showing 'some tokens of approaching Christmas'. A decade later, in 1867, *The Times* was carrying its Christmas advertisements and reviews for children's books ten days earlier, on 11 December. This date held for some time: women's magazines did not to run advertisements for seasonal goods until mid-December in the 1880s. But by the 1890s the *Lady* had articles on Christmas shopping at the end of November, and *The Times* began its Christmas advertising on the same date. By the turn of the century, Gamage's department store had its Christmas catalogue printed by October.[50]

In the early part of the century, it was food that had preoccupied many who were shopping for Christmas: as the meal was the heart of the home celebration, so food was the centre of the preparatory shopping. Manby Smith was rhapsodic about the displays:

> There are apples of all hues and sizes, among which the brown russet, the golden bob, and the Ribston pippins, are pre-eminent. Among the pears are the huge winter-pear, the delicious Charmontel, and the bishop's-thumb. Then there are foreign and hot-house grapes ... large English pine-apples, pomegranates, brown biffins from Norfolk, and baskets of soft medlars; Kent cob-nuts, filberts and foreign nuts ... all gaily mingled and mixed up with flowers of all hues, natural and artificial.

He was less enthusiastic, however, about the other types of shopping that were appearing: '"Christmas presents" forms a monster line in the posters on the walls and in the shop-windows. Infantine appeals in gigantic type cover the hoardings. "Do, Papa, Buy Me" so-and-so . . .'[51]

As the century progressed presents came to the fore, and in particular more and more presents were specifically marketed for Christmas: the connection of Christmas with presents was also moving into the world of the shop-bought. New Year's gifts had been common, as were 'boxes' (tips) for servants and tradesmen. But gifts before the early nineteenth century revolved around food or, to a lesser degree, small gifts for children. Perhaps the very first advertisement to suggest that a purchase should be made specifically as 'a present at Christmas' (although it adds the more conventional 'or a New Year's gift') appeared as early as 1728, when 'Famous Anodyne Necklaces' were suggested for 'All God-Fathers, God-Mothers, Relations, Friends, and Acquaintances to give to CHILDREN . . . approved of by the Great Dr Chamberlen for Children's teething fits, fevers convulsions, &c.'[52]

Some New Year's gifts made the move to Christmas quite easily, and some created a niche market of their own. As early as the 1740s books such as *The Merry Medley; or, Christmas-box for Gay Gallants and Good Companions* and *A Christmas-box for Masters and Misses, Consisting of Stories to Improve the Minds of Children* were advertised.[53] But it was not until improved printing technology – especially for the illustrations – arrived in the nineteenth century that gift books became standard Christmas gifts. In 1823 the book- and print-seller Rudolph Ackermann published *Forget Me Not, A Christmas and New Year's Present for 1823*. It was a great success, and by 1825 there was competition from another nine annuals; by 1831 there were sixty-two. The content of all the annuals was similar – literary pieces, whether essays, stories or poetry, often commissioned from some of the most famous writers of the period; travel writing; and pretty engravings. The selling point was not really the contents. Instead, the annuals sold because they were beautifully bound, often with silk ribbon markers, and with the engravings printed lavishly on expensive paper. It was as luxury objects that they became ubiquitous in fashionable homes. The *Keepsake*, one of the most successful, had a presentation plate at the front, which made it clear that these books were entirely to be given as gifts. A review of another, *The Winter's Wreath*, in the *Athenaeum* commended it for having a binding 'that excels that of any Annual which we have yet seen; and, considering that not the least honourable office of an Annual is to adorn the tables of drawing rooms, this is far from

One of innumerable catalogues showing how Christmas had become a child-centred season by the end of the century. By this time, some catalogues had begun to appear as early as October.

slight praise'.[54] The annuals managed to convey the idea that they were personal presents while being mass-produced, and this helped them achieve great success. In 1825 Alaric Watts ('the Father of the Annuals') produced the *Literary Souvenir*, which sold 6,000 copies in the first two weeks of publication; in the next year it sold 10,000 copies, and annually thereafter he expected sales of 15,000 while the annuals remained in fashion.[55] (For equivalent sales figures for non-gift books, see pp. 167–8.)

There were also annuals for children, such as *The Juvenile Forget Me Not*, which appeared from 1830. This was followed by annuals for those whose lives took a more religious bent. *The Christmas Tree: A Book of Instruction and Amusement for All Young People* was published for over a decade, and had essays with titles like 'The Vanity of Earthly Things', as well as stories about children whose mothers had died. ('They talked over all the circumstances of that last day of their dear mother's life; and the mention of her name only seemed to inspire them with good and gentle thoughts. "If we had a Bible, we might read that psalm papa told us she asked him to read to her just before she died." But the twins needed no book; their minds were well stored with holy things . . .')[56] Secular children's magazines joined in the annual publishing frenzy. One example was the magazine *Youth's Monthly Visitor*, which in the 1820s began to bind up its year's output as *Youth's Miscellany of Knowledge and Entertainment*. Rather than stories about beautiful religious deaths, *Youth's Miscellany* specialized in useful knowledge: arithmetic, optics, how many pores a body contained, and how coal was mined.[57] For, outside the niche market for elegant anthologies, as late as the 1840s Christmas presents were still for the most part for children. In *A Christmas Carol*, the husband of Scrooge's ex-fiancée comes home bearing 'Christmas toys and presents' for the children only. When it was noted that Prince Albert liked 'the agreeable accompaniment of Christmas presents' for adults as well as children, it was unusual enough to comment on.[58]

In 1870, when Lewis's Bon Marché in Liverpool set up a separate, 'snow'-filled Christmas Fairyland – which became an annual event – the emphasis on children became even stronger. In 1888 Roberts' Stores in Stratford also had an annual Christmas grotto, with both Cinderella and Santa Claus appearing. The *Draper's Record* said that 17,000 children had been to see Santa: this was, apparently, his first outing to a department store, but by 1889 he was making multiple appearances across the country, promoting shopping for children.[59] By 1906 Gamage's advertised that it held a stock of 500,000 toy soldiers, 'but owing to the exceptional demand at Christmastime, customers are urged to give their orders as early as possible'.[60] Gordon Selfridge claimed to have originated the phrase 'Only — days until Christmas',[61] and if it was not he, and not first promoted in a department store, it ought to have been.

Advertisers without Christmas products to promote were not left behind. By the end of the nineteenth century, many ran seasonal advertisements anyway: Eno's Fruit Salts had a picture of three people dancing, and the strapline 'Happy Xmas. We feel jolly and well, Thanks to Eno's Fruit Salts'; Pear's Soap had a picture of a small child hiding under an overturned bathtub, with the heading 'Oh! Here's a Merry Christmas'.[62] There were also a large number of marketing campaigns designed to get each company's sales material into as many homes as possible. By the end of the century, Beecham's Pills gave away a 'Music Portfolio' with

December purchases, while Colman's Mustard splashed the slogan 'J. & J. Colman's Xmas Greetings 1896. To their young friends all over the world' across the front of copies of *Little Red Riding Hood*. Bryant and May matches produced almanacs printed with illustrations and quotations from Shakespeare, and Express Dairies' promotion was a pop-up model of a kitchen, complete with nursemaid and children drinking milk, and giving more milk to a kitten. Borwick's Baking Powder produced a series of cards that were folded to produce twelve pictures illustrating nursery rhymes. The Sen-Sen Cachou Co. was rather less domestic, producing 'The Sen-Sen War Puzzle', a board game in which players raced to be first to beat the Boers.[63]

This dose of 'Empire' was a visible eruption of the more generally invisible internationalism that went to make up a British Christmas: Germany had supplied the trees, the USA had exported both Santa Claus and mass advertising; the Dutch had provided the origin of Santa Claus's name, and also their shoes to hold presents (even though somehow, in the transmission, the shoes had turned into stockings). By the end of the century the traditional Christmas, that luxurious moment of home-grown tradition, was produced by manufacturers, delivered by railways, advertised by newspapers and magazines. Christmas books, Christmas travel, Christmas pantomimes, Christmas concerts, Christmas exhibitions: Prince Albert's 'products of all quarters of the globe', from which 'we have only to choose which is the best and cheapest for our purposes', had now been reshaped, reordered, repackaged and delivered to create an image not of the industrial age, but of the age of domesticity.

APPENDICES

APPENDIX 1

Currency

Pounds, shillings and pence were the divisions of the currency. One shilling was made up of 12 pence; one pound of 20 shillings, i.e. 240 pence. Pounds were represented by the £ symbol, shillings as '*s*.', and pence as '*d*.' (from the Latin *denarius*). 'One pound, one shilling and one penny' was written as £1.1.1. or £1 1s. 1*d*. 'One shilling and sixpence', referred to in speech as 'One and six', was written 1/6 or 1s. 6*d*.

A guinea was a coin to the value of £1 1*s* (The coin was not circulated after 1813, although the term remained and tended to be reserved for luxury goods.) A sovereign was a 20-shilling coin, a half-sovereign a 10-shilling coin. A crown was 5 shillings, half a crown 2*s*. 6*d*., and the remaining coins were a florin (2 shillings), sixpence, a groat (4 pence), a threepenny bit (pronounced 'thrup'ny bit'), twopence (pronounced tuppence), a penny, a halfpenny (pronounced hayp'ny), a farthing (¼ of a penny) and a half a farthing (⅛ of penny).

There were many slang names for various sums of money: a pound was (and is) a 'quid', while a shilling was a 'bob', sixpence a 'tanner', and a £5 note a 'finnif' or 'finnuf'. These were the most common, although there were many other terms, including the confusing 'half a dollar' for 2*s*. 6*d*. (A 'dollar' for 5*s*. seems to have been rather less common.)

Relative values have altered so substantially that attempts to convert nineteenth-century prices into contemporary ones are usually futile. As I am usually discussing the costs of everyday articles, some sense of the value of goods should be apprehended. However, if a more precise attempt to convert is wanted, the website http://www.ex.ac.uk/~RDavies/arian/current/howmuch.html is useful.

APPENDIX 2

Department stores (and other large shops) and their opening dates

KEY
* Survives today
† Survived into the second half of the twentieth century
Italics Not a department store

1776   Flint and Clark; in 1813 became Clark and Debenham, later Debenhams*

1790   Dickins and Smith; in 1835 became Dickins, Son and Stevens, later Dickins and Jones (closed 2006)†

1812   Swan and Edgar†

1813   Benjamin Harvey, later Harvey Nichols*

1817   Shoolbred's

1821   Manchester Bazaar, from 1836 Kendal, Milne*

1826   Pullars of Perth

1830   Jolly's of Bath*

1832   *Lilly and Skinner**

1833   *Peter Robinson*†

1837   Marshall and Wilson; in 1848 became Marshall and Snelgrove†
Bainbridge's of Newcastle*

1839   *The Scotch House* (closed *c*.2004)†

1840   *Heal's**

1842   *Maple's*†

1849   Harrod's*

1851   Bax and Co., later Emary and Co., now Aquascutum*

1856   Burberry's of Basingstoke, later Thomas Burberry and Co.*
Lewis's of Liverpool*

1858   Gorringe's†

1862   Derry and Toms†

1863   Whiteley's*

1864 John Lewis, Oxford Street*
1866 Civil Service Supply Association†
1867 Bentall's, Kingston upon Thames*
       Handley's of Southsea
1870 Barker's† (closed 2006)
1871 Peter Jones*
1871 Army and Navy Cooperative†
1873 Pontings†
1875 *Liberty and Co.**
       *The Irish Linen Co.**
1877 Bon Marché, Brixton
1879 D. H. Evans†
1882 *Fenwick's*, Newcastle*
1883 *Penberthy's*†
       *Jaeger**
1887 Bobby's, Margate
1894 Bourne and Hollingsworth†
1897 *Calman Links**
1909 Selfridge's*

APPENDIX 3

Holidays 'kept at the Exchequer, Stamp-Office, Excise-Office, Custom-House, Bank, East-India, and South-Sea House'

From [Thomas Mortimer], *'Pholanthropos', Every Man His Own Broker Or, A Guide to Exchange-Alley.* (London, S. Hopper at Caesar's Head, 1761; rev. ed. 1801)

	1761	1801
January	1 (New Year)	1
	6 (Epiphany)	6
		18
	25* (St Paul)	25
	30 (King Charles the Martyr)	30
February	2 (Purification of the Virgin Mary)	2
	3 (Shrove Tuesday)	
	4 (Ash Wednesday)	
	14 (St Valentine)	
	24 (St Mathias)	24
March	1 (St David)	
	20 (Good Friday)	
	23 (Easter Monday)	
	24 (Easter Tuesday)	
	25 (Lady Day)	25

	1761	1801
April	23 (St George)	
	25 (St Mark)	25
	26 (Duke of Cumberland's Birthday)	
	30 (Ascension Day)	
May	1 (Sts Philip and Jacob)	1
	11 (Whit Monday)	
	12 (Whit Tuesday)	
	13 (Whit Wednesday)	
		17
	29* (Restoration of Charles II)	29
June	4* (George III's birthday)	4
	10 (Princess Amelia's birthday)	
	11 (St Barnabas)	11
	24 (St John)	24
	29 (Sts Peter and Paul)	29
July	15 (St Swithin)	
	25 (St James)	25
August	1 (Lammas Day)	
		12
	24 (St Bartholomew)	24
September	2* (Commemoration of the Great Fire of London)	2
	14 (Holy Rood)	

	1761	1801
	21 (St Matthew)	21
		22
	29 (St Michael)	29
October	18 (St Luke)	18
		25
	26 (George III proclaimed king)	26
	28 (Sts Simon and Jude)	28
November	1 (All Saints' Day)	1
	2 (All Souls' Day)	
	4 (William III's birthday)	4
	5 (Guy Fawkes Day)	5
	9* (Lord Mayor's Show)	9
	28 (Accession of Elizabeth I)	
	30 (Prince of Wales's birthday)	30
December	21 (St Thomas)	21
	25	25
	26	26
	27 (St John)	27
	28 (Innocents)	28
Total	**51 days a year**	**37 days a year**

* Holidays with an asterisk are, if they fall on a Sunday, observed the following day.

SELECT BIBLIOGRAPHY

ORIGINAL DOCUMENTS AND EPHEMERA

A number of collections of printed ephemera have been particularly useful:

Bodleian Library:

  The John Johnson Collection of Printed Ephemera

  The Fillingham Collection (on pleasure gardens)

British Library:

  Playbills: London III: Miscellaneous Institutions, Societies and Other Bodies – 12 vols. 351–363; PB-MIC C13137 PLAYBILL 377 0–3; RAM 792.95; Daniel Lysons Collectanea, C.103.k.1112 and C.103.c.16; Sarah Banks Collection: L.R.301.h.2–11 and 937.g.96

  The Pantheon: 840. m.30

  Marylebone Gardens, 840.m.29

  Ranelagh, L. R. 282.b.7; and 840.m.28

  Vauxhall Gardens: Cup. 401.k.7

  Garrick's Stratford Jubilee: [Daniel George], c.61.e.2

Guildhall Library: Scrapbook of cuttings on Vauxhall Gardens, C.27

PARLIAMENTARY REPORTS

[House of Commons], *Report from the Select Committee of the House of Commons on the Earl of Elgin's Collection of Sculptures Marbles &c.* (London, Murray, 1816)

1825: Committee on Petition of Trustees of the British Museum Relative to the Rich Collection, 1825; vol. 107

1836: Report from the Select Committee on the Arts, and their Connection with Manufacturers

1849: Accounts of Income and Expenditures of the British Museum, vol. 30

1850: Accounts of Income and Expenditures of the British Museum, vol. 33

1850: Royal Commission to Inquire into the Constitution and Government of the British Museum, vol. 34.1

1852–3: Select Committee on the National Gallery, 1852–3, vol. 35

1860: Report of the Select Committee on Public Institutions, vol. 16

1863: Return on Number of Visitors to British Museum Collections from the Date of its Establishment to March 1863, vol. 29

PRIMARY SOURCES

Anon., *An Account of the British Institution for Promoting the Fine Arts in the United Kingdom* (London, 1805)

——, 'Advertisements', *Quarterly Review*, 97 (June and September 1855), 222

——, *The Birmingham Saturday Half Holiday-Guide, with a Map* (Birmingham, William Walker, [1871])

——, *The Book of the Old Edinburgh Club for the Year[s] 1808, 1809, 1810* (3 vols., Edinburgh, T. & A. Constable, 1907–10)

——, *Cassell's Handy Guide to the Sea-Side. Illustrated. A Description of all the principal English sea watering-places, with their relative advantages to the tourist and resident* (2nd ed., London, Cassell, Petter, and Galpin, [1865])

——, *The Christmas Book. Christmas in the Olden Time: Its Customs and their Origin* (London, James Pattie, 1859)

——, *The Christmas Tree: A Book of Instruction and Amusement for all Young People* (London, James Blackwood, editions in 1856, 1858, 1859, 1860)

——, *The Christmas Tree, A Present from Germany* (London, Darton & Clark, 1844)

——, 'The Circulating Libraries and Publishers', *Pall Mall Gazette*, 59 (July 1894), 3

——, *The Crystal Palace: A Little Book for Little Boys* (London, James Nisbet, 1851)

——, *Cupid's Garland, or, Love's Annual Resource, A Collection of Original Valentine Verses, Written expressly for the Work, for Ladies to Declare their Sentiments to Gentlemen, in language pleasing and amusing* (London, Thomas Hughes, [?1820])

——, *A Description of Vaux-hall Gardens. Being a proper companion and guide for all who visit that place* (London, S. Hooper, 1762)

——[W.T.], *The Express and Herald Original Bath Guide, Historical and Descriptive* (Bath, William Lewis, Express and County Herald, [1870?])

——, *Fireside Facts from the Great Exhibition* (London, [n.p.] [1851]) (no title page: information from British Library catalogue) (incorporates much material from *Little Henry's Holiday*, below])

——, *George Sandford; or, The Draper's Assistant. By One who has Stood Behind the Counter* (Edinburgh, Thomas Grant, 1853)

——, 'The [Great Exhibition's] Catalogue's Account of Itself', *Household Words*, 74 (1851), 519

——, 'The Great Exhibition and the Little One', *Household Words*, 67 (1851), 356–60

——, *Hymen's Rhapsodies, or Lover's Themes, A Collection of Original Valentine Verse, Written expressly for this Work, for Gentlemen to Address Ladies in Sonnets, Superior to any other* (London, Thomas Hughes, [?1820])

——, *Jimmy Trebilcock; or, the Humorous Adventures of a Cornish Miner, at the*

Great Exhibition, What he Saw and What he didn't See (Camborne, T. T. Whear, 1862)

——, 'The Labourer's Reading-Room', *Household Words*, 3 (1851), 581–5

——['by the author of "Pleasant Pages"'], *Little Henry's Holiday at the Great Exhibition* (London, Houston & Stoneman, [1851])

——, *Mama's Visit with her Little Ones, to the Great Exhibition* (London, [n.p.], 1852)

——, *Mr Goggleye's Visit to the Exhibition of National Industry to be Held in London on the 1st of April 1851* (London, 'Tim Takem'in', [?1851])

——, *Mr Punch at the Seaside, as pictured by Charles Keene, John Leech, George du Maurier, Phil May, L. Raven-Hill, J. Bernard Patridge, Gordon Browne, E. T. Reed, and Others . . .* ([no place of publication], Educational Book Co., [n.d.])

——[T. MacKinlay?], *Mrs Cornely's [sic] Entertainments at Carlisle House, Soho Square* (Bradford, Blackburn, [1840?])

——, *The New Amusing and Instructive Valentine Writer; or The Lover's Dumb Signs. A Selection of the Newest and Best Valentine Verses, &c. for the Use of Ladies & Gentlemen who wish to learn The Art of Making Love* (Edinburgh, W. Smith, [?1830])

——, *Official Descriptive and Illustrated Catalogue* (London, Spicer Bros, 1851)

——, *The Original Bath Guide, Considerably Enlarged and Improved* (Bath, J. Savage and Meyler and Son, 1811)

——, *The Plan of an Academy for the Better Cultivation, Improvement and Encouragement of Painting, Sculpture, Architecture, and the Arts of Design in General* (London, [n.p.], 1755)

——, *Premiums Offered by the Society Instituted at London for the Encouragement of Arts, Manufactures and Commerce* (London, [n.p.], 1768–75, 1783–90)

——, *Puffs and Mysteries; or, The Romance of Advertising* (London, W. Kent, 1855)

——, *The Quizzing Valentine Writer, A Collection of Original Verses, Written expressly for this Work, and calculated to Excite Risibility in all Countenances. Adapted for Both Sexes* (London, Thomas Hughes, [1820])

——, *The Satirical Valentine Writer, Being a Collection of Original Saterising [sic] Verses, Written expressly for this Work, on Various Characters, Calculated to meet the Ideas of all Descriptions of Writers* (London, Thomas Hughes, [1820])

——, *The Seaside Library of Penny Fiction* (Weymouth, Sherren & Son, 1887, 'New and Enlarged Edition', 1897)

——, *A Sketch of the Spring Gardens, Vauxhall. In a Letter to a Noble Lord* (London, G. Woodfall, 1752)

——[A Tea Dealer], *Tsiology, a discourse on Tea* (London, [n.p.], 1826)

——, 'The Unstamped Press in London', *Tait's Edinburgh Magazine*, 1 (1834)

——, *A Visit to the Bazaar* (London, J. Harris, 1818)

——, 'A Visit to Mudie's', *Pall Mall Gazette*, 39 (11 March 1884), 11

[Ablett, W. H., ed.], *Reminiscences of an Old Draper* (London, Sampson Low, Marston, Searle & Rivington, 1876)

Ackermann, Rudolph, *The Microcosm of London* (3 vols., London, Ackermann, 1808–9)

——, *The Repository of Arts, Literature, Commerce, Manufactures, Fashions and Politics* (London, Ackermann, 1808–28)

——, ed., *Ackermann's Costume Plates: Women's Fashions in England, 1818–28*, ed. Stella Blum (London, Constable, 1978)

[Adams, W. B., as], 'Helix', 'The Industrial Exhibition of 1851', *Westminster Review*, April 1850, 97

Aflalo, F. G., ed., *The Cost of Sport* (London, John Murray, 1899)

Amory, Thomas, *The Life and Opinions of John Buncle Esquire* (1756), ed. Ernest A. Baker (London, George Routledge and Sons, 1904)

Andrews, William, *Master and Artisan in Victorian England: The Diary of William Andrews and the Autobiography of Joseph Gutteridge*, ed. Valerie E. Chancellor (London, Evelyn, Adams & Mackay, 1969)

Archenholz, Johann Wilhelm von, *A Picture of England: Containing a Description of the Laws, Customs, and Manners of England*, tr. from the French (Dublin, P. Byrne, 1791)

Austen, Jane, *Jane Austen's Letters to her Sister Cassandra and Others*, ed. R. W. Chapman (Oxford, Clarendon Press, 1932)

——, *Northanger Abbey* [1818]; *Lady Susan; The Watsons; Sanditon*, ed. James Kinsley and John Davie; intro. and notes, Claudia L. Johnson (Oxford, Oxford University Press, 2003)

Babbage, Charles, *The Exposition of 1851* (London, John Murray, 1851)

Bamford, Samuel, *The Autobiography of Samuel Bamford*, ed. W. H. Chaloner (London, Frank Cass & Co., 1967)

Barry, James, *An Inquiry into the Real and Imaginary Observations to the Acquisition of the Arts in England* (London, [n.p.], 1775)

Bartlett, David, *What I Saw in London; or, Men and Things in the Great Metropolis* (London, Auburn, 1852)

La Belle Assemblée, or, Bell's Court and Fashionable Magazine, 1805–32, also as *La Belle Assemblée, or, Court and Fashionable Magazine; containing Interesting and Original Literature and Records of the Beau-Monde* and *The Court Magazine, and Belle Assemblée*

Bennett, John B., *The Power, Interest, and Duty of the Public to Effect an Abridgment of House of Business. A Prize Address* (London, George Barclay, 'by order of the Metropolitan Early Closing Association', 1848)

Bentley, Thomas, *A view of the advantages of inland navigations: with a plan of a navigable canal, intended for a communication between the ports of Liverpool and Hull* (London, Becket & De Hondt, 1765) (part written by Erasmus Darwin)

Booth, J. B., *The Old Pink 'Un Days* (London, Grant Richards, 1924)

——, *A 'Pink 'Un' Remembers* (London, Werner Laurie, 1937)

——, *Sporting Times: The 'Pink 'Un' World* (London, Werner Laurie, 1938)

Boucicault, Dion, *London Assurance* (1841), ed. James L. Smith (London, Adam & Charles Black, 1984)

——, *Plays by Dion Boucicault*, ed. Peter Thomson (Cambridge, Cambridge University Press, 1984)

Brontë, Charlotte, *Jane Eyre* (1847), ed. Michael Mason (Harmondsworth, Penguin, 1996)

Brown, J., *Tourist Rambles in Yorkshire, Lincolnshire, Durham, . . .* (London, Simpkin Marshall, 1878)

Bunn, Alfred, *The Stage: Both Before and Behind the Curtain* (London, Bentley, 1840)

Burgess, Fred W., *The Practical Retail Draper: A Complete Guide for the Draper and Allied Trades* (5 vols., London, Virtue & Co., [1912])

[Burn, James Dawson], *The Language of the Walls: And a Voice from the Shop Windows, Or, The Mirror of Commercial Roguery*, by One Who Thinks Aloud (Manchester, Abel Heywood, 1855)

Burney, Fanny, *Cecilia, or, Memoirs of an Heiress* (1782), ed. Peter Sabor and Margaret Anne Doody (Oxford, Oxford University Press, 1999)

——, *Evelina, or, The History of a Young Lady's Entrance in the World* (1778), ed. Margaret Anne Doody (Harmondsworth, Penguin, 1994)

——, *The Journals and Letters of Frances Burney (Mme D'Arblay)*, ed. Joyce Hemlow et al., (12 vols., Oxford, Clarendon Press, 1972–89)

——, *The Wanderer; or, Female Difficulties* (1814), ed. Margaret Anne Doody, Robert L. Mack and Peter Sabor (Oxford, Oxford University Press, 2001)

Byng, John, Viscount Torrington, *The Torrington Diaries*, ed. C. Bruyn Andrews (London, Methuen, 1970)

Campbell, Thomas, *Diary of a Visit to England in 1775*, ed. James L. Clifford (Cambridge, Cambridge University Press, 1947)

Cockburn, Henry, *Journal of Henry Cockburn, Being a Continuation of the Memorials of his Time, 1831–1854* (Edinburgh, Edmonston & Douglas, 1874)

Collins, Louis, *The Advertisers Guardian (and Advertisement Agents' Guide)* (London, [n.p.], 1885) (published annually from 1885 to 1902, except 1900, 1901)

[Colman, George], *Man and Wife; or, The Shakespeare Jubilee* (Dublin, for A. Leathley, S. Powell, P. and W. Wilson, et al., 1770)

Cook, Dutton, *Nights at the Play* (London, Chatto & Windus, 1883)

Cook, Thomas, *A Hand Book of the Trip from Leicester, Nottingham, and Derby to Liverpool and the Coast of North Wales* (1845), intro. Paul Smith (London, Routledge/Thoemmes Press, 1998)

Cross, J. C., *Circusiana, or A Collection of the Most Favourite Ballets, Spectacles, Melo-drames, &c., Performed at the Royal Circus, St George's Fields* (2 vols., London, Lackington, Allen & Co., 1809)

Cust, Lionel Henry, compiler, Sidney Colvin, ed., *History of the Society of Dilettanti* (London, [n.p.], 1898)

Darwin, Erasmus, *Essential Writings of Erasmus Darwin*, ed. Desmond King-Hele (Cambridge, Cambridge University Press, 1981)

——, *The Letters of Erasmus Darwin*, ed. Desmond King-Hele (Cambridge, Cambridge University Press, 1981)

Davies, Thomas, *Memoirs of the Life of David Garrick, Esq.* (Dublin, J. Williams, 1780)

Defoe, Daniel, *The Complete English Tradesman* (2 vols., Rivington, 1726–7)

——, *A Plan of the English Commerce* (1731) (Oxford, Basil Blackwell, 1927)

——, *A Tour through the Whole Island of Great Britain* (1724), ed. P. N. Furbank, W. R. Owens, and A. J. Coulson (London, Yale University Press, 1991)

Dennis, John, *The Pioneer of Progress; or, The Early Closing Movement in Relation to the Saturday Half-Holiday and the Early Payment of Wages* (London, Hamilton, Adams, & Co., [1861])

Dent, Robert K., *Old and New Birmingham, A History of the Town and its People* (Birmingham, Houghton and Hammond, 1880)

Dickens, Charles, *The Christmas Books*, vol. 1: *A Christmas Carol and The Chimes* (1843, 1844), ed. Michael Slater (Harmondsworth, Penguin, 1985)

——, 'The King of the Billstickers', *Household Words*, 22 March 1851

Doré, Gustave, and Blanchard Jerrold, *London, A Pilgrimage* (London, Grant & Co., 1872)

Edgeworth, Maria, *The Absentee* (1812), ed. W. J. McCormack and Kim Walker (Oxford, Oxford University Press, 2001)

——, *Belinda* (1801) (London, Johnson & Co., 1811)

——, *Castle Rackrent* and *Ennui* (1800; 1809), ed. Marilyn Butler (Harmondsworth, Penguin, 1992)

——, *The Life and Letters of Maria Edgeworth*, ed. Augustus Hare, ([London], Edward Arnold, 1894)

Egan, Pierce, *Walks through Bath* (Bath, Meyler and Sons, 1819)

Engels, Friedrich, *The Condition of the Working Classes in England* (1845), tr. and ed. W. O. Henderson and W. H. Chaloner (Stanford, Cal., Stanford University Press, 1968)

Felkin, William, *The Exhibition in 1851, of the Products and Industry of All Nations. Its Probable Influence upon Labour and Commerce* (London, Arthur Hall, Virtue, 1851)

Fergusson, James, *Observations on the British Museum, National Gallery and National Records Office, with Suggestions for their Improvement* (London, [n.p.], 1849)

Ffyfe, William Wallace, *Christmas: Its Customs and Carols. With Compressed Vocal Score of Select Choral Illustrations* (London, James Blackwood, [1860])

FitzGerald, John, *The Duty of Procuring More Rest for the Labouring Classes; the Earlier Closing of Shops, and the Saturday Half-holiday* (London, W. H. Dalton, 1856)

Fitzgerald, Percy, *Music Hall Land: An account of the natives, male and female, pastimes, songs, antics, and general oddities of that strange country* (London, Ward and Downey, 1890)

——, *Principles of Comedy and Dramatic Effect* (London, Tinsley Brothers, 1870)

——, *The Savoy Opera and the Savoyards* (London, Chatto & Windus, 1894)

——, *The Story of 'Bradshaw's Guide'* (London, Field & Tuer, 1890)

——, *The World Behind the Scenes* (London, Chatto & Windus, 1881)

Fosbroke, Thomas Dudley, *The Tourist's Grammar; or, rules relating to the scenery and antiquities incident to travellers; compiled from the best authorities and including an epitome of Gilpin's Principles of the Picturesque* (London, [n.p.], 1826)

Friswell, J. Hain, 'Circulating Libraries: Their Contents and their Readers', *London Society*, 20 (December 1871), 514–24

Gascoyne, Caroline, *Recollections of the Crystal Palace* (London, [n.p.], 1852)

Gaspey, William, *The Great Exhibition of the World's Industry held in London in 1851* (London, [n.p.], [1852?–1861?])

Gilbart, James William, *A Practical Treatise on Banking* . . . (London, E. Wilson, 1828)

Gilpin, William, *An Essay on Prints, containing remarks upon the principles of picturesque beauty* (2nd ed., London, J. Robson, 1768)

——, *My dearest Betsy. A Self-Portrait of William Gilpin 1756–1848, Schoolmaster and Parson, from his Letters and Notebooks*, ed. Peter Benson (London, Dobson, 1981)

——, *Observations on the River Wye . . . and South Wales* (1782) (Oxford, Woodstock Books, 1991)

——, *Observations relative chiefly to Picturesque Beauty . . . particularly the Highlands of Scotland* (London, R. Blamire, 1789)

——, *Observations relative chiefly to Picturesque Beauty . . . particularly the Mountains and Lakes of Cumberland and Westmoreland* (1786) (Poole, Woodstock Books, 1996)

——, *Three Essays: – on Picturesque Beauty; – on Picturesque Travel; – and, on Sketching Landscape* . . . (London, R. Blamire, 1792)

Goldsmith, Oliver, *The Vicar of Wakefield* (1766), ed. Stephen Coote (Harmondsworth, Penguin, 1986)

Goodall, G. W., *Advertising: A Study of a Modern Business Power* (London, Constable, 1914)

Grant, Elizabeth, *Memoirs of a Highland Lady*, ed. Andrew Tod (Edinburgh, Canongate, 1992)

Gray, Thomas, *The Correspondence of Gray, Walpole, West and Ashton (1733–1771)*, ed. Paget Toynbee (Oxford, Clarendon Press, 1915)

——, *A Supplement to the Tour of Great Britain* . . . (London, G. Kearsley, 1787)

Greeley, Horace, *Glances at Europe: In a Series of Letters from Great Britain, France, Italy, Switzerland, &c., during the Summer of 1851, including notices of the Great Exhibition, or World's Fair* (New York, Dewitt & Davenport, 1851)

Hallé, Charles, *The Life and Letters of Sir Charles Hallé, being an autobiography, 1816–1860, with correspondence and diaries*, ed. C. E. Hallé and Marie Hallé (London, Smith Elder & Co., 1896)

Hayes, J. W., *The Draper and Haberdasher: A Guide to the General Drapery Trade* (London, Houlston, 1878)

[Hayward, Abraham], 'The Advertising System', *Edinburgh Review*, 77 (February 1843), 1–43

Hervey, Thomas K., *The Book of Christmas* (London, William Spooner, 1836)

——, *The Book of Christmas* (London, Frederick Warne, 1888)

Hindley, Charles, *Curiosities of Street Literature* (1871) (Welwyn Gardens City, Seven Dials Press, 1969)

——, *The History of the Catnach Press, at Berwick-upon Tweed, Alnwick and Newcastle-upon-Tyne, in Northumberland, and Seven Dials, London* (London, Charles Hindley, 1886)

——, *The Life and Times of James Catnach, (late of Seven Dials), Ballad Monger* (London, Reeves and Turner, 1878)

[——], *'The Catnach Press'. A Collection of the Books and Woodcuts of James Catnach, late of Seven Dials, Printer;* with *The Full, True, & Particular Account of the Life: Trial, Character, Confession, and Behaviour, Together with an Authentic Copy of the will, or Last Dying Speech of Old Jemmy Catnach, Late of Seven Dials, Printer* [by Charles Hindley] (London, Reeves and Turner, [1869])

Hodgkinson, Richard, *A Lancashire Gentleman: The Letters and Journals of Richard Hodgkinson, 1763–1847*, ed. F. and K. Wood (Stroud, Alan Sutton, 1992)

Hole, James, *An Essay on the History and Management of Literary, Scientific, and Mechanics' Institutes* (London, [n.p.], 1853)

Holyoake, George J., *The History of the Rochdale Pioneers* (10th rev. ed., [London], Allen & Unwin, 1893)

——, *Self-help by the People: History of Co-operation in Rochdale* (London, [n.p.], 1858)

Hunt, Richard, *Hunt's Hand-Book to the Official Catalogues [of the Great Exhibition]* (London, Spicer, 1851)

Hutton, Catherine, *Reminiscences of a Gentlewoman of the Last Century: Letters of Catherine Hutton*, ed. C. H. Beale (Birmingham, Cornish Bros, 1891)

Jackson, Peter, ed., *George Scharf's London: Sketches and Watercolours of a Changing City, 1829–1850* (London, John Murray, 1987)

——, *John Tallis's London Street Views, 1838–1840: Together with the Revised and Enlarged Views of 1847* (Richmond, London Topographical Society, 2002)

James, Henry, *The Spoils of Poynton* (1897), ed. David Lodge (Harmondsworth, Penguin, 1987)

Jerrold, Douglas, *The Brownrigg Papers*, ed. Blanchard Jerrold (London, John Camden Hotten, 1860)

Jerrold, W. Blanchard, *How to See the British Museum. In Four Visits* (London, Bradbury and Evans, 1852)

Johnson, Barbara, *Barbara Johnson's Album of Fashions and Fabrics*, ed. Natalie Rothstein (London, Thames and Hudson, 1987)

Johnson, Samuel, *A Journey to the Western Isles of Scotland* (1775), ed. Peter Levi (Harmondsworth, Penguin, 1984)

Kenrick, W., *An Address to the Artists and Manufacturers of Great Britain* (London, [n.p.], 1774)

Knight, Charles, *Cyclopaedia of London* (London, Knight, 1851)

——, *Knight's Excursion Companion: Excursions from London* (London, Knight, 1851)

——, *Passages of a Working Life during Half a Century* (2 vols., London, Bradbury and Evans, 1864–5)

——, ed., *London* (London, Knight, 1841–4, 1851)

——, ed., *London*, rev. E. Walford (London, Knight, 1875–7)

Knight, Joseph, *Theatrical Notes* (London, Lawrence & Bullen, 1893)

Lackington, James, *Memoirs of the First Forty-Five Years of the Life of James Lackington* (rev. ed., London, 'Printed for the Author', 1792)

[Langford, J. A., as] 'J. A. L.', *A Century of Birmingham Life: A Chronicle of Local Events, from 1741 to 1841* (rev. ed., Birmingham, [n.p.], 1868)

La Roche, Sophie von, *Sophie in London, 1786, being the Diary of Sophie v. la Roche*, tr. Clare Williams (London, Jonathan Cape, 1933)

Latham, Richard, *The Account Book of Richard Latham, 1724–1767*, ed. Lorna

Weatherill (Oxford, for the British Academy by the Oxford University Press, 1990)

Leifchild, William, *Royal Gardens, Vauxhall. Particulars and conditions of sale . . . of that . . . property . . . which will be sold by auction . . . at Garraway's Coffee-House* (auction notice) (London, [n.p.], [1841])

Lichtenberg, Georg Christoph, *Lichtenberg's Visits to England as Described in his Letters and Diaries*, tr. Margaret L. Mare and W. H. Quarrell (Oxford, Clarendon Press, 1938)

Lilwall, John, *The Half-Holiday Question Considered, with Some Thoughts on the Instructive and Healthful Recreations of the Industrial Classes* (London, Kent & Co., 1856)

[Lockman, J.], *A Sketch of Spring-Gardens, Vaux-Hall. In a Letter to a Noble Lord* (London, [n.p.], [1752])

Lybbe Powys, Mrs Philip, *Passages from the Diaries of Mrs Philip Lybbe Powys, of Herwick House, Oxon, 1756–1808*, ed. Emily J. Climenson (London, Longmans, Green and Co., 1899)

McColloch, J. R., *Observations on the influence of the East India Company's monopoly on the price and supply of tea and on the commerce with India, China, &c.* (London, Longman, Rees, Orme, Brown, & Green, 1831)

Manby Smith, Charles, *Curiosities of London Life, or Phases, Physiological and Social, of the Great Metropolis* (London, William and Frederick G. Cash, 1853)

——, *The Little World of London; or, Pictures in Little of London Life* (London, Arthur Hall, Virtue, and Co., 1857)

Mandeville, Bernard, *The Fable of the Bees* (1714), ed. Philip Harth (Harmondsworth, Penguin, 1970)

Manners, John [Duke of Rutland], *A Plea for National Holy-Days* (London, [n.p.], 1843])

Marx, Karl, *The Marx–Engels Reader*, ed. Robert C. Tucker (New York, W. W. Norton, 1978)

Mayett, Joseph, *The Autobiography of Joseph Mayett of Quainton, 1783–1839*, ed. Ann Kussmaul (Cambridge, Buckinghamshire Record Society, 1986)

Mayhew, Edward, *Stage Effect: or, The Principles which Command Dramatic Success in the Theatre* (London, C. Mitchell, 1840)

Mayhew, Henry, *London Labour and the London Poor: A cyclopedia of the conditions and earnings of those that will work, those that cannot work, and those that will not work* (London, Woodfall, 1851)

——, *The Unknown Mayhew: Selections from the Morning Chronicle, 1849–50*, ed. E. P. Thompson and Eileen Yeo (Harmondsworth, Penguin, 1984)

——, and George Cruikshank, *1851: or, The Adventures of Mr and Mrs Sandboys and Family, Who Came Up to London to 'Enjoy Themselves', and to See the Great Exhibition* (London, George Newbold, [1851])

Mogg, Edward, *Paterson's Roads: Being an entirely original and accurate description of all the Direct and Principal Cross Roads in England and Wales, with part of the roads of Scotland* (16th ed., London, Longman, Hurst, Bees, Orme, and Brown, et al., 1822)

Montagu, Elizabeth, *Mrs Montagu, 'Queen of the Blues', Her Letters and Friendships from 1762 to 1800*, ed. Reginald Blunt and E. J. Climenson (2 vols., London, Constable, 1923)

Morell, Jemima, *Miss Jemima's Swiss Journal: The First Conducted Tour of Switzerland* (London, Routledge/Thoemmes Press, 1998)

Morley, Henry, *The Journal of a London Playgoer* (2nd ed., 1891) (Leicester, Leicester University Press, 1974)

[Mortimer, Thomas], *'Pholanthropos', Every Man His Own Broker: Or, A Guide to Exchange-Alley, in which the Nature of the several FUNDS, vulgarly called the STOCKS, is clearly explained; and the Mystery and Iniquity of STOCK-JOBBING laid before the Public in a New and Impartial Light . . .* (London, S. Hopper at Caesar's Head, 1761; rev. ed. 1801)

Moses, Elias, and Son, *Fashions for 1857: Spring and Summer Manual; The Record of Public Sentiments; The Herald of the Seasons; The Commercial Cornucopia* (price lists) (London, [n.p.], 1849–57)

——, *The Growth of an Important Branch of British Industry (The Ready-Made Clothing System* (London, [n.p.], 1860)

——, *On Modern Costume. A Sequel to 'Gossip on Dress'* (London, [n.p.], 1863)

[Murray, John], *A Handbook for Travellers in Switzerland . . .* (London, John Murray, eds. of 1838, 1843, 1892)

Packwood, George, *Packwood's Whim. The Goldfinch's Nest; or, The Way to Get Money and be Happy* (London, [n.p.], 1796)

Papworth, John W., *Museums, Libraries, and Picture Galleries* (London, Chapman and Hall, 1853)

[Pardon, George Frederick], *The London Conductor; Being a Guide for Visitors to the Great Industrial Exhibition, through the principal portions of the metropolis; including a brief history and description of the palaces, parks, churches; government, legal, and commercial buildings; bridges, statues, museums, hospitals, club-houses, theatres, and streets of London; and the remarkable places in its vicinity* (London, John Cassell, 1851; reprint, Kilkenny, Boethius, 1984)

Payn, James, 'Penny Fiction', *The Nineteenth Century*, 9, 47 (January 1881), 145–54

Peek, H., *The Badminton Library of Sports and Pastimes: The Poetry of Sport* (London, Badminton Press, 1896)

Pepys, Samuel, *The Diary of Samuel Pepys*, ed. Robert Latham and William Matthews (11 vols., London, Bell & Hyman, 1970–83)

Place, Francis, *The Autobiography of Francis Place (1771–1854)*, ed. Mary Thale (London, Cambridge University Press, 1972)

Planché, James Robinson, *The Extravaganzas of J. R. Planché, Esq., Somerset Herald, 1825–1871*, ed. T. F. Dillon Croker and Stephen Tucker (5 vols., London, Samuel French, 1879)

——, *The New Haymarket Spring Meeting. A New Easter Extravaganza* (London, Thomas Hailes Lacy, [1855])

——, *Pieces of Pleasantry for Private Performance during the Christmas Holidays* (London, Thomas Hailes Lacy, [1868])

——, *The Recollections and Reflections of J. R. Planché (Somerset Herald). A Professional Autobiography* (2 vols., London, Tinsley Brothers, 1872)

Plumptre, James, *James Plumptre's Britain: The Journals of a Tourist in the 1790s*, ed. Ian Ousby (London, Hutchinson, 1992)

[——], *The Lakers: A Comic Opera* (London, W. Clarke, 1798)

Postlethwayt, Malachy, *Britain's Commercial Interest Explained and Improved* . . . (London, [n.p.], 1757)

Prentice, Archibald, *Historical Sketches and Personal Recollections of Manchester* . . . ([no place of publication], Gilpin, 1851)

Pückler-Muskau, Prince, *Puckler's Progress: The Adventures of Prince Pückler-Muskau in England, Wales and Ireland, as told in letters to his former wife, 1826–9*, tr. Flora Brennan (London, Collins, 1987)

Pye, John, *Evidence Relating to the Art of Engraving, taken before the Select Committee of the House of Commons, on Arts, 1836; and the Committee's Report made to the House Thereon* (London, Longman, Rees, Orme, Brown, Green, and Longman, 1836)

——, *Patronage of British Art: An Historical Sketch* (London, Longman, Brown, Green, and Longmans, 1845)

Rae, George, *The Country Banker; His Clients, Cares, and Work from an Experience of Forty Years* (London, John Murray, 1885; reprinted London, Routledge, 1999)

[Ralph, James], *The Case of Authors by Profession or Trade, stated, with regard to booksellers, the stage, and the public. No matter by whom* (London, R. Griffiths, 1758)

Razzell, P. E., and R. W. Wainwright, *The Victorian Working Class: Selections from Letters to the Morning Chronicle* (London, Cass, 1973)

Redding, Cyrus, *The Stranger in London; or, Visitor's Companion to the Metropolis and its Environs. With an historical and descriptive sketch of the Great Exhibition* (London, Henry G. Bohn, 1851)

Richardson, Samuel, *Selected Letters of Samuel Richardson*, ed. John Carroll (Oxford, Clarendon Press, 1964)

Sala, George Augustus, *Gaslight and Daylight, with Some London Scenes they Shine Upon* (London, Chapman & Hall, 1859)

——, *London Up to Date* (London, Adam & Charles Black, 1894)

——, *Twice Round the Clock; or, the Hours of the Day and Night in London* (London, Houlston & Wright, 1859)

——[as 'Vates Secundus'], *Great Exhibition: 'Wot is to Be', or, Probable Results of the Industry of All Nations in the Year '51. Showing What is to be Exhibited, Who is to Exhibit, in short, How it's all Going to be Done* (London, The Committee for Keeping Things in their Places, 1850)

Sampson, Henry, *A History of Advertising from the Earliest Times* (London, Chatto & Windus, 1874)

——, *Successful Advertising: Its Secrets Explained* (London, Smith's Advertising Agency, 1886)

Sanger, George, *Seventy Years a Showman: My Life and Adventures in Camp and Caravan the World Over* (London, C. A. Pearson, 1910)

Schimmelpenninck, Mary Anne, *Life of Mary Anne Schimmelpenninck*, ed. Christiana C. Hankin (3rd ed., 2 vols., London, [n.p.], 1859)

Schinkel, Karl Friedrich, *The English Journey: Journal of a visit to France and Britain in 1826*, ed. David Bindman and Gottfried Riemann, tr. G. Gayna Walls (London, Paul Mellon Centre for Studies in British Art, Yale University Press, 1993)

Schopenhauer, Johanna, *A Lady Travels: Journeys in England and Scotland, from the Diaries of Johanna Schopenhauer*, tr. Ruth Michaelis-Jena and Willy Merson (London, Routledge, 1988)

Shiercliff, E., *The Bristol and Hotwell Guide* (Bristol, Bulgin and Rosser, 1793)

[Shillito, Charles], *The Country Book-Club. A Poem* (London, 'Printed for the Author', 1788)

Smith, Adam, *Lectures in Jurisprudence* (1762–3, 1766), ed. R. L. Meek, D. D. Raphael and P. G. Stein (Oxford, Clarendon Press, 1978)

——, *The Theory of Moral Sentiments* (1790), ed. D. D. Raphael and A. L. Macfie (Oxford, Clarendon Press, 1976)

——, *The Wealth of Nations* ([1776], Glasgow, [n.p.], 1805)

Smith, Adolph, and John Thomson, *Street Life in London* (London, [n.p.], 1877)

Smith, James L., ed., *Victorian Melodramas: Seven English, French and American Melodramas* (London, Dent, 1976)

Smith, William, *Advertise. How? When? Where?* (London, Routledge, Warne, and Routledge, 1863)

Strang, John, *Glasgow and its Clubs; or, glimpses of the condition, manners, characters & oddities of the city during the past & present century* (London and Glasgow, R. Griffin, 1856)

'Syntax, Dr' [William Combe], *The Tour of Dr Syntax in Search of the Picturesque* (5th ed., London, R. Ackermann, 1815)

Taylor, J. R., *Government, Legal, and General Saturday Half-Holiday, and the Closing of the courts of Law and Equity Entirely on that Day. Report of the*

Great Public Meeting, held in the Guildhall of the City of London, on the 15th of August, 1855 . . . (London, V. & R. Stevens and G. S. Norton, 1857)

[Temple, Sir William, as] I—B—, M. D., *A Vindication of Commerce and the Arts; proving that they are the source of the greatness, power, riches and populousness of a state* . . . (London, J. Nourse, 1758)

Thompson, Alfred, *Linda of Chamouni, or, Not Formosa, An Operatic Incongruity, in Three Scenes and a Sensation* (London, n.p., first produced at the Gaiety 1869)

Timbs, John, *Club Life of London* ([London], Richard Bentley, 1866)

Trollope, Anthony, *London Tradesmen* (originally appeared in the *Pall Mall Gazette*, 10 July to 7 September, 1880) (London, Elkin Mathews & Marrot, 1927)

——, 'The National Gallery', *St James's Magazine*, June 1861 (reprinted in *Miscellaneous Essays and Reviews*, New York, Arno Press, 1981)

Turner, J., *The New English Valentine Writer, or the High Road to Love; for Both Sexes. Containing A Complete Set of Valentines, Proper for almost every Trade in Town or Country, with their Answers* (London, T. Sabine, 1784)

Uzanne, Octave, *The Sunshade, the Glove, the Muff* (London, J. C. Nimmo and Bain, 1883)

Vertue, George, *Notebooks* (6 vols., Walpole Society, 1930–55)

Walpole, Horace, *Anecdotes of Painting in England* . . . (4 vols., Strawberry Hill, 1762–71)

——, *Horace Walpole's Journals of Visits to Country Seats, &c.*, ed. Paget Toynbee ([no place of publication], Walpole Society, 1927–28)

——, *The Yale Edition of Horace Walpole's Correspondence*, ed. W. W. Lewis (48 vols., New Haven, Yale University Press, 1937–83)

West, Thomas, *A Guide to the Lakes: dedicated to the Lovers of Landscape Studies, and to all who have visited or intend to visit the Lakes* . . . (London, Richardson and Urquhart, 1778)

[Wissett, R.], *A View of the Rise, Progress, and Present State of the Tea Trade in Europe* ([London?], [n.p.], 1801)

Wroth, Warwick, *Cremorne and the Later London Gardens* (London, Elliot Stock, 1907)

——, assisted by Arthur Edgar Wroth, *The London Pleasure Gardens of the Eighteenth Century* (London, Macmillan and Co., 1896)

Young, Arthur, *The Farmer's Tour through the East of England* . . . (4 vols., London, W. Strahan, 1771)

——, *A Six Months Tour through the North of England* . . . (4 vols., London, W. Strahan, 1770)

——, *A Six Weeks Tour through the Southern Counties of England and Wales* (2nd ed., London, W. Strahan, 1769)

Zola, Emile, *Au bonheur des dames (The Ladies' Paradise)* (1883), tr. and ed. Robin Buss (Harmondsworth, Penguin, 2001)

SECONDARY SOURCES

Anon., *'Noble and Patriotic': The Beaumont Gift, 1828* (London, National Gallery, 1988)

Adburgham, Alison, *Liberty's: A Biography of a Shop* (London, George Allen & Unwin, 1975)

——, *Shopping in Style: London from the Restoration to Edwardian Elegance* (London, Thames and Hudson, 1979)

——, *Shops and Shopping, 1800–1914: Where, and in What Manner the Well-Dressed Englishwoman Bought her Clothes* (London, George Allen & Unwin, 1981)

Ainger, Michael, *Gilbert and Sullivan: A Dual Biography* (Oxford, Oxford University Press, 2002)

Albert, William, *The Turnpike Road System in England, 1663–1840* (Cambridge, Cambridge University Press, 1972)

Alborn, Timothy, *Conceiving Companies: Joint-Stock Politics in Victorian England* (London, Routledge, 1998)

Aldcroft, Derek H., and Michael J. Freeman, *Transport in the Industrial Revolution* (Manchester, Manchester University Press, 1983)

Alderson, Frederick, *Bicycling: A History* (Newton Abbot, David and Charles, 1972)

——, *The Inland Resorts and Spas of Britain* (Newton Abbot, David and Charles, 1973)

Alexander, David, *Retailing in England during the Industrial Revolution* (London, Athlone Press, 1970)

Alexander, Nicholas, and Gary Akehurst, eds., *The Emergence of Modern Retailing, 1750–1950* (London, Frank Cass, 1999)

——, eds., 'Introduction: The Emergence of Modern Retailing, 1750–1950', *Business History*, 'Special issue on the Emergence of Modern Retailing, 1750–1950', 40, 4 (1998), 1–15

Allen, Brian, *Francis Hayman* (London, Yale University Press, 1987)

——, ed., *Towards a Modern Art World*, Studies in British Art 1 (New Haven, Yale University Press, 1995)

Allen, Reginald, ed., *The First Night Gilbert and Sullivan* (London, Chappell, 1958)

Alsop, Joseph, *The Rare Arts Traditions: The History of Art Collecting and its Linked Phenomena* (London, Thames and Hudson, 1982)

Altick, Richard D., *The English Common Reader: A Social History of the Mass Reading Public, 1800–1900* (Chicago, University of Chicago Press, 1957)

——, *The Shows of London* (Cambridge, Mass., The Belknap Press, 1978)

Anderson, B. L., and P. L. Cottrell, *Money and Banking in England: The Development of the Banking System, 1694–1914* (Newton Abbot, David and Charles, 1974)

Anderson, Gregory, *Victorian Clerks* (Manchester, Manchester University Press, 1976)

Anderson, Patricia, *The Printed Image and the Transformation of Popular Culture, 1790–1860* (Oxford, Clarendon Press, 1991)

Andrews, Malcolm, *The Search for the Picturesque: Landscape Aesthetics and Tourism in Britain, 1760–1800* (Aldershot, Scolar Press, 1989)

Appadurai, Arjun, ed., *The Social Life of Things: Commodities in Cultural Perspective* (Cambridge, Cambridge University Press, 1986)

Appleton, William W., *Madame Vestris and the London Stage* (New York, Columbia University Press, 1974)

Ashworth, William J., *Customs and Excise: Trade, Production, and Consumption in England, 1640–1845* (Oxford, Oxford University Press, 2003)

Auerbach, Jeffrey A., *The Great Exhibition of 1851: A Nation on Display* (London, Yale University Press, 1999)

Backsheider, Paula R., *Spectacular Politics: Theatrical Power and Mass Culture in Early Modern England* (Baltimore, Johns Hopkins University Press, 1993)

Bagwell, Philip S., *The Railway Clearing House in the British Economy, 1842–1922* (London, George Allen & Unwin, 1968)

——, *The Transport Revolution* (2nd ed., London, Routledge, 1988)

Bailey, Peter, *Leisure and Class in Victorian England: Rational Recreation and the Contest for Control* (London, Methuen, 1978)

——, *Popular Culture and Performance in the Victorian City* (Cambridge, Cambridge University Press, 1998)

——, 'A Mingled Mass of Perfectly Legitimate Pleasures: The Victorian Middle Class and the Problem of Leisure', *Victorian Studies*, 21 (1997), 7–28

——, ed., *Music Hall: The Business of Pleasure* (Milton Keynes, Open University Press, 1986)

Baines, Paul, *The House of Forgery in Eighteenth-Century Britain* (Aldershot, Ashgate, 1999)

Baker, Robert, Dorothy Porter, and Roy Porter, eds., *The Codification of Medical Morality: Historical and Philosophical Studies of the Formalization of Western Medical Morality in the Eighteenth and Nineteenth Centuries*, vol. 1: *Medical Ethics and Etiquette in the Eighteenth Century* (Dordrecht and London, Kluwer Academic, 1993)

Barish, Jonas A., *The Antitheatrical Prejudice* (Berkeley, University of California Press, 1981)

Barnes, James J., *Free Trade in Books: A Study of the London Book Trade since 1800* (Oxford, Clarendon Press, 1964)

Barnsby, G., 'The Standard of Living in the Black Country during the 19th Century', *Business History Review*, 24 (1971), 220–39

Barry, Jonathan, and Christopher Brooks, eds., *The Middling Sort of People: Culture, Society and Politics in England, 1550–1800* (Basingstoke, Macmillan, 1994)

Basalla, George, *The Evolution of Technology* (Cambridge, Cambridge University Press, 1988)

Bashford, Christina, and Leanne Langley, eds., *Music and British Culture, 1785–1914* (Oxford, Oxford University Press, 2000)

Baudrillard, Jean, *For a Critique of the Political Economy of the Sign* (St Louis, Telos, 1981)

Beaver, Patrick, *The Crystal Palace: A Portrait of Victorian Enterprise* (2nd ed., London, Phillimore, 1986)

Beetham, Margaret, *A Magazine of her Own?: Domesticity and Desire in the Woman's Magazine, 1800–1914* (London, Routledge, 1996)

——, and Kay Boardman, eds., *Victorian Women's Magazines: An Anthology* (Manchester, Manchester University Press, 2001)

Bennett, Scott, 'Victorian Newspaper Advertising: Counting What Counts', *Publishing History*, 8 (1980), 5–18

Bennett, Tony, *The Birth of the Museum: History, Theory, Politics* (London, Routledge, 1995)

——, John Golby and Ruth Finnegan, 'Christmas and Ideology', *Popular Culture: Themes and Issues*, Block 1, Units 1/2: 'Christmas: A Case Study' (Milton Keynes, Open University Press, 1981)

Benson, John, *The Penny Capitalists: A Study of Nineteenth-Century Working-Class Entrepreneurs* (Dublin, Gill and Macmillan, 1983)

——, *The Rise of Consumer Society in Britain, 1880–1980* (New York, Longman, 1984)

——, and Gareth Shaw, eds., *The Evolution of Retail Systems, c.1800–1914* (Leicester, Leicester University Press, 1992)

——, eds., *The Retailing Industry* (3 vols., London, I. B. Tauris, 1999), vol. 2: *The Coming of the Mass Market, 1800–1945*

——, and Laura Ugolini, eds., *A Nation of Shopkeepers: Five Centuries of British Retailing* (London, I. B. Tauris, 2003)

Berg, Maxine, *The Age of Manufactures, 1700–1820: Industry, Innovation and Work in Britain* (rev. ed., London, Routledge, 1994)

——, 'From Imitation to Invention: Creating Commodities in 18th-Century Britain', *Economic History Review*, 55 (2002), 1–30

——, 'Women's Consumption and the Industrial Classes of 18th-Century England', *Journal of Social History*, 30, 2 (1996), 415–34

——, and Kristine Bruland, eds., *Technological Revolutions in Europe: Historical Perspectives* (Cheltenham, Edward Elgar, 1998)

——, and Helen Clifford, eds., *Consumers and Luxury: Consumer Culture in Europe, 1650–1850* (Manchester, Manchester University Press, 1999)

——, and Elizabeth Eger, eds., *Luxury in the Eighteenth Century: Debates, Desires and Delectable Goods* (Basingstoke, Palgrave Macmillan, 2003)

Bermingham, Ann, *Landscape and Ideology: The English Rustic Tradition, 1740–1860* (Berkeley, University of California Press, 1986)

——, and John Brewer, eds., *The Consumption of Culture, 1600–1800: Image, Object, Text* (Routledge, London, 1995)

Berry, Christopher J., *The Idea of Luxury: A Conceptual and Historical Investigation* (Cambridge, Cambridge University Press, 1994)

Bianchi, Marina, 'Collecting as a Paradigm of Consumption', *Journal of Cultural Economics*, 21, 4 (1997), 275–89

——, ed., *The Active Consumer: Novelty and Surprise in Consumer Choice* (London, Routledge, 1998)

Bicknell, Peter, *Gilpin to Ruskin: Drawing Masters and their Manuals, 1800–1860* (Cambridge, Fitzwilliam Museum, 1988)

Bingham, A. Walker, *The Snake-Oil Syndrome: Patent Medicine and Advertising* (Hanover, Mass., Christopher Publishing House, 1994)

Birchall, Johnston, *The International Co-operative Movement* (Manchester, Manchester University Press, 1997)

Birley, Derek, *Land of Sport and Glory: Sport and British Society, 1887–1910* (Manchester, Manchester University Press, 1995)

——, *Sport and the Making of Britain* (Manchester, Manchester University Press, 1993)

Bissell, Don, *The First Conglomerate: 45 Years of the Singer Sewing Machine Company* (Brunswick, Me., Audenreed, 1999)

Black, Barbara J, *On Exhibit: Victorians and their Museums* (Charlottesville, University Press of Virginia, 2000)

Black, Jeremy, *The British Abroad: The Grand Tour in the Eighteenth Century* (Stroud, Alan Sutton, 1992)

Blackman, Janet, 'The Development of the Retail Grocery Trade in the Nineteenth Century', *Business History*, 9, 2 (1967), 110–17

——, 'The Food Supply of an Industrial Town: A Study of Sheffield's Public Markets, 1780–1900', *Business History*, 9, (1963), 83–97

Blakey, Dorothy, *The Minerva Press, 1790–1820* ([Oxford?], 'Printed for the Bibliographical Society by Oxford University Press', [1935])

Bonnell, Thomas, 'Bookselling and Canon-Making: The Trade Rivalry over the English Poets, 1776–1783', *Studies in Eighteenth-Century Culture*, 19 (1989), 53–69

Bonner, Arnold, *British Co-operation: The History, Principles, and Organisation of the British Co-operative Movement* (rev. ed., Manchester, Co-operative Union, 1970)

Bonner, Thomas Neville, *Becoming a Physician: Medical Education in Britain, France, Germany, and the United States, 1750–1945* (New York, Oxford University Press, 1995)

Bonython, Elizabeth, *King Cole: A Picture Portrait of Sir Henry Cole, KCB, 1808–1882* (London, Victoria & Albert Museum, [1982])

——, and Anthony Burton, *The Great Exhibitor: The Life and Work of Henry Cole* (London, Victoria & Albert Museum, 2003)

Booth, Michael R., *Theatre in the Victorian Age* (Cambridge, Cambridge University Press, 1991)

——, *Victorian Spectacular Theatre: 1850–1910* (London, Routledge & Kegan Paul, 1981)

——, ed., *Victorian Theatrical Trades: Articles from The Stage, 1883–1884* (London, Society for Theatre Research, 1981)

Borsay, Peter, *The English Urban Renaissance: Culture and Society in the Provincial Town, 1660–1770* (Oxford, Clarendon Press, 1989)

——, 'The English Urban Renaissance: The Development of Provincial Urban Culture, *c.*1680–*c.*1760', *Social History*, 5 (1977), 581–98

——, *The Image of Georgian Bath, 1700–2000: Towns, Heritage and History* (Oxford, Oxford University Press, 2000)

——, ed., *The Eighteenth-Century Town: A Reader in English Urban History, 1688–1820* (London, Longman, 1990)

——, and Angus McInnes, 'The Emergence of a Leisure Town: Or an Urban Renaissance?', *Past and Present*, 126 (1990), 189–202

Brown, Jonathan, *The English Market Town: A Social and Economic History, 1750–1914* (Marlborough, Crowood, 1986)

Brown, P. S., 'The Vendors of Medicines in Eighteenth-Century Bath Newspapers', *Medical History*, 19 (1975), 352–69

Bourdieu, Pierre, *Distinction: A Social Critique of the Judgement of Taste*, tr. Richard Nice (Cambridge, Mass., Harvard University Press, 1986)

——, *The Field of Cultural Production: Essays on Art and Literature*, ed. Randal Johnson (Cambridge, Polity, 1993)

Boyce, Benjamin, *The Benevolent Man: A Life of Ralph Allen of Bath* (Oxford, Oxford University Press, 1967)

Boyce, George, James Curran and Pauline Wingate, eds., *Newspaper History from the Seventeenth Century to the Present Day* (London, Constable, 1978)

Bradley, Ian, ed., *The Complete Annotated Gilbert and Sullivan* (Oxford, Oxford University Press, 1996)

Brake, Laurel, *Print in Transition, 1850–1910: Studies in Media and Book History* (Basingstoke, Palgrave, 2001)

——, A. Jones and L. Madden, eds., *Investigating Victorian Journalism* (Basingstoke, Macmillan, 1990)

——, B. Bell and D. Finkelstein, eds., *Nineteenth-Century Media and the Construction of Identities* (Basingstoke, Palgrave, 2000)

Brailsford, Dennis, *British Sport: A Social History* (Cambridge, Lutterworth Press, 1992)

——, *Sport, Time and Society: The British at Play* (London, Routledge, 1991)

——, *A Taste for Diversions: Sport in Georgian England* (Cambridge, Lutterworth Press, 1999)

Bratton, Jacky, *New Readings in Theatre History* (Cambridge, Cambridge University Press, 2003)

——, ed., *Music Hall: Performance and Style* (Milton Keynes, Open University Press, 1986)

Bredvold, Louis I., *The Natural History of Sensibility* (Detroit, Wayne State University Press, 1962)

Brendon, Piers, *Thomas Cook: 150 Years of Popular Tourism* (London, Secker & Warburg, 1991)

Breward, Christopher, *The Culture of Fashion* (Manchester, Manchester University Press, 1995)

——, *The Hidden Consumer: Masculinities, Fashion and City Life, 1860–1914* (Manchester, Manchester University Press, 1999)

Brewer, John, *The Pleasures of the Imagination: English Culture in the Eighteenth Century* (London, HarperCollins, 1997)

——, and Roy Porter, eds., *Consumption and the World of Goods* (London, Routledge, 1993)

——, and Susan Staves, eds., *Early Modern Conceptions of Property: Consumption and Culture in the 17th and 18th Centuries* (London, Routledge, 1995)

Briggs, Asa, *Friends of the People: The Centenary History of Lewis's* (London, B. T. Batsford, 1956)

Briggs, Peter, 'News from the Little World: A Critical Glance at Eighteenth-Century British Advertising', *Studies in Eighteenth-Century Culture*, 23 (1993), 29–45

Brigstocke, Hugh, *William Buchanan and the 19th-Century Art Trade: 100 Letters to his Agents in London and Italy* ([London], Paul Mellon Centre for Studies in British Art, 1982)

Brown, Ivor, and George Fearon, *Amazing Monument: A Short History of the Shakespeare Industry* (London, Heinemann, 1939)

Bruntjen, Sven H. A., *John Boydell, 1719–1804: A Study of Art Patronage and Publishing in Georgian London* (New York, Garland, 1985)

Buchanan, B. J., 'The Evolution of the English Turnpike Trusts: Lessons from a Case Study', *Economic History Review*, 2nd ser., 39, 2 (1986), 223–43

Buck, Anne, 'Buying Clothes in Bedfordshire: Customers and Tradesmen, 1700–1800', *Textile History*, 22, 2 (1991), 211–37

——, *Victorian Costumes and Costume Accessories* (London, Herbert Jenkins, 1961)

——, and H. Matthews, 'Pocket Guides to Fashion: Ladies' Pocket Books Published in England, 1760–1830', *Costume*, 18 (1984), 241–57

Buck, John D., 'The Motives of Puffing: John Newberry's Advertisements, 1742–1767', *Studies in Bibliography*, 30 (1977), 196–210

Buday, George, *The History of the Christmas Card* (London, Spring Books, 1964)

Burnby, Juanita, 'Printer's Ink and Patent Medicines: The Story of the Diceys', *Pharmaceutical Journal*, August 1982, 162–4

Burton, Anthony and Pip, *The Green Bag Travellers: Britain's First Tourists* (London, André Deutsch, 1978)

Bynum, W. F., Stephen Lock and Roy Porter, *Medical Journals and Medical Knowledge: Historical Essays* (London, Routledge, 1992)

Bynum, W. F., and Roy Porter, eds., *Medical Fringe and Medical Orthodoxy, 1750–1850* (London, Croom Helm, 1987)

Byrde, Penelope, *The Male Image: Men's Fashion in Britain, 1300–1970* (London, B. T. Batsford, 1979)

Cain, Louis P. and Paul J. Uselding, eds., *Business Enterprise and Economic Change: Essays in Honor of Harold F. Williamson* ([no place of publication], Kent State University Press, 1973)

Callery, Sean, *Harrods Knightsbridge: The Story of Society's Favourite Store* (London, Ebury, 1991)

Campbell, Colin, *The Romantic Ethic and the Spirit of Modern Consumerism* (Oxford, Basil Blackwell, 1987)

Campbell Orr, Clarissa, ed., *Women in the Victorian Art World* (Manchester, Manchester University Press, 1995)

Cardwell, D. S. L., ed., *Artisan to Graduate: Essays to Commemorate the Foundation in 1824 of the Manchester Mechanics' Institution* . . . (Manchester, Manchester University Press, 1974)

Carlson, C. L., 'Edward Cave's Club and its Project for a Literary Review', *Philological Quarterly*, 17 (1938), 115–19

Carpenter, Kenneth E., ed., *Books and Society in History: Papers of the Association of College and Research Libraries Rare Books and Manuscripts Preconference* (New York, R. R. Bowker, 1983)

Carr-Saunders, A. M., and P. A. Wilson, *The Professions* (Oxford, Clarendon Press, 1933)

Carter, John, ed., *New Paths in Book Collecting* (reprint; Freeport, NY, Books for Libraries Press, 1967)

Caygill, Marjorie, and Christopher Date, *Building the British Museum* (London, British Museum Press, 1999)

Certeau, Michel de, *The Practice of Everyday Life*, tr. Steven Rendall (Berkeley, University of California Press, 1988)

Chalkin, C. W., 'Capital Expenditure on Building for Cultural Purposes in Provincial England, 1730–1780', *Business History*, 22 (1980), 51–70

Chapman, Stanley, *The Early Factory Masters: The Transition to the Factory System in the Midland Textile Industry* (London, Gregg Revivals, 1992)

——, 'The Innovating Entrepreneurs in the British Ready-Made Clothing Industry', *Textile History*, 24, 1 (1993), 5–25

——, *Merchant Enterprise in Britain, from the Industrial Revolution to World War I* (Cambridge, Cambridge University Press, 1992)

Chartres, J. A., *Markets and Fairs in England and Wales, 1500 to 1860* (Leeds, University of Leeds, School of Business and Economic Studies, 1993)

Chaudhuri, K. N., *The Trading World of Asia and the English East India Company* (Cambridge, Cambridge University Press, 1978)

Church, R., *Kenricks in Hardware. A Family Business, 1791–1966* (Newton Abbot, David and Charles, 1969)

Clark, Peter, *British Clubs and Societies, 1580–1800: The Origins of an Associational World* (Oxford, Clarendon Press, 2000)

——, *The English Alehouse. A Social History, 1200–1830* (London, Longman, 1983)

——, *Sociability and Urbanity: Clubs and Societies in the Eighteenth-Century City*, H. J. Dyos Memorial Lecture (Leicester, University of Leicester, 1986)

—— and Jean Hosking, *Population Estimates of English Small Towns 1550–1851* (rev. ed., Leicester, Centre for Urban History, University of Leicester, 1993)

——, ed., *The Cambridge Urban History of Britain*, vol. 2: *Culture and Leisure, 1540–1840* (Cambridge, Cambridge University Press, 2000)

——, ed., *Country Towns in Pre-Industrial England* (Leicester, Leicester University Press, 1981)

——, ed., *The Early Modern Town: A Reader* (London, Longman, 1976)

——, ed., *The Transformation of English Provincial Towns, 1600–1800* (Hutchinson, London, 1984)

——, and Penelope Corfield, eds., *Industry and Urbanisation in Eighteenth Century England*, Papers from the ESRC Colloquia held at University College, London, January 1993 and The Centre for Urban History, University of Leicester, February 1994 (Leicester, Centre for Urban History, University of Leicester, 1994)

——, and Bernard Lepetit, eds., *Capital Cities and their Hinterlands in Early Modern Europe* (Aldershot, Scolar Press, 1996)

Clarke, Bob, *From Grub Street to Fleet Street: An Illustrated History of English Newspapers to 1899* (Aldershot, Ashgate, 2004)

Clarke, John, and Charles Critcher, *The Devil Makes Work: Leisure in Capitalist Britain* (Basingstoke, Macmillan, 1985)

Clear, Gwen, *The Story of W. H. Smith and Son, '. . .* based on earlier editions by G. R. Pocklington (1921) and F. E. K. Foat (1932 and 1937)' (London, private publication, 1949)

Cockburn, Harry A., *A History of the New Club, Edinburgh, 1787–1937* (London, W. & R. Chambers, 1938)

——, *Taverns and Clubs of Old Edinburgh* (Reprint, [no place of publication], *Scots Magazine*, 1935)

Codell, Julie F., 'Marion Harry Spielmann and the Role of the Press in the Professionalization of Artists', *Victorian Periodicals Review*, 22, 1 (1989), 7–15

Cohen, G. A., *Karl Marx's Theory of History: A Defence* (Oxford, Clarendon Press, 1978)

Coke, David, *The Muse's Bower: Vauxhall Gardens, 1728–1786* ([Sudbury, Gainsborough's House, 1978])

Cole, G. D. H., *A Century of Co-operation* (London, George Allen & Unwin, 1947)

Cole, Richard Cargill, *Irish Booksellers and English Writers, 1740–1800* (London, Mansell, 1986)

Coleman, D. C., 'Adam Smith, Businessmen, and the Mercantile System in England', *History of European Ideas*, 9, 2 (1988), 161–70

——, *The British Paper Industry, 1495–1860: A Study in Industrial Growth* (Oxford, Clarendon Press, 1958)

——, 'An Innovation and its Diffusion: The New Draperies', *Economic History Review*, 2nd ser., 22 (1969), 417–29

Colley, Linda, *Britons: Forging the Nation 1707–1837* (London, Pimlico, 1994)

Collins, Michael, *Banks and Industrial Finance in Britain, 1800–1939* (Basingstoke, Macmillan Educational, 1991)

——, *Money and Banking in the U.K.: A History* (London, Croom Helm, 1988)

Collins, Tony, and Wray Vamplew, *Mud, Sweat and Beers: A Cultural History of Sport and Alcohol* (Oxford, Berg, 2002)

——, 'The Pub, the Drinks Trade and the Early Years of Modern Football', *Sports Historian*, 20, 1 (2000), 1–17

Collison, Robert, *The Story of Street Literature: Forerunner of the Popular Press* (London, J. M. Dent & Sons, 1973)

Coltham, Stephen, 'English Working-Class Newspapers in 1867', *Victorian Studies*, 13 (1969), 158–80

Conway, Hazel, *People's Parks: The Design and Development of Victorian Parks in Britain* (Cambridge, Cambridge University Press, 1991)

Copeland, John, *Roads and their Traffic, 1750–1850* (Newton Abbot, David and Charles, 1968)

Cordery, Simon, *British Friendly Societies* (New York, Palgrave Macmillan, 2003)

——, 'Friendly Societies and the Discourse of Respectability in Britain, 1825–1875', *Journal of Business Studies*, 34 (1995), 35–58

Corfield, Penelope J., *The Impact of English Towns, 1700–1800* (Oxford, Oxford University Press, 1982)

——, *Power and the Professions in Britain, 1700–1850* (London, Routledge, 1995)

Corina, Maurice, *Fine Silks and Oak Counters: Debenhams, 1778–1978* (London, Hutchinson Benham, 1978)

Corley, T. A. B., *Quaker Enterprise in Biscuits: Huntley and Palmers of Reading, 1822–1972* (London, Hutchinson, 1972)

Cox, John D., and David Scott Kastan, *A New History of Early English Drama* (New York, Columbia University Press, 1997)

Cox, Nancy, *The Complete Tradesman: A Study of Retailing, 1550–1820* (Aldershot, Ashgate, 2000)

Craske, Matthew, *Art in Europe, 1700–1830: A History of the Visual Arts in an Era of Unprecedented Urban Economic Growth* (Oxford, Oxford University Press, 1997)

Crossick, Geoffrey, and Serge Jaumain, eds., *Cathedrals of Consumption: The European Department Story, 1850–1939* (Aldershot, Ashgate, 1999)

Crouzet, François, ed., *Capital Formation in the Industrial Revolution* (London, Methuen, 1972)

Crowley, John, *The Invention of Comfort: Sensibilities and Design in Early Modern Britain and Early America* (Baltimore, Johns Hopkins University Press, 2000)

——, 'The Sensibility of Comfort', *American Historical Review*, 104 (1999), 749–82

Csikszentmihalyi, Mihaly, and Eugene Rochberg-Halton, *The Meaning of Things: Domestic Symbols and the Self* (New York, Columbia University Press, 1981)

Cunningham, H., *Leisure in the Industrial Revolution, c. 1780–c.1880* (London, Croom Helm, 1980)

Cunnington, Phillis, and Alan Mansfield, *English Costumes for Sports and Outdoor Recreation: From the Sixteenth to the Nineteenth Centuries* (London, Adam & Charles Black, 1969)

Curtis, T. C., and W. A. Speck, 'The Societies for the Reformation of Manners: A Case Study in the Theory and Practice of Moral Reform', *Literature and History*, 3 (1976), 45–64

Dale, Antony, *Fashionable Brighton, 1820–1860* (2nd ed., London, Oriel Press, 1987)

Dale, Tim, *Harrods: A Palace in Knightsbridge* (London, Harrods Publishing, 1995)

——, *Harrods: The Store and the Legend* (London, Pan, 1981)

Davenport-Hines, R. P. T., ed., *Markets and Bagmen: Studies in the History of Marketing and British Industrial Performance, 1830–1939* (Aldershot, Gower, 1986)

——, and Jonathan Liebenau, eds., *Business in the Age of Reason* (London, Frank Cass, 1987)

Davis, Arthur K., 'Veblen on the Decline of the Protestant Ethic', *Social Forces*, 22 (1944), 282–6

Davis, Dorothy, *A History of Shopping* (London, Routledge & Kegan Paul, 1966)

Davis, Graham, and Penny Bonsall, *Bath: A New History* (Keele, Keele University Press, 1996)

Davis, Jim, and Victor Emeljanow, *Reflecting the Audience: London Theatre Audiences, 1840–1880* (Iowa City, University of Iowa Press, 2001)

Dearborn, Dorothy, 'Christmas Cards through the Years', *Atlantic Advocate*, 66 (December 1975), 21–3

Dearmer, Percy, R. Vaughan Williams and Martin Shaw, *The Oxford Book of Carols* (London, Oxford University Press, 1928)

Deelman, Christian, *The Great Shakespeare Jubilee* (London, Michael Joseph, 1964)

Devine, T. M., *The Tobacco Lords: A Study of the Tobacco Merchants of Glasgow and their Trading Activities, c.1740–90* (Edinburgh, John Donald, 1975)

Diamond, Michael, *Victorian Sensation, Or, the Spectacular, the Shocking and the Scandalous in Nineteenth-Century Britain* (London, Anthem Press, 2003)

Digby, Anne, *The Evolution of British General Practice, 1850–1948* (Oxford, Oxford University Press, 1999)

——, *Making a Medical Living: Doctors and Patients in the English Market for Medicine, 1720–1911* (Cambridge, Cambridge University Press, 1994)

Dillard, Philip H., *How Quaint the Ways of Paradox! An Annotated Gilbert & Sullivan Bibliography* (Metuchen, NJ, Scarecrow Press, 1991)

Dingle, R. E., 'Drink and Working-Class Living Standards in Britain, 1870–1914', *Business History Review*, 25 (1972), 608–22

Dolan, Brian, *Josiah Wedgwood: Entrepreneur to the Enlightenment* (London, HarperCollins, 2004)

Donoghue, Frank, *The Fame Machine: Book Reviewing and Eighteenth-Century Literary Careers* (Stanford, Cal., Stanford University Press, 1996)

Doody, Margaret Anne, *Frances Burney: The Life in the Works* (New Brunswick, NJ, Rutgers University Press, 1988)

Drayton, Richard, *Nature's Government: Science, Imperial Britain, and the 'Improvement' of the World* (New Haven, Yale University Press, 2000)

Drinkwater, John, ed., *The Eighteen-Sixties: Essays by Fellows of the Royal Society of Literature* (Cambridge, Cambridge University Press, 1932)

Drotner, Kirsten, *English Children and their Magazines, 1751–1945* (New Haven, Yale University Press, 1988)

Drummond, P., 'The Royal Society of Musicians in the Eighteenth Century', *Music and Letters*, 59 (1978), 268–78

Dunae, Patrick, 'Boy's Own Paper: Origin and Editorial Policies', *The Private Library*, 2nd ser., 9, 4 (1976), 125–58

——, 'Penny Dreadfuls: Late 19th-Century Boys' Literature and Crime', *Victorian Studies*, 22, 2 (1979), 133–50

Duncan, Carol, and Alan Wallach, 'The Universal Survey Museum', *Art History*, 3, 4 (1980), 448–69

Dyos, H. J., and Michael Wolff, eds., *The Victorian City: Images and Reality* (London, Routledge & Kegan Paul, 1973)

Dyson, Anthony, *Pictures to Print: The Nineteenth-Century Engraving Trade* (London, Farrand, 1984)

Earle, Edward, 'The Effect of Romanticism on the 19th Century Development of Copyright Law', *Intellectual Property Journal*, 6 (1991), 269–90

Eaves, Morris, *The Counter-Arts Conspiracy: Art and Industry in the Age of Blake* (Ithaca, Cornell University Press, 1992)

Edelstein, T. J., *Vauxhall Gardens* (New Haven, Yale Center for British Art, 1983)

Ehrlich, Cyril, *The Music Profession in Britain since the Eighteenth Century: A Social History* (Oxford, Clarendon Press, 1985)

——, *The Piano: A History* (rev. ed., Oxford, Clarendon Press, 1990)

——, *Social Emulation and Industrial Progress – the Victorian Piano* (Belfast, Queen's University, 1975)

Eliot, Simon, *Some Patterns and Trends in British Publishing, 1800–1919* (London, Bibliographical Society, 1994)

——and John Sutherland, *The Publishers' Circular 1837–1900: A Guide to the Microfiche Edition* ([Cambridge], Chadwyck-Healey, [1988])

Ellis, Aytoun, *The Penny Universities: A History of the Coffee-Houses* (London, Secker & Warburg, 1956)

Engel, A. J., *From Clergyman to Don: The Rise of the Academic Profession in Nineteenth-Century Oxford* (Oxford, Clarendon Press, 1983)

Everitt, Alan, ed., *Perspectives in English Urban History* (Basingstoke, Macmillan, 1973)

Fawcett, Trevor, *Bath Entertain'd: Amusements, Recreations and Gambling at the 18th-Century Spa* (Bath, Ruton, 1998)

——, 'Eighteenth-Century Shops and the Luxury Trade', *Bath History*, 3 (1990), 49–75

——, 'Hospital, Casino, Holiday Resort, Heritage Site: The Eighteenth-Century Transformation of Bath', *The Historian*, 59 (1998), 4–8

——, *The Rise of English Provincial Art: Artists, Patrons, and Institutions outside London, 1800–1830* (Oxford, Clarendon Press, 1974)

——, and M. Inskip, 'The Making of Orange Grove', *Bath History*, 5 (1994), 24–50

Fawkes, Richard, *Dion Boucicault: A Biography* (London, Quartet, 1979)

Faxon, Frederick W., *Literary Annuals and Gift Books: A Bibliography, 1823–1903*, with a supplementary essay by Eleanore Jamieson and Iain Bain (reprint, Pinner, Private Libraries Association, 1973)

Fay, C. R., *Palace of Industry, 1851: A Study of the Great Exhibition and its Fruits* (Cambridge, Cambridge University Press, 1951)

Feather, John, 'British Publishing in the 18th Century: A Preliminary Subject Analysis', *Library*, 6th ser., 8 (1986), 32–46

——, *The English Provincial Book Trade before 1850: A Checklist of Secondary Sources* (Oxford, Oxford Bibliographical Society, 1981)

——, *A History of British Publishing* (London, Croom Helm, 1988)

——, *The Provincial Book Trade in Eighteenth-Century England* (Cambridge, Cambridge University Press, 1985)

——, 'The Publishers and the Pirates: British Copyright Law in Theory and Practice, 1710–1775', *Publishing History*, 22 (1987), 5–32

——, 'Publishers and Politicians: The Remaking of the Law of Copyright in Britain, 1775–1842. Part I: Legal Deposit and the Battle of the Library Tax', *Publishing History*, 24 (1988), 49–76

——, *Publishing, Piracy and Politics: An Historical Study of Copyright in Britain* (London, Mansell, 1994)

Feltes, Norman, *Modes of Production of Victorian Novels* (Chicago, University of Chicago Press, 1986)

Fergus, J., '18th-Century Readers in Provincial England: The Customers of Samuel Clay's Circulating Library and Bookshop in Warwick, 1770–72', *Papers of the Bibliographic Society of America*, 78 (1984), 155–213

Ferry, John William, *A History of the Department Store* (New York, Macmillan, 1960)

ffrench, Yvonne, *The Great Exhibition: 1851* (London, Harvill, 1950)

Fine, Ben, and Ellen Leopold, 'Consumerism and the Industrial Revolution', *Social History*, 15, 2 (1990), 151–79

Finkelstein, David, 'The Secret: British Publishers and Mudie's Struggle for Economic Survival, 1861–64', *Publishing History*, 34 (1993), 21–50

Flavell, M. Kay, 'The Enlightened Reader and the New Industrial Towns: A Study of the Liverpool Library, 1758–1790', *British Journal for 18th-Century Studies*, 8 (1985), 17–35

Flinn, M. W., 'Trends in Real Wages, 1750–1850', *Business History Review*, 2nd ser., 27 (1974), 395–411

Flint, Kate, *The Woman Reader, 1837–1914* (Oxford, Clarendon Press, 1993)

Folkenflik, Robert, 'Macpherson, Chatterton, Blake, and the Great Age of Literary Forgery', *Centennial Review*, 18 (1974), 378–91

Fontaines, Una des, 'Wedgwood's London Showrooms', *Proceedings of the Wedgwood Society*, 8 (1970), 193–212

Fordham, Sir Herbert George, *'Paterson's Roads': Daniel Paterson, His Maps and Itineraries, 1738–1825* (London, Oxford University Press, for the Transactions of the Bibliographical Society, 1925)

Forrest, Denys, *Tea for the British: The Social and Economic History of a Famous Trade* (London, Chatto & Windus, 1973)

Forty, Adrian, *Objects of Desire: Design and Society 1750–1980* (London, Thames and Hudson, 1986)

Foss, Michael, *The Art of Patronage: The Arts in Society, 1660–1750* (London, Hamilton, 1971)

Foucault, Michel, *The Order of Things: An Archaeology of the Human Sciences* (London, Routledge, 2001)

Fox, Celina, *Graphic Journalism in England during the 1830s and 1840s* (London, Garland, 1988)

Fox, M. R., *Dye-Makers of Great Britain, 1856–1976: A History of Chemists, Companies, Products and Changes* (Manchester, ICI, 1987)

Fraser, A., 'John Murray's Colonial and Home Library', *Papers of the Bibliographic Society of America*, 91 (1997), 339–408

——, 'A Publishing House and its Readers, 1841–1880: The Murrays and the Miltons', *Papers of the Bibliographic Society of America*, 90 (1996), 5–47

Fraser, W. Hamish, *The Coming of the Mass Market, 1850–1914* (Basingstoke, Macmillan, 1981)

Freeman, Michael, *Railways and the Victorian Imagination* (New Haven, Yale University Press, 1999)

——, and Derek H. Aldcroft, eds., *Transport in Victorian Britain* (Manchester, Manchester University Press, 1988)

Fri, James L., 'This Business of Christmas: Toys', *Current Trends*, 47 (1937), 53–6

Fullerton, Peter, 'Patronage and Pedagogy: The British Institution in the Early Nineteenth Century', *Art History*, 5, 1 (1982), 59–72

Gadd, David, *Georgian Summer: Bath in the Eighteenth Century* (Bath, Adams and Dart, 1971)

Gaskill, Howard, 'What did James Macpherson Really Leave on Display at his Publisher's Shop in 1762?', *Scottish Gaelic Studies*, 16 (1990), 67–89

——, ed., *Ossian Revisited* (Edinburgh, Edinburgh University Press, 1991)

Gerhold, Dorian, *Road Transport before the Railways: Russell's London Flying Waggons* (Cambridge, Cambridge University Press, 1993)

Gernsheim, Alison, *Victorian and Edwardian Fashion: A Photographic Survey* (New York, Dover, 1981; republication of *Fashion and Reality* [1963])

Gibbs-Smith, C. H., *The Great Exhibition of 1851* (2nd ed., London, HMSO, 1981)

Ginsburg, Madeleine, 'Rags to Riches: The Secondhand Clothes Trade, 1700–1978', *Costume*, 14 (1980), 121–35

——, 'The Tailoring and Dressmaking Trades, 1700–1850', *Costume*, 6 (1972), 64–9

Golby, J. M., and A. W. Purdue, *The Civilisation of the Crowd: Popular Culture in England, 1750–1900* (rev. ed., Stroud, Sutton, 1999)

——, *The Making of the Modern Christmas* (rev. ed., Stroud, Sutton, 2000)

Goodbar, Octavia, 'The Business of Christmas: Cards', *Current Trends*, 47 (1937), 56–8

Goodman, Andrew, *Gilbert and Sullivan at Law* (East Brunswick, NJ, Associated Universities Presses, 1983)

Goody, J., *Literacy in Traditional Societies* (Cambridge, Cambridge University Press, 1975)

Gosden, Peter H. J. H., *The Friendly Societies in England, 1815–1875* (Manchester, Manchester University Press, 1961)

——, *Self-Help: Voluntary Association in the 19th Century* (London, Batsford, 1973)

Goulstone, John, *Football's Secret History* (Upminster, 3–2 Books, 2001)

——, 'The Working-Class Origins of Modern Football: An Examination of the Influence of Folk Football on the Development of the Association and Rugby Codes' (typescript deposited in the British Library, 1997)

Gourvish, T. R., *Railways and the British Economy, 1830–1914* (London, Macmillan, 1980)

——, and Alan O'Day, eds., *Later Victorian Britain, 1867–1900* (Basingstoke, Macmillan, 1988)

Graham, Walter, *The Beginnings of the English Literary Periodicals* (Oxford, Clarendon, 1926)

Greenhalgh, P., *Ephemeral Vistas: The Expositions Universelles, Great Exhibitions and World's Fairs, 1851–1939* (Manchester, Manchester University Press, 1988)

Greenwood, Jeremy, *Newspapers and the Post Office, 1635–1834* ([no place of publication], Postal History Society, 1971)

Gretton, Thomas, *Murders and Moralities: English Catchpenny Prints, 1800–1860* (London, Colonnade Book, British Museum Publications, 1980)

Griest, Guinevere L., *Mudie's Circulating Library and the Victorian Novel* (Newton Abbot, David and Charles, 1970)

Gross, John, *The Rise and Fall of the Man of Letters: Aspects of English Literary Life since 1800* (London, Weidenfeld & Nicolson, 1969)

Guttmann, Allen, *Sports Spectators* (New York, Columbia University Press, 1986)

Haber, L. F., *The Chemical Industry during the Nineteenth Century: A Study of the Economic Aspect of Applied Chemistry in Europe and North America* (Oxford, Clarendon Press, 1958)

Hadfield, Miles and John, *The Twelve Days of Christmas* (London, Cassell, 1961)

Haining, Peter, ed., *The Penny Dreadful: Or, Strange, Horrid and Sensational Tales* (London, Gollancz, 1975)

Haley, Bruce, *The Healthy Body and Victorian Culture* (Cambridge, Mass., Harvard University Press, 1978)

Halliday, F. E., *The Cult of Shakespeare* (London, Duckworth, 1957)

Hannavy, John, *The English Seaside in Victorian and Edwardian Times* (Princes Risborough, Shire, 2003)

Hargreaves, John, *Sport, Power and Culture: A Social and Historical Analysis of Popular Sports in Britain* (Cambridge, Polity, 1986)

Harris, Michael, and Alan Lee, eds., *The Press in English Society from the Seventeenth to the Nineteenth Centuries* (London, Associated Universities Presses, 1986)

Harrison, M., 'The Ordering of the Urban Environment: Time, Work and the Occurrence of Crowds, 1790–1835', *Past and Present*, 110 (1986), 134–68

Hart, Kevin, *Samuel Johnson and the Culture of Property* (Cambridge, Cambridge University Press, 1999)

Hartwell, R. M., ed., *The Causes of the Industrial Revolution in England* (London, Methuen, 1967)

Harvey, Adrian, *The Beginnings of a Commercial Sporting Culture in Britain, 1793–1850* (Aldershot, Ashgate, 2004)

Haskell, Francis, *Past and Present in Art and Taste: Selected Essays* (London, Yale University Press, 1987)

——, and Nicholas Penny, *Taste and the Antique: The Lure of Classical Sculpture, 1500–1900* (London, Yale University Press, 1981)

Havenhand, Greville, *A Nation of Shopkeepers* (London, Eyre & Spottiswoode, 1970)

Hawke, Gary R., *Railways and Economic Growth in England and Wales, 1840–1970* (Oxford, Clarendon Press, 1970)

Hembry, Phyllis, *The English Spa, 1560–1815: A Social History* (London, Athlone Press, 1980)

——, completed by Leonard W. Cowie and Evelyn E. Cowie, *British Spas from 1815 to the Present: A Social History* (London, Athlone Press, 1997)

Herlihy, David V., *Bicycle: The History* (New Haven, Yale University Press, 2004)

Hern, Anthony, *The Seaside Holiday: The History of the English Seaside Resort* (London, Cresset, 1967)

Hills, Richard L., and W. H. Brock, eds., *Chemistry and the Chemical Industry in the 19th Century: The Henrys of Manchester and other Studies* (Aldershot, Variorum, 1997)

Hindley, Diana and Geoffrey, *Advertising in Victorian England, 1837–1901* (London, Wayland, 1972)

Hindley, Geoffrey, *A History of Roads* (London, Peter Davies, 1971)

Hole, Christina, *Christmas and its Customs* (London, Richard Bell, [1957])

Holmes, Charles, and C. H. Collins Baker, *The Making of the National Gallery, 1824–1924* (London, The National Gallery, 1924)

Holt, Elizabeth Gilmore, ed., *The Triumph of Art for the Public: The Emerging Role of Exhibitions and Critics* (Washington, DC, Decatur House, 1980)

Holt, Richard, *Sport and the British: A Modern History* (Oxford, Clarendon Press, 1989)

Honeycombe, Gordon, *Selfridges: Seventy-five Years: The Story of the Store, 1909–1984* (London, Park Lane Press, 1984)

Honeyman, Katrina, *Origins of Enterprise: Business Leadership in the Industrial Revolution* (Manchester, Manchester University Press, 1982)

——, *Well Suited: A History of the Leeds Clothing Industry, 1850–1990* (Oxford, Oxford University Press, 2000)

Hood, Julia, and B. S. Yamey, 'The Middle-Class Co-operative Retailing Societies in London, 1864–1900', *Oxford Economic Papers*, 9 (1957), 309–22

Hooper-Greenhill, Eilean, *Museums and the Shaping of Knowledge* (London, Routledge, 1992)

Hoppen, K. Theodore, *The Mid-Victorian Generation, 1846–1886* (Oxford, Clarendon Press, 1998)

Horrell, Sara, 'Home Demand and British Industrialization', *Journal of Economic History*, 56 (1996), 561–605

Hosgood, Christopher P., 'Mercantile Monasteries: Shops, Shop Assistants and Shop Life in Late Victorian and Edwardian Britain', *Journal of British Studies*, 38 (1999), 322–52

Houston, R. A., 'The Development of Literacy: Northern England, 1640–1750', *Economic History Review*, 2nd ser., 35 (1982), 199–216

——, *Social Change in the Age of Enlightenment: Edinburgh, 1660–1760* (Oxford, Clarendon Press, 1994)

Hudson, Derek, and Kenneth W. Luckhurst, *The Royal Society of Arts, 1754–1954* (London, John Murray, 1954)

Hudson, Kenneth, *Patriotism with Profit: British Agricultural Societies in the Eighteenth and Nineteenth Centuries* (London, Hugh Evelyn, 1972)

——, *A Social History of Museums: What the Visitors Thought* (London, Macmillan, 1975)

Hughes, G. Bernard, 'Furniture for the Regency Traveller', *Country Life*, March 1967, 452–3

Hughes, Linda K., and Michael Lund, *The Victorian Serial* (Charlottesville, University Press of Virginia, 1991)

Hughes, Peter, and David Williams, eds., *The Varied Pattern: Studies in the 18th Century* (Toronto, A. M. Hakkert, 1971)

Hughes, Winifred, *The Maniac in the Cellar: Sensation Novels of the 1860s* (Princeton, Princeton University Press, 1981)

Hugill, Antony, *Sugar and All That . . . A History of Tate and Lyle* (London, Gentry Books, 1978)

Huggins, Mike, *Flat Racing and British Society, 1790–1914: A Social and Economic History* (London, Frank Cass, 2000)

——, *The Victorians and Sport* (London, Hambledon and London, 2004)

Humphries, Charles, and William C. Smith, *Music Publishing in the British Isles, from the Beginning until the Middle of the Nineteenth Century: A Dictionary of Engravers, Printers, Publishers and Music Sellers, with a Historical Introduction* (2nd ed., Oxford, Basil Blackwell, 1970)

Hunt, J. Dixon, 'Theatres, Gardens and Garden-theatres', *Essays and Studies*, 33 (1980), 95–118

Hunt, R. W., I. G. Philip and R. J. Roberts, eds., *Studies in the Book Trade in Honour of Graham Pollard* (Oxford, Oxford Bibliographical Society, 1975)

Hunt, Tristram, *Building Jerusalem: The Rise and Fall of the Victorian City* (London, Weidenfeld & Nicolson, 2004)

Hutchinson, Sidney C., *The History of the Royal Academy, 1768–1968* (2nd ed., London, Robert Royce, 1968)

Isaac, Peter, and Barry McKay, eds., *The Mighty Engine: The Printing Press and its Impact* (Winchester, St Paul's Bibliographies, 2000)

——, eds., *The Reach of Print: Making, Selling and Using Books* (Winchester, St Paul's Bibliographies, 1998)

Jackson-Stops, Gervase, ed., *Treasure Houses of Britain: 500 Years of Private Patronage and Art Collecting* (London, Yale University Press, 1985)

Jacob, Margaret C., *Scientific Culture and the Making of the Industrial West* (Oxford, Oxford University Press, 1997)

James, Louis, '"Economic" Literature: The Emergence of Popular Journalism', *Victorian Periodicals Newsletter*, 14 (1972), 13–20

——, *Fiction for the Working Man, 1830–1850: A Study of the Literature Produced for the Working Classes in Early Victorian Urban England* (Harmondsworth, Penguin, 1974)

——, *Print and the People 1819–1851* (London, Allen Lane, 1976)

Jefferys, James B., *Retail Trading in Britain, 1850–1950: A Study of Trends in Retailing with Special Reference to the Development of Co-operative, Multiple Shop and Department Store Methods of Trading* (Cambridge, Cambridge University Press, 1954)

Johnson, James H., and Colin G. Pooley, eds., *The Structure of Nineteenth Century Cities* (London, Croom Helm, 1982)

Jones, Aled, 'Tillotson's Fiction Bureau: The Manchester Manuscripts', *Victorian Periodicals Review*, 17, 1 and 2 (1984), 43–9

Jones, Hurford, *Two Centuries: The Story of David Lloyd Pigott and Company of London, Tea and Coffee Merchants, 1760–1960* (London, Harley, n.d.)

Jordan, John O., and Robert L. Patten, eds., *Literature in the Marketplace: Nineteenth-Century British Publishing and Reading Practices* (Cambridge, Cambridge University Press, 1995)

Joyce, Patrick, *Work, Society and Politics: The Culture of the Factory in Later Victorian England* (London, Gregg Revivals, 1991)

Kaplan, Joel H., and Sheila Stowell, *Theatre and Fashion: Oscar Wilde to the Suffragettes* (Cambridge, Cambridge University Press, 1994)

Kaufman, Paul, *Borrowings from the Bristol Library, 1773–1784: A Unique Record of Reading Vogues* (Charlottesville, Bibliographical Society of the University of Virginia, 1960)

——, 'English Book Clubs and their Role in Social History', *Libri*, 14, 1 (1964), 1–31

——, *Libraries and their Users: Collected Papers in Library History* (London, The Library Association, 1969)

Kearns, Gerry, and Chris Philo, eds., *Selling Places: The City as Cultural Capital, Past and Present* (Oxford, Pergamon, 1993)

Keith, Sarah, 'Mudie's Circulating Library', *Nineteenth-Century Fiction*, 11 (1956), 156–7

Kellett, John R., *Railways and Victorian Cities* (London, Routledge & Kegan Paul, 1979; 1st published 1969 as *The Impact of the Railways on Victorian Cities*)

Kelly, John Alexander, *German Visitors to English Theatres in the Eighteenth Century* (Princeton, Princeton University Press, 1936)

Kern, Stephen, *The Culture of Time and Space, 1880–1914* (London, Weidenfeld & Nicolson, 1983)

King, Andrew, *The London Journal, 1845–83: Periodicals, Production and Gender* (Aldershot, Ashgate, 2004)

——, and John Plunkett, eds., *Popular Print Media, 1820–1900* (London, Routledge, 2004)

King-Hele, Desmond, *Erasmus Darwin: A Life of Unequalled Achievement* (London, Giles de la Mare, 1999)

Klingender, Francis D., *Art and the Industrial Revolution* (London, Evelyn, Adams & Mackay, 1968)

Knott, J., 'Circulating Libraries in Newcastle in the 18th and 19th Centuries,' *Library History*, 2, 6 (1972), 227–49

Koehn, Nancy F., *Brand New: How Entrepreneurs Earned Consumers' Trust from Wedgwood to Dell* (Boston, Harvard Business School Press, 2001)

Korshin, Paul, 'Types of 18th-Century Literary Patronage', *Eighteenth-Century Studies*, 7, 4 (1974), 453–69

Kowaleski-Wallace, Elizabeth, *Consuming Subjects: Women, Shopping, and Business in the Eighteenth Century* (New York, Columbia University Press, 1997)

Krause, Elliott A., *Death of the Guilds: Professions, States, and the Advance of Capitalism, 1930 to the Present* (New Haven, Yale University Press, 1996)

Lamb, Andrew, 'Gilbert and Sullivan and the Gaiety', *Musical Times*, 112 (1971), 1162–4

Lancaster, Bill, *The Department Store: A Social History* (London, Leicester University Press, 1995)

Langdon, Philip, 'Great Exhibitions: Representations of the Crystal Palace in Mayhew, Dickens, and Dostoyevsky', *Nineteenth-Century Contexts*, 20 (1997), 27–59

Langford, Paul, *A Polite and Commercial People: England, 1727–1783* (Oxford, Oxford University Press, 1989; p/b 1992)

Lansdell, Avril, *Fashion à la Carte, 1860–1900: A Study of Fashion through Cartes-de-Visite* (Princes Risborough, Shire, 1985)

——, *Seaside Fashions 1860–1939: A Study of Clothes Worn in or beside the Sea* (Princes Risborough, Shire, 1990)

Laqueur, T. W., *Religion and Respectability: Sunday Schools and Working Class Culture, 1780–1850* (London, Yale University Press, 1976)

Lead, Peter, *The Trent and Mersey Canal* (Ashbourne, Moorland, 1980)

Lee, Alan J., *The Origins of the Popular Press, 1855–1914* (London, Croom Helm, 1976)

Leiss, William, Stephen Kline and Sut Jhally, *Social Communication in Advertising: Persons, Products and Images of Well-Being* (London, Methuen, 1986)

Lemire, Beverly, 'Developing Consumerism and the Ready-Made Clothing Trade in Britain, 1750–1800', *Textile History*, 15, 1 (1984), 21–44

——, *Dress, Culture and Commerce: The English Clothing Trade before the Factory, 1660–1800* (Basingstoke, Macmillan, 1997)

——, *Fashion's Favourite: The Cotton Trade and the Consumer in Britain 1660–1800* (Oxford, Oxford University Press 1991)

——, '"A Good Stock of Cloathes": The Changing Market for Cotton Clothing in Britain, 1750–1800', *Textile History*, 22, 2 (1991), 311–28

Levitt, Sarah,'Cheap Mass-produced Men's Clothing in the Nineteenth and Early Twentieth Centuries', *Textile History*, 22, 2 (1991), 179–92

——, 'Manchester Mackintoshes: A History of the Rubberized Garment Trade in Manchester', *Textile History*, 17, 1 (1986), 51–69

——, *Victorians Unbuttoned: Registered Designs for Clothing, their Makers and Wearers, 1839–1900* (London, George Allen & Unwin, 1986)

——, and Jane Tozer, *Fabric of Society: A Century of People and their Clothes, 1770–1870* (Carno, Powys, Laura Ashley, 1983)

Lewis, Lawrence, *The Advertisements of The Spectator* (London, Archibald Constable & Co., 1909)

Ley, J. W. T., 'The Apostle of Christmas', *The Dickensian*, 2 (December 1906), 324–6

Lindsay, J., *The Trent and Mersey Canal* (Newton Abbot, David and Charles, 1979)

Lipking, Lawrence, *The Ordering of the Arts in Eighteenth-Century England* (Princeton, Princeton University Press, 1970)

Lippincott, Louise, *Selling Art in Georgian London: The Rise of Arthur Pond* (London, Yale University Press, 1983)

Loeb, Lori Anne, *Consuming Angels: Advertising and Victorian Women* (New York, Oxford University Press, 1994)

Loesser, Arthur, *Men, Women and Pianos: A Social History* (New York, Dover, 1990)

Longrigg, Roger, *The History of Horse Racing* (London, Macmillan, 1972)

Loudon, Irvine, *Medical Care and the General Practitioner, 1750–1850* (Oxford, Clarendon Press, 1986)

——, 'The Origins of the General Practitioner', *Journal of the Royal College of General Practitioners*, 33 (1983), 13–18

Loveridge, Pat, *A Calendar of Fairs and Markets Held in the Nineteenth Century* ([no place of publication], Romany and Traveller Family History Society, 2003)

Lowerson, John, *Sport and the English Middle Classes: 1870–1914* (Manchester, Manchester University Press, 1993)

——, and John Myerscough, *Time to Spare in Victorian England* (Hassocks, Harvester, 1977)

Lutchmansingh, Larry D., 'Commodity Exhibitionism at the London Great Exhibition of 1851', *Annals of Scholarship*, 7 (1990), 203–16

Lysack, Krista, 'Goblin Markets: Victorian Women Shoppers at Liberty's Oriental Bazaar', *Nineteenth-Century Contexts*, 27, 2 (2005), 139–65

Maas, Jeremy, *Gambart, Prince of the Victorian Art World* (London, Barrie & Jenkins, 1975)

MacCannell, Dean, *The Tourist: A New Theory of the Leisure Class* (London, Macmillan, 1976)

McDowell, Paula, 'Consuming Women: The Life of the "Literary Lady" as Popular Culture in Eighteenth-Century Britain', *Genre*, 26 (1993), 219–52

McElroy, Davis D., *Scotland's Age of Improvement: A Survey of Eighteenth-Century Literary Clubs and Societies* (Pullman, Wash., Washington State University Press, 1969)

McInnes, A., 'The Emergence of a Leisure Town: Shrewsbury, 1660–1760', *Past and Present*, 120 (1988), 60–64

McIntyre, Ian, *Garrick* (Harmondsworth, Penguin, 1999)

Mackay, James, *The Man Who Invented Himself: A Life of Sir Thomas Lipton* (Edinburgh, Mainstream, 1998)

McKendrick, Neil, 'Josiah Wedgwood: An Eighteenth-Century Entrepreneur in Salesmanship and Marketing Techniques', *Economic History Review*, 2nd ser., 12, 3 (1960), 408–33

——, 'Josiah Wedgwood and Cost Accounting in the Industrial Revolution', *Economic History Review*, 2nd ser., 23, 1 (1970), 45–67

——, 'Josiah Wedgwood and Factory Discipline', *Historical Journal*, 4, 1 (1961), 30–55

——, 'Josiah Wedgwood and George Stubbs', *History Today*, 7 (1957), 504–14

——, 'Josiah Wedgwood and Thomas Bentley: An Inventor–Entrepreneur Partnership in the Industrial Revolution', *Transactions of the Royal Historical Society*, 5th ser., 14 (1964), 1–33

——, John Brewer and J. H. Plumb, *The Birth of a Consumer Society: The Commercialization of Eighteenth-Century England* (London, Europa, 1982)

——, ed., *Historical Perspectives: Studies in English Thought and Society, in Honour of J. H. Plumb* (London, Europa, 1974)

——, and R. B. Outhwaite, eds., *Business Life and Public Policy: Essays in Honour of D. C. Coleman* (Cambridge, Cambridge University Press, 1986)

Mackerness, E. D., *A Social History of English Music* (London, Routledge & Kegan Paul, 1964)

Macleod, Dianne Sachko, *Art and the Victorian Middle Class: Money and the Making of Cultural Identity* (Cambridge, Cambridge University Press, 1996)

McVeagh, John, *Tradefull Merchants: The Portrayal of the Capitalist in Literature* (London, Routledge & Kegan Paul, 1981)

McVeigh, Simon, *Concert Life in London from Mozart to Haydn* (Cambridge, Cambridge University Press, 1993)

Maidment, Brian, *Into the 1830s: Some Origins of Victorian Illustrated Journalism. Cheap Octavo Magazines of the 1820s and their Influence* (Manchester, Manchester Polytechnic Library, 1992)

Malcolmson, Robert W., *Popular Recreations in English Society, 1700–1850* (Cambridge, Cambridge University Press, 1973)

Malet, Hugh, *The Canal Duke: A Biography of Francis, 3rd Duke of Bridgewater* (Newton Abbot, David and Charles, 1961)

Malley, Shawn, 'Austen Henry Layard and the Periodical Press: Middle-Eastern Archaeology and the Excavation of Cultural Identity in Mid-19th-Century Britain', *Victorian Review*, 22 (1996), 171–89

——, 'Shipping the Bull: Staging Assyria in the British Museum', *Nineteenth-Century Contexts*, 26, 1 (2004), 1–27

Mangan, J. A., ed., *Reformers, Sport, Modernizers: Middle-Class Revolutionaries* (London, Frank Cass, 2002)

Mann, Julia de Lacey, *The Cloth Industry in the West of England from 1640 to 1880* (Oxford, Clarendon Press, 1971)

Marchand, Leslie A., *The Athenaeum: A Mirror of Victorian Culture* (Chapel Hill, University of North Carolina Press, 1941)

Margetson, Stella, *Leisure and Pleasure in the Eighteenth Century* (London, Cassell, 1970)

Marillier, H. C., *Christie's, 1766–1925* (London, Constable & Co., 1926)

Marriott, John, ed., *Unknown London: Early Modernist Visions of the Metropolis, 1815–1845* (6 vols., [no place of publication], Pickering & Chatto, 2000)

Marrus, Michael R., ed., *The Emergence of Leisure* (New York, Harper Torchbooks, 1974)

Marshall, Gail, and Adrian Poole, eds., *Victorian Shakespeare*, vol. 1: *Theatre, Drama and Performance* (Basingstoke, Palgrave, 2003)

Marwick, W. H., 'Shops in Eighteenth- and Nineteenth-Century Edinburgh', *Book of the Old Edinburgh Club*, 30 (1959), 119–41

Mason, Tony, *Association Football and English Society, 1863–1915* (Brighton, Harvester, 1980)

Mathias, Peter, *The Brewing Industry in England, 1700–1830* (Cambridge, Cambridge University Press, 1959)

——, *Retailing Revolution: A History of Multiple Retailing in the Food Trades based upon the Allied Suppliers Group of Companies* (London, Longmans, Green and Co., 1967)

——, *The Transformation of England: Essays in the Economic and Social History of England in the Eighteenth Century* (London, Methuen, 1979)

Matthews, Leslie G., *History of Pharmacy in Britain* (Edinburgh and London, E. & S. Livingstone, 1962)

Mayer, David, III, *Harlequin in his Element: The English Pantomime, 1806–1836* (Cambridge, Mass., Harvard University Press, 1969)

Meisel, Martin, *Realizations: Narrative, Pictorial and Theatrical Arts in Nineteenth-Century England* (Princeton, Princeton University Press, 1983)

Meldola, Raphael, et al., eds., *Jubilee of the Discovery of Mauve and the Foundation of the Coal-Tar Industry by Sir W. H. Perking* (London, George Edward Wright, 1907)

Meller, H. E., *Leisure and the Changing City, 1870–1914* (London, Routledge & Kegan Paul, 1976)

Merwe, Pieter van der, *The Spectacular Career of Clarkson Stanfield, 1793–1867* (Tyne and Wear, Tyne and Wear County Council Museum, 1979)

Micklethwaite, John, and Adrian Wooldridge, *The Company: A Short History of a Revolutionary Idea* (London, Weidenfeld & Nicolson, 2004)

Miles, Clement A., *Christmas Customs and Traditions: Their History and Significance* (London, T. Fisher Unwin, 1912)

Miller, Daniel, ed., *Unwrapping Christmas* (Clarendon Press, Oxford, 1993)

Miller, Edward, *That Noble Cabinet: A History of the British Museum* (London, André Deutsch, 1973)

Miller, Michael B., *The Bon Marché: Bourgeois Culture and the Department Store, 1869–1920* (London, George Allen & Unwin, 1981)

Mineka, Francis E., *The Dissidence of Dissent: The Monthly Repository, 1806– 1838* (Chapel Hill, University of North Carolina Press, 1944)

Minihan, Janet, *The Nationalization of Culture: The Development of State Subsidies to the Arts in Great Britain* (New York, New York University Press, 1977)

Mitchell, C. J., 'Provincial Printing in Eighteenth-Century Britain', *Publishing History*, 21 (1987), 20–21

Moir, Esther, *The Discovery of Britain: The English Tourists, 1540–1840* (London, Routledge & Kegan Paul, 1964)

Money, John, *Experience and Identity: Birmingham and the West Midlands, 1760–1800* (Manchester, Manchester University Press, 1977)

Moody, Jane, *Illegitimate Theatre in London, 1770–1840* (Cambridge, Cambridge University Press, 2000)

Moore, Andrew W., *Norfolk and the Grand Tour: 18th-Century Travellers Abroad and their Souvenirs* (Norwich, Norfolk Museums Service, 1985)

Mordaunt Crook, Joseph, *The British Museum* (London, Allen Lane, 1972)

Morris, R. J., 'Voluntary Societies and British Urban Elites, 1780–1850', *Historical Journal*, 26 (1983), 95–118

Morrison, Kathryn A., *English Shops and Shopping: An Architectural History* (London, Yale University Press, 2003)

Mui, Hoh-Cheung, and Lorna H. Mui, *Shops and Shopkeeping in Eighteenth-Century England* (London, Routledge, 1989)

Murphy, Peter T., *Poetry as an Occupation and an Art in Britain, 1760–1830* (Cambridge, Cambridge University Press, 1993)

Musson, A. E., 'Newspaper Printing in the Industrial Revolution', *Economic History Review*, 2nd ser., 10 (1957–8), 411–26

——, and Eric Robinson, *Science and Technology in the Industrial Revolution* (Manchester, Manchester University Press, [1969])

Myers, Robin, and Michael Harris, eds., *Author/Publisher Relations during the Eighteenth and Nineteenth Centuries* (Oxford, Oxford Polytechnic Press, 1983)

——, eds., *Development of the English Book Trade, 1700–1899* (Oxford, Oxford Polytechnic Press, 1981)

——, eds., *Economics of the British Booktrade, 1605–1939* (Cambridge, Chadwyck Healy, 1985)

——, eds., *A Genius for Letters: Booksellers and Bookselling from the 16th to the 20th Century* (Winchester, St Paul's Bibliographies, 1995)

——, eds., *Journeys through the Market: Travel, Travellers and the Book Trade* (Folkestone, St Paul's Bibliographies, 1999)

——, eds., *Medicine, Mortality and the Book Trade* (Folkestone, St Paul's Bibliographies, 1998)

——, eds., *Sale and Distribution of Books from 1700* (Oxford, Oxford Polytechnic, 1984)

——, eds., *Serials and their Readers, 1620–1914* (Winchester, St Paul's Bibliographies, 1993)

——, eds., *Spreading the Word: The Distribution Networks of Print, 1550–1850* (Winchester, St Paul's Bibliographies, 1990)

——, and Giles Mandelbrote, eds., *The London Book Trade: Topographies of Print in the Metropolis from the Sixteenth Century* (London, British Library, 2003)

Natan, Alex, ed., *Silver Renaissance: Essays in Eighteenth-Century English History* (London, Macmillan, 1961)

Nead, Lynda, *Victorian Babylon: People, Streets and Images in Nineteenth-Century London* (London, Yale University Press, 2000)

Neale, R. S., *Bath, 1680–1850: A Social History, or, A Valley of Pleasure, Yet a Sink of Iniquity* (London, Routledge & Kegan Paul, 1981)

——, 'The Standard of Living 1780–1844: A Regional and Class Study', *Business History Review*, 2nd ser., 19 (1966), 590–606

Nenadic, Stana, 'Middle-Rank Consumers and Domestic Culture in Edinburgh and Glasgow, 1729–1840', *Past and Present*, 145 (1994), 122–56

Neuburg, Victor E., *The Penny Histories: A Study of Chapbooks for Young Readers over Two Centuries* (London, Oxford University Press, 1965)

——, *Popular Literature: A History and Guide, from the Beginning of Printing to the Year 1897* (London, Woburn Press, 1977)

Neve, Mica, 'Consumerism and its Contradictions', *Cultural Studies*, 1 (1987), 204–10

Nevett, T. R., *Advertising in Britain: A History* (London, Heinemann, 1982)

——, and Stanley C. Hollander, *Marketing in Three Eras: Proceedings of the Third Conference on Historical Research in Marketing* (East Lansing, Michigan State University, 1987)

Nicholson, Norman, *The Lakers: The Adventures of the First Tourists* (London, Robert Hale, 1955)

Nord, Deborah Epstein, *Walking the Victorian Streets: Women, Representation, and the City* (Ithaca, Cornell University Press, 1995)

North, Michael, and David Ormrod, eds., *Art Markets in Europe, 1400–1800* (Aldershot, Ashgate, 1998)

Olsen, Donald J., *Town Planning in London: The Eighteenth and Nineteenth Centuries* (New Haven, Yale University Press, 1982)

Ousby, Ian, *The Englishman's England: Taste, Travel and the Rise of Tourism* (London, Pimlico, 2002)

Owen, Felicity, and David Blayney Brown, *Collector of Genius: A Life of Sir George Beaumont* (London, Yale University Press, 1988)

Parks, Stephen, ed., *Four Tracts on Freedom of the Press, 1790–1821* (New York, Garland, 1974)

Parry, Noel, and José Parry, *The Rise of the Medical Profession: A Study of Collective Social Mobility* (London, Croom Helm, 1976)

Pavitt, Jane, ed., *Brand New* (London, Victoria & Albert Museum, 2000)

Perkin, Harold, *The Rise of Professional Society: England since 1880* (London, Routledge, 1989)

Peterson, M. Jeanne, *The Medical Profession in Mid-Victorian London* (Berkeley, University of California Press, 1978)

Pick, John, *The West End: Mismanagement and Snobbery* (Eastbourne, John Offord, 1983)

Pimlott, J. A. R., *The Englishman's Christmas: A Social History* (Hassocks, Harvester, 1978)

——, *The Englishman's Holiday: A Social History* (London, Faber, 1947)

Plant, Marjorie, *The English Book Trade: An Economic History of the Making and Sale of Books* (2nd ed., London, George Allen & Unwin, 1965)

Plumb, J. H., *The Commercialization of Leisure in 18th-Century England*, Stenton Lecture (Reading, University of Reading, 1973)

——, *Georgian Delights* (London, Weidenfeld & Nicolson, 1980)

Pocklington, G. R., *The Story of W. H. Smith & Son* (London, privately printed, 1921)

Pointon, Marcia, 'Portrait Painting as a Business Enterprise in London in the 1780s', *Art History*, 7, 2 (1984), 187–205

——, *Strategies for Showing: Women, Possession and Representation in English Visual Culture, 1665–1800* (Oxford, Oxford University Press, 1997)

Poovey, Mary, ed., *The Financial System in Nineteenth-Century Britain* (New York, Oxford University Press, 2003)

Porter, J. H., 'The Development of a Provincial Department Store, 1870–1939', *Business History*, 13, 1 (1971), 64–71

Porter, Roy, *Bodies Politic: Disease, Death and the Doctors in Britain, 1650–1900* (London, Reaktion, 2001)

——, *Doctor of Society: Thomas Beddoes and the Sick Trade in Late-Enlightenment England* (London, Routledge, 1992)

——, *Quacks: Fakers and Charlatans in English Medicine* (illustrated ed. of *Health for Sale: Quackery in England, 1650–1850*, 1989), (Stroud, Tempus, 2000)

——, ed., 'The Medical History of Waters and Spas', Supplement no. 10 to *Medical History*, 1990 (London, Wellcome Institute, 1990)

——, ed., *Patients and Practitioners: Lay Perceptions of Medicine in Pre-Industrial Society* (Cambridge, Cambridge University Press, 1985)

——, and Marie Mulvey Roberts, eds., *Pleasure in the Eighteenth Century* (Basingstoke, Macmillan, 1996)

Price, J. M., 'What Did Merchants Do? Reflections on British Overseas Trade, 1660–1790', *Journal of Economic History*, 49 (1989), 267–84

Prouty, Charles T., 'The Copyright of Shakespeare's Dramatic Works', in *Studies in Honor of A. H. R. Fairchild*, vol. 21, no. 1, ed. Giles E. Dawson (University of Missouri, Columbia, Mo., 1946)

Pykett, Lyn, *The Sensation Novel: From The Woman in White to The Moonstone* (Plymouth, Northcote House, 1994)

Quickenden, Kenneth, 'Boulton and Fothergill Silver: Business Plans and Miscalculations', *Art History*, 3, 3 (1980), 274–94

Rappaport, Erika Diane, *Shopping for Pleasure: Women in the Making of London's West End* (Princeton, Princeton University Press, 2000)

Raven, James, *Judging New Wealth: Popular Publishing and Responses to Commerce in England, 1750–1800* (Oxford, Clarendon Press, 1992)

Raymond, Joad, ed., *News, Newspapers and Society in Early Modern Britain* (London, Frank Cass, 1999)

Rees, Terence, *Theatre Lighting in the Age of Gas* (London, Society for Theatre Research, 1978)

——, and David Wilmore, *British Theatrical Patents* (London, Society for Theatre Research, 1996)

Reid, D. A. 'The Decline of St Monday, 1766–1876', *Past and Present*, 71 (1976), 76–101

Reilly, Robin, *Josiah Wedgwood, 1730–1795* (London, Macmillan, 1992)

Reitlinger, Gerald, *The Economics of Taste*, vol. 1: *The Rise and Fall of Picture Prices, 1760–1960*; vol. 2: *The Rise and Fall of Objets d'Art Prices since 1750*; vol. 3: *The Art Market in the 1960s* (London, Barrie & Rockliff, 1961–70)

Renier, Anne, *Friendship's Offering: An Essay on the Annuals and Gift Books of the 19th Century* (London, Private Libraries Association, 1964)

Richards, Jeffrey, *Sir Henry Irving: A Victorian Actor and his World* (London, Hambledon and London, 2005)

Richards, Thomas, *The Commodity Culture of Victorian England: Advertising and Spectacle, 1851–1914* (Stanford, Cal., Stanford University Press, 1990)

Richardson, Alan, *Literature, Education, and Romanticism: Reading as Social Practice, 1780–1832* (Cambridge, Cambridge University Press, 1994)

Ring, Jim, *How the English Made the Alps* (London, John Murray, 2000)

Rivers, Isabel, *Books and their Readers in Eighteenth-Century England: New Essays* (London, Leicester University Press, 2001)

——, ed., *Books and their Readers in Eighteenth-Century England* ([Leicester?], Leicester University Press, 1982)

Robertson, David, *Sir Charles Eastlake and the Victorian Art World* (Princeton, Princeton University Press, 1978)

Robinson, Dwight E., 'Eighteenth-Century Commerce and Fashion: Matthew Boulton's Marketing Techniques', *Economic History Review*, 2nd ser., 16, 1 (1963), 39–60

——, 'The Importance of Fashions in Taste to Business History: An Introductory Essay', *Business History Review*, 37, 1 (1963), 5–36

——, 'The Styling and Transmission of Fashions Historically Considered', *Journal of Economic History* 20, 4 (1960), 576–87

Robinson, Howard, *Britain's Post Office: A History of Development from the Beginnings to the Present Day* (London, Oxford University Press, 1953)

Robson, Robert, *The Attorney in Eighteenth-Century England* (Cambridge, Cambridge University Press, 1959)

Rodrick, Anne B., *Self Help and Civic Culture: Citizenship in Victorian Birmingham* (Aldershot, Ashgate, 2004)

Rollins, Cyril, and R. John Witts, eds., *The D'Oyly Carte Opera Company in Gilbert and Sullivan Operas: A Record of Productions, 1875–1961* (London, Michael Joseph, 1962)

Rose, Jonathan, 'Rereading the English Common Reader: A Preface to a History of Audiences', *Journal of the History of Ideas*, 53, 1 (1992), 47–70

Rose, Mark, 'The Author in Court, Pope v. Curll, 1741', *Cardozo Arts and Entertainment Law Journal*, 10 (1992), 475–93

——, 'The Author as Proprietor: Donaldson v. Becket and the Genealogy of Modern Authorship', *Representations*, 23 (1988), 51–85

——, *Authors and Owners: The Invention of Copyright* (Cambridge, Mass., Harvard University Press, 1993)

[Rosenfeld, S., ed.], *Anatomy of an Illusion: Studies in Nineteenth-Century Scene Design: Lectures of the Fourth International Congress on Theatre Research* (Amsterdam, International Federation for Theatre Research, 1969)

Ross, Trevor, 'Copyright and the Invention of Tradition', *Eighteenth-Century Studies*, 26 (1992), 1–27

Rowell, George, *The Victorian Theatre, 1792–1914: A Survey* (2nd ed., Cambridge, Cambridge University Press, 1978)

Rowland, William G., Jr., *Literature and the Marketplace: Romantic Writers and their Audiences in Great Britain and the United States* (Lincoln, University of Nebraska Press, 1996)

Rubinstein, David, 'Cycling in the 1890s', *Victorian Studies*, 21, 1 (1977), 47–71

Rubinstein, W. D., *Men of Property: The Very Wealthy in Britain since the Industrial Revolution* (London, Croom Helm, 1981)

Russell, Norman, *The Novelist and Mammon: Literary Responses to the World of Commerce in the Nineteenth Century* (Oxford, Clarendon Press, 1986)

Sadie, Stanley, 'Concert Life in Eighteenth-Century England', *Proceedings of the Royal Musical Association*, 78 (1958–9), 17–30

St Clair, William, *The Reading Nation in the Romantic Period* (Cambridge, Cambridge University Press, 2004)

Samuelson, Sue, *Christmas, An Annotated Bibliography* (New York, Garland, 1982)

Sands, Mollie, *The Eighteenth-Century Pleasure Gardens of Marylebone, 1737–1777* (London, Society for Theatre Research, 1987)

Sansom, William, *Christmas* (London, Weidenfeld & Nicolson, 1968)

Saunders, David, *Authorship and Copyright* (London, Routledge, 1992)

Saunders, J. W., *The Profession of English Letters* (London, Routledge & Kegan Paul, 1964)

Saxon, A. H., *Enter Foot and Horse: A History of Hippodrama in England and France* (New Haven, Yale University Press, 1968)

——, *The Life and Art of Andrew Ducrow and the Romantic Age of the English Circus* (Hamden, Conn., Archon, 1978)

Schivelbusch, Wolfgang, *Disenchanted Night: The Industrialization of Light in the Nineteenth Century*, tr. Angela Davies (Berkeley, University of California Press, 1995)

——, *The Railway Journey: The Industrialization of Time and Space in the 19th Century* (Leamington Spa, Berg, 1986)

Schofield, R. S., 'Dimensions of Illiteracy, 1750–1850', *Explorations in Economic History*, 10 (1972–3), 437–54

Scola, R., *Feeding the Victorian City: The Food Supply of Manchester, 1770–1870*, ed. W. A. Armstrong and Pauline Scola (Manchester, Manchester University Press, 1992)

——, 'Food Markets and Shops in Manchester, 1770–1870', *Journal of Historical Geography*, 1 (1975), 153–4

Scott, W. S., *Green Retreats: The Story of Vauxhall Gardens, 1661–1859* (London, Odhams Press, 1955)

Senelick, L., 'Politics as Entertainment: Victorian Music Hall Songs', *Victorian Studies*, 19 (1975), 149–80

Shannon, Brent, 'ReFashioning Men: Fashion, Masculinity, and the Cultivation of the Male Consumer in Britain, 1860–1914', *Victorian Studies*, 46, 4 (2004), 597–630

Sharpe, Pamela, 'Cheapness and Economy: Manufacturing and Retailing Ready-Made Clothing in London and Essex, 1830–50', *Textile History*, 26, 2 (1995), 203–13

Shattock, Joanne, and Michael Wolff, eds., *The Victorian Periodical Press: Samplings and Soundings* (Leicester, Leicester University Press, 1982)

Shaw, Gareth, and M. T. Wild, 'Retail Patterns in the Victorian City', *Transactions of the Institute of British Geographers*, 4 (1979), 278–91

Shepard, Leslie, *The History of Street Literature: The Story of Broadside Ballads, Chapbooks, Proclamations, News-Sheets, Election Bills, Tracts, Pamphlets, Cocks, Catchpennies, and other Ephemera* (Newton Abbot, David and Charles, 1973)

——, *John Pitts, Ballad Printer of Seven Dials, 1765–1844* (Pinner, Private Libraries Association, 1969)

Simmons, Jack, *The Victorian Railway* (London, Thames and Hudson, 1995)

——, 'Railways, Hotels, and Tourism in Great Britain, 1839–1914', *Journal of Contemporary History*, 19, 2 (1984), 201–22

Slater, T. R., 'Family, Society and the Ornamental villa on the Fringes of English Country Towns', *Journal of Historical Geography*, 4 (1978), 129–44

Slaughter, M. M., 'The Development of Common Law Defamation Privileges: From Communitarian Society to Market Society', *Cardozo Arts and Entertainment Law Journal*, 14 (1992), 351–406

Smout, Christopher, 'Tours in the Scottish Highlands from the Eighteenth to the Twentieth Centuries', *Northern Scotland*, 5, 2 (1983), 99–121

Snyder, P. V., *The Christmas Tree Book: The History of the Christmas Tree and Antique Christmas Tree Ornaments* (Harmondsworth, Penguin, 1977)

Solkin, David, *Painting for Money: The Visual Arts and the Public Sphere in Eighteenth-Century England* (New Haven, Yale University Press, 1993)

Southworth, James Granville, *Vauxhall Gardens: A Chapter in the Social History of England* (New York, Columbia University Press, 1941)

Spadafora, David, *The Idea of Progress in Eighteenth-Century Britain* (New Haven, Yale University Press, 1990)

Stochholm, Johanne M., *Garrick's Folly: The Shakespeare Jubilee of 1769 at Stratford and Drury Lane* (London, Methuen, 1964)

Storch, R., ed., *Popular Culture and Custom in Nineteenth-Century England* (London, Croom Helm, 1982)

Stratton, Michael, and Barrie Trinder, 'The Foundations of a Textile Community: Sir Robert Peel at Fazeley', *Textile History*, 26, 2 (1995), 185–201

Styles, John, 'Clothing the North: The Supply of Non-Elite Clothing in the Eighteenth-Century North of England', *Textile History*, 25, 2 (1994), 139–66

——, 'Involuntary Consumers: Servants and their Clothes in Eighteenth-Century England', *Textile History*, 33 (2002), 9–21

Sutherland, John A., *Fiction and the Fiction Industry* (London, Athlone Press, 1978)

——, *Victorian Fiction: Writers, Publishers, Readers* (Basingstoke, Macmillan, 1995)

——, *Victorian Novelists and Publishers* (Chicago, University of Chicago Press, 1976)

Sutton, G. B, 'The Marketing of Ready Made Footwear in the Nineteenth Century: A Study of the Firm of C. & J. Clark', *Business History*, 6, 2 (1964), 93–112

Swinglehurst, Edmund, *Cook's Tours: The Story of Popular Travel* (Poole, Blandford, 1982)

——, *The Romantic Journey: The Story of Thomas Cook and Victorian Travel* (London, Pica, 1974)

Teich, Mikulás, and Roy Porter, eds., *The Industrial Revolution in National Context: Europe and the USA* (Cambridge, Cambridge University Press, 1996)

Temperley, Nicholas, ed., *Music in Britain: The Romantic Age, 1800–1914*, vol. 5 of *The Blackwell History of Music in Britain*, gen. ed. Ian Spink (Oxford, Blackwell, 1988)

Temple, Kathryn, *Scandal Nation: Law and Authorship in Britain, 1750–1832* (Ithaca and London, Cornell University Press, 2003)

Thompson, E. P., 'The Moral Economy of the English Crowd in the Eighteenth Century', *Past and Present*, 50 (1971), 76–136

——, 'Time, Work Discipline and Industrial Capitalism', *Past and Present*, 38 (1967), 56–97

Thompson, F. M. L., ed., *The Cambridge Social History of Britain, 1750–1950*, vol. 3: *Social Agencies and Institutions* (Cambridge, Cambridge University Press, 1990)

——, ed., *The Rise of Suburbia* (Leicester, Leicester University Press, 1982)

Tilly, L., 'Food Entitlement, Famine, and Conflict', *Journal of Interdisciplinary History*, 14, 2 (1983), 333–49

Tischler, Steven, *Footballers and Businessmen: The Origins of Professional Football in England* (London, Holmes & Meier, 1981)

Tinniswood, Adrian, *A History of Country House Visiting: Five Centuries of Tourism and Taste* (Oxford, Basil Blackwood and the National Trust, 1989)

Towner, John, 'The Grand Tour: A Key Phase in the History of Tourism', *Annals of Tourism Research*, 12, 3 (1985), 297–333

Tranter, Neil, *Sport, Economy and Society in Britain, 1750–1914* (Cambridge, Cambridge University Press, 1998)

Travis, Anthony S., *The Rainbow Makers: The Origins of the Synthetic Dyestuffs Industry in Western Europe* (Bethlehem, Pa., Lehigh University, Associated Universities Presses, 1993)

Tylecote, Mabel, *The Mechanics' Institutes of Lancashire and Yorkshire before 1851* (Manchester, Manchester University Press, 1957)

Uglow, Jenny, *The Lunar Men: The Friends Who Made the Future, 1730–1810* (London, Faber, 2002)

Vamplew, Wray, *Pay Up and Play the Game: Professional Sport in Britain, 1875–1914* (Cambridge, Cambridge University Press, 1988)

——, *The Turf: A Social and Economic History of Horse Racing* (London, Allen Lane, 1976)

Vaughan, J., *The English Guide Book, c.1780–1870* (Newton Abbot, David and Charles, 1974)

Vicinus, Martha, ed., *A Widening Sphere: Changing Roles of Victorian Women* (Bloomington, Indiana University Press, 1977)

Vickery, Amanda, *The Gentleman's Daughter: Women's Lives in Georgian England* (London, Yale University Press, 1998)

Vries, J. de, 'The Industrial Revolution and the Industrious Revolution', *Journal of Economic History*, 54 (1994), 249–70

Vries, Leonard de, *Victorian Advertisements* (London, John Murray, [1968])

Walkley, Christina, *Dressed to Impress: 1840–1914* (London, Batsford, 1989)

——, *The Way to Wear 'Em: 150 Years of Punch on Fashion* (London, Peter Owen, 1985)

——, and Vanda Foster, *Crinolines and Crimping Irons: Victorian Clothes: How They were Cleaned and Cared For* (London, Peter Owen, 1978)

Walkowitz, Judith, *City of Dreadful Delight* (London, Virago, 1992)

Waller, Philip, ed., *The English Urban Landscape* (Oxford, Oxford University Press, 2000)

Walsh, Claire, 'Shop Design and the Display of Goods in Eighteenth-Century London', *Journal of Design History*, 8, 3 (1995), 157–76

Walton, John K., *Wonderlands by the Waves: A History of the Seaside Resorts of Lancashire* (Preston, Lancashire County Books, 1992)

Walvin, James, *Football and the Decline of Britain* (Basingstoke, Macmillan, 1986)

——, *Fruits of Empire: Exotic Produce and British Taste, 1660–1800* (New York, New York University Press, 1997)

——, *Leisure and Society, 1830–1950* (London, Longman, 1978)

——, *The People's Game: The History of Football Revisited* (Edinburgh, Mainstream, 1994)

——and J. K. Walton, eds., *Leisure in Britain, 1780–1939* (Manchester, Manchester University Press, 1983)

Ward, Stephen V., *Selling Places: The Marketing and Promotion of Towns and Cities, 1850–2000* (London, E. & F. N. Spon, 1998)

Waterfield, Giles, ed., *Palaces of Art: Art Galleries in Britain, 1790–1990* (London, Dulwich Picture Gallery, 1991)

Waugh, Norah, *The Cut of Men's Clothes, 1600–1900* (New York, Theatre Arts Books, 1964)

——, *The Cut of Women's Clothes 1600–1930* (London, Faber, 1968)

Weatherill, Lorna, *Consumer Behaviour and Material Culture in Britain, 1660–1760* (London, Routledge, 1988)

Webb, Igor, *From Custom to Capital: The English Novel and the Industrial Revolution* (Ithaca, Cornell University Press, 1981)

Weber, William, 'Mass Culture and the Reshaping of European Musical Taste, 1770–1870', *International Review of the Aesthetics and Sociology of Music,* 8 (1977), 5–22

——, *Music and the Middle Class: The Social Structure of Concert Life in London, Paris and Vienna* (London, Croom Helm, 1975)

——, *The Rise of Musical Classics in Eighteenth-Century England: A Study in Canon, Ritual, and Ideology* (Oxford, Clarendon Press, 1992)

Weightman, Gavin, and Steve Humphries, *Christmas Past* (London, Sidgwick & Jackson, 1987)

White, Cynthia L., *Women's Magazines, 1693–1968* (London, Michael Joseph, 1970)

Wilensky, Harold L., 'The Professionalization of Everyone?', *American Journal of Sociology,* 70 (1964), 137–58

Wilk, R., 'Consumer Goods as a Dialogue about Development', *Culture and History,* 7 (1990), 79–100

Williamson, Geoffrey, *Wheels within Wheels: The Story of the Starleys of Coventry* (London, Geoffrey Bles, 1966)

Wilmot, Sarah, *'The Business of Improvement': Agriculture and Scientific Culture in Britain, c.1770–c.1870* (Bristol, Historical Geography Research Series, no. 24, 1990)

Wilson, A. E., *Christmas Pantomime: The Story of an English Institution* (London, George Allen & Unwin, 1934)

Wilson, Elizabeth, *The Sphinx in the City: Urban Life, the Control of Disorder, and Women* (London, Virago, 1991)

Wilson, R. G., *Gentlemen Merchants: The Merchant Community in Leeds, 1700–1830* (Manchester, Manchester University Press, 1971)

Wilton, Andrew, and Ilaria Bignamini, eds., *The Grand Tour: The Lure of Italy in the 18th Century* (London, Tate, 1996)

Wind, E., 'The Revolution of History Painting', *Journal of the Warburg Institute,* 2 (1938–9), 116–27

Winstanley, Michael J., *The Shopkeeper's World, 1830–1914* (Manchester, Manchester University Press, 1983)

Wise, Sarah, *The Italian Boy: Murder and Grave-Robbery in 1830s London* (London, Jonathan Cape, 2004)

Wolff, Janet, and John Seed, eds., *The Culture of Capital: Art, Power and the Nineteenth-Century Middle Class* (Manchester, Manchester University Press, 1988)

Womack, Peter, *Improvement and Romance: Constructing the Myth of the Highlands* (Basingstoke, Macmillan, 1989)

Woodforde, John, *The Story of the Bicycle* (London, Routledge & Kegan Paul, 1970)

Woodmansee, Martha, *The Author, Art and the Market: Rereading the History of Aesthetics* (New York, Columbia University Press, 1994)

——, 'The Genius and the Copyright: Economic and Legal Conditions of the Emergence of the "Author"', *Eighteenth-Century Studies*, 17, 4 (1984), 425–48

——, and Peter Jaszi, eds., *The Construction of Authorship: Textual Appropriation in Law and Literature* (Durham, NC, Duke University Press, 1991)

Wright, Gwendolyn, ed., *The Formation of National Collections of Art and Archaeology*, Studies in the History of Art, 47, Center for Advanced Study in the Visual Arts, Symposium Papers 27 (Washington, DC, National Gallery of Art, 1996)

Yanni, Carla, *Nature's Museums: Victorian Science and the Architecture of Display* (Baltimore, Johns Hopkins University Press, 1999)

Zachs, William, *The First John Murray and the Late 18th-Century Book Trade* (Oxford, Oxford University Press, 1998)

Zionkowski, Linda, 'Territorial Disputes in the Republic of Letters: Canon Formation and the Literary Profession', *The Eighteenth Century: Theory and Interpretation*, 31 (1990), 3–22

Ziter, Edward, *The Orient on the Victorian Stage* (Cambridge, Cambridge University Press, 2003)

NOTES

Preface

1 Samuel Johnson, *A Journey to the Western Isles of Scotland* (1775), ed. Peter Levi (Harmondsworth, Penguin, 1984), p. 48.

2 James Pope-Hennessy, *Queen Mary: 1867–1953* (London, Unwin, 1959), pp. 277–8.

3 Edward Gibbon, *The History of the Decline and Fall of the Roman Empire* (1776–88), ed. David Womersley (Harmondsworth, Allen Lane, 1994), vol. 2, ch. 31, p. 174.

1: *From Arcadia to Arcade: The Great Exhibition*

1 This was from a speech given at the Mansion House, 21 March 1850 and reported in *The Times*, 22 March 1850, p. 5, col. b.

2 Marie Mulvey Roberts, 'Pleasures Engendered by Gender: Homosociality and the Club', in Roy Porter and Marie Mulvey Roberts, eds., *Pleasure in the Eighteenth Century* (Basingstoke, Macmillan, 1996), p. 48.

3 Joseph Addison, *The Spectators*, ed. Donald F. Bond (Oxford, Clarendon Press, 1965), vol. 1, p. 34.

4 Pat Rogers, 'Joseph Addison', in *Oxford Dictionary of National Biography*, Oxford University Press, 2004.

5 John Brewer, *The Pleasures of the Imagination: English Culture in the Eighteenth Century* (London, HarperCollins, 1997), p. 35.

6 Addison, *The Spectators*, Spectator 9, p. 42.

7 Peter Clark, *British Clubs and Societies, 1580–1800: The Origins of an Associational World* (Oxford, Clarendon Press, 2000), p. 89.

8 Ibid., pp. 67–8.

9 The information on the formation of the RSA, and its finances, comes from Derek Hudson and Kenneth W. Luckhurst, *The Royal Society of Arts, 1754–1954* (London, John Murray, 1954), pp. 6–11, 41.

10 R. Campbell, *The London Tradesman, being a compendious view of all the trades, professions, arts, both liberal and mechanic, now practised in the cities of London and Westminster* (London, T. Gardner, 1747), pp. 103, 110, 108, 106.

11 Sarah Lowengard, 'Colours and colour making in the eighteenth century', in Maxine Berg and Helen Clifford, eds., *Consumers and Luxury: Consumer Culture in Europe, 1650–1850* (Manchester, Manchester University Press, 1999), pp. 104–5.

12 Cited in Jeffrey A. Auerbach, *The Great Exhibition of 1851: A Nation on Display* (London, Yale University Press, 1999), p. 12.

13 Toys described in George Buday, *The History of the Christmas Card* (London, Spring Books, 1964), pp. 7–8.

14 Auerbach, *The Great Exhibition*, pp. 70, 57, 65.

15 Cited in ibid., p. 64.

16 P. Greenhalgh, *Ephemeral Vistas: The Expositions Universelles, Great Exhibitions and World's Fairs, 1851–1939* (Manchester, Manchester University Press, 1988), pp. 28–9.

17 From the *Official Descriptive and Illustrated Catalogue* (London, Spicer Bros., 1851), contents pages.

18 William Felkin, *The Exhibition in 1851, of the Products and Industry of All Nations. Its Probable Influence upon Labour and Commerce* (London, Arthur Hall, Virtue, 1851), pp. 5, 8.

19 Horace Greeley, *Glances at Europe: In a Series of Letters from Great Britain,*

France, Italy, Switzerland, &c., during the Summer of 1851, including notices of the Great Exhibition, or World's Fair (New York, Dewitt & Davenport, 1851), p. 22.

20 Cited in Auerbach, *The Great Exhibition*, p. 108.

21 The episode, and interpretation, are highlighted in ibid., p. 96.

22 Blotters, letter-openers, perspective view and cigar boxes: John Johnson Collection of Ephemera, Bodleian Library, JJ Great Exhibition Artefacts 3, 4. Handkerchief: ibid., JJ Printed Fabrics, 1. Gloves: Sarah Levitt, *Victorians Unbuttoned: Registered Designs for Clothing, their Makers and Wearers, 1839–1900* (London, George Allen & Unwin, 1986), p. 20.

23 John Johnson Collection, JJ Tea & Coffee 2.

24 *Official Catalogue*, vol. 2, section 11, Cotton, entry 51.

25 Knives and cutlery from *Official Catalogue*, vol. 2, section 21, entry 690. Vase described in Auerbach, *The Great Exhibition*, pp. 112–13.

26 Levitt, *Victorians Unbuttoned*, pp. 106–7.

27 The anti-concussion hat: Patrick Beaver, *The Crystal Palace: A Portrait of Victorian Enterprise* (2nd ed., London, Phillimore, 1986), p. 51. Yachting clothes and doctor's suit: Alison Adburgham, *Shops and Shopping, 1800–1914: Where, and in What Manner the Well-Dressed Englishwoman Bought her Clothes* (London, George Allen & Unwin, 1981), p. 92. 'Duplexa' coat: *Official Catalogue*, vol. 2, section 20, entry 69.

28 Adburgham, *Shops and Shopping*, p. 92.

29 Auerbach, *The Great Exhibition*, p. 110; Beaver, *The Crystal Palace*, p. 52.

30 *Official Catalogue*, vol. 2, sections 10 and 26, entries 468, 477a, 484, 496. Smyth and Roberts's piano, Cyril Ehrlich, *The Piano: A History* (rev. ed., Oxford, Clarendon Press, 1990), p. 28.

31 *Official Catalogue*, vol. 2, section 10, entries 480, 487.

32 *Illustrated London News*, 14 June 1851, p. 570.

33 Henry Mayhew and George Cruikshank, *1851: or, The Adventures of Mr and Mrs Sandboys and Family, Who Came Up to London to 'Enjoy Themselves', and to See the Great Exhibition* (London, George Newbold, [1851]), p. 1.

34 Cited in Thomas Richards, *The Commodity Culture of Victorian England: Advertising and Spectacle, 1851–1914* (Stanford, Cal., Stanford University Press, 1990), p. 29. The original source is unclear, as there is a confusion in the footnote.

35 Paul Langford, *A Polite and Commercial People: England, 1727–1783* (Oxford, Oxford University Press, 1989; p/b 1992), pp. 68–9.

36 Ibid., p. 70.

37 Lorna Weatherill, *Consumer Behaviour and Material Culture in Britain, 1660–1760* (London, Routledge, 1988), p. 25.

38 Neil McKendrick, 'The Consumer Revolution in Eighteenth-Century England', in Neil McKendrick, John Brewer and J. H. Plumb, *The Birth of a Consumer Society: The Commercialization of Eighteenth-Century England* (London, Europa, 1982), p. 26.

39 Weatherill, *Consumer Behaviour*, p. 25.

40 George Colman and David Garrick, *The Clandestine Marriage*, in William Jones, *Jones's British Theatre* (Dublin, John Chambers, 1795), vol. 9, p. 40.

41 Peter Mathias, *The Transformation of England: Essays in the Economic and Social History of England in the Eighteenth Century* (London, Methuen, 1979), p. 162.

42 *Punch*, 30 October 1880, p. 194.

43 Cited in Lori Anne Loeb, *Consuming Angels: Advertising and Victorian Women* (New York, Oxford University Press, 1994), p. 26.

44 Cited in Dianne Sachko Macleod, *Art and the Victorian Middle Class: Money and the Making of Cultural Identity* (Cambridge, Cambridge University Press, 1996), p. 274.

45 Cited in ibid., p. 275.

46 'Helix' [W. B. Adams], 'The Industrial Exhibition of 1851', *Westminster Review*, April 1850, p. 97.

47 Walter Benjamin, *Charles Baudelaire: A Lyric Poet in the Era of High Capitalism* (London, Verso, 1983), p. 166.

48 *The Letters of Queen Victoria: A Selection from Her Majesty's Correspondence between the Years 1837 and 1861*, ed. Arthur Christopher Benson and Viscount Esher (London, John Murray, 1908), vol. 2, p. 317.

49 Cited in Greenhalgh, *Ephemeral Vistas*, p. 31.

50 *Punch*, 1851, p. 43.

51 *Illustrated London News*, 31 May 1851, p. 501.

52 *The Times*, 2 May 1851, p. 5, col. a.

53 Auerbach, *The Great Exhibition*, p. 138.

54 Jenny Uglow, *The Lunar Men: The Friends Who Made the Future, 1730–1810* (London, Faber, 2002), p. 216.

55 Statutes at Large, XVI, 388–94, cited in Clark, *British Clubs and Societies*, p. 351.

56 Ibid., pp. 350–51.

57 Richard D. Altick, *The English Common Reader: A Social History of the Mass Reading Public, 1800–1900* (Chicago, University of Chicago Press, 1957), p. 205.

58 Ibid., p. 202.

59 Cited in John Seed, 'Commerce and the Liberal Arts: The Political Economy of Art in Manchester, 1775–1860', in Janet Wolff and John Seed, eds., *The Culture of Capital: Art, Power and the Nineteenth-Century Middle Class* (Manchester, Manchester University Press, 1988), p. 69.

60 H. Cunningham, *Leisure in the Industrial Revolution, c. 1780–c.1880* (London, Croom Helm, 1980), p. 101.

61 Jack Simmons, *The Victorian Railway* (London, Thames and Hudson, 1995), p. 272.

62 Michael Freeman, *Railways and the Victorian Imagination* (New Haven, Yale University Press, 1999), p. 114.

63 Auerbach, *The Great Exhibition*, p. 139.

64 Cited in Piers Brendon, *Thomas Cook: 150 Years of Popular Tourism* (London, Secker & Warburg, 1991), p. 58.

65 Ibid., p. 57.

66 Ibid., p. 63.

67 Cited in Auerbach, *The Great Exhibition*, p. 136.

68 Ibid., pp. 141–2.

69 Mayhew, *1851*, p. 15.

70 Simmons, *The Victorian Railway*, p. 275; Philip S. Bagwell, *The Transport Revolution* (2nd ed., London, Routledge, 1988), p. 116.

71 Auerbach, *The Great Exhibition*, p. 135.

72 Ibid., p. 142.

73 [George Frederick Pardon], *The London Conductor; Being a Guide for Visitors to the Great Industrial Exhibition . . .* (London, John Cassell, 1851; reprint, Kilkenny, Boethius, 1984), n.p.

74 Christopher Breward, *The Hidden Consumer: Masculinities, Fashion and City Life, 1860–1914* (Manchester, Manchester University Press, 1999), pp. 132–3.

75 Richard D. Altick, *The Shows of London* (Cambridge, Mass., The Belknap Press, 1978), pp. 462, 464–5, 426.

76 James Robinson Planché, *The Extravaganzas of J. R. Planché, Esq., Somerset Herald, 1825–1871*, ed. T. F. Dillon Croker and Stephen Tucker (5 vols., London, Samuel French, 1879). Mr Buckstone appears in vol. 5, pp. 5–34.

77 Brendon, *Thomas Cook*, p. 57.

78 *The Times*, 29 May 1851, p. 8, col. a.

2: 'A Nation of Shopkeepers':
The Eighteenth-century Shop

1 *Idler*, 56 (12 May 1759), in Samuel Johnson, *Idler and Adventurer*, Yale Edition of the Works of Samuel Johnson, vol. 2 (New Haven, Yale University Press, 1963), p. 175.

2 Cited in Michael J. Winstanley, *The Shopkeeper's World, 1830–1914* (Manchester, Manchester University Press, 1983), pp. 12–13.

3 Hoh-Cheung Mui and Lorna H. Mui, *Shops and Shopkeeping in Eighteenth-*

Century England (London, Routledge, 1989), p. 5.

4 Nancy Cox, *The Complete Tradesman: A Study of Retailing, 1550–1820* (Aldershot, Ashgate, 2000), p. 39.

5 Ibid., p. 42.

6 Ibid., pp. 36, 45, 44; Mui and Mui, *Shops and Shopkeeping*, pp. 108–10.

7 Winstanley, *Shopkeeper's World*, p. 15.

8 Cox, *Complete Tradesman*, pp. 77–9, 98.

9 Mui and Mui, *Shops and Shopkeeping*, p. 47.

10 Ibid., p. 47.

11 Cox, *Complete Tradesman*, pp. 89–90.

12 Ibid., p. 129.

13 Mui and Mui, *Shops and Shopkeeping*, pp. 207–8.

14 Cox, *Complete Tradesman*, p. 121.

15 Cited in Mui and Mui, *Shops and Shopkeeping*, p. 225.

16 Robin Reilly, *Josiah Wedgwood, 1730–1795* (London, Macmillan, 1992), p. 213.

17 Uglow, *Lunar Men*, p. 64.

18 Neil McKendrick, 'The Commercialization of Fashion', in McKendrick, Brewer, Plumb, *Birth of a Consumer Society*, p. 68.

19 Cited in Mui and Mui, *Shops and Shopkeeping*, p. 14.

20 Cited in Cox, *Complete Tradesman*, pp. 110–12.

21 Ibid., p. 94.

22 Cited in ibid., pp. 90–92.

23 Cited in McKendrick, 'The Commercialization of Fashion', in McKendrick, Brewer, Plumb, *Birth of a Consumer Society*, p. 85.

24 Claire Walsh, 'The Newness of the Department Store: A View from the Eighteenth Century', in Geoffrey Crossick and Serge Jaumain, eds., *Cathedrals of Consumption: The European Department Story, 1850–1939* (Aldershot, Ashgate, 1999), p. 49.

25 Reilly, *Josiah Wedgwood*, pp. 120–21.

26 Brenda J. Scragg, 'James Lackington', in *Oxford Dictionary of National Biography*.

27 Cited in Mui and Mui, *Shops and Shopkeeping*, pp. 17–18.

28 Cited in Kenneth Quickenden, 'Boulton and Fothergill Silver: Business Plans and Miscalculations', *Art History*, 3, 3 (September 1980), p. 284.

29 Hildyard, *Leeds Mercury*, 5 March 1751; Davenport and Co., ibid., 14 May 1751. Both cited in Mui and Mui, *Shops and Shopkeeping*, pp. 231, 232–3.

30 Cited in ibid., pp. 14–15.

31 Jeremy Bentham, *An Introduction to the Principles of Morals and Legislation* (London, T. Payne and Son, 1789), xviii. §17 note.

32 Sir Joshua Reynolds, *The Discourses of Sir Joshua Reynolds*, ed. Edmund Gosse (London, Kegan, Paul, Trench & Co., 1884), p. i.

33 'A Methodized Journal, 1773–1786', Huntington Library, HM31201, p. 60, cited in Elizabeth Eger, 'Luxury, Industry and Charity: Bluestocking Culture Displayed', in Maxine Berg and Elizabeth Eger, eds., *Luxury in the Eighteenth Century: Debates, Desires and Delectable Goods* (Basingstoke, Palgrave Macmillan, 2003), p. 202n.

34 Karl Marx and Friedrich Engels, *The German Ideology* (Moscow, Progress Publishers, 1976), p. 48.

35 Colin Jones and Rebecca Spang, 'Sans-culottes, *sans café, sans tabac*: Shifting Realms of Necessity and Luxury in Eighteenth-Century France', in Berg and Clifford, *Consumers and Luxury*, p. 38.

36 William J. Ashworth, *Customs and Excise: Trade, Production, and Consumption in England, 1640–1845* (Oxford, Oxford University Press, 2003), pp. 40, 1–2, 10.

37 Both advertisements cited in Denys Forrest, *Tea for the British: The Social and Economic History of a Famous Trade* (London, Chatto & Windus, 1973), p. 23.

38 Ibid., pp. 33–4.

39 Ibid., p. 54.

40 Mui and Mui, *Shops and Shopkeeping*, pp. 250–51.

41 McKendrick, 'The Consumer Revolution', in McKendrick, Brewer, Plumb, *Birth of Consumer Society*, p. 29; James Walvin, *Fruits of Empire: Exotic Produce and British Taste,*

1660–1800 (New York, New York University Press, 1997), pp. 25, 30; and Peter Mathias, *Retailing Revolution: A History of Multiple Retailing in the Food Trades based upon the Allied Suppliers Group of Companies* (London, Longmans, Green and Co., 1967), p. 24.

42 Cox, *Complete Tradesman*, pp. 204–5; Mui and Mui, *Shops and Shopkeeping*, p. 148.

43 Mui and Mui, *Shops and Shopkeeping*, p. 174.

44 Ashworth, *Customs and Excise*, p. 47; Walvin, *Fruits of Empire*, p. 119.

45 Walvin, *Fruits of Empire*, pp. 119–120.

46 Uglow, *Lunar Men*, p. 412.

47 Mui and Mui, *Shops and Shopkeeping*, pp. 256–9.

48 Ibid., pp. 262–72.

49 Ibid., pp. 273–5.

50 Weatherill, *Consumer Behaviour*, p. 25.

51 Walvin, *Fruits of Empire*, p. 27.

52 Cited in Uglow, *Lunar Men*, p. 96.

53 Ibid., p. 219.

54 Reilly, *Josiah Wedgwood*, pp. 10–14.

55 Cited in ibid., p. 87.

56 Cited in Neil McKendrick, 'Josiah Wedgwood and the Commercialization of the Potteries', in McKendrick, Brewer, Plumb, *Birth of a Consumer Society*, p. 141.

57 Cited in Neil McKendrick, 'Josiah Wedgwood: An Eighteenth-Century Entrepreneur in Salesmanship and Marketing Techniques', *Economic History Review*, 2nd series, 12, 3 (1960), p. 415.

58 Ibid., pp. 414–15.

59 Cited in Reilly, *Josiah Wedgwood*, p. 206.

60 Cited in McKendrick, 'Josiah Wedgwood and the Commercialization of the Potteries', in McKendrick, Brewer, Plumb, *Birth of a Consumer Society*, p. 112.

61 Cited in Brian Dolan, *Josiah Wedgwood: Entrepreneur to the Enlightenment* (London, HarperCollins, 2004), p. 267.

62 McKendrick, 'Josiah Wedgwood and the Commercialization of the Potteries', in McKendrick, Brewer,

Plumb, *Birth of a Consumer Society*, p. 121.

63 Cited in Uglow, *Lunar Men*, p. 201.

64 Cited in Cox, *Complete Tradesman*, pp. 109–10.

65 Cited in McKendrick, 'Josiah Wedgwood and the Commercialization of the Potteries', in McKendrick, Brewer, Plumb, *Birth of a Consumer Society*, p. 125.

66 Cited in Dolan, *Josiah Wedgwood*, p. 216.

67 McKendrick, 'Josiah Wedgwood and the Commercialization of the Potteries', in McKendrick, Brewer, Plumb, *Birth of a Consumer Society*, pp. 130–31.

68 Ibid., p. 126.

69 Cited in ibid., p. 118.

70 Cited in Una des Fontaines, 'Wedgwood's London Showrooms', *Proceedings of the Wedgwood Society*, 8 (1970), p. 197.

71 Simeon Shaw, *A History of the Staffordshire Potteries and the Rise and Progress of the Manufacture of Pottery and Porcelain* (Hanley, [n.p.], 1829), p. 124.

72 Reilly, *Josiah Wedgwood*, p. 21.

73 Ibid., p. 48.

74 The information in this paragraph is derived from Bagwell, *Transport Revolution*, pp. 23–6.

75 Reilly, *Josiah Wedgwood*, pp. 46–7.

76 Bagwell, *Transport Revolution*, pp. 29–30.

77 The information in these two paragraphs is from Bagwell, *Transport Revolution*, pp. 31–7 and 45, except the information about Kirkby Stephen, which is in Mui and Mui, *Shops and Shopkeeping*, p. 12.

78 Bagwell, *Transport Revolution*, p. 45.

79 Adam Smith, *The Wealth of Nations* [1776], Glasgow, [no publisher], 1805), vol. I, pp. 25, 202.

80 Peter Borsay, *The English Urban Renaissance: Culture and Society in the Provincial Town, 1660–1770* (Oxford, Clarendon Press, 1989), p. 22.

81 Bagwell, *Transport Revolution*, pp. 1–4.

82 Francis D. Klingender, *Art and the Industrial Revolution* (London, Evelyn, Adams & Mackay, 1968), pp. 15–16.

83 Cited in Uglow, *Lunar Men*, pp. 142–3.

84 Reilly, *Josiah Wedgwood*, pp. 50, 52, 55, 58.

85 These two paragraphs are based on Stanley Chapman, *The Early Factory Masters: The Transition to the Factory System in the Midland Textile Industry* (London, Gregg Revivals, 1992), pp. 85–91.

86 Roger Scola, *Feeding the Victorian City: The Food Supply of Manchester, 1770–1870*, ed. W. A. Armstrong and Pauline Scola (Manchester, Manchester University Press, 1992), pp. 202–4.

87 Christina Fowler, 'Changes in Provincial Retail Practice during the Eighteenth Century, with Particular Reference to Central-Southern England,' in Nicholas Alexander and Gary Akehurst, eds., *The Emergence of Modern Retailing, 1750–1950* (London, Frank Cass, 1999), p. 41.

88 Mui and Mui, *Shops and Shopkeeping*, p. 76.

89 McKendrick, 'The Commercialization of Fashion', in McKendrick, Brewer, Plumb, *Birth of a Consumer Society*, p. 88.

90 James Woodforde, *The Diary of a Country Parson, 1740–1803* (Oxford, Oxford University Press, 1924–31), vol. 1, p. 332.

91 Henry Mayhew, *London Labour and the London Poor* (London, Woodfall, 1851), vol. I, p. 27.

92 Cited in Dorothy Davis, *A History of Shopping* (London, Routledge & Kegan Paul, 1966), p. 245.

93 Beverly Lemire, *Fashion's Favourite: The Cotton Trade and the Consumer in Britain 1660–1800* (Oxford, Oxford University Press, 1991), p. 136.

3: *The Ladies' (and Gents') Paradise: The Nineteenth-century Shop*

1 Scola, *Feeding the Victorian City*, pp. 206–8.

2 Ralph Hancock, 'Sugar', in Alan Davidson, ed., *The Penguin Companion to Food* (Harmondsworth, Penguin, 2002), pp. 917–21.

3 James B. Jefferys, *Retail Trading in Britain, 1850–1950: A Study of Trends in Retailing with Special Reference to the Development of Co-operative, Multiple Shop and Department Store Methods of Trading* (Cambridge, Cambridge University Press, 1954), p. 2.

4 Alexander and Akehurst, *The Emergence of Modern Retailing*, pp. 16–20.

5 Cited in Arnold Bonner, *British Co-operation: The History, Principles, and Organisation of the British Co-operative Movement* (rev. ed., Manchester, Co-operative Union, 1970), pp. 22–3.

6 The information in the previous three paragraphs comes from Bonner, *British Co-operation*, pp. 28, 44, 45, 49–51, 51–2, 73, 103–4.

7 Julia Hood and B. S. Yamey, 'The Middle-Class Co-operative Retailing Societies in London, 1864–1900', *Oxford Economic Papers*, 9 (1957), p. 311.

8 Ibid.

9 Winstanley, *Shopkeeper's World*, pp. 36–7.

10 Mathias, *Retailing Revolution*, p. 36.

11 Ibid., pp. 96–7.

12 Francis Goodall, 'Marketing Consumer Products before 1914: Rowntrees and Elect Cocoa', in R. P. T. Davenport-Hines, ed., *Markets and Bagmen: Studies in the History of Marketing and British Industrial Performance, 1830–1939* (Aldershot, Gower, 1986), p. 19.

13 Mathias, *Retailing Revolution*, p. 48.

14 Ibid., pp. 45–6.

15 Said by me among others. This is the peril of thinking that the middle classes represented everyman (and woman).

16 Mui and Mui, *Shops and Shopkeeping*, p. 238.

17 Ibid., p. 239.

18 Stanley Chapman, 'The Innovating Entrepreneurs in the British Ready-Made Clothing Industry', *Textile History*, 24, 1 (1993), p. 5.

19 *A Visit to the Bazaar* (London, J. Harris, 1818), pp. 72–3.

20 Katrina Honeyman, *Well Suited: A History of the Leeds Clothing Industry, 1850–1990* (Oxford, Oxford University Press, 2000), pp. 10–11.

21 Daniel Kirwan, *Palace and Hovel, or, Phases of London Life* (Hartford, Conn., Belknap & Bliss, 1871), p. 91; cited in Breward, *Hidden Consumer,* p. 125.

22 Kirwan, *Palace and Hovel,* p. 140; cited in Breward, *Hidden Consumer,* p. 123.

23 George Augustus Sala, *Twice Round the Clock; or, the Hours of the Day and Night in London* (London, Houlston & Wright, 1859), pp. 83–6.

24 *Official Catalogue,* vol. 2, section 3, sub-section 20, entry 135a, p. 585.

25 Norah Waugh, *The Cut of Men's Clothes, 1600–1900* (New York, Theatre Arts Books, 1964), p. 131.

26 Adburgham, *Shops and Shopping,* p. 123.

27 Honeyman, *Well Suited,* p. 15.

28 Ibid., pp. 12–14.

29 Ibid., pp. 21–2.

30 Don Bissell, *The First Conglomerate: 45 Years of the Singer Sewing Machine Company* (Brunswick, Me., Audenreed, 1999), pp. 21, 25.

31 Ibid., pp. 26–7.

32 Levitt, *Victorians Unbuttoned,* p. 15.

33 Honeyman, *Well Suited,* p. 14.

34 Sarah Levitt, 'Manchester Mackintoshes: A History of the Rubberized Garment Trade in Manchester', *Textile History,* 17, 1 (1986), pp. 51–2.

35 Chapman, 'The Innovating Entrepreneurs', *Textile History,* 24, 1 (1993), p. 10.

36 Thomas Hancock, *Personal narrative of the original and progress of the caoutchouc or india rubber manufacture in England* ([no publisher or place of publication], 1857), p. 55; cited in Levitt, 'Manchester Mackintoshes', *Textile History,* 17, 1 (1986), p. 52.

37 Cited in ibid., p. 53.

38 George Augustus Sala, *Gaslight and Daylight, with Some London Scenes they Shine Upon* (London, Chapman & Hall, 1859), p. 59.

39 Levitt, *Victorians Unbuttoned,* p. 53.

40 Cited in G. B. Sutton, 'The Marketing of Ready Made Footwear in the Nineteenth Century: A Study of the Firm of C. & J. Clark', *Business History,* 6, 2 (1964), pp. 94–5.

41 Penelope Byrde, *The Male Image: Men's Fashion in Britain, 1300–1970* (London, B. T. Batsford, 1979), p. 200.

42 Mui and Mui, *Shops and Shopkeeping,* p. 240.

43 Byrde, *Male Image,* pp. 200–201; Sutton, 'The Marketing of Ready Made Footwear', *Business History,* 6, 2 (1964), p. 96.

44 Sutton, 'The Marketing of Ready Made Footwear', *Business History,* 6, 2 (1964), pp. 96–7.

45 Alison Gernsheim, *Victorian and Edwardian Fashion: A Photographic Survey* (New York, Dover, 1981), p. 38.

46 Chapman, 'The Innovating Entrepreneurs', *Textile History,* 24, 1 (1993), pp. 16–17.

47 All in the John Johnson Collection of Ephemera, Bodleian Library, Oxford.

48 Cited in Altick, *Shows of London,* p. 221.

49 Cited in Chapman, 'The Innovating Entrepreneurs', *Textile History,* 24, 1 (1993), pp. 19–20.

50 Cited in Breward, *Hidden Consumer,* p. 158.

51 Cited in ibid., p. 156.

52 Ibid., p. 125.

53 Terry Nevett, 'Advertising and Editorial Integrity in the Nineteenth Century', in Michael Harris and Alan Lee, eds., *The Press in English Society from the Seventeenth to the Nineteenth Centuries* (London, Associated Universities Presses, 1986), pp. 151–2.

54 Adburgham, *Shops and Shopping,* p. 12.

55 Cited in David Alexander, *Retailing in England during the Industrial Revolution* (London, Athlone Press, 1970), p. 10.

56 I owe the omnibus information in the three preceding paragraphs to Derek H. Aldcroft and Michael J. Freeman, *Transport in the Industrial Revolution* (Manchester, Manchester University Press, 1983), pp. 135, 139–40.

57 Ibid., pp. 143–4, 153–5.

58 Bagwell, *Transport Revolution,* pp. 140–41.

59 Aldcroft and Freeman, *Transport in the Industrial Revolution*, pp. 144–5.

60 Bagwell, *Transport Revolution*, p. 123.

61 Cited in Cox, *Complete Tradesman*, p. 96.

62 Grant Thorburn, *Men and Manners in Britain* (New York, [no publisher], 1834), pp. 35–6, cited in Altick, *Shows of London*, p. 226.

63 Francis Place, *The Autobiography of Francis Place (1771–1854)*, ed. Mary Thale (London, Cambridge University Press, 1972), vol. 2, p. 123.

64 Charles Manby Smith, *The Little World of London; or, Pictures in Little of London Life* (London, Arthur Hall, Virtue, and Co., 1857), pp. 19–24.

65 Sophie von la Roche, *Sophie in London, 1786, being the Diary of Sophie v. la Roche*, tr. Clare Williams (London, Jonathan Cape, 1933), pp. 237–9.

66 Ibid., p. 87.

67 Place, *Autobiography*, vol. 2, p. 123.

68 Cited in Crossick and Jaumain, *Cathedrals of Consumption*, p. 55.

69 [W. H. Ablett, ed.], *Reminiscences of an Old Draper* (London, Sampson Low, Marston, Searle & Rivington, 1876), p. 18.

70 Ibid., pp. 201–2.

71 The two sets of streets are named in *Picture of London*, 1803, cited in McKendrick, 'The Commercialization of Fashion', in McKendrick, Brewer, Plumb, *Birth of a Consumer Society*, p. 78.

72 Robert Southey, *Letters from England* (1807), ed. Jack Simmons (London, Cresset Press, 1951), pp. 49–50.

73 Listed in Adburgham, *Shops and Shopping*, p. 14.

74 Friedrich Engels, *The Condition of the Working Classes in England* (1845), tr. and ed. W. O. Henderson and W. H. Chaloner (Stanford, Cal., Stanford University Press, 1968), p. 56.

75 Michael Winstanley, 'Temples of Commerce: Revolutions in Shopping and Banking', in Philip Waller, ed., *The English Urban Landscape* (Oxford, Oxford University Press, 2000), p. 154.

76 Cited in Adburgham, *Shops and Shopping*, p. 207.

77 Ibid.

78 Bill Lancaster, *The Department Store: A Social History* (London, Leicester University Press, 1995), p. 75.

79 Cited in Cox, *Complete Tradesman*, pp. 142–3.

80 Cited in Walsh, 'The Newness of the Department Store', in Crossick and Jaumain, *Cathedrals of Consumption*, p. 58.

81 Maria Edgeworth, *Castle Rackrent* and *Ennui* (1800; 1809), ed. Marilyn Butler (Harmondsworth, Penguin, 1992), p. 147.

82 Frances Burney, *The Wanderer; or, Female Difficulties* (1814), ed. Margaret Anne Doody, Robert L. Mack and Peter Sabor (Oxford, Oxford University Press, 2001), p. 426.

83 Frances Burney, *Evelina, or, The History of a Young Lady's Entrance in the World* (1778), ed. Margaret Anne Doody (Harmondsworth, Penguin, 1994), p. 456, n. 48.

84 Cited in Adburgham, *Shops and Shopping*, p. 18.

85 Ibid., p. 22.

86 Altick, *Shows of London*, pp. 38–9.

87 Sala, *Twice Round the Clock*, p. 175.

88 *A Visit to the Bazaar*, pp. 3–5.

89 Cited in Adburgham, *Shops and Shopping*, p. 19.

90 Emil Zola, *Au Bonheur des Dames* (*The Ladies' Paradise*) (1883), tr. and ed. Robin Buss (Harmondsworth, Penguin, 2001), p. 188.

91 Wolfgang Schivelbusch, *The Railway Journey: The Industrialization of Time and Space in the 19th Century* (Leamington Spa, Berg, 1986), p. 188.

92 Fowler, 'Changes in Provincial Retail Practice', in Alexander and Akehurst, *The Emergence of Modern Retailing*, p. 50.

93 Gareth Shaw, 'The Evolution and Impact of Large-Scale Retailing in Britain', in John Benson and Gareth Shaw, eds., *The Evolution of Retail Systems, c.1800–1914* (Leicester, Leicester University Press, 1992), p. 138.

94 Lancaster, *The Department Store*, pp. 48–50.

95 Ibid., pp. 34–6.

96 Ibid., p. 51.

97 Cited in Erika Diane Rappaport, *Shopping for Pleasure: Women in the Making of London's West End* (Princeton, Princeton University Press, 2000), p. 82.

98 Brent Shannon, 'ReFashioning Men: Fashion, Masculinity, and the Cultivation of the Male Consumer in Britain, 1860–1914', in *Victorian Studies*, 46, 4 (2004), p. 611.

99 Asa Briggs, *Friends of the People: The Centenary History of Lewis's* (London, B. T. Batsford, 1956), pp. 28–9, 38, 43, except the information about the Two-shilling Tea, which appears in Forrest, *Tea for the British*, pp. 175–6.

100 Briggs, *Friends of the People*, p. 37.

101 K. Theodore Hoppen, *The Mid-Victorian Generation, 1846–1886* (Oxford, Clarendon Press, 1998), p. 352; Winstanley, 'Temples of Commerce', in Waller, *The English Urban Landscape*, p. 164.

102 Briggs, *Friends of the People*, p. 77.

103 Listed in Adburgham, *Shops and Shopping*, p. 278.

104 Shaw, 'The Evolution and Impact of Large-Scale Retailing in Britain', in Benson and Shaw, *Retailing Industry*, p. 239.

105 Ian Nairn, *Nairn's London* (Harmondsworth, Penguin, 1966), pp. 165–6.

106 Adburgham, *Shops and Shopping*, pp. 152–3.

107 Rappaport, *Shopping for Pleasure*, p. 150.

108 Zola, *Au Bonheur des dames*, pp. 407–8.

109 The information on the murders is to be found in Robert and Isabelle Tombs, *That Sweet Enemy: The French and the British from the Sun King to the Present* (London, Heinemann, 2006), p. 382; the evaluation of Pilotelle's Marat collection is from the preface of Ernest Balfour Bax, *Jean-Paul Marat: The People's Friend*, which can be found on the Marxists Internet Archive, at www.marxists.org/archive/bax/1900/marat/preface.htm.

110 All from Alison Adburgham, *Liberty's: A Biography of a Shop* (London, George Allen & Unwin, 1975), pp. 12–17, 21–2, 30–31, 35–45.

111 Lancaster, *The Department Store*, pp. 55–6.

112 1900 figures: Jefferys, *Retail Trading in Britain*, p. 29. 1910 figures: Geoffrey Crossick and Serge Jaumain, 'The World of the Department Store: Distribution, Culture and Social Change', in Crossick and Jaumain, *Cathedrals of Consumption*, p. 5. The conclusion is, however, my own.

113 Gordon Honeycombe, *Selfridges: Seventy-five Years: The Story of the Store, 1909–1984* (London, Park Lane Press, 1984), pp. 22–4.

114 [Ablett], *Reminiscences of an Old Draper*, pp. 30ff.

115 Honeycombe, *Selfridges*, pp. 25–6.

116 This paragraph relies on Lancaster, *The Department Store*, pp. 72, 75, except the information about the Selfridge's livery, from Adburgham, *Shops and Shopping*, p. 274.

117 Cited in Rappaport, *Shopping for Pleasure*, pp. 155, 158–9.

118 Honeycombe, *Selfridges*, pp. 13–14.

119 Mathias, *Retailing Revolution*, pp. 100–101, 108.

120 Honeycombe, *Selfridges*, p. 12; Lancaster, *The Department Store*, p. 72.

121 Rappaport, *Shopping for Pleasure*, p. 157.

122 Adburgham, *Shops and Shopping*, p. 276.

4: *Read All About It: Buying the News*

1 John Brewer is the author of the phrase 'legislative accident', *Pleasures of the Imagination*, p. 131.

2 Clark, *British Clubs and Societies*, p. 40; Roy Porter, 'Material Pleasure in the Consumer Society', in Porter and Roberts, *Pleasure in the Eighteenth Century*, p. 24; Borsay, *English Urban Renaissance*, p. 129.

3 Porter and Roberts, *Pleasure in the Eighteenth Century*, p. 24.

4 French, English, Scottish and Welsh (English-language) newspapers: Linda Colley, *Britons: Forging the Nation 1707–1837* (London, Pimlico, 1994), pp. 41, 220; Ireland: Richard Cargill Cole, *Irish Booksellers and English Writers, 1740–1800* (London, Mansell, 1986), pp. 15–17; Welsh-language newspaper: John Feather, *The Provincial Book Trade in Eighteenth-Century England* (Cambridge, Cambridge University Press, 1985), p. 16.

5 Diana Dixon, 'Newspapers in Huntingdonshire in the Eighteenth and Nineteenth Centuries', in Peter Isaac and Barry McKay, eds., *The Mighty Engine: The Printing Press and its Impact* (Winchester, St Paul's Bibliographies, 2000), pp. 143–4; *Northampton Mercury*, 31 May 1720.

6 Bob Clarke, *From Grub Street to Fleet Street: An Illustrated History of English Newspapers to 1899* (Aldershot, Ashgate, 2004), pp. 114–15.

7 James Raven, 'The Book Trades', in Isabel Rivers, ed., *Books and their Readers in Eighteenth-Century England* ([Leicester?], Leicester University Press, 1982), p. 24.

8 Cited in William St Clair, *The Reading Nation in the Romantic Period* (Cambridge, Cambridge University Press, 2004), pp. 309–11.

9 T. R. Nevett, *Advertising in Britain: A History* (London, Heinemann, 1982), p. 51.

10 Altick, *English Common Reader*, p. 323.

11 Clark, *British Clubs and Societies*, p. 69.

12 Cited in Brewer, *Pleasures of the Imagination*, pp. 183–4.

13 Nevett, *Advertising in Britain*, p. 51.

14 R. Bradley, *The Virtue and Use of Coffee . . .* (London, 1772), cited in Walvin, *Fruits of Empire*, p. 37.

15 Nevett, *Advertising in Britain*, p. 51.

16 Cited in Borsay, *English Urban Renaissance*, pp. 133–4.

17 Jeremy Greenwood, *Newspapers and the Post Office, 1635–1834* ([no place of publication], Postal History Society, 1971), unpaginated.

18 Howard Robinson, *Britain's Post Office: A History of Development from the Beginnings to the Present Day* (London, Oxford University Press, 1953), p. 65.

19 Bagwell, *Transport Revolution*, p. 40.

20 Robinson, *Britain's Post Office*, pp. 102, 104–6, 114.

21 Bagwell, *Transport Revolution*, p. 41.

22 Robinson, *Britain's Post Office*, p. 121.

23 Feather, *Provincial Book Trade*, p. 48.

24 Colley, *Britons*, p. 220.

25 Clarke, *From Grub Street to Fleet Street*, pp. 96, 100.

26 Feather, *Provincial Book Trade*, p. 17.

27 la Roche, *Sophie in London*, pp. 95–100.

28 Neil McKendrick, 'George Packwood and the Commercialization of Shaving', in McKendrick, Brewer, Plumb, *Birth of a Consumer Society*, pp. 176–7.

29 Ian Mitchell, 'The Development of Urban Retailing, 1700–1815', in Peter Clark, ed., *The Transformation of English Provincial Towns, 1600–1800* (London, Hutchinson, 1984), pp. 261–2, 267, 271–6.

30 Barry O'Connor, 'Sir John Hill', in *Oxford Dictionary of National Biography*.

31 Cited in Roy Porter, *Quacks: Fakers and Charlatans in English Medicine* (Stroud, Tempus, 2000), p. 111.

32 Kirsten Drotner, *English Children and their Magazines, 1751–1945* (New Haven, Yale University Press, 1988), p. 17.

33 Cited in Porter, *Quacks*, p. 55.

34 Cited in Robin Myers and Michael Harris, eds., *Author/Publisher Relations during the Eighteenth and Nineteenth Centuries* (Oxford, Oxford Polytechnic Press, 1983), p. 38.

35 Cited in Mui and Mui, *Shops and Shopkeeping*, pp. 230, 229.

36 Robinson, *Britain's Post Office*, pp. 96, 122.

37 Porter, *Quacks*, pp. 83–4.

38 Cited in Uglow, *Lunar Men*, p. 37.

39 Porter, *Quacks*, pp. 21–2.

40 Roy Porter, *Bodies Politic: Disease, Death and the Doctors in Britain, 1650–1900* (London, Reaktion, 2001), pp. 207–8.

41 Stephen Paget, *John Hunter, Man of*

Science and Surgeon (1728–1793) (London, T. Fisher Unwin, 1897), p. 165.

42 Cited in Henry Sampson, *A History of Advertising from the Earliest Times* (London, Chatto & Windus, 1874), pp. 411–18.

43 Cited in McKendrick, 'George Packwood and the Commercialization of Shaving', in McKendrick, Brewer, Plumb, *Birth of a Consumer Society*, pp. 150–51.

44 Brewer, *Pleasures of the Imagination*, p. 167.

45 Cox, *Complete Tradesman*, p. 150.

46 William St Clair, *Reading Nation*, pp. 10–11.

47 Feather, *Provincial Book Trade*, pp. 33–4.

48 Ibid., pp. 36–7.

49 Ibid., p. 151.

50 Altick, *English Common Reader*, pp. 73–5.

51 T. W. Laqueur, *Religion and Respectability: Sunday Schools and Working Class Culture, 1780–1850* (London, Yale University Press, 1976), p. 44 (and also for the figure for 1851 later in the paragraph).

52 Adam Smith, *The Wealth of Nations*, vol. II, p. 202.

53 Altick, *English Common Reader*, p. 330.

54 Charles Kingsley, *Yeast: A Problem* (London, John W. Parker, 1851), pp. 229–30.

55 Altick, *English Common Reader*, p. 329; Nevett, *Advertising in Britain*, p. 41.

56 'The Newspaper Press', *Quarterly Review*, 150 (1880), p. 521.

57 This is a paraphrase, from J. M. Golby and A. W. Purdue, *The Civilisation of the Crowd: Popular Culture in England, 1750–1900* (rev. ed., Stroud, Sutton, 1999), p. 133.

58 Virginia Berridge, 'Popular Sunday Papers and mid-Victorian Society', in George Boyce, James Curran and Pauline Wingate, eds., *Newspaper History from the Seventeenth Century to the Present Day* (London, Constable, 1978), p. 257.

59 The analysis of the content of these

three papers was tabulated in ibid., pp. 256–8.

60 Ibid., pp. 327–31.

61 Frederick Pollock, *The Law of Torts* (3rd ed., London, Stevens and Sons, 1892).

62 Donald J. Gray, 'Early Victorian Scandalous Journalism: Renton Nicholson's *The Town* (1837–42)', in Joanne Shattock and Michael Wolff, eds., *The Victorian Periodical Press: Samplings and Soundings* (Leicester, Leicester University Press, 1982), pp. 318–19, 322–3.

63 Graham Pollard, 'Serial Fiction', in John Carter, ed., *New Paths in Book Collecting* (reprint; Freeport, NY, Books for Libraries Press, 1967), p. 265.

64 Henry Vizetelly, *Glances Back through Seventy Years* (London, Kegan, Paul & Co., 1893), pp. 13, 11–12.

65 'Cheap Literature', *British Quarterly Review*, 29 (1859), pp. 333ff., cited in Patricia Anderson, *The Printed Image and the Transformation of Popular Culture, 1790–1860* (Oxford, Clarendon Press, 1991), p. 102.

66 Aled Jones, 'Tillotson's Fiction Bureau: The Manchester Manuscripts', *Victorian Periodicals Review*, 17, 1 and 2 (1984), pp. 44–6.

67 Graham Pollard, 'Serial Fiction', in Carter, *New Paths in Book Collecting*, p. 269.

68 1 & 2 Vict. Cap. 98; cited in Simmons, *The Victorian Railway*, p. 222.

69 Ibid. pp. 220, 222.

70 Ibid., p. 117.

71 Gwen Clear, *The Story of W. H. Smith and Son* (London, private publication, 1949), pp. 3–4, 6, 7–8.

72 Ibid., p. 9.

73 Simmons, *The Victorian Railway*, p. 240.

74 Altick, *English Common Reader*, pp. 354–5.

75 D. C. Coleman, *The British Paper Industry, 1495–1860: A Study in Industrial Growth* (Oxford, Clarendon Press, 1958), pp. 91–3.

76 Ibid., pp. 111–12, 113–17.

77 Ibid., pp. 180–81, 191–5.

78 Cynthia L. White, *Women's Magazines,*

1693–1968 (London, Michael Joseph, 1970), pp. 60–61.

79 Altick, *English Common Reader*, p. 357.

80 White, *Women's Magazines*, p. 61.

81 Obituary of John Walter, *The Times*, 29 July 1847, p. 7, cols. c–d.

82 The Applegarth: Nevett, *Advertising in Britain*, p. 40, and also Dilwyn Porter, 'John Walter (1818–1894)', in *Oxford Dictionary of National Biography*. The Hoe and *Lloyd's*: Drotner, *English Children and their Magazines*, p. 66. The Hoe and *The Times*: White, *Women's Magazines*, p. 62.

83 Nevett, *Advertising in Britain*, p. 79.

84 Altick, *English Common Reader*, p. 356.

85 Clarke, *From Grub Street to Fleet Street*, pp. 130–32.

86 Adrian Harvey, *The Beginnings of a Commercial Sporting Culture in Britain, 1793–1850* (Aldershot, Ashgate, 2004), p. 32.

87 Tony Mason, 'Sporting News, 1860–1914', in Harris and Lee, *The Press in English Society*, p. 178.

88 Robinson, *Britain's Post Office*, p. 99.

89 Harvey, *Commercial Sporting Culture*, p. 45.

90 Tony Mason, 'Sporting News', in Harris and Lee, *The Press in English Society*, p. 172; Tony Mason, *Association Football and English Society, 1863–1915* (Brighton, Harvester, 1980), pp. 188–9.

91 Harvey, *Commercial Sporting Culture*, p. 46.

92 Ibid., pp. 43, 46.

93 Cited in Mason, 'Sporting News', in Harris and Lee, *The Press in English Society*, p. 171.

94 Ibid., pp. 169–72.

95 Harvey, *Commercial Sporting Culture*, pp. 47–8.

96 Mike Huggins, *The Victorians and Sport* (London, Hambledon and London, 2004), p. 150.

97 Ibid., p. 153; Mason, 'Sporting News', in Harris and Lee, *The Press in English Society*, pp. 174, 176.

98 Ibid., pp. 177–8.

99 Louis James, *Fiction for the Working Man, 1830–1850: A Study of the Literature Produced for the Working Classes in Early Victorian Urban England* (Harmondsworth, Penguin, 1974), p. 49.

100 Anderson, *Printed Image*, pp. 46–7.

101 Ibid., pp. 54–7.

102 Cited in 'Introduction', Andrew King and John Plunkett, eds., *Popular Print Media, 1820–1900* (London, Routledge, 2004), vol. 1, p. 10.

103 Listed in Altick, *English Common Reader*, p. 338.

104 Anderson, *Printed Image*, pp. 94–5.

105 White, *Women's Magazines*, p. 30.

106 Margaret Beetham, *A Magazine of her Own?: Domesticity and Desire in the Woman's Magazine, 1800–1914* (London, Routledge, 1996), pp. 17, 27.

107 *La Belle Assemblée*, February–April 1806.

108 Ibid., January–June 1832.

109 Ibid.

110 'March Fashions', *Punch*, 1848, p. 91.

111 Loeb, *Consuming Angels*, p. 78.

112 Margaret Beetham and Kay Boardman, eds., *Victorian Women's Magazines: An Anthology* (Manchester, Manchester University Press, 2001), p. 159.

113 Cited in White, *Women's Magazines*, p. 44.

114 *Englishwoman's Domestic Magazine*, supplements IX, 1864; III, 1863; cited in Beetham, *A Magazine of her Own?*, pp. 75–8.

115 Cited in Beetham and Boardman, *Victorian Women's Magazines*, p. 90.

116 Sampson, *History of Advertising*, p. 15.

117 Noted by the House of Commons Select Committee on Patent Medicines, 1912–14, Q3897, Q3898.

118 Berridge, 'Popular Sunday Papers', in Boyce et al., *Newspaper History*, p. 250.

119 Cited in White, *Women's Magazines*, p. 65.

120 Louis Collins, *The Advertisers Guardian (and Advertisement Agents' Guide)* (London, [no publisher], 1885), p. 20.

121 Beetham, *A Magazine of her Own?*, pp. 96–7.

5: *Penny a Line:*
Books and the Reading Public

1 Brewer, *Pleasures of the Imagination*,
pp. 169, 186.

2 Jane Austen, *Northanger Abbey* [1818];
Lady Susan; The Watsons; Sanditon, ed.
James Kinsley and John Davie; intro.
and notes, Claudia L. Johnson
(Oxford, Oxford University Press,
2003), p. 26.

3 Samuel Richardson to Bishop
Hildersley, 1761, John Carroll, ed.,
Selected Letters of Samuel Richardson
(Oxford, Clarendon Press, 1964),
p. 341.

4 Cited in Feather, *Provincial Book
Trade*, p. 65.

5 Frances Burney, *Cecilia, or, Memoirs of
an Heiress* (1782), ed. Peter Sabor and
Margaret Anne Doody (Oxford,
Oxford University Press, 1999),
p. 722.

6 Charles Babbage, *On the Economy of
Machinery and Manufactures* (3rd ed.,
[no place of publication], Charles
Knight, 1833), p. 315.

7 Borsay, *English Urban Renaissance*,
p. 131.

8 Brewer, *Pleasures of the Imagination*,
p. 137.

9 Ibid., p. 175.

10 Cited in St Clair, *Reading Nation*,
p. 143.

11 Shakespeare: Marcus Walsh, 'Literary
Scholarship and the Life of Editing',
in Isabel Rivers, *Books and their
Readers in Eighteenth-Century England:
New Essays* (London, Leicester
University Press, 2001), pp. 209–10.
New novels: David Saunders,
Authorship and Copyright (London,
Routledge, 1992), p. 136. Byron:
St Clair, *Reading Nation*, p. 194.
Incomes: James Raven, *Judging New
Wealth: Popular Publishing and
Responses to Commerce in England,
1750–1800* (Oxford, Clarendon
Press, 1992), p. 58.

12 St Clair, *Reading Nation*, pp. 623–4.

13 Cited in ibid., p. 309; the figures for
Godwin and Paine are found in
appendix 9, pp. 600 and 623–4.

14 Figures for Fielding and the *Rambler*:
Altick, *English Common Reader*,

pp. 49, 50. Byron: St Clair, *Reading
Nation*, p. 586.

15 Borsay, *English Urban Renaissance*,
p. 132.

16 Michael Powell and Terry Wyke,
'Penny Capitalism in the Manchester
Book Trade: The Case of James
Weatherley', in Peter Isaac and Barry
McKay, eds., *The Reach of Print:
Making, Selling and Using Books*
(Winchester, St Paul's Bibliographies,
1998), pp. 135–56, *passim*.

17 Paul Kaufman, *Libraries and their
Users: Collected Papers in Library
History* (London, The Library
Association, 1969), pp. 116–18.

18 Louis, *Fiction for the Working Man*,
p. 8.

19 Kaufman, *Libraries and their Users*,
p. 44.

20 R. J. Morris, 'Clubs, Societies and
Associations', in F. M. L. Thompson,
ed., *The Cambridge Social History of
Britain, 1750–1950*, vol. 3: *Social
Agencies and Institutions* (Cambridge,
Cambridge University Press, 1990),
p. 406.

21 Cited in Kaufman, *Libraries and their
Users*, p. 36.

22 Ibid., p. 37.

23 Borsay, *English Urban Renaissance*,
pp. 133–4.

24 Brewer, *Pleasures of the Imagination*,
p. 180.

25 Cited in Kaufman, *Libraries and their
Users*, p. 17.

26 Ibid., pp. 210–15.

27 Phyllis Hembry, *British Spas from
1815 to the Present: A Social History*
(London, Athlone Press, 1997), p. 4.

28 Brewer, *Pleasures of the Imagination*,
p. 177.

29 Ibid., pp. 177–8.

30 Cited in Louis, *Fiction for the Working
Man*, p. 6.

31 'Moral Statistics of Parishes in
Westminster', *Journal of the Statistical
Society*, 1 (1838), p. 485.

32 St Clair, *Reading Nation*, p. 244.

33 Victor E. Neuburg, *Popular Literature:
A History and Guide, from the
Beginning of Printing to the Year 1897*
(London, Woburn Press, 1977),
p. 172.

34 James J. Barnes, 'Depression and

Innovation in the British and American Book Trade, 1819–1939', in Kenneth E. Carpenter, ed., *Books and Society in History: Papers of the Association of College and Research Libraries Rare Books and Manuscripts Preconference* (New York, R. R. Bowker, 1983), p. 237.

35 Louis, *Fiction for the Working Man*, p. 38.

36 James J. Barnes, *Free Trade in Books: A Study of the London Book Trade since 1800* (Oxford, Clarendon Press, 1964), p. 116.

37 Listed in Anderson, *Printed Image*, p. 162.

38 John A. Sutherland, *Victorian Novelists and Publishers* (Chicago, University of Chicago Press, 1976), p. 5.

39 Robert Collison, *The Story of Street Literature: Forerunner of the Popular Press* (London, J. M. Dent & Sons, 1973), p. 11, p. 23.

40 Neuburg, *Popular Literature*, p. 26.

41 Sarah Wise, *The Italian Boy: Murder and Grave-Robbery in 1830s London* (London, Jonathan Cape, 2004), pp. 241, 244.

42 Charles Hindley, *The History of the Catnach Press, at Berwick-upon Tweed, Alnwick and Newcastle-upon-Tyne, in Northumberland, and Seven Dials, London* (London, Charles Hindley, 1886), pp. 65–8.

43 This is cited in ibid., p. 77, but unfortunately there is no indication of the source.

44 Ibid., pp. 52ff.

45 Angus Fraser, 'John Thurtell', in *Oxford Dictionary of National Biography*; Alsager Vian, rev. J. Gilliland, 'William Corder', ibid.; information on Bartholomew Fair, in Altick, *Shows of London*, p. 420.

46 Altick, *English Common Reader*, p. 288.

47 Sutherland, *Victorian Novelists*, p. 75.

48 Marjorie Plant, *The English Book Trade: An Economic History of the Making and Sale of Books* (2nd ed., London, George Allen & Unwin, 1965), pp. 299–300.

49 Ibid., pp. 345–7, 350, 352, 353.

50 Altick, *English Common Reader*, p. 200.

51 *Athenaeum*, 2 January 1828.

52 Cited in Guinevere L. Griest, *Mudie's Circulating Library and the Victorian Novel* (Newton Abbot, David and Charles, 1970), p. 82.

53 For the information on Mudie's in the previous four paragraphs, ibid., pp. 17–21, 25, 28, 39, 62.

54 *Quarterly Review*, 42 (1830), p. 384.

55 Passenger numbers: Bagwell *Transport Revolution*, pp. 95, 97; T. R. Gourvish, *Railways and the British Economy, 1830–1914* (London, Macmillan, 1980), p. 26. Track mileage: Bagwell, *Transport Revolution*, pp. 81–2.

56 Altick, *English Common Reader*, p. 337.

57 Sutherland, *Victorian Novelists*, pp. 20–21.

58 Altick, *English Common Reader*, p. 290.

59 Sutherland, *Victorian Novelists*, pp. 32–3.

60 Ibid., pp. 30–31.

61 Simmons, *The Victorian Railway*, pp. 245–7.

62 Schivelbusch, *The Railway Journey*, p. 65.

63 'Railway Circulating Libraries', *Punch*, 1849, p. 61.

64 Freeman, *Railways and the Victorian Imagination*, p. 89.

65 Saunders, *Authorship and Copyright*, p. 140.

66 Altick, *English Common Reader*, pp. 308–9.

67 'Empedocles', in *The Oxford Companion to English Literature*, ed. Margaret Drabble (Oxford, Oxford University Press, 2000).

68 Simmons, *The Victorian Railway*, p. 247.

69 This was not published until the twentieth century, however. Anthony Trollope, *The New Zealander*, ed. N. John Hall (Oxford, Clarendon Press, 1972), p. 183.

70 Brendon, *Thomas Cook*, p. 16.

71 I am grateful for this information to Jan Morris, who has passed it on to me from Sir Kyffin Williams, RA.

72 Freeman, *Railways and the Victorian Imagination*, p. 46.

73 Simmons, *The Victorian Railway*, pp. 345–6.

74 Thomas Cook, *A Hand Book of the Trip from Leicester, Nottingham, and Derby to Liverpool and the Coast of North Wales* (1845), intro. Paul Smith (London, Routledge/Thoemmes Press, 1998), p. 7.

75 John Gadsby, *Notes and Queries*, 3 January 1885.

76 Percy Fitzgerald, *The Story of 'Bradshaw's Guide'* (London, Field & Tuer, 1890), pp. 8, 15, 22, 29, 35.

77 Collins, *Advertisers Guardian*, 1885, pp. 146ff.

78 *The Times*, 8 October 1861, p. 6.

79 *Punch*, 1864, p. 217 (and *Punch*, never one to let a good joke go, carries the saga over two further pages).

80 Cited in Felicity A. Nussbaum, Polygamy, *Pamela*, and the Prerogative of Empire', in Birmingham and Brewer, Consumption of Culture, p. 217.

81 Cited in Brewer, *Pleasures of the Imagination*, p. 634.

82 Langford, *Polite and Commercial People*, p. 508.

83 St Clair, *Reading Nation*, p. 233.

84 Altick, *Shows of London*, pp. 244–5.

85 St Clair, *Reading Nation*, p. 214.

86 I have drawn on Shawn Malley, 'Shipping the Bull: Staging Assyria in the British Museum', *Nineteenth-Century Contexts*, 26, 1 (2004), for this account, especially pp. 3–5.

87 Planché, *Mr Buckstone's Voyage Round the Globe (in Leicester Square)*, in *The Extravaganzas of J. R. Planché*, vol. 5, p. 12.

88 Ian Ousby, *The Englishman's England: Taste, Travel and the Rise of Tourism* (London, Pimlico, 2002), p. 13.

89 Sir Herbert George Fordham, *'Paterson's Roads': Daniel Paterson, His Maps and Itineraries, 1738–1825* (London, Oxford University Press, for the Transactions of the Bibliographical Society, 1925), pp. 333–5.

90 Edward Mogg, *Paterson's Roads* ... (16th ed., London, Longman, Hurst, Bees, Orme, and Brown, et al., 1822).

91 Ousby, *Englishman's England*, pp. 61–2; Adrian Tinniswood, *A History of Country House Visiting: Five Centuries of Tourism and Taste* (Oxford, Basil Blackwood and the National Trust, 1989), p. 94.

92 Cited in Ousby, *Englishman's England*, pp. 12–13.

93 Audrey Cooper, 'George Nicholson and his Cambrian Traveller's Guide', in Isaacs and McKay, *Mighty Engine*, pp. 48, 51–2.

94 Ousby, *Englishman's England*, pp. 122–3.

95 Cited in Esther Moir, *The Discovery of Britain: The English Tourists, 1540–1840* (London, Routledge & Kegan Paul, 1964), p. 142.

96 *The Birmingham Saturday Half Holiday-Guide, with a Map* (Birmingham, William Walker, [1871]), *passim*.

97 Huggins, *Victorians and Sport*, p. 157; Neil Tranter, *Sport, Economy and Society in Britain, 1750–1914* (Cambridge, Cambridge University Press, 1998), p. 22.

6: *To Travel Hopefully: Holidays and Tourism*

1 George Eliot, *Adam Bede* (1859), ed. Stephen Gill (Harmondsworth, Penguin, 1985), p. 557.

2 This society is named in Liza Picard, *Victorian London: The Life of a City, 1840–1870* (London, Weidenfeld & Nicolson, 2005), p. 106, but unfortunately no source is given.

3 Cunningham, *Leisure in the Industrial Revolution*, p. 42.

4 All cited in Neil McKendrick, 'Josiah Wedgwood and Factory Discipline', *Historical Journal*, 4, 1 (1961), p. 46.

5 Cunningham, *Leisure in the Industrial Revolution*, pp. 146–7.

6 Ibid., pp. 64–5.

7 Charles Dickens, *The Christmas Books*, vol. 1: *A Christmas Carol and The Chimes* (1843, 1844), ed. Michael Slater (Harmondsworth, Penguin, 1985), p. 53.

8 Cunningham, *Leisure in the Industrial Revolution*, p. 61.

9 St Monday and working days a year:

Hans-Joachim Voth, 'Work and the Sirens of Consumption in Eighteenth-Century London', in Marina Bianchi, ed., *The Active Consumer: Novelty and Surprise in Consumer Choice* (London, Routledge, 1998), pp. 146–7. Fairs: Mark Judd, ' "The oddest combination of town and country": Popular Culture and the London Fairs, 1800–60', in James Walvin and J. K. Walton, eds., *Leisure in Britain, 1780–1939* (Manchester, Manchester University Press, 1983), p. 15.

10 Cunningham, *Leisure in the Industrial Revolution*, p. 64.

11 Gregory Anderson, *Victorian Clerks* (Manchester, Manchester University Press, 1976), p. 16.

12 Shop times and 'we never closed at all': Winstanley, *Shopkeeper's World*, pp. 57–8; except Liberty's: Adburgham, *Liberty's*, p. 36, and Harrod's: Sean Callery, *Harrods Knightsbridge: The Story of Society's Favourite Store* (London, Ebury, 1991), p. 41.

13 Cunningham, *Leisure in the Industrial Revolution*, p. 143.

14 J. R. Taylor, *Government, Legal, and General Saturday Half-Holiday . . . Report of the Great Public Meeting, held in the Guildhall of the City of London, on the 15th of August, 1855 . . .* (London, V. & R. Stevens and G. S. Norton, 1857), p. 12.

15 Cited in Altick, *Shows of London*, p. 471.

16 Cited in Cunningham, *Leisure in the Industrial Revolution*, p. 62.

17 Cited in W. G. Hoskins, *Devon* (Newton Abbot, David and Charles, 1972), p. 152.

18 Colley, *Britons*, p. 172.

19 Cited in Tinniswood, *Country House Visiting*, p. 67.

20 Jane Austen, *Pride and Prejudice* (1813), ed. Vivien Jones (rev. ed., Harmondsworth, Penguin, 2003), pp. 231–2.

21 Mrs Philip Lybbe Powys, *Passages from the Diaries of Mrs Philip Lybbe Powys, of Herwick House, Oxon, 1756–1808*, ed. Emily J. Climenson (London, Longmans, Green and Co., 1899), p. 18.

22 Ousby, *Englishman's England*, p. 61.

23 Cited in ibid., pp. 50, 57.

24 Lybbe Powys, *Diaries*, p. 167.

25 John Byng, Viscount Torrington, *The Torrington Diaries*, ed. C. Bruyn Andrews (London, Methuen, 1970), vol. 2, p. 204.

26 Cited in Brewer, *Pleasures of the Imagination*, p. 219.

27 Cited in Tinniswood, *Country House Visiting*, pp. 93–4.

28 Lybbe Powys, *Diaries*, p. 7.

29 Brewer, *Pleasures of the Imagination*, p. 303.

30 Lybbe Powys, *Diaries*, pp. 165, 168.

31 Cited in Ousby, *Englishman's England*, pp. 63–4.

32 Charles Dickens, *Bleak House* (1853), ed. Norman Page (Harmondsworth, Penguin, 1985), p. 137.

33 Cost of travel, Brendon, *Thomas Cook*, p. 14. Income for journeymen: Elizabeth Waterman Gilboy, 'Demand as a Factor in the Industrial Revolution', in R. M. Hartwell, ed., *The Causes of the Industrial Revolution in England* (London, Methuen, 1967), p. 131.

34 Lake District in 1630s: *A Short Survey of England*, cited in Ousby, *Englishman's England*, p. 100. Defoe: cited in Norman Nicholson, *The Lakers: The Adventures of the First Tourists* (London, Robert Hale, 1955), p. 24. Scotland: Edward Burt, *Letters from a Gentleman in the North of Scotland*, cited in Peter Womack, *Improvement and Romance: Constructing the Myth of the Highlands* (Basingstoke, Macmillan, 1989), p. 1; Johnson, *A Journey to the Western Isles*, p. 60.

35 Thomas Amory, *The Life and Opinions of John Buncle Esquire* (1756), ed. Ernest A. Baker (London, George Routledge and Sons, 1904), p. 76.

36 *The Works of the Right Honorable Edward Burke*, vol. 1 (London, John C. Nimmo, 1887), part 4, section 7, p. 216.

37 William Gilpin, *An Essay on Prints, containing remarks upon the principles*

of picturesque beauty (2nd ed., London, J. Robson, 1768), p. 2.

38 Cited in Malcolm Andrews, *The Search for the Picturesque: Landscape Aesthetics and Tourism in Britain, 1760–1800* (Aldershot, Scolar Press, 1989), p. vii.

39 Austen, *Northanger Abbey*, p. 81.

40 Langford, *Polite and Commercial People*, p. 476.

41 James Plumptre, *The Lakers: A Comic Opera* (London, W. Clarke, 1798), p. 2.

42 Cited in Ousby, *Englishman's England*, pp. 111, 117.

43 Edgeworth, *Castle Rackrent* and *Ennui*, p. 251.

44 Kathryn Temple, *Scandal Nation: Law and Authorship in Britain, 1750–1832* (Ithaca and London, Cornell University Press, 2003), pp. 74–5.

45 Tobias Smollett, *Humphry Clinker* (1771), ed. James L. Thorson (New York, W. W. Norton, 1983), p. 230.

46 All cited in Paul Baines, *The House of Forgery in Eighteenth-Century Britain* (Aldershot, Ashgate, 1999) p. 107.

47 Altick, *Shows of London*, p. 237.

48 Arthur Loesser, *Men, Women and Pianos: A Social History* (New York, Dover, 1990), p. 257.

49 Byron: St Clair, *Reading Nation*, pp. 333–4.

50 Stana Nenadic, 'Romanticism and the Urge to Consume in the First Half of the Nineteenth Century', in Berg and Clifford, *Consumers and Luxury*, p. 215.

51 Brewer, *Pleasures of the Imagination*, p. 457.

52 *Court Magazine*, July–December 1832, *passim*.

53 Adburgham, *Shops and Shopping*, p. 85.

54 Ibid., pp. 51, 65, 71–2.

55 *Official Catalogue*, vol. 2, classes 12 and 15, entry 15, p. 486.

56 Cited in Moir, *Discovery of Britain*, p. 143.

57 Plumptre, *The Lakers*, pp. 19, 58.

58 Ibid., pp. 6, 12, 16.

59 *Official Catalogue*, vol. 2, 'Advertiser', p. 23.

60 Andrews, *Search for the Picturesque*, pp. 67, 74–5.

61 Cited in Cooper, 'George Nicholson', in Isaacs and McKay, *Mighty Engine*, p. 51.

62 *The Times*, 8 March 1827, p. 4. I am grateful to Keith Ramsey for this reference, and to Michael Hargreave Mawson for further information on rhodium.

63 Cited in Anthony and Pip Burton, *The Green Bag Travellers: Britain's First Tourists* (London, André Deutsch, 1978), p. 25.

64 It is Andrews, in *Search for the Picturesque*, p. 11, who notices the change from Latin to English, but he gives a different interpretation for the reason behind it.

65 Parliamentary Papers, Select Committee on Public Houses, 1853–4.

66 Brendon, *Thomas Cook*, pp. 33, 36–7; Cook, *A Hand Book*, pp. 7ff.

67 Brendon, *Thomas Cook*, pp. 39–40.

68 Ibid, p. 50.

69 Ibid., p. 64.

70 Ibid., p. 65.

71 Jim Ring, *How the English Made the Alps* (London, John Murray, 2000), p. 53.

72 Frederic Harrison, *Memories and Thoughts: Men – Books – Cities – Art* (London, Macmillan, 1906), p. 240.

73 Christopher Smout, 'Tours in the Scottish Highlands from the Eighteenth to the Twentieth Centuries', *Northern Scotland*, 5, 2 (1983), pp. 114–15.

74 Simmons, *The Victorian Railway*, p. 41.

75 Ring, *How the English Made the Alps*, pp. 46–7.

76 John Ruskin, 'On the Old Road', in *The Works of John Ruskin* (London, George Allen, Library Edition, 1887–1912), vol. 34, p. 140.

77 All cited in Brendon, *Thomas Cook*, pp. 81, 89, 90.

78 Cook, *Excursionist* magazine, 6 June 1864.

79 Cunningham, *Leisure in the Industrial Revolution*, p. 162.

80 James Walvin, *Leisure and Society*,

1830–1950 (London, Longman, 1978), p. 19.

81 John Hannavy, *The English Seaside in Victorian and Edwardian Times* (Princes Risborough, Shire, 2003), p. 9.

82 John Lowerson and John Myerscough, *Time to Spare in Victorian England* (Hassocks, Harvester, 1977), p. 33.

83 Jane Austen, *Emma* (1815), ed. Fiona Stafford (Harmondsworth, Penguin, 2003), pp. 97, 101.

84 Graham Davis and Penny Bonsall, *Bath: A New History* (Keele, Keele University Press, 1996), pp. 29, 40.

85 Borsay, *English Urban Renaissance*, p. 31; Cyril Ehrlich, *The Music Profession in Britain since the Eighteenth Century: A Social History* (Oxford, Clarendon Press, 1985), pp. 23–4.

86 Davis and Bonsall, *Bath*, pp. 53–5.

87 Borsay, *English Urban Renaissance*, p. 35.

88 Pierce Egan, *Walks through Bath* (Bath, Meyler and Sons, 1819), pp. 68–9.

89 Adburgham, *Shops and Shopping*, pp. 45–6.

90 Trevor Fawcett, *Bath Entertain'd: Amusements, Recreations and Gambling at the 18th-Century Spa* (Bath, Ruton, 1998), pp. 57–9.

91 Ehrlich, *Music Profession in Britain*, pp. 23–4.

92 *The Original Bath Guide, Considerably Enlarged and Improved* (Bath, J. Savage and Meyler and Son, 1811), pp. 103–4, 111.

93 Cited in Peter Borsay, *The Image of Georgian Bath, 1700–2000: Towns, Heritage and History* (Oxford, Oxford University Press, 2000), p. 27.

94 Jane Austen, *Persuasion* (1818), ed. Gillian Beer (Harmondsworth, Penguin, 1998), p. 15.

95 Davis and Bonsall, *Bath*, pp. 81, 72–3.

96 [W.T.], *The Express and Herald Original Bath Guide, Historical and Descriptive* (Bath, William Lewis, Express and County Herald, [1870?]), *passim*.

97 Hembry, *British Spas from 1815*, pp. 1–2.

98 Ibid., pp. 10–11, 33–4.

99 Ibid., p. 16.

100 Cited in P. M. Horsley, 'George Keate and the Voltaire–Shakespeare Controversy', *Comparative Literature Studies*, 16 (1945), p. 7.

101 Cited in Ousby, *Englishman's England*, p. 32.

102 *Lloyd's Evening Post* in Ian McIntyre, *Garrick* (Harmondsworth, Penguin, 1999), p. 548; Boswell cited in Brewer, *Pleasures of the Imagination*, pp. 326–7.

103 Cited in McIntyre, *Garrick*, p. 351.

104 [George Colman], *Man and Wife; or, The Shakespeare Jubilee* (Dublin, for A. Leathley, S. Powell, P. and W. Wilson, et al., 1770), pp. 6–7.

105 From her obituary in the *Gentleman's Magazine*, March 1815, p. 284.

106 This description has been taken from Christian Deelman, *The Great Shakespeare Jubilee* (London, Michael Joseph, 1964), p. 284.

107 Samuel Foote, cited in ibid., p. 285.

108 Deelman, *The Great Shakespeare Jubilee*, pp. 274–5.

109 Byng, *Torrington Diaries*, vol. 1, p. 224.

110 For the facts and also their interpretation, Ousby, *Englishman's England*, p. 28.

111 Ibid., p. 36.

112 Ibid., pp. 38–9.

113 Cunningham, *Leisure in the Industrial Revolution*, pp. 85, 160.

114 [Pardon], *The London Conductor*, pp. 53–4, 56.

115 Smout, 'Tours in the Scottish Highlands', *Northern Scotland*, 5, 2 (1983), p. 107; Sir Walter Scott, 'The Lord of the Isles', appendix K, in *The Poetical Works of Sir Walter Scott* (Boston, Little, Brown & Co., 1857), vol. 5, p. 325.

116 Smout, 'Tours in the Scottish Highlands', *Northern Scotland*, 5, 2 (1983), p. 112.

117 Walvin, *Leisure and Society*, pp. 22–3.

118 Cunningham, *Leisure in the Industrial Revolution*, p. 162.

119 Avril Lansdell, *Seaside Fashions 1860–1939: A Study of Clothes Worn in or beside the Sea* (Princes

Risborough, Shire, 1990),
pp. 16–17.
120 Cited in Adburgham, *Shops and Shopping*, p. 125.
121 Lansdell, *Seaside Fashions*, pp. 5–6.
122 Ibid., pp. 15, 19.
123 Ibid., pp. 19, 24–5, 27, 29–30; Phillis Cunnington and Alan Mansfield, *English Costumes for Sports and Outdoor Recreation: From the Sixteenth to the Nineteenth Centuries* (London, Adam & Charles Black 1969), pp. 264–6.
124 Freeman, *Railways and the Victorian Imagination*, p. 116.
125 Hannavy, *The English Seaside*, pp. 9–10.
126 I am indebted for this concept, as well as for the material that follows in the next six paragraphs, to Richard Roberts, 'The Corporation as Impresario: The Municipal Provision of Entertainment in Victorian and Edwardian Britain', in Walvin and Walton, *Leisure in Britain*, pp. 136–57.
127 Ehrlich, *Music Profession in Britain*, p. 64.
128 Ibid., pp. 56, 64.
129 Cited in Schivelbusch, *The Railway Journey*, p. 61.

7: The Greatest Shows on Earth?

1 It is impossible to write about the shows of London without bringing in Richard Altick's seminal *The Shows of London* at every turn. I must therefore stress my debt to Altick here, and simply indicate my areas of heaviest reliance: for architectural models, pp. 113–15; art exhibitions, p. 409; automata, pp. 60, 69, 357–8; de Loutherbourg, pp. 119–25; dioramas, pp. 163–5; ethnographic shows, pp. 45–6; Charles Mathews, pp. 222–4; Napoleon, pp. 222, 238–40, 396; panoramas, pp. 129, 136–7, 167, 176–7, 199, 203–4, 208–9, 410; photography, pp. 376–8; science exhibitions, pp. 81, 84–5, 371–2; sightseeing, pp. 434–7; toys, pp. 232–3; waxworks, p. 51; zoos and menageries, pp. 307–15,

317–18. For the evangelical response to shows and theatres, pp. 207, 228–9. Where citations in this chapter are not directly credited, these pages are the source.
2 James Robinson Planché, *The Drama at Home; or, An Evening with Puff* (London, S. G. Fairbrother, 1844), p. 20.
3 Burney, *Evelina*, p. 85.
4 Andrews, *Search for the Picturesque*, p. 30.
5 Terence Rees, *Theatre Lighting in the Age of Gas* (London, Society for Theatre Research, 1978), p. 84.
6 Samuel Pepys, *The Diary of Samuel Pepys*, ed. Robert Latham and William Matthews (11 vols., London, Bell & Hyman, 1970–83), vol. 7, p. 333.
7 Planché, The Drama at Home, p. 20.
8 James Fenimore Cooper, *England. With Sketches of Society in the Metropolis* (London, Richard Bentley, 1837), vol. 2, pp. 47–8.
9 This table is drawn from figures cited in Altick, *Shows of London*, pp. 454, 467.
10 Tinniswood, *Country House Visiting*, p. 132.
11 Ibid., p. 130.
12 Prince Pückler-Müskau, *Pückler's Progress: The Adventures of Prince Pückler-Muskau in England, Wales and Ireland, as told in letters to his former wife, 1826–9*, tr. Flora Brennan (London, Collins, 1987), pp. 133, 137.
13 From 'the new turnpike' to the Lancaster assize: Amanda Vickery, *The Gentleman's Daughter: Women's Lives in Georgian England* (London, Yale University Press, 1998), p. 252. The Bridgewater Canal, silver plating and iron smelting: Uglow, *Lunar Men*, p. 139–41; Lybbe Powys, *Diaries*, pp. 20, 65, 126.
14 Trevor Fawcett, *The Rise of English Provincial Art: Artists, Patrons, and Institutions outside London, 1800–1830* (Oxford, Clarendon Press, 1974), p. 156.
15 William Wordsworth, *The Prelude, or, Growth of a Poet's Mind*, in *Wordsworth's Poetical Works*, ed.

William Knight (London, Macmillan & Co., 1896), vol. 3, VII, pp. 230–59.

16 Fawcett, *Rise of English Provincial Art*, pp. 153–4.

17 Pückler-Muskau, *Pückler's Progress*, p. 129.

18 Barbara J. Black, *On Exhibit: Victorians and their Museums* (Charlottesville, University Press of Virginia, 2000), pp. 67–8.

19 Playbill cited in Jane Moody, *Illegitimate Theatre in London, 1770–1840* (Cambridge, Cambridge University Press, 2000), p. 133.

20 Martin Meisel, *Realizations: Narrative, Pictorial and Theatrical Arts in Nineteenth-Century England* (Princeton, Princeton University Press, 1983), pp. 217–18, 221.

21 Petipa cited in Roland John Wiley, *Tchaikovsky's Ballets: Swan Lake, Sleeping Beauty, Nutcracker* (Oxford, Clarendon Press, 1985), p. 183.

22 Sybil Rosenfeld, 'The Grieve Family', in [S. Rosenfeld, ed.], *Anatomy of an Illusion: Studies in Nineteenth-Century Scene Design: Lectures of the Fourth International Congress on Theatre Research* (Amsterdam, International Federation for Theatre Research, 1969), p. 42.

23 R. Derek Wood, 'The Diorama in Great Britain in the 1820s', *History of Photography*, 17, 3, *passim*.

24 Klingender, *Art and the Industrial Revolution*, p. 145.

25 Burney, *Evelina*, p. 122.

26 Brendon, *Thomas Cook*, p. 20.

27 William Thackeray, *The Newcomes: Memoirs of a Most Respectable Family* (1853–5), ed. Andrew Sanders (Oxford, Oxford University Press, 1995), p. 209.

28 R. Davenport-Hines, 'William Palmer', in *Oxford Dictionary of National Biography*.

29 Jim Steinmeyer, *Hiding the Elephant: How Magicians Invented the Impossible* (London, Arrow, 2004), pp. 29–31.

30 James Robinson Planché, *The New Planet; or, Harlequinade Out of Place* (London, S. G. Fairbrother, 1847), *passim*.

31 Cited by Undine Concannon in 'Anna Maria Tussaud', in *Oxford Dictionary of National Biography*.

32 [Charles Lamb], 'The Old and the New Schoolmaster', *London Magazine*, 3 (1821), p. 495.

33 Cited in Meisel, *Realizations*, p. 63.

34 [Pardon], *The London Conductor*, pp. 46–7.

35 All these pieces of sheet music can be found in the British Library.

36 Cited in Altick, *English Common Reader*, p. 114.

37 Cited in Francis E. Mineka, *The Dissidence of Dissent: The Monthly Repository, 1806–1838* (Chapel Hill, University of North Carolina Press, 1944), p. 57.

38 *The Times*, 23 September 1809.

39 Cited in A. H. Saxon, *Enter Foot and Horse: A History of Hippodrama in England and France* (New Haven, Yale University Press, 1968), p. 104.

40 Pepys, *Diary*, vol. 8, p. 240.

41 *A Description of Vauxhall Gardens. Being a proper companion and guide for all who visit that place* (London, 1762), pp. 9, 32.

42 Ibid., p. 9.

43 'Descriptions of Southwark, Lambeth, Newington &c.', [1796], in the collection made by Henry Jacob Burn and held at the British Library as 'Vauxhall Gardens: A Collection of tickets, bills of performances, pamphlets, MS notes, engravings and extracts and cuttings from books and periodicals relating to Vauxhall Gardens, originally made by Jacob Henry Burn'. It is worth noting that substantial portions of this 1796 pamphlet are lifted wholesale from the anonymous *A Description of Vauxhall Gardens* of 1762 cited above.

44 Ibid., p. 23.

45 W. S. Scott, *Green Retreats: The Story of Vauxhall Gardens, 1661–1859* (London, Odhams Press, 1955), p. 86.

46 Pückler-Muskau, *Pückler's Progress*, pp. 128–9.

47 Cited in Scott, *Green Retreats*, p. 95.

48 Mollie Sands, *The Eighteenth-Century Pleasure Gardens of Marylebone, 1737–1777* (London, Society for Theatre Research, 1987), p. 94.

49 Burney, *Evelina*, p. 471.

50 T. J. Edelstein, *Vauxhall Gardens* (New Haven, Yale Center for British Art, 1983), p. 15.

51 Burney, *Evelina*, pp. 209–10.

52 Most of these spas, with descriptions, appear in Edelstein, *Vauxhall Gardens*, *passim*.

53 Joseph Strutt, *The Sports and Pastimes of the People of England*, 'a new edition much enlarged and corrected' by J. Charles Cox (London, Methuen and Co., 1903), pp. 200–201.

54 Mark Judd, 'The Oddest Combination of Town and Country', in Walvin and Walton, *Leisure in Britain*, p. 15.

55 Cunningham, *Leisure in the Industrial Revolution*, p. 173.

56 Wordsworth, *The Prelude*, VII, pp. 695–723.

57 Michael J. Turner, 'Abraham Thornton', in *Oxford Dictionary of National Biography*.

58 My thanks to Jill Grey, Keith Ramsey and Sheldon Goldfarb for supplying the crucial links to this murder case.

59 All fair exhibitors listed in Judd, 'The Oddest Combination of Town and Country', in Walvin and Walton, *Leisure in Britain*, pp. 19–21; the conclusion about the concurrent spread of newspapers and increasing representation of crime is my own.

60 [G. A. Sala], 'Leicester Square', *Household Words*, 7 (1853), pp. 64–5.

61 Max Schlesinger, *Saunterings in and About London*, tr. Otto Wenckstein (London, Nathaniel Cook, 1853), pp. 18–20.

62 Nevett, *Advertising in Britain*, pp. 20–21, 53.

63 Cited in Clear, *The Story of W. H. Smith*, p. 14.

64 Sampson, *History of Advertising*, p. 27.

65 Ibid., p. 31.

8 : *Penny Plain, Tuppence Coloured: The Theatrical Spectacular*

1 Brewer, *Pleasures of the Imagination*, p. 49.

2 Vickery, *Gentleman's Daughter*, pp. 234–5.

3 Borsay, *English Urban Renaissance*, pp. 119–20.

4 Booth, *Theatre in the Victorian Age*, p. 16.

5 Borsay, *English Urban Renaissance*, p. 148; J. H. Plumb, 'The Commercialization of Leisure', in McKendrick, Brewer, Plumb, *Birth of a Consumer Society*, p. 277.

6 Fawcett, *Bath Entertain'd*, pp. 82–3.

7 Hembry, *British Spas from 1815*, p. 3.

8 Brewer, *Pleasures of the Imagination*, pp. 60–61.

9 Fawcett, *Rise of English Provincial Art*, p. 158.

10 Cited in Brewer, *Pleasures of the Imagination*, p. 385.

11 Fawcett, *Rise of English Provincial Art*, p. 166.

12 Booth, *Theatre in the Victorian Age*, p. 6.

13 Jacky Bratton, *New Readings in Theatre History* (Cambridge, Cambridge University Press, 2003), p. 55.

14 J. Ewing Ritchie, *Here and There in London* (London, W. Tweedie, 1859), p. 111–16.

15 Bratton, *New Readings in Theatre History*, p. 49.

16 Rappaport, *Shopping for Pleasure*, p. 182.

17 Maria Edgeworth, *The Absentee* (1812), ed. W. J. McCormack and Kim Walker (Oxford, Oxford University Press, 2001), p. 98.

18 Booth, *Theatre in the Victorian Age*, p. 62.

19 Cited in Rees, *Theatre Lighting in the Age of Gas*, p. 188.

20 Cited in ibid., pp. 175–6.

21 Moody, *Illegitimate Theatre*, p. 172.

22 This figure, a conflation of Charles Booth and Walter Besant, is suggested by Booth, *Theatre in the Victorian Age*, p. 4.

23 Ibid.

24 Ibid., p. 13.

25 Wolfgang Schivelbusch, *Disenchanted Night: The Industrialization of Light in the Nineteenth Century*, tr. Angela Davies (Berkeley, University of California Press, 1995), p. 31.

26 Sala, *Gaslight and Daylight*, p. 159.

27 Cyril Rollins and R. John Witts, eds., *The D'Oyly Carte Opera Company in Gilbert and Sullivan Operas: A Record of Productions, 1875–1961* (London, Michael Joseph, 1962), p. 23.

28 Booth, *Theatre in the Victorian Age*, pp. 18–19.

29 Peter Thomson, 'Henry James Byron', in *Oxford Dictionary of National Biography*.

30 Kean and Byron: Booth, *Theatre in the Victorian Age*, p. 13. The remaining figures: John Pick, *The West End: Mismanagement and Snobbery* (Eastbourne, John Offord, 1983), p. 31.

31 Booth, *Theatre in the Victorian Age*, p. 35.

32 Brewer, *Pleasures of the Imagination*, pp. 328–9.

33 *La Belle Assemblée*, almanac for 1842, p. 7.

34 Altick, *Shows of London*, p. 185.

35 Bratton, *New Readings in Theatre History*, p. 40.

36 Terence Rees and David Wilmore, *British Theatrical Patents* (London, Society for Theatre Research, 1996), pp. 18ff.; Booth, *Theatre in the Victorian Age*, p. 38.

37 Rees and Wilmore, *British Theatrical Patents*, pp. 7ff.

38 Booth, *Theatre in the Victorian Age*, p. 1.

39 Citd in ibid., pp. 36, 18.

40 *Midsummer Night's Dream* and fairy-tale literature: Michael R. Booth, *Victorian Spectacular Theatre: 1850–1910* (London, Routledge & Kegan Paul, 1981), pp. 37–8, 36. W. S. Gilbert: cited in Rees, *Theatre Lighting in the Age of Gas*, p. 181.

41 Pückler-Muskau, *Pückler's Progress*, pp. 79–81.

42 Planché, *The Extravaganzas of J. R. Planché*, vol. I, p. 46.

43 Summary derived from Booth, *Theatre in the Victorian Age*, p. 195, with additional information from Pick, *The West End*, p. 31.

44 Charles Dickens, *David Copperfield* (1850), ed. Jeremy Tambling (Harmondsworth, Penguin, 1996), p. 270.

45 Rosenfeld, 'The Grieve Family', in [Rosenfeld, ed.], *Anatomy of an Illusion*, p. 40.

46 Rees, *Theatre Lighting in the Age of Gas*, pp. 44–5, 84, 49.

47 Maureen Dillon, "Like a Glow-worm who had lost its Glow", The Invention of the Incandescent Electric Lamp and the Development of Artificial Silk and Electric Jewellery', *Costume*, 35 (2001), p. 78.

48 Rees, *Theatre Lighting in the Age of Gas*, pp. 181–2.

49 Booth, *Victorian Spectacular Theatre*, pp. 82–3.

50 Booth, *Theatre in the Victorian Age*, pp. 34–5.

51 J. C. Cross, *Circusiana, or A Collection of the Most Favourite Ballets, Spectacles, Melo-drames, &c., Performed at the Royal Circus, St George's Fields* (2 vols., London, Lackington, Allen & Co., 1809), pp. 93–4.

52 *Paris in Uproar, The Champ de Mars* and *Bagshot-Heath Camp*: Moody, *Illegitimate Theatre*, pp. 27–8. The British Glory in Egypt and ad: Altick, *Shows of London*, p. 176.

53 Moody, *Illegitimate Theatre*, pp. 27–9.

54 *The Times*, 2 June 1800, p. 1, col. a.

55 I have relied heavily on A. H. Saxon's two books, *Enter Foot and Horse* and *The Life and Art of Andrew Ducrow and the Romantic Age of the English Circus* (Hamden, Conn., Archon, 1978) for much of the information on hippodrama, except where otherwise stated. The Royal Circus advertisement: *Enter Foot and Horse*, pp. 39–40.

56 Saxon, *Enter Foot and Horse*, p. 49.

57 Ibid., pp. 45, 49.

58 Cited in ibid., pp. 83–7.

59 Ibid., pp. 89, 96.

60 Ibid., p. 90.

61 Pückler-Muskau, *Pückler's Progress*, pp. 66–7.

62 Saxon, *Enter Foot and Horse*, p. 94.

63 Saxon, *Andrew Ducrow*, pp. 239–41.

64 Bratton, *New Readings in Theatre History*, pp. 41, 50.

65 *The Times*, 6 November 1823, p. 1; Saxon, *Enter Foot and Horse*, pp. 99–100.

66 Saxon, *Enter Foot and Horse*, pp. 134, 137–8.

67 Meisel, *Realizations*, p. 218.

68 *Mazeppa*, in James L. Smith, ed., *Victorian Melodramas: Seven English, French and American Melodramas* (London, Dent, 1976), pp. 18–19.

69 Saxon, *Enter Foot and Horse*, p. 182.

70 Altick, *Shows of London*, p. 201.

71 J. Gilliland, 'Adah Isaacs Menken', in *Oxford Dictionary of National Biography*.

72 All cited in Fawcett, *Rise of English Provincial Art*, pp. 158–9, 161–2.

73 Alfred Bunn, *The Stage: Both Before and Behind the Curtain* (London, Bentley, 1840), vol. 1, pp. 224–5.

74 Percy Fitzgerald, *Principles of Comedy and Dramatic Effect* (London, Tinsley Brothers, 1870), p. 15.

75 Cited in Meisel, *Realizations*, p. 115.

76 Maria Edgeworth, *Belinda* (London, Johnson & Co., 1811), vol. 3, pp. 350–51.

77 Meisel, *Realizations*, pp. 99ff, 111–12.

78 Cited in ibid., pp. 148–9, 157.

79 Henry James, *Notes on Acting and the Drama, 1872–1901*, ed. Allan Wade (London, Rupert Hart-Davis, 1949), p. 148.

80 Cited in Meisel, *Realizations*, p. 174.

81 Cited in Booth, *Victorian Spectacular Theatre*, p. 20.

82 *Dramatic Essays [of Leigh Hunt, W. Hazlitt, John Forster and George H. Lewes]*, ed. William Archer and R. W. Lowe (London, Walter Scott, 1894–6), pp. 250–51.

83 Booth, *Victorian Spectacular Theatre*, pp. 32, 57.

84 Alfred Darbyshire, *The Art of the Victorian Stage*, cited in Booth, *Theatre in the Victorian Age*, p. 49.

85 Brewer, *Pleasures of the Imagination*, p. 392.

86 Moody, *Illegitimate Theatre*, pp. 139–40, 130–31, 134; except rhyming couplet: Saxon, *Enter Foot and Horse*, p. 5.

87 Moody, *Illegitimate Theatre*, p. 135.

88 The citations and interpretation from Richard W. Schoch, 'Shakespeare Mad', in Gail Marshall and Adrian Poole, eds., *Victorian Shakespeare*, vol. 1: *Theatre, Drama and Performance* (Basingstoke, Palgrave, 2003), pp. 73–4, 76, 78.

89 Harley Granville-Barker, 'Exit Planché – Enter Gilbert', in John Drinkwater, ed., *The Eighteen-Sixties: Essays by Fellows of the Royal Society of Literature* (Cambridge, Cambridge University Press, 1932), p. 118.

90 Cited in ibid., pp. 114–15, 117.

91 Moody, *Illegitimate Theatre*, pp. 34–7.

92 St Clair, *Reading Nation*, p. 371.

93 Ibid., pp. 368–70.

94 Smith, *Victorian Melodramas*, p. xviii.

95 Cited in Booth, *Victorian Spectacular Theatre*, pp. 2, 69.

96 Cited in Fawcett, *Rise of English Provincial Art*, p. 161.

97 Smith, *Victorian Melodramas*, p. 22.

98 Ibid., pp. 220, 239.

99 Ibid.

100 Alfred Thompson, *Linda of Chamouni, or, Not Formosa, An Operatic Incongruity, in Three Scenes and a Sensation* (London, n.p., n.d. [after 1869]), pp. 25–6.

101 Smith, *Victorian Melodramas*, pp. 157, 168, 174.

102 Cited in Richard Fawkes, *Dion Boucicault: A Biography* (London, Quartet, 1979), p. 71.

103 Schoch, 'Shakespeare Mad', in Marshall and Poole, *Victorian Shakespeare*, pp. 74, 76, 79.

104 Booth, *Victorian Spectacular Theatre*, p. 63.

105 Fawkes, *Boucicault*, p. 107.

106 Michael Diamond, *Victorian Sensation, Or, the Spectacular, the Shocking and the Scandalous in Nineteenth-Century Britain* (London, Anthem Press, 2003), p. 222.

107 Smith, *Victorian Melodramas*, p. xx; Booth, *Victorian Spectacular Theatre*, pp. 68–9, 72.

108 Henry Morley, *The Journal of a London Playgoer* (2nd ed., 1891) (Leicester, Leicester University Press, 1974), p. 316.

109 Diamond, *Victorian Sensation*, p. 225.

110 Morley, *Journal of a London Playgoer*, p. 258.

111 Fawkes, *Boucicault*, p. 123.

112 Ibid., p. 148; Diamond, *Victorian Sensation*, pp. 229–30.

113 [Squire and Marie Bancroft], *Mr and Mrs Bancroft on and off the Stage, by themselves* (4th ed., London, Richard Bentley, 1888), vol. 2, p. 308.

114 Edward Ziter, *The Orient on the*

Victorian Stage (Cambridge, Cambridge University Press, 2003), p. 1.

115 Morley, *Journal of a London Playgoer*, p. 111.

116 Cited in Reginald Allen, ed., *The First Night Gilbert and Sullivan* (London, Chappell, 1958), pp. 379–80.

117 Rappaport, *Shopping for Pleasure*, pp. 187, 186.

118 Cited in Joel H. Kaplan and Sheila Stowell, *Theatre and Fashion: Oscar Wilde to the Suffragettes* (Cambridge, Cambridge University Press, 1994), p. 8.

119 Ibid., pp. 8, 19–20.

120 Cited in Erika D. Rappaport, 'Acts of Consumption: Musical Comedy and the Desire of Exchange', in Crossick and Jaumain, *Cathedrals of Consumption*, pp. 192–3.

121 Cited in ibid., p. 194.

9: *Going for a Song: The Music Market*

1 Cited in Ehrlich, *Music Profession in Britain*, p. 5.

2 Douglas A. Reid, 'Thomas Britton', in *Oxford Dictionary of National Biography*.

3 Borsay, *English Urban Renaissance*, p. 123.

4 Cited in Brewer, *Pleasures of the Imagination*, p. 366.

5 Plumb, 'The Commercialization of Leisure', in McKendrick, Brewer, Plumb, *Birth of a Consumer Society*, p. 279.

6 Simon McVeigh, *Concert Life in London from Mozart to Haydn* (Cambridge, Cambridge University Press, 1993), p. 32.

7 Cited in Brewer, *Pleasures of the Imagination*, pp. 400–401.

8 William Weber, *The Rise of Musical Classics in Eighteenth-Century England: A Study in Canon, Ritual, and Ideology* (Oxford, Clarendon Press, 1992), p. 19.

9 McVeigh, *Concert Life in London*, p. 75.

10 This is cited in Borsay, *English Urban Renaissance*, pp. 114–15, although it

is not clear from the source if that includes the number of Italian composers in Italy as well as in the rest of Europe.

11 Brewer, *Pleasures of the Imagination*, p. 570.

12 Ehrlich, *Music Profession in Britain*, pp. 19–20.

13 Brewer, *Pleasures of the Imagination*, p. 568.

14 Colley, *Britons*, p. 199.

15 Vickery, *Gentleman's Daughter*, p. 230.

16 Cited in Brewer, *Pleasures of the Imagination*, p. 63.

17 Ibid., pp. 25–8.

18 Burney, *Evelina*, p. 116.

19 McVeigh, *Concert Life in London*, p. 15.

20 Ehrlich: *Music Profession in Britain*, p. 6.

21 Sands, *Pleasure Gardens of Marylebone*, pp. 25, 29.

22 Brewer, *Pleasures of the Imagination*, p. 379; McVeigh, *Concert Life in London*, pp. 111–13.

23 Cited in McVeigh, *Concert Life in London*, pp. 47–8.

24 Burn, 'Vauxhall Gardens' pamphlet collection, p. 186.

25 Cited in E. D. Mackerness, *A Social History of English Music* (London, Routledge & Kegan Paul, 1964), p. 108.

26 Cited in Vickery, *Gentleman's Daughter*, p. 126.

27 Oliver Goldsmith, *The Vicar of Wakefield* (1766), ed. Stephen Coote (Harmondsworth, Penguin, 1986), p. 106.

28 Sands, *Pleasure Gardens of Marylebone*, pp. 57, 69.

29 McVeigh, *Concert Life in London*, p. 67.

30 Richard Leppert, 'Social Order and the Domestic Consumption of Music', in Ann Bermingham and John Brewer, eds., *The Consumption of Culture, 1600–1850: Image, Object, Text* (Routledge, London, 1995), p. 521.

31 Cited in the *Oxford English Dictionary*.

32 Loesser, *Men, Women and Pianos*, pp. 220–21, 223.

33 Ibid., pp. 224–7, 241.

34 Ibid., pp. 227–8.

35 Weber, *Rise of Musical Classics*, p. 18.
36 D. W. Drummel, 'Music Publishing', in Nicholas Temperley, ed., *Music in Britain: The Romantic Age, 1800–1914*, vol. 5 of *The Blackwell History of Music in Britain*, gen. ed. Ian Spink (Oxford, Blackwell, 1988), p. 48.
37 Loesser, *Men, Women and Pianos*, p. 252.
38 Plant, *English Book Trade*, pp. 306–7.
39 Loesser, *Men, Women and Pianos*, pp. 251, 229.
40 Mackerness, *Social History of English Music*, p. 107.
41 Loesser, *Men, Women and Pianos*, pp. 252–3.
42 Ibid., p. 251.
43 Ibid., p. 235; Brewer, *Pleasures of the Imagination*, p. 535.
44 Loesser, *Men, Women and Pianos*, pp. 234–5.
45 Ibid., pp. 248–50.
46 Altick, *English Common Reader*, p. 306.
47 Ehrlich, *The Piano*, p. 40.
48 Mathias, *Retailing Revolution*, p. 13.
49 Ehrlich, *The Piano*, pp. 34–6.
50 The Broadwood entries are at no. 518 in the *Official Catalogue*, vol. 2, section 10; William Rolfe and Sons at no. 472; a wide range of pianos can also be found in entries 464a, 467–502.
51 Ehrlich, *The Piano*, pp. 38–9.
52 Ibid., p. 32.
53 Ibid., p. 50.
54 All cited in ibid., p. 100. The 60-guinea piano appears to have incurred no mark-up, according to Ehrlich, but I have not been able to locate a copy of the *Bethnal Green Times* to verify this.
55 Davis and Bonsall, *Bath*, p. 95.
56 Ehrlich, *The Piano*, pp. 69, 71–3, 88.
57 Ehrlich, *Social Emulation and Industrial Progress – the Victorian Piano* (Belfast, Queen's University, 1975), p. 7.
58 Ibid.
59 Ehrlich, *Music Profession in Britain*, p. 53.
60 Peter Clark and R. A. Houston, 'Culture and Leisure, 1700–1840', in Peter Clark, ed., *The Cambridge Urban History of Britain*, vol. 2: *Culture and Leisure, 1540–1840* (Cambridge, Cambridge University Press, 2000), p. 581.
61 William Weber, *Music and the Middle Class: The Social Structure of Concert Life in London, Paris and Vienna* (London, Croom Helm, 1975), pp. 63–4.
62 Ibid., p. 31.
63 Ibid., p. 16.
64 Ehrlich, *Music Profession in Britain*, pp. 54–5.
65 John Rosselli, 'Louis Jullien', in *Oxford Dictionary of National Biography*; Ehrlich, *Music Profession in Britain*, p. 60; Altick, *Shows of London*, p. 330.
66 Hoppen, *Mid-Victorian Generation*, p. 400.
67 Ehrlich, *Music Profession in Britain*, pp. 61–2.
68 Charles Hallé, *The Life and Letters of Sir Charles Hallé, being an autobiography, 1816–1860, with correspondence and diaries*, ed. C. E. Hallé and Marie Hallé (London, Smith Elder & Co., 1896), p. 111.
69 Dave Russell, 'Musicians in the English Provincial City: Manchester, c.1860–1914', in Christina Bashford and Leanne Langley, eds., *Music and British Culture, 1785–1914* (Oxford, Oxford University Press, 2000), pp. 238, 239–40; Ehrlich, *Music Profession in Britain*, p. 62.
70 Russell, 'Musicians in the English Provincial City', in Bashford and Langley, *Music and British Culture*, p. 236.
71 Cited in Ehrlich, *Music Profession in Britain*, p. 63.
72 Ibid., p. 62.
73 Russell, 'Musicians in the English Provincial City', in Bashford and Langley, *Music and British Culture*, p. 236.
74 Ehrlich, *Music Profession in Britain*, p. 51.
75 Cunningham, *Leisure in the Industrial Revolution*, pp. 167–8.
76 Bratton, *New Readings in Theatre History*, pp. 55, 58.
77 Warwick Wroth, *Cremorne and the Later London Gardens* (London, Elliot Stock, 1907), pp. 57, 60.

78 Altick, *Shows of London*, p. 502.
79 Cunningham, *Leisure in the Industrial Revolution*, pp. 167–8.
80 Ibid., pp. 168–9.
81 Peter Bailey, ed., *Music Hall: The Business of Pleasure* (Milton Keynes, Open University Press, 1986), intro, p. ix; Ehrlich, *Music Profession in Britain*, p. 57.
82 John Earl, 'Building the Halls', in Bailey, *Music Hall*, pp. 2–4.
83 Cunningham, *Leisure in the Industrial Revolution*, p. 170.
84 Ibid., p. 170.
85 Bailey, *Music Hall*, intro, p. xi.
86 Percy Fitzgerald, *Music Hall Land* (London, Ward and Downey, 1890), p. 4.
87 H. Chance Newton, *Idols of the Halls, being my Music-hall Memories* (London, Heath Cranton, 1928), p. 59.
88 Peter Bailey, 'George Leybourne', in *Oxford Dictionary of National Biography*.
89 V. de Frece [Vesta Tilley], *Recollections of Vesta Tilley, Lady de Frece* (London, Hutchinson and Co., 1934), p. 125.

10: *Going, Going: Art and the Market*

1 Altick, *Shows of London*, p. 101.
2 Cited in Brewer, *Pleasures of the Imagination*, p. 223.
3 Cited in Jeremy Black, *The British Abroad: The Grand Tour in the Eighteenth Century* (Stroud, Alan Sutton, 1992), p. 260.
4 Ibid., p. 266.
5 Cited in Brewer, *Pleasures of the Imagination*, p. 256.
6 Robert Strange, *An Inquiry into the Rise and Establishment of the Royal Academy of Arts* (London, n.p., 1775), p. 62.
7 Saunders, *Authorship and Copyright*, p. 41.
8 Brewer, *Pleasures of the Imagination*, p. 163. John Arbuthnot and Alexander Pope, *The Memoirs of the Extraordinary Life, Works, and Discoveries of Martinus Scriblerus* (1741), ed. Charles Kerby-Miller (New Haven, Yale University Press, 1950), p. 105.
9 Cited in Brewer, *Pleasures of the Imagination*, p. 252.
10 Hudson and Luckhurst, *The Royal Society of Arts*, pp. 34–5, 39.
11 Sidney C. Hutchinson, *The History of the Royal Academy, 1768–1968* (2nd ed., London, Robert Royce, 1968), pp. 24–6, 31, 33.
12 H. C. Marillier, *Christie's, 1766–1925* (London, Constable & Co., 1926), pp. 8, 12.
13 Brewer, *Pleasures of the Imagination*, p. 223.
14 Joshua Reynolds, *Discourses on Art*, ed. Robert R. Wark (San Marino, Cal., Huntington Library, 1959), p. 43.
15 Brewer, *Pleasures of the Imagination*, pp. 238–9.
16 Colley, *Britons*, pp. 206–7.
17 Cited in Hutchinson, *History of the Royal Academy*, pp. 37–8.
18 Ibid., p. 53.
19 Ibid.
20 Louise Lippincott, 'Expanding on Portraiture: The Market, the Public, and the Hierarchy of Genres in Eighteenth-Century Britain', in Bermingham and Brewer, *The Consumption of Culture*, p. 78.
21 Altick, *Shows of London*, p. 105.
22 Gilpin, *An Essay on Prints*, p. 2.
23 Brewer, *Pleasures of the Imagination*, pp. 455, 452.
24 I have relied on Sven H. A. Bruntjen, *John Boydell, 1719–1804: A Study of Art Patronage and Publishing in Georgian London* (New York, Garland, 1985), *passim*, for my account of Boydell and his gallery, except where otherwise noted.
25 Altick, *Shows of London*, p. 106.
26 Ibid., p. 108.
27 Lybbe Powys, *Diaries*, pp. 299–300.
28 *Noble and Patriotic: The Beaumont Gift, 1828* (London, National Gallery, 1988), p. 8.
29 Cited in Colley, *Britons*, pp. 174–5.
30 Altick, *Shows of London*, p. 405.
31 Peter Fullerton, 'Patronage and Pedagogy: The British Institution in the Early Nineteenth Century', *Art History*, 5, 1 (1982), p. 60.

32 Cited in Morris Eaves, *The Counter-Arts Conspiracy: Art and Industry in the Age of Blake* (Ithaca, Cornell University Press,1992), p. 75.

33 Fullerton, 'Patronage and Pedagogy', *Art History*, 5, 1 (1982), pp. 67.

34 Colley, *Britons*, p. 176.

35 Ibid.

36 Walpole, 14 February 1753, *Letters of Horace Walpole, Earl of Orford, to Sir Horace Mann*, (London, Richard Bentley, 1833), vol. III, p. 32.

37 Marjorie Caygill and Christopher Date, *Building the British Museum* (London, British Museum Press, 1999), p. 13.

38 Kenneth Hudson, *A Social History of Museums: What the Visitors Thought* (London, Macmillan, 1975), pp. 9-10.

39 William Hutton, *A Journey to London* (2nd ed., London, n.p., 1818), pp. 112-16.

40 I have not made this up. The catalogue is reproduced in *Chambers Book of Days, A Miscellany of Popular Antiquity*, ed. R. Chambers (Edinburgh and London, W. & R. Chambers, [1866?]) p. 608.

41 Altick, *Shows of London*, p. 440.

42 Caygill and Date, *Building the British Museum*, pp. 15-16.

43 Altick, *Shows of London*, p. 429.

44 Cited in Edward Miller, *That Noble Cabinet: A History of the British Museum* (London, André Deutsch, 1973), p. 26.

45 Cited in Hudson and Luckhurst, *The Royal Society of Arts*, pp. 34-5.

46 Cited in Altick, *Shows of London*, p. 406.

47 St Clair, *Reading Nation*, pp. 194-5.

48 Cited in Fawcett, *Rise of English Provincial Art*, p. 5.

49 Cited in Black, *On Exhibit*, p. 105.

50 Ibid., p. 3.

51 Ibid., p. 5.

52 Cited in *Noble and Patriotic*, p. 10.

53 Cited in Charlotte Klonk, 'The National Gallery in London and its Public', in Berg and Clifford, *Consumers and Luxury*, pp. 228-9.

54 Ibid., p. 11.

55 Janet Minihan, *The Nationalization of Culture: The Development of State Subsidies to the Arts in Great Britain* (New York, New York University Press, 1977), pp. 23-4.

56 'Report from the Select Committee on the Arts, and their Connection with Manufacturers', *Reports*, House of Commons, 1836, 19.1, 10.1.

57 Klonk, 'The National Gallery', in Berg and Clifford, *Consumers and Luxury*, p. 234.

58 Select Committee on the Arts, 108.

59 Altick, *Shows of London*, pp. 444-5.

60 Carol Duncan, 'Putting the "Nation" in London's National Gallery', in Gwendolyn Wright, ed., *The Formation of National Collections of Art and Archaeology*, Studies in the History of Art, 47, Center for Advanced Study in the Visual Arts, Symposium Papers 27 (Washington, DC, National Gallery of Art, 1996), pp. 108-9.

61 Charles Holmes and C. H. Collins Baker, *The Making of the National Gallery, 1824-1924* (London, The National Gallery, 1924), pp. 24-5.

62 David Robertson, 'Sir Charles Lock Eastlake', in *Oxford Dictionary of National Biography*.

63 Altick, *Shows of London*, pp. 454, 467; and Klonk, 'The National Gallery', in Berg and Clifford, *Consumers and Luxury*, p. 237.

64 Sir Henry Cole, *Fifty Years of Public Work of Sir Henry Cole, accounted for in his deeds, speeches and writings* ([London], Bell, 1884), vol. 2, p. 368.

65 Cited in Tony Bennett, *The Birth of the Museum: History, Theory, Politics* (London, Routledge, 1995), p. 71.

66 [Henry Cole], 'Public Galleries and Irresponsible Boards', *Edinburgh Review*, 251 (January 1866), p. 69.

67 Cited in Black, *On Exhibit*, p. 101.

68 Ibid., pp. 32-3, 200.

69 Fawcett, *Rise of English Provincial Art*, pp. 1, 113, 168-9, 184-5.

70 Seed, '"Commerce and the Liberal Arts"', in Wolff and Seed, *Culture of Capital*, pp. 47, 65.

71 Altick, *Shows of London*, p. 405; Klonk, 'The National Gallery', in Berg and Clifford, *Consumers and Luxury*, p. 231.

72 Cited in Macleod, *Art and the Victorian Middle Class*, pp. 96–7.

73 Seed, ' "Commerce and the Liberal Arts" ', in Wolff and Seed, *Culture of Capital*, pp. 69–70; Macleod, *Art and the Victorian Middle Class*, p. 98.

74 Brendon, *Thomas Cook*, p. 64.

75 Cited in Macleod, *Art and the Victorian Middle Class*, pp. 101–4.

76 Brewer, *Pleasures of the Imagination*, p. 202.

77 Louise Lippincott, *Selling Art in Georgian London: The Rise of Arthur Pond* (London, Yale University Press, 1983), pp. 31, 38, 50, 56, 132–4, 142.

78 Goldsmith, *The Vicar of Wakefield*, p. 130.

79 Gerald Reitlinger, *The Economics of Taste*, vol. 1: *The Rise and Fall of Picture Prices, 1760–1960* (London, Barrie & Rockliff, 1961), pp. 30–31.

80 Macleod, *Art and the Victorian Middle Class*, p. 40.

81 Ibid., p. 232.

82 Cited in Fawcett, *Rise of English Provincial Art*, p. 151.

83 Seed, ' "Commerce and the Liberal Arts" ', in Wolff and Seed, *Culture of Capital*, pp. 52–4.

84 Macleod, *Art and the Victorian Middle Class*, p. 234.

85 Jeremy Maas, *Gambart, Prince of the Victorian Art World* (London, Barrie & Jenkins, 1975), pp. 22, 31, 39.

86 Ibid., pp. 38, 39.

87 Ibid., pp. 30, 99.

88 Altick, *Shows of London*, p. 412.

89 Macleod, *Art and the Victorian Middle Class*, p. 239.

90 Ibid., pp. 310–11.

91 Linda Merrill, 'Charles Augustus Howell', in *Oxford Dictionary of National Biography*.

92 *Punch*, 21 July 1888, p. 30.

93 Julie F. Codell, 'Marion Harry Spielmann and the Role of the Press in the Professionalization of Artists', *Victorian Periodicals Review*, 22, 1 (1989), pp. 7–13.

11: *Sporting Life*

1 Peter Gaskell, *The Moral and Physical Condition of the Manufacturing Population . . .* (London, John W. Parker, 1836), pp. 181, 248.

2 Samuel Bamford, *The Autobiography of Samuel Bamford*, ed. W. H. Chaloner (London, Frank Cass & Co., 1967), vol. 1, pp. 137ff.

3 Dennis Brailsford, *A Taste for Diversions: Sport in Georgian England* (Cambridge, Lutterworth Press, 1999), pp. 15ff.

4 Ibid., pp. 23, 20–21.

5 Bamford, *Autobiography*, vol. 1, p. 141.

6 Brailsford, *A Taste for Diversions*, p. 187.

7 Ibid., pp. 24–5.

8 Borsay, *English Urban Renaissance*, p. 186.

9 Ibid., pp. 185, 181.

10 Brailsford, *A Taste for Diversions*, p. 25.

11 Borsay, *English Urban Renaissance*, pp. 218–19.

12 Ibid., p. 192.

13 Lybbe Powys, *Diaries*, pp. 24–5.

14 Ibid., pp. 134–5.

15 Cited in Borsay, *English Urban Renaissance*, p. 183.

16 Ibid., pp. 303–4.

17 Roger Longrigg, *The History of Horse Racing* (London, Macmillan, 1972), pp. 91–2.

18 Plumb, 'The Commercialization of Leisure', in McKendrick, Brewer, Plumb, *Birth of a Consumer Society*, pp. 280–81; Harvey, *Commercial Sporting Culture*, p. 32.

19 Brailsford, *A Taste for Diversions*, p. 26.

20 Longrigg, *History of Horse Racing*, pp. 89–90; Brailsford, *A Taste for Diversions*, p. 161.

21 Harriet Ritvo, 'Possessing Mother Nature: Genetic Capital in Eighteenth-Century Britain', in John Brewer and Susan Staves, eds., *Early Modern Conceptions of Property: Consumption and Culture in the 17th and 18th Centuries* (London, Routledge, 1995), pp. 415–16.

22 Borsay, *English Urban Renaissance*, p. 218.

23 Wray Vamplew, 'Tattersall family', in *Oxford Dictionary of National Biography.*

24 Ibid.

25 Except where otherwise noted, the information on the Weatherby and Tattersall dynasties comes from Mike Huggins, 'A Tranquil Transformation: Middle-Class Racing "Revolutionaries" in Nineteenth-Century England', in J. A. Mangan, ed., *Reformers, Sport, Modernizers: Middle-Class Revolutionaries* (London, Frank Cass, 2002), pp. 43–4, 45–7.

26 Brailsford, *A Taste for Diversions*, p. 26.

27 Ibid., p. 27.

28 Walvin, *Leisure and Society*, p. 24.

29 Simmons, *The Victorian Railway*, p. 272.

30 Wray Vamplew, *The Turf: A Social and Economic History of Horse Racing* (London, Allen Lane, 1976), p. 29; Simmons, *The Victorian Railway*, p. 273.

31 Simmons, *The Victorian Railway*, p. 301.

32 Ibid.

33 Vamplew, *The Turf*, pp. 30–31.

34 Ibid., p. 35.

35 Mike Huggins, *Flat Racing and British Society, 1790–1914: A Social and Economic History* (London, Frank Cass, 2000), pp. 31–2.

36 Dennis Brailsford, *British Sport: A Social History* (Cambridge, Lutterworth Press, 1992), p. 85.

37 Harvey, *Commercial Sporting Culture*, p. 20.

38 Huggins, *Victorians and Sport*, p. 148.

39 Huggins, *Flat Racing and British Society*, pp. 27–8.

40 Wray Vamplew, *Pay Up and Play the Game: Professional Sport in Britain, 1875–1914* (Cambridge, Cambridge University Press, 1988), p. 55.

41 Ibid., p. 152.

42 Tranter, *Sport, Economy and Society*, p. 20.

43 Vamplew, *The Turf*, p. 38.

44 Vamplew, *Pay Up and Play the Game*, pp. 57–8.

45 Ibid., p. 101.

46 Ibid., pp. 56–7.

47 Huggins, *Flat Racing and British Society*, p. 154.

48 Cited in Cunningham, *Leisure in the Industrial Revolution*, p. 82.

49 Cited in ibid., p. 92.

50 Ibid., pp. 93, 96.

51 Ibid., p. 93; Altick, *Shows of London*, p. 87.

52 Cunningham, *Leisure in the Industrial Revolution*, p. 151.

53 Ibid., p. 152.

54 Robert W. Malcolmson, *Popular Recreations in English Society, 1700–1850* (Cambridge, Cambridge University Press, 1973), p. 36.

55 Ibid., pp. 34–5.

56 John Goulstone, *Football's Secret History* (Upminster, 3–2 Books, 2001), p. 27.

57 Richard Holt, *Sport and the British: A Modern History* (Oxford, Clarendon Press, 1989), p. 151; Peter Bailey, *Leisure and Class in Victorian England: Rational Recreation and the Contest for Control* (London, Methuen, 1978), p. 147; Mason, *Association Football*, pp. 26–7, 48–9, 51.

58 Holt, *Sport and the British*, p. 150.

59 Bailey, *Leisure and Class*, p. 147; Brailsford, *British Sport*, p. 96.

60 Mason, *Association Football*, pp. 48–9.

61 Hoppen, *Mid-Victorian Generation*, p. 362; Holt, *Sport and the British*, p. 152.

62 Holt, *Sport and the British*, p. 150.

63 Ibid., p. 31.

64 Mason, *Association Football*, p. 22.

65 Goulstone, *Football's Secret History*, pp. 28–33.

66 Cited in ibid., pp. 47–8.

67 Holt, *Sport and the British*, p. 85.

68 Cited in Goulstone, *Football's Secret History*, p. 48.

69 Tranter, *Sport, Economy and Society*, p. 15.

70 Ibid., pp. 24–5.

71 Ibid.; Mason, *Association Football*, pp. 15–16.

72 Huggins, *Victorians and Sport*, p. 63.

73 Mason, *Association Football*, pp. 69–72.

74 Hoppen, *Mid-Victorian Generation*, p. 363.

75 Golby and Purdue, *The Civilisation of the Crowd*, p. 110.

76 Blackman, Janet, 'The Development of the Retail Grocery Trade in the Nineteenth Century', *Business History*, 9, 2 (1967), p. 110.

77 Cited in Mason, *Association Football*, p. 73.

78 Bailey, *Leisure and Class*, p. 150.

79 Ibid.; Huggins, *Victorians and Sport*, pp. 63–6.

80 Mason, *Association Football*, p. 74.

81 *Punch*, 3 November 1888, pp. 206–7; Mason, *Association Football*, p. 75.

82 Ibid., p. 66.

83 Ibid., pp. 34–5.

84 Ibid., p. 141; Tranter, *Sport, Economy and Society*, p. 17.

85 Mason, *Association Football*, pp. 146–7; Simmons, *The Victorian Railway*, p. 302.

86 Tony Collins and Wray Vamplew, 'The Pub, the Drinks Trade and the Early Years of Modern Football', *Sports Historian*, 20, 1 (2000), pp. 7–11.

87 Mason, *Association Football*, p. 35.

88 Ibid., pp. 39–42.

89 Cited in Cunningham, *Leisure in the Industrial Revolution*, pp. 115–16.

90 Cited in Bailey, *Leisure and Class*, pp. 83–4.

91 David V. Herlihy, *Bicycle: The History* (New Haven, Yale University Press, 2004), pp. 75, 147, 150; Bagwell, *Transport Revolution*, pp. 137–8.

92 Herlihy, *Bicycle*, pp. 165, 216, 246, 251.

93 John Lowerson, *Sport and the English Middle Classes: 1870–1914* (Manchester, Manchester University Press, 1993), p. 234.

94 David Rubinstein, 'Cycling in the 1890s', *Victorian Studies*, 21, 1 (1977), pp. 51, 57.

95 Simmons, *The Victorian Railway*, p. 305.

96 Frederick Alderson, *Bicycling: A History* (Newton Abbot, David and Charles, 1972), p. 103.

97 F. G. Aflalo, ed., *The Cost of Sport* (London, John Murray, 1899), pp. 326–7.

98 Alderson, *Bicycling*, p. 73.

99 Ibid., pp. 102–3.

100 Ibid., pp. 43–5.

101 Bagwell, *Transport Revolution*, p. 138.

102 Rubinstein, 'Cycling in the 1890s', *Victorian Studies*, 21, 1 (1977), p. 49.

103 Cited in Huggins, *Victorians and Sport*, p. 153.

104 Grant Allen, *Hilda Wade: A Woman with Tenacity of Purpose* (London and New York, G. P. Putnam's Sons, [1899]), *passim*. My thanks to my Victoria mailbase colleagues for their contributions to this list of 'cycling' stories.

105 Huggins, *Victorians and Sport*, p. 162.

106 Loeb, *Consuming Angels*, p. 43; Shannon, 'ReFashioning Men', *Victorian Studies*, 46, 4 (2004), p. 603.

107 *Official Catalogue*, vol. 2, classes 12 and 15, no. 15, p. 486.

108 Cunnington and Mansfield, *English Costumes for Sports*, pp. 49–54.

109 Levitt, *Victorians Unbuttoned*, p. 206.

110 Mason, *Association Football*, p. 32.

111 Cited in Holt, *Sport and the British*, p. 127.

112 Levitt, *Victorians Unbuttoned*, p. 199.

113 Cited in Cunnington and Mansfield, *English Costumes for Sports*, pp. 229–30.

114 'Pastimes for Ladies. On Three Wheels', *Woman's World*, 6 (1887), pp. 423–4, cited in Beetham and Boardman, *Victorian Women's Magazines*, pp. 41–2.

115 Adburgham, *Shops and Shopping*, pp. 264–5.

116 Ibid., p. 203; Breward, *Hidden Consumer*, pp. 141–2.

117 Tranter, *Sport, Economy and Society*, p. 33.

118 Smout, 'Tours in the Scottish Highlands', *Northern Scotland*, 5, 2 (1983), pp. 110–11.

119 Vamplew, *Pay Up and Play the Game*, p. 55.

12: *Visions of Sugar Plums: A Christmas Coda*

1 Charles Dickens, *Sketches by Boz*, vol. 1, ed. Andrew Lang (London, Gadshill Edition, vol. 26, Chapman and Hall, 1898), 'Characters', pp. 258–62.

2 J. M. Golby and A. W. Purdue, *The*

Making of the Modern Christmas (rev. ed., Stroud, Sutton, 2000), p. 40.

3 Tony Bennett, John Golby and Ruth Finnegan, 'Christmas and Ideology', in *Popular Culture: Themes and Issues*, Block 1, Units 1/2: 'Christmas: A Case Study' (Milton Keynes, Open University Press, 1981), p. 19.

4 J. A. R. Pimlott, *The Englishman's Christmas: A Social History* (Hassocks, Harvester, 1978), p. 80.

5 Cited in Gavin Weightman and Steve Humphries, *Christmas Past* (London, Sidgwick & Jackson, 1987), pp. 46–7.

6 *The Amberley Papers: Letters and Diaries of Lord and Lady Amberley*, ed. Bertrand and Patricia Russell (London, Hogarth Press, 1937), vol. 2, pp. 388, 426.

7 Pimlott, *Englishman's Christmas*, pp. 98–9.

8 *The Christmas Tree, A Present from Germany* (London, Darton & Clark, 1844), pp. 1–2.

9 *Illustrated London News*, 27 December 1845, p. 405.

10 Ibid., Christmas Supplement, 1848, p. 409.

11 Charles Manby Smith, *Curiosities of London Life, or Phases, Physiological and Social, of the Great Metropolis* (London, William and Frederick G. Cash, 1853), pp. 323–5.

12 Cited in Weightman and Humphries, *Christmas Past*, pp. 107–9.

13 Ibid., pp. 112–13.

14 William Wallace Ffyfe, *Christmas: Its Customs and Carols. With Compressed Vocal Score of Select Choral Illustrations* (London, James Blackwood, [1860]), p. 22.

15 Golby and Purdue, *Modern Christmas*, p. 51.

16 David Philip Miller, 'Davies Gilbert', *Oxford Dictionary of Biography*.

17 Percy Dearmer, R. Vaughan Williams and Martin Shaw, *The Oxford Book of Carols* (London, Oxford University Press, 1928), pp. x–xi.

18 Hindley, *History of the Catnach Press*, pp. 242–3.

19 Dearmer et al., *Oxford Book of Carols*, pp. x–xi.

20 Hannah Cullwick, *The Diaries of Hannah Cullwick, Victorian Maidservant*, ed. Liz Stanley (London, Virago, 1984), p. 261.

21 Golby and Purdue, *Modern Christmas*, p. 76; Pimlott, *Englishman's Christmas*, p. 77.

22 Weightman and Humphries, *Christmas Past*, p. 85.

23 James Robinson Planché, *Pieces of Pleasantry for Private Performance during the Christmas Holidays* (London, Thomas Hailes Lacy, [1868]), *passim*.

24 Weightman and Humphries, *Christmas Past*, pp. 143, 145.

25 Ibid., p. 81.

26 Pimlott, *Englishman's Christmas*, p. 90.

27 Weightman and Humphries, *Christmas Past*, p. 62.

28 Kathleen R. Farrar, 'The Mechanics' Saturnalia', in D. S. L. Cardwell, ed., *Artisan to Graduate: Essays to Commemorate the Foundation in 1824 of the Manchester Mechanics' Institution* . . . (Manchester, Manchester University Press, 1974), pp. 99–114, *passim*.

29 Pimlott, *Englishman's Christmas*, p. 92.

30 Drotner, *English Children and their Magazines*, p. 143.

31 *The Times*, 22 December 1877, p. 5, col. f.

32 Manby Smith, *Curiosities of London Life*, p. 250.

33 Cited in Pimlott, *Englishman's Christmas*, p. 69.

34 Weightman and Humphries, *Christmas Past*, pp. 125, 129.

35 Ibid., p. 43.

36 Cited in ibid., p. 111.

37 Copies of all these can be found in the British Library.

38 Manby Smith, *Little World of London*, p. 261.

39 Charles Dickens, *The Posthumous Papers of the Pickwick Club* (1836–7), ed. Mark Wormald (Harmondsworth, Penguin, 1999), p. 431.

40 Buday, *Christmas Card*, pp. 45–7.

41 Golby and Purdue, *Modern Christmas*, p. 69.

42 Buday, *Christmas Card*, pp. 53–5.

43 Weightman and Humphries, *Christmas Past*, p. 56.

44 Golby and Purdue, *Modern Christmas*, p. 15.

45 Buday, *Christmas Card*, pp. 6, 15, 53–9, 88–9.
46 Pimlott, *Englishman's Christmas*, pp. 104–5.
47 Ibid., p. 102.
48 Ibid., p. 124.
49 Weightman and Humphries, *Christmas Past*, p. 111.
50 Bennett, Golby, Finnegan, 'Christmas and Ideology', in *Popular Culture: Themes and Issues*, p. 18; Weightman and Humphries, *Christmas Past*, p. 160.
51 Manby Smith, *Curiosities of London Life*, pp. 323, 320.
52 Cited in Pimlott, *Englishman's Christmas*, p. 74.
53 Ibid., p. 74.
54 Cited in Frederick W. Faxon, *Literary Annuals and Gift Books: A Bibliography, 1823–1903* (reprint, Pinner, Private Libraries Association, 1973), p. 10.
55 Peter J. Manning, 'Wordsworth in the Keepsake', in John O. Jordan and Robert L. Patten, eds., *Literature in the Marketplace: Nineteenth-Century British Publishing and Reading Practices* (Cambridge, Cambridge University Press, 1995), pp. 44–5.
56 *The Christmas Tree: A Book of Instruction and Amusement for all Young People* (London, James Blackwood, 1860), p. 30.
57 Drotner, *English Children and their Magazines*, p. 63.
58 Dickens, *A Christmas Carol*, p. 82; Pimlott, *Englishman's Christmas*, p. 122.
59 Briggs, *Friends of the People*, p. 38; Lancaster, *The Department Store*, pp. 23–4, 51.
60 Weightman and Humphries, *Christmas Past*, p. 160.
61 Honeycombe, *Selfridges*, p. 26.
62 Cited in Golby and Purdue, *Modern Christmas*, pp. 16–17.
63 All cited in Diana and Geoffrey Hindley, *Advertising in Victorian England, 1837–1901* (London, Wayland, 1972), entries 2.7–2.13.

INDEX